THE BEST PLAYS OF 1970–1971

THE

BURNS MANTLE

YEARBOOK

THE
BEST PLAYS
OF 1970-1971

EDITED BY OTIS L. GUERNSEY JR.

Illustrated with photographs and
with drawings by HIRSCHFELD

DODD, MEAD & COMPANY

NEW YORK • TORONTO

Copyright © 1971 by Dodd, Mead & Company, Inc.
ISBN 0-396-06429-9
Library of Congress Catalog Card Number: 20-21432

Printed in the United States of America

EDITOR'S NOTE

THERE WERE 111 PRODUCTIONS this year of the new play *The Night Thoreau Spent in Jail* by Jerome Lawrence and Robert E. Lee—and not one performance of one production took place in New York City. This script was staged all across the United States by university and regional theater groups in the membership of the American Playwrights Theater, and it exemplifies the growing importance and even influence of the coast-to-coast theater. Time and again plays reach New York after an American or even world premiere in Los Angeles *(The Trial of the Catonsville Nine)*, Houston *(The Effect of Gamma Rays on Man-in-the-Moon Marigolds)*, Washington *(The Great White Hope)*, New Haven *(A Place Without Doors)*, etc.

It is *Best Plays* policy to keep in step with our theater wherever it leads at whatever pace it sets, so we have expanded our coverage of "The Season Around the United States" in 1971. We carry a complete Directory of programs presented in the more than 50 professional regional theaters in the United States and Canada in alphabetical order from Abingdon, Va. to Winnipeg, Manitoba, prepared by Ella A. Malin; and now in this 1970-71 volume Miss Malin has prepared an expanded listing, with complete cast and credits, for each world or American premiere production of a new script on the coast-to-coast circuit. For added insight, this section on "The Theater Around the United States" is introduced with an article by the abovementioned distinguished playwrights Messrs. Lawrence and Lee, describing what it was like and what it means to be produced 111 times outside New York.

Other articles enhancing our factual and critical coverage in *The Best Plays of 1970-71* are those of John Mortimer—playwright, critic and, by the way, busy Q.C.—who describes the London theater season; and of Ossia Trilling, our European editor, who annually provides a comprehensive critique of the theater on the European continent, as well as listings of Paris and London highlights, with the assistance of Heather Maisner.

Robert Schroeder evaluates still another year of off-off-Broadway fermentation and also provides a catalogue of the more important tributary New York production organizations and their major productions—a greater number than ever in this volume. This year, the borderline between "off" and "off off" was beginning to waver here and there. A few off-off shows that didn't wholly qualify technically for off status were nevertheless making it in the commercial theater with long runs, attracting commercial-theater audiences and showing up on commercial-theater lists of record like those of *Variety* and *Theater Information Bulletin*. We've included some of these borderline cases in our "Plays Produced off Broadway" list (while noting that they are exceptions), and if we have erred on the side of inclusion, so much the better. Our Broadway and off-Broadway listings are, as usual, a complete record of New York professional theater production for the twelve-month period covered by this volume.

Stanley Green, author of *Ring Bells! Sing Songs!,* a history of Broadway musicals in the 1930s, has prepared and expanded the section on cast replacements in long-run New York shows and on tour, so that it is an ever more comprehensive record of major acting assignments. Bernard Simon, editor of *Simon's Directory,* the definitive compendium of theatrical material, services and other data, has supplied the details of bus-and-truck-tour production and casting. Rue Canvin prepared the listings of theater publications and necrology and helped out with numerous other trouble-shooting assignments. Al Hirschfeld's drawings add the official "look" of the season to our *Best Plays* coverage, and we are most grateful to the distinguished designers of scenery and costumes who loaned us their sketches for publication in the photo section as a representation of the year's best work.

This volume is the result of careful and generous attention by Jonathan Dodd on behalf of the publisher, Dodd, Mead & Company; by the editor's wife in the long pre-publication weeks of checking programs and proofs; by Henry Hewes of the *Saturday Review,* Mimi Horowitz of *Playbill,* Hobe Morrison of *Variety,* Clara Rotter of the New York *Times,* Ralph Newman of the Drama Book Shop and literally hundreds of helpful and encouraging experts in theatrical production and communications: and by the many photographers in New York and elsewhere who devote their attention and talent to the stage, including Martha Swope, Van Williams, Ted Yaple, Bert Andrews, Zodiac Photographers, Bill Yoscary, Steve Schapiro, Alan B. Tepper, Nat Messik, Martha Holmes, William L. Smith, Fletcher Drake and Douglas Spillane.

Last and most, we extend our appreciation along with our most sincere admiration to the writers, actors and other stage artists who made a gift of courage and dedication and time and talent as they pressed on through still another New York theater season. We are thankful for the ten Best Plays and equally for the 150 which didn't quite or didn't by a long shot make the best list. Whatever their individual merits, together they succeed in maintaining our theater as a continuing and compelling adornment, even a necessity, of our life and times.

OTIS L. GUERNSEY Jr.

June 1, 1971

CONTENTS

Drawings by HIRSCHFELD

SUMMARIES
OF THE
SEASONS

○
○
○

THE SEASON IN NEW YORK

○ *By Otis L. Guernsey Jr.*
○
○

NOSTALGIA WAS A CONSPICUOUS INGREDIENT of the New York theater season of 1970-71. On the surface, many signs pointed in the same direction: backward. We entered 1970-71 from seasons in which *You Can't Take It With You* and *The Show-Off* had been big hits, and with *The Front Page* fresh in memory. The dominating musical hit for most of the winter was *No, No, Nanette,* a bit of fluff from the 1920s with Ruby Keeler as the star. Then along came its biggest rival on the musical scene with a title that at least sounded nostalgic—*Follies.*

Among straight plays, the Ibsen repertory starring Claire Bloom in *Hedda Gabler* and *A Doll's House* were two of the three hottest tickets in town, quoted at $40 a pair on the black market. Add to all of this the first English-language version of Molière's *The School for Wives* in Broadway history, the *Story Theater* episodes from Grimm's Fairy Tales and a British play about Queen Victoria's Empire soldiers in India, and it is all too easy to jump to the conclusion that this was a season of auld lang syne.

Certainly nostalgia made the scene in 1970-71, but it didn't manage to steal the scene or even a major part of it. The New York stage in 1970-71 wasn't a moth-eaten, warmed-over product of tired or aging artists; on the contrary, most of our leading playwrights took the year off, and most of the best new scripts represent new growth, a greening rather than a yellowing. *Sleuth* is a first play by Anthony Shaffer. Yes, *Conduct Unbecoming* is ostensibly a nostalgic collection of scarlet-uniformed pukka sahib characters, but its real subject is highly contemporaneous—the cruelty deep-rooted in man's nature—and it was its author's, Barry England's, first major professional stage production. *The Philanthropist* was Christopher Hampton's Broadway debut with a new play (his Ibsen adaptations preceded it by a few weeks). *The Gingerbread Lady* is the first Neil Simon play with a cutting edge as well as a sharp point. *The House of Blue Leaves* is John Guare's first full-length play. *Home* was David Storey's American theater debut. *Follies* may have a nostalgic title, but it is not so by any means; written by James Goldman and Stephen Sondheim, it is brilliant and innovative. *Steambath* may be Bruce Jay Friedman's second Best Play, but it's the first anywhere in which God has been personified as a Puerto Rican steam room attendant.

And lest anyone suppose that in a time of social and political unrest new

3

The 1970-71 Season on Broadway

REVIVALS (15)

Charley's Aunt
Othello
Lincoln Center Rep
The Good Woman of
  Setzuan
The Playboy of the
  Western World
An Enemy of the People
Antigone
Hay Fever
Ibsen Rep
A Doll's House
Hedda Gabler
Hamlet
No, No, Nanette
A Midsummer Night's
  Dream
The School for Wives
Johnny Johnson
Dance of Death

PLAYS (14)

Opium
Gandhi
Les Blancs
The Castro Complex
The Candyapple
Foreplay
THE GINGERBREAD
  LADY
Happy Birthday,
  Wanda June
Four on a Garden
And Miss Reardon Drinks
  a Little
Father's Day
All Over
Scratch
Lenny

MUSICALS (11)

The Rothschilds
Two by Two
The Me Nobody Knows
Lovely Ladies, Kind
  Gentlemen
Soon
Ari
Oh! Calcutta!
FOLLIES
70, Girls, 70
Frank Merriwell
Earl of Ruston

SPECIALTIES (4)

Bob and Ray—the Two
  and Only
Paul Sills
  Story Theater
  Metamorphoses
Emlyn Williams as Charles
  Dickens

HOLDOVER SHOWS
WHICH BECAME HITS
DURING 1970-71

Applause
Company

FOREIGN PLAYS
IN ENGLISH (8)

CONDUCT
  UNBECOMING
Not Now, Darling
SLEUTH
HOME
A Place Without Doors
Abelard & Heloise
THE PHILANTHROPIST
How the Other Half Loves

FOREIGN-LANGUAGE
PRODUCTIONS (4)

Light, Lively and Yiddish
The President's Daughter
Orlando Furioso
National Theaters of Japan

Categorized above are all the plays listed in the "Plays Produced on Broadway" section of this volume.
Plays listed in CAPITAL LETTERS have been designated Best Plays of 1970-71.
Plays listed in **bold face type** were classified as hits in *Variety's* annual list of hits and flops published June 9, 1971.
Plays listed in *italics* were still running June 1, 1971.

New York theater was an ostrich burying its head in detective stories, marital/ alcoholic tensions and beach ball production numbers, we point to the fact that one of our Best Play co-authors—Father Daniel Berrigan—is in jail this summer of 1971 for anti-war protest "crimes" including the actions described in the Berrigan-Saul Levitt dramatization *The Trial of the Catonsville Nine*. Still another Best Play author, Athol Fugard—whose *Boesman and Lena* is a piercing example of the human condition on the receiving end of racial preju- dice—is considered a troublemaker in his native South Africa, which denied him a passport to come to New York for rehearsals of his play in June.

Five of the plays on this year's best list were foreign scripts (four British, one South African). Equally, five—including the musical and three off-Broad- way plays—were American. The foreign scripts predominated on Broadway and caused it to outweigh off Broadway on the ten best list, six to four.

Yes, the number of shows produced on Broadway declined to 56 produc- tions of record during 1970-71 (see the one-page summary accompanying this report) from 68 last year, 76 the year before and 84 the year before that. This figure is all the more distressing because the new-American-play category suf- fered the greatest decline. There were only 14 new American straight play programs produced on Broadway this season along with the 11 musicals, com- pared with 21-14 last year, 24-12 the year before and 25-10 the year before that. What's more, or rather less, of these 14 new plays six were Limited Broadway productions under the new "middle theater" agreement (of which more anon), so that there were only eight—count 'em on your fingers—eight American plays produced in 1970-71 in the old Broadway sense of the word production.

Is "distressing" a strong enough word for this development? Wouldn't "alarming" be more accurate? I make bold to say no at this time. There is no great attentuation of playwriting—the 39 new American straight-play pro- grams produced off Broadway this season tell us clearly where our replacement playwrights are, and the New York audience continues to make hits out of the best material that comes to Broadway, even at today's prices. As long as there is a sizeable playwriting and audience potential, there is the condition for a healthy theater. Production statistics don't tell the whole story. Those who yearn for the good old 200-play seasons of the 1920s should go back to the old Burns Mantle *Best Plays* volumes and read some of the descriptions of the plots with third-act resolutions brought about by remorse, suicide, fortuitous heart attacks, etc. Why don't we have all these plays today? Maybe we do, on daytime TV.

Meanwhile, the problem of high production costs, consequently an ever- more-limiting ticket price increase, linked with the high-risk factor inherent in the power of the New York *Times* daily reviews, poisons the environment. Luckily, the art form itself is vigorously healthy, and it is surviving. And the theater as an institution is not just sitting there; it is working hard to solve its problems, which is another good sign. The new 7:30 p.m. curtain for the convenience of commuters and the "middle theater" arrangement for encour- aging producers are evidence of the effort the theater is making to change with the times and lifestyles of its patrons. In the meantime—as the figures distressingly show—many Broadway playwrights and producers are holding off, waiting for conditions to improve.

In 1970-71, the going rate for the best seat at a Broadway musical (fifth row center at *Follies,* say, on a Friday night) was $15, with musical matinees pegged anywhere from $7 to $9 a seat and the cheapest seat at midweek going for $5 or $6. For a straight play on Broadway $8.50 was the usual price for a top ticket; prices above $9 were in existence, but rare. Off Broadway, prices varied somewhat according to degree of popular appeal and even of subsidy, but a young man taking his Friday night date to an off-Broadway show would have been well advised to expect to pay $7.50 each for front row seats and $4 in the last row.

It's almost embarrassing to report, here in the midst of all the modern theater's difficulties, that the *Variety*-estimated total Broadway theater gross for 1970-71 was a healthy $54,941,023, an increase over last year's $53 million, possibly creeping back toward that record high of $59 million in 1967-68. Road productions of Broadway shows continued to do better than ever, grossing $50,079,434 compared to last year's $48 million (and thus giving Broadway its fourth $100-million-plus season in a row: $105 million plus, the highest on record). In the matter of playing weeks (if ten shows play ten weeks that's 100 playing weeks) Broadway registered 1,099 this season compared with 1,047 last year and 1,200-odd in the four previous years. The high 1970-71 gross is explained not by great activity, therefore, but by higher ticket prices and longer runs for the high-priced holdovers. The two longest-running musicals in Broadway history were both playing in 1970-71: *Hello, Dolly!* which set a new record of 2,844 performances before it closed, and *Fiddler on the Roof* which in turn would break *Dolly's* record in July, 1971.

Within the overall figures there were conspicuous individual triumphs and tragedies. The Alan Jay Lerner musical *Lolita, My Love* folded in Boston to the tune of a $900,000 loss, while *Dolly* was reporting a $9,000,000 net profit on its $350,000 investment and still counting. Some of the year's ongoing successes, according to *Variety* reports, were *Hair* ($2,098,000 on $150,000), *Coco* with Katharine Hepburn (which grossed $206,131 in a single week on the road, in Chicago), *Sleuth* ($160,314 net on $150,000 at season's end and still going strong), *Fiddler on the Roof* (about $7 million net on $350,000), *Man of La Mancha* ($5 million on $200,000) and *The Boys in the Band* ($580,000 net on $20,000 in New York, $120,000 on $70,000 in national companies). According to an estimate published by the theatrical financing division of the New York State attorney general's office, "average capitalization" for shows was $300,000 for Broadway and $47,000 off Broadway. But an "average" figure is meaningless in a situation in which a small-scale straight play can squeak onto Broadway for $110,000 whereas an unsuccessful *Lovely Ladies, Kind Gentlemen* could cost $600,000 to produce and lose more than that in an unprofitable tryout.

Personal triumph and tragedy abounded, too, within the overall statistics. An international pride of gifted actors and actresses imprinted their portraits on our memory of the season: Bob and Ray with their wonderful vignettes . . . Ruby Dee as Lena and James Earl Jones (followed by Zakes Mokae) as the burdened Boesman . . . . . Maureen Stapleton as an alcoholic, Betsy von Furstenberg as a rejected love object . . . Jeremy Clyde as a British subaltern and Donald Pickering as his nemesis . . . Cliff Gorman as Lenny Bruce . . . Mildred Dunnock as a murderess . . . Danny Kaye as Noah . . . Vincent Gardenia as a rejected male parent . . . Claire Bloom as Nora and Hedda . . . Anthony Quayle and Keith Baxter as cat and mouse . . . Harold Gould as a zookeeper . . . Ruby Keeler, Bobby Van, Helen Gallagher and Jack Gilford as themselves at their best in *No, No, Nanette* . . . Sir John and Sir Ralph joining forces in *Home* . . . Ditto Carol Channing and Sid Caesar in *Four on a Garden* . . . Brian Bedford's Arnolphe . . . Alec McCowen's philologist . . . Estelle Parsons, Julie Harris and Nancy Marchand as sisters . . . Phil Silvers as an unsuspecting husband . . . Alexis Smith as a neglected wife and Dorothy Collins as an errant one . . . Hal Linden as Rothschild vs. Keene Curtis as his titled opponents . . . Hamid Hamilton Camp as a crow in *Story Theater,* and as various gods in *Metamorphoses.*

As a matter of fact, if our season did not run a complete metaphysical gamut it at least touched both ends at A and Z with effective personifications onstage of both God and Satan. As we have noted, God appeared in *Steambath* in the form of an authoritative, awesome Puerto Rican, guardian of the anteroom to eternity, played by Hector Elizondo. Satan appeared in the form of a small-town Yankee lawyer as portrayed by Will Geer in Archibald MacLeish's short-lived *Scratch.* Both were highly successful, formidable portrayals—put them onto the same stage, and *there* would be a play.

The directors could point with pride to Peter Brook, who found a whole new way of doing *A Midsummer Night's Dream;* directors and producers to Harold Prince, who followed last season's pacesetting *Company* with 1970-71's pacesetting *Follies.* Among other producers who both dared and succeeded in this perilous interval were Morton Gottlieb and Helen Bonfils, David Merrick (of course), Hillard Elkins (who brought *Oh! Calcutta!* uptown into the respectable neighborhood of his *A Doll's House* and *Hedda Gabler*), Saint Subber, Alexander H. Cohen (who produced a dandy Tony Awards TV show in collaboration with his wife, Hildy Parks, and then went on to win the Critics Award with *Home*), Zev Bufman, T. Edward Hambleton (still astride his Phoenix as it rose from the ashes) and the remarkable Joseph Papp who now has five auditoriums in working order at the Public Theater on Lafayette Street, put on ten shows (not counting experimental stagings) this season and, when he fell as usual into financial difficulties, summoned the City of New York to his rescue.

Among those who fared less felicitously in 1970-71 were Joseph Kipness and Lawrence Kasha who produced and then immediately closed Oliver Hailey's *Father's Day* after only one performance, following an unfavorable *Times* review—though high praise soon began pouring in from other sources including major weeklies, and the continuing profits from *Applause* might well have influenced the producers to take a longer chance on *Father's Day* (to be fair, Mr. Kipness has since commented that maybe he could have used a little hindsight at the right moment). The Hailey play, about three divorced women meeting their ex-husbands for cocktails, has already been produced again, by the Washington, D.C. Theater Club, and will undoubtedly survive its New York experience. There were 11 other one-performance unfortunates on and off Broadway this season:—*The Nuns, Children in the Rain, My House Is Your House, The Immaculate Misconception, The Shrinking Bride, The Red White and Black, And Whose Little Boy Are You?, Gandhi, The Candyapple, Johnny Johnson* and *Frank Merriwell*—but no other such *succes d'estime* as *Father's Day*.

Another of the year's major playwriting disappointments was Edward Albee's *All Over,* an effort to dramatize the importance and significance of life in the contrasting situation of a death watch, with friends and family hovering around a dying man and indulging their own impulses and emotions. It seemed formless, almost purposeless, with the John Gielgud staging hurling the spoken observations out into empty, echoing space without any compression. It should be reported, however, that *All Over* attracted adherents who praised it highly; it was the first choice of Clive Barnes, Harold Clurman, William Glover and Edward S. Hipp for best play and of George Oppenheimer for best American play in the Drama Critics Circle voting.

The considerable Gallic fascination of Danielle Darrieux proved unable to carry the heavy weight of *Coco* after Katharine Hepburn left it to go on tour, and the gross dropped by $70,000 the first week the one star replaced the other in the Broadway cast. Shelley Winters made an unsuccessful foray into playwriting with three one-acters on a program entitled *One Night Stands of a Noisy Passenger,* romantic shipboard episodes. Judith Anderson tried playing Hamlet for a couple of special performances at Carnegie Hall, neither the first time the Prince of Denmark has been portrayed by an actress, nor the most effective. The Roundabout tried an off-Broadway *Hamlet* with an all-*male* cast including the actor playing Gertrude. Still another *Hamlet,* an amateur one mounted by the combined efforts of the Oxford and Cambridge drama societies under Jonathan Miller's direction, was brought over here for a brief tour.

Probably the year's most conspicuous individual waste of time and talent was Norman Wisdom's in a tasteless sex farce called *Not Now, Darling* dragged all the way from England even though we have a continuing domestic surplus of this commodity. Shirley Booth wrestled with Noel Coward stylization in a revival of *Hay Fever* and didn't quite manage a draw. After the success of *No, No, Nanette* it must have seemed a good idea to bring back a collection of Gershwin numbers as an off-Broadway musical, but *Do It Again!* failed to attract much attention.

Titles like *Foreplay* (one actor refused a role in this show because he would not play a nude homosexual love scene), *The Immaculate Misconception, Score* and *Stag Movie* found the theater still trying to sell sex in one form or another, more often than not in some fun-house-mirror distortion. It didn't succeed without an additionally supportive quality like the satirical viewpoint of *The Dirtiest Show in Town,* the innocence of the commune characters in *Touch* or the consuming emotions of a historical love affair in *Abelard & Heloise,* which included a nude love scene played by Keith Michell and Diana Rigg in the title roles.

There were two adroit manipulations of spacetime onstage, one of them in *Follies* (of which more later in this report) and another in the British comedy *How the Other Half Loves,* thoroughly Americanized on Broadway under the direction of Gene Saks, with Phil Silvers and Sandy Dennis as neighbors whose spouses are making it, not quite clandestinely enough. The spacetime trick is that a single living-room set serves for both households. The couples aren't aware of each other, of course; they are supposed to be in separate houses, but the audience sees them as two couples inhabiting the same room at the same time. The chef d'oeuvre of this play by Alan Ayckbourn, which happened to be the season's best light comedy fare, is a dinner party, or rather *two* dinner parties taking place at the same table with the same guests on two succeeding nights—one party a success and the other a disaster.

In the deep water where the currents run slow they were setting in the same directions as in recent seasons. 1970-71 continued to be a time of change, we hope of development, within the theater art. Audience tastes continued fragmenting into a group of audiences instead of a great monolith. There was one audience for *No, No, Nanette,* another for *Home,* another for the manic-depressive *Alice,* and so forth. More and more obviously, it seemed, the New York theater was dividing into two theaters like some unicellular creature overcome with an impulse to grow; not the Broadway/off Broadway separation, not straight/musical, not even square/far out, but a comfortable/uncomfortable theater division which crossed all other dividing lines; the comfortable theater as we have always known it existing side-by-side with the uncomfortable theater as it is bound to become, stretching our minds until it strains our imagination, stimulating our senses to the threshold of pain.

The "uncomfortable" new theater has abandoned the old rubber-tired ride in favor of roller-coaster speed and excitement. It continued to experiment with forms of theater that tear down that reassuring fourth wall and reach out for direct contact with the audience. As Walter Kerr put it in a Sunday *Times* article, "The audience has got to have more rehearsal time. It is being asked to do so many things these days." It was asked to touch elbow-tips as a symbolic taking-part in the affectionate activities of the off-Broadway musical *Kiss Now.* At *Commune,* it was asked to share the experience of collectivism by removing shoes upon entering the theater and creating a huge pile of footwear symbolizing community and togetherness, along with the inconvenience of trying to find your own shoes after the show. In John Guare's fine *The House of Blue Leaves* the characters kept telling the audience more about themselves than they would tell each other, but this was more in the nature of extended stage asides than a radical form of stagecraft.

New styles of playwriting were flashing like colored lights all over the city. *Follies* was breaking new ground, and so was Paul Sills's *Story Theater* and *Metamorphoses,* adapting myths and fairy tales to the stage with an unusual mix of narration, mime, a few words of dialogue and a musical background. This was a form of collaborative rather than literary theater with all the tricks of stagecraft used to punch up the ironies of fairyland: the sky really *is* falling as near as makes no difference, and the gods *will* use mortals as their playthings, and it is the lot of human kind to put up with its tortured destiny.

There were many variations on the subliminal style practised so expertly by Harold Pinter and Samuel Beckett and so assiduously by others, a style like a negative impression of a photo image, in which the actual words spoken are a counterpoint to the unspoken meaning, in which the words that count are the words between the lines bringing images to mind after the image expressed. David Storey's New York Drama Critics Circle best-play-award-winning *Home* was an example of this stylistic development, and also of the fact that it runs great risks of noncommunication between playwright and audience. Suppose the audience does *not* hear the words between the spoken lines, what then is left on the stage? The two Pinter one-acters *Landscape* and *Silence* revived this year by Lincoln Center Repertory at the Forum Theater are problematical in this respect, even though their author is a master of the medium. *Home, too,* is stylistically curious but perilously inarticulate with its insistent groping, and almost always missing hold, through the murky memories and cliche-ridden habits of speech of two old fogies who, granted, are brain-damaged by senility or some other tragedy of the psyche (Storey is never clear on this or any other point) but who, judging from the scraps of conversation left to them, would have bored the bejesus out of everybody on the best day they ever had. I am one of those to whom *Home* communicates very little except a modicum of compassion for the human condition; about as much, say, as an average segment of *Marcus Welby, M.D.* True, with Ralph Richardson and John Gielgud playing the two staring old men there is for a while the illusion that, yes, something important *is* being said between the lines and happening in the pauses, because of the brilliant inventiveness of character detail which these two perfectly polished, highly reflective artists bring to their roles. Obviously, there are some to whom *Home* communicates—New York's distinguished drama critics, for example, ranked it the best play of the year, bar none. Well, my choice for the best is *Follies,* or for one without music *Sleuth.* As for *Home,* I include it here among the Best Plays of 1970-71 for journalistic rather than esthetic reasons. I was not moved or even held by it, but as the Critics Award winner it deserves special consideration for a place in the running record as a Best Play selection.

In substance as well as in form and style the currents of the "uncomfortable" new theater were running the patterns of recent seasons. A sense of outrage is pushing most other subjective concepts off the stage; not invented outrage, but feedback of outrage plucked from life like an ugly *objet trouvé* and shaped by the playwright into recognizable dramatic form. Look at the subjects of some of season's most effective work. *Boesman and Lena* pictures human beings reduced to the status of swamp animals. *The House of Blue Leaves* is an oil-and-water mixture of intimate human agony and a black-comedy effort to murder the Pope. *Alice in Wonderland* becomes a horror tale in which the Dormouse at the Mad Hatter's tea party crams his mouth and smears his face with food in a stomach-turning image of degraded appetite. *Follies* gambols in the wreckage of exposed and shattered pretenses. *The Trial of the Catonsville Nine* is a polite protest in courtroom-scene form, but its outrage is—and there is no greater outrage anywhere among the louder theatrical noises of 1970-71—that the facts and events it represents onstage really happened. Even the Broadway theater's numero uno, Neil Simon, was writing in *The Gingerbread Lady* about an alcoholic nymphomaniac and her friends the homosexual and the narcississist.

Within all this artistic turmoil the "comfortable" theater continued to exist, however, and even to flourish. There is no shadow of a doubt that a large segment of the audience continued to demand and enjoy the likes of *Sleuth*, *No, No, Nanette* and the Ibsen repertory. Artistic changes and changing audience tastes are mirror images of each other, though there may be some chicken-and-egg debate about which comes first. The theater as we have known it and the theater as it is becoming are drifting farther and farther apart, because the old theater is anchored fast, and so are the tastes and styles of some audiences. The increasing gap is one of the factors that is creating the illusion of an era of nostalgia—the new theater is making old-style theater *seem* nostalgic.

Taking a wide-angle view of the season of 1970-71, we see that our versatile theater is capable of assimilating both *Sleuth* and *Home,* both *Follies* and *Nanette,* and of recruiting an audience for each; but while our new theater is developing and gaining strength, our old theater as of this date is still in the ascendancy, economically at least, and its partisans still in the majority. Coming out of *Follies,* I overheard an elderly dissatisfied customer, a square audience peg in the roundest hole of the season (and with a title like *Follies* they must get a lot of those), complain to his companion: "They haven't had *my* kind of musical since *Suzie Wong.*" Very well, sir, you're entitled to your opinion, your taste and your enjoyment, and you are still in the majority— but you are *not* entitled to pretend that the New York stage belongs in the grip of some sort of retrogressive impulse like nostalgia, rather than in the main stream of the steady, sometimes uncomfortable but inexorable progress toward the more exciting theater of the future.

Broadway

A "hit" in the true Broadway meaning of the word isn't just a show that is hard to get into on a Friday night in December, but a show which pays off its production cost (it may be easy to get into but become a "hit" by virtue of a big movie sale). In recent seasons, however, the term "hit" has been losing some of its magic. Very often, Broadway doesn't have either the first or the last word on a playscript, as it once did. Plays come to Broadway from previous regional or foreign production which has already established their position in world theater before New York ever sees them. A good script ignored on Broadway for some special reason may take on an illustrious life of its own in theaters around the world or in other media (remember that *The Lion in Winter* was a 92-performance flop by the old Broadway standards). So we make no special point in this resume, as we have in the past, about which 1970-71 offerings were "hits" and which were "flops" except that this information is recorded in the one-page summary of the Broadway season accompanying this article.

The ultimate insignia of New York professional theater achievement (we insist) is not the instant popularity of the hit list, but selection as a Best Play in these volumes. Such selection is made with the script itself as the primary consideration, for the reason (as we have stated in previous volumes) that the script is the very spirit of the theater, the soul in its physical body. The script is not only the quintessence of the present, it is most of what endures into the future.

So the Best Plays are the best scripts. As little weight as is humanly possible is given to comparative production values. The choice is made without any regard whatever to a play's type—musical, comedy or drama—or origin on or off Broadway, or popularity at the box office or lack of same.

The Best Plays of 1970-71 were the following, listed in the order in which they opened (an asterisk * with the performance number signifies that the play was still running on June 1, 1971):

Boesman and Lena
    (off Broadway; 205 perfs.)
Steambath
    (off Broadway; 128 perfs.)
Conduct Unbecoming
    (Broadway; 144 perfs.)
Sleuth
    (Broadway; 229* perfs.)
Home
    (Broadway; 110 perfs.)

The Gingerbread Lady
    (Broadway; 193 perfs.)
The Trial of the Catonsville Nine
    (off Broadway; 130* perfs.)
The House of Blue Leaves
    (off Broadway; 126* perfs.)
The Philanthropist
    (Broadway; 72 perfs.)
Follies
    (Broadway; 66* perfs.)

The best of the 1970-71 straight plays in the opinion of the *Best Plays* editor was *Sleuth;* not the most poetic *(Boesman and Lena),* nor the most significant *(The Trial of the Catonsville Nine),* nor the farthest out *(Blue Leaves),* but the best play; the best made, the most entertaining, the most effective use of the medium, and certainly not without meaningful overtones emanating from its suspense-story form. On the surface, *Sleuth* is a menacing confrontation between a snobbish intellectual (the detective story writer played by Anthony Quayle) and his wife's proletarian and persistent lover (a charmless but quick-witted young man played by Keith Baxter). The dangerous games they play with each other in jealous rivalry, trying with frightening masquerades to unman each other, are most cleverly conceived in Anthony Shaffer's script and executed by the cast. The author is the twin brother of the much-cited playwright Peter Shaffer—at least we've been led to believe so, but we must admit we've never seen them standing together side by side, and this Anthony Shaffer is a tricky fellow. Under the symbolical games-playing of his script (his first to be produced professionally) there's a much larger situation implied: a distinguished but crumbling old order being hastened to its grave by the importunities of a brash new breed. Carl Toms's set was one of the year's most interesting, and Clifford Williams's direction was a meticulous execution of Shaffer's ingenious plot.

Sleuth was the most conspicuous of many works by British authors which dominated the straight-play scene on Broadway this season. *Home* has been covered earlier in this report, as have *Abelard & Heloise* and *How the Other Half Loves,* which enhanced the Broadway scene. A third British play on the Best Plays list is *Conduct Unbecoming,* the London-New York playwriting debut of a new author, Barry England. His was a colorful tale of warped values among the British officer caste of an Indian regiment in Her Majesty Queen Victoria's Imperial army in the late 1800s. One of these proud, scarlet-uniformed, pig-sticking pukka sahibs commits a clandestine act of most ungentlemanly violence, and the play's problem is to discover who is the guilty party, in a formal midnight inquiry in the officers' mess. The performances of Donald Pickering as the spit-and-polish adjutant who conducts the trial, and of Jeremy Clyde as a tipsy, new-fledged subaltern who would like nothing better than to be kicked out of all this and sent home, were noteworthy vignettes within an ensemble of notable performances by the British cast. Again, there are the fibers of reality running through what is ostensibly a simple, theatrical tale of suspense in a highly colorful setting. Barry England's play is also a dramatic demonstration that callous and unspeakable violence against dumb animals can lead to callous and unspeakable violence against human beings and is in fact an extension of the same reprehensible impulse to shed blood—a truth that can't be overstressed, either in Imperial India or here and now in the land of the free and the home of the brave.

A fourth British play on the Best Plays list is Christopher Hampton's *The Philanthropist,* a provoking piece of work which opens by spattering blood all over the wall in the incident of a suicide, leaving the audience in shock and in quaking anticipation of what may happen next. Nothing similar ever does; what follows is the polite and deferential self-destruction of an intellectual who sells his manhood for a mess of good manners and an uncontrollable impulse to accommodate everybody. The script is a character study of a philology professor who has succumbed to early training and is now buried alive in attentive mannerisms and the literal meanings of words. Hungry women, egotistical authors, concerned friends revolve around him; he always pays attention but cannot understand. He is bound to destroy his romance, his friendships and himself, not with a bang but with impeccable courtesy, without raising his voice or using a word wrongly. Alec McCowen gave one of his perfectly detailed performances, sustaining every quirk and whimsy of this professor, and he was nobly assisted by Ed Zimmermann as a friend on the faculty, Penelope Wilton as a sexual virago, Jane Asher as a bewildered fiancee and Victor Spinetti as a novelist whose ego is sometimes battered but never broken.

Hampton's adaptations of Ibsen's *A Doll's House* and *Hedda Gabler* were hot tickets even before *The Philanthropist* arrived; again, a happy combination of playwriting and acting skill, with Claire Bloom in vibrant and career-expanding interpretations of Nora and Hedda. Hampton's *When Did You Last See My Mother?* off Broadway in 1967 was one of the first of the new-era dramas of sexual involvement. His is an established and expanding career which, with this first flowering of an original full-length play on Broadway, is in its early and most promising spring.

Turning to the American list, our choice for the best would have to be *Follies,* the musical that not only had widely varied effects on the fragmenting audience, but even fragmented its own enthusiasts. There are those who hated *Follies* and those who loved it; and even among those who loved it, there were some who shrugged off its book. I am not one of them. To me *Follies* was uniformly imaginative, varying never in quality but only in intensity from scene to scene. Remember that its title is *Follies,* not *The Follies;* it wasn't a girlie show, but a haunting and emotionally moving treatment of the foolishness and heartache of human pretenses. The theater itself being a kind of pretense, the appropriate setting for *Follies* was a bare, ruined stage where once the sweet showgirls sang, now littered with the rubble of plaster ornamentation, its half-demolished roof open to the sky. In this dead pretense of a theater there takes place a reunion of middle-aged former show people who are themselves the living results of the pretenses, the "follies," projected by their 20-year-old selves when they were young and playing on Broadway. These memory-images of youth were present onstage as actual people, in black and white to contrast with the grown-up characters, haunting the mature characters with their past selves. Seldom did the memory-figures make direct contact with their future selves; they were true to the strange principles of spacetime governing the relationship between memory and reality.

Each of the leading characters has been indulging his or her folly, brought to a critical state by this boozy reunion and finally and achingly exposed in an ironic "Loveland" sequence staged in Valentine lace, with beribboned showgirls and chorus boys in powdered periwigs. At the heart of the matter was the pervasively sad and increasing *felt* story of two promising marriages gone to seed: the stately Alexis Smith with a coldly successful politician-diplomat, John McMartin, and the wistful Dorothy Collins with a traveling man, Gene Nelson, who loves her but cheats on her. They and their problems are symbols, certainly, but the symbols are appropriate to our times and circumstances, and extremely empathetic. When all their follies have been mercilessly exposed in the ironies of "Loveland;" when the youth-figures have disappeared in the wings; when the party is over and the married couples are left alone to face one another in the dawn coming through the holes in the roof of Boris Aronson's magnificently haunted setting, a form of emotional catharsis has taken place, seldom if ever before experienced in the musical theater—less than tragic, perhaps, but strangely akin to the emotional mood of the burial scene in *Death of a Salesman.*

The very concept of *Follies* was partly responsible for its distinction as this season's best-of-bests, but it also inspired each of its contributors to a best effort, and therefore it took fire from many torches. The powerful book was written by James Goldman, author of *The Lion in Winter;* the lyrics and music had the stinging precision of the Stephen Sondheim we already admired in *Company* (*Follies* is *Company* once more, with feeling). Alexis Smith has matured into a star of the first magnitude who was equally capable of carrying the show with unbending poise, or of stopping it with a barelegged "Loveland" number called "The Saga of Lucy and Jessie." Yvonne De Carlo, Ethel Shutta and Mary McCarty also supplied show-stopping interludes. All of the foregoing adds up to a tribute to the producing-directing expertise of Harold Prince and Michael Bennett. Whoever did what at what moment, it was all done brilliantly for *Follies,* a pacesetting musical for our new theater.

The best American straight play of the Broadway season was Neil Simon's *The Gingerbread Lady,* a head taller (it seemed to me) in a group of interesting if imperfect works that included *Les Blancs, Happy Birthday, Wanda June, And Miss Reardon Drinks a Little, Scratch* and *All Over.* Simon, easily the most successful playwright of his generation—and deservedly so, on the basis of his comic insights—has moved slowly from the bright optimism of *Barefoot in the Park* toward the shadows of *Visitor from Mamaroneck* (in *Plaza Suite*) and *Last of the Red Hot Lovers,* finally to arrive at the dark corner of *The Gingerbread Lady.* The lady of Simon's title is an alcoholic nymphomaniac whose two well-meaning best friends—a homosexual actor and a narcissistic ex-beauty queen—keep stumbling against her, driving her ever closer to the brink of self-destruction. What saves her, and indeed the play itself, is the character's (and Simon's) sense of humor, her tendency to veer in the direction of irony rather than self-pity. Simon's wit rescued his indifferently-made play (which is somewhat distorted in construction, owing to extensive rewrites). Maureen Stapleton played the lady as the most perceptive spectator as well as the most involved participant in her own fight to survive, in the season's outstanding performance by an actress in a straight play. This fight was lost in the first tryout version of *The Gingerbread Lady,* which must have been as suspenseful as a stone's fall to the ground; in the final rewritten version it was beginning to be won, maybe, with the help of a daughter (played by Ayn Ruymen) who simply refuses to give up on her alcoholic mother. This script was a logical progression in Neil Simon's developing mood as a playwright, and, with a few flaws, a worthy addition to the Simon canon.

Paul Zindel too was contemplating lost ladies in his *And Miss Reardon Drinks a Little,* a study of three sisters, all school teachers, one married, one (not the drinker) more than a little neurotic, all somewhat alienated from reality, which finally invades their privacy in the form of the married couple downstairs. Zindel won the 1971 Pulitzer Prize for last season's off-Broadway *The Effect of Gamma Rays on Man-in-the-Moon Marigolds;* in his second produced play the passion is all there but the play not quite, though it enjoyed an extraordinarily capable ensemble of performances including those of Estelle Parsons (as the drinking Miss Reardon), Julie Harris as the neurotic and Nancy Marchand as the married one, the take-charge type.

The late Lorraine Hansberry's work-in-progress *Les Blancs,* with text prepared for production by her husband Robert Nemiroff, was a dramatized textbook of the black dilemma. It centered on James Earl Jones as a completely Western-civilized, citified African who visits his native village to attend his father's funeral and resists letting himself be caught up in the local web of revolt and violence. He wants nothing so much as to get back to his white wife in respectable London—possibly with some reason, because the people in his native village, white and black, tend to be attitude symbols. Another of the season's noteworthy serious efforts was Archibald MacLeish's *Scratch,* a play suggested by Stephen Vincent Benet's story *The Devil and Daniel Webster,* in which Webster (Patrick Magee) confronts Old Scratch (Will Geer) in a mock-trial contest for the forsworn soul of a Yankee farmer. In the first act, MacLeish the poet faces us with the fact of an America in which even a good man like Daniel Webster might yield to the devilish temptation to preserve the Union at the price of Liberty—individual liberty, for example, by supporting the Fugitive Slave Act to appease the Southern voters. This was an image of potentially tremendous impact and might have been worth exploring more deeply than the final act, a colorful but conventionally theatrical trial scene, was capable of doing.

Another slice of Americana on Broadway was *Lenny,* a dramatic celebration of the life and works of the controversial night club comedian Lenny Bruce, who was willing to use any means up to and beyond obscenity, blasphemy, etc., to expose the hypocrisies of the late 1950s and early 1960s, when he made himself equally conspicuous on stages and in the courts. This show was not so much of a documentary as a poetic idealization, with Lenny presented as a champion of freedom of speech (or, rather, the victim of our sometimes fear and hatred of really free speech), much sinned against and scarcely sinning at all. I'm in no position to judge its veracity; I can only say that Julian Barry's script, which seemed to be made in large part out of Bruce's night club monologues, aroused my interest in the character without letting me believe in him as a personification of ruthless honesty. What I did believe in thoroughly, thanks to a memorable performance by Cliff Gorman as Lenny, was a vital personality, a racing engine impossible to control and guaranteed to self-destruct. Gorman played the camping Emory in *The Boys in the Band* to perfection on stage and screen; as Lenny he pulled out all the stops, including even a little camp, of a highly sophisticated and powerful acting talent, and the music came out loud and clear from one end of the scale to the other. The 1970-71 drama season made a star out of Cliff Gorman, and that may prove to be one of its outstanding contributions to theater history.

On the lighter side, Kurt Vonnegut Jr.'s playwriting debut with *Happy Birthday, Wanda June* was an auspicious one. With Kevin McCarthy as a modern Hemingway-like Ulysses who returns home to find his Penelope married to a doctor, the play is a put-down of adventurous hero types. Many of its scenes and character vignettes were very funny in broad farcical style, notably the performance of William Hickey as the mighty hunter's side-kick, the somewhat simple minded "Looseleaf Harper." Another long reach for farce was made in *Four on a Garden,* four man-and-woman comedy skits credited to Abe Burrows, with Carol Channing and Sid Caesar in good form as the lady and the house painter, the old couple trying a last fling, etc.

Happy Birthday, Wanda June was one of several shows transferred to or produced on Broadway under the new agreement covering smaller playhouses in the Times Square area. It used to be referred to as a "Middle Theater" arrangement. Now it's "Limited Gross Broadway Theater Agreement"—we call it "Limited Broadway" in this volume—enabling shows in playhouses near Broadway to come in with union concessions and generally lowered production costs, in order to minimize the risk of and thereby encourage experimentation. *A Place Without Doors,* the Barbara Bray translation of Marguerite Duras's study of a murderess, was brought from its American premiere at the Long Wharf in New Haven to a Limited Broadway house. With Mildred Dunnock as an interrogated prisoner explaining but never elucidating the reasons that drove her to kill, this was exactly the kind of theater novelty that the Limited Broadway arrangement was designed to encourage. (The French version of this play, *L'Amante Anglaise,* was produced off Broadway this year by the visiting Tréteau de Paris, with Madeleine Renaud as the murderess and Claude Dauphin as the interrogator.

Except for this French play and *Wanda June,* however, the new arrangement produced nothing but disappointments: the short-lived *Opium* based on Jean Cocteau's diaries, *Gandhi* with Jack MacGowran in episodes of the great Indian leader's life and career, *The Castro Complex* about sex fetishism, *The Candyapple* with a comedy of Roman Catholic attitudes and *Soon,* a rock musical romance. The Limited Broadway deal was designed to apply not only to the middle-sized theaters between 299 (off Broadway) and 600 (Broadway) capacity; it aimed also to encourage Limited Broadway production in large houses with auditoriums roped off to limit the seating and consequently the potential weekly gross. No show took advantage of this part of the opportunity in 1970-71, but it is expected that Limited Broadway production in regular Broadway houses will get under way next year. The one-performance musical *Frank Merriwell, or Honor Challenged,* based on the Burt L. Standish stories, was widely reported as a Limited Broadway show, but it was not—it opened under a regular Broadway contract.

For most of the season the list of new Broadway musicals was dominated, not by *Follies* which came along late, but by two hefty early-season shows, *Two by Two* and *The Rothschilds.* Top individual efforts in *Two by Two* (the story of Noah adapted by Peter Stone from Clifford Odets's play *The Flowering Peach*) included Richard Rodgers's score, with Martin Charnin's lyrics suiting the Rodgers musical style; and Danny Kaye's Noah who at the beginning of the play is too old to do God's will but shakes off his years to become spry enough to command his unwilling family to their fateful voyage. This was an outstanding performance by a skilled and experienced musical comedy star (I am speaking of the Kaye performance at the beginning of the show's run, before he suffered a muscle injury and decided to adapt his role and indeed the whole show to his infirmity, abandoning much of Noah and filling in with more and more straight Danny Kaye in his new performance). David Hays's setting of weathered boards and light projections provided a rugged Old Testament atmosphere for the story of a famous Jewish family in a historically tough spot.

The same might be said for *The Rothschilds,* which traced the fortunes of the banking family from the ghettos to the courts of Europe. Rothschilds are treated with good humor and affection in Sherman Yellen's light-hearted book, to which Keene Curtis gave strong support in performing all the smiling anti-Rothschild villains from the local nobleman to Prince Metternich. Another musical with a strong book was *70, Girls, 70* about a group of enterprising senior citizens—led by Mildred Natwick, Hans Conried and Lillian Roth—who steal for profit and fun, suggested by the story of the film *Make Mine Mink,* in a stage version prepared by Fred Ebb, Norman L. Martin and Joseph Masteroff.

Two off-Broadway musical hits moved uptown and became part of the Broadway scene: *The Me Nobody Knows,* the charming show based on the writings of underprivileged city children, and the fabulous *Oh! Calcutta!* (and *You're a Good Man Charlie Brown* reappeared on Broadway in June as a new season began). Leon Uris's *Ari,* an effort to make a musical out of episodes in his novel *Exodus* about Jewish refugees struggling to reach the promised land of Israel, was short-lived. So was *Earl of Ruston,* a rock musical by C.C. Courtney and Peter Link (author of last season's excellent *Salvation*) and C.C.'s brother Ragan Courtney. This show was an arrogantly daring effort to push out the frontiers of the musical stage with the re-enactment of the life of a small-town misfit, the Courtneys' cousin Earl Woods, who died young after a hapless life spent partly in mental institutions. Earl's mother, Leecy R. Woods Moore, was actually present onstage to comment about her son. Earl himself was played by the Courtney brothers, two actors playing one character who communicates with himself a lot. It was an imaginative, stimulating musical which, finally and unhappily, wasn't able to put over its leading character as a tragic figure or even as a compelling *raison d'être* for all this talented commotion. The Courtneys and Link will certainly be heard from again in future, and those who saw one of the five performances of *Earl of Ruston* can congratulate themselves on having witnessed a stage in the progress of these gifted young musical authors.

Specialty shows supplied more than their ordinary share of flavor to the Broadway season. *Bob and Ray—the Two and Only* brought Bob Elliott and Ray Goulding (TV and radio comedians and satirists whose work has included the popular cartoon ad characters Bert and Harry Piel) in a collection of their tongue-in-cheek interviews and characterizations. There was *Story Theater,* discussed earlier in this report. Emlyn Williams stopped off briefly at Lincoln Center's Alice Tully Hall with his famous impersonation of Charles Dickens, in an evening of excerpts from that author's works. Among foreign-language productions, the Italian romantic adventure extravaganza *Orlando Furicso* was an early-autumn arrival on the entertainment scene (classify it Broadway, off Broadway or what you will—it was produced in a huge air-bubble auditorium raised for the occasion in Bryant Park). The production list also included two Yiddish-language musicals, Ben Bonus's *Light, Lively and Yiddish* (a romantic contrast between the folk of the old and new worlds) and the sentimental romance *The President's Daughter*. And the National Theaters of Japan gave three performances each of Noh and Kyogen plays, demonstrating these forms of traditional Japanese theater to New York audiences at Carnegie Hall.

So it was a season in which the exceptional creative achievement like *Follies,* Peter Brook's *Dream* or Cliff Gorman's Lenny stood out from a dwindling but still vital and varied supply of full-scale legitimate stage production. Good or otherwise for the theater as an institution, it was of course a good year for many individual artists, and here is where we list the *Best Plays* choices for the bests among the individual work of 1970-71. In the category of so-called "supporting" performances, clear distinctions cannot possibly be made on the basis of official billing, in which an actor's agent may bargain him into a contract as a "star" following the title (which is not true star billing) or as an "also starring" star, or any of the other typographical gimmicks. Here in these volumes we divide the acting into "primary" and "secondary" roles, a primary role being one which carries a major responsibility for the play; *one which might some day cause a star to inspire a revival in order to appear in that role.* All others, be they vivid as Mercutio, are classed by us as secondary.

Here, then, are the *Best Plays* bests of 1970-71:

PLAYS

BEST PLAY: *Sleuth* by Anthony Shaffer
ACTOR IN A PRIMARY ROLE: Cliff Gorman as Lenny Bruce in *Lenny*
ACTRESS IN A PRIMARY ROLE: Maureen Stapleton as Evy Meara in *The Gingerbread Lady*
ACTOR IN A SECONDARY ROLE: Hamid Hamilton Camp as various characters in *Story Theater* and *Metamorphoses*
ACTRESS IN A SECONDARY ROLE: Estelle Parsons as Catherine Reardon in *And Miss Reardon Drinks a Little*
DIRECTOR: Peter Brook for *A Midsummer Night's Dream*
SCENERY: Sally Jacobs for *A Midsummer Night's Dream*
COSTUMES: Stephanie Kline for *Story Theater*

MUSICALS

BEST MUSICAL: *Follies* by James Goldman
ACTOR IN A PRIMARY ROLE: Danny Kaye as Noah in *Two by Two*
ACTRESS IN A PRIMARY ROLE: Alexis Smith as Phyllis Stone in *Follies*
ACTOR IN A SECONDARY ROLE: Keene Curtis as various characters in *The Rothschilds*

ACTRESS IN A SECONDARY ROLE: Dorothy Collins as Sally Durant Plummer
in *Follies*
DIRECTOR: Harold Prince and Michael Bennett for *Follies*
SCENERY: Boris Aronson for *Follies*
COSTUMES: Florence Klotz for *Follies*
CHOREOGRAPHY: Donald Saddler for *No, No, Nanette*
LYRICS: Stephen Sondheim for *Follies*
MUSIC: Richard Rodgers for *Two by Two*

Revivals on and off Broadway

This season was a vintage year for revivals. The number was somewhere
near average—15 on Broadway and 20 off—but here and there among them
the excitement ran exceptionally high. We mentioned earlier in this report
that the Christopher Hampton-adapted Ibsen repertory starring Claire Bloom
ran with no moss on the old scripts but plenty of ice on the Friday night
tickets. An even bigger hit—the hit of the Broadway season, in fact—was the
revival of the Otto Harbach-Frank Mandel-Vincent Youmans *No, No, Nanette*
with its hit tunes "Tea for Two" and "I Want to Be Happy" and its airy book
about a Bible manufacturer who can't resist offering aid and comfort to lonely
young girls—platonic comfort, that is. There's nothing about *Nanette* to suggest that it might make a special appeal to audiences of the 1970s, or strike a
particular spark of fond recollection. The nostalgia in this show was superimposed on the material rather than evoked from it. Charming Ruby Keeler was
recruited to smile engagingly in scene after scene as Nanette's mother, and
to stop the show in Act I with a selection of tap routines that summoned up
innocent Saturday afternoon visions of *Forty-second Street*. Patsy Kelly was
cast as a maid locked in battle with her hated enemies the vacuum cleaner
and the doorbell. Raoul Pene du Bois's costumes and scenery were exactly as
we could hope the 1920s looked, as affectionate a caricature as were Donald
Saddler's dances and Busby Berkeley's production numbers. Burt Shevelove
adapted and directed *Nanette* for flair rather than condescending camp, so
that the sharper performances like those of Bobby Van and Helen Gallagher
blended well with the smoother, more nostalgic ones of Miss Keeler and Jack
Gilford as the benevolent Bible man. *Nanette* was a supremely skillful coup
of theater which inspired the loose talk about a "nostalgic" trend which others
will undoubtedly try to imitate before long.

One of the season's most contemporary works of stage art was based on
one of the theater's most glowingly patinaed treasures—William Shakespeare's
A Midsummer Night's Dream as produced by the Royal Shakespeare Company and directed by Peter Brook, brought to Broadway for a limited engagement (thank you, David Merrick Arts Foundation). The contemporary theater, many believe, is moving away from a playwrights' and toward a directors'
medium, and certainly this revival is one of the shows that could support that
belief. As presented with unfailing directorial imagination, the play seemed

almost brand new; the fairy tale was no longer etherial, no more sprites with gauzy wings, but an intensely *physical* magic. Against Sally Jacobs's glaring white three-walled setting, the actors in their orange and purple robes were psychedelically present, as though dressed in day-glo. They moved three-dimensionally, climbing ladders and swinging from trapezes. They clung and twined in acts of love at ground level; here, love is a physical enchantment, and Titania's infatuation for Bottom is based entirely on her imagination of his sexual prowess, so that their relationship takes on the flavor of a joke about the traveling salesman and the farmer's daughter. Brook's version of *A Midsummer Night's Dream* had the quality of a chemical trip rather than a poetic one. Done in this way it was still great theater—and you needed the comedy of Bottom and his joiners and bricklayers doing their silly play about Pyramus and Thisbe in the court scene at the end, to bring you back to earth, to the proportions of reality. Brook and the company chose to interrelate the court and forest scenes of this *Dream* by means of dual casting, i.e.: the actor and actress playing Theseus and Hippolyta also played Oberon and Titania. This helped integrate the play and corresponded neatly with the ensemble style of the British acting company, who made many contributions to the show but never tried to preempt it. This was a director's triumph and one of the Broadway season's major entertainments.

Another example of the high level of excellence attained by many of the season's revivals was the Tony Award for best actor to Brian Bedford as Arnolphe in the Phoenix's production of Molière's *The School for Wives*. This is the role played in New York by Louis Jouvet in a previous Broadway production, in French, in 1951. The *Best Plays* record lists no previous New York production in English, but Lewis Harmon remembers an English-language production of *The School for Wives* off Broadway more than 20 years ago, before the complete off-Broadway production schedule became a matter of record in these volumes.

Shakespeare was well represented with *A Midsummer Night's Dream;* three *Hamlets;* the American Shakespeare Festival *Othello* with Moses Gunn, which visited Broadway briefly; a popular off-Broadway *Macbeth* rearranged by the director, Dino DeFilippi, so that the action took place as though in Macbeth's imagination—he didn't take direct part in the action; and, of course, the perennially wonderful Shakespeare-in-Central-Park mounted under Joseph Papp's eagle eye. This year he gave us a three-play "Wars of the Roses" consisting of *Henry VI* in two full-length parts followed by *Richard III* on the third evening, tracing the violent quarrels of the York and Lancaster factions through the bloody murders to the "glorious summer" of the first Tudor, Henry VII. As an act of special dedication, Papp put on the three plays together, continuously, for one all-night performance beginning at dusk on Saturday, June 27 and running till dawn Sunday, June 28. Three thousand enthralled New Yorkers packed the Delacorte Theater and heard, to their added delight, Richmond's question at Bosworth Field "How far into the morning is it, lords?" answered "Upon the stroke of four" at exactly 4:03 a.m. When the three-play marathon ended in the dawn's early light, the audience gave the players a ten-minute standing ovation. Later on in the season, Papp's indoor New York Shakespeare Festival organization at the Public Theater scored with a very well-received revival of Pirandello's *Trelawny of the "Wells"*.

Lincoln Center Repertory enjoyed a season of distinguished revivals in the large Vivian Beaumont Theater. Productions were skilled, and the plays chosen were tough-fibered: Brecht's *The Good Woman of Setzuan,* Synge's *The Playboy of the Western World* (marking the centennial of the author's birth), Sophocles's *Antigone* and Arthur Miller's adaptation of Ibsen's *An Enemy of the People*—the only American work, alas. On its smaller Forum Theater stage, Lincoln Center Rep revived Harold Pinter's *The Birthday Party, Landscape* and *Silence* and Paul Shyre's version of Sean O'Casey's autobiographical *Pictures in the Hallway* on a schedule which also brought two new playscripts, of which more later.

Off-Broadway revivals of unusual interest included the Roundabout Theater's *Uncle Vanya* and *She Stoops to Conquer* as well as its previously mentioned all-male *Hamlet*. Beckett's *Waiting for Godot* was expertly revived under Alan Schneider's direction. Eugene O'Neill's *Long Day's Journey Into Night* was one of the hits of the off-Broadway season as staged by Arvin Brown and acted by Robert Ryan, Geraldine Fitzgerald, Stacy Keach and James Naughton and Paddy Croft. Dale Wasserman's *One Flew Over the Cuckoo's Nest,* about a patient resisting but finally overwhelmed by the terrors and cruelties of a mental institution—played on Broadway by Kirk Douglas in 1963 and now off Broadway by William Devane—was successfully revived in a partially rewritten version. And both *Dames at Sea* and *Colette* played return engagements off Broadway this season, the former in cabaret at Plaza 9. *Woyzeck* appeared, too, but only briefly and without much distinction.

On Broadway, the revival season began with a limp *Charley's Aunt* and ended with short-lived efforts to bring back *Johnny Johnson* and *The Dance of Death*. In between, however, was a banner season for the old scripts. It was easy to fall into the habit of forgetting all about Elizabethans and remembering Peter Brook's *A Midsummer Night's Dream* as one of the most exciting new plays of the season. And I was asked several times, "Are you going to pick *No, No, Nanette* as one of the ten best?" (Being a revival, it isn't eligible.) These productions were more than just museum-piece curiosities. Like the living theater that created them originally, they retain that spark of eternal fire ready to flame for the artist who learns their secret.

New off Broadway

Where did all the American plays go? Well, many of them went off Broadway in search of lower production costs and more venturesome audiences. The production area which is termed "off Broadway"—the Equity-cast show in a 299-seat mid-Manhattan theater which sets a regular schedule of performances and offers itself to public scrutiny and critical review—has grown stead-

The 1970-71 Season off Broadway

PLAYS (39)

The Cage
The Dirtiest Show in Town
STEAMBATH
The Emerald Slippers
Three by Ferlinghetti
Children in the Rain
Public Theater
The Happiness Cage
Subject to Fits
Underground
Candide
The Basic Training of Pavlo Hummel
Happy Birthday, Wanda June
Alice in Wonderland
My House Is Your House
American Place
Sunday Dinner
The Carpenters
Pinkville
Roundabout
Tug of War
Chas. Abbott & Son
The Immaculate Misconception
Score
A Dream Out of Time
Negro Ensemble
Perry's Mission & Rosalee Pritchett
Ride a Black Horse
Commune
One Night Stands of a Noisy Passenger
The Shrinking Bride
In New England Winter

SPECIALTIES (7)

MacGowran in the Works of Beckett
Here Are Ladies
Baird Marionettes
Whistling Wizard & Sultan of Tuffet
Ali Baba
Winnie the Pooh
Theater of the Balustrade
Tarot

MUSICALS (13)

Whispers on the Wind
Blood
Sensations
Touch
Ododo
Stag Movie
The Survival of St. Joan
Look Where I'm At
A Day in the Life of Just About Everyone
The Red White and Black
Kiss Now
The Ballad of Johnny Pot
Godspell

Istanboul
Scenes From American Life
THE TRIAL OF THE CATONSVILLE NINE
THE HOUSE OF BLUE LEAVES
Acrobats & Line
Things That Almost Happen
Behold! Cometh the Vanderkellans
The Olathe Response
King Heroin
And Whose Little Boy Are You?
Any Resemblance to Persons Living or Dead . . .

REVIVALS (20)

N.Y. Shakespeare
The Chronicles of King Henry VI, Part 1
The Chronicles of King Henry VI, Part 2
Richard III
Sambo (mobile)
Dames at Sea
Trelawny of the "Wells"
Colette
Roundabout
Hamlet
Uncle Vanya
She Stoops to Conquer
Hamlet (Ox-Camb)
Macbeth
Waiting for Godot
Forum Theater
The Birthday Party
Landscape & Silence
Pictures in the Hallway

One Flew Over the Cuckoo's Nest
Long Day's Journey Into Night
The Homecoming
Woyzeck

REVUES (6)

To Be or Not to Be—What Kind of a Question Is That?
Earthlight
Cooler Near the Lake
Do It Again!
The Proposition
Six

FOREIGN PLAYS IN ENGLISH (6)

The Nuns
BOESMAN AND LENA
Slag
Saved
The Dream on Monkey Mountain
Ac/Dc

FOREIGN-LANGUAGE PRODUCTIONS (4)

Golden Bat
Die Brücke
Amphitryon
Kurve & Kleinbürger-hochzeit
L'Amante Anglaise

Categorized above are all the plays listed in the "Plays Produced off Broadway" section of this volume.
Plays listed in CAPITAL letters have been designated Best Plays of 1970-71.
Plays listed in *italics* were still running June 1, 1971.

ily in importance and expertise over the last two decades until, with the advent of international hits like *You're a Good Man Charlie Brown* or *The Boys in the Band,* and the increase in the price of a hit ticket to $10, it can no longer be classified merely as some sort of junior Broadway. Its production costs often rise above the "experimental" level—loft troupes and performance groups have taken over that function in New York. Off Broadway is now moderately professional, generally intimate theater whose authors and audiences tend to be younger and more flexible than those at the bigger playhouses uptown, but no less enthusiastic. They demand an extra dimension of imagination in their entertainment, and of themselves as witnesses to it, and they will tolerate such extravagances as audience participation, sulphurous language and explicit sex scenes.

Where have all the new American plays gone? They have gone off Broadway, where the action is, where Charles Gordone's *No Place to Be Somebody* and Paul Zindel's *The Effect of Gamma Rays on Man-in-the-Moon Marigolds* have carried away the Pulitzer Prize two years in a row. If American playwrights were content to spend their efforts on works for the "comfortable" theater, they'd be on Broadway with the British playwrights—but they're not, they're writing new-theater scripts which get a hearing more readily in the smaller playhouses. There are 39 new American play programs in the "Plays Produced off Broadway" list for 1970-71 (see the one-page summary accompanying this article). This is a lot of action; somewhat less than last year's flood of 53 (costs are going up and risks are slightly higher these days off Broadway, too) but still an impressive volume of creative effort.

The quality results are also comparable to last year: four Best Plays off Broadway in both seasons, three American and one foreign. The foreign script on the 1970-71 best list was Athol Fugard's haunting *Boesman and Lena,* about a "hotnot" couple (in Apartheid parlance this identifies their degree of blackness) of shack dwellers chivvied from place to place at the whim of the white *baas,* living not only *on* the white man's cast-off trash but *as* the white man's cast-off trash, in a lean-to in the mud of a river estuary. Lena is weary and resentful, Boesman weary and frightened, brought to almost unbearable reality in the performance of Ruby Dee as Lena and first James Earl Jones, then Zakes Mokae, as Boesman. Fugard, a white South African playwright, director and actor, who established an international reputation a few seasons ago with *The Blood Knot,* and who has been active in black theater enterprises in his own country, was denied a passport by South Africa to come to New York to attend rehearsals of his play because, in Fugard's words, "The government thinks I'm a potential source of trouble"—an exquisite form of trouble, if *Boesman and Lena* is a sample.

The first of the season's American off-Broadway Best Plays to open was *Steambath,* a dark comedy by Bruce Jay Friedman, author of the previous Best Play *Scuba Duba.* In his new script Friedman is joking about life from the point of view of death. His protagonist is a young man (played by Anthony Perkins, who also directed) who finds himself dead and waiting for eternity in a sort of anteroom which in Friedman's imagination takes the form of a steam room attended by a nervously energetic Puerto Rican who is God. Now, God is a busy man who has his floors to mop, his towels to wash and his auto crashes on the freeways to supervise; but he takes time to listen to his customers' strange tales before he hustles them out of the door that leads to forever. The play is about the young man's protests that he must go back, his life is unfinished (in reality, there was nothing in his life worth going back to, and he will realize this in the next second or two after the curtain comes down). Hector Elizondo's personification of God was one of the season's notable acting achievements, and Friedman's saw-toothed edge of humor was as sharp as ever, in a painfully funny show.

John Guare's *The House of Blue Leaves* was another outstanding new script, also a black comedy, also toying with religious imagery, but somewhat more bitter than Friedman's. Guare, like Friedman, senses life as a comedy even in its most painful or exalted moments. His play is about a middle-aged sufferer, a zookeeper whose mentally disturbed wife seems like part of his menagerie, who dreams of escape from his piteous niche in Queens by means of writing and selling songs to a friend who makes movies in Hollywood. The play takes place on the day of Pope Paul's visit to New York in 1965, which through Guare's eyes becomes an analogy of muddled values, with nun and starlet equally the object of respect and scorn, and with suffering humanity— exemplified by the poor mind-wandering wife—the least of anybody's worries. The zookeeper becomes a figure of compelling sympathy as played by Harold Gould, a brave swimmer drowning in one of the Gowanus Canals of life. His girl friend in the apartment below, whose idea of hell is Sandra Dee losing her hair curlers the night before her first movie, is a vivid caricature of *Reader's Digest* values. The characters in *The House of Blue Leaves* often feel the need to speak to the audience directly; and in many other ways, too, this guaranteed sugar-free script is one for our new theater. It burns as it goes down like a good shot of rye whisky, and it richly deserved its New York Drama Critics Circle citation as the year's best American play.

The fourth of the off-Broadway Best Plays, the third by American authors, was *The Trial of the Catonsville Nine,* written by one of the nine who lived it, Father Daniel Berrigan, and adapted for New York production by Saul Levitt. It was constructed as a poetic condensation of the trial of the Berrigan brothers, both of them Roman Catholic priests, and seven others for seizing handfuls of draft board files and burning them in the public square at Catonsville, Md., on May 17, 1968, as an act of protest against the Vietnam war (the defendants were found guilty and sentenced to two to three and one-half years' imprisonment). As the judge and lawyers go about their business and the defendants state their motives and justifications and protest an oppressive United States presence not only in Vietnam but in such other parts of the world as Guatemala, the play grew on you like a fine painting of an historical event. Father Daniel Berrigan is an often-published poet, and the script quotes many passages from his works. The play had scant physical action but increasing sympathy for everyone caught in this moral and legal cobweb. The Berrigans (impersonated by Ed Flanders and Michael Kane) and their friends don't want to go to jail, but they want us all to understand fully that dropping napalm on children is a horribly and unmitigatedly evil act. The Federal judge (William Schallert) doesn't want these Christian soldiers punished in a real prison for their symbolic "crime"; but under the law he has no option to exercise his personal sympathies. Neither does the prosecuting attorney (Davis Roberts), a black man in this re-enactment as at the real trial; he bears the defendants no malice, but he never compromises with the facts of his open-and-shut case. The jury too is charged to make its decision on the basis of law, not sympathy. Staged with scrupulous attention to clear communication by Gordon Davidson of the Mark Taper Forum in Los Angeles, where the play was first performed, *The Trial of the Catonsville Nine* was a combination documentary play and practical demonstration of our present political and moral dilemma. The Berrigans did what they had to do; the Court did what it had to do, and we the jury are witness to events over which we have no direct control but for which we too are called to account (and after the end of the play we watched a stark black and white newsreel of the events at Catonsville, leaving the audience with an image of the pitiful reality of the protest). Staged in a church which huddles near the travertine ostentation of the Lincoln Center complex (and transferred from there to Broadway just after season's end), here was a piece of highly effective theater for our time, as relevant as a body count.

Turning from the sublime to the frequently ridiculous, off Broadway is where they began taking it all off a few seasons ago; where *Oh! Calcutta!* first flourished; where yeasty four-syllable obscenities became household words; where the Marquis de Sade became the most-trammeled source for theatrical material since Holinshed. Off Broadway was beginning to emerge from this blue period in 1970-71, but some vestiges remained. Tom Eyen's facetiously-titled *The Dirtiest Show in Town* facetiously represented itself to be about pollution. It was a satire on various conspicuous aberrations of our society including both pollution and sex deviation, a collection of pungent caricatures flawed by witless efforts to represent naked sex acts explicitly on the stage. Naked sex acts invariably shatter whatever illusion a show has been able to create; there are no longer any characters or play up there on the stage, merely bare actors in an exhibition for voyeurs. Stripped (if you will excuse the expression) of its extraneous orgies, *The Dirtiest Show in Town* would have been and indeed was one of the season's most flavorful evenings of episodic theater. What critics were beginning to call "the obligatory naked scene" was still in evidence this season, on Broadway and off (for example, there was a shower bath scene with a pretty blonde in *Steambath* which had no roots in the play and had no effect on it one way or the other), but no show since *Oh! Calcutta!* has succeeded on this one quality alone.

Each of the organized off-Broadway producing groups made its special mark, with Joseph Papp's New York Shakespeare Festival Public theater the standout in both quantity and quality. Papp was living precariously and energetically in 1970-71, perhaps a little more so that usual in both categories. The season had scarcely begun when he let it be known that he needed extra financial help to complete his season of summer Shakespeare in Central Park. No sooner did he get past this crisis than an even greater one loomed: construction costs of creating several theaters in the former Astor Library building on Lafayette Street had mounted over the $2 million mark, and the whole project was in severe financial jeopardy. Meanwhile, in his five auditoriums (the Estelle R. Parsons, the Florence S. Anspacher, the Other Stage, Martinson and South Halls) Papp mounted one show after another of challenging, not always successful but always provocative theater—ten programs including musicals, specialties, revivals and new work that demonstrated eloquently the energy, the taste, the dedication of this gifted impresario, and above all the real usefulness of *all* these auditoriums to him and to the theatergoing public. Clearly, Papp and his Shakespeare Festival operation are among the richest of the city's (and the state's, and for that matter the nation's) cultural treasures, comparable to England's Royal Shakespeare, Royal Court and National Theaters in demonstrating the possibilities of subsidized or semi-supported theater. Papp appealed to the city to help him out, supporting his argument (it was reliably rumored) with an English translation of the word used so effectively by Cambronne at Waterloo. In any case, Mayor John V. Lindsay's impoverished municipality somehow found the money to buy the Public Theater building (paying off the remodeling costs) and leasing it back to Joseph Papp. This was a decision which will do credit to those involved in making it, roughly in the same proportion as that which has accrued to Secretary Seward for insisting on the purchase of Alaska.

Papp didn't come up with a *Hair* or a *No Place to Be Somebody* in his city-owned building this season, but his ten-show program pulsated with imagination, from Dennis J. Reardon's new script *The Happiness Cage,* which began Papp's 1970-71 season with a fantasy about medical experiments in inducing human happiness, to David Rabe's strong new script *The Basic Training of Pavlo Hummel,* which ended it on a contemporary note about an unhappy young man doomed to serve in the army in the Vietnam war and to die in a Saigon fragging. In between were the hit revival of *Trelawny of the "Wells"* and a *Candide* constructed from improvisations by the Organic Theater Company of Chicago; two fascinating solo shows, Siobhan McKenna's *Here Are Ladies* portraying heroines of Irish literature, and homage to an illustrious talent with *Jack MacGowran in the Works of Samuel Beckett;* a musical *Blood* loosely based on the *Oresteia* and done by the same young people who did last year's *Stomp* but not quite a match for their previous inspiration; a pair of new one-acters about the black condition, by Walter Jones and Edgar White, under the portmanteau title *Underground;* and *Slag* by David Hare, a British script presented in London by the Royal Court, about the last three teachers remaining at a moribund girls' school, a metaphor of British society.

Finally, and by no means least challengingly, the Public Theater came up with *Subject to Fits,* described by its young author Robert Montgomery (no relation) in a program note as follows: *"Subject to Fits* is neither adaptation, dramatization nor translation of Dostoevsky's inimitable novel *The Idiot.* The greatness of Dostoevsky's masterpiece is inseparable from its novelistic form, and any attempt to literally transpose it into another art form could not help but undermine its wholeness and alienate its power. *Subject to Fits* is a response to *The Idiot;* it is absolutely unfaithful to the novel; it uses the novel for its own selfish purposes; it does not hold the novel responsible. As such, it is entirely original—smacking of *The Idiot,* dreaming of *The Idiot,* but mostly taking off from where *The Idiot* drove it."

Whatever the roots of *Subject to Fits* may be, what appeared on the stage was a kind of realized nightmare of demented effusion and forlorn hopes, with Andy Robinson in a juicy performance of Prince Myshkin and with a rock score throbbing painfully behind the fantasies which emerged from the Dostoevsky work. The play is a kind of object-lesson critique of Dostoevsky, an acrobatic and juggling act of words, ideas and poses. It either grabbed you or it didn't; it grabbed enough critics to take sixth place in the best-play voting (and it was the first choice of two critics, Martin Gottfried and Jack Kroll). Love it or leave it, *Subject to Fits* was a progressive work of new theater, typical of Joseph Papp's imaginative production policy and the standout of his 1970-71 season.

Wynn Handman's American Place Theater was as always a showcase for playwrights. Its most interesting 1970-71 work was *The Carpenters,* a first professionally-produced play by a new author, Steven Tesich, who was born in Yugoslavia and emigrated to America at age 14. His play was a strong, if pessimistic, image of the generation gap. A hard-working husband and father (Vincent Gardenia) decides to take a day off from work, and in staying home finds that he is unwanted by his wife and hapless children, one of whom is going to kill him if he can. His family is coming apart like the home that shelters them, and there is no carpenter capable of making repairs. The father's contribution to the home (in the light of Tesich's play), which is security and authority, is no longer of any importance to grim, self-centered, directionless new America. Tesich's judgment was harsh but his perception keen, and we eagerly await more scripts from this promising new source.

Family guilt and recrimination also was the subject of another American Place production, Joyce Carol Oates's symbolic *Sunday Dinner,* about a ritual feast at the graveside of a family's departed mother. George Tabori considered the brutalizing effect of military training and the Vietnam war in *Pinkville.* American Place's season ended with a work-in-progress, Sam Shepard's *Back Bog Beast Bait,* which was not submitted for review at the playwright's request—a privilege available to all American Place authors and sometimes exercised, in circumstances designed to give the playwright the greatest possible encouragement and opportunity while subjecting him to the least possible pressure.

The development of black theater is the aim of the Negro Ensemble Company, and presumably its season can be accounted a success because its series of programs was offered under the portmanteau title "Themes of Black Struggle," and one of them offended a lot of people. This was *Ododo* (the Yoruba word for "truth"), a musical review of the black man's history in North America viewed as repeated episodes of hate and injustice leading to a present status as an inevitable revolutionary—a kind of release of pent-up fury on the stage. Perhaps it satisfied some inner longing in black members of the audience; but Clive Barnes of the New York *Times* may have been speaking for a large segment of theatergoers when he wrote in his review: "The black nationalism of shows like *Ododo* makes me realize that I am white . . . . . it is a purely racist show, and I am not prepared to feel deliciously masochistic guilt for crimes I did not commit."

In the course of its season under the direction of Douglas Turner Ward and Robert Hooks, the Negro Ensemble Company also brought in *Perry's Mission* and *Rosalee Pritchett*, a pair of one-acters about the contemporary black condition; *The Dream on Monkey Mountain*, a play by a Trinidadian, Derek Walcott, a poetic image in the form of a black convict's dreams; and, finally, *Ride a Black Horse*, the dramatization by an Ohio professor, John Scott, of the emerging conflict between the black liberal-intellectual community (personified in the play by a college teacher) and the radical impulses of the ghetto leaders.

The Chelsea Theater Center staged a schedule of interesting productions in its loft over at the Brooklyn Academy of Music, and two of them were eventually brought across the river for brief runs in Manhattan. One of the latter was Edward Bond's *Saved*, one of the darkest and most controversial of the dark British plays, containing the now-famous scene in which a baby is stoned to death. It was directed by Alan Schneider in its American premiere. The other production transported from Brooklyn to Manhattan was *Tarot*, a rock musical pantomime with tarot card deck characters playing out the adventures of The Fool. In the course of its season the Chelsea Theater Center imported Heathcote Williams's *AC/DC*, about pinball machines, TV sets and other electronic contraptions as hallucinations of our time, to Brooklyn but not to Manhattan.

On its small Forum Theater stage, Lincoln Center Repertory presented A.R. Gurney Jr.'s close scrutiny of America, *Scenes From American Life*, a time machine that traveled from the Depression years through our present travails into what the playwright conceives to be an inevitably Orwellian future. Lincoln Center Rep was also preparing another new play—new to America, that is—for production in the Forum. It was Friedrich Duerrenmatt's adaptation of Strindberg's *The Dance of Death*, entitled *Play Strindberg*, which was in previews as the season ended.

Elsewhere in off Broadway's new-play production list, a highlight was Israel Horovitz's *Line*, about five ill-assorted people jockeying for position in a line waiting for we know not what, insulting and loving each other to pass the time. A young musician (Richard Dreyfuss) manages to outwit the others much of the time, monopolizing first place, in a metaphor of the artist's drive to succeed. The play is witty and perceptive in the writing and was capably acted by a good cast throughout its one-hour running time. Horovitz also supplied an amusing curtain-raising sketch entitled *Acrobats*, about a husband-and-wife team having a family quarrel during their balancing act.

Irv Bauer's *A Dream Out of Time* was another standout, one which suffered an interference of its run by the strike of off-Broadway actors in mid-season. It contrasted two generations of a Jewish family in New York, with Sam Levene representing a generation which worked its way out of the Lower East Side, and James J. Sloyan as the brightly promising modern young man radicalized by the failures of the American dream. There was a drama of prison life, *The Cage,* written by an ex-lifer Rick Cluchey and performed by a cast of ex-inmates. In another part of the forest, Ed Bullins is working on a 20-play cycle about the black experience in the industrial areas of America's North and West. The second of them, *In New England Winter,* surfaced briefly at the Henry Street Playhouse (the first was *In the Wine Time* depicting a world of winos, petty holdups and general hopelessness). Bullins's plays are getting harder and harder to see, as he arranges to have them produced farther and farther out on the edges of the New York professional theater. This is too bad for most theatergoers, because he is a major playwrighting talent who ought to have a wide hearing. Another of the year's achievements in the tributaries was *King Heroin,* a drama of drug abuse written, directed and produced by Al Fann at St. Philip's Community Theater in Harlem.

The potpourri of 1970-71 off-Broadway entertainment included the satisfying ingredient of the Bil Baird Marionettes in three programs from the repertory. Of the six revues, only the improvisational *The Proposition* caught on for any length of time; the new edition of Second City, *Cooler Near the Lake,* did not. A glorious Japanese rock musical enlivened the earlier part of the season: *Golden Bat,* brought over here by the Tokyo Kid Brothers who describe themselves as "La Mama, Tokyo" and the Golden Bat itself as "a popular Japanese comic strip character who, like a phoenix, died and was reborn . . . . . a symbol of *matsuri*—the hopes, dreams and will of the young generation."

Of the 13 home-grown musicals produced off Broadway this season, only *Godspell* and *Touch* were hits. *Godspell* was a rock musical takeout of the Gospel according to St. Matthew, with Jesus in clown makeup as a folk hero, and with an irresistable mood of innocent wonder in the stylized re-enactment of his life and sacrifice as adapted and musicalized by Stephen Schwartz and John-Michael Tebelak (with one additional number by Jay Hamburger and Peggy Gordon). *Touch* was something else, a joyous musical celebration of the communal way of life of contemporary young people, written by Kenn Long, Amy Saltz and Jim Crozier. Another of the off-Broadway musicals, *The Ballad of Johnny Pot,* about a Johnny Appleseed character who scatters cannabis instead of pippins, took extraordinary measures following lukewarm reviews: it staged an admission-free performance. The theater was jammed even on a rainy night, with turn-aways accommodated on later evenings (so much for the myth that you can't give away tickets to a show that isn't a hit). The experiment was curious but ultimately ineffective. When the show returned to charging admission, action at the box office was scant and it closed after a two-week run.

Such was the off-Broadway theatergoing experience in 1970-71: a modest abundance of average skill and considerable variety, hitting its share of the high spots which rise out of the seething effort in any New York theater season. It was often relevant to contemporary life, and vice versa; off Broadway may have had some small effect on our times with telling programs like *The Trial of the Catonsville Nine*, and in return our troubled times were having some effect on off Broadway. Certainly some portion of the potential audience was kept away from the tributary theater, or at least rendered very cautious, by the increasing upset in the city streets. The bright-light, theater-cluster areas like Lower Second Avenue, Sheridan Square or the East Seventies weren't much affected, but off-Broadway theatergoers thought twice about seeking entertainment at some lone theater up a dark and taxiless side street. A recent off-Broadway theater-building boom came to an abrupt halt, as the planners reassessed their plans in a troubled city. The off-Broadway theater is calculated to survive any number of artistic revolutions. But it is highly susceptible to the side effects of civil unrest and urban blight, and it is ardently to be hoped that this threat will disappear in better days to come.

Offstage

Whatever may be the problems of the New York legitimate theater as compared with its golden age a few decades ago, 1971 was a year in which theater people were taking action to meet and solve them.

This was the season in which the 7:30 curtain became a reality. The League of New York Theaters under Richard Barr's leadership had approved changing the Broadway curtain time from 8:30 to 7:30 p.m., and so had David Merrick (who brought a 1960 experiment in a one-day-a-week early showing to an abrupt end by switching his shows back to 8:30). The reason for moving the curtain time up was, in Barr's words, "to reduce the time span between the end of the business day and the start of performances, to allow our audiences to get home an hour earlier."

It had been argued that even an 8:30 curtain didn't allow Manhattanites time for a truly leisurely dinner before the theater. With the earlier curtain time, they could have supper afterwards as many Londoners do, and the suburbanites wouldn't have that long 5:30-to-8:30 wait for the shows to begin, and they might be able to get the baby sitter home before midnight. Besides (it was whispered), there was street crime in the Broadway area as elsewhere in the city, and it might be well to get the public home an hour earlier.

Some objection to the new curtain time was voiced by theater party brokers, who argued that their patrons needed the longer pre-curtain time to attend dinners, etc., before the show, but the League decided to go ahead. On Dec. 1 a campaign to inform the public of the early 7:30 curtain (and 2 instead of 2:30 at matinees) was launched. It included posters all over town and program inserts, one of which is reproduced nearby in these pages. On Jan. 4, 1971 the curtains rose at 7:30 p.m. and estimates of the results were soon pouring in. Theatergoers seemed to like the new arrangement. There was no immediate dramatic effect on the box office, but at season's end it was estimated that the new curtain time may have increased ticket sales by as much as 17 per cent. Some restaurateurs complained of loss of business; others said they had gained. Vincent Sardi Jr. of Sardi's reported to *Variety* that the increase in supper business more than made up for the loss in dinner business: "The net result is we're doing much better than before." Carol Channing and Sid Caesar, stars of *Four on a Garden* reported to a luncheon meeting at the Algonquin Hotel sponsored by *Playbill* that their early-curtain audiences seemed sharper and more responsive than the 8:30 audiences, possibly because they had ingested more lightly of both food and drink. Finally, Ted Kalem, *Time's* drama critic, put forward a suggestion taken up by nobody so far that the theater keep its new 7:30 curtain for commuters and other early birds on weekdays but provide a *late* curtain at 9 or even 9:30 on weekends for city-dwelling night owls.

THEATREGOERS

PLEASE NOTE!

Beginning Jan. 4, 1971

Evening Performances

of All Broadway Shows

will start

at 7:30 P.M.

Wed. & Sat. Mats.

at 2:00 P.M.

Another much-discussed dream implemented into contractual reality in 1971 was the Limited Gross Broadway Theater Agreement (previously called "middle theater" and referred to generally in this *Best Plays* volume as "Limited Broadway"). Technically speaking, the term "Broadway" with its scales of salaries and percentages to artists, technicians, rentals, etc., applies to theaters seating more than 600. "Off Broadway" with its different scales applies to those seating 299 or fewer. Thus there is an area between which is now defined as "middle theater" or "Limited Broadway"—and there are houses right in the Broadway area like the Edison Theater which come under these new rules. But even more importantly for the future, it is hoped, the "Limited Broadway" rules are also designed to permit a producer to rope off some of the seats in a regular-sized Broadway house so that his maximum weekly gross would not exceed $25,000 at a top reduced to $5. Under these conditions, he could mount a show with Limited Broadway cost concessions. If he finds he has a smash hit on his hands, the producer may elect to remove the ropes and move up to full Broadway status (and cost levels) after four weeks (but a show scaled originally to Broadway cannot move *down* to Limited Broadway).

It is hoped that this new arrangement will encourage production of unconventional, avant garde, more risky material on the Broadway scene to attract those adventurous spirits, particularly young people, who are no longer satisfied with conventional Broadway fare, or who cannot pay the ever-increasing Broadway ticket price. Broadway theaters available for Limited Broadway production include the Ambassador, Belasco, Billy Rose, Biltmore, Brooks Atkinson, Ethel Barrymore, Eugene O'Neill, Golden, Helen Hayes, Longacre and Lyceum. No Limited Broadway productions appeared in these theaters in 1971, though there were several in the 500-seat houses in the area; for example, *Happy Birthday, Wanda June* moved from off to Limited Broadway. Theater buffs will be waiting to see what effect the new arrangement will have on 1972 production.

Other efforts to improve the general condition of the theater included the movement by the League of New York Theaters and others formally to establish the Times Square area as a "special district," with a high saturation of police and other municipal attentions including taxi lines, in order to create an environment favorable to theatergoing. Mayor John V. Lindsay gave his approval to this effort, particularly as it might apply to extending the zoning area in which office-tower builders would be encouraged to include theaters in their structures. Experiments in the computerization of ticket sales continued, with Ticketron taking over the Macy's box office and expanding its remote-location operation to include all but four Broadway shows in addition to various games and concerts. The first New York theater club modeled on the London pattern—a private club with professionally-produced plays for members only—was planned for the 177-seat Stage 73 Playhouse on East 73d Street. It is to be called the Actors and Playwrights Theater and will include a restaurant.

The theater was watching closely the first halting steps of the infant video cassette industry, the processes (there are five major ones) by which a library of recorded entertainment may be played at will through your TV set. It may be a while before the average citizen owns a cassette library the way he now owns a collection of LP records, but not a long while. One of the competing, incompatible, major processes will probably win out eventually, just as the LP record won in competition with other long-play systems, and when this happens it is expected that the video cassette market will settle down to standardized prosperity. This could "revolutionize" (that's the word they're using) legitimate theater economics, because even an unsuccessful show might be taped for sale on cassettes in a market that will eventually be as starved for fresh material—after the old movies have finally been cassetted and sold—as commercial TV is today.

One of the season's most trying events was an Actors Equity strike of off-Broadway actors and stage managers which began on Monday, Nov. 16, involved 200 people in 17 struck shows and lasted for 31 days through Wednesday, Dec. 16 (but most of the 13 shows that resumed didn't get going again until the following week; two never reopened and two had transferred out of the strike jurisdiction to Broadway and Limited Broadway). The strike ended when Equity and the League of Off-Broadway Theaters and Producers, whose spokesman was Paul Libin, agreed to send major issues including salary, welfare and pensions to arbitration. Salary minimums for actors before the strike were $75-$150 depending on the weekly gross of each off-Broadway production. The League offered $90-$165 and Equity was demanding $125-$265. The arbitrator fixed the sum at $100-$175 this year rising to $125-$200 in 1974, and Libin commented on the arbitrated package: "It will mean the slow death of off Broadway as we know it" because of increased production costs. The shows that closed during the strike were *What the Butler Saw* after a long run and *Score* after a short one; and in addition the play *A Dream Out of Time,* which had only just opened to favorable notices, never regained its momentum.

Such controversy as arose offstage in the course of the 1970-71 season was of the sputtering, rather than the raging, variety. *Hair* ran into censorship problems in Indianapolis, South Bend and Evansville, Ill., St. Paul, Minn., San Antonio, Tex. and Madrid in Spain, but nothing as severe as last year's banned-in-Boston episode. *Oh! Calcutta!* also raised moderate objections in Ottawa, Canada and Cambridge, Mass. and turned a few mid-Western noses blue in a closed-circuit TV version.

There were hassles over the critics with Clive Barnes, the daily drama reviewer of the New York *Times* in the center of the turbulence because of the economic power of the paper's reviews, a matter of life or death to most productions. The Dramatists Guild—the organization of playwrights, librettists, composers and lyricists on and off Broadway—made an effort under the leadership of its then president Frank D. Gilroy to persuade the *Times* to do something, *anything,* about this situation which the paper's own critics have often characterized as repugnant even to them. In a meeting and an exchange of correspondence with A.H. Rosenthal, the paper's managing editor, the dramatists suggested such possible mitigations as a box score of other critics run along with the *Times's* daily review, or a panel of guest critics who might offer additional opinions. The *Times* found all the suggestions unworkable, though expressing sympathy for the problem of playwrights whose work lives or dies with the views of only one man (it was never suggested that Clive

Barnes was the wrong man, or that his reviews be inhibited in any way, only that some means be found to take some of the economic curse off them).

The *Times* critic went the extra mile with the dramatists; he sat down un-armed and unescorted with 70 of them at Guild headquarters one afternoon in an open discussion and fielded all questions up to and including "What are your qualifications, Mr. Barnes?" (His reply was, "What are your qualifica-tions as a playwright? Chiefly you do the job.") At one point in this exchange he explained that power is almost as disconcerting to a dedicated critic as it is to those he is reviewing—it is *influence* the critic strives to exercise, not power, Barnes told the gathering. Meanwhile the intolerable situation remains.

There was a flurry of excitement over drama criticism in Boston in the spring, when Archibald MacLeish's *Scratch* opened there for its pre-Broad-way tryout. The Boston *Globe's* reviewer didn't like the play much, and the editorial page editor apparently felt that their man should have approached the play, not with the traditional iconoclastic objectivity of the drama critic, but with a historian's respectful awe. The paper took issue with its own critic on the editorial page the next day in these terms: "When America's greatest living poet—and perhaps her very greatest, living or dead—writes a play about the state of the Union, it is not a matter to be taken lightly."

Joseph Papp's New York Shakespeare Festival was only one of many noble theater endeavors that suffered financial difficulties in 1970-71. The Charles Playhouse in Boston had to close its doors after its subscription list dwindled and money ran out. The Tyrone Guthrie Theater in Minneapolis had its worst season ever. Lincoln Center Repertory was confronting the hard fact that perhaps the type of theater operation originally envisioned at the Vivian Beaumont is becoming less and less feasible, artistically as well as econom-ically, and plans were being made for others to use some of the extra space originally provided to accommodate and store multiple repertory productions —others including New York City Center and movie theaters which would help to carry the costs of operation.

The instinct to reach out toward subsidy grew in reverse proportion to the weakening performing-arts economy. The National Endowment continued to function under the direction of Nancy Hanks, President Nixon's appointee, granting $731,750 to 26 resident professional theaters in 24 cities, and $207,500 to 22 experimental groups like Cafe La Mama, Chelsea Theater Center, etc., in eight cities. This was only a drop in the bucket of need. The Theater Development Fund continued to sustain the professional New York theater in its especially effective and double-barreled way of coming to the aid of shows *after* they are produced. Selected productions are helped over the first rough weeks of their run by the purchase of significant blocks of tickets which are then distributed at reduced rates to audiences of students, etc., who might not be able to see a play otherwise—thus giving the show a much-needed economic boost on the one hand and helping to recruit new audiences on the other. The following 1970-71 productions received a helping hand from TDF in one way or another: *Conduct Unbecoming, Story Theater, Othello, Hay Fever, Jack MacGowran in the Works of Samuel Beckett, Touch,*

A Midsummer Night's Dream, Happy Birthday, Wanda June, The School for Wives, The Playboy of the Western World, The Trial of the Catonsville Nine, An Enemy of the People, Trelawny of the "Wells," All Over, Antigone, The House of Blue Leaves and *Subject to Fits.*

Our public and private efforts to support the theater are commendable, but they shouldn't obscure the fact that in the United States we have no such subsidized organizations as England's National Theater, Royal Shakespeare Company and Royal Court, from whence come a considerable number of those excellent plays which steal the limelight of our Broadway seasons, some of them risky concepts which might never have reached full-scale production in an unsubsidized, private commercial theater. But even London's fine publicly-financed theaters are a mere detail. Here's one figure that says it all. West Germany spends $2.42 per person annually in government support for the arts; Sweden and Austria $2 per person; Canada $1.40; Israel $1.34; England with its great subsidized theaters a measly $1.23. Here in the United States, where we spent $1,125 per person on highways in 1970, the annual per capita support of the arts is 7½ cents.

Finally, the season's most poignant offstage event took place only just offstage, in a Philadelphia theater. On Friday night, March 12, David Burns collapsed on the stage of the Forrest just after his big Act II number in the musical *70, Girls, 70.* He died a few moments later in the wings, of a heart ailment that had been troubling him for some time. He had lived the life of an actor, and he made such a mark on the entertainment scene that he already enjoyed, if that is the word, the sincerest type of adulation in the many bald imitations of his technique and personality to be found all over the media. The sad occurrence of his final exit was so remarkable in its sheer theatricality that we must note it here. Without stepping out of character, David Burns died the death of an actor, on the stage in a starring role, at the height of a distinguished career, on a Friday night with a good house, his big number finished, nothing in his ears but the sound of applause.

As though taking its cue from the popularity of *No, No, Nanette,* the 1971 TV show celebrating the 25th anniversary of the Antoinette Perry (Tony) Awards presented a cavalcade of numbers from the Tony Award-winning musicals over the years. This was a much more entertaining show than the Academy, Emmy or other 1971 awards programs on television, as the Broadway musical stars of the past and present sang and danced 25 years of show-stopping numbers from Rodgers & Hammerstein to Strouse & Adams by way of Lerner & Loewe, Bock & Harnick, Frank Loesser, Meredith Willson, Leonard Bernstein, Jerry Herman, Stephen Sondheim and all the others.

Like the 1970-71 drama season itself, this musical cavalcade was not merely a nostalgic savoring of the past, it was also a progress right up, into and through the present toward the future. Certainly the Rodgers & Hammerstein songs sounded wonderful—they always will, and by the way this very season's Broadway musical stage was brightened by still another lilting Rodgers love song, "I Do Not Know a Day I Did Not Love You" from *Two by Two.* But the significant point is that Broadway enjoyed wearing the laurels of *Carousel, My Fair Lady* and *Guys and Dolls* without standing on them. "Oh What a Beautiful Morning" or "This Was a Real Nice Clambake" may not be titles immediately relevant to our time, but for our time Broadway has come up with "Another Hundred People Just Got off the Train" from *Company* or "I'm Still Here" from *Follies.*

As the Tony Awards cavalcade of musicals demonstrated, the theater's past has been glorious—but in 1970-71 it is ringing out as many echoes of the future as echoes of the past. The New York theater is beset with economic, sociological, journalistic and even real estate difficulties, as we have outlined. It is caught in a tide rip of violent artistic change at a moment when the quiet backwaters of the comfortable past offer not even the illusion of safety from the turbulent present. Our theater is in all kinds of difficulty except the worst kind of all: stagnation. It is puzzled and perverse and at times discouraged, but—to borrow a line from the 1971 Tony Award winner *Applause*—"But alive, that's the thing! But alive!"

THE 1970-71 OFF-OFF-BROADWAY SEASON

By Robert Schroeder

ONCE TOUTED AS A PRIME ARENA for the experimentation that was to reconstitute the American theater, off off Broadway has settled into an elitist groove—if not a rut—that effectively shelters its practitioners from either criticism or acclaim, and consequently precludes their becoming actually influential. The most "successful" of this season's productions, the Andre Gregory version of *Alice in Wonderland,* played to an audience measured in multiples of tens, not hundreds, four times a week. The most "successful" off-off-Broadway theater, La Mama, played the most popular of its productions only ten times, to audiences again measured in tens, not hundreds. While spasmodic, not-in-the-least comprehensive reviews of off-off-Broadway shows appeared from time to time in the New York *Post* and the *Times* and in a few other periodicals (even *The Village Voice* has materially reduced its coverage), the presentations were treated more as feature-story phenomena than as the subject of serious critical evaluation. *The Daily News* does not bother its head, or its five million readers, with off-off-Broadway theater.

Much was made in the feature-story treatments of off on Broadway's search for a "tribal ritual" pertinent to Americans today. The Performance Group's *Commune,* The Judson Poets' Theater's *Dracula Sabbat,* La Mama's *The Red Horse Animation* and *Pork,* the National Black Theater's *Ritual,* The Open Theater's *Terminal,* the Soul and Latin Theater's *Walls* and *The Block,* Theater Genesis's *Mad Dog Blues* and *Grand Mal Crick* and many others exemplified this continuing trend. Characterized by group-mime, carefully choreographed and non-individualized performances, and insistently avoiding linear plot development, concentration upon the plight of an individual with whom an audience can identify, or any sort of premeditated and sustained tug at the heart strings, these offerings must have constituted the most isolated and lonely "tribal rituals" in anthropological history.

The nudie and sex-exploitation shows similarly failed to excite the interest of any significant segment of the public. A few of the established porno houses —Dramatis Personae was the prime example—played to a small but steady trade, but most of the season's porno offerings were fast fados.

There has been a marked increase in minority-group theater in New York. The Agrupacion de Arte Latinamericano (ADAL), The Greenwich Mews Spanish Theater and the New York Theater of the Americas presented a great many more plays in Spanish, and translated from the Spanish, than have been available in the recent past. And the Afro-American Studio, Al Fann's Theatrical Ensemble, the East River Players, the National Black Theater, the New Federal Theater, The New Lafayette Theater, the Soul and Latin Theater, and the Urban Arts Corps and other troupes made an increasing number of plays and improvisations of particular interest to blacks, and to the ghetto communities, available in both Brooklyn and Manhattan.

Among the most interesting and esthetically pleasing offerings this season was *Deafman Glance,* conceived and directed by Robert Wilson and presented by his Byrd Hoffman School of Byrds at the Brooklyn Academy of Music. Imagine a slow-motion cartoon movie in soft pastel, feature-length, and sketched not by the Disney factory but by Salvador Dali in a soaring mood, with a cast of seeming thousands of living beings (the grossest I saw was a pregnant, nude, dancing woman, and the smallest a turtle—but I was sitting pretty far back), and you'll have a starting conception of this opulent, if snail-paced, extravaganza.

Camp was stricken this year. Of the many former purveyors of the foolish and the foppish, only Charles Ludlam's Ridiculous Theatrical Company remained active, performing a repertory of two Ludlam ridiculoscripts starring, of course, and directed by, of course, Ludlam.

Altogether lacking in off off Broadway's 1970-71 season was actual experimentation. The Performance Group's *Commune* was a not-even-more-communal re-hash of *Dionysus in 69; Alice in Wonderland* amounted to Andre Gregory's previous *Endgame* and *Beclch* stews stirred into a sprinkling of Grotowski, and basted in Lewis Carroll. The Chelsea Theater Center's *AC/DC* was the Electric Circus with dialogue. Even the laudible *Deafman Glance* was a sequel to last season's (and the same troupe's) more innovative *The Life and Death of Sigmund Freud.* Whatever may be its political importance or even effectiveness, the National Black Theater's *Ritual* is, esthetically, a demeaning burlesque of traditional black religious expression, Garveyism, and the mature Malcolm X. The Open Theater's *Terminal* simply terminated its superior *The Serpent;* and off off Broadway's great white hope, Sam Shepard, became, in his *Mad Dog Blues,* more rock performer than playwright. If the seminal new-theater discovery did occur during the 1970-71 season, it did not take place in New York, off-off-Broadway.

O
O
O

THE SEASON AROUND THE UNITED STATES

with

A DIRECTORY OF PROFESSIONAL REGIONAL THEATER

O
O
O

INTRODUCTION: A "NEW BROADWAY" COAST TO COAST

By Jerome Lawrence and Robert E. Lee

Authors of *Inherit the Wind, Mame, The Night Thoreau Spent in Jail* and many other plays. Much of this article previously appeared as a state-of-the-art report to playwrights in the *Dramatists Guild Quarterly*

OUR 13TH PRODUCED PLAY, *The Night Thoreau Spent in Jail,* has been the most stimulating and exciting experience of our playwriting lives Yet, it has never come close to those parochial few blocks of real estate known as Broadway.

This was intentional. As of June, 1971, there have been 111 different productions of our play in major resident, community and university theaters throughout the country under the auspices of American Playwrights Theater; everywhere, in fact, from Thoreau's home town (Concord, Mass.) to Nixon's home town (Whittier, Calif.). By December 31, 1971, when the license to American Playwrights Theater ends, David Ayers (executive secretary of APT) estimates there will have been 150 productions—each with a different cast, director, designer, and a different "theater home." This has never happened before with a play not bearing the stamp of a Broadway or a London "hit". Perhaps, like Thoreau himself, American playwrights are beginning to hear a different drummer.

With the withering of Broadway as the seed-ground for new plays, particularly plays of *ideas,* the birth of a truly *national* theater in the form of APT

39

was not only necessary, but inevitable. It all began with a question from the floor at an American Educational Theater Association convention in Eugene, Ore. eight years ago. "Why can't we have your plays first?", an indignant member asked. "Why do we have to wait for important plays until three to five years after they see the light of Manhattan?"

There had always been suspicion, distrust, arm's-length behavior *on both sides* between the tributary theater and the so-called professionals of Broadway. Why not build a bridge between them? This was necessary, we felt, not only as a service to those hungry and waiting theaters (too long confined to museum pieces or delayed carbon copies of established "hits"). America's practising playwrights needed an alternate and entirely new platform where their works could touch audiences *not* on the road to Broadway, not as mere try-outs for Broadway. APT is *instead* of Broadway.

We went to work. Ohio State University gave APT a home. ANTA and AETA gave us their blessing. The Dramatists Guild helped us draw up a working contract, largely written by the late Elmer Rice. Robert Anderson was daring enough to put forth the first play, *The Days Between.* Others followed: George Sklar with *And People All Around;* Jerome Weidman and James Yaffee with *Ivory Tower;* Ron Cowen with *Summertree.*

The purpose was simple: to bring fresh and vital new plays to a national audience. At the time, we wrote: "We need a new Broadway, a national Broadway, a Broadway which is better than Broadway, a platform for plays where the value sense is not corrupted by economic hysteria, a petrified tradition, and administration bedlam."

Well, it's happened. The new Broadway stretches a long way, far from the madding crowd of Shubert Alley. Does the playwright-in-labor only want his creative baby born where the powers that be can crown it one day with a Pulitzer Prize or inclusion in the *Best Plays* volume? Perhaps some day prize-givers and best-play-selectors will lift their eyes beyond the valley of the shadow of the Shuberts. (The Pulitzer Committee doesn't confine its newspaper prizes to the N.Y. *Times, Post* and *Daily News.*)

But this seeming discrimination is due to a lack of awareness of what APT has achieved. From a literary point of view, it is our only genuinely national theater. Through APT, playwrights have a chance to see their works take on a multitude of forms—instead of the life-or-death one-shot of Broadway. And for thousands of resident, community and on-campus theaters across America, the door is now open wide to material which, before APT, was totally beyond their reach.

How are the plays chosen? The governing board includes an equal number of playwrights and tributary producers. It was decided, however, that the playwrights should not pass judgment on the works of their fellow-authors. The producer-members, who must mount the individual productions, decide which plays will be most challenging to the audiences they serve.

An APT play may come from a well known theater name or from a totally new dramatist. (Ron Cowen was a student in one of our classes at UCLA just a few years ago.) Twenty-five member theaters must agree to present the play before it is officially activated. The playwright who longs to communicate will find new and unexpected stimulation through APT. This has surely been our experience.

Examples: At Kent State, the audience rushed onto the stage at the final curtain call, embracing the actors; veterans of the National Guard madness just a year before wept openly and subscribed to Henry David Thoreau's dedicated non-rock-throwing non-violence.

At the Old Globe in San Diego, Ron Heller, playing the lead, was playing himself really; he was out on bail for being the leader of a group which, peacefully, Thoreau-fashion, had taken over the ROTC Building at San Diego State. His personal conviction electrified every line he spoke.

In Chicago, Christopher Walken was Henry, Douglas Campbell was Emerson, and Anne Casson (Sybil Thorndyke's daughter) was Mrs. Thoreau, with inspired direction by Patrick Henry. Goodman Theater's production chalked up the biggest audience in the 45-year history of that distinguished playhouse.

In Whittier, Calif., with Jean Korf directing an all-student cast, every line blasting the President (it was James Polk in the play, of course), caused not only cheers in the audience, but stomping on the floor, whistles, an ovation as if Merman were coming down those red stairs in *Hello, Dolly!* All this in What's-His-Name's home territory!

Concord, Mass. let the play come "home." In Thoreau country, Thoreau came doubly alive. Emerson wore Emerson's own nightshirt. Ellen Sewell wrote with one of Thoreau's own pencils. When Henry David pointed to Concord Bridge in the play, he was *really* pointing to Concord Bridge. Ghosts came to life in Veteran's Hall in Concord, just down the street from the Alcott and the Emerson homes. The Concord Players have now abandoned *Little Women* as their annual "passion play." A brand new play about their local folk-hero has taken its place.

UCLA experimented for the first time in the melding of a professional and student cast. Directed by the Lee half of this team, the play was an adventure and a discovery for both Equity members and so-called amateurs (incidentally, the root of that word means "lovers"). There were standing ovations for Guy Stockwell, True Boardman, Larry Simpasa, and faculty members Dorothy Folger and Ralph Freud (after whom the theater at UCLA is named). The run had to be repeated in the fall with 1,000 people turned away.

In each production, we made discoveries as playwrights—valuable nuances, subtleties in character relationships, staging devices—which were passed on to the next production. These refinements and developments did not take place under the pressure of a half-million-dollar investment, under the threat of a possible out-of-town closing, under a shaky producer saddled with insecurity and Johnny-come-lately wisenheimer advisors. The play was the thing. The physical production at UCLA cost less than $1,800; it would be difficult to find any $750,000 Broadway presentation that looked as professional, as effective.

At Dallas Theater Center, Paul Baker dedicated himself to a production which would be "everything the playwrights dreamed it could be." He flew in David Ayers, who had originated the Thoreau role in Ohio State's pilot production for the University's centennial, to coach his actors, to pass on what had been learned to date from other presentations of the play. Frank Lloyd Wright, who designed their theater, was a Thoreauvian, so the physical production was done in the spirit of both men: Baker assigned a Wright student to design not merely the set but the total ambiance of the theater. The moment you entered the lobby, you were plunged into a bird-filled green forest, you seemed to be at the very shore of Walden Pond.

There were many other notable and effective productions: Kenneth Graham's imaginative staging at Minnesota, Jean Arthur's direction at Vassar, Greg Falls's production at ACT in Seattle, Alliance Theater in Atlanta, Alley in Houston, Arena in Washington, the Quonset Hut Theater at Ohio Wesleyan, and, appropriately enough, the 100th production at State College of New York at Geneseo, where the Thoreau Society is headquartered. (There Walter Harding, *the* Thoreau authority, has sent his multiple blessings out to the performances all over the country.)

Were there any ineffective productions? Of course there were. We have not seen all of them and it's the chance you take. But each has a character and a flavor of its own (and it's been done proscenium, in the round, in horseshoe, in thrust, indoors and out). A few times the play has not worked. The difficulty, it seems to us, has been a director who was more interested in the director than in the subject matter. He produced *himself* instead of the play. But that very often happens on Broadway, too.

The future of American Playwrights Theater depends on the daring, the gambling spirit of both playwrights and producing members. We deplore the theater which refuses to do a new play unless they get it exclusively. We are equally sad about the dramatist whose eyes are solely set on the Broadhurst or the Plymouth or the Morosco in Manhattan. Playwright and producing members must join at the middle of this new bridge.

Let us give you some astonishing figures. Our *Inherit the Wind* ran three years on Broadway. (And would it be produced there today with a cast of 65? Absolutely not. But they'd grab it at APT.) Our *Mame* ran more than 1,500 performances at the Winter Garden and the Broadway. But *The Night Thoreau Spent in Jail* will have had more performances in *one year* than both *Inherit* and *Mame* added together. If you want to reach people, try the *new* Broadway. There is a waiting audience. Their reactions are like beautiful thunder.

A DIRECTORY OF PROFESSIONAL REGIONAL THEATER

*Including selected Canadian programs
and selected programs for children*

Professional 1970-71 programs and repertory productions by leading resident companies around the United States, plus major Shakespeare festivals including that of Stratford, Ontario (Canada), are grouped in alphabetical order of their locations and listed in date order from late May, 1970 to June, 1971. This list does not include Broadway, off-Broadway or touring New York shows, summer theaters, single productions by commercial producers or college or other non-professional productions. The directory was compiled by Ella A. Malin for *The Best Plays of 1970-71* from information provided by the resident producing organizations at Miss Malin's request. First productions of new plays—American or world premieres—in regional theaters are listed with full casting and credits, as available. Figures in parentheses following titles give number of performances and date given is opening date, included whenever a record of these facts was obtainable from the producing managements.

Summary

This Directory lists 323 productions (including programs of one-acters and workshop productions) presented by 39 groups in 53 theaters in 37 cities during the 1970-71 season. Of these, 141 were American plays in 112 full productions and 29 workshop productions. 57 programs were world premieres, 9 were American or North American Continental premieres.

Frequency of production of individual scripts was as follows:

    2 plays received 5 productions (*Little Murders, Othello*)

    8 plays received 4 productions (*The Fantasticks, A Day In the Death of Joe Egg, Indians, Long Day's Journey Into Night, The Merchant of Venice, The Night Thoreau Spent in Jail, The Price, The Skin of Our Teeth.*)

  10 plays received 3 productions (*Arsenic and Old Lace, The Comedy of Errors, Harvey, Life With Father, Plaza Suite, Richard II, Rosencrantz and Guildenstern Are Dead, The Tempest, The Threepenny Opera, Twelfth Night.*)

  34 plays received 2 productions

208 plays received 1 production

Listed below are the playwrights who received the greatest number of productions. The first figure is the number of productions; the second figure (in parentheses) is the number of plays produced, including one-acters.

Shakespeare	38 (15)	O'Neill	7 (4)
Brecht	9 (6)	Feiffer	7 (3)
Shaw	8 (7)	Beckett	6 (5)
Miller	8 (4)	Wilder	6 (2)
Pinter	7 (6)	Molière	5 (4)

Kilty	4	(2)	Ibsen	3	(3)
Simon	4	(2)	Arrabal	3	(2)
Jones/Schmidt	4	(1)	Corwin	3	(2)
Kopit	4	(1)	Ionesco	3	(2)
Lawrence and Lee	4	(1)	Chase	3	(1)
Nichols (Peter)	4	(1)	Kesselring	3	(1)
Chekhov	3	(3)	Lindsay and Crouse	3	(1)
Coward	3	(3)	Stoppard	3	(1)

ABINGDON, VA.

Barter Theater

THE WORLD OF CARL SANDBURG (32). Adapted from the work of Carl Sandburg by Norman Corwin. June 2, 1970. Director, Owen Phillips; lighting, Robert Marshall; costumes, Lynn Sams. With Dale Carter Cooper, Jeff Dalton, Ronald Hale, Michael Rives.

THE LION IN WINTER (25). By James Goldman. June 23, 1970. Director, Owen Phillips; lighting, Robert Marshall; costumes, Lynn Sams. With Antonie Becker, Jane Cronin, Roger Brown.

THE PETRIFIED FOREST (42). By Robert E. Sherwood. July 7, 1970. Director, Robert Porterfield; scenery, Bennet Averyt; lighting, Robert Marshall; costumes, Lynn Sams. With Sheila Bevan, Ronald Hale, Richard Snow, Milton Tarver.

ARSENIC AND OLD LACE (48). By Joseph Kesselring. July 21, 1970. Director, Owen Phillips; scenery, Bennet Averyt; lighting, Robert Marshall; costumes, Martha Kelly. With Dale Carter Cooper, William Schilling, Jane Cronin, Ronald Hale.

RAT RACE (34). By Paul Dellinger. August 14, 1970 (world premiere). Director, Owen Phillips; scenery, Bennet Averyt; lighting, Robert Marshall; costumes, Lynn Sams.
Doc Dugan .... William Schilling
Liz Whitlock .... Dale Carter Cooper
Walter Driscoll .... Ronald Hale
Dottie Dugan .... Nan Macy
Senator J. Myles Kilgore ..... Milton Tarver
Mal Kilgore .... Michael Rives
Murphy .... Bill Evans
Peterson; The Voice .... Jeff Dalton
The scene is the living room of Doc Dugan.

Act I: Evening. Act II, Scene 1: That night. Scene 2: Early the next morning.

THE STAR-SPANGLED GIRL (50). By Neil Simon. September 15, 1970. Director, Owen Phillips; scenery, Bennet Averyt; lighting, Robert Marshall. With Milton Tarver, Ronald Hale, Anna Stuart.

MUCH ADO ABOUT NOTHING (34). By William Shakespeare. May 4, 1971. Director, Owen Phillips; scenery, Bennet Averyt; costumes, Martha Kelly. With Ginger Bowen, Robert Foley, Liz Ingleson, John Milligan, Michael Norell.

A STAND IN THE MOUNTAINS (34). By Peter Taylor. May 25, 1971 (world premiere). Director, Michael Norell; scenery, Kathrin Moore; lighting, Frank Moss; costumes, Martha Kelly.
Louisa Weaver .... Dale Carter Cooper
Will Weaver .... James Sargent
Zack Weaver .... Milton Tarver
Thelma Campbell .... Cindy Tarver
Mina .... Ginger Bowen
Harry Weaver .... Jerry Oddo
Lucille Weaver .... Marlene Caryl
Georgia Di Lupa .... Liz Ingleson
Dr. Smith .... Robert Foley
Constable .... William Schilling
Act I, Scene 1: Sitting room of the Weaver cottage at Owl Mountain, the morning of the Fourth of July, 1940. Scene 2: Will Weaver's room in the cottage. Scene 3: Front porch of the cottage. Act II, Scene 4: Will's room, three weeks later. Scene 5: Sitting room, after lunch the same day. Scene 6: Sitting room, perhaps two weeks later. Scene 7: Will's room, late afternoon two weeks later.

ANN ARBOR, MICH.

University of Michigan Professional Theater Program: The Actors Company

IN THE MATTER OF J. ROBERT OPPEN-HEIMER (8). By Heinar Kipphardt; translated by Ruth Speirs. October 13, 1970. Director, Allen Fletcher; scenery and costumes, William D. Roberts; lighting, Mark S. Krause. With Josef Sommer, Chester Smith, Patrick Gorman, Stanley Anderson, Theodore Sorel, Clayton Corzatte.

SUMMERTREE (8). By Ron Cowen. October 20, 1970. Director, Clayton Corzatte; scenery and costumes, William D. Roberts; lighting, Mark S. Krause. With Dirk Benedict, Eve Roberts, William Myers, Jacqueline Coslow.

LITTLE MURDERS (8). By Jules Feiffer. October 27, 1970. Directors, Allen Fletcher, Josef Sommer; scenery and costumes, William D. Roberts; lighting, Mark S. Krause. With Angela Paton, Stanley Anderson, Patricia Hamilton, Theodore Sorel.

University of Michigan Professional Theater Program: Phoenix Theater Company

THE SCHOOL FOR WIVES (16). By Molière; English verse translation by Richard Wilbur. January 26, 1971. Director, Stephen Porter; scenery and lighting, James Tilton; costumes, Nancy Potts. With Brian Bedford, Joan Van Ark, Paul Ballantyne, David Dukes, Gordon Gould, James Greene, George Pentecost, Peggy Pope, Mario Siletti.

University of Michigan Professional Theater Program: New Play-in-Progress

SIAMESE CONNECTIONS (8). By Dennis J. Reardon. March 16, 1971 (world premiere). Director, Arthur Storch; designer, James Tilton; costumes, Dennis Parker.

Granny .... Fay Sappington
Tom Jensen .... Chester Smith
Minister; Auctioneer .... Robert Porter
Frank Kroner Sr. .... Ward Costello
James Kroner .... John Savage
Kate Kroner .... Helen Stenborg
Frank Kroner Jr. .... Ronny Cox
Gretchen .... Bonnie Gallup
    Scene: An American farm. Act I, Scene 1: An afternoon in late autumn. Scene 2: Very early the next morning. Act II, Scene 1: Three months later, late afternoon, early evening. Scene 2: One month later, a day sometime between winter and spring.

ASHLAND, ORE.

The Oregon Shakespearean Festival: Outdoor Theater

THE MERCHANT OF VENICE (53). By William Shakespeare. May 22, 1970. Director, Angus L. Bowmer; scenery, Clayton L. Karkosh; lighting, Steven L. Maze; costumes, Jean Schultz Davidson. With Michael Winters, Michael O'Sullivan, Fredi Olster, Dorothy French.

ROSENCRANTZ AND GUILDENSTERN ARE DEAD (16). By Tom Stoppard. May 23, 1970. Director, Angus L. Bowmer; scenery, Clayton L. Karkosh; lighting, Steven L. Maze; costumes, Jean Schultz Davidson. With Larry Carpenter, Roger Kozol, Loyd Williamson.

THE COMEDY OF ERRORS (27). By William Shakespeare. June 27, 1970. Director, Nagle Jackson; scenery, Clayton L. Karkosh; lighting, Steven L. Maze; costumes, Jean Schultz Davidson. With Larry Carpenter, Mark D. Murphey, Ric Hamilton, Rick Newman, Candace Birk, Catherine Lincoln.

JULIUS CAESAR (26). By William Shakespeare. June 28, 1970. Director, Larry Oliver; scenery, Clayton L. Karkosh; lighting, Steven L. Maze; costumes, Jean Schultz Davidson. With Philip Davidson, Ric Hamilton, Raye Birk, John Arnone, Candace Birk, Vivian Sally Kemp.

RICHARD II (26). By William Shakespeare. June 29, 1970. Director, Nagle Jackson; scenery, Clayton L. Karkosh; lighting, Steven L. Maze; costumes, Jean Schultz Davidson. With Michael O'Sullivan, Julian Lopez-Morillas, Kit Carson, Philip Davidson, Dorothy French, Fredi Olster, Diana Bellamy.

THE IMAGINARY INVALID (11). By Molière; translated by Morris Bishop. August 13, 1970. Director, Raye Birk; scenery, Clayton L. Karkosh; lighting, Steven L. Maze; costumes, Jean Schultz Davidson. With John Arnone, Vivian Sally Kemp, Roger Kozol, John Sheehan, Ron Boussom.

The Oregon Shakespearean Festival: Angus Bowmer Theater

A MIDSUMMER NIGHT'S DREAM (12). By William Shakespeare. March 19, 1971. Director, Raye Birk; scenery, Richard L. Hay; lighting, Steven A. Maze; costumes, Jean Schultz Davidson. With Shirley Patton. Will Huddleston, Rick Hamilton, Fredi Olster, Larry Martin, Candace Birk, J. Steven White.

UNDER MILK WOOD (11). By Dylan Thomas. March 20, 1971. Director, Larry Oliver; scenery, Richard L. Hay; lighting, Steven A. Maze; costumes, Jean Schultz Davidson. With Larry Martin, Garry Moore.

ARSENIC AND OLD LACE (11). By Joseph Kesselring. March 20, 1971. Director, Philip Davidson; scenery, Richard L. Hay; lighting, Steven A. Maze; costumes, Patte Moon. With Diana Bellamy, Harry Kinney, Candace Birk.

A MAN FOR ALL SEASONS (11). By Robert Bolt. March 21, 1971. Director, Pat Patton; scenery, Richard L. Hay; lighting, Steven A. Maze; costumes, Jean Schultz Davidson. With Raye Birk, Diana Bellamy, Martha J. Tippin, Tom Donaldson.

BALTIMORE

Center Stage

A CRY OF PLAYERS (38). By William Gibson. October 23, 1970. Director, John Stix; scenery, Eldon Elder, lighting, Charles Vanderpool; costumes, Jay Scott. With Rae Allen, Peter Strauss, Carolan Daniels, Peter Bailey Britton.

MARAT/SADE (27). By Peter Weiss; English version by Geoffrey Skelton; verse adaptation by Adrian Mitchell. November 27, 1970. Director, Peter W. Culman; scenery, Charles Vanderpool; lighting, Dennis Shenk; costumes, Jay Scott. With Peter Bailey Britton, Carolan Daniels, Barbara Frank, Hurd Hatfield.

TWELFTH NIGHT (38). By William Shakespeare. January 1, 1971. Director, Shelton Patinkin; scenery, Preston Sisk; lighting, Joan Olsson; costumes, Jay Scott. With Carolan Daniels, Barbara Frank, Steven Gilborn, Wil Love, Betsy Stoll, Henry Strozier.

THE LOVER and THE COLLECTION (27).

By Harold Pinter. February 5, 1971. Director, Robert Lewis; scenery and lighting, Leo Kerz; costumes, Jay Scott. With Valerie French, Wil Love, Margaret Phillips, Jonathan Slade, Henry Strozier, John Tillinger.

CEREMONIES IN DARK OLD MEN (29). By Lonne Elder III. March 5, 1971. Director, Richard Ward; scenery, Whitney J. LeBlanc; lighting, Joan Olsson; costumes, Jay Scott. With Darryl Croxton, Bob Delegall, Bette Howard, Eric Kilpatrick, Gail Moses, Irv Turner, Richard Ward.

FIRE IN THE MINDHOUSE (27). Words by Arnold Borget; music by Lance Mulcahy. April 2, 1971 (world premiere). Director, John Stix; designer, David Mitchell; lighting, Joan Olsson; costumes, Jay Scott; musical director, William Bland; visuals, Thom Lafferty. With Lee Allen, Robert Guillaume, Carol Fox Prescott, Nell Carter, Ken Gilman.

BUFFALO

Studio Arena Theater

DAMES AT SEA (30). Book and lyrics by George Haimsohn and Robin Miller; music by Jim Wise. September 29, 1970. Director, Don Price; scenery and costumes, John Wright Stevens; lighting, David Zierk; musical director, Stuart Hamilton; choreography, Don Price. With Brenda Broome, Richard Balin, Tommy Breslin, Jerry Grant.

SCENES FROM AMERICAN LIFE (8). By A. R. Gurney, Jr. October 27, 1970 (world premiere). Director, Warren Enters; scenery and costumes, Stephen J. Hendrickson; lighting, David Zierk. With Bill Abrams, Terry Burns, Nancy Donohue, Robert Einenkel, Jane Hallaren, Roy London, Caroline McWilliams, Steve Nelson, Patricia O'Connell.

The play is a collage of scenes taking place in Buffalo from 1930 to 1985. One intermission.

THE SURVIVAL OF ST. JOAN (30). Book and lyrics, James Lineberger; music by Hank and Gary Ruffin. November 5, 1970 (world premiere). Director, Chuck Gnys; scenery and costumes, Peter Harvey; lighting, David Zierk; musical coordinator, Stephen Schwartz; music performed by Ruffin.

Joan .... Gretchen Corbett
Farmer .... Dennis Lipscomb
1st Friar; Swineherd; Physician Corporal;
  Philippe; Friar with
  Penitents .... F. Murray Abraham

Bishop's Monk; Soldier; Leper;
    Penitent ....Bill Braden
4th Witch; Barmaid; Whore; Phillip's
    Mother; 1st Nun ....Mary Carter
Prison Monk; Soldier; Penitent;
    Leper ....Tom Carter
Jailer; Farmhand; English Soldier;
    Bishop ....John A. Coe
Child with Mother;
    Farmer's Child ....Patrick Ford
2d Witch; Farmhand's Wife; Whore;
    Joan's Mother; Fortune Teller;
    Penitent ....Judith Granite
Hanged Soldier; Deserter; Young Monk;
    Penitent; Leper ....Peter Lazer
3d Witch; Poet; Soldier; Joan's Brother;
    Penitent ....Mac McMack
Bishop; Colonel; Lieutenant;
    Man ....George Pentecost
1st Witch; Mother with Child;
    Court Lady; Whore; Nun; Penitent;
    Leper Woman ....Janet Sarno
Young Witch; Court Lady; Girl with
    English Soldier; Whore;
    Villager ....Julia Willis
Act I: Overture plus 18 scenes. Act II: 17
scenes. A "medieval rock opera."

THE PRICE (30). By Arthur Miller. December 3, 1970. Director, Warren Enters; scenery, Larry Aumen; lighting, David Zierk; costumes, Duane Andersen. With Jack Gilford, Shepperd Strudwick, Richard McKenzie, Eve Collyer.

L.A. UNDER SIEGE (8). By Mayo Simon. December 29, 1970 (world premiere). Director, Warren Enters; scenery, Douglas Higgins; lighting, Peter J. Gill; costumes, Carrie F. Robbins.

Lenore ....Cathryn Damon
Howard ....Bill Moor
Rosalind ....Janet Dowd
Jack ....Michael (M.P.) Murphy
Mitzi ....Trinity Thompson
Saul ....Tom Rosqui
Girl and Salesgirl ....Christine Joyce
Doctor; Norman ....Peter Gorwin
    One intermission.

OTHELLO (30). By William Shakespeare. February 4, 1971. Director, Louis Criss; scenery, Stephen J. Hendrickson; lighting, David Zierk; costumes, Timothy Miller. With Clebert Ford, Nicholas Kepros, Erika A. Slezak.

THE EFFECT OF GAMMA RAYS ON MAN-IN-THE-MOON MARIGOLDS (30). By Paul Zindel. March 4, 1971. Director, Warren Enters; scenery, Larry Aumen; lighting, David Zierk; costumes, Duane Andersen. With Jo Van Fleet, Kathryn Baumann, Pamela Kingsley, Elizabeth Sanders, Ethel Woodruff.

SCUBA DUBA (30). By Bruce Jay Friedman. April 1, 1971. Director, Clarke Gordon; scenery, Larry Aumen; lighting, Peter J. Gill. With F. Murray Abraham, Clarke Gordon, Elizabeth Perry, Kelly Swartz.

INDIANS (30). By Arthur Kopit. May 6, 1971. Director, Neal Du Brock; scenery, Douglas Lebrecht; lighting, David Zierk; music, Richard Peaslee; Sun Dance choreography, Renata Strauss. With Stan Porter, Alan Mixon, Robert Darnell, Leslie Woolf, Muni Seroff.

Studio Arena Theater: Albright-Knox Art Gallery

THE NEPHEW (7). By Neal Du Brock; adapted from the novel by James Purdy. March 24, 1971 (world premiere). Director, Warren Enters; scenery, Douglas Lebrecht; lighting, David Zierk; costumes, Duane Andersen; incidental music, Ned Rorem.
The Author ....James Patterson
Boyd Mason ....Wallace Rooney
Mrs. Barrington ....Margaret Brewster
Alma Mason ....Margaret Hamilton
Clara Himbaugh ....Mary Bell

Faye Laird ....Laurinda Barrett
Mrs. Laird ....Barbara Sharpe
Willard Baker ....Spencer Davis
Vernon Miller ....Page Johnson
Professor Mannheim ....Roger De Koven
Rosa ....Sally Rubin
    The action of the play takes place from one Memorial Day to the next and occurs in and around Alma Mason's house on a leafy residential street in Rainbow Center, Ohio. The time is the recent past.

Studio Arena Theater: Guest Production

JACQUES BREL IS ALIVE AND WELL AND LIVING IN PARIS (37). January 5,

1971 and again April 28, 1971.

Studio Arena Theater: Children's Theater

ALADDIN! (5). By Aina Niemela and Joe Servello; adapted from *The Arabian Nights.* November 27, 1970. Director, Maynard Burgess; scenery, Edward Patton; costumes, Christine Benzino; choreography, Renata Strauss. With Ted Bouton, Christine Joyce, Luke Pauly.

THE DOCTOR IN SPITE OF HIMSELF (7). By Molière; adapted by Steve Andersen.

December 30, 1970. Directors, Richard and Aza McKenzie; scenery, Douglas LeBrecht; costumes, Christine Benzino. With Betty Lutes, Jim Menke, Ensley (sic).

THE PIED PIPER OF HAMELIN (7). By William Glennon. April 14, 1970. Director, Norman Leger, scenery, Peter Politanoff; costumes, Christine Benzino. With June Duell, Ted Bouton, Jim Menke.

BURLINGTON, VT.

Champlain Shakespeare Festival

TWELFTH NIGHT (15). By William Shakespeare. July 21, 1970. Director, Anthony Wiles; scenery, W. M. Schenk; lighting, Stephen Anderson; costumes, Julie Schwalow.

TROILUS AND CRESSIDA (12). By William Shakespeare. July 23, 1970. Director, James J. Thesing; scenery, W. M. Schenk; lighting, Stephen Anderson; costumes, Julie Schwalow.

EDWARD II (11). By Christopher Marlowe. July 28, 1970. Director, Edward Feidner; scenery, W. M. Schenk; lighting, Stephen Anderson; costumes, Julie Schwalow.

With Betty Smith, Wayne Grace, Anthony Wiles, Ric Zank, Rob Collins, and members of the company.

CHICAGO

The Goodman Resident Theater Company: Goodman Memorial Theater

THE THREEPENNY OPERA (34). Book and lyrics by Bertolt Brecht; music by Kurt Weill; English adaptation by Marc Blitzstein. October 12, 1970. Director, Douglas Seale; scenery, James Maronek; lighting, G. E. Naselius; costumes, Virgil Johnson; musical director, Ronald Jones; choreographer, Wilbert Bradley. With Ann Casson, Richard Curnock, Susan Batson, Leonardo Cimino, Loyse Anderson, LuAnn Post.

TWELFTH NIGHT (34). By William Shakespeare. November 30, 1970. Director, Douglas Seale; scenery, Sandro La Ferla; lighting, Jerrold Gorrell; costumes, Alicia Finkel. With Eric Berry, Ann Casson, Donald Woods, Jo Henderson, Max Howard.

THE NIGHT THOREAU SPENT IN JAIL (36). By Jerome Lawrence and Robert E. Lee. January 18, 1971. Director, Patrick Henry; scenery, James Maronek; lighting, Bengt Nygren; costumes, Daniel Pugh. With Douglas Campbell, Jo Henderson, Ann Casson, Christopher Walken, Douglas Mellor.

MARCHING SONG (34). By John Whiting. March 1, 1971. Director, Douglas Seale; scenery, Sandro La Ferla; lighting, Jerrold Gorrell; costumes, Alicia Finkel. With Richard Curnock, Rebecca Taylor, Ann Casson, Douglas Campbell, Leonardo Cimino.

POOR BITOS (34). By Jean Anouilh; translated by Lucienne Hill. April 12, 1971. Director, Douglas Campbell; scenery, Marc Cohen; lighting, Wayne Tignor; costumes, Virgil Johnson. With Leonardo Cimino, Joseph Shaw, Richard Curnock, Ann Casson, Maurice Copeland, Vincent Park.

LADY AUDLEY'S SECRET (34). By Douglas Seale; adapted from the novel by Mary Elizabeth Braddon; music by George Goehring; lyrics by John Kuntz. May 24, 1971. Director, Douglas Seale; scenery and costumes, Alicia Finkel; lighting, Jerrold Gorrell; choreographer, Jerry Tullos. With LuAnn Post, Max Howard, Donna Curtis, Leonardo Cimino, June Gable, Russell Nype, Terry Lomax.

Goodman Memorial Theater: Studio Theater Company

THE AMOROUS FLEA, musical based on Molière's *The School for Wives,* October 12, 1970; THE TRIAL by Andre Gide and Jean-Louis Barrault, based on Franz Kafka's novel, November 2, 1970; A SCENT OF FLOWERS by James Saunders, December 7, 1970; ALL THAT FALL and PLAY by Samuel Beckett, February 1, 1971; THE MEMORANDUM by Vaclav Havel, translated by Vera Blackwell, February 22, 1971; THE CHERRY

ORCHARD by Anton Chekhov, translated by Tyrone Guthrie and Leonid Kipnis, April 5, 1971; NARROW ROAD TO THE DEEP NORTH by Edward Bond, April 26, 1971;

THE LAUNDRY by David Guerdon, May 18, 1971. Each of these productions ran for 12 performances.

Goodman Memorial Theater: Resident Children's Theater Company

THE PANDA AND THE SPY (25) by Mary Virginia Heinlein, directed by Kelly Danford, June 29, 1970; SACRAMENTO FIFTY MILES (34) by Eleanor and Ray Harder based on *The Brementown Musicians*, directed by Jack Jones, September 19, 1970; ALI BABA AND THE MAGIC CAVE (24) by William Glennon, directed by Bella Itkin, November 21, 1970; A THREEPENNY CHRISTMAS OR THE LEGEND OF NICK

THE SAINT (26) book and lyrics by Stephen Lehner, music by Kenneth Wannberg, directed by Kelly Danford, December 19, 1970; ALICE IN WONDERLAND (30) by Thom Racina, musical based on the story by Lewis Carroll, directed by Thom Racina, January 30, 1971; AESOP'S FALABLES (30), rock musical, book by Ed Gracyzk; music by John Hogan and Henry Moran; lyrics by Marty Conine and Ed Graczyk, March 27, 1971.

Note: Goodman Memorial Theater's professional touring company presented the following during the 1970-71 season in schools and community centers. *The Thwarting of Baron Bolligrew* by Robert Bolt; *How the First Letter Was Written* by Aurand Harris, from Rudyard Kipling's *Just So Stories; The Hide and Seek Odyssey of Madeline Gimple* by Frank Gagliano; *As You Like It* by William Shakespeare.

CINCINNATI

Playhouse In the Park: Robert S. Marx Theater

MANY HAPPY RETURNS: A RE-VIEW OF REVUES (25). Sketches and lyrics by Howard Dietz; music by Arthur Schwartz. June 18, 1970. Director, Word Baker; scenery, Holly Haas Donaldson; lighting, Jay Depenbrock; costumes, Caley Summers; choreographers, Ken Jansen and Word Baker; musical director and arranger, Worth Gardner. With Jack Fletcher, John Towey, John Glover, Bill McClaren, David Huffman, Ceil Cabot, De-Ann Mears, Madelyn Cain, Mary Lynn Melton, Tonia Smith, Richard Ooms.

COME BACK, LITTLE SHEBA (42). By William Inge. July 16, 1970. Director, Eugene Lesser; scenery and lighting, Jay Depenbrock; costumes, Annie Peacock. With Gil Rogers, Charlotte Rae.

HE WHO GETS SLAPPED (25). By Leonid Andreyev. August 27, 1970. Director, Brooks Jones; scenery, Ed Wittstein; lighting, Jay Depenbrock; costumes, Caley Summers. With Laura Esterman, Ken Jenkins, Lester Rawlins, Paul Benedict.

TOBACCO ROAD (30). By Jack Kirkland, based on the novel by Erskine Caldwell. September 24, 1970. Directors, Word Baker and Dan Early; scenery, Stuart Wurtzel; lighting, Jay Depenbrock; costumes, Caley Summers.

With Frank Raiter, Michael Stoddard, Leora Dana, Anita Dangler.

AS YOU LIKE IT (24). By William Shakespeare. October 27, 1970. Directors, Michael Flanagan and Word Baker; scenery, Stuart Wurtzel; lighting, Jay Depenbrock; costumes, Caley Summers; choreographer, Zachary Solov; music, Stone Fox. With Dan Gantry, Gastone Rossilli, Garry George, Ian Wilder.

THE BLACKS (16). By Jean Genet. November 18, 1970. Director, Marc Primus; scenery, Stuart Wurtzel; lighting, Jay Depenbrock; costumes, Patrizia Von Brandenstein. With Gilbert Lewis, Harold Miller, Beatrice Winde, Marlene Warfield.

ANGEL STREET (54). By Patrick Hamilton. April 1, 1971. Director, Anthony Perkins; scenery, Ed Wittstein; lighting, Lee Bonamy; costumes, Caley Summers. With Roni Dengel, Bill Moor.

SLOW DANCE ON THE KILLING GROUND (27). By William Hanley. May 1, 1971. Director, Dan Early; scenery, Tom Oldendick, lighting, Leo Bonamy; costumes, Caley Summers. With Roger De Koven, Robert Stocking, Lori Heineman.

Playhouse In the Park: Shelter House Theater

KRAPP'S LAST TAPE and EH, JOE (12). By Samuel Beckett. June 25, 1970. With William Hansen.

Playhouse In the Park: Guest Production

JACQUES BREL IS ALIVE AND WELL   1971. March 1,
AND LIVING IN PARIS (31).

CLEVELAND

Cleveland Play House: Euclid-77th Theater

DON JUAN IN HELL (22). By George Bernard Shaw. September 9, 1970. Director, Stuart Levin; lighting, Steve Waxler, Jeffrey Dallas; costumes, Joe Dale Lunday. With Robert Thorson, John Buck Jr., Elizabeth Lowry, Robert Moak.

THE THREEPENNY OPERA (40). Book and lyrics by Bertolt Brecht; music by Kurt Weill; English adaptation by Marc Blitzstein. October 16, 1970. Director, John Going; scenery and costumes, Joe Dale Lunday; lighting, Paul Stenbock; musical director, Donna Renton. With Richard Halverson, Edith Owen, David Frazier, Michelle Reilley, Mary Shelley.

LYSISTRATA (4). By Aristophanes; translated by Douglass Parker. December 4, 1970. Director, John Going; scenery and costumes, Joe Dale Lunday; lighting, Paul Stenbock. With June Gibbons, Myrna Kaye, Myriam Lipari, Ronald Greene.

YOU KNOW I CAN'T HEAR YOU WHEN THE WATER'S RUNNING (26). By Robert Anderson. December 18, 1970. Director, John Going; scenery and costumes, Joe Dale Lunday; lighting, Paul Stenbock. With Robert Allman, David Berman, David Frazier, June Gibbons, Ron Greene, Richard Halverson, Myrna Kaye, Allen Leatherman, Edith Owen.

SUMMER AND SMOKE (33). By Tennessee Williams. January 22, 1971. Director, John Going; scenery and costumes, Joe Dale Lunday; lighting, Jeffrey Dallas. With Shelia Russell, Jonathan Bolt, Robert Snook, Richard Halverson, Edith Owen.

THE DEVIL'S DISCIPLE (18). By George Bernard Shaw. March 4, 1971. Director, John Going; scenery and costumes, Joe Dale Lunday; lighting, Jeffrey Dallas. With Jonathan Bolt, Jean Barrett, Robert Thorson, Richard Halverson.

PLAZA SUITE (14). By Neil Simon. May 7, 1971. Director, John Going; scenery, Paul Rodgers; lighting, Jeffrey Dallas; costumes, Joe Dale Lunday. With David Berman, David Frazier, June Gibbons, Mary Shelley, Vivienne Stotter.

Cleveland Play House: Drury Theater

WHATEVER HAPPENED TO HUGGING AND KISSING? and THE HUFF AND THE PUFF (24). By Norman Wexler. September 11, 1970. Director, Robert Snook; scenery and lighting, Marla Nedelman; costumes, Joe Dale Lunday. With David Berman, Mary Gallagher, Stuart Levin, Vivienne Stotter, Marcie Ross.

FALLEN ANGELS (40). By Noel Coward. October 23, 1970. Director, Richard Oberlin; scenery and costumes, Eugene Hare; lighting, Paul Stenbock. With June Gibbons, Robert Allman, Allen Leatherman, Marjorie Dawe.

EXCEPT FOR SUSIE FINKEL (38). By Joe Manchester. December 11, 1970 (world premiere). Director, Jonathan Bolt; scenery, Marla Nedelman; lighting, Paul Stenbock; costumes, Harriet Cone.
Sunshine .... Robert Thorson
Jonas Fox .... Tom Keena
Shoshana .... Mary Shelley

Mike .... Susan Burkhalter
Dr. Spiegle .... Ben Letter
   The action of the play takes place in Jonas Fox's apartment on the West Side of New York. Act I, Scene 1: A Sunday morning in spring. Scene 2: That afternoon. Scene 3: Late morning, the following Friday. Act II: Early evening, the following Sunday.

THE WHITE HOUSE MURDER CASE (33). By Jules Feiffer. January 29, 1971. Director, Richard Oberlin; scenery, Eugine Hare; lighting, Paul Stenbock; costumes, Diane Dalton Smith. With Ben Letter, Allen Leatherman, Mary Shelley, Leif Ancker, Ted Hallaman, Robert Thorson.

THE PROMISE (17). By Aleksei Arbuzov; translated by Ariadne Nicolaeff. April 30, 1971. Director, Jonathan Bolt; scenery, Joe Dale Lunday; lighting, Jeffrey Dallas. With John Buck Jr., Myriam Lipari, Robert Thorson.

Cleveland Play House: Brooks Theater

GALLOWS HUMOR (21). By Jack Richardson. October 30, 1970. Director, Jonathan Bolt; scenery and costumes, Marla Nedelman; lighting, Paul Stenbock. With Cleo Holladay, Bob Moak.

ENDGAME (32). By Samuel Beckett. October 31, 1970. Director, Larry Tarrant; scenery and costumes, Marla Nedelman; lighting, Paul Stenbock. With Jonathan Bolt, Cleo Holiday, Bob Moak, Robert Thorson.

SPOON RIVER ANTHOLOGY (29). By Edgar Lee Masters; conceived and adapted by Charles Aidman; music, Naomi Caryl Hirshhorn; lyrics, Charles Aidman. December 25, 1970. Director, Robert Snook; lighting, Orison Bedell; costumes, Diane Dalton Smith. With Jean Barrett, John Buck Jr., Tom Carson, Evie McElroy, Mary Gallagher.

BEYOND THE FRINGE (27). By Alan Bennett, Peter Cook, Jonathan Miller, Dudley Moore. February 5, 1971. Director, Robert Snook; scenery and lighting, Orison Bedell; costumes, Harriet Cone. With David Berman, John Buck Jr., David O. Frazier, Bob Moak.

Cleveland Play House: Guest Production

SONGS FROM MILK WOOD, adapted from Dylan Thomas' *Under Milk Wood;* JOURNEYS, collected by Richard Lewis; WOYZECK by Georg Buchner, translated by Henry J. Schmidt (8). March 8, 1971. National Theater of the Deaf.

DALLAS

Dallas Theater Center: Kalita Humphreys Theater

THE BOYS FROM SYRACUSE (33). Book by George Abbott, based on *The Comedy of Errors* by William Shakespeare; music by Richard Rodgers; lyrics by Lorenz Hart. July 2, 1970. Director, David Pursley; scenery and costumes, David Pursley; lighting, Randy Moore. With Randolph Tallman, Louise Mosley, John Figlmiller, Maureen O'Brian, Margaret Yount.

FARCE 'N FLICK (a magic cine scene production) by B. M. Svoboda and FANTOCCINI (a mime show) by Sally Netzel (15). September 15, 1970. Directors, B. M. Svoboda and Frank Schaefer; designers, Kveta Bartak and Yoichi Aoki. *Fantoccini* lighting, Margaret Yount; cameramen for *Farce 'n Flick,* Manuel De Aumente, John Mahoney, Frank Schaefer. With members of the Dallas Theater Center Company.

HAMLET ESP (34). By Paul Baker; a new concept of William Shakespeare's *Hamlet.* October 27, 1970. Director, Paul Baker; scenery and costumes, Mary Sue Jones; lighting, Randy Moore. With Reginald Montgomery, Randolph Tallman, Gene Leggett.

PETER PAN (29). Book by James M. Barrie; music by Mark Charlap; lyrics by Carolyn Leigh; additional music by Jule Styne; additional lyrics by Betty Comden and Adolph Green. December 8, 1970. Director, Ryland Merkey; scenery and costumes, Michael Wray; lighting, Linda Blase, Robyn Baker Flatt; musical direction, Beatrice Heikkila, choreography, Cheryl Tyre. With Albert Insinnia, Norma Levin, John Henson, Chequita Jackson.

THE SEAGULL (21). By Anton Chekhov; translated by David Magarshack. January 12, 1971. Director, Paul Baker; scenery, Marian Smith-Martin, Johanna Stalker; lighting, Jim Progar; costumes, Sally Baker Laurie. Based on the production score by K. S. Stanislavsky for the Moscow Art Theater. With Mary Sue Jones, Christopher Hendrie, Michael Wray, Sharon Jeffries, Chelcie Ross.

HARVEY (21). By Mary Chase. February 23, 1971. Director, Ken Latimer; scenery, Johanna Stalker; lighting, Ken Harden. With Ryland Merkey, Ella-Mae Brainard, John Figlmiller, Barry Hope, Nancy Jones.

THE NIGHT THOREAU SPENT IN JAIL (39). By Jerome Lawrence and Robert E. Lee. April 7, 1971. Directors, Paul Baker, David H. Ayers, Kaki Dowling; scenery, David George; lighting, Randy Moore; costumes, John Henson. With Randolph Tallman, Steven Mackenroth and members of the company.

Dallas Theater Center: Down Center Stage

A DAY IN THE DEATH OF JOE EGG (30). By Peter Nichols. July 7, 1970. Director, Campbell Thomas; scenery and costumes, Johanna Stalker; lighting, Larry Wheeler. With David Pursley, Betty June Lary, Preston Jones, Elizabeth Lumpkin, Lynn Trammell.

THE LATE CHRISTOPHER BEAN (40). By Sidney Howard. October 6, 1970. Director, Sally Netzel; designer, Johanna Stalker; lighting, Paul John Smith. With Judith Davis, Ken Latimer, Synthia Rogers.

WAITING FOR GODOT (26). By Samuel Beckett. December 15, 1970. Director, Ken Latimer; designer, Kathleen Latimer; lighting, Sally Netzel. With Randy Moore, Allen Hibbard, Steven Mackenroth, Michael Dendy.

ANNA CHRISTIE (28). By Eugene O'Neill. February 2, 1971. Director, Campbell Thomas; scenery, Russell Guinn; lighting, Allen Hibbard; costumes, Mary Ann Colia. With Kaki Dowling, Preston Jones, William L. Denney, Sally Netzel.

DEAR LIAR (15). By Jerome Kilty; adapted from the correspondence of George Bernard Shaw and Mrs. Patrick Campbell. March 23, 1971. Director, Edward Herrmann; designer, Lynn Lester; lighting, Sally Netzel. With Campbell Thomas, Jacque Thomas.

THE ATTENDANT (13). By Stratis Karras; translated by Evangelos Voutsinas. May 11, 1971 (American premiere). Director, Stratis Karras; designer, Nellie Diaks; lighting, Sam Nance.

Lalakis ....Ryland Merkey
Loukoumas ....Gene Leggett
Makis ....Bryant J. Reynolds
Savvas ....Mac Williams
Old Woman ....Joan Meister

DETROIT

Oakland University Professional Theater Program: Detroit Institute of Art

THE SKIN OF OUR TEETH (7). By Thornton Wilder. November 25, 1970. Director, Terence Kilburn; scenery and lighting, Richard Davis; costumes, Veronica Gustaff. With Glynis Bell, Harry Ellerbe, Elisabeth Orion, Barbara Quinn.

LIFE WITH FATHER (7). By Howard Lindsay and Russel Crouse. December 30, 1970. Director, Joseph Shaw; scenery and lighting, Richard Davis; costumes, Veronica Gustaff. With William LeMassena, Elisabeth Orion.

THE CRUCIBLE (7). By Arthur Miller. January 27, 1971. Director, Terence Kilburn; scenery and lighting, Richard Davis; costumes, Veronica Gustaff. With Glynis Bell, Peter Brandon, Elisabeth Orion, Toby Tompkins.

TARTUFFE (7). By Molière; English translation by Richard Wilbur. February 24, 1971. Director, Terence Kilburn; scenery and lighting, Richard Davis; costumes, Veronica Gustaff. With Diane Bugas, William LeMassena, Joseph Shaw.

THE RAINMAKER (7). By N. Richard

Nash. March 24, 1971. Director, Terence Kilburn; scenery and lighting, Richard Davis; costumes, Veronica Gustaff. With Diane Bugas, David Himes, Philip Mallet.

WHO'S AFRAID OF VIRGINIA WOOLF? (7). By Edward Albee. April 21, 1971. Director, John Ulmer; scenery and lighting, Richard Davis; costumes, Veronica Gustaff. With Peter Brandon, Priscilla Morrill, Elizabeth Oustinoff, Toby Tompkins.

A THOUSAND CLOWNS (7). By Herb Gardner. May 12, 1971. Director, Terence Kilburn; scenery, James D. Hansen; lighting, Katherine Ann Turco; costumes, Veronica Gustaff. With William LeMassena, Teddy Moniak, Howard Morton, Susan Thorne.

THE FANTASTICKS (7). Book and lyrics by Harvey Schmidt; music by Tom Jones; based on Edmond Rostand's *Les Romantiques*. June 16, 1971. Director, Christopher Hewett; scenery, James D. Hansen; lighting, Katherine Ann Turco; costumes, Veronica Gustaff. With Joe Bellomo, Robert Englund, Erik Howell, Jennifer Williams.

HALIFAX, NOVA SCOTIA (CANADA)

Neptune Theater: Summer Season, Main Stage

DEATH OF A SALESMAN (19). By Arthur Miller. July 3, 1970. Director, Keith Turnbull; scenery, Antony Dimitrov; lighting, David Hinks; costumes, Olga Dimitrov.

ANY WEDNESDAY (22). By Muriel Resnick. July 7, 1970. Director, Heinar Piller; scenery, Fred Allen; lighting, David Hinks; costumes, Olga Dimitrov.

THE EGG (18). By Felicien Marceau. July

14, 1970. Director, Keith Turnbull; scenery, Antony Dimitrov; lighting, David Hinks; costumes, Olga Dimitrov.

Summer 1970 Neptune Theater Company included Liza Creighton, Jerry Franken, Ron Hastings, Patricia Ludwick, Margaret Macleod, Jack Medley, Kenneth Pogue, Rosemary Radcliffe, David Renton, Terry Tweed, Faith Ward, Sandy Webster, Kenneth Wickes.

Neptune Theater: Winter Season

RUMPLE STILTSKIN (18). By Diane Stapley and Ronald Chudley. December 26, 1970. Director, Heinar Piller; scenery, Antony Dimitrov; lighting, David Hinks; costumes, Olga Dimitrov. With Barbara Bryne, Gracie Finley, George Jordan, David Renton, Lionel Simmons, Kenneth Wickes.

A MIDSUMMER NIGHT'S DREAM (15). By William Shakespeare. January 28, 1971. Director, Heinar Piller; scenery, Antony Dimitrov; lighting, David Hinks, costumes, Olga Dimitrov. With Don Allison, Diana Barrington, Denise Fergusson, Briain Petchey, Kenneth Pogue, Margot Sweeny, Carolyn Younger.

LONG DAY'S JOURNEY INTO NIGHT (15). By Eugene O'Neill. February 18, 1971. Director, William Davis; scenery, Antony Dimitrov; lighting, David Hinks; costumes, Olga

Dimitrov. With David Dodimead, Lynne Gorman, Patricia Ludwick, Briain Petchey, Kenneth Pogue.

THE CARETAKER (15). By Harold Pinter. March 11, 1971. Director, Eric Salmon; scenery, Antony Dimitrov; lighting, David Hinks; costumes, Olga Dimitrov. With Patrick Boxill, Kenneth Pogue, David Renton.

THE FANTASTICKS (21). Book and lyrics by Harvey Schmidt; music by Tom Jones; based on Edmond Rostand's Les Romantiques. April 1, 1971. Director, Alan Lund; scenery, Antony Dimitrov; lighting, David Hinks; costumes, Olga Dimitrov; choreography, Alan Lund; musical director, Alan Lund. With Bob Ainslie, Douglas Chamberlain, Beth Anne Cole, Bill Cole, Jeff Hyslop, Jack Northmore, David Renton, Kenneth Wickes.

HARTFORD, CONN.

The Hartford Stage Company

ROSENCRANTZ AND GUILDENSTERN ARE DEAD (44). By Tom Stoppard. October 16, 1970. Director, Paul Weidner; scenery and costumes, Santo Loquasto; lighting, Joe Pacitti. With Jeremiah Sullivan, John Colenback, Tana Hicken, John MacAllan.

RING ROUND THE MOON (44). By Jean Anouilh; translated by Christopher Fry. November 27, 1970. Director, Philip Minor; scenery, Santo Loquasto; lighting, John Wright Stevens; costumes, Linda Fisher. With Jeremiah Sullivan, Jill Tanner, Katherine Houghton.

A GUN PLAY (44). By Yale M. Udoff. January 8, 1971 (world premiere). Director, Paul Weidner; scenery, Santo Loquasto; lighting, Larry Crimmins, costumes, Colleen Callahan.
Stan .... David O. Petersen
Orlando .... Henry Thomas
Wallace .... Ted Graeber
Lita .... Charlotte Moore
Linden .... Robert Moberly
Jack .... James Valentine
Norma .... Darthy Blair
1st Motorcycle Officer ..... James Carruthers
George .... Ron Frazier

Melinda .... Tana Hicken
Fashion Model .... Delores Brown
2d Motorcycle Officer .. Christopher Andrews
Young Girl .... Robin Murphy
Johnni .... Michael Esterson
The action of the play takes place in a small club in a large American city, without an intermission.

LONG DAY'S JOURNEY INTO NIGHT (44). By Eugene O'Neill. February 19, 1971. Director, Jacques Cartier; scenery and costumes, Santo Loquasto; lighting, Peter Hunt. With Robert Pastene, Teresa Wright, Tom Atkins, John Glover.

BLITHE SPIRIT (44). By Noel Coward. April 2, 1971. Director, Nagle Jackson; scenery and costumes, Lawrence King; lighting, Larry Crimmins. With Lois de Banzie, Peter Duncan, Darthy Blair, Charlotte Moore.

THE BOYS IN THE BAND (44). By Mart Crowley. May 14, 1971. Director, Paul Weidner; scenery, Lawrence King; lighting, Larry Crimmins; costumes, Colleen Callahan. With Ron Frazier, Anthony Heald, Mark Dempsey, Henry Thomas.

HOUSTON

Alley Theater: Large Stage

DEAR LOVE (14). By Jerome Kilty; adapted from the correspondence of Elizabeth Barrett and Robert Browning. September 17, 1970

(world premiere). Director, Burry Fredrick.
Elizabeth Barrett .... Myrna Loy
Robert Browning .... Jerome Kilty

MOURNING BECOMES ELECTRA (38). By Eugene O'Neill. October 22, 1970. Director, Nina Vance; scenery and costumes, Jerry Williams; lighting, Richard D. Cortright. With Lillian Evans, Nancy Evans Leonard, William Hardy, William Trotman, Ray Stricklyn.

RING ROUND THE BATHTUB (38). By Jane Trahey. December 3, 1970 (world premiere). Director, William Hardy; scenery and costumes, Jerry Williams; lighting, John Hagan.

Darcy .... Mary K. Isaacs
Gran .... Gertrude Flynn
Maggie Train .... Jeannette Clift
Dan Train .... James Broderick
Esme .... Melissa Weaver
Aunt Bea .... Lillian Evans
Uncle Louis .... Joe Finkelstein
Cousin Esther .... Bettye Fitzpatrick
Mr. Valpone .... Rutherford Cravens
Mr. Roccanova ..... James Richard Morgan
Telephone Man .... Woody Skaggs
Mr. Enright .... George Ebeling
Captain Featherwhistle ...... I. M. Hobson
Nurse Samson .... Nancy Evans Leonard
Salvation Army Singers ..R. Edward Leonard,
Beth Sanford, Donna O'Connor, Karen Filer
The entire action of the play takes place at the Train home in Chicago. The time is between October and Christmas of a year in the early 1930's when the Depression was in full swing. Act I, Scene 1: A late afternoon in October. Scene 2: The last Sunday in October.

Act II, Scene 1: The morning after Election Day. Scene 2: Late that night. Act III, Scene 1: Afternoon of December 24. Scene 2: That night.

THE NIGHT THOREAU SPENT IN JAIL (38). By Jerome Lawrence and Robert E. Lee. January 14, 1971. Director, Beth Sanford; scenery, Jerry Williams; lighting, John Hagan. With Michael Moriarity, Grace Chapman, Kendall Clark, Lillian Evans.

OUR TOWN (38). By Thornton Wilder. February 25, 1971. Director, R. Edward Leonard; scenery and costumes, Jerry Williams; lighting, Jonathan Duff. With George Ebeling, Clint Anderson, Kendall Clark, Grace Chapman, Bettye Fitzpatrick, Joel Stedman, Nancy Evans Leonard.

THE PRIME OF MISS JEAN BRODIE (38). By Jay Presson Allen; adapted from the novel by Muriel Spark. April 8, 1971. Director, Bob Leonard; scenery and costumes, Jerry Williams; lighting, John Hagan. With Jeannette Clift, John Milford, Patricia Pearcy, Bob Larkin, Nancy Evans Leonard.

DIAL "M" FOR MURDER (38). By Frederick Knott. May 20, 1971. Director, Burry Fredrick; scenery and costumes, Jerry Williams; lighting, John Hagan. With Lillian Evans, Garry Phillips, William Hardy, Jack Bell.

Alley Theater: Arena Stage

TANGO (11). By Slawomir Mrozek; translated by Ralph Manheim and Teresa Dzieduscycka. May 21, 1971. Director, Beth Sanford; scenery and lighting, Richard H. Graham Jr.; costumes, Jerry Williams. With Jack Stedman, I. M. Hobson, Donna O'Connor, Woody Skaggs, Karen Filer.

Alley Theater: Children's Theater

THE ADVENTURES OF WINNIE-THE-POOH (10). By Beth Sanford; adapted from the book by A. A. Milne. June 10, 1970. Director, Beth Sanford. With Bettye Fitzpatrick, Donna O'Connor, Karen Filer, Rutherford Cravens.

THE YELLOW BRICK ROAD (8). By Iris Siff. January 23, 1971.

TOM SAWYER'S TRIP ABROAD (4). By Sam Havens; music by George Morganstern.

KANSAS CITY, MO.

Missouri Repertory Theater

THE SKIN OF OUR TEETH (16). By Thornton Wilder. July 2, 1970. Director, John O'Shaughnessy; scenery, Max Beatty; lighting, Lee Watson; costumes, Richard Hieronymus. With Molly McGreevy, Rebecca Engelking, Leslie Pollock, Edward Stevlingson, Harriet Levitt.

HARVEY (16). By Mary Chase. July 9, 1970. Director, Patricia McIlrath; scenery, James

Blackwood, lighting, Lee Watson, costumes, Vincent Scassellati. With JoElla Deffenbaugh, Robin Humphrey, James Burr.

INDIANS (15). By Arthur Kopit. July 16, 1970. Director, John O'Shaughnessy; scenery, Jack Montgomery; lighting, Lee Watson; costumes, Vincent Scassellati. With Alvah Stanley, Edward Stevlingson, Ray Aranha, Robert Scogin, Robert Elliott, Philip Christopher.

EXIT THE KING (14). By Eugene Ionesco; translated by Donald Watson. July 23, 1970. Director, Rod Alexander; scenery, Max Beatty; lighting, Lee Watson; costumes, Vincent Scassellati. With Robert Elliott, Harriet Levitt, Robin Humphrey, Alvah Stanley.

THE TEMPEST (15). By William Shakespeare. August 6, 1970. Director, William Woodman; scenery, Jack Montgomery; lighting, Lee Watson; costumes, Vincent Scassel-lati. With Alvah Stanley, Robert Scogin, Robert Elliott, Ray Aranha, Sally Gordon, James Burr.

ARMS AND THE MAN (12). By George Bernard Shaw. August 13, 1970. Director, Robin Humphrey; scenery, J. Morton Walker; lighting, Lee Watson. With Sally Gordon, Jo-Ella Deffenbaugh, Robert Elliott, Art Ellison, Robert Scogin.

LAKEWOOD, OHIO

Great Lakes Shakespeare Festival

THE MERCHANT OF VENICE (18). By William Shakespeare. July 10, 1970. Director, Lawrence Carra; scenery, Milton Howarth; lighting, Frederic Youens; costumes, William French. With Durward B. McDonald, Robert Allman, Anne Draper, Kate Webster.

R.U.R. (ROSSUM'S UNIVERSAL ROBOTS) (18). By Karel Capek; English version by Paul Selver and Nigel Playfair. July 15, 1970. Director, Joseph J. Garry Jr.; scenery, Milton Howarth; lighting, Frederic Youens; costumes, William French. With Kermit Brown, Anne Draper, Robert Allman, Kate Webster, Norma Joseph.

JULIUS CAESAR (18). By William Shakespeare. July 29, 1970. Director, Lawrence Carra; scenery, Milton Howarth; lighting, Frederic Youens; costumes, William French. With Keith Mackey, Robert G. Denison, John Milligan, Robert Allman, Anne Draper, Norma Joseph.

VOLPONE (12). By Ben Jonson. August 12, 1970. Director, Lawrence Carra; scenery, Milton Howarth; lighting, Frederic Youens; costumes, William French. With John Milligan, Roy Clary, Norma Joseph.

THE COMEDY OF ERRORS (8). By William Shakespeare. August 26, 1970. Director, Robert Benedetti; scenery, Milton Howarth; lighting, Frederic Youens; costumes, William French. With William McLuckey, Robert Browning, Kate Webster, Anne Draper, Norma Joseph.

LOS ANGELES

Center Theater Group of the Mark Taper Forum

STORY THEATER (54). Devised by Paul Sills from Grimm's Fairy Tales. June 18, 1970. Director, Paul Sills; designer, Michael Devine; lighting, H. R. Poindexter; costumes, Stephanie Kline. With Peter Bonerz, Hamid Hamilton Camp, Melinda Dillon, Mary Frann, Valerie Harper, Richard Libertini, Paul Sand, Richard Schaal, Lewis Arquette.

THE DREAM ON MONKEY MOUNTAIN (54). By Derek Walcott. August 27, 1970 (world premiere). Director, Michael A. Schultz; scenery, Edward Burbridge; lighting, Tharon Musser; costumes, Lewis Brown; choreography, Mary Barnett.
Tigre ....Herbert Jefferson Jr.
Souris ....Afolabi Ajayi
Corporal Lestrade ....Ron O'Neal
Makak ....Roscoe Lee Browne
The Apparition ....Anne Worthington
Moustique ....Antonio Fargas
Basil ....James A. Watson Jr.
Market Wife ....Esther Rolle
Market Inspector
  Pamphilion ....Charles Turner

Principal Drummer ....Andrew Beddeau
  Musicians: K. Lawrence Dunham, Santiago A. Gonzalez III. Village Women, Wives of Makak: Deborah Brooks, Charlette Cooke, Philomena Nowlin, Esther Rolle, Freda Vanterpool. Village Men, Warriors: Cinque Attucks, Fred Grey, Ed Mock, Charles Turner.
  Time: The present. Place: A West Indian island. Prologue: Quatre Chemin Jail. Part I: Makak's hut; a country road; a village market. Part II: The cell; the forest; apotheosis. Epilogue: Quatre Chemin Jail.

ROSEBLOOM (54). By Harvey Perr. November 5, 1970 (world premiere). Director, Gordon Davidson; scenery, Michael Devine; lighting, Tharon Musser; costumes, Peter Wexler; songs, Randy Newman.
Sylvie ....Sheree North
Enola Gay ....Carrie Snodgress
Mark ....Ron Rifkin
Harry Rosebloom ....Nehemia Persoff
  The action of the play takes place in the living room of Mark and Enola Gay Rose-

bloom. The time is the present. One intermission.

METAMORPHOSES (54). A Story Theater production conceived by Paul Sills from Ovid's *Metamorphoses;* translated, adapted with lyrics by Arnold Weinstein. February 4, 1971. Director, Paul Sills; scenery, James Trittipo; lighting, H. R. Poindexter; costumes, Noel Taylor; music, Country Joe McDonald; additional music, David Cohen. With Susan

Anspach, Bill Callaway, Bernie Casey, George Gaynes, Michael Greene, Paula Kelly, George Morgan, Trina Parks, John Rubinstein, Avery Schreiber, Lesley Warren, Judi West.

OTHELLO (54). By William Shakespeare. April 8, 1971. Director, John Berry; scenery, Peter Larkin; lighting, Martin Aronstein; costumes, Dorothy Jeakins. With James Earl Jones, Anthony Zerbe, Jill Clayburgh, Penelope Allen.

Note: Center Theater Group's 1971 season at the Mark Taper Forum will also include *A New Musical Entertainment* featuring the lyrics of E.Y. Harburg, June 17, 1971, directed by Michael A. Schultz; the American premiere of Peter Nichols's *The National Health or Nurse Norton's Affair,* August 26, 1971, directed by Gordon Davidson; George Bernard Shaw's *Major Barbara,* November 4, 1971, directed by Edward Parone.

New Theater for Now Workshop of the Mark Taper Forum

June 1, 1970 through May 31, 1971. Each program usually receives about 6 performances.

L.A. UNDER SIEGE by Mayo Simon. Director, Edward Parone; designers, Michael Devine, Tharon Musser, Pete Menefee, Don Morand, Tom A. Larson. With Frank Aletter, Helen Page Camp, Naomi Hirshhorn, Allyn Ann McLerie, Fredricka Myers, David Sachs, Brian Taggert, Malachi Throne, Douglass Watson.

THE TRIAL OF THE CATONSVILLE NINE by Daniel Berrigan, S. J. Director, Gordon Davidson; designers, Michael Devine, Tharon Musser; music, Joseph Byrd; film sequences, Sterling Johnson, Patrick Crawford and Group One Productions, Inc. With Gwen Arner, Beau Bridges, Paul Carr, Matt Clark, Mariclare Costello, James Daly, Mary Jackson, John Lasell, Davis Roberts, William Schallert, Peter Strauss, Tom Troupe, Anthony Zerbe.

FATHER'S DAY (a work-in-progress) by

Oliver Hailey. Director, Michael Monte; designers, Robert Moore, Michael Garrett, Jeffrey Jones. With Barbara Colby, Ellen Geer, Donald Moffat, Lawrence Pressman, John Saxon, Diana Webster.

CAFETERIA STYLE LUNCH by David Trainer, MOMSIE AND THE MIDNIGHT BRIDE by Alan Ormsby, directed by Wallace Chappell. BLACK JUDAS by Robert Valine, directed by Alfred Rossi. Designers, Robert Morre, Michael Garrett, Jeffrey Jones; music, Santiago A. Gonzales III; choreographer, Maryellen Clemons. With Helen Page Camp, Steve Franken, Santiago A. Gonalez III, Ben Hammer, Kelly Jean Peters, Barbara Press, John Ritter, Paul Winfield.

WHO WANTS TO BE THE LONE RANGER by Lee Kalcheim. Director, Edward Parone; designers, Donald Harris, Tharon Musser, William Barbe. With Bob Balaban, Bill Callaway, Helen Page Camp, Dana Elcar, Diana Ewing, Pippa Scott, Joyce Van Patten, Judi West.

LOUISVILLE, KY.

Actors Theater of Louisville

THE TAMING OF THE SHREW (15). By William Shakespeare. September 24, 1970. Director, Jon Jory; scenery and costumes, James Edmund Brady; lighting, Johnny Walker. With George Ede, William Swetland, Ken Jenkins, Katharine Houghton, Lee Anne Fahey.

CHARLEY'S AUNT (26). By Brandon Thomas. October 15, 1970. Director, Jon Jory; scenery, Grady Larkins; lighting, Johnny Walker; costumes, Bill Walker. With Max Wright, David C. Burrow, Christopher Murney, Judith Long, Lee Anne Fahey.

OUR TOWN (26). By Thornton Wilder. November 12, 1970. Director, Jon Jory; scenery and lighting, Johnny Walker; costumes, Bill Walker. With Victor Jory, George Ede, Jean Inness, Adale O'Brien, Roger Miller, Lee Anne Fahey.

THE LION IN WINTER (24). By James Goldman. December 10, 1970. Director, Ken Jenkins; scenery and costumes, John Jensen; lighting, Johnny Walker. With Stanley Anderson, Judith Long, Adale O'Brien.

A THURBER CARNIVAL (24). By James Thurber. December 10, 1970. Director, Sue

Lawless; scenery, John Jensen; lighting, Johnny Walker; costumes, Bill Walker. With Hugh Alexander, Peggy Cowles, George Ede, Lee Anne Fahey, Jean Inness, Victor Jory and members of the company.

THE TENTH MAN (24). By Paddy Chayefsky. January 7, 1971. Director, Jon Jory; scenery, Grady Larkins; lighting, Geoffrey T. Cunningham; costumes, Bill Walker. With Max Wright, Peggy Cowles, Joe Hindy, Paul Villani.

FEIFFER'S PEOPLE (24) By Jules Feiffer. February 4, 1971. Director, Dennis Rosa; scenery, Hal Tine; lighting, Johnny Walker; costumes, Bill Walker. With Stanley Anderson, Lee Anne Fahey, Sandy McCallum, Wathen Montgomery, Gretchen Oehler.

A DAY IN THE DEATH OF JOE EGG (24). By Peter Nichols. February 4, 1971. Director, Ken Jenkins; scenery, Hal Tine; lighting, Johnny Walker; costumes, Bill Walker. With Max Wright, Judith Long, Lucy Welch, Eleanor Wilson.

MAJOR BARBARA (23). By George Bernard Shaw. March 4, 1971. Director, Jon Jory; scenery, Hal Tine; lighting, Johnny Walker; costumes, Bill Walker. With Katharine Houghton, Paul Villani, Ken Jenkins, Stanley Anderson.

DRACULA (37). By Hamilton Deane and John L. Balderston; from the novel by Bram Stoker. April 1, 1971. Director, Christopher Murney; scenery, Hal Tine; lighting, Johnny Walker; costumes, Bill Walker. With George Ede, Paul Villani, Lee Anne Fahey.

MILWAUKEE

Milwaukee Repertory Theater Company: Todd Wehr Theater

MEDEA (44). By Euripides; translated by Philip Vellacott. September 25, 1970. Director, Tunc Yalman; scenery and costumes, William James Wall; lighting, William Mintzer. With Sirin Devrim, William McKereghan, Alan Zampese.

YOU CAN'T TAKE IT WITH YOU (44). By Moss Hart and George S. Kaufman. November 6, 1970. Director, Ronald L. Hufham; scenery, Christopher M. Idoine; lighting, William Mintzer; costumes, Janet C. Warren. With Anne Shropshire, Linda Carlson, Stuart Kendall, Dale J. Bellaire.

AS YOU LIKE IT (44). By William Shakespeare. December 18, 1970. Director, Timothy S. Mayer; scenery and costumes, William James Wall; lighting, William Mintzer. With Dale J. Bellaire, Charles E. Siegel, Kevin O'Connor, Linda Carlson, Judith Light.

SPOON RIVER ANTHOLOGY (44). By Edgar Lee Masters; conceived, adapted, and arranged by Charles Aidman. January 29, 1971. Director, John Pasquin; scenery, William James Wall; lighting, William Mintzer. With members of the Company.

THE LIAR (44). By Carlo Goldoni; new version by Tunc Yalman. March 12, 1971. Director, Paul Weidner; scenery, Christopher M. Idoine; lighting, William Mintzer; costumes, Janet C. Warren. With Charles E. Siegel, Linda Carlson, Gary Bayer, Jim Jansen, Philip Mackenzie.

A DOLL'S HOUSE (44). By Henrik Ibsen, translated by Eva Le Gallienne. April 23, 1971. Director, Tunc Yalman; scenery and costumes, William James Wall; lighting, William Mintzer. With Charles Kimbrough, Mary Jane Kimbrough, William McKereghan, Elizabeth Franz.

MINNEAPOLIS

The Guthrie Theater Company: Guthrie Theater

THE VENETIAN TWINS (33). By Carlo Goldoni; translated by Robert David MacDonald. June 18, 1970. Director, Robert David MacDonald; scenery and costumes, Gordon Micunis; lighting, Robert Scales. With Fern Sloan, Michele Shay, Paul Ballantyne, Emery Battis, Briain Petchey, Robert Pastene, Katherine Ferrand.

CEREMONIES IN DARK OLD MEN (34). By Lonne Elder III. June 19, 1970. Director, Israel Hicks; scenery, John Jensen; lighting, Robert Scales; costumes, Geraldine Cain.

With Maxwell Glanville, Gerry Black, Ron Glass, Arnold Wilderson, Bette Howard, Ed Bernard.

THE TEMPEST (28). By William Shakespeare. June 20, 1970. Director, Philip Minor; scenery and costumes, John Jensen; lighting, Robert Scales; music, John Gessner. With Robert Pastene, Joseph Culliton, Charles Keating, Linda Kelsey, Arnold Wilkerson.

A MAN'S A MAN (38). By Bertolt Brecht; translated by Gerhard Nellhaus. August 11,

1970. Director, John Hirsch; scenery and costumes, Eoin Sprott; lighting, Robert Scales. With Biff McGuire, Fern Sloan, Emery Battis, Barbara Byrne, Robert Benson.

A PLAY BY ALEKSANDR SOLZHENIT-SYN (57). Adapted by Paul Avila Mayer; translated by Nicholas Benthell and David Burg. October 13, 1970 (world premiere). Director, Michael Langham; scenery and costumes, John Jensen; lighting, Robert Scales; music arranged by David Karr and Maury Bernstein; advisor on labor camp life, Olaf Tammark; interpretive consultant on Russian language, Ellin Gorky; fight staged by David Feldshuh. Produced by arrangement with George W. George and Joel W. Schenker; supported by a grant from the National Endowment for the Arts, Washington, D. C.

Prisoners
Rodion Nemov .... Briain Petchey
Pavel Gai .... Robert Pastene
Lyuba Nyegnevitskaya .... Fern Sloan
Granya Agrafena Zybina ...... Michele Shay
Boris Khomich .... Charles Keating
Timofey Mereshchun ..... James J. Lawless
Nikolay Hakhimchuk .... Kenneth Pogue
Makar Munitz .... Paul Ballantine
Grishka Chegenyov .... Ron Glass
Dimka .... Lance Davis
Ohmula .... Timothy Casey
Kostya .... Peter Michael Goetz
Pososhkov .... Eric House
Dorofyev .... Warren Frost
Camille Leopoldovich
    Gontoir .... Emery Battis

Shurochka Soymina .... Ellin Gorky
Bella .... Barbara Bryne
1st Girl Student .... Allison Giglio
2d Girl Student .... Linda Kelsey
Goldtooth .... Ross Bickell
Georgi .... Arnold Wilkerson
Angel; 3d Bricklayer .... Marc Rush
Head Cook; 1st Bricklayer ....David Felshuh
2d Bricklayer .... Gerry Black
4th Bricklayer .... Allan Estes
Gangleader of
    Machineshop .... Joseph Culliton
1st Female Drudge .... Bette Howard
2d Female Drudge ......Katherine Ferrand
Accordionist .... Maury Bernstein
Free Citizens
Arnold Yefimovich
    Gurvich .... Robert Benson
Vasili Onufrevich Brylov ....Jon Cranney
Machine Shop Foreman .....Michael Parish
Bricklayers' Foreman ....William Levis
Plasterers' Foreman .... Marc Rush
Cai's Wife .... Katherine Ferrand
Camp Guards
Lieutenant Ovchukhov ....Sandor Szabo
Junior Sergeant Kolody .....Allen Hamilton
Wardress .... Noel McCoy
Visiting Warder ....Maxwell Glanville
Check Point Guard .... Michael Parish
Tower Guards ....Ed Barnard, William Levis
Escort Guards .... Stephen Keep,
                            Leroy McDonald
    The action of the play takes place in a Stalinist correctional labor camp in 1945. Two intermissions.

The Guthrie Theater Company: Other Place Theater

SILENCE and LANDSCAPE by Harold Pinter. August 5, 1970. Director, Dan Bly; scenery and lighting, John Stark; costumes, Diana Grilli. With Emery Battis, Timothy Casey, Katherine Ferrand, Fern Sloan.

THE LABYRINTH by Fernando Arrabal. August 5, 1970. Director, Milt Commons; scenery and lighting, John Stark, Paul Daniels; costumes, Arnold Levine. With Ross Bickell, Allan Estes, Michele Shay, Jon Cranney, Timothy Casey.

WINNERS by Brian Friel. August 13, 1970. Director, Dan Bly. With Dan Bly, Linda Kelsey, William Levis.

ENCORE, FOOD FOR THOUGHT and A

MILD CASE OF DEATH by David Korr. August 15, 1970. With Dan Bly, William Levis, Stephen Keep, Katherine Ferrand, Linda Kelsey, Allison Giglio.

MADAM POPOV and WET DREAM BY GOD by Gladden Schrock. August 20, 1970. Director, Dan Bly; scenery, John Stark; lighting, Dennis Dorn; costumes, Diana Grilli. With Allison Giglio, Gerry Black, William Levis, Stephen Keep, Dan Bly, Briain Petchey.

BAAL by Bertolt Brecht; translated by Ralph Manheim and William E. Smith. August 22, 1970. Director, David Feldshuh; designer, Ron Hall. With Charles Keating, Ross Bickell, Allison Giglio, Peter Michael Goetz.

MONTREAL, QUE. (CANADA)

Centaur Theater Company

A TOUCH OF THE POET (34). By Eugene O'Neill. October 14, 1970. Director, Maurice Podbrey; scenery, Michael Eagan; lighting,

Vladimir Svetlovsky; costumes, Janet Logan. With Sandra Nicholls, Myra Benson, Gerard Parkes, Dana Ivey.

OTHELLO (34). By William Shakespeare. November 18, 1970. Director, John Juliani; scenery, Alan Barlow; lighting, Vladimir Svetlovsky. With Robert Kya-Hill, Maurice Podbrey, Sandra Nicholls, Dana Ivey.

THE ARCHITECT AND THE EMPEROR OF ASSYRIA (26). By Fernando Arrabal. January 6, 1971. Concept and *mise en scene*, Savage God (working name for the approach developed by John Juliani); scenery, costumes and lighting, Mousseau. With Roger Blay, Errol Sitahal.

UNCLE VANYA (33). By Anton Chekhov. February 3, 1971. Director, Jean-Pierre Ronford; scenery, Germain; lighting, Vladimir Svetlovsky. With Maurice Podbrey, Paul Craig, Nonnie Griffin, Dana Ivey.

THE DEATH OF BESSIE SMITH by Edward Albee, directed by William Davis and THE ELECTRONIC NIGGER by Ed Bullins, directed by Maurice Podbrey (26). March 10, 1971. Scenery, Michael Eagan; lighting, Vladimir Svetlovsky; costumes, Norma McNaughton. With Ardon Bess, Griffith Brewer, Tom Carew, Marcia Eleccion, Dana Ivey, Irene Lasdin, John McCurry, Errol Slue.

THE HOMECOMING (33). By Harold Pinter. April 7, 1971. Director, Elsa Bolam; scenery, Mark Negin; lighting, Vladimir Svetlovsky; costumes, Norma McNaughton. With Tom Carew, Peter Elliott, Richard Donat, Dana Ivey.

REVENGE (27). By Howard Brenton. May 12, 1971 (Continental premiere). Director, Maurice Podbrey; scenery, Gerald Potterton; lighting, Vladimir Svetlovsky; costumes, Norma McNaughton.
Adam Hepple; Asst. Commissioner;
  Archibald MacLeish .....Barrie Baldaro
Voice of Brixton Gaol ....Maurice Podbrey
Rot ....Griffith Brewer
Bung ....Richard Donat
P.C. George ....Peter Elliott
P.C. Albert; Ghost of P.C. Albert;
  Cowhand ....Tom Carew
Liz; Dorothy MacLeish ....Dana Ivey
Jane; Daisy ....Jill Frappier
A bizarre comedy-thriller in two acts.

NEW HAVEN, CONN.

Long Wharf Theater

THE SKIN OF OUR TEETH (25). By Thornton Wilder. October 23, 1970. Director, Jeff Bleckner; scenery, John Conklin; lighting, Ronald Wallace; costumes, Santo Loquasto. With Olivia Cole, Joyce Ebert, Richard Venture, Martha Schlamme.

A PLACE WITHOUT DOORS (25). By Marguerite Duras; translated by Barbara Bray from *L'Amante Anglaise*. November 20, 1970 (American premiere). Director, Brian Murray; scenery, John Conklin; lighting, Ronald Wallace.
The Questioner ....Alvin Epstein
Pierre Lannes ....Richard A. Dysart
Claire Lannes ....Mildred Dunnock

YEGOR BULICHOV (25). By Maxim Gorky; translated and adapted by Joan Isserman. December 18, 1970 (American premiere). Director, Arvin Brown; scenery, Elmon Webb and Virginia Dancy; lighting, Ronald Wallace; costumes, Whitney Blausen.
Aksinya ....Carol Teitel
Glafira (Glasha) ....Martha Schlamme
Shura ....Patricia Pearcy
Varvara ....Carol Morell
Andrey Zvontzov ....Tom Atkins
Yegor Bulichov ....Morris Carnovsky
Pavlin ....William Swetland
Donat ....Paul Henry Itkin
Antonina ....Marjorie Lynne Feiner

Alexey ....Will Fenno
Stepan Tyatin ....Tom Crawley
Doctor ....William Cwikowski
Mokey Bashkin ....Charles Cioffi
Yakov Laptev ....John Cazale
Taisya ....Heidi Mefford
Melanya ....Joyce Ebert
Trumpet Player ....John Glover
Mokroussov ....Michael Procaccino
Prokopy ....Richard Venture
Two intermissions.

SHE STOOPS TO CONQUER (24). By Oliver Goldsmith. January 15, 1971. Director, Isaac Schambelan; scenery, Hal Tine; lighting, Ronald Wallace; costumes, Lewis Rampino. With Richard Venture, Emery Battis, Tom Atkins, Joyce Ebert, Olivia Cole, Patricia Pearcy.

SOLITAIRE/DOUBLE SOLITAIRE (25). By Robert Anderson. February 12, 1971 (world premiere). Director, Arvin Brown; scenery, Kert Lundell; lighting, Ronald Wallace; costumes, Lewis Rampino.
Double Solitaire
Charley ....Richard Venture
Barbara ....Joyce Ebert
Mrs. Potter ....Ruth Nelson
Mr. Potter ....John Cromwell
Sylvia ....Martha Schlamme
George ....William Swetland

Peter ....Will Fenno
Solitaire
Sam Bradley ....Richard Venture
Madam ....Ruth Nelson
Daughter ....Patricia Pearcy
Brother ....Will Fenno
Wife ....Joyce Ebert
Father ....John Cromwell
Captain ....William Swetland

THE BLOOD KNOT (25). By Athol Fugard. March 12, 1971. Director, Ted Cornell; scenery, Elmon Webb and Virginia Dancy; lighting, Ronald Wallace; costumes, Louisa Ian-

Yale Repertory Theater

STORY THEATER: GIMPEL THE FOOL by Isaac Bashevis Singer; adaptation by Larry Arrick; lyrics by Barbara Damashek. SAINT JULIAN THE HOSPITALER by Gustave Flaubert; adaptation and lyrics by Kenneth Cavander. OLYMPIAN GAMES written and composed by Kenneth Cavander and Barbara Damashek; based on Ovid's *Metamorphoses* (22). October 8, 1970. Director, Larry Arrick; scenery and costumes, Santo Loquasto; lighting, Edgar Swift. With Alvin Epstein, Carmen De Lavallade, Elizabeth Parrish, James Naughton, Jeremy Geidt.

THE REVENGER'S TRAGEDY (22). By Cyril Tourneur. November 19, 1970. Director, Robert Brustein; scenery, Santo Loquasto; lighting, William B. Warfel; costumes, Ariel Ballif. With Kenneth Haigh, Lee Richardson, Elizabeth Parrish, Jeremy Geidt, Carmen De Lavallade.

WHERE HAS TOMMY FLOWERS GONE? (22). By Terrence McNally. January 7, 1971 (world premiere). Director, Larry Arrick; scenery and costumes, Steven Rubin; lighting and graphics coordinator, William B. Warfel; lighting, Dennis G. Daluiso; slides, Michael Shane; music arranger, Barbara Damashek; sound, Eugene Kimball.
Tommy Flowers ....Robert Drivas
Greta Rapp ....Barbara Damashek
Showgirl ....Lydia Fisher
Nedda Lemon ....Sarah Albertson
Bunny Barnum ....Katherine De Hetre
Tommy's Mother; First Lady;
    Woman Customer ....Elizabeth Parrish
Tommy's Brother ....James Naughton
Tommy's Nephew;
    Photographer ....Henry Winkler
Ben Delight ....Jeremy Geidt
Arnold ....Steve Van Benschoten
Taxi Driver; Moderator .....David Ackroyd
Man at Prison; Howard Johnson's
    Soda Jerk ....Louis Plante
Policeman; New York Athletic Club Man;

notti. With Zakes Mokae, David Clennon.

HEARTBREAK HOUSE (25). By George Bernard Shaw. April 9, 1971. Director, Edward Gilbert; scenery and costumes, Peter Wingate; lighting, Judy Rasmuson. With Laurie Kennedy, William Swetland, Martha Schlamme, Joyce Ebert, Ronald Bishop.

THE PRICE (25). By Arthur Miller. May 7, 1971. Director, Gilbert Cates; scenery, Elmon Webb, Virginia Dancy; lighting, Ronald Wallace; costumes, Louisa Iannotti. With Richard Venture, Joyce Ebert, Will Lee, William Swetland.

Another Man at Prison ....Charles Turner
Prexy's Soda Jerk ....Peter Covette
Reporter
    Interviewing Marilyn ....James Brick
Girl in Taxi Scene; Voice From Rear;
    Waitress; Shoplifter ....Maxine Lieberman
Lady in the Hat;
    Lady Columnist ....Lisa Carling
    The time of the play is now. The places of the play are here, there, and everywhere. One intermission.

MACBETH (22). By William Shakespeare. February 18, 1971. Director, Robert Brustein; scenery, Leo Yoshimura; lighting, William B. Warfel; costumes, Ariel Ballif. With Jeremy Geidt, Lee Richardson, David Ackroyd, Elizabeth Parrish, Carmen De Lavallade.

WOYZECK by Georg Buchner and PLAY by Samuel Beckett (22). April 1, 1971. Director, Tom Haas; scenery, Michael Yeargan; lighting, Paul Butler; costumes, Kenneth Thompson. With Sarah Albertson, David Ackroyd, Elizabeth Parrish, Alvin Epstein, Charlene Bletson.

THE LITTLE MAHAGONNY (22). By Bertolt Brecht; music by Kurt Weill; translated by Michael Feingold. May 13, 1971 (American premiere). Director, Michael Posnick; scenery and costumes, Santo Loquasto; lighting, Robert W. Scheeler; musical director, Gustav Meier.
Bessie ....Maxine Lieberman
Jessie ....Stephanie Cotsirilos
Charlie ....Jack Litten
Billy ....Theodore Ravinett
Bobby ....H. Ray Downer
Jimmy ....William Duvall
Master of
    Ceremonies ..Henry Winkler, Jeremy Geidt

THE SEVEN DEADLY SINS (22). By Bertolt Brecht; music by Kurt Weill; translated by H. W. Auden and Chester Kallman. May 13, 1971. Director, Alvin Epstein; scenery and costumes, Santo Loquasto; lighting, Robert W. Scheeler; musical director, Gustav Meier.

With Elizabeth Parrish, Stephanie Cotsirilos, Robert Benedetti, Stephen Van Benschoten.

Yale Repertory Theater: Sunday Experiments Series

ESSIE MAE and AFTER THE PARTY, by Lainie London, November 22, 1970; POP-CORN, by David Epstein, January 24, 1971; THE GIANTS IN THE EARTH, by Kenneth Bernard, March 7, 1971; An original play by African playwright Emmanuel Yirenchi, April 18, 1971; TAKE ME TO YOUR PADDY WAGON, by Ken Eisler, May 16, 1971. Director of series, Eve Vizy.

Yale Repertory Theater: Children's Theater

JAMES AND THE GIANT PEACH (4). By Roald Dahl; adapted by Sue Lawless; music and lyrics by Leni Stern. February 21 and 28, 1971. Director, Frank S. Torok.

Note: the Yale Repertory Theater and Drama School also present a Workshop Series; Yale Cabaret; Studio Projects and Main Stage Productions with students, members of the Repertory Theater and faculty members.

OKLAHOMA CITY

The Mummers Theater

A MAN FOR ALL SEASONS (28). By Robert Bolt. December 4, 1970. Director, Porter Van Zandt; scenery, Robert Steinberg; costumes, William Schroder. With Benjamin Slack, Edward Mulhare, Mary Michaels, Christopher Shelton.

DEAR LIAR, (28). By Jerome Kilty; adapted from the correspondence of George Bernard Shaw and Mrs. Patrick Campbell. December 17, 1970. Director, Mack Scism; scenery, Robert Steinberg; lighting, Richard Harden; costumes, William Schroder. With Mack Scism, Angela Wood.

THE RIVALRY (28). By Norman Corwin. January 1, 1971. Director, John Wylie; scenery, Robert Steinberg; lighting, Richard Harden; costumes, Pamela Scofield. With Earl Hindman, Clarence Felder, Jane Marla Robbins, Susan Tanner.

THE WORLD OF CARL SANDBURG (28). By Norman Corwin; from the work of Carl Sandburg. February 9, 1971. Director, Saylor Creswell; scenery, Robert Steinberg; lighting, Richard Harden; costumes, Pamela Scofield. With Charles Berendt, Nick Roberts, Anne Ault.

BEDTIME STORY by Sean O'Casey, and A PHOENIX TOO FREQUENT by Christopher Fry (28). February 12, 1971. Director, John Wylie; scenery, Robert Steinberg; lighting, Richard Harden; costumes, William Schroder. With Robert Machray, Mary Michaels, Rudolph Willrich, Angela Wood, Mary Ed Porter.

ARSENIC AND OLD LACE (28). By Joseph Kesselring. March 4, 1971. Director, John Wylie; scenery, William Schroder; lighting, Robert Steinberg; costumes, Pamela Scofield. With Jessie Lee Fulton, John Wylie, Benjamin Slack, Florence Garner, Scott Porter, Tom Carson.

THE STAR-SPANGLED GIRL (28). By Neil Simon. March 25, 1971. Director, Mack Scism; scenery, Stephen A. Milam; lighting, Rick Harden; costumes, William Schroder. With Christopher Shelton, Tom Carson, Mary Michaels.

SEE HOW THEY RUN (28). By Philip King. April 15, 1971. Director, John Wylie; scenery, Robert Steinberg; lighting, Richard Harden; costumes, William Schroder. With Anne Ault, Tom Carson, Mary Ed Porter, Scott Porter.

PRINCETON, N. J.

McCarter Theater

ALL MY SONS (5). By Arthur Miller. October 16, 1970. Director, Arthur Lithgow; scenery, Bil Mikulewicz; lighting, F. Mitchell Dana; costumes, James Edmund Brady. With Seymour Penzner, Robert Blackburn, Dorothy Chace, Tom Brennan.

A RAISIN IN THE SUN (5). By Lorraine Hansberry. October 30, 1970. Director, Eric Krebs; scenery, Bil Mikulewicz; lighting, F. Mitchell Dana; costumes, James Edmund Brady. With Sylvia Soares, Darryl Grisham, Sam Stokes, Fred Morsell, Jan Davis, Delores Martin.

THE SHOW-OFF (6). By George Kelly. November 13, 1970. Director, Robert Blackburn; scenery, Bil Mikulewicz; lighting, F. Mitchell

Dana; costumes, James Edmund Brady. With Tom Brennan, Dorothy Chace, Ruth Dixon, Robert Blackburn.

MACBETH (3). By William Shakespeare. January 31, 1971. Director, Russell L. Treyz; scenery, Grady Larkins; lighting, F. Mitchell Dana; costumes, James Edmund Brady. With Arthur W. Lithgow, Fred Morsell, W. G. McMillan, Joan Weisberg, Beth Dixon.

CAESAR AT THE RUBICON (6). By Theodore H. White. February 12, 1971 (world premiere). Director, Arthur W. Lithgow; scenery, Grady Larkins; lighting, F. Mitchell Dana; costumes, James Edmund Brady; music, Frank Lewin.

G. Julius Caesar .... Robert Blackburn
B. Asinius Pollio .... Richard Pilcher
Aulus Hirtius .... Tom Brennan
Titus Labienus .... Seymour Penzner
Mark Antony .... Donald Gantry
Cornelius Balbus .... Fred Morsell
Scribonius Curio .... Brendan Burke
Vercingetorix .... W.G. McMillan
Tailor .... Loyd Williamson

Commander of the Guard .. Richard Jamieson
Soldiers, Slaves: Tennyson Moore, Brock Putnam, Bob Schmidbauer, Jack Tate, Tazewell Thompson.

LITTLE MURDERS (6). By Jules Feiffer. February 26, 1971. Director, Russell L. Treyz; scenery, Bil Mikulewicz; lighting, F. Mitchell Dana; costumes, James Edmund Brady. With Lee Wallace, Scotty Bloch, Richard Pilcher, Joan Weisberg, W. G. McMillan.

THE IMPORTANCE OF BEING EARNEST (6). By Oscar Wilde. March 19, 1971. Director, Russell L. Treyz; scenery, David Jenkins; lighting, F. Mitchell Dana; costumes, James Edmund Brady. With Richard Pilcher, Richard Jamieson, Leila Cannon, Beth Dixon, Alice Elliott.

THE HOMECOMING (6). By Harold Pinter. April 2, 1971. Director, Louis Criss; scenery, David Jenkins; lighting, F. Mitchell Dana; costumes, Charles Blackburn. With Lee Wallace, Donald Gantry, Brendan Burke, W. G. McMillan, Richard Jamieson, Joan Weisberg.

PROVIDENCE, R. I.

Trinity Square Repertory Company: Trinity Square Playhouse

YOU CAN'T TAKE IT WITH YOU (28). By Moss Hart and George S. Kaufman. October 14, 1970. Director, Adrian Hall; scenery and lighting, Eugene Lee; costumes, John Lehmeyer. With Marguerite Lenert, Donald Somers, James Gallery, George Martin, Richard Kavanaugh, Cynthia Wells.

LITTLE MURDERS (28). By Jules Feiffer. November 25, 1970. Director, William Cain; scenery and lighting, Robert D. Soule; costumes, John Lehmeyer. With Beatrice Ballance, David C. Jones, Marguerite Lenert, George Martin, James Gallery.

ADAPTATION by Elaine May and NEXT by Terrence McNally (28). January 6, 1971. Director, Wayne Carson; scenery and lighting, Robert D. Soule; costumes, John Lehmeyer. With Martin Molson, Richard Kavanaugh, David Davies, Beatrice Ballance, James Gallery, Marguerite Lenert.

THE GOOD AND BAD TIMES OF CADY FRANCIS MCCULLUM AND FRIENDS (28). By Portia Bohn. February 17, 1971 (world premiere). Director, Adrian Hall; scenery and lighting, Eugene Lee; costumes, Franne Lee; music and lyrics, Richard Cumming.

Act I
Woman .... Marion Mercer
The Vegetable .... Elizabeth Moore

Attendant .... Richard Kneeland
Attendant .... Ed Hall
Great River, Montana: A country school
Miss Andrews .... Elizabeth Moore
Young Cady .... Thomas Mason
Young Dinah .... Joanna Williams
Mickey O'Brien .... David Kennett
A Wedding Reception
Cady Francis McCullum .. Richard Kneeland
Dinah Darling .... Marian Mercer
New York City: A gynecologist's offie
Tio Tomas .... Ed Hall
Cady Francis McCullum .. Richard Kneeland
Dinah Darling .... Marian Mercer
Richard E. Moneyman ....David C. Jones
Tom Darling .... Robert Black
Babs Moneyman .... Elizabeth Moore
Jason Emory .... Jon Kimbell
Ancient Mariner .... David Kennett
Act II: A cold water flat
Landlady .... Elizabeth Moore
Cady Francis McCullum .. Richard Kneeland
Dinah Darling .... Marian Mercer
Tio Tomas .... Ed Hall
Hitting the campaign trail
Mario Caputo ad Manager .. David Kennett
                              and Robert Black
The Plaza
Cady Francis McCullum .. Richard Kneeland
Dinah Darling .... Marian Mercer
Tio Tomas .... Ed Hall
    Additional scenes: The trial and Many years later.

HARVEY (28). By Mary Chase. April 7, 1971. Director, Philip Minor; scenery and lighting, Robert D. Soule; costumes, John Lehmeyer. With William Cain, Dortha Duckworth, Richard Kavanaugh, James Gallery, Mina Manente.

Trinity Square Repertory Company: Rhode Island School of Design Theater

SON OF MAN AND THE FAMILY (40). By Timothy Taylor and Adrian Hall; music, Richard Cumming and Terrence Vesey. November 18, 1970 (world premiere). Director, Adrian Hall; scenery, Eugene Lee; lighting, Roger Morgan; costumes, John Lehmeyer.
The beginning
Storyteller .... Martin Molson
The Mother .... Barbara Orson
The Father .... David Kennett
Aunt .... Barbara Meek
Uncle .... Donald Somers
Jesus .... James Eichelberger
Gibault School .... William Damkoehler
George Powers .... Richard Kavanaugh
The Board .... Robert J. Colonna,
      Richard Kavanaugh, Martin Molson,
                          Donald Somers
Haight-Ashbury, a rock concert
Robert Black .... Al McCreery
William Damkoehler .... Terence Vesey
The ritual
The Family . . Richard Jenkins, David Kennett,
      Jon Kimbell, Mina Manente, Thomas
      Mason, Barbara Meek, Barbara Orson,
          Cynthia Wells, Joanna Williams
Improvisation .... Robert J. Colonna,
                        James Eichelberger
Initiation
Initiate .... Joanna Williams
Myths
Storyteller .... Robert J. Colonna
Crucifixion
Charles Manson .... James Eichelberger
Act II: The Hinman case
Attorney .... Martin Molson
Danny DiCarlo .... Jon Kimbell
Attorney .... Richard Kavanaugh
Miss Lutesinger .... Barbara Meek
Attorney .... William Damkoehler
Sadie Mae Glutz .... Cynthia Wells
The Victim .... James Eichelberger
The Killers .... Robert Black, Mina Manente,
          Thomas Mason, Joanna Williams
The Sharon Tate Murders
Susan Atkins .... Cynthia Wells
The Killers . . David Kennett, Mina Manente,
                          Joanna Williams

The Victims .... William Damkoehler,
          Jon Kimbell, Thomas Mason,
          Barbara Meek, Barbara Orson
Leno and Rosemary La Bianca
Storyteller .... David Kennett
The Killers .... Robert Black, Mina Manente,
          Thomas Mason, Joanna Williams
The raid on Spahn Ranch
William Damkoehler, Richard Kavanagh
*The family visits the Barker Ranch in the
  Mojave Desert*
Juan Flynn
The Boys . . Robert Black, James Eichelberger,
          Richard Jenkins, David Kennett
The Girls ...... Jon Kimbell, Thomas Mason,
          Mina Manente, Cynthia Wells,
                          Joanna Williams
Press Interview
Police Chief Davis .... Donald Somers
The End. The Beginning
Statements of Fear .... William Damkoehler,
      Barbara Meek, James Eichelberger, Richard
      Kavanaugh, Donald Somers, Martin Molson, Barbara Orson, Robert J. Colonna

THE TAMING OF THE SHREW (40). By William Shakespeare. December 30, 1970. Director, Adrian Hall; scenery and lighting, Eugene Lee; costumes, John Lehmeyer. With Marian Mercer, William Cain, David C. Jones, Cynthia Wells.

LOVE FOR LOVE (40). By William Congreve. February 10, 1971. Director, Philip Minor; scenery, Robert D. Soule; lighting, Eugene Lee; costumes, John Lehmeyer. With Richard Kavanaugh, Jill Tanner, Cynthia Wells, James Gallery, William Cain, Robert J. Colonna.

THE THREEPENNY OPERA (40). Book and lyrics by Bertolt Brecht; music by Kurt Weill; English translation by Marc Blitzstein. March 24, 1971. Director, Adrian Hall; musical director, Richard Cumming; scenery and lighting, Eugene Lee; costumes, John Lehmeyer. With Richard Kneeland, Cynthia Wells, Barbara Orson, Robert J. Colonna, David C. Jones.

ROCHESTER, MINN.

Oakland University Professional Theater Program: Meadow Brook Theater

THE SKIN OF OUR TEETH (20). By Thornton Wilder. November 5, 1970. Director, Terence Kilburn; scenery and lighting, Richard Davis; costumes, Veronica Gustaff. With Glynis Bell, Harry Ellerbe, Elisabeth Orion, Barbara Quinn.

LIFE WITH FATHER (20). By Howard Lindsay and Russel Crouse. December 3, 1970. Director, Joseph Shaw; scenery and lighting, Richard Davis; costumes, Veronica Gustaff. With William LeMassena, Elisabeth Orion.

THE CRUCIBLE (20). By Arthur Miller. January 7, 1971. Director, Terence Kilburn; scenery and lighting, Richard Davis; costumes, Veronica Gustaff. With Glynis Bell, Peter Brandon, Elisabeth Orion, Toby Tompkins.

TARTUFFE (20). By Molière; English translation by Richard Wilbur. February 4, 1971. Director, Terence Kilburn; scenery and lighting, Richard Davis; costumes, Veronica Gustaff. With Diane Bugas, William LeMassena, Joseph Shaw.

THE RAINMAKER (20). By N. Richard Nash. March 4, 1971. Director, Terence Kilburn; scenery and lighting, Richard Davis; costumes, Veronica Gustaff. With Diane Bugas, David Himes, Philip Mallet.

WHO'S AFRAID OF VIRGINIA WOOLF? (20). By Edward Albee. April 1, 1971. Director, John Ulmer; scenery and lighting, Richard Davis; costumes, Veronica Gustaff. With Peter Brandon, Priscilla Morrill, Elizabeth Oustinoff, Toby Tompkins.

A THOUSAND CLOWNS (20). By Herb Gardner. April 29, 1971. Director, Terence Kilburn; scenery, James D. Hansen; lighting, Katherine Ann Turco; costumes, Veronica Gustaff. With William LeMassena, Teddy Moniak, Howard Morton, Susan Thorne.

THE FANTASTICKS (20). Book and lyrics by Harvey Schmidt, music by Tom Jones; based on Edmond Rostand's Les Romantiques. May 27, 1971. Director, Christopher Hewett; scenery, James D. Hansen; lighting, Katherine Ann Turco; costumes, Veronica Gustaff. With Joe Bellomo, Robert Englund, Erik Howell, Jennifer Williams.

SAN DIEGO

San Diego Shakespeare Festival: Globe Theater

MUCH ADO ABOUT NOTHING (50). By William Shakespeare. June 9, 1970. Director, Pirie MacDonald; designer, John Conklin; lighting, Bruce Kelley. With Theodore Sorel, Moira Wylie.

RICHARD II (40). By William Shakespeare. June 12, 1970. Director, Stephen Porter; de-

signer, Peggy Kellner; lighting, Bruce Kelley. With Richard Kneeland, Stephen D. Newman.

CYMBELINE (30). By William Shakespeare. July 9, 1970. Director, Louis Criss; designer, Douglas Russell; lighting, Bruce Kelley. With Ellen Geer, Tom Toner.

SAN FRANCISCO

American Conservatory Theater (ACT): Geary Theater

THE MERCHANT OF VENICE (47). By William Shakespeare. November 14, 1970. Director, Ellis Rabb; scenery, lighting and projections, James Tilton; costumes, Ann Roth. With Mark Bramhall, Peter Donat, Michael Learned, Ken Ruta, Deborah Sussel.

HADRIAN VII (20). By Peter Luke; based on works by Fr. Rolfe (Baron Corvo). November 18, 1970. Director, Allen Fletcher; scenery and costumes, Robert Fletcher; lighting, Ward Russell. With Peter Donat, Jay Doyle, Winifred Mann, William Patterson, G. Wood.

THE RELAPSE (23). By John Vanbrugh. December 8, 1970. Director, Edward Hastings; scenery and costumes, Robert Fletcher; lighting, Ward Russell. With Mark Bramhall, Robert Fletcher, Michael Learned, Lee McCain, William Patterson, Ken Ruta, Scott Thomas.

THE TEMPEST (15). By William Shakespeare. December 21, 1970. Director, William

Ball; scenery and costumes, Robert Fletcher; lighting, Ward Russell; original music, Lee Hoiby. With Suzanne Collins, David Gilliam, John Hancock, Ken Ruta, Mark Wheeler.

THE LATENT HETEROSEXUAL (28). By Paddy Chayefsky. January 12, 1971. Director, Allen Fletcher; scenery, Robert Darling; lighting, Ward Russell; costumes, Walter Watson. With Joseph Bird, Lee McCain, Josef Sommer, G. Wood.

THE TIME OF YOUR LIFE (26). By William Saroyan. February 2, 1971. Director, Edward Hastings; scenery, Jackson De Govia; lighting, Ward Russell; costumes, Elizabeth Covey. With Jim Baker, Joy Carlin, William Patterson, Ken Ruta, Scott Thomas.

AN ENEMY OF THE PEOPLE (25). By Henrik Ibsen; translated by Allen Fletcher. March 2, 1971. Director, Allen Fletcher; scenery, Robert Fletcher; lighting, Ward Russell;

costumes, Walter Watson. With Peter Donat, Jay Doyle, Winifred Mann, Deborah Sussel.

THE SELLING OF THE PRESIDENT (24). A musical vaudeville suggested by a book by Joe McGinness; stage script, Stuart Hample; music and lyrics, Bob James and Jack O'Brien. March 30, 1971 (world premiere). Director, Ellis Rabb; scenery, lighting and still projections, James Tilton; costumes, Elizabeth Covey; musical director; Vaughn Aubrey; orchestrations and choral arrangements, Bob James; sound designed by Charles Richmond; associate director, Jack O'Brien; film sequences, American Zoetrope; film director, Michael Jackson.

The American Flag
Megan ....Carolyn Blakey
Lotus ....Nancy Blossom

Beige ....Light Brown
RandyMann ....Michael Cavanaugh
Cochise ....Jeff Chandler
King George ....John Hancock
Roxie Rideout ....Lee McCain
Chunky Berman ....Deborah Sussel
Canibus Sativa ....Ann Weldon
Steven Tudd ....Mark Wheeler
George Smith ....G. Wood
Irene Jantzen ....Michael Learned
Ted Bacon ....Josef Sommer
Ward Nichols ....Scott Thomas
Walter ....Joseph Bird
George Mason ....Peter Donat
Gracie Mason ....Joy Carlin
Norman Bille
Emerson ....William Patterson
Marty "Smiles"
Faranghetti ....Martin Berman

SARASOTA, FLA.

Asolo Theater Festival: The State Theater Company

LIFE WITH FATHER (26). By Howard Lindsay and Russel Crouse. June 19, 1970. Director, Richard G. Fallon; scenery and costumes, Holmes Easley; lighting, John D. Gowans. With Robert Britton, Isa Thomas, William Pitts, Mary Skinner.

ALL'S WELL THAT ENDS WELL (19). By William Shakespeare. July 10, 1970. Director, Eberle Thomas; scenery, William King; lighting, John D. Gowans. With Barbara Redmond, Henry Strozier, Patrick Egan, Richard Hopkins.

THE PRICE (12). By Arthur Miller. July 31, 1970. Director, Richard Meyer; scenery and costumes, Holmes Easley; lighting, John D. Gowans. With Barbara Redmond, Bradford Wallace, Henry Strozier, Stuart Culpepper.

BORN YESTERDAY (29). By Garson Kanin. February 18, 1971. Director, Howard J. Millman; scenery, Henry Swanson; lighting, James Meade; costumes, Flozanne John. With William Leach, Walter Rhodes, Sharon Spelman.

CANDIDA (19). By George Bernard Shaw. February 20, 1971. Director, Eberle Thomas; scenery, Holmes Easley; lighting, James Meade; costumes, Catherine King. With Walter Rhodes, Polly Holliday, James L. Sutorius.

A DAY IN THE DEATH OF JOE EGG (19). By Peter Nichols. February 26, 1971. Director, Jon Spelman; scenery, Ray Perry; lighting, James Meade; costumes, Catherine King. With Patrick Egan, Kathleen O'Meara Noone, Devora Millman.

THE COMEDY OF ERRORS (30). By William Shakespeare. March 5, 1971. Director, Bradford Wallace, scenery, Henry Swanson; lighting, James Meade; costumes, Catherine King. With Richard Hopkins, William Leach, Robert Lanchester, James L. Sutorius, Barbara Redmond, Sharon Spelman.

LOVE FOR LOVE (31). By William Congreve. April 9, 1971. Director, Robert Strane; scenery, Henry Swanson; lighting, James Meade; costumes, Catherine King. With Walter Rhodes, Patrick Egan, Bill E. Noone, William Leach, Kathleen O'Meara Noone.

THE SUBJECT WAS ROSES (26). By Frank D. Gilroy. May 7, 1971. Director, Richard Meyer; scenery, John M. Wilson; lighting, James Meade; costumes, Catherine King. With William Leach, Polly Holliday.

CHARLEY'S AUNT (26). By Brandon Thomas. May 21, 1971. Director, Robert Lanchester; scenery, James Tilton; lighting, James Meade; costumes, Catherine King. With Richard Hopkins, Bill E. Noone, James L. Sutorius, Sharon Spelman, Susan Sandler.

Asolo Theater Festival: Children's Theater

THE TORTOISE AND THE HARE by Alan Broadhurst. August 7, 1970. Director, Moses Goldberg.

ANDROCLES AND THE LION by Aurand Harris. December 19, 1970. Director, Moses Goldberg.

SEATTLE

Seattle Repertory Theater

INDIANS (19). By Arthur Kopit. October 21, 1970. Director, Arne Zaslove; scenery, Jason Phillips; lighting, Mark S. Krause; costumes, Ritchie M. Spencer. With Douglass Watson, Manu Tupou, Ted D'Arms, Robert Loper.

A FLEA IN HER EAR (20). By George Feydeau; English version by Carol Johnston. November 11, 1970. Director, Duncan Ross; scenery, Jason Phillips; lighting, Mark S. Krause; costumes, Ritchie M. Spencer. With Geraldine Court, Clayton Corzatte, Ted D'Arms, Anne Murray, Robert Loper.

THE MISER (19). By Molière; translated by Nagle Jackson. December 9, 1970. Director, Nagle Jackson; scenery, Jason Phillips; lighting, Steven Maze; costumes, Ritchie M. Spencer. With Michael O'Sullivan, Sian Barbara Allen, Gary Reineke, Clayton Corzatte, Joan White.

HAY FEVER (19). By Noel Coward. December 30, 1970. Director, Arthur Storch; scenery, Ritchie M. Spencer; lighting, Steven Maze;

costumes, Jason Phillips. With Maureen O'Sullivan, Clayton Corzatte, Sian Barbara Allen, Randall Rickman.

THE PRICE (19). By Arthur Miller. January 20, 1971. Director, Robert Loper; scenery, Jason Phillips; lighting, William Mintzer; costumes, James York. With Ted D'Arms, Clayton Corzatte, Eve Roberts, Albert M. Ottenheimer.

HAPPY ENDING and DAY OF ABSENCE (21). By Douglas Turner Ward. February 10, 1971. Director, Israel Hicks; scenery, Jason Phillips; lighting, William Mintzer. With Hilda Haynes, Beatrice Winde, Ron Glass, Joe Fields.

RICHARD II (55). By William Shakespeare. March 6, 1971. Director, Duncan Ross; scenery, Jason Phillips; lighting, William Mintzer; costumes, Ritchie M. Spencer. With Richard Chamberlain, Douglass Watson, Jeffrey Tambor, Clayton Corzatte, Ted D'Arms, Sian Barbara Allen.

Seattle Repertory Theater: Guest Productions

DEAR LOVE (4). October 1, 1970. By Jerome Kilty; adapted from the correspondence of Elizabeth Barrett and Robert Browning. With Myrna Loy, Jerome Kilty.

EMLYN WILLIAMS AS CHARLES DICKENS (2). February 28, 1971.

STRATFORD, CONN.

American Shakespeare Festival Theater

ALL'S WELL THAT ENDS WELL (32). By William Shakespeare. June 16, 1970 evening. Director, Michael Kahn; scenery, Marsha L. Eck; lighting, John Gleason; costumes, Jane Greenwood. With Eva Le Gallienne, Roberta Maxwell, Joseph Maher, Josef Sommer, Peter Thompson.

OTHELLO (33). By William Shakespeare. June 17, 1970 matinee. Director, Michael Kahn; scenery, Karl Eigsti; lighting, John

Gleason; costumes, Jane Greenwood. With Moses Gunn, Lee Richardson, Roberta Maxwell, Jan Miner.

THE DEVIL'S DISCIPLE (31). By George Bernard Shaw. June 19, 1970 evening. Director, Cyril Ritchard; scenery, William Ritman; lighting, John Gleason; costumes, Jane Greenwood. With Cyril Ritchard, Margaret Hamilton, Lee Richardson, David Selby.

STRATFORD, ONT. (CANADA)

Stratford Festival: Festival Theater

THE MERCHANT OF VENICE (37). By William Shakespeare. June 8, 1970. Director, Jean Gascon; designer, Desmond Heeley. With Leo Ciceri, Donald Davis, Maureen O'Brien, Helen Carey.

THE SCHOOL FOR SCANDAL (36). By Richard Brinsley Sheridan. June 9, 1970. Director, Michael Langham; designers, Leslie

Hurry, Jack King; lighting, Gil Wechsler. With Robin Gammell, Stephen Murray, Mervyn Blake, Helen Carey, Barry MacGregor.

HEDDA GABLER (22). By Henrik Ibsen; new version by Christopher Hampton. June 10, 1970. Director, Peter Gill; designer, Deirdre Clancy; lighting, Gil Wechsler.
Miss Juliana Tesman ....Anne Ives

Berte ....Christine Bennett
George Tesman ....Gordon Jackson
Hedda Tesman ....Irene Worth
Mrs. Elvsted ....Gillian Martell
Judge Brack ....Donald Davis
Eilert Lovborg ....Leo Ciceri
    The action takes place in Tesman's villa in

Stratford Festival: Avon Theater

THE ARCHITECT AND THE EMPEROR
OF ASSYRIA (11). By Fernando Arrabal.
July 20, 1970 (Canadian premiere). Director,
Chattie Salaman; designer, Jean Baptiste Ma-
nessier. Lighting, Gil Wechsler; music, Louis
Applebaum. With Roger Blay, Arnold Sobo-
loff.

THE FRIENDS (24). By Arnold Wesker.
July 22, 1970 (Continental premiere). Direc-
tor, Kurt Reis; designer, Peter Wingate; light-
ing, Gil Wechsler; song; Wilfred Josephs.
Esther ....Kate Reid
Manfred ....William Needles
Crispin ....Roland Hewgill
Tessa ....Zulema Dene
Simone ....Dolores Sutton
Macey ....Salem Ludwig
Roland ....Richard Curnock
    The scene is England and the time, the pres-
ent. One intermission.

VATZLAV (18). By Slawomir Mrozek; translated by Ralph Manheim. August 11, 1970

the west end of town. Two intermissions.

CYMBELINE (17). By William Shakespeare.
July 21, 1970. Director, Jean Gascon; de-
signer, Tanya Moiseiwitsch; lighting, Gil
Wechsler. With Powys Thomas, Maureen
O'Brien, Robin Gammell, Leo Ciceri, Mervyn
Blake.

(Continental premiere). Director, Colin
George; designer, Brian Jackson; lighting, Gil
Wechsler; music, Louis Applebaum.
Vatzlav ....Douglas Campbell
The Lackey ....Joseph Rutten
Mr. Bat ....Arnold Soboloff
Mrs. Bat ....Kate Reid
Bobbie ....William Needles
Quail ....Eric House
Sassafras ....Donald Ewer
The Genius ....James Edmond
Justine ....Carolyn Younger
Oedipus ....Roland Hewgill
The Guide ....John Gardiner
The Officer ....Ken Tomlin
General Barbaro ....Richard Curnock
The Executioner ....Dominic Hogan
    Soldiers: I.M. Findlay, John Gardiner,
Dominic Hogan, Denis Jestadt, Tim Leary.
    The action takes place on a platform in-
clined toward the audience. The play, which
lasts approximately one and three-quarter
hours, is written to be performed without an
intermission.

Stratford Festival Guest Artist Program: Avon Theater

THE SUN NEVER SETS (4). By Patrick
Crean; from the works of Rudyard Kipling.
July 2, 1970. Director, Powys Thomas; light-
ing, Gil Wechsler. With Patrick Crean.

STYLE PANTOMIMES and BIP PANTO-
MIMES (8). Created by Marcel Marceau.
July 6, 1970. With Marcel Marceau and his
partner, Don Diego Christian.

SYRACUSE, N. Y.

Syracuse Repertory Theater

THE FANTASTICKS (9). Book and lyrics
by Tom Jones; music by Harvey Schmidt;
based on Edmond Rostand's Les Romantiques. March 5, 1971. Director, Gary Gage;
scenery, Leonard Dryansky; lighting, Robert
Alexander; costumes, Richard Hieronymus.
With Joe Bellomo, Valerie Lee, Gary Gage,
Sandy McCallum, David Deardorff, Ron
Prather, Samuel As-Said, John Thomas Waite.

INDIANS (9). By Arthur Kopit. March 19,
1971. Director, Rex Henriot; scenery, Leonard Dryansky; lighting, Robert Alexander;
costumes, Richard Hieronymus. With Gerald
Richards, Clayton Corbin, Victor Raider-Wex-
ler, David Moody, Patrick Desmond, Gary
Gage.

THE TIME OF YOUR LIFE (9). By William Saroyan. April 2, 1971. Director, Rex

Henriot; scenery, Robert Lewis Smith; lighting, Robert Alexander; costumes, Richard
Hieronymus. With Jack Collard, Patrick Desmond, Zoaunne Henriot, Samuel As-Said.

THE TAVERN (9). By George M. Cohan.
April 16, 1971. Director, Rex Henriot; scenery, Leonard Dryansky; lighting, Robert Alexander; costumes, Richard Hieronymus. With
Sandy McCallum, John Thomas Waite, Zoaunne Henriot, Gary Gage, Joyce Krempel.

ROOM SERVICE (9). By John Murray and
Allen Boretz. April 30, 1971. Director, Rex
Henriot; scenery, Robert Lewis Smith; light-
ing, Robert Alexander; costumes, Richard
Hieronymus. With James Callahan, Ron
Prather, Gary Gage, Jack Collard, Sandy
McCallum, Zoaunne Henriot.

VANCOUVER, B.C. (CANADA)

The Playhouse Theater Company: Main Stage

THE SECRETARY BIRD (21). By William Douglas Home. September 30, 1970. Director, Paxton Whitehead; scenery, Brian H. Jackson; lighting, Dick Bylin; costumes, Margaret Ryan. With Tony Van Bridge, Patricia Gage, Micki Maunsell, Susan Ringwood, Paxton Whitehead.

ROSENCRANTZ AND GUILDENSTERN ARE DEAD (21). By Tom Stoppard. October 28, 1970. Director, David Gardner; scenery, Brian H. Jackson; lighting, Dick Bylin; costumes, Margaret Ryan. With Neil Dainard, Alan Scarfe, Paxton Whitehead, Frank Maraden, Angela Slater.

A DAY IN THE DEATH OF JOE EGG (21). By Peter Nichols. November 25, 1970. Director, Tom Kerr; scenery and costumes, Cameron Porteous; lighting, Dick Bylin. With

Neil Dainard, Anne Butler, Ellen Lyn Brown.

OTHELLO (21). By William Shakespeare. January 6, 1971. Director, David Gardner; scenery and costumes, Brian Jackson; lighting, Dick Bylin. With Arthur Burghardt, Alan Scarfe, Annie Scarfe, Anne Butler.

PLAZA SUITE (21). By Neil Simon. February 3, 1971. Director, John Brockington; scenery, Cameron Porteous; lighting, Dick Bylin; costumes, Margaret Ryan. With Tod Andrews, Vera Lockwood, Linda Sorensen, Glenn MacDonald, Alan Wallis.

HOBSON'S CHOICE (21). By Harold Brighouse. March 3, 1971. Director, Malcolm Black; scenery, Maurice Strike; lighting, Gil Wechsler; costumes, Tiina Lipp. With Tony Van Bridge, Anne Wakefield, William Christopher.

WALTHAM, MASS.

Brandeis University: Spingold Theater

THE DEVILS (11). By John Whiting. January 8, 1971. Director, Charles Werner Moore; scenery, William Mickley; lighting, Bruce West. With K. Lype O'Dell, Mervyn Williams, David Palmer, Leslie Groper.

BEYOND WORDS with Kenyon Martin and the National Pantomime Theater and FAUST, conceived by Kenyon Martin (11). February 10, 1971 (world premiere). Director, Kenyon Martin; scenery and lighting, Bruce West; costumes and masks, Charles Berliner; slide projections, Paulette Spruill, Corinna Taylor; film sequences, Sara Elder and Brian Heller.

Faust ....David Palmer
Valentine ....David A. Zucker
Gretchen ....Virginia Finegold
Mephistopheles ....Bart McCarthy
Devil Dwarf ....Eugenia Dromey
Sloth ....Sharon Landes
Pride ....Howland Chamberlain
Envy ....Donna Harris
Wrath ....Pamela Fubler
Greed ....Richard A. Rubin
Gluttony ....Dean Haglin
Lust ....Georgiana Spelvin

GETTING MARRIED (11). By George Bernard Shaw. March 24, 1971. Director, Peter Sander; scenery, Victor A. Becker; lighting,

Henry Sparks; costumes, Julie Weiss. With Mervyn Williams, Howland Chamberlain, K. Lype O'Dell, Ellen Olian-Bate.

THE FIFTY YEAR GAME OF GIN RUMMY by David Feldman; directed by Paul Nelsen and NOCTURNES by Richard Reichman; directed by Ted Davis (11). May 5, 1971 (world premiere). Scenery, Charles Berliner; lighting, Michael F. Hottois; costumes, Betsy Leichliter.

The Fifty Year Game of Gin Rummy
Rabinowitz ....Gil Schwartz
Boris ....Martin Halpern
Steinberg ....Louis Golden
Nocturnes
Barbara ....Arva Holt
Teddy ....Richard A. Rubin
Susan ....Virginia Feingold
Jim ....Donald Silva
Fred ....Joseph Proctor
Louise ....Linda Varvel
1st golfer ....Dean Haglin
2d golfer ....John Clarke
Nova ....Leslie Groper
Narrator ....Ellen Olian-Bate
Soldier ....David Zucker
    Chorus: Janet Lewis, Victoria Lippman, Laure Mattos and the company.

Note: New plays presented in the Laurie Premiere Theater were *The Truce* by Martin Hogan; *John Brown's Body* by Stephen Vincent Benet in a new chamber theater adaptation by Ted Davis and Sharyn Abramhoff; *Imprisoned* by Ira Bernstein; *Darline's Mystery* by George Masselam; *Machine* and *Journey to the Underword* by Jim Lucason; *Pleasure Palace* by Sharyn Abramhoff.

WASHINGTON, D.C.

Arena Stage: Arena Theater

THE NIGHT THOREAU SPENT IN JAIL (39). By Jerome Lawrence and Robert E. Lee. October 23, 1970 (world professional premiere). Director, Norman Gevanthor; scenery, Ming Cho Lee; lighting, Lee Watson; costumes, Marjorie Slaiman.

Waldo .... Richard Bauer
Lydian .... Leslie Cass
Mother .... Grayce Grant
Henry .... Michael Fairman
John .... Donegan Smith
Bailey .... Ned Beatty
Deacon Ball .... Michael Tucker
Ellen .... Jill Eikenberry
Sam Staples .... Howard Witt
Edward .... Christopher Gladstone, Larry Friedman
Farmer .... Richard Sanders
Woman .... Joan Ulmer
Williams .... Theodore Wilson
    Townspeople: Morris Engle, Mark D'Angelo, Belinha Rowley, Greg Yaroch. One intermission.

MOTHER COURAGE (39). By Bertolt Brecht; American version by George Tabori. December 4, 1970. Director, Gilbert Moses; designers, Eugene Lee, Franne Newman; music, Paul Dessau. With Viveca Lindfors, Jane Alexander, Donegan Smith, Michael Tucker, Howard Witt.

PUEBLO (39). By Stanley R. Greenberg. February 26, 1971 (world premiere). Director, Gene Frankel; scenery, David R. Ballou; lighting, Lee Watson; costumes, Marjorie Slaiman; electronic and concrete sound, Paul Betjeman; movement sequences coach, Virginia Freeman.
Commander Lloyd
    Mark Bucher .... Shepperd Strudwick
Rose .... Joan Ulmer
Court of Inquiry
    Presiding Officer .... Humphrey Davis
    Court Counsel .... Donegan Smith
    Additional Members ... Richard Bernstein, Russell Carr, Dick David
Congressional Committee
    Chairman .... Ben Kapen

Arena Stage: Kreeger Theater

THE RULING CLASS (39). By Peter Barnes. January 15, 1971 (American premiere). Director, David William; scenery, Leo Kerz; lighting, Hugh Lester; costumes, Marjorie Slaiman.
13th Earl of Gurney .... Robert Prosky
Toastmaster .... Michael Fairman
Daniel Tucker .... Eric House
Bishop Lampton .... Al Corbin
Sir Charles Gurney .... Michael Lewis

Congressman .... Richard Bauer
Additional Members .... Jerry Mopps, Sam Rosenman
Rear Adm.
    Frank L. Johnson .... Robert Prosky
Adm. Thomas H. Moorer .... Richard Dix
Super C .... Ned Beatty
Officers and Crew of the USS Pueblo
Chief Warrant Officer
    Gene Howard Lacy ... Michael Fairman
Chief Engineman
    Monroe Onel Goldman .... Howard Witt
Ens. Timothy Leon Harris ... Dan Ahearn
Lt. Stephen Harris .... Tom Klunis
Chief Communications Technician
    James F. Kell .... Bruce Weitz
Quartermaster 1st Class
    Charles Benton Law ... Richard Sanders
Seaman .... Greg Yaroch
Boatswain's Mate 3d Class
    Willis C. Bussell .... Don Sutton
Radio Operator .... Michael Tucker
Signalman .... Christopher Leahy
Lt. Frederick
    Carl Schumacher .... Tom Leopold
Fireman Duane Hodges ... Mark D'Angelo
    Others: .. Tim Burnham, David Evans, Ted Hannan Peter Roidakis, John Heard
North Korean Officer .... Alvin Lum
North Korean Guards .... Tim Burnham, Mark D'Angelo, David Evans, Ted Hannan, John Heard, Peter Roidakis
Cmdr. Chuck Clark .... Richard Sanders
Lt. General
    Seth J. McKee .... Brooks Rogers
Rear Adm.
    Joseph B. McDevitt .... Morris Engle
Negotiator .... Michael Lewis
Navy Secretary Chafee ...... Brooks Rogers
    Performed without an intermission.

AWAKE AND SING (39). By Clifford Odets. April 30, 1971. Director, Norman Gevanthor; scenery, Bennet Averyt; lighting, Henry R. Gorfein; costumes, Marjorie Slaiman. With Eda Reiss Merin, Gene Gross, Robert Prosky, Armand Assante, Jill Eikenberry.

Pall Bearers .... Lee Clark, Mark D'Angelo, Morris Engle, Donegan Smith
Dinsdale Gurney .... Richard Sanders
Lady Claire Gurney ...... Pauline Flanagan
Mathew Peake .... Michael Tucker
14th Earl of Gurney .... Douglas Rain
Dr. Paul Herder .... Richard Bauer
Mrs. Treadwell .... Betty Sinclair
Mrs. Piggot-Jones .... Grayce Grant

Grace Shelley ....Leslie Cass
McKyle ....Michael Fairman
McKyle's Assistant ....Mark D'Angelo
The Monster ....Art Beatty
Kelso Truscott, O.C. ....Howard Witt
Detective Inspector
  Brockett ....Ned Beatty
Detective Sergeant Fraser ...Donegan Smith
1st Lord ....Michael Tucker
2d Lord ....Morris Engle
3d Lord ....Lee Clark
  The action of the play takes place in and
near Gurney Manor, Dr. Herder's Clinic, and
the House of Lords. One intermission.

WIPE-OUT GAMES (39). By Eugene Ionesco; translated by Donald Watson. April 9,
1971 (American premiere). Director, Mel

Shapiro; scenery, Santo Loquasto; lighting,
Lee Watson; costumes, Linda Fisher.
  Various characters in sixteen separate set-
pieces played by Art Beatty, Anne Ives, Joan
Ulmer, Dorothea Hammond, Belinha Rowley,
Grayce Grant, Leslie Cass, Louise Heath, Ann
Sachs, Don Sutton, Richard Sanders, Donegan
Smith, Bruce Weitz, Richard Bauer, Michael
Lewis, Ned Beatty, Michael Tucker, Michael
Fairman, Mark D'Angelo, Greg Yaroch.
Played without an intermission.

WHAT THE BUTLER SAW (39). By Joe
Orton. May 21, 1971. Director, David William; scenery, John Conklin; lighting, Vance
Sorrells; costumes, Gwynne Clark. With Ronald Drake, Richard Bauer, Niki Flacks, Elizabeth Shepherd, Donald Warfield, Michael
Lewis.

Arena Stage: Guest Production

JACK MACGOWRAN IN THE WORKS OF
SAMUEL BECKETT (14). Text adapted by

Jack MacGowran with the approval and advice of Samuel Beckett. March 6, 1971.

Note: the 1970-71 season concludes with *The Sign In Sidney Brustein's Window* by Lorraine
Hansberry, June 11, 1971.

Washington Theater Club

EXIT THE KING (35). By Eugene Ionesco.
June 3, 1970. Director, Davey Marlin-Jones;
scenery and costumes, James Parker; lighting
and visual design, Robert H. Leonard, William Eggleston. With Ned Beatty, Bob Spencer, Anne Chodoff, Trinity Thompson, Howard Jerome, Marcia Wood.

BEFORE YOU GO (35). By Lawrence Hol-
ofcener. July 8, 1970. Director, Davey Marlin-
Jones; scenery and lighting, T. C. Behrens;
costumes, Joyce Wilsie. With Ralph Strait,
Marcia Wood.

THE EFFECT OF GAMMA RAYS ON
MAN-IN-THE-MOON MARIGOLDS (39).
By Paul Zindel. September 23, 1970. Director,
Davey Marlin-Jones; scenery and lighting,
T. C. Behrens; costumes, Gail Singer. With
Helena Carrol, Fran Brill, Marie Carroll,
Francesca James, Patricia Pearcy.

THE LAST SWEET DAYS OF ISAAC (39).
Book and lyrics by Gretchen Cryer; music,
Nancy Ford. November 11, 1970. Director,
Davey Marlin-Jones; scenery, Paul Parady;
lighting, T. C. Behrens; costumes, Gail Singer.
With Christian Grey, Carole Prandis.

A FIFTH OF SPREAD EAGLE (39). By
The Company; material compiled by Sue Law-
less. December 16, 1970 (world premiere).
Director and choreographer, Judith Haskell;
scenery and lighting, T. C. Behrens; costumes,
Gail Singer; musical director, Bob Vigoda.

ACT I: Opening (music, Bob Vigoda, lyrics,
Judith Haskell)—Company; Spiro and Judy
Show (by Stephen Lesher)—Jamil Zakkai,
Laura Waterbury, Brendan Hanlon; "The
Silent Majority Waltz" (music and lyrics, Les-
ley Davidson)—Company; Stewardess (by
Breck Wall)—Delores St. Amand; A History
Lesson (by Alex Fraser)—Brendan Hanlon,
Mickey Hartnett, Jamil Zakkai, Laura Water-
bury, Michael Forella; Rat Poison (anony-
mous)—Brendan Hanlon, Delores St. Amand;
TV Integration (by Marvin Himelfarb)—
Jamil Zakkai, Michael Forella, Laura Water-
bury, Mickey Hartnett, Brendan Hanlon.
"Comfort Me With Apples" (music, Bob
Vigoda, lyrics, Shirley Grossman)—Laura
Waterbury; Aesop in Washington (by Eve
Merriam)—Company. Intermission. The Met-
roliner (by Jeremy Stevens)—Michael Fo-
rella, Jamil Zakkai; Gift Package (by Bren-
dan Hanlon)—Brendan Hanlon; Sic Transit
(by Irv Goldberg, Hod Ogden)—Company;
"That Nixon Feeling" (music and lyrics,
David Finkle and Bill Weeden)—Delores St.
Amand; Group Analysis (by Ben Bagley)—
Company. "Praise Be the Lord" (music and
lyrics, Don Tucker)—Michael Forella, Com-
pany.
  ACT II: "Hard Hat Soft Shoe" (music,
Leni Stern, lyrics, Lewy Olfson)—Company;
Red, White and Very Blue (by Robert Koe-
sis)—Mickey Hartnett, Michael Forella, Brendan Hanlon; "She's Your Woman" (music
and lyrics, Carol Hannan)—Laura Waterbury;
A Fine Romance (anonymous)—Michael

Forella, Delores St. Amand; Inside Sketch (by Marvin Himmelfarb)—Laura Waterbury, Brendan Hanlon, Michael Forella; "Academy Awards" (music, Bob Vigoda, lyrics, June Stevens)—Mickey Hartnett, Company; "Festival Kings" (music and lyrics, June Stevens) —Brendan Hanlon, Michael Forella, Jamil Zakkai; Truth in Advertising (by Carol Hannan)—Mickey Hartnett, Laura Waterbury; Noses (by Jean Maljean)—Jamil Zakkai, Delores St. Amand, Mickey Hartnett, Michael Forella; "The Ketchup, Indiana, Blues" (music and lyrics, Brendan Hanlon and Oatis Stevens)—Brendan Hanlon; Identification (by Michael Forella)—Delores St. Amand, Jamil Zakkai, Michael Forella; Integration in Jim Hogg County (by Mike Heimberg)—Jamil Zakkai, Brendan Hanlon, Mickey Hartnett, Laura Waterbury; Working His Way Through (by Eve Merriam)—Brendan Hanlon; "Middle of the Road" (music and lyrics, Shirley Grossman)—Delores St. Amand, Company; Pax (by Irv Goldberg and Hog Ogden)— Brendan Hanlon, Jamil Zakkai, Michael Forella; "I Want to Play a Tune on My Tambourine" (music and lyrics, Michael Brown) —Company; Finale—Company.

LITTLE BOXES: THE COFFEE LACE and TREVOR (39). By John Bowen. January 20, 1971. Director, Davey Marlin-Jones; scenery, Paul Parady, lighting, T. C. Behrens; cos-

tumes, Gail Singer. With Ronald Dawson, Pat Gebhard, Brendan Hanlon, J. S. Johnson, Margaret Winn, Jamil Zakkai.

THE WEB AND THE ROCK (39). By Delores Sutton; based on Thomas Wolfe's novel. February 24, 1971 (world premiere). Director, Davey Marlin-Jones; scenery and lighting, T. C. Behrens; costumes, Gail Singer.

Usher; Joe; Policeman ....Jamil Zakkai
Esther Jack ....Dolores Sutton
Julia Weober ....Ruth Maynard
George Webber ....Stephen McHattie
Jim Plemmons; Max ......Michael Forella
Lily Farrell; Sylvie ....Margaret Winn
Mary Morgan; Woman ......Suzanne Zenor
Fritz Jack ....J. S. Johnson
One Intermission.

THE CHINESE and DR. FISH (39). By Murray Schisgal. March 31, 1971. Director, Leland Ball; scenery, Paul Parady; lighting, Bruce Lancaster; costumes, Gail Singer. With Marie Carroll, Michael Forella, Sally-Jane Heit, J. S. Johnson, Suzanne Zenor.

FATHER'S DAY (39). By Oliver Hailey. May 5, 1971. Director, Davey Marlin-Jones; scenery and lighting, T. C. Behrens; costumes, Gail Singer. With Carole Cook, Anne Meacham, Michael Prince, Ken Kercheval, Peter Palmer, Garn Stephens.

Washington Theater Club: Monday Night Staged Readings

THE GREAT CHINESE REVOLUTION. By Anthony Scully, S.J. November 30, 1970. Director, Louis Scheeder. SOMEONE'S CRYING. By Jasper Oddo. December 21, 1970, NET network. Director, Jack Samath. CLAW MAN. By Leon Gillen. February 1, 1971. Director, Louis W. Scheeder. SLEEP and PUT ON YOUR POTATO JACKET. By Sam Smiley. February 22, 1971. Director, B. C.

May. CLOWN. By Jack Gonzales. March 15, 1971. Director. Davey Marlin-Jones. OUT OF SIGHT. By David Calliccio. April 12, 1971. Director, Steve Macht. THE PRESENTATION, SUNDAYS AREN'T WHAT THEY USED TO BE, LADIES DAY. By Marvin Himelfarb. May 17, 1971. Directors, Mickey Hartnett, Fredric Lee, Paul Bennett.

Note: Washington Theater Club's 1970-71 season concludes with *Whores, Wars And Tin Pan Alley,* June 9, 1971.

WINNIPEG, MANITOBA (CANADA)

Manitoba Theater Center: Main Stage

A MAN'S A MAN (24). By Bertolt Brecht. November 2, 1970. Director, John Hirsch; designer, Eoin Sprott; lighting, Robert Reinholdt. With Biff McGuire, Evelyne Anderson, Monique Mercure.

LONG DAY'S JOURNEY INTO NIGHT (24). By Eugene O'Neill. November 30, 1970. Director, Keith Turnbull; scenery, William Ritman; lighting, Robert Reinholdt; costumes, Cuthbert Jackson. With David Dodimead, Frances Hyland, Robert Fields, Neil Vipond, Nancy Beatty.

SALVATION (24). Book, music and lyrics by Peter Link and C. C. Courtney. January 11, 1971. Director, Keith Turnbull; designer, Tiina Lipp; lighting, Robert Reinholds; musical director, Victor Davies; choreographer, James Clouser. With Yolande Bavan, P. M. Howard, Andrea Martin, Brian McKay, Dorothy Poste, Michele Shay, Dennis A. L. Simpson, Alan Weeks and Merry-Go-Round Orchestra.

HOBSON'S CHOICE (24). By Harold Brighouse. February 8, 1971. Director, Malcolm

Black; scenery, Maurice Strike; lighting, Gil Wechsler; costumes, Tiina Lipp. With Anne Wakefield, Tony Van Bridge, William Christopher.

WAR AND PEACE (24). Adapted by Alfred Neumann, Edwin Piscator and Guntram Prufer; from the novel by Leo Tolstoy; English version by Robert David MacDonald. March 8, 1971. Director, Edward Gilbert; designer, Peter Wingate; lighting, Robert Reinholdt. With James Valentine, Henry Ramer, Deborah Kipp, Dale Helward.

LITTLE MURDERS (24). By Jules Feiffer. April 5, 1971. Director, Keith Turnbull; scenery, William Ritman; lighting, Bill Williams; costumes, Doreen Brown. With Lillian Lewis, Joseph Warren, Peggy Mahon, Dick Reicheg.

Manitoba Theater Center: The Warehouse—Special Productions

BRECHT ON BRECHT arranged and adapted by George Tabori; THE SUN NEVER SETS with Patrick Crean; AUNT CAROLINE'S WILL by Albert Roussel; A LITTLE HARLEQUINADE by Antonio Salieri; LONG DAY'S JOURNEY INTO NIGHT by Eugene O'Neill.

Manitoba Theater Center: Children's Theater

POPCORN MAN (10). By Dodi Robb and Pat Patterson. December 28. Director, John Wood; designer, John Ferguson.

THE SEASON IN LONDON

By John Mortimer

Playwright and critic, author of *Voyage Round My Father* and the adaptation of *The Captain of Köpenick* produced in London this season.

DURING THE PAST YEAR the British theater has, in spite of rising costs and falling audiences, remained the best place for a writer to work without undue interference or commercial pressure and with the aid of the best actors in the world. The Royal Court, once thought to be the home of theatrical revolution (this was always a myth; from the time of the early Osbornes the Court plays were always dramatically conventional), turned out most of the West End hits. The National continued its useful career as a public library, although some complained of the obscurity of the works displayed. The Royal Shakespeare adhered to its own style of sparse and somewhat gloomy production. These nationally subsidized theaters were all faced with the problems of inflation and it's clear that considerably more government money than anyone thought will be needed to establish the National with its two companies in its new home on the South Bank of the Thames.

No great new writer appeared during the year, which is not really remarkable. What great new writer has appeared in the world since the death of Camus or the tardy discovery of Jorge Luis Borges? No great intellect was displayed in the theater, but its critics have never thought the drama a place for intellectuals; and since Shaw and Pirandello there has been no dramatist with whom one would care to spend an evening in argument. The best of theater has always been magic and conjuring, such as Peter Brook's circus production of *A Midsummer Night's Dream,* founded on a Parisian idea and beautifully translated to bewitch English and American audiences. And in the pyrotechnics of great acting Olivier, Gielgud, Richardson and Scofield have all been seen at their monumental best; and only the most ungrateful would comment that three of these names would no doubt head any review of the British theater in the 1930s.

If possible our theater grew more middle class and respectable during the year; Sir Laurence Olivier became the first actor to enter the House of Lords, no doubt causing intense jealousy among the ghosts of Irving and Gerald du Maurier; and *Oh! Calcutta!* settled down as accepted family entertainment for coach parties. Not only did the theater abandon any political attack on the establishment, but the fashion for black, anarchic farce, aimed to pull the rug from under an audience's accepted conventions, seems to have changed. Writers, mostly with quiet competence, have cultivated their own gardens; many of us have looked into our pasts. The new Conservative government,

73

which most playwrights find extremely distasteful, has not been insulted with the zestful glee of satire in the Macmillan era. It has been totally ignored.

The protective power of the Lord Chamberlain (a Court official who controlled the morals of the theater for hundreds of years) having been abolished, we are still waiting for a prosecution of a play for obscenity. In spite of a somewhat hysterical Puritan backlash encouraged by certain public figures, no play has yet been attacked by the Director of Public Prosecutions. A private prosecution of *The Council of Love* for blasphemy failed. The play, translated from the French, dealt with the Christian deity's introduction of venereal disease as a punishment for vice at the Papal Court. The gods principally offended were the Gods of Wit.

Musicals, the staple fare and great creation of the American theater, have not figured greatly in England this year; a fact which I personally welcome as I cannot believe in the reality of any character who can suddenly burst into song, backed by 20 strings playing music which is neither pop nor classical but something that exists only in the sweet, soupy world of orchestra pits. However, the National intends to pay tribute to Broadway by reviving *Guys and Dolls* and Drury Lane has been filled with the tunes of Johann Strauss.

Shakespeare, who remains our best writer, has suffered a good deal at the hands of directors who formed fascinating theories about his texts before even reading them. Jonathan Miller directed Shylock as a 19th century Rothschild, apparently not having noticed his speech about slaves which were not, to my recollection, to be bought or sold on the Paris Bourse. In spite of a Jessica played for laughs and an Antonio given as a sad Baron Charlus, this *The Merchant of Venice* was distinguished by an electric performance by Olivier. Later two of Brecht's disciples attempted to demonstrate that the Roman populace is the hero of *Coriolanus*, with predictably unfortunate results. The absence of reliable accounts of Shakespeare's plays for today's audiences has been in part filled by the Young Vic, where the seats are hard but the productions simple and energetic. It's a lot cheaper than most cinemas.

The traditional feeling of this year in the British theater was emphasized by two plays by Terence Rattigan, one a revival; a revival of *The Chalk Garden;* a new play by Christopher Fry, a writer who was exaggeratedly praised and as exaggeratedly ignored in the last two decades; and *Vivat! Vivat Regina!* a work by Robert Bolt pregnant with all the excitement of school broadcasting in the 1930s. There was a first-class revival of *Mrs. Warren's Profession* at the National and a new production by Ingmar Bergman of *Hedda Gabler* which, with a play designed to show the skull beneath the skin, gave us only the skull.

Of the new writers, Heathcote Williams in *AC/DC* showed the most talent, closely followed by E.A. Whitehead whose *The Foursome* was a carefully modulated and artfully constructed work on the theme of cosmetics, a subject which has fascinated fine writers from Swift to Max Beerbohm. Christopher Hampton wrote *The Philanthropist* which had to recommend it a most stunning first act and intelligent people talking quite intelligently, a rare relief after many years of earnest proletarian drama. Peter Nichols enjoyed a love-hate relationship with his past in *Forget-Me-Not Lane,* as did I in a play called *A Voyage Round My Father*. Both plays were first produced at the beautiful new Greenwich Theater, by now one of London's best "off-Broadway" houses. These plays were compared constantly, but in fact have no point in common except a determination by both Mr. Nichols and myself to ignore all theatrical trends and find out about ourselves.

Things to be grateful for: *After Haggerty,* David Mercer's best play ringing with testy eloquence and appealing egotism; the Stratford *The Winter's Tale,* a deep dream about jealousy and forgiveness, directed with a film's freedom in time by Trevor Nunn; Paul Scofield's performance as the astonished practical joker in *The Captain of Köpenick,* the greatest-ever example of an actor acting a man acting; everyone's contribution to *Home,* including the untitled performers; and all the evenings I didn't go to the theater but spent quietly alive and not longing for the interval.

So what is a year in the theater? A hundred individuals trying hard to express their own fears, loves, hates, terrors and obsessions, not at all united by the common misfortune of having to do it in 1970-71.

Highlights of the London Season

Selected and compiled by Ossia Trilling

OUTSTANDING PERFORMANCES

MAGGIE SMITH as Hedda Tesman in *Hedda Gabler*	JOHN GIELGUD as Harry in *Home*	JUDI DENCH as Grace Harkaway in *London Assurance*
EMRYS JAMES as the Boss in *The Plebeians Rehearse the Uprising*	LYNN REDGRAVE in four roles in *The Two of Us*	ROBERT MORLEY as Frank Foster in *How the Other Half Loves*
ALEC McCOWEN as Philip in *The Philanthropist*	ANGELA PLEASENCE as Joan in *Saint Joan*	ZOE CALDWELL as Lady Hamilton in *A Bequest to the Nation*
PAUL ROGERS as Andrew (replacement) in *Sleuth*	EILEEN ATKINS as Elizabeth I in *Vivat! Vivat Regina!*	DONALD SINDEN as Henry VIII in *Henry VIII*
ALAN BADEL as Kean in *Kean*	INGRID BERGMAN as Lady Wayneflete in *Captain Brassbound's Conversion*	PAUL SCOFIELD as Voight in *The Captain of Köpenick*

OUTSTANDING DIRECTORS

HAROLD PINTER *Exiles*	INGMAR BERGMAN *Hedda Gabler*	FRANK DUNLOP *The Captain of Köpenick*

OUTSTANDING DESIGNERS

MALCOLM PRIDE *Catch My Soul*	MATIAS *Rabelais*	RICHARD PILBROW *Meet Me in London*

OUTSTANDING NEW BRITISH PLAYS

(D)—Playwright's London debut. Figure in parentheses is number of performances; plus sign (+) indicates play was still running on June 1, 1971

HOME by David Storey. A troubling study of mental disturbance. With John Gielgud, Ralph Richardson. (40)

THE IDIOT by Simon Gray. National Theater's dramatization of the Dostoevsky novel. With Derek Jacobi, Diane Cilento, Tom Baker. (32+ in repertory)

THE PHILANTHROPIST by Christopher Hampton. Philip loves his fellow men too wisely and too well. With Alec McCowen (later George Cole), Jane Asher, Charles Gray. (312+)

A YARD OF SUN by Christopher Fry. Transfer of Nottingham Playhouse production: family reconciliations in post-war Italy. With Frank Middlemass, Eithne Dunne, Lucy Fleming. (8)

VIVAT! VIVAT REGINA! by Robert Bolt. Reworking of the Elizabeth I-Mary Stuart conflict, from the Chichester Festival. With Richard Pearson, Sarah Miles, Eileen Atkins (later Judy Parfitt, Margaret Tyzack). (276+)

THE DISORDERLY WOMEN by John Bowen. Revised version of the Manchester Stables Theater production of the Bacchae legend set in modern times. With William Roache, Joan Heal. (26)

A VOYAGE ROUND MY FATHER by John Mortimer. The author looks back over his shoulder at his youth. With Mark Dignam, David Wood. (26)

NO ONE WAS SAVED by Howard Barker. Dramatization of the Beatles' song Eleanor Rigby and Father Mackenzie. With Mike D'Abo, Maureen Lipman. (30)

MORALITY by Michael O'Neill and Jeremy Seabrook. The self-interest of ambitious parents overcomes their petty-bourgeois prejudices. With Joan Hickson, Bernard Gallagher, Edward Petherbridge, Diane Hart. (1)

THE FOURSOME by E. A. Whitehead (D). Two teenage couples and a tumble in the sand. With Paul Angelis, Philip Donaghy, Claire Sutcliffe, Sharon Duce. (48+)

FORGET-ME-NOT LANE by Peter Nichols. The author looks back over his shoulder nostalgically at his youth. With Anton Rodgers, Joan Hickson, Michael Bates. (62+)

ONE AT NIGHT by Dennis Cannan. Middle-aged sexual offender justifies his Lolita complex. With Frances Cuka, Roy Dotrice. (48+)

LIMITED RUNS OF INTERESTING NEW BRITISH PLAYS

THE OPEN DOOR by Claude Duneton. Fantasy conversation about a man's obsessions and loneliness. With David Calderisi. (10)

SAMSON by David Selbourne. Dramatization of father-son conflict. With Graham Roberts, Emma Stevens. (11)

MR KILT AND THE GREAT I AM by Kenneth Ross (D). When is a murderer not a murderer? With Brian Smith, Peter Bayliss. (24)

THE ISLAND THAT WAS FAR AWAY by Caryl Jenner. Fantasy about an old sea captain and his dream. With the Caryl Jenner Productions Company. (6)

KEEP OUT, LOVE IN PROGRESS by Walter Hall. Comedy of sex and murder, real or game playing? With Robert Gillespie, Alex Marshall. (3)

BILLY'S LAST STAND by Barry Hines. Old brawn vanquishes young brains. With John Barrett, Ian McKellen. (17)

THE OTHERS by David Mowat. Middle-aged businessman reforms his family. With the Questors Theater Company. (4)

ALL THE LONELY PEOPLE by David Pearson (D). Social fantasies in a derelict house. With the Questors Theater Company. (4)

A FACE FOR ALL OCCASIONS compiled by Michael Darlow and Christine Fox from the writings of Charles Dickens and others. With Bill Maynard. (21)

THE LIFE AND DEATH OF ALMOST EVERYBODY by David Campton. The march of history in one act. With Robert Byrne. (4)

NUMBER THREE by John Grillo. Who are the sane, who the insane in a psychiatric ward? With Henry Woolf, the author. (16)

MY DARLING DAISY by Christopher Taylor. How a famous Edwardian beauty tried to blackmail King George V and failed. With Coral Browne, Roland Culver, Victor Maddern. (24)

THANKYOU AND GOOD EVENING by Michael Konrad Harding. TV quiz program in which the roles of the participants are reversed. With Carl Forgione, David Peart, Irene Gawne, Mike Daley. (11)

TEN YEARS HARD by Peter Myers. A topical revue, topically presented. With Michael Flanders, Sally Smith. (32)

THE WAITING ROOM by John Bowen. Two people's pasts come together in the waiting-room of a morgue. With Anna Cropper, Robert Morris. (11)

DOLL! DOLL! by Robin Smythe. Two tramps become the victims of a lecherous night watchman and a petty thief. With Henry Woolf, Julie Somers, George Innes, Gabor Vernon. (3)

MACBETH by William Shakespeare, adapted by Charles Marowitz. Three Macbeths, as the reflection of the three weird sisters, make the plot trebly clear. With Thelma Holt, Nikolas Simmonds. (20)

MACBETH by William Shakespeare, directed by Steven Berkoff. Revival of the tragedy in the round. With Steven Berkoff, Eliza Ward. (14)

HERE ARE LADIES compiled by Siobhan McKenna. One-woman show of her favorite Irish heroines. With the author. (20)

THE LORD BYRON SHOW by Richard Digby Day. An open-air-theater production about Byron. With Gary Bond. (14)

THE THEATER OF DEATH by Phillip Martin. Script-writer awaiting trial creates film scripts out of his anxieties. With Charles Houston, George Innes. (10)

A DISCUSSION by David Halliwell. How verbal mountains can be made out of grammatical molehills. With Ronald Oliver, John Clive. (10) On a double bill with *Foursome* by Eugene Ionesco (see Foreign Plays Produced in London).

WHITE POEM by David Mercer. Dramatic monologue of a Rhodesian farmer. With Bruce Myles. (24) On a double bill with *Black Pieces* by Mustapha Matura (see Foreign Plays Produced in London).

SPRING HEELED JACK by Peter Terson. Story of a latter-day Jack the Ripper. With the National Youth Theater Company. (15)

SEE THE PRETTY LIGHTS by Alan Plater. Wallflower girl meets her wallflower man. With Susan Glanville, Gil Sutherland. (10)

LIE DOWN I THINK I LOVE YOU by Ceredig Davies. Drop-out youth musical. With Ray Brooks, Vanessa Miles, Malcolm Reynolds. (22)

LORNA AND TED by John Hale. Problems of an oddly married couple. With Rita Tushingham, Ray McAnally. (27)

ALBERT'S BRIDGE by Tom Stoppard. Stage version of Prix Italia prizewinning drama of a workman and his bridge. With Michael Mundell. (10)

CHEEK by Howard Barker. Ill-fated attempt at seduction by fecklessness. With Tom Chadbon, Ken Cranham, Diane Hart. (15)

THE GENTLE KNIGHT by Willis Hall. Story of a knight with squeaking armor who meets a wheezing dragon. With the Caryl Jenner Productions Company. (17) On a double bill with *No Talking* by Olwen Wymark (see American Plays Produced in London).

SUPERMAN by Pip Simmons. Modern superman mythology debunked. With the Pip Simmons Theater Group. (15)

26 EFFORTS AT PORNOGRAPHY by Carey Harrison. Schoolmaster's attempt to understand his pupil's erotic writing reveals his own loneliness and sense of failure. With John Bott, Keith Dewhurst. (10)

THE GOLDEN GOOSE by Marged Smith, dramatization of the well known story; and MR. PUNCH AT HOME by Wilfred Harvey, private life of the characters of a Punch and Judy Show. With the Caryl Jenner Productions Company. (15)

THE PERSUADER by Alan Partington (D). Tramp's fatal meeting with a park-bench couple. With Joan Hemingway, Jackie Pallio Jr., Mark Johnson. (10)

FRUIT by Howard Brenton. An attack on the corrupting effect of power. With Paul Brooks. (14)

WHAT HAPPENED TO BLAKE by David Hare. A dramatic portrait of the poet. With Colin McCormack. (14)

THE SERVANTS AND THE SNOW by Iris Murdoch. Typical Murdoch mixture of horror and love, feudalism versus democracy. With Philip Bond, Maxine Audley, Adrienne Corri. (27)

FORWARD UP YOUR END by Kenneth Hill (D). Comedy about civic malpractices in Birmingham. With Bill Wallis, Peter Armitage, Trudi Van Doorn. (52)

THE NIGHT OF THE RODENTS by John Walsh. Two intruders defeated. With John Higgins, John Railton, Lon Satton. (10)

COME TOGETHER including *Playback 65* by Leopold Mahler and N.F. Simpson, confrontation between actor in the flesh and on TV sets, and *A Celebration for Due Process* by Stuart Brisley, an unusual attack on the law (3); *AC/DC* by Heathcote Williams, a revival of the prizewinning sexual drama (2); *1861 Whitby Lifeboat Disaster* by Peter Terson, documentary about a historic disaster (2); and *The Journey* by Naftali Tavin (2).

STUFF by Roger McGough. Satirical revue. With Polly James, the Scaffold. (18)

THE CHICAGO CONSPIRACY by John Burgess (D). Documentary indictment of a miscarriage of justice. With William S. Burroughs. (2)

SHACK-SHACK and SIT QUIETLY ON THE BAULK by Richard Metallus (D). Experimental investigations into violence and the color problem. With Rick James, Chrissie Shrimpton, Carl Wildman. (11)

THE CONTINUING STORY OF ALFRED by Carl Forgione. Young man tries to free himself from his mother. With James Warl, Drewe Wood, David Langdon, Sally-Jane Spencer, Sue Best. (10)

THE TERRIBLE FISK MACHINE by Diana Wynne-Jones. Female scientist diminishes human beings with her Fisk machine. With the Caryl Jenner Productions Company. (16)

COCKY by Jack Ronder. One-man show about the Scottish advocate Henry Cockburn. With Russell Hunter. (18)

PALACH by Alan Burns. Why a Czech student committed suicide in Wenceslas Square in 1968. With Nikolas Simmonds, Henry Soskin. (15)

MR JOYCE IS LEAVING PARIS by Tom Gallagher (D). An episode in the Irish author's life. With Robert Bernal. (10)

GILGAMESH, KING OF URUK by Frederick Proud. Dramatic story about the ancient Assyrian monarch. With Paul Gregory, Roger Green. (3)

FUNERAL GAMES by Joe Orton. Stage premiere of TV black comedy about a phony religious setup. With John Bott, Drewe Henley, Patrick Carter, Kate O'Mara. (10)

THE WAKEFIELD NATIVITY. Selectively adapted version of medieval mystery dramas. With the Young Vic Theater Company. (22 in repertory)

PIRATES by Keith Dewhurst. Rollicking musical about life on the ocean wave. With Patrick O'Connell, Robert Powell. (1)

THE WAGES OF THIN by Trevor Griffiths (D). Black one-acter about a case of victimization. With Walter Hall, David Jarrett, Shane Connaughton. (8)

A TALE OF THREE BROTHERS by Merula Salaman. Granny's will reveals three unusual presents for her grandsons. With Cleo Sylvestre, Nigel Humphries. (20)

THE KING STAG by Carlo Gozzi, adapted by Carl Wildman. New production of classical comedy with which the Young Vic's defunct namesake opened 25 years back. With Nickie Henson, Denise Coffey. (24 in repertory)

JOHN GOULD SHOW by various authors. One-man show. With John Gould. (11)

BYRON—THE NAKED PEACOCK by Misha Williams (D). A new view of Byron and explanation for his conduct. With Frank Barrie. (4 in repertory)

B.S. JOHNSON VERSUS GOD by B.S. Johnson (D). Program of two plays: *Whose Dog Are You?* and *You're Human Like the Rest of Them.* Anti-church satire on the Church today and the exploitation of man by religion. With Michael Deacon, Elizabeth Proud. (10)

BRISTOW by Frank Dickens (D) and Michael Blakewell. Dramatized British comicstrip from the *Evening News.* With Freddie Jones, Anna Quayle. (20)

AN HOUR OF EMBARRASSMENT comprising *The Reasons For Flying, Variable Lengths, Watch the Bucket, Does It Make Your Cheeks Ache* by Henry Livings. With Jim Hiley, Geoff Hoyle, Patrick Barlow. (11)

CURTAINS by Tom Mallin. The sex war dramatized. With Antonia Pemberton, Nigel Hawthorne. (15)

THREE ONE-ACTERS: INTERSECTION by David Calderisi, youth and middle age argue it out, with Peter King, Roy Martin (8); A LAST BELCH FOR THE GREAT AUK by David Halliwell, a two-hander on incompatibility, with Anthony May, Susan Tracy (18); DUEL by Phillip Martin, wild-west fantasy, with David Dixon, Andrew Carr, Diana Patrick (later Geoffrey Housliffe, Tina Packer (18).

MEETING AT NIGHT by James Bridie. The late Scottish author's unperformed Highland comedy about graft finally reaches London. With Wilfrid Hyde White, Sydney Tafler, Renee Houston. (43)

HAVE YOU MET OUR RABBIT? by Michael Stevens (D). With Prunella Scales, Robert Coleby. On a triple bill with *Black Mass* by Edward Bond (revival) and *Offending the Audience* by Peter Handke (see Foreign Plays Produced in London). With the Other Company. (18)

THE COLLECTOR by David Parker (D). Adaptation of John Fowles's novel about a butterfly-collecting impotent sexual dreamer. With Brian McDermott, Annette André. (18)

THE TWO KINDS OF ANGEL by David Edgar (D). Two girls' lives parallel those of Rosa Luxemburg and Marilyn Monroe. With Patricia Cartland, Alex Marshall. (10)

GAMES/AFTER LIVERPOOL by David Snodin (D). Sexual games among mixed-up kids. With Timothy Dalton, Edward Jewesbury, Judy Loe. (18)

MISTER by Stanley Eveling. Retired old salt receives unwelcome guests of both sexes with fatal results. With Freddie Jones, Esmond Knight, Delia Lindsay. (20)

GUM AND GOO by Howard Brenton. Young girl's fantasy about murder and rape. With Miles Anderson, Christopher Biggins. (12)

PIGNIGHT by Snoo Wilson (D). The pigs take over the world. With Paul Freeman, Daryl Kovann. (4)

THE GOOD AND FAITHFUL SERVANT by Joe Orton. Dramatization of TV play about the exploiting power of the Establishment. With John Rutland, Vivienne Burgess. (14)

JOHN FORD'S CUBAN MISSILE CRISIS by Albert Hunt (D) and a group from the Bradford Art College. With the Group. (18)

CHILDREN OF THE WOLF by John Peacock. Irish author's modern variant on the legend of Electra's revenge. With Yvonne Mitchell. (30)

LIQUID by David Mowat. Glib military fantasy. With Crispin Gilbard. On a double-bill with THE GYMNASIUM by Olwen Wymark (see American Plays Produced in London). (2 each)

SAVOURY MERINGUE by James Saunders. Satire on traditional theater. With Prunella Scales, Robert English. (10)

CONN AND THE CONQUERORS OF SPACE by Bill Morrison. A medley of space fantasy and Irish mythology. With the Caryl Jenner Productions Company. (14)

MAX ADRIAN in two full-length one-man shows: *GBS* by Michael Voysey and *Gilbert and Sullivan*. (8 each)

PASSION by Edward Bond. The passion of the Son of Man brought up to date. With Penelope Wilton, Nigel Hawthorne, Susan Engel. (1)

BLUBBER by John Grillo. The huge fantasy of the "little" man. With Gay Soper, Darryl Kavann, Nigel Anthony. (18)

THE UNCOMFORTABLE QUEEN by Wilfred Harvey. A young queen becomes "uncomfortable." With the Caryl Jenner Productions Company. (12)

THE OBJECT by Giles Cooper. Space-capsule upsets the apple cart. With Roger Lloyd Pack, Barrie Shore, Anthony Jacobs. (10)

DOWN UPPER STREET by various authors. A topical revue set in North London. With John Gould, Joyce Rae. (24)

ANARCHIST by Michael Almaz. Bakunin's influence on Russian history and the coming revolution. With John Grillo, John Malcolm, Gillian Brown. (17)

FOOD and ZONK by John Grillo. Double bill about sex variations. With the Portable Theater Company. (7)

SHELTER by Alun Owen. Unhappy woman seeks shelter from the rain and finds greater unhappiness. With Tom Kempinski, Ann Mitchell. (9)

DISABLED by Peter Ransley. Adapted former TV drama asks: When is a cripple not a cripple? With Leonard Rossiter, Peter McEnery, Pauline Yates. (20)

A NEW COMMUNION FOR FREAKS, PROPHETS AND WITCHES by Jane Arden. Women's Lib through the eyes of mental patients. Sheila Allen, Liz Kustow, the author. (3)

INQUISITION by Michael Almaz. Strip-cartoon of the Spanish Inquisition. With John Grillo. (14)

CORUNNA by Keith Dewhurst. Musical about the Peninsular War. With Juliet Ackroyd, Mark McManus, Steeleye Span. (15)

THE NINE DAYS IN MAY. Program of laboratory theater from home and abroad including: *Dangerous Mission* by Dalt Wonk, with the Bird in Hand Theater of New York (4); *The People Show* (3); *King Lear* (not Shakespeare's version) by and with Mario Ricci's Theater of the Tiber, Rome (2); *Harlequin and Columbine* by and with The Freehold (3); *People/Time, Space* by and with Roland Miller, Shirley Cameron (2); *The One Eyed King* by Eric Price, with the Chamelion Theater, Southampton (1); *Mitsutaki Ishii* experimental dance and mime from Japan (2); *Duet With Three Others* by Rio Fanning, with the Actors Present Company (1); *Who Killed Lester Kaufmann* by and with the Incubus Company (2); *Guns and Butter* by and with the Cervantes Players (1).

THE POSITION GROTESQUE by Stanley Rice. Comedy of sexual misunderstanding.

With Anthony Jacobs, Moray Watson, Katherine Schofield. (10)

WE'RE LOOKING FOR MARY PICKFORD by David Henry Wilson (D). A psychological fantasy farce of two imprisoned brothers in search of freedom. With Norman Mitchell, Michael Malnik. (7+)

THE CRITIC AS ARTIST by Oscar Wilde. Dramatized and staged by Charles Marowitz. With Timothy West. (5+)

NIGHT SCHOOL by Harold Pinter. Stage premiere of TV play. With John White, Shelagh Fraser, Rosamund Greenwood, Harry Landis. (7+)

POPULAR ATTRACTIONS

BLINDSIGHT by Anne Wolridge-Gordon (D). Moral Rearmament propaganda play. With Philip Friend, Philip Newman, Michael Malnick, Joyce Heron, Mary Jones. (116)

THE HOSTAGE by Brendan Behan. Revival of Behan's world-famous drama about modern Ireland. With Robin Wentworth, Romy Baskerville. (27)

THE TEMPEST by William Shakespeare. Jonathan Miller's production at Mermaid with black players in unexpected roles. With Graham Crowden, Angela Pleasence. (52)

THE BED by Paul Raymond. Sexual titillation for its own sake. With Tony Bateman, John Higgins. (120)

LONDON ASSURANCE by Dion Boucicault, adapted by Ronald Eyre. Century-old comedy about social ambition and an almost thwarted love affair. With Donald Sinden, Judi Dench, Elizabeth Spriggs. (55 in repertory)

LADY FREDERICK by W. Somerset Maugham. Stylish revival of comedy. With Margaret Lockwood, Tony Britton, Heather Chason. (104)

THE FORGOTTEN FACTOR by Alan Thornhill. Revival of 25-year-old Moral Rearmament propaganda play. With Philip Friend, Philip Newman, Joyce Heron, Mary Jones. (92)

THE WINTER'S TALE by William Shakespeare. Transfer of Trevor Nunn's unorthodox Stratford production. With Barrie Ingham, Judi Dench, Elizabeth Spriggs. (44 in repertory)

THE GREAT WALTZ by Erich Korngold and Jerome Chodorov. Old Viennese operetta

without the cobwebs. With Sari Barabas, Leo Fuchs, Walter Cassel (later Ina de Wiata). (371+)

MUCH ADO ABOUT NOTHING by William Shakespeare. Regents Park open-air-theater production. With Irena Mayeska, Gary Bond. (54)

BLITHE SPIRIT by Noel Coward. Revival of Coward's smash hit comedy compares well with original. With Beryl Reid, Amanda Reiss. (204)

THE TWO OF US by Michael Frayn. A four-play vehicle for two clever quick-change artists. With Lynn Redgrave, Richard Briers. (186)

THE WELL OF THE SAINTS by J. M. Synge. Dublin Abbey Theater production visits London. With Kathleen Barrington, John Kavanagh, Eamonn Kelly, Pat Laffan, Maira O'Donnell. (8)

HOW THE OTHER HALF LOVES by Alan Ayckbourn. Two rival couples and their friends hilariously intertwined in time and place. With Robert Morley, Heather Sears, Joan Tetzel (later Jan Holden). (349+)

TWELFTH NIGHT by William Shakespeare. John Barton's hilarious Stratford production comes to town. With Judi Dench, Donald Sinden, Elizabeth Spriggs, Barrie Ingham, Emrys James, Leslie Sands. (50 in repertory)

SAINT JOAN by Bernard Shaw. The poor man's reach-me-down revival at the Mermaid. With Angela Pleasence, George Benson, John Tordoff. (77)

TEA PARTY/THE BASEMENT by Harold Pinter. Dramatization of two successful T.V. plays. With Donald Pleasence, Barry Foster, Vivien Merchant. (83)

A BEQUEST TO THE NATION by Terence Rattigan. Nelson's sensual affair with Emma Hamilton leads to a fatal decision. With Ian Holm, Zoe Caldwell, Leueen MacGrath. (125)

WAITING FOR GODOT by Samuel Beckett. Popular revival of modern classic for Young Vic audiences. With Gavin Reed, Desmond McNamara, Nicky Henson. (41+ in repertory)

THE JOCKEY CLUB STAKES by William Douglas Home. Crime and corruption among the followers of the Sport of Kings. With Julia Lockwood, Alastair Sim (later Wilfrid Hyde White). (261+)

THE DUCHESS OF MALFI by John Webster. Award-winning adaptation that impressed on its trans-European tour. With The Freehold Company. (10)

MAJOR BARBARA by George Bernard Shaw. Royal Shakespeare Company's first, creditable essay in Shavian play-acting. With Judi Dench, Brewster Mason, Elizabeth Spriggs. (44 in repertory)

DOWN THE ARCHES by Ewan Hooper. Documentary about Greenwich in its own theater. With Bill Stewart, Sally Mates, Derek Griffiths. (27)

THEATER GO ROUND including *When Thou Art King,* Shakespeare history cycle adapted by John Barton, with Brewster Mason, Michael Williams, Juliet Aykroyd (11); *Arden of Faversham* by unknown 16th century author, with Dorothy Tutin, Emrys James (19); *King John* by William Shakespeare, with Patrick Stewart, Norman Rodway (7); *Dr. Faustus* by Christopher Marlowe. With David Waller, Alan Howard (3); *A Midsummer Night's Dream* by William Shakespeare, a studio performance of Peter Brook's production (1); *Richard III* by William Shakespeare, a studio performance of Terry Hands's production, with Norman Rodway (1); *Hamlet* by William Shakespeare, a studio performance of Trevor Nunn's production, with Alan Howard (1); *The Elizabethans,* a studio production of Shakespeare's England in song and verse (5).

AC/DC by Heathcote Williams. Revival of prizewinning drama. With Henry Woolf, Victor Henry, Sheila Scott-Wilkinson. (16)

THE WINSLOW BOY by Terence Rattigan. Revival of 25-year-old drama of a man's fight for his son's good name. With Steven Pacey, Megs Jenkins, Annette Crosbie, Kenneth More. (243+)

THE PROJECTOR by William Rufus Chetwood. Joan Littlewood and John Wells dip into the past and come up with something new. With Bill Wallis, Trudi Van Doorn. (70)

EXILES by James Joyce. Harold Pinter directs a Pinterish play before its time. With John Wood, Vivien Merchant, Timothy West. (36)

THE TAMING OF THE SHREW by William Shakespeare. Partially modernized to fit the stage and young audience at the Young Vic. With Jim Dale, Jane Lapotaire. (38+ in repertory)

WHEN WE ARE MARRIED by J.B. Priestley. Transfer of the Yvonne Arnaud Theater, Guilford, production. With Peggy Mount, Gwen Cherrell, Fred Emney. (232+)

GAME PLAYS including *Moonmen* (38), *Comics* (21), *Epic* (13), *Skule Rool* (12), *Eskimos* (15), *Marching Orders* (21) by the Dogg's Troupe. With the authors.

PARTICIPATORY PLAYS including *Revolution Workshop* by the Dogg's Troupe, with the authors (45); *Work in Progress* by the Dogg's Troupe, with Jim Hiley, Geoff Hoyle, Patrick Barlow (7); *Mushrooms and Toadstools* by Henry Livings, with Jim Hiley, Geoff Hoyle, Patrick Barlow (19).

ACT-IN by the Dogg's Troupe. An indoor and outdoor event. With the authors. (42)

TONIGHT AT EIGHT (formerly *Tonight at 8:30*) by Noel Coward. Coward's famous triple playbill revived. With Millicent Martin, Alan MacNaughtan, Gary Bond. (95)

HENRY VIII by William Shakespeare. Brief London transfer of Trevor Nunn's hit production. With Donald Sinden, Peggy Ashcroft, Brewster Mason. (4)

DICK TURPIN by Anthony Loynes and Ron Pember. Mocking dramatization of Britain's most famous highwayman. With Mark Burns, Richard Wordsworth, Rohan McCullough. (78)

THE SECRET UNDER THE STAIRS by Gregory Marshall. Who are really the baddies in a 15th century priory? With the Caryl Jenner Productions Company. (28)

CATCH MY SOUL by Jack Good (D). Rock version of *Othello* story set in the middle west. With Lance Le Gault, P.J. Proby, Sharon Gurney, the author. (80)

THE TWO GENTLEMEN OF VERONA by William Shakespeare. Robin Phillips's Stratford hit comes to town for a brief spell. With Ian Richardson, Patrick Stewart, Sebastian Shaw, Helen Mirren, Sheila Burell. (12)

MRS WARREN'S PROFESSION by George Bernard Shaw. The National Theater's first, creditable essay in Shavian play-acting. With Coral Browne, Bill Fraser, Sarah Badel. (34+ in repertory)

HAMLET by William Shakespeare. Transfer of Anthony Page's Nottingham Playhouse production. With Alan Bates, Celia Johnson, Douglas Wilmer, Angela Scoular. (28)

THE DUCHESS OF MALFI by John Webster. Experimental interpretation of Jacobean horror comic. With Judy Parfitt, Victor Henry, Desmond Gill. (38)

THE FORMATION DANCERS by Frank Marcus. Updated revival of author's early sexual comedy. With Anton Rodgers, Anna Calder-Marshall, Barbara Leigh-Hunt, Lyndon Brook. (26)

ENDGAME by Samuel Beckett. Young Vic's second attempt to please youthful audiences with "difficult" theater. With Denise Coffey, Harold Innocent, Same Kelly, Desmond McNamara. (27+ in repertory)

AFTER HAGGERTY by David Mercer. Royal Shakespeare Company's production re-cast, rewritten and successfully restaged in a commercial theater. With Frank Finlay (later Barry Foster), Billie Whitelaw, Leslie Sands. (131+)

DON'T START WITHOUT ME by Joyce Rayburn. Quadrangular sex farce in which wife-swapping plot is foiled. With Paul Daneman, Jan Waters, Brian Cox, Lucy Fleming. (125+)

THE PRINCE AND THE HENGIRL (author unknown), mixed media play about a Hengirl's journey to rescue a Prince from a Dark Lady; and THERE WAS ONCE THIS MAN . . . by Marged Smith, story of a squeak that begins in a man's shoe and ends up in a teddy bear. With the Caryl Jenner Productions Company. (22)

THE LICENTIOUS FLY by Huntly Harding. A sexually hungry country widower on the rampage. With Christopher Benjamin, Queenie Watts, Larry Noble, Antonia Pemberton. (48)

CAPTAIN BRASSBOUND'S CONVERSION by George Bernard Shaw. Star-studded commercial revival of little-done comedy Shaw wrote for Ellen Terry. With Ingrid Bergman, Joss Ackland, Kenneth Williams. (115+)

MACBETH by William Shakespeare. Greenwich Theater's ambitious production of Shakespeare's tragedy. With Alan Dobie, Hildegard Neil. (43)

SPOILED by Simon Gray. A pupil wreaks havoc in a married schoolmaster's home. With Anna Massey, Jeremy Kemp, Simon Ward. (38)

ELLEN by Peter Ransley (D). Dramatization of the true-life story of a down-and-out intruder. With Mary Merrall, Ian McShane. (26)

MOVE OVER MRS MARKHAM by Ray Cooney and John Chapman. A farcical sexual wild goose chase ends happily. With Moira Lister, Lana Morris, Tony Britton, Cicely Courtneidge. (86+)

HANKY PARK by Walter Greenwood. Dramatization of autobiographical novel about Northern England in the hungry between-wars period. With Jack Tweddle, Sally Miles. (29)

VINCENT by W. Gordon Smith (D). One-man show about Vincent van Gogh. With Tom Fleming. (16)

MEASURE FOR MEASURE by William Shakespeare. The Young Vic's second foray into Shakespeare for young people. With Ronald Pickup, Jane Lapotaire. (17+ in repertory)

A WOMAN KILLED WITH KINDNESS by Thomas Heywood. Spectacular National Theater revival of Jacobean middle class tragedy. With Joan Plowright, Anthony Hopkins, Louise Purnell, Derek Jacobi. (8+ in repertory)

THE CHALK GARDEN by Enid Bagnold. Transfer of Yvonne Arnaud Theater, Guilford, revival. With Gladys Cooper, Joan Greenwood, Michael Goodliffe. (40+)

LITTLE MALCOLM AND HIS STRUGGLE AGAINST THE EUNUCHS (also titled Hail Scrawdyke!) by David Halliwell. Revival for benefit of Young Vic patrons. With Una Stubbs, Sam Kelly. (11+ in repertory)

CORIOLANUS by William Shakespeare. Berliner Ensemble's four-man directing and designing team turns Shakespeare into Brecht without altering the text. With Anthony Hopkins, Constance Cummings. (10+ in repertory)

UNDER MILK WOOD by Dylan Thomas. Revival of staged radio play about life in a Welsh town. With Glyn Houston, Marion Grimaldi, Nell Curran, Clive Merrison. (24)

JOHN BULL'S OTHER ISLAND by George Bernard Shaw. Revival of rarely-performed

Alexis Smith as Phyllis Stone, *right*, accompanied by her memory
figure (Virginia Sandifur) in the musical *Follies*

Maureen Stapleton as Evy Meara in *The Gingerbread Lady*

Cliff Gorman as Lenny Bruce in *Lenny* (FAR RIGHT)

Ralph Richardson (FAR LEFT) and John Gielgud in *Home*

James Earl Jones as Tshembe Matoseh in *Les Blancs*

Hamid Hamilton Camp in *Story Theater* (FAR RIGHT)

Ruby Dee as Lena i[n] *Boesman and Lena* (FA[R] LEFT)

Jeremy Clyde as 2d Lt Edward Millington i[n] *Conduct Unbecoming*

Claire Bloom as Hedda in *Hedda Gabler*

Danny Kaye as Noah in *Two by Two* (FAR RIGHT)

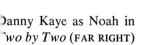

Brian Bedford as Arnolphe in *The School for Wives* (FAR LEFT)

Hector Elizondo as Attendant in *Steambath*

Alec McCowen as Philip in *The Philanthropist*

Keene Curtis as Joseph Fouche in *The Rothschilds* (FAR RIGHT)

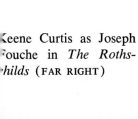

Ruby Keeler as Sue Smith in *No, No, Nanette* (FAR LEFT)

Harold Gould as Artie Shaughnessy in *The House of Blue Leaves*

SLEUTH—*Above*, the British manor-house setting designed by Carl Toms. *Left*, Keith Baxter and Anthony Quayle in a scene from the cat-and-mouse thriller by Anthony Shaffer

Ralph Richardson and John Gielgud in *Home*, the Critics Award winner

Betsy von Furstenberg is toasted by Ayn Ruymen, Maureen Stapleton and Michael Lombard in Neil Simon's *The Gingerbread Lady*

THE PHILANTHROPIST—A professor and his tearful fiancee (Alec McCowen and Jane Asher) break off their engagement with a goodbye kiss

CONDUCT UNBECOMING—Participants in court martial include Donald Pickering as the Adjutant (seated in middle of table, *center*), Elizabeth Shepherd as a complainant, Michael Barrington as the Colonel (standing, *right*) and Jeremy Clyde as the defendant (seated at extreme *right*)

Bob (Bob Elliott) *and Ray* (Ray Goulding, at top) *the Two and Only* on Broadway

Sid Caesar and Carol Channing in one of the four playlets of Abe Burrows's *Four on a Garden*

AND MISS REARDON DRINKS A LITTLE—Estelle Parsons, Julie Harris and Nancy Marchand as sisters in the play by Paul Zindel

Below, Will Geer in the title role of Archibald MacLeish's *Scratch*

STORY THEATER & METAMOR-PHOSES—At top, Valerie Harper, Richard Schaal, Hamid Hamilton Camp, Melinda Dillon and Paul Sand in *Henny Penny*, one of the Grimm's tales adapted for the stage by Paul Sills. *Directly above*, the *Baucis and Philomen* segment of the troupe's rendition of Ovid's tales, with the Messrs. Camp, Sand, Miss Harper and Avery Schreiber.

Above, Bernice Massi, Phil Silvers, Sandy Dennis and Richard Mulligan in *How the Other Half Loves*

Below, James Earl Jones with African tribesmen in the late Lorraine Hansberry's *Les Blancs*

Above, Richard Dysart and Mildred Dunnock in *A Place Without Doors*

Showgirls in elaborate costumes designed by Florence Klotz parade in the ironic "Loveland" sequence of *Follies*

Boris Aronson sketch of his prizewinning *Follies* scenery design

Below, the *Follies* principals: Phyllis and Benjamin Stone (Alexis Smith and John McMartin, *left*) and Sally and Buddy Plummer (Dorothy Collins and Gene Nelson, *right*)

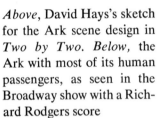

Above, David Hays's sketch for the Ark scene design in *Two by Two*. *Below,* the Ark with most of its human passengers, as seen in the Broadway show with a Richard Rodgers score

Right, Danny Kaye as Noah in the musical *Two by Two*

THE ROTHSCHILDS—Amshel (Timothy Jerome), Jacob (Chris Sarandon), father Mayer (Hal Linden), Nathan (Paul Hecht), Solomon (David Garfield) and Kalman (Allan Gruet) in the "Rothschild and Sons" musical number

70, GIRLS, 70—Mildred Natwick (on moon) and her fellow conspirators

NO, NO, NANETTE—Helen Gallagher and Bobby Van in leading roles of the musical

Below, Nanette balances on a beach ball (Susan Watson, second from right) with her friends in Atlantic City scene of *No, No, Nanette*, adapted by Burt Shevelove from 1925 Vincent Youmans musical, with Donald Saddler dances

Sketches by Raoul Pene du Bois of three of his
1920s costume designs for *No, No, Nanette*

A DOLL'S HOUSE—Donald Madden, Patricia Elliott and Claire
Bloom in Christopher Hampton's adaptation of Ibsen

A MIDSUMMER NIGHT'S DREAM—Above, Sally Jacobs's model for the set of the Royal Shakespeare Company production directed by Peter Brook (Stratford-Upon-Avon 1970, North America 1971, London 1971). *Below*, the airborne cast in action with Titania (Sara Kestelman, center) resting in her bower, surrounded by her coterie of faithful sprites

THE SCHOOL FOR WIVES—Right, Brian Bedford as Arnolphe upends David Dukes as Horace in Molière's comedy

AN ENEMY OF THE PEOPLE—Below, in foreground, Barbara Cason, Stephen Elliott and Tandy Cronyn in Lincoln Center Repertory production of the Ibsen classic, as adapted by Arthur Miller

BOESMAN AND LENA—Ruby Dee as Lena and Zakes Mokae (who replaced James Earl Jones) as Boesman in Athol Fugard's play

OFF BROADWAY

STEAMBATH—Right, Hector Elizondo as Attendant and Anthony Perkins as Tandy in Bruce Jay Friedman's comedy

THE HOUSE OF BLUE LEAVES—William Atherton, Tom Flynn, Anne Meara (as Bunny), Katherine Helmond (as Bananas), Harold Gould (as Artie), Carl Hunt, Margaret Linn (on knees, as Corinna), Carl Hunt, Frank Converse, Rita Karin, Alix Elias and Kay Michaels in the play by John Guare

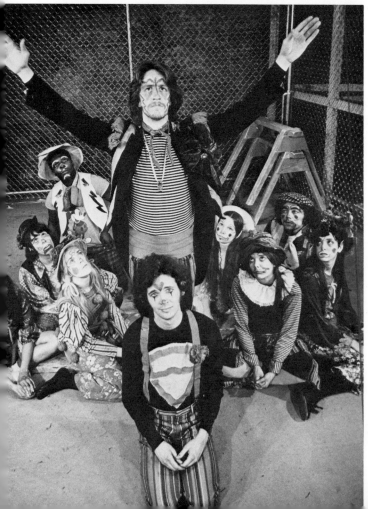

ROCK MUSICALS—
Above, Plowright Players in a scene from *Touch*. *Left*, Stephen Nathan (front), David Haskell (arms upraised) and others in the cast of *Godspell*

Right, Stacy Keach, James Naughton, Geraldine Fitzgerald and Robert Ryan (seated) in O'Neill's *Long Day's Journey Into Night*

Left, Sam Levene, James J. Sloyan and Clara Heller in Irv Bauer's *A Dream Out of Time*. *Below*, a scene from Israel Horovitz's *Line* with John Randolph, John Cazale, Richard Dreyfuss and Barnard Hughes

On these facing pages, a sampling of this season's N.Y. Shakespeare Festival shows, both indoor and outdoor

Above, Andy Robinson as Prince Myshkin (in box) and company in *Subject to Fits. Right*, Siobhan Mc-Kenna in *Here Are Ladies. Below*, Jack MacGowran in the *Works of Samuel Beckett*

Above, Nicholas Kepros in title role of *Henry VI* in outdoor Shakespeare. *Left*, Robert Ronan and Sasha von Scherler indoors at the Public Theater in *Trelawny of the "Wells."* *Below*, the cast of David Rabe's new play *The Basic Training of Pavlo Hummel*

CHELSEA THEATER CENTER—The baby carriage scene in the American premiere of Edward Bond's *Saved*

NEGRO ENSEMBLE COMPANY—*Below*, Antonio Fargas and Roscoe Lee Browne in *The Dream on Monkey Mountain* by Derek Walcott

ROUNDABOUT THEATER—*Above*, Fred Stuthman and Robert G. Murch in *Chas. Abbott and Son*

OFF-BROADWAY

ENSEMBLES

THEATER OF THE EYE
—*Right*, clockwise from
top, Madeleine le Roux,
Ellen Gurin, Sommer Sally
and Nana Winter in *The
Dirtiest Show in Town*,
sometimes about pollution

BIL BAIRD'S MARIONETTES—A scene from
Holiday on Strings, Winter receives a message from
Spring

AMERICAN PLACE—
Above, son (John Karkes)
confronts father (Vincent
Gardenia) and mother (Alice
Drummond) in *The Carpenters*, new play by Steven
Tesich

FORUM THEATER, LINCOLN CENTER—
Above, Christopher Walken, Priscilla Pointer,
Elizabeth Huddle and James Broderick in A.R.
Gurney Jr's *Scenes From American Life*. *Left*, Miss
Pointer, Conrad Bain and Robert Symonds in Duerrenmatt's *Play Strindberg*, in rehearsal as season
ended

Above, Tim Pelt, Victor Mims and Vernee Watson in Al Fann's *King Heroin*

Left, Henderson Forsythe as Didi and Paul B. Price as Gogo in long-run off-Broadway revival of Beckett's *Waiting for Godot*

A SAMPLING OF NEW PLAYS

IN REGIONAL THEATERS

PROVIDENCE, R.I.—Members of the Trinity Square Repertory Company in a scene from their world premiere production of *Son of Man and Family*

LOS ANGELES—*Above*, at Mark Taper Forum, Carrie Snodgrass, Sheree North, Nehemiah Persoff and Ron Rifkin in Harvey Perr's *Rosebloom*. *Left*, Tom Troupe and James Daly as the Berrigan brothers in the world premiere production of *The Trial of the Catonsville Nine* in the Mark Taper's "New Theater for Now" series under the direction of Gordon Davidson, who also staged it later in its Best Play version in N.Y.

WASHINGTON, D.C.—
The season at Arena Stage
included the American premiere of Ionesco's *Wipe-Out
Games* (*right*, with Ned
Beatty seated); the world
premiere of Stanley R.
Greenberg's *Pueblo* (*left*,
with Tom Klunis, Tom Leo-
pold, Shepperd Strudwick,
Daniel Ahearn, Alvin Lum
and Mr. Beatty); and the
world professional premiere
of Lawrence & Lee's *The
Night Thoreau Spent in Jail*
(*below*, with Jill Eikenberry
and Michael Fairman)

WASHINGTON, D.C.—The Washington Theater Club
Season included the world premiere of *The Web and the
Rock* adapted from Thomas Wolfe's novel by Dolores
Sutton, with (*below*) Stephen McHattie, Michael Forella,
Miss Sutton (the author) and Margaret Winn

STRATFORD, CANADA—Fernando Arrabal's *The Architect and the Emperor of Assyria* (*left*) with Roger Blay and Arnold Soboloff in the title roles

MINNEAPOLIS—*Below,* Minnesota Theater Company's production of Aleksandr Solzhenitsyn's *A Play* with Briain Petchey, Linda Kelsey, Allison Giglio, Maxwell Glanville and Peter Michael Goetz

comedy about the "throubles" in Ireland. With Christopher Benjamin, Anna Cropper, Edward Petherbridge. (23+)

SLAG by David Hare. Royal Court revival of Hampstead Theater Club's drama. With Lynn Redgrave, Anna Massey, Barbara Ferris. (7+)

SOME FOREIGN PLAYS PRODUCED IN LONDON

THE CREDITORS by August Strindberg. With the Portable Theater Company. (6)

ON THE HARMFULNESS OF TOBACCO and SWAN SONG by Anton Chekhov. With Stanley Lebor. (6)

HEDDA GABLER by Henrik Ibsen. With Maggie Smith, Jeremy Brett, Robert Stephens, John Moffat. (64 in repertory)

THE PLEBEIANS REHEARSE THE UPRISING by Gunter Grass. With Emrys James, Peggy Ashcroft, Geoffrey Hutchings. (27)

BLACK PIECES by Mustapha Matura. With T-Bone Wilson, Alfred Fagon, Oscar James. (25) On a double bill with *White Poem* by David Mercer (see Limited Runs of Interesting New British Plays).

COUNCIL OF LOVE by Oscar Panizza. With Warren Mitchell, Peter Bayliss, John Trigger, Lally Bowers. (83)

INEDITS IONESCO by Eugene Ionesco. With Jean Rougerie, Andre Chaumeau. (6)

FOURSOME by Eugene Ionesco. With John Clive, Ronald Oliver. On a double bill with *A Discussion* by David Halliwell (see Limited Runs of Interesting New British Plays). (10)

SCAPINO OR THE CHEATS OF SCAPIN, adapted from Molière. With Jim Dale, Nicky Henson, Anna Carteret, John Moffatt, Jane Lapotaire. (27+ in repertory)

OEDIPUS by Sophocles. With Ronald Pickup. (26+ in repertory)

THE SOLDIER'S TALE by Igor Stravinsky. With Gordon Jackson, Nicky Henson, Una Stubbs, Desmond McNamara. (13+ in repertory)

KRAPP'S LAST TAPE by Samuel Beckett. With George Innes. (10)

A MODERN PROFOUND AND IMPORTANT RESEARCH INTO THE FOSSILS OF THE 25TH GEOLOGICAL ERA by Abbas Naalbandian. With the Shakin Sarkisian Group. (1)

ARREST by Victor Corti (D). World premiere of Canadian author's environmental drama about censorship and the reaction of the audience to intervention. With Norman Beaton, Caroline Gilmore. On a double bill with *It Bees Dat Way* by Ed Bullins (See American Plays Produced in London). (15)

THE NET by Alan Poolman. With Damien Thomas, Karin Fernald. (16)

CYRANO by Edmond Rostand, adapted by Patrick Garland. With Edward Woodward, Anthony Nicholls, Anna Carteret, Gerald James. (42+ in repertory)

DRACULA by Alfredo Rodriguez Arias, with Marucha Bo, Facundo Bo, the author; and GODDESS by Javier Arroyuelo, with Facundo Bo, Marucha Bo. (6)

THE HISTORY OF THE THEATER by Javier Arroyuelo and Raphael Lopez Sanchez. With the TSE Company of Argentine. (9)

THE WILD DUCK by Henrik Ibsen. With Michael Denison, Dulcie Gray, Hayley Mills, Alfred Lynch. (46)

LULU by Frank Barnes, adapted from *Earth Spirits* and *Pandora's Box* by Frank Wedekind. With Julia Foster, John Phillips, Edward Petherbridge, Sheila Ballantine. (111)

THE EMPIRE BUILDERS by Boris Vian. With John Preston, Mimi Whitford. (24)

THE KING STAG by Carlo Gozzi. With Harold Innocent, Denise Coffey, Andrew Robertson. (24 in repertory)

THE DRAGON by Yevgeny Schwarz. With the Unity Theater Company. (15)

KEAN by Jean-Paul Sartre, adapted by Frank Hauser. With Alan Badel, Lisa Daniely, Felicity Kendal, Ken Wynne. (121+)

THE ARCHITECT AND THE EMPEROR OF ASSYRIA by Fernando Arrabal. With Jim Dale, Anthony Hopkins. (15+ in repertory)

OFFENDING THE AUDIENCE by Peter Handke. With The Other Company. On a triple bill with *Black Mass* by Edward Bond, and *Have You Met Our Rabbit* by Michael Stevens (see Limited Runs of Interesting New British Plays). (26)

THE BABY ELEPHANT by Bertolt Brecht. With Mark McManus, Tim Curry. (6)

MAN IS MAN by Bertolt Brecht. With Henry Woolf, Susan Williamson, Trevor Peacock, Georgia Brown. (38)

THE INFORMER by Bertolt Brecht. With Ken Parry, Jackie Ellis. (13)

REQUIEM FOR ROMEO AND JULIET (8), QUO VADIS (4) and FUSION (4) by the Tréteaux Libres Company.

THE CAPTAIN OF KÖPENICK by Carl Zuckmayer, adapted by John Mortimer. With Paul Scofield, Hazel Hughes, Jim Dale, John Moffatt, Bill Fraser. (24+ in repertory)

RABELAIS by Jean-Louis Barrault. With Gerald Harper, Joe Melia, Bernard Horsfall, Bernard Bresslaw, Ian Trigger. (45)

PLAYBAG consisting of The Niece Wife by Eugene Ionesco, The Unsatisfactory Supper by Tennesee Williams and Our Girls Are Famous by Carl Forgione. With Leonard Field, Miranda Forbes, Roger Lloyd Pack, Edward Phillips, Michael Craze. (9)

CALIGULA by Albert Camus. With the Tréteau de Paris. (7)

THE LADY FROM THE SEA by Henrik Ibsen. With Fulton Mackay, Ann Lynn. (25)

ENCHANTED NIGHT by Slawomir Mrozek. With Edward de Souza, Gordon Sterne, Irene Gorst (13).

CONFRONTATION by Hans Keuls. World premiere of Dutch author's English play about the murder of the Kennedy brothers and that of two Gracchi in ancient Rome. With Paul Massie, Margaretta Scott, Peter Madden. (15)

WORLD THEATER SEASON 1970—Moscow Art Theater in The Seagull by Anton Chekhov (12) and The Third Pathétique by Nicolai Pogodin. (4)

WORLD THEATER SEASON 1971—Théâtre Michel in La Ville Dont le Prince Est un Enfant (20); Royal Dramatic Theater, Stockholm, in The Dream Play (8); Schiller Theater in Yvonne, Princess of Burgundy (4) and Krapp's Last Tape with Endgame (4); Genoa Stabile Theater in The Venetian Twins (8); Dormen Theater, Turkey, in A Tale of Istanbul (8); Nuria Espert Company, Spain, in The Maids (8).

SOME AMERICAN PLAYS PRODUCED IN LONDON

1776 (musical) based on a conception of Sherman Edwards, book by Peter Stone. With Ronald Radd, Richard Huggett, Harold Kasket. (168)

THE HERETIC by Morris West. World premiere of historical drama about the martyrdom of Giordano Bruno. With Leonard Rossiter, Joseph O'Conor. (82)

OH! CALCUTTA! (revue) by various authors, devised by Kenneth Tynan. With a changing cast. (359+)

THE BAPTISM by Leroi Jones. With Marie Adams, Bill Bailey, Michael Da Costa. (12)

CANCER by Michael Weller (D). World premiere of Royal Court commissioned play about American university students on the eve of graduation. With Seth Allen, Mari Gorman, Al Mancini. (36)

NO TALKING by Olwen Wymark. With the Caryl Jenner Productions Company. On a double bill with The Gentle Knight by Willis Hall (see Limited Runs of Interesting New British Plays). (17)

CHIAROSCURO by Israel Horovitz. With Marcella Markham, David Baron. (11)

STOMP (musical) by the Texas University group. With the authors. (10)

CREATURES OF THE CHASE by Walter Manus. With Bobbie Byers, Stephen Barker. (9)

IT BEES DAT WAY by Ed Bullins. With Oliver Norman, Corinne Skinner, Alfred Fagon. On a double bill with Arrest by Victor Corti (see Some Foreign Plays Produced in London). (15)

BUTTERFLIES ARE FREE by Leonard Gershe. With Keir Dullea, Barbara Ferris, Eileen Heckart. (40)

NATIVITY PLAY by Billy Hoffman. With the Wherehouse La Mama Company. (9)

ISABEL'S A JEZEBEL (musical) by Galt MacDermot and William Dumaresq. World premiere of rewrite of 1970 tryout. With Carole Hayman, Nicholas Ball. (64)

THE HIGH BID by Henry James. With Eartha Kitt, Charles Carson, Gary Watson. (40)

BIRDBATH by Leonard Melfi. With Carl Forgione, Julie Somers. (10)

CAPTAIN JACK'S REVENGE by Michael Smith. With Michael Pennington, Anthony Corlan, Edward Jewesbury. (16)

THE DECLINE AND FALL OF LESLIE WEST by Dalt Wonk. With the off-Broadway Bird in Hand Company. (16)

SPIDER RABBIT by Michael McClure. With Amanda Lear, P. J. Proby. (14)

FLASH GORDON AND THE ANGELS by David Zane Mairowitz. World premiere about a send-up of the popular science fiction convention. With William S. Burroughs (on film), Manning Redwood. (16)

CHILD'S PLAY by Robert Marasco. With Laurence Harvey, Rupert Davies. (79+)

ICARUS'S MOTHER by Sam Shepard. With Christopher Biggins, Marc Alexander. (18)

I RISE IN FLAME, CRIED THE PHOENIX by Tennessee Williams. With Graham Lines, Barbara Laurenson, Yvonne Bonnamy. (9)

GRANT'S MOVIE by Mike Weller. World premiere about three youngsters who kidnap a cop, torture him and act out his aggressions. With Tony Sibbald, Cedric Scott. (16)

NEITHER HERE NOR THERE by Olwen Wymark. The mental passion of six girls. With Cleo Sylvestre, Diana Patrick. (13)

THE DIFFERENCE by Peter Bergman. With Gypsie Kemp, Clive Endersby. (8)

TIRA TELLS ALL THERE IS TO KNOW ABOUT HERSELF by Mike Weller. World premiere. With Maureen Lipman, Richard Kane. (13)

THE GLASS MENAGERIE by Tennessee Williams. With Helen Cherry, Ann Penfold, Bruce Myles, Steven Berkoff. (5+)

THE DIRTIEST SHOW IN TOWN by Tom Eyen. With Paul-Matthew Eckhart, Jeffrey Herman, Bradford Riley, Madeleine le Roux, Sommer Sally. (25+)

THE GYMNASIUM by Olwen Wymark. With Crispin Gilbard. On a double bill with *Liquid* by David Mowat (see Limited Runs of Interesting New British Plays). (2)

O
O
O

THE SEASON ELSEWHERE IN EUROPE

O   *By Ossia Trilling*
O
O

THE REPETITIOUSNESS WITH WHICH I introduce my annual review of the European scene by stressing the dominance of the German-speaking theater is a habit my readers will by now have gotten used to. It can't be helped. Germany, Switzerland and even Austria hold the critic's attention first and foremost, even were he to spend more time than he can afford in other parts of the Continent. The theater in German-speaking Europe is a magnet whose attraction grows stronger year by year. Above all, and at long last, there's an undeniable upsurge of new writers who, for the first time, can vie on equal terms with their colleagues across the borders and the waters.

A grievous loss was the death of Fritz Kortner, not the youngest but certainly the most spiritually youthful of all Europe's directors. Another name that has passed from the world scene is that of Helene Weigel, who died a few days after appearing in the title role of the Brecht-Gorki *The Mother* in Paris, which the Berliner Ensemble—left with no titular head as of this writing—took there in May for the centenary celebrations of the Commune.

The ferment in all departments continued unabated. Heads rolled. Musical chairs was the parlor game played regularly by city theater boards and managers, and not a few scandals again burst into the headlines. With August Everding nominated to leave the Munich Kammerspiele for the Hamburg State Opera, and his former literary manager Ivan Nagel, a drama critic of international repute, billed to follow Heinz Lietzau (of whom more anon) at the Hamburg Schauspielhaus, dissent erupted in Munich. Gunter Grass resigned after a dismal spell as literary adviser in Frankfurt, and shortly afterward he attacked his Munich counterpart, Heinar Kipphardt, in print. This led to Kipphardt's dismissal by the city authorities on what were avowedly grounds of political bias. The German-speaking theater's spokesmen rose in protest and Everding's entire acting crew threatened to resign.

Irony was heaped on the scandal by the echo of a similar controversy in Berlin, when the Christian Democratic city caucus voted to withhold the annual subsidy from the radically-oriented Schaubühne, only to provoke virtually unanimous criticism from champions of free speech of all parties and of all professions. Thanks to socialist in-fighting, the subsidy was restored, but

86

not without damage to the smooth working of the duumvirate of Claus Peymann (who resigned) and Peter Stein (whose continued leadership there was
for long in the balance). As for Lietzau in Hamburg, after losing the confidence of the city fathers and 3.5 million Deutschmarks in 15 months, he
simply pulled out, leaving the Schauspielhaus adrift with nobody at the helm
until Rolf Liebermann, from the neighboring State Opera, agreed to lend a
temporary hand. This did not prevent the theater from mounting one of the
season's most impressive productions, that of Christopher Hampton's *The
Philanthropist,* directed by Dieter Dorn and starring Helmut Griem as Philip,
which won wide acclaim at the annual Berlin Theater Review against the stiff-
est artistic competition. From Stuttgart at the Review, the Berlin-born British
director Peter Zadek broke several records with his spectacular adaptation of
Sean O'Casey's anti-war tragedy *The Silver Tassie,* in the manner of a Joan
Littlewood musical. This was not only his second, and very different, version
of the same play previously mounted in Wuppertal and also invited to Berlin,
but also the fourth time a play staged by him could be seen at the Review.
His forthcoming appointment as manager in Bochum leaves one in great ex-
pectation of things to come in that city's theater. The hope that Frankfurt's
waning fortunes might soon turn is strengthened by the appointment of Peter
Palitzsch as the new manager of the drama there next season, with Wilfried
Minks, Germany's leading designer, as part of his new team.

At Stuttgart the year's outstanding new work was Martin Walser's *Child's
Play* (not to be confused with Robert Marasco's American script with the
same title), staged not by Palitzsch, however, but by the talented young Alfred
Kirchner, due to become Stuttgart's chief director when Hans Peter Doll takes
over the State Theaters' management. Walser's play is part poetic and part
allegorical; its background is the present revolutionary ferment and disorien-
tation of the young. In a Lilliputian decor two young people play out a disastrous game with their well-meaning, liberal-minded parents. The climax is
duly horrific. Palitzsch himself made theatrical history with a three-hour-long
version of *Waiting for Godot,* precisely acted and ingeniously clowned. If
nothing else, he proved that he can be relied on to stage a non-Marxist drama
faithfully in the teeth of his political convictions.

At Dusseldorf Karlheinz Stroux, about to retire in favor of Ulrich Brecht
(from Kassel), paraded an imposing list of works old and new, as well as the
expected list of guest directors. We saw the third part of Martin Sperr's anti-
bourgeois trilogy *Munich Freedom,* staged by Michael Kehlmann, which
exposes the hatreds and prejudices of people in a large city; when left-wing
students protest against the encroachment of big brewery interests on the security of the dwellers of a dormitory area, the fat is in the fire, and the liberal
brewer—not too persuasively—commits suicide. Wolfgang Hildesheimer's
Mary Stuart, staged by Polish guest director Konrad Swinarski, had the Swiss
star Maria Becker back on a West German stage in the title role of a new view
of the Elizabethan power struggle. From Paris, the expatriate Wolfgang
Mehring came to stage Pablo Neruda's *Splendor and Glory of Joaquin Muri-
eto* in a spectacular oratorio-like production with three choruses and no

soloists. Here, too, Friedrich Duerrenmatt's latest dramatic exploration into the human psyche, *Portrait of a Planet,* saw the light of day in a thought-provoking in-the-round production by Erwin Axer, designed by his country-woman from Warsaw, Eva Starowieyska. It recalls the strip-cartoon technique and in some ways the theme of Thornton Wilder's *The Skin of Our Teeth* and denounces mankind's abject meanness in an evangelical cavalcade of 25 short sketches. The author himself staged the play some months later for its Swiss premiere in Zurich but only partly seems to have heeded the warnings of the lukewarm notices that followed the Dusseldorf world premiere. More successful was Stroux's fashionably strident production of the Swiss drama-tist's updated version of Shakespeare's *Titus Andronicus,* which not only had Tamora in a topless costume but also managed to scandalize the mayor and several well-dressed worthies in the front stalls, not because of the stage nudity, but, to judge from their exclamations and demonstrative storming-out midway in the performance, because of the atrocities (all borrowed from the original text) which evidently reminded many of them too sharply of similarly hor-rendous happenings in Germany in the not too distant past.

Before turning our attention to the two parts of Berlin, a word is due about a handful of productions in less-well-known playhouses, like Jorge Lavelli's characteristically scabrous handling, in Max Bignen's decor, of Witold Gombrowicz's *Operetta* in Bochum; French author Armand Gatti's *Rosa Collective,* world premiered in Kassel, a discussion drama in the overwhelm-ingly prolix convention this writer affects, in which the story of the murder of the titular revolutionary (Rosa Luxemburg) is stylistically intertwined with that of the Black Panthers and the Tupamaros; the professional premiere, 19 years after it was written, of Peter Weiss's *The Insurance* in Essen, in which the director Hans Neuenfels combines allusive sexual elements of the per-missive age with the author's surrealistic anti-bourgeois message; Leonard Steckel's directorial swan song, just before losing his life in a railroad acci-dent, at Hamburg's Thalia Theater; or Harry Buckwitz's inspired, festive guest production, starring Ernst Schröder, of Brecht's *The Life of Galileo,* in Minks's sumptuous Giottoesque decors, in Nuremberg, as part of the Durer quincentenary junketing.

West Berlin

In West Berlin it was the Schaubühne which began to steal the thunder with the 1970 festival production of the Brecht-Gorki *The Mother,* starring Therese Giehse, a production that later figured officially in the annual Review in 1971, by the only theater with two offerings. For this Peter Stein, heading a collective directing team, had gutted the auditorium, leaving the audience on three sides of a central stage flanked by huge portraits and scenes from the life of Lenin. Despite the Schaubühne's two official entries, the other being Claus Peymann's wily interpretation of Peter Handke's latest foray into the world of linguistics and philosophical hair-splitting *The Ride Over Lake Constance,* it was Peter Stein's multifariously inventive rendering of Ibsen's *Peer Gynt,* in a seven-hour-long version playing on two consecutive nights, that created the season's most memorable theatrical landmark. The title role was divided among six actors and Stein managed to pull every kind of trick out of his theatrical hat, to the general delight of the audience seated on two sides of a 25-yard-long rectangular arena stage, without sacrificing anything of the play's poetic verve or its implicit political, social and philosophical message.

In the private theater sector, history was made by the septuagenarian guest director Elisabeth Bergner, who chose a French farce for her widely-praised directorial debut. Another foreign visitor was Clifford Williams, whose productions of *Oh! Calcutta!,* after Hamburg, Paris and Berlin, began to cover the face of the commercial stage like a scarlet rash. Notable at the Schiller (the West Berlin State Theater) and its ancillary stages were Ernst Schröder's production of Gombrowicz's surrealistic *Yvonne* (later much applauded at London's World Theater Season); his neatly packaged version of the two parts of Shakespeare's *Henry IV* in a single evening, featuring Martin Held as Falstaff, in a version by the East Berlin dramatist Peter Hacks; Karl Paryla's version of Conor Cruise O'Brien's *Murderous Angels;* the Berlin premiere of Wolfgang Bauer's *Change,* an Austrian black comedy of a sadistic plot that fails, and the world premiere of a first play by yet another Austrian, *Hanserl* by Franz Buchrieser, a one-act tragedy in which a feckless youth slays his uncomprehending ex-Nazi widowed father in a fit of unmotivated pique. At the Free People's Theater, Hansjörg Utzerath fumbled Rolf Hochhuth's *Guerrillas* despite a bravely deliberate attempt to slant it critically against the author's misguided intentions; but his acutely observed version of Duerrenmatt's *Play Strindberg,* starring Hans Dieter Zeidler, ranked among his best work and was outshone only by the Berlin premiere of Dieter Forte's *Martin Luther and Thomas Muntzer,* which had world-premiered in Basle. This poetic essay, debunking hallowed traditions, acquired critical contours that won back for Utzerath's theater much of its ebbing renown.

East Berlin

No visit to East Berlin is complete without an experience of Walter Felsenstein's "Komisch Oper," where "musical theater" rather than "opera" proper is the watchword. Two technically non-operatic masterpieces were Götz Friedrich's stunning production of *Porgy and Bess,* starring Rudolf Asmus, the first production that owes nothing to its New York prototype. Designed by two Muscovite Jews (Valeri Levental and Marina Sokolova) and with some changes in text and score (snatches of authentic Jewish folk-songs added), this enthusiastically-applauded production sells out at each performance. I cannot believe that the public is unaware of the mingling of the echoes of onstage Tsarist anti-semitism and official Communist policy towards "Zionism" in East Berlin on these occasions.

Though far fewer plays reach the stages of East Berlin, by contrast with the work of western colleagues, there is much that is up to date in the repertory and it is eagerly lapped up. Even an old timer like Valetin Katayev's 40-year-old *Avantgarde,* staged by one of Benno Besson's young proteges at the People's Theater, is listened to with rapt attention. On the other hand, its public appeal is limited compared with such a popular revival as Besson's knock-about version of Molière's *The Doctor in Spite of Himself* which shows off Rolf Ludwig's comic talent to perfection. The center of gravity remains firmly rooted at Besson's theater, which has been promised a face-lift and a new single-tier amphitheater to replace the hangar-like, off-putting old auditorium with its bad acoustics and luckless sight-lines. Here, too the young ex-Berliner Ensemble directing team of Manfred Karge and Matthias Langhoff scored another success with an anti-naturalistic, neo-expressionist updating of Schiller's *The Brigands,* with the text altered, characters cut, and the whole acquiring an unexpected actuality recalling the angry young men and protesting students of western re-readings of the classics. By contrast, the Berliner Ensemble's novelty, Sean O'Casey's *Cock-a-Doodle-Dandy* directed by Werner Hecht and Hans-Georg Voigt, strikes a mediocre note—not an epithet usually associated with Brecht's old theater. Even Ruth Berghaus, the interim head until a successor to Helene Weigel is found, managed to give *In the Jungle of Cities* a new look that was strictly limited in appeal, Ekkehard Schall's artificial delivery and sinuous posturing as the scapegrace Shlink notwithstanding.

Switzerland and Austria

Harry Buckwitz's new regime in Zurich paid handsome dividends, both artistically and in audience attendance figures. The rot of the last few years seems to have been stopped with no loss of artistic quality. Two novelties were Alfred Muschg's rewrite of Goethe's fragmentary *The Agitated Ones (Die Aufgeregten),* whose portrait of class-conscious aristocrats anxious to avoid taking sides in the divisive situation of the French Revolution acquires an ironic topicality; and Duerrenmatt's own iconclastic view of the same author's *Urfaust,* set on a medieval-type trestle stage and acted with an impish permissiveness. Another controversial production (aside from Durrenmatt's of his own *Portrait of a Planet,* mentioned earlier) was the European premiere of Joseph Papp's *Naked Hamlet,* staged by Günther Büch. Basle survived the year without spectacularity (other than the premature death of Hans Bauer). Werner Düggelin's production of *Twelfth Night* was notable for the plentiful use of fanciful props, while Hans Hollmann's of *The Lady From Maxim's* provided the modicum of social criticism we have come to expect from this Austrian-born *enfant terrible* among German directors. The world premiere of Heinrich Henkel's *Iron Painters,* a two-hander about the drudgery of work, marked the arrival of an important new discovery in the realistic tradition and has since been either staged or announced by 30 German playhouses.

The new wave of Austrian playwriting centered chiefly around Graz, which had spawned Peter Handke, Wolfgang Bauer, Harald Sommer, Frank Buchrieser (mentioned above) and others. Wolfgang Bauer's latest full-length play, *New Year's Eve, or Mass-Murder in the Hotel Sacher,* written as a vehicle for the comedian Helmut Qualtinger and carrying oblique echoes of such controversial topics as the Mylai massacre, failed to reach the stage of the Vienna People's Theater, owing to the star's last-minute sickness. A public reading of the text by Herr Qualtinger some weeks earlier, however, provided a foretaste of a provocative new work now destined for the ensuing season. A new play here was Peter Turrini's *The Rat Race.* It had two escapists shot down like the rats they are themselves trying to exterminate. A visit of the La Mama players encouraged Gustav Manker to stage Wilhelm Pevny's *Sprintogasmics* at the same theater, but this only led to a mass walk-out half way through.

Gerhard Klingenberg, newly appointed head of the Burg Theater when Paul Hoffmann retires next year, staged *Julius Caesar,* starring O.E. Hasse, in modern dress—white coattails versus S.S. uniforms—a production that found somewhat less favor than Ostrovski's *The Forest,* starring Käthe Gold and staged in a convincing Slav ambiance by Czech guest director Jaroslav Dudek and Czech guest designer Zybnek Kolar, or Ernst Haeussermann's new adaptation, staged by himself, of the Schnitzler stream-of-consciousness short story *Miss Elsa,* about a young girl who takes her own life rather than submit to the advances of an elderly roue. In the subtly recreated pre-World War I Viennese atmosphere Attila Horbiger and the lovely Erika Pluhar were unforgettable. It was agreeable to welcome back to Vienna after countless years of absence in Hollywood the Hungarian stage and film star Hans Jaray, in a revival of Hermann Bahr's 55-year-old *The Concert,* as it was sad to bid goodbye forever to the 77-year-old genius of Viennese cabaret, Robert Farkas.

France

The new Paris season began auspiciously with Pierre Dux taking over the reins of the Comédie Française and announcing several short seasons of one-act plays by authors, known and unknown, thereby creating a precedent and fulfilling a lifetime ambition to pull France's oldest national theater out of its tradition-bound rut right into the middle of the second half of the 20th century. Dux was also put in charge of Théâtre de France, without lead or discretion since Jean-Louis Barrault's dismissal in 1968, to be used partly as a second stage for the Comédie Française and partly for visiting troupes, a purpose for which it had already been used in the first months of the period under review. It was here that the only item in a much reduced Theater of the Nations season was to be seen: *XX* was its name and Luca Ronconi, responsible for last season's *Orlando Furioso,* its "onlie begetter." Five hundred spectators were huddled into 25 booths on two levels, each section watching a seemingly independent and unrehearsed theatrical event mimed or acted often with careless abandon in several tongues, mostly incomprehensible, even when identified as French or Italian. After two hours the dividing partitions were flown and the audience was asked to troop out peacefully—since the police, one was invited to believe, had taken over the country! It was a small point, made with more thunder than illumination. For Ariane Mnouchkine's *1789,* a multimedia, rip-roaring documentary about the taking of the Bastille— staged, on its opening night, in the prohibitive sub-zero temperature of an abandoned government factory—one also had to stand throughout, but the performance at least was riveting.

This production, incidentally, was first presented in Milan, since Miss Mnouchkine found no backer and no manager to house her show in the French capital. When the new Cultural Minister, Jacques Duhamel, eventually offered it a roof in the Cartoucherie de Vincennes, it became an overnight smash hit, the indisputably outstanding performance of the year. Monsieur Duhamel's subsequent popularity suffered a severe blow when he tried to interfere (as Malraux had done successfully two years before in the case of the scheduled Théâtre National Populaire production of Gatti's anti-Franquista drama *The Passion of General Franco)* with the same company's production of *Murderous Angels,* for which Georges Wilson had invited Joan Littlewood to make her bow as a French-speaking director. O'Brien and the cast stood firm and this time won against a state censorship that had taken exception to the portrayal of the King of the Belgians in the play, no doubt to avoid giving offense to a reigning monarch. No such considerations affected the T.N.P. production of Edward Bond's *Early Morning,* in which royal personages were as dead as the denizens of the third-act purgatory that Bond imagined for them.

The remaining repertory of the subsidized theaters was largely uneventful, with the single exception of Strindberg's *The Dream Play,* to which Raymond Rouleau, who had played the Officer in Antonin Artaud's original 1928 staging, gave the expressionistic feel of the earlier production. Jacques Fabbri fooled deliciously in his own version of *An Italian Straw Hat* at the City Theater, where an imposing revival of Giraudoux's anti-war *Tiger at the Gates* rivaled it in popularity. Billetdoux's new play with the untranslatable title *Rintru Par Trou Tar Hin* (well, I might have a go at finding an English equivalent for it: *Doanch Yubee Leightin Ternite)* was a jumble of serious and light-hearted reflections on the topics of the day. The Théâtre de l'Est Parisien's (T.E.P.'s) main contribution was a nicely-balanced attempt to make Gorki's *The Enemies* ring true even today.

Barrault lost all the money he had won on *Rabelais* in staging *Jerry on the Butte* in the same wrestling ring, a colorful sequel that mysteriously failed to draw, while his wife Madeleine Renaud gave one of her most cruelly perceptive performances in the title role of Stanislaw Ignacy Witkiewicz's disturbing parable *The Mother* which Claude Régy staged with proper attention to its Artaudian overtones. Equally disturbing was Jorge Lavelli's handling of Ionesco's *Death Games* at Lars Schmidt's Montparnasse Theater. Like the Planchon season a year before, it lost him money but he made it up on the smash hit version of *Hadrian VII* starring Claude Riche. Other boulevard successes were Anouilh's third hit in two years, *Don't Wake the Mistress,* a backstage tragicomedy in flashback form about an egotistical actor-manager with a bad conscience and a flair for sending up the classics; a noteworthy revival of *Death of a Salesman* starring Claude Dauphin; Maria Casarès—straight from playing Queen Victoria at the T.N.P.—and Sami Frey in Carlos Fuentes's two-hander *The One-Eyed Man Is King* that Lavelli had previously staged with them at the Avignon and Vienna festivals; Romain Weingarten's absurdist Gallic extension of the dream world of Lewis Carroll, *Alice in the Luxemburg Gardens,* and Remo Forlani's mock-poetic critique of the student revolt, *At the Dogs' Ball,* cynically set in the Paris sewers.

André Bourseiller's own multimedia collage, assisted by Eldridge Cleaver, on present-day U.S.A. and inspired by his transatlantic visit in 1970, with the catchpenny title of *Oh! America!,* was brought for a season to the Théâtre de France, where, seated on cushions in the "parterre," one was able to admire or abhor, depending on one's position (political as well as physical), a raucous but cunningly devised piece of anti-American propaganda. Thierry Maulnier's pseudo-historical study of Anglo-French relations in 1066 or thereabouts, entitled *The Conqueror's Eve,* achieved the distinction of earning one, and only one, favorable notice in the press, and that was in the daily paper to which he is a regular contributor. Victor Haïm's monodrama *Skin of a Fruit on a Rotten Tree* starring Etienne Berry (a study of fascism in terms of a South American politician on the run) was the latest new work at the Poche-Montparnasse and followed Bernard da Costa's breakthrough to the commercial avant-garde theater (after a struggle through Paris's cafe-theaters and the like) named *The Grandduchess's Farewells.* A provincial production of Romeo and Juliet at the Théâtre de France was adversely criticized in the press, but the widely-praised Jean-Louis Trintignant *Hamlet* proved so poverty-stricken in every department that I regretted having chosen it in preference (influenced by the star's name, no doubt) and decided that French critics are no reliable guides to Shakespearean production.

Italy

My theatergoing in Italy was severely cut this season but I was lucky to catch Giorgio Strehler's beautifully lit and marvellously orchestrated, sensational and thought-provoking adaptation of Gorki's *The Lower Depths.* It was given an abstract treatment, with the 17 inmates of the asylum disposed to a trestle stage, and Satin and the Baron breaking through the fourth wall to preach their respective philosophies of hope and resignation in a palpably theatrically-conscious convention. His long-awaited production of *Saint Joan of the Stockyards,* with Valentina Cortese in the title role, was launched at the previous Florence Festival before making its appearance—with dramatic irony—at the theater Strehler had earlier abandoned, the Milan Piccolo. In Genoa, Luigi Squarzina scored three signal successes: a composite version of Molière's Tartuffe and Bulgakov's Molière, with its implied criticism of the Soviet censor's methods by analogy with the ban on *Tartuffe* by Louis XIV; a documentary drama *September 8, 1943* by Enzo de Bernart, Ruggero Zangrandi and the director, dealing with the duplicity of the Italian command after the Allied landings in Sicily; and a revival of Goldoni's *The Venetian Twins* which welcomed the Protean Alberto Lionello back into the fold and got a gratifying response at the 1971 World Theater Season in London. Another milestone in Italian theatrical history was the reopening of the modernized Teatro Argentina in Rome with a splendidly mounted and star-studded production by Giorgio De Lullo of *Julius Caesar,* with himself as Marc Antony, Renzo Ricci as Caesar, Romolo Valli as Brutus, and the rest of disbanded Compagnia de Giovani to boot. Despite this, Rome is still without a permanent company.

Belgium and Holland

The Belgian theater seemed to be dominated by a repertory of Anglo-Saxon importations. Several of the main productions were done by foreign guests, such as Frank Dunlop from Britain's National Theater, who staged de Ghelderode's *Pantagleize,* and Otomar Krejca, who put on his familiar version of *Three Sisters* in Brussels, both at the Belgian National Theater. A curiosity was the first production (at the Théâtre du Rideau) outside France of Montherlant's drama of hidden passions in a Jesuit college entitled *The City Whose Prince Is a Child,* staged by Jean Meyer, whose original production from Paris inaugurated the 1971 World Theater Season. The Flemish writer, Hugo Claus, preferred to have his works staged in Holland first—his drama of incest, *Friday,* and his allegorical anti-imperialist satire on Belgian politics *The Life and Works of Leopold II,* directed by himself with aplomb at the Amsterdam City Theater. The Dutch touring group, Centrum, had an eye-catching production of *Young Kees,* adapted from a well known novel of adolescence, which became the undisputed artistic hit of the season.

Scandinavia

Paavo Haaviko fulfilled last season's promise with a reflective patriotic drama *The Brotterus Family* at the Helsinki National Theater. Otherwise, Finnish theater politics were clouded by resignations and closures. In Oslo, too, the threatened closure of the experimental Chat Noir Theater provided ammunition for much invective. In Denmark a superb production of Peter Barnes's *The Ruling Class* was sold out nightly at the Royal Theater in Copenhagen, while in Aalborg an unusual *Peer Gynt,* with the players doing double duty as cast and scenery, heralded the arrival of a bright new directorial talent in Kaspar Rostrup. The Swedish actor Lars Passgaard played Gynt to critical acclaim, but his return to Aalborg in *Romeo and Juliet* a few months later proved less happy.

At the Stockholm City Theater, under Vivica Bandler, several first plays and experimental productions caught the public fancy, including one on the theme of ecology during which the audience went on a conducted bus ride through the town. The Royal Dramatic's highlights included a first documentary play on the shooting of strikers in 1932 in Adalen; Alf Sjoberg's production of Strindberg's semi-autobiographical short play *The Burnt House,* starring Max von Sydow as the autobiographical Stranger, which the director turned into a full evening's entertainment by the addition of an interlude with songs and the reciting of Strindberg's poems; and, not least, Ingmar Bergman's first stage production for twelve months, Lars Forssell's neo-Strindbergian poetic tragedy of an anarchistic entertainer, called *Show* and modeled on the tragic story of Lenny Bruce, dressed in an apt if horrifyingly surrealistic decor by Gunilla Palmstierna-Weiss and topped by a moving performance by Allan Edwall as the nonconformist and persecuted loner.

Eastern Europe

The first visit of a professional Turkish troupe to England was that of the 15-year-old privately owned Dormen Theater from Istanbul, which took Haldun Dormen's witty production of the native musical *A Tale of Istanbul* to the World Theater Season. The performance of Anthony Shaffer's *Sleuth* by two members of the company displayed another facet of their versatility. So did a further version of Arthur Miller's *The Price,* which I added to my growing collection in Istanbul. Turkish theater may lag behind Europe's in general standards and quality, but it is second to none in quantity and enthusiasm. The works of the late Nazim Hikmet, banned for years as a Communist, are at last being done everywhere, and several studio theaters in Ankara and Istanbul are not afraid to tackle material that is controversial both politically and artistsically. Witness the revival of the late Sermet Cagan's provocative socio-critical drama *The Leg and Foot Factory* by the enterprising Guner Sumer in an overtly proletarian district of Istanbul, or the frankness with which the execution of Ethel and Julius Rosenberg may be openly discussed on the stage by one group while another puts on a drama of absurdist cruelty by Turkey's most prolific dramatist, Aziz Nesin.

How sad, then, to travel eastward and find repression and censorship raising their ugly heads again. Shortly after Otomar Krejca's composite version of *Oedipus* and *Antigone* reached the boards at the Theater Behind the Gate in Prague as a denunciation of state tyranny, the world famous actor-director was removed from the leadership of the theater he had founded five years back, and the authorities refused to let him take his own production of *Three Sisters* abroad with him (so that the company's visit to the 1971 World Theater Season was cancelled, with other European dates). A letter of protest bearing the signatures of more than 200 leading European theater people was sent to Prague.

In Poland, after the resignation of Gomulka, a new wind blowing through cultural corridors was warmly welcomed on all sides. Kazimierz Dejmek was invited to return; and if it is too soon to expect the works of Slawomir Mrozek or Gombrowicz, so long proscribed, to reappear this year, at least a revival of interest in Witkiewicz, heralded by Erwin Axer's striking production of *The Mother* at the Contemporary Theater, is at hand. And the opening of a brand new building for the Jewish State Theater, imposing in its modernity, is also a sign of the general thaw.

In Rumania the theatrical thaw set in a long time ago and shows no sign of abating. A controversial anti-illusionistic production by Radu Penciulescu of *King Lear,* starring George Constantin, marked Radu Beligan's debut as the National Theater's new head. The Bulandra City Theater has been providing a platform for a new wave of absurdist writers, including Iosif Naghiu with *The Hood,* about a man who is intellectually blind, and Maria Sorescu, author of *Jonah,* who has written two more short plays of poetic content about different facets of the human condition. The first full-length play by Alexandru Popescu, a pseudo-historical drama *The Great Tailor of Wallachia,* was staged at the Comedy Theater, where Lucian Giurchescu also put on Brecht's early drama of identity *Man Is Man* as *Galy Gay.* Elsewhere, the regulars—Horia Lovinescu, Aurel Baranga, Al Mirodan, Paul Everac—all delivered what has come to be known as their "annual play." Mirodan's *The Moon Mayor and His Sweetheart,* staged by Ion Kozar at the Little Theater, was of course inspired by the American moon landings.

Russia

The year of the 24th Party Congress saw a spate of plays dealing with communist uplift and patriotic encouragement. They included dramas portraying Russian village life at the Maly Theater, plays about The Unknown Soldier, the electrification of the U.S.S.R., Siberian power stations and similar inspiriting themes. Another play dealt with the heroism of girls of the Young Communist League in the Great Patriotic War. This was the theme of Boris Vassilyev's *Tomorrow It Will Be Quiet,* which was done simultaneously at the Soviet Army Theater and in a thrilling production at Liubimov's Taganka Theater. Aleksei Arbuzov had a new play staged by Anatoli Efros at the Malaya Bronnaya Theater called *Fairy Tales of Old Arbat,* about an artist who realizes late in life that solidarity is better than solitude. At the Mayakovsky Theater Andrei Goncharov directed the first Moscow production of Tennessee Williams's *A Streetcar Named Desire* with Svetlana Mizeri as Blanche, a production that was attacked in *Soviet Culture* on ideological grounds. The wave of documentaries has given ground before a wave of biographical dramas, based on the published correspondence of their protagonists: thus, after *Dear Liar* about Shaw, *Elegy* about Turgenev and the popular dramatization of Chekhov's letters, Moscow has come up with a dramatization of the life of Nicolai Ostrovsky based on letters and documents, and, most recently, a drama about Tschaikovsky entitled *Unseen Friend* and based on the letters that passed between the composer and Nadezhda von Meck, the woman he never met.

Highlights of the Paris Season

Selected and compiled by Ossia Trilling

OUTSTANDING PERFORMANCES

ROBERT HIRSCH as George Dandin in *George Dandin*	EDWIGE FEUILLÈRE as Betty in *The Regular Guys*	CLAUDE GÉNIA in several roles in *Death Games*
FRANÇOIS PÉRIER as Julien in *Don't Wake the Mistress*	JEAN-PIERRE GRANVAL as Jarry in *Jarry on the Butte*	MARIA CASARÈS as Queen Victoria in *Early Morning*
CLAUDE RICH as Frederick William Rolfe in *Hadrian VII*	JACQUES FABBRI as Fadinand in *An Italian Straw Hat*	MADELEINE RENAUD as The Mother in *The Mother*
CLAUDE WINTER as Agnès in *The Dream Play*	CATHERINE HUBEAU as Juliet in *Romeo and Juliet*	LOLEH BELLON as Tatiana in *The Enemies*
CLAUDE DAUPHIN as Willy Loman in *Death of a Salesman*	FRANCINE BERGÉ as Andromaque in *Tiger at the Gates*	JEAN-PIERRE AUMONT as Dag Hammarskjold in *Murderous Angels*

OUTSTANDING DIRECTORS

JEAN-LOUIS BARRAULT *Jarry on the Butte*	JOAN LITTLEWOOD *Murderous Angels*	JORGE LAVELLI *The One-Eyed Man Is King*

OUTSTANDING DESIGNERS

JACQUES LE MARQUET *The Mother*	YANNIS KOKKOS *Tiger at the Gates*	NESTOR DE ARZADUN *XX, or The Wheel*

OUTSTANDING NEW FRENCH PLAYS

(D)—Playwright's Paris debut

JEUX DE MASSACRE (Death Games) by Eugène Ionesco. Death stalks a modern city beleagured by the plague. With Claude Génia, André Julien, André Cazalas.

ALICE DANS LES JARDINS DU LUXEMBOURG (Alice in the Luxemburg Gardens) by Romain Weingarten. A childhood comment on the terrifying world of adults. With Hermine Karagheuz, Michel Bouquet, Loleh Bellon.

OCTOBRE À ANGOULÊME (October in Angoulême) by Jean Thévenin (D). The events of May 1968 transposed in time and place. With Michel Ruhl, Madeleine Gines.

NE REVEILLEZ PAS MADAME (Don't Wake The Mistress) by Jean Anouilh. An actor-manager looks back on his private and public life. With François Périer, Danielle Lebrun, Jean Parédès, Claude Nicot, Luce Garcia-Ville, Monita Derrieux.

JARRY SUR LA BUTTE by Jean-Louis Barrault, based on the works of Alfred Jarry. An exuberant satire on war, religion, politics and, of course, sex. With Jean-Pierre Granval, Robert Etcheverry, Anny Duperey, the author.

OH! AMERICA! by André Bourseiller and Eldridge Cleaver. A rock cavalcade of America today seen through French eyes. With the Action Culturelle du Sud-Est Company.

LE SOIR DU CONQUÉRANT (The Conqueror's Eve) by Thiérry Maulnier. The dynastic squabbles of William the Conqueror. With Jean Davy, Michel le Royer, Louise Conte.

1789 by the Théâtre du Soleil. A spectacular documentary on the storming of the Bastille and the implications of revolution. With the Théâtre du Soleil.

MME. JONAS DANS LA BALEINE (Mrs Jonah in the Whale) by René Barjeval (D). Mr. and Mrs. Jonah hide in a deep shelter on the eve of the final cataclysm. With Marie Pacôme, François Maistre, Jacques Jouanneau.

AU BAL DES CHIENS (At the Dogs' Ball) by Remo Forlani. Alexandrine comedy, four concierges caught in the Paris sewers during the student riots. With Véronique Silver, Ginette Garcin, Aline Bertrand, Françoise Pavy, Jacques Gripel.

RINTRU PA TROU TAR HIN! by François

Billetdoux. When menaced, adult man will look for scapegoats. With Jean Mercure, Pierre Byland, Monique Tarbès, Virginie Billetdoux, the author.

LA CIGOGNE (The Stork) by Armand Gatti. The effects of the atom bomb on Nagasaki. With Jean-Pierre Jorris, Pascale de Boysson.

POPULAR ATTRACTIONS

SOGNO, MA FORSE NO (I'm Dreaming or Maybe Not) by Luigi Pirandello, LE TOMBEAU D'ACHILLE (Achilles's Tomb) by André Roussin and LE NOUVEAU LOCATAIRE (The New Tenant) by Eugène Ionesco. Three contrasting one-acters. With Arlette Thomas, Henri Labussière.

DOUBLE JEU (Double Game) by Robert Thomas. A murder mystery with two brothers, or only one? With Simone Valère, Jean Desailly.

LE CONTRAT (The Contract) by Francis Veber. The rivalry between an assassin and a would-be suicide in the same hotel room. With Jean Le Poulain, Raymond Gérôme.

HOSANNA by Jean Vartet. Flighty wife compromises husband and two lovers to help a third, a murderer, to make good his escape. With Jacques Jouanneau, Geneviève Fontanel, Pierre Vernier, Jean Leuvrais.

UNE POIGNÉE D'ORTIES (A Handful of Nettles) by Marc-Gilbert Sauvajon. The environment turns out to be more to blame than the suspect. With Pierre Michel, Georges Marchal, Claire Maurier.

UN PIANO DANS L'HERBE (A Piano in the Grass) by Françoise Sagan. Middle-age tries fruitlessly to recapture its youth. With Françoise Christophe, Daniel Ivernel.

HAUTE SURVEILLANCE (Death Watch) by Jean Genet. New adaptation of Genet's play, set not behind bars, but in and around them. With Arcady, Paul Barge, Jean-Pierre Chevallier, Bernard Rousselet.

DOUCE-AMER (Bitter-Sweet) by Jean Poiret. Adulterous wife is taken back by her husband. With Nicole Courcel, Daniel Ceccaldi, the author.

IL NE FAUT JURER DE RIEN (You Can't Be Sure of Anything) by Alfred de Musset and GEORGE DANDIN by Molière. Comédie Française's new updated productions of two classics. With Michel Duchaussoy, Robert Hirsch.

LES BONSHOMMES (The Regular Guys) by Françoise Dorin. A selfish brute trespasses on the privacy of three women. With Edwige

Feuillère, Mony Dalmès, Yvonne Clech, Michel Serrault.

LES ADIEUX DE LA GRANDE DUCHESSE (The Grand Duchess's Farewells) by Bernard da Costa. In three sketches a young man falls victim to the absurdist machinations of an older couple. With Tsilla Chelton, Jacques Mauclair, Daniel Colas.

VOULEZ-VOUS JOUER AVEC MOA? (Will You Play With Me?) by Marcel Achard. Revival of a famous poetic fantasy. With the Loic Volard-Jacques Rosny Company.

UN CHAPEAU DE PAILLE D'ITALIE (An Italian Straw Hat) by Eugène Labiche. Famous vaudeville newly adapted. With Jacques Fabbri, Isa Mercure, Claudine Collas.

L'IDIOTE (A Shot in the Dark) by Marcel Achard. Revival of popular success about a seemingly innocent country girl. With Dany Carrel, François Guérin.

LE GRAIN DE BEAUTÉ (The Beauty Spot) by Raphael Delpard. Complications that arise from the determination of a would-be grandfather. With Perrette Pradier, Claude Rollet, Patrick Préjean, Elyane Borras, Louis Arbessier.

INDIEN VAUT MIEUX QUE DEUX TU L'AURAS (A Scalp In the Hand Is Worth Two In the Bush) by Jacques Mareuil, Jean Le Poulain and Jean Marsan. A French girl uses her TV prize money to visit a crazy Red Indian reservation in U.S.A. With Annie Cordy, Pierre Dorris.

LOUISIANE MES AMOURS (Louisiana My Loves) by Henri Bourtayre and Jacques Plante. Operetta adaptation of Gone With the Wind. With Bernard Muracciole, Francis Linel.

LA VOYANTE (The Clairvoyant) by André Roussin. Revival of Roussin's rip-roaring farce. With Elvire Popesco, Jean Chevrier, Gisèle Casadesus.

L'ART D'AIMER (The Art of Love) by Jean-Marc Tennberg. Ovid's poem adapted. With the author.

LILI VERTU (Lili the Virtuous) by Roger Normand. Easy virtue enrolled in the service of respectability, with songs. With Colette Renard, Yves Llobregat.

NICOMÈDE by Corneille. New Comédie Française production of the comedy. With Louis Seigner, Annie Ducaux.

DIEU ABOIE-T-IL? (Does God Bark?), re-titled Adorable Pucelle (Darling Virgin) by François Boyer. Modern Cassandra sows havoc for the establishment to reap. With Jean-Pierre Darras, Anne Alvaro, Yves-Marie Maurin.

LA GUERRE DE TROI N'AURA PAS LIEU (The Trojan War Will Not Take Place, or Tiger at the Gates) by Jean Giraudoux. Stunning new City Theater production of Giraudoux's anti-war fantasy. With José-Maria Flotats, Michel de Ré, Annie Duperey, Francine Bergé, Anne Doat, Jean Mercure.

LE GOBE-DOUILLE (The Sucker), bitter-sweet sketches and one-acters (including old ones) by Roland Dubillard; MIC, a critique of labels by Jean-Claude Grumberg; MORT DE LORD CHATTERLEY (Death of Lord Chatterley), black comedy by Christopher Frank (D), and two déjà-vus by Guy Foissy. With Luce Garcia-Ville, Danielle Lebrun, Roland Bertin; later with France Darry, Clotilde Juano, Oliver Lebeaut.

LES PRODIGES (The Marvels) by Jean Vauthier. New production of verbal duel of absurdity. With Georges Wilson, Andrée Tainsy, Judith Magre.

LA LOGEUSE (The Landlady) by Jacques Audiberti. Revival of scatological comedy. With Jacqueline Gauthier, Max Viale, Jacqueline Coué, Henry Labussière.

PAUVRE FRANCE! (Norman, Is That You?) adapted by Jean Cau from Ron Clarke and Sam Bobrick. French father discovers that his son is not what he seems. With Jacques Fabbri, Bernard Giraudeau.

IL FAUT QUE LE SYCAMORE COULE (The Sycamore Must Sink) by Jean-Michel Ribes. Philosophical lucky-dip bubbling over with illustrations of the human paradox. With Renée Saint Cyr, Luc Cendrier.

LE BAS ET LE HAUT (The Low and the High) by Jean-Loup Philippe. An intruder in a bachelor's apartment. With Maïa Simon, Laurence Himbert, Philippe Nottin, the author.

LES BONNES (The Maids) by Jean Genet. Revival of Genet's symbolical drama with three actresses: Sylvie Belai, Elizabeth Kaza, Michèle Oppenot.

LES BONNES (The Maids) by Jean Genet. Revival of symbolical drama with three actors in the female roles. With Michel Baudinat, Jean-Jacques Leconte, Jean-Marie Patte.

LE MISANTHROPE by Molière. New view, by Antoine Bourseiller, of a classic. With the Company of Action Dramatique du Sud-Est.

LES POUBELLES (The Ashcans) by Jean Bouchaud. A series of satirical sketches on the world as it is. With Danièle Girard, Georges Beller, the author.

PIÈGE POUR UN HOMME SEUL (Trap for a Lonely Man) by Robert Thomas. Revival of famous thriller. With Gaby Sylvia, Philippe Vallauris, the author.

PASSION EN BLEU, BLANC, ROUGE (Passion under the Tricolor) by Jean-Pierre Bisson. France's great heroes pass by again. With the author.

VOS GUEULES, LES MOUETTES! (Shut Up, Seagulls!) by Robert Dhéry. Fun and games, with music, on the Breton fishing coast supervised by a lighthouse keeper. With Jean Lefebvre, Colette Brosset, Robert Castel, the author.

MON FAUST (My Faust) by Paul Valéry. Revival of dramatization of the Faust story. With Pierre Fresnay, Danièle Delorme, Jean Bertheau.

LA JALOUSIE (Jealousy) by Sacha Guitry and MAIS N'TE PROMÈNE DONC PAS TOUTE NUE (But Don't Run About With Nothing On) by Georges Feydeau. Comédie Française's revival of two popular plays. With Micheline Boudet, Jacques Charon, Geneviève Casile.

LA COMMUNE DE PARIS (The Paris Commune) by Gérard Dournel. Soup of blood from the past. With Simone Bartel.

MON ISMÉNIE by Eugène Labiche on a double bill with LE TOMBEAU D'ACHILLE (Achilles's Tomb) by André Roussin. Revival of a popular double bill. With Pierre Peyrou.

FAISONS UN RÊVE (Let's Make a Dream) by Sacha Guitry. Revival of successful comedy.

ÉLECTRE by Jean Giraudoux. Comédie Française revival of famous drama. With Geneviève Casile, François Chaumette, Annie Ducaux.

L'ÉTOILE AU FRONT (The Starred Forehead) by Raymond Roussel. Pre-surrealistic kaleidoscope. With Jean Rougerie, Brigitte Degaire.

LA VIE DE MOLIÈRE (The Life of Molière) adapted from the book by the Sieur de Grimarest. With Sylvain and Jean Rougerie, Sylvaine Charley.

LIMITED RUNS OF INTERESTING NEW FRENCH PLAYS

J'AI REGNÉ CETTE NUIT (I Reigned That Night) by Pierre Sabatier. The Borgias unmasked. With Dora Doll, Jean Davy, Michel Le Royer.

LES MOROT-CHANDONNEUR (The Morot-Chandonneurs) by Philippe Jullian and Bernard Minoret. Scandalous story of a French family from the Marquis of Sade's times to the present day. With Julia Dancourt, Gérard Maro.

COMME LA PIERRE (Like Stone) by Romain Weingarten. The poetic visions of a convict. With Michel Aumont.

SI CAMILLE ME VOYAIT . . . (If Camille Could See Me Now . . .) by Roland Dubillard. A series of humorous verse duologues about a mystified young lady. With Myriam Colombi, Bernard Dhéran.

FEMMES PARALLÈLES (Parallel Ladies) by François Billetdoux. Contrasting retrospections of three girls. With Denise Gence, Christine Ferson, Catherine Samie.

JE FUS CET ENFANT-LÀ (I Was That Child) by Yan Brian, after Roger Vitrac. Multimedia production about a young man's deprivations. With Dirk Sanders, Laura Proença.

POURQUOI T'AS FAIT ÇA? (Why Did You Do That?) by Philippe Avron and Claude Evrard. Dramatic musical questioning the world around us. With the authors.

LA MORT DE BUECHNER (Buechner's Death) by Wolfram Mehring. What made Büchner tick. With Judith Amias, the author.

SAVONAROLE by Michel Suffran (D). Drama of the Florentine martyr. With the Theater Center of Limoges Company.

L'HOMME COUCHÉ (The Prostrate Man) by Carlos Semprun-Maura. Reality and fantasy mingle in a detective thriller. With Laurent Terzieff, Pascale de Boysson.

TOI ET TES NUAGES (You and Your Clouds) by Eric Westphal (D). Two sisters live out a tragic experience in self-imposed seclusion. With Anna Karina, Eléonore Hirt, François Darbon.

LE MONTREUR (The Demonstrator) by Andrée Chedid (D). Poetic Lebanese drama suspended between night and day. With Berengère Dautun, Michel Bernardy.

COEUR À DEUX (Heart for Two) by Guy Foissy. Young couple alienated by admass. With Alain Pralon, Ludmila Mikaël.

UNE SAISON EN ENFER (A Season in Hell) by Arthur Rimbaud. The poet's works dramatized. With Jacques Roux.

LE REPAS DES DINOSAURES (The Dinosaurs' Dinner) by Charles-Henri Barras. Satire of class distinction seen through the eyes of a fast-disappearing aristocratic clan. With René Clermont, Mary Marquet, Jacques Dumesnil, Gaby Sylvia.

IL NOUS FAUT DES FOUS (We Need Madmen) by Gérard Louault (D). A dramatic exercise in non-violence. With Chantal Touzet, Jean-Loup Bourel, Gérard Probst.

BUBUTZ by Alain Cuniot (D). An adulterous husband loses his mistress. With Simone Couderc, Simone Faget, the author.

L'ESCALIER DE SILAS (Silas' Staircase) by Geneviève Serreau (D). Group of people in search of an elusive stranger. With Gérard Croce, Marion Pecqueur.

C'EST TROIS FOISSY ! ! ! (Three Times Foissy ! ! !) by Guy Foissy. Women and cars that encumber our lives. With Gérard Borland, Luc Ritz, Gérard Laureau.

LE CLIENT (The Customer) by Jean-Claude Carrière. Customers of a bar stake all in a bid to save it from bankruptcy. With Jean Lauvrais, Christine Minazzoli.

LA DESCENTE SUR RÉCIFE (Going Down to Récife) by Gabriel Cousin. Starvation in Brazil. With Georges Aminel, Christine Fersen.

LE GENERAL INCONNU (The Unknown General) by René de Obaldia. A new production. With François Chaumette, Ludmila Mikaël.

RIXE (The Brawl) by Jean-Claude Grumberg. The phobias of a married couple. With Jean-Paul Roussillon. Berengère Dautun.

LES EVASIONS DE MONSIEUR VOISIN (Mr. Voisin's Evasions) by the Aquarium Theater Company. Finaglings of a wily accountant. With the Aquarium Theater Company.

OLYMPIAS by Marcel Jouhandeau. The rise and fall of Alexander the Great. With Francine Blaison, Géraldine Klein.

ADIEU VÉRONIQUE and BABEL 75 by Serge Béhar (D). Two one-acters about youth in the acquisitive society and the dangers of non-communication. With Danièle Volle, Olivier Hussenot, Pierre Constant.

VOX POPULI adapted from Aristophanes's *The Knights* by Jacques Mirat. With Fabrice Nadar, the author.

SI LES CERISES. . . . . . AVAIENT LE TEMPS (If Cherries . . . Had Time) by Claude Cortesi. Self-guying satirical fantasy revue. With Yon de Murguia, Consuelo Ibanez, Liliane Geney.

L'HOMME QUI RIT (The Laughing Man)

adapted from Victor Hugo's novel by Yves Gasc. With the Villiers company.

LE DÉMON RESSUSCITÉ (The Demon returns) by Jean Nicolas (D). The devil runs amok. With the Comédiens de Paris company.

THÉRÈSE EST TRISTE OU ATTENTION TROP TARD (Theresa is Sad or Careful too Late) by the Vrai Chic Parisien. A collective production. With the Vrai Chic Parisien.

LES GLACES (The Mirrors) by René Tholy (D). Pursuit of love mirrored in a score of ways. With Pascaline Aubert, Philippe Duclos.

LA PEAU D'UN FRUIT SUR UN ARBRE POURRI (The Skin of a Fruit on a Rotten Tree) by Victor Haim. A monodrama that explores the fascist mind. With Étienne Berry.

SOME AMERICAN PLAYS PRODUCED IN PARIS

THE HOLY GHOSTLY and MELODRAMA PLAY by Sam Shepard. With the New Troupe, New York.

THE SERPENT by Jean-Claude van Itallie. With the Solow-Chabert Workshop.

HAIR (musical) by Gerome Ragni and James Rado. With the Atelje 212 Company. Belgrade.

SWEET CHARITY (musical) by Neil Simon. With Magali Noël, Jacques Duby, Colette Marchand.

PROLOG by Robert Wilson. With the Byrd Hoffman School of Byrds.

DEAFMAN GLANCE by Robert Wilson. With the Byrd Hoffman School of Byrds.

MINUS ONE by Lawrence Parke. World premiere of new play about the sensuous needs and desires of human beings. With the Theater Today company from Hollywood.

FIRE by the Bread and Puppet Theater. With the Bread and Puppet Theater.

DEATH OF A SALESMAN by Arthur Miller. With Claude Dauphin, Helena Bossis, Maurice Sarfati.

ROSE-MARIE (musical) by Otto Harbach and Oscar Hammerstein II. With Bernard Sinclair, Angelina Cristi.

BUTTERFLIES ARE FREE by Leonard Gershe. With Lise Delamare, Martine Kelly.

TOM PAINE by Paul Foster. With Henri Virlojeux, Annick Fougery, Jacques Lalande.

THE MILK TRAIN DOESN'T STOP HERE ANY MORE by Tennessee Williams. With Claude Génia, Claude Titre, Denise Grey.

THE INDIAN WANTS THE BRONX and IT'S CALLED THE SUGAR PLUM (Sucre d'Orge) by Israel Horovitz. With Colette Castel, Laurent Terzieff, Marcel Dalio.

NORMAN, IS THAT YOU? by Ron Clarke and Sam Bobrick, adapted by Jean Cau as *Pauvre France* (see Popular Attractions). With Jacques Fabbri, Bernard Giraudeau.

DAMES ON BROADWAY (musical) by George Haimsohn and Robin Miller. With Sheila White.

CHIAROSCURO by Israel Horovitz. With Odette Barrois, Georges Aubert.

THIS PROPERTY IS CONDEMNED and TALK TO ME LIKE THE RAIN AND MAKE ME LISTEN by Tennessee Williams. With Stephen Meldegg, France Girard.

OH! CALCUTTA! by various authors. With Daisy Maias, Victor Bagnière.

SOME OTHER FOREIGN PLAYS PRODUCED IN PARIS

THEATER OF THE NATIONS SEASON 1971 consisted of *XX, or The Wheel* by Rodolfo Juan Wilcock and Luca Ronconi. With the Teatro Libero of Rome and l'Action Culturelle du Sud-Est.

BONE BY BONE ALIVE by David Benedictus. With the Wherehouse La Mama, London, Company.

SOGNO, MA FORSE NO (I'm Dreaming or Maybe Not) by Luigi Pirandello. Part of a triple bill. With Arlette Thomas, Henri Labussière.

DON JUAN RETURNS FROM THE WARS by Odön von Harvath. With the Theater 9 Company.

IVANOV by Anton Chekhov. With Michel Vitold.

RELATIVELY SPEAKING (Pantoufle) by Alan Ayckbourn. With Guy Tréjan, Micheline Luccioni, Alain Douty.

WHY DID YOU PUT ME ON THE LANDING (Pourquoi M'Avez-Vous Posée Sur le Palier) by Peter Scott (D). Premiere of pseudonymous English author's thriller. With Caroline Cellier, Henry Garçin.

HADRIAN VII by Peter Luke. With Claude Rich, Dominique Blanchar, Maurice Teynac, Pierre Bertin.

THE MISTRESS OF THE INN by Carlo Goldoni. With Georges Toussaint, Jacques Ardonin, Annie Sinigalia.

THE KARAMAZOV TRIAL by Diego Fabbri. With Henri Crémieux, Claude Brosset, Dominique Rozan.

CHRISTOPHE COLOMBE by Michel de Ghelderode. With the Mouffetard Theater Company.

THE NAKED KING by Yevgeni Shvarts. With Claude Bouchery, François Guiller, Arièle Sémenoff.

THE FOURPOSTER by Jan de Hartog. With Jean-Claude Brialy, Caroline Cellier.

THE DAWNING DAY by Arieh Chen. With Hélène Hily, Robert Kimmich.

THE TEMPEST by William Shakespeare. With the Tréteaux de Sologne.

THE MOTHER by Stanislaw Ignacy Witkiewicz. With Madeleine Renaud, Michel Lonsdale.

WOYZECK by Georg Buechner. With Judith Amias, Michaël Deckner, Wolfram Mehring.

LA MOSCHETA by Ruzzante. By the Du Cothurne Company.

EARLY MORNING by Edward Bond. With Maria Casarès, Françoise Brion, Gabriel Cattand, José-Maria Flotats, Georges Wilson.

DEAR JANET (ROSENBERG), DEAR MR. KOONING by Stanley Eveling. With Evelyne Ker, Jean Toport.

MASSACRING VIVALDI by David Mercer and THE CRABS by Roland Dubillard. With Bernard Fresson, Lucienne Hamon, Maria Machado, Roland Dubillard.

THE DREAM PLAY by August Strindberg. With Claude Winter, Georges Descrières, Jean Piat, Denise Gence, Jacques Toja.

THE WORKHOUSE DONKEY by John Arden. With Dora Doll, Victor Garrivier.

SLEUTH by Anthony Shaffer. With Pierre Fresnay, Henri Garcin.

THE ONLY JEALOUSY OF EMER by William Butler Yeats and RENARD by Igor Stravinsky. With the La Mama Company.

THE END OF SUMMER by Tadeusz Rittner. With Anne Carrère, Catherine le Couey, Myriam Anissimov, Michel Auclair.

HAMLET by William Shakespeare. With Jean-Louis Trintignant, Bulle Ogier.

THE KNIGHT OF THE BURNING PESTLE by Beaumont and Fletcher. With Victor Lanoux, Pierre Alain.

UNDER MILK WOOD by Dylan Thomas. With the Tripot Company.

ROMEO AND JULIET by William Shakespeare. With the Company du Cothurne of Lyons. With Catherine Hubeau.

LOOK BACK IN ANGER by John Osborne. With the Tréteaux du Sud-Parisien.

THE ENEMIES by Maxim Gorky. With Gabriel Cattand, Loleh Bellon, Victor Garrivier.

THE BUTTERFLY GAME by Jerzy Dobrzanski. With the Poule Noire-François Larose Company.

THE MOUSETRAP by Agatha Christie. With Madeleine Clervanne, Jean-Paul Cisife, Sady Rebbot.

HOW THE OTHER HALF LOVES by Alan Ayckbourn. With Marie Daems, Claude Brasseur, Darry Cowl, Claude Piéplu, Pascale Roberts.

THE BRIGANDS by Friedrich von Schiller. With René-Marie Feret, Jean-Claude Jay.

THE HAPPY APPLE by Jack Pulman. With Henri Tisot, Evelyne Ker.

CREDITORS by August Strindberg. With Hélène Roussel, Michel Derain, André Cellier.

THE AUDIENCE by Frederico Garcia Lorca. With l'Atalier Zero.

ECHO ALPHA by Ahmed El Maanouni. With the Théâtre de l'Héliotrope.

THE THREEPENNY OPERA (musical) by Bertolt Brecht. With Arlette Téphany, Maurice Barrier.

THE STORY OF THE THEATER by Javier Arreyuelo and Rafael Lopez Sanchez. With the T.S.E. Company of Argentina.

MURDEROUS ANGELS by Conor Cruise O'Brien. With Jean-Pierre Aumont, Wole Soyinka, Georges Anderson, Jacques Baillon, James Campbell.

SECOND HELPING by Slawomir Mrozek. With Uta Taeger, Georges Riquier.

THE ONE-EYED MAN IS KING by Carlos Fuentes. With Sami Frey, Maria Casarès.

CELESTINA by Fernando de Rojas. With the Prologue Company.

AFTER HAGGERTY by David Mercer. With Maria Machado, Roland Dubillard, Pierre Arditi, Claude Brosset.

WIR SPIELEN FRIEDEN (We're Playing at Peace) by and with Die Komödianten from Vienna.

TURN, WALK OR DIE by Joseph Mundy (D). World premiere of Israeli play (in French) in which Herzl's and Kafka's ideas clash. With Hazel Carr, Gérard Desalles, Jean Edmond.

LA GUERRE, YES SIR! by Roch Carrier and TARTUFFE by Molière. With the Company of the Théâtre du Nouveau Monde of Montreal.

THE SECRETARY BIRD (Le Canard à l'Orange) by William Douglas Home. With Genevieve Page, Jean Poiret, Hélène Duc.

MARY IN MINKS by Shuji Terayama. With the Tenjosajiki company from Tokyo.

THE SOLDIERS by Carlos-José Reyes, and THE HELL FILE by Enrique Buenaventura. With the Experimental Cali Theater Company from Colombia.

THE FAIR by Miroslav Krleza. With the Cavella Company from Zagreb.

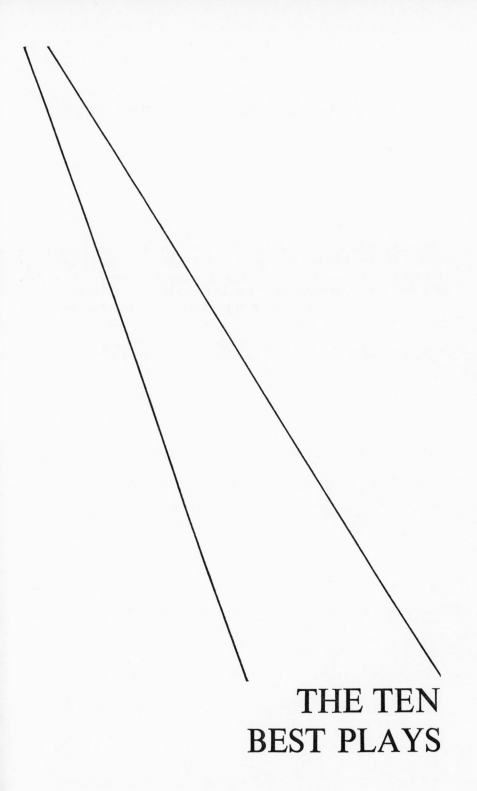

THE TEN
BEST PLAYS

In the following synopses of 1970-71's Best Plays, scenes and lines of dialogue, stage directions and description quoted from the script appear *exactly* as in the stage version of the play unless (in a very few instances, for technical reasons) an abridgement is indicated by five dots (. . . . .). The appearance of three dots (. . .) is the script's own punctuation to denote the timing of a spoken line.

BOESMAN AND LENA

A Play in One Act

BY ATHOL FUGARD

Cast and credits appear on page 323

ATHOL FUGARD was born June 11, 1932 in the semi-desert Karoo country of South Africa. His mother was an Afrikaner, his father of Irish and Hugenot descent. He studied in Port Elizabeth and the University of Cape Town and spent two years at sea, mostly in the Far East. He married an actress, Sheila Meiring, and for a time they ran an experimental theater in Cape Town.

Fugard's first plays were No Good Friday, Nogogo *and* The Blood Knot *which won its author an international reputation and reached these shores in an off-Broadway production starring James Earl Jones March 1, 1964 for 240 performances (it is about two black half-brothers, one light-skinned and the other dark). His next play,* People Are Living There, *was done in Glasgow in 1968. His next,* Hello and Goodbye, *was produced off Broadway last season for 45 performances.*

Fugard now lives at Schoenmakerskop near Port Elizabeth with his wife and daughter Lisa-Maria. Some of his training for his triple profession of actor-director-writer was acquired at Rehearsal Room, in Johannesburg's Dorkay House (the headquarters of South Africa's Union Artists, the organization that cares for the cultural interests of non-Europeans in the Transvaal). Later, as resident director of Dorkay House, he staged the works of many modern playwrights including Steinbeck and Pinter. He has also been associated for a number of years with the Serpent Players of New Brighton, a theater workshop for black Africans. When Boesman and Lena *was placed in New York re-hearsal last spring, Fugard was denied a passport by his government to visit the production because, in his own words, "The government thinks I'm a source of trouble . . . The ironic thing about the whole business is that the state has made a considerable profit out of two of my plays which have run at state-sponsored theaters."*

The following sypnosis of Boesman and Lena *has been prepared by com-bining the South African and American versions of the script. The dialogue appears exactly as in the off-Broadway production, which incorporated a few minor changes in the spoken words and substituted English for many of the Afrikaans phrases. Also, the off-Broadway play devised actual speeches for the character of the Old African, whereas in the original script Fugard indicates only when the Old African speaks (in Xhosa language), not what he says. All stage directions and other quotations of descriptive material (in italics) are taken from the original version of the script as published in South Africa.*

Time: The present

Place: The mud flats of the river Swartkops, South Africa

SYNOPSIS: A heavily burdened *"Colored man"* in South African parlance, Boesman, comes onto a stage that is bare except for the suggestion of a hill and a dumping ground, including pieces of a junked automobile. He is drag-ging an old sheet of corrugated iron and carrying the necessities of his life: old mattress, blanket, battered cooking utensils, threadbare clothing. *"He chooses a spot, then drops the corrugated iron, sets down his load and slumps to the ground beside it. He has obviously walked very far."*

After Boesman comes his wife Lena, similarly *"a Colored woman"* and similarly burdened, similarly fatigued, barefoot, a bundle of firewood under one arm, *"wearing one of those sad dresses that reduce the body to an angu-lar, gaunt cipher of poverty. A life of hardship and dissipation obscures their ages, but they are most probably in their 50s. Boesman looks up slowly as Lena appears. He watches her with a hard, cruel objectivity. He says nothing. She has been reduced to a dumb, animal-like submission by the weight of her burden and the long walk behind them and in this condition almost misses him sitting to one side, propped up against his bundle. Realizing she has passed him, she stops but does not turn to face him in case they have to walk still further."*

Lena drops the firewood and her bundle and sits down slowly, in intense relief.

LENA: Here? Mud! Swartkops! Too late now. No. There's one.
Pause. Staring at a bird.

Bastard! Clear out, bastard! So slowly . . . ! Must be a feeling hey. Even your shadow is so heavy you leave it on the ground. Tomorrow they'll hang up there in the wind and laugh. We'll be in the mud. I hate them.

She looks at Boesman.

Why did you walk so hard? In a hurry to get here? Jesus, Boesman! What's here? This . . . *(The mud between her fingers.)* . . . and tomorrow. And that will be like this! Rot! This piece of world is rotten. Put down your foot and you're in it up to your knee. That last spell was hard. Against the wind. I thought you were never going to stop. Heavier and heavier. Every step. This afternoon heavier than this morning. This time heavier than last time. And there's other times coming. *"Vat jou goed en trek!"* Whiteman says "Clear out!" *Eina!*

Boesman is watching her with undisguised animosity and disgust.

Remember the old times? Quick march! Even run when they chased us. Don't make trouble for us here Boesman. I can't run anymore. Quiet hey! Get out the bottle man, let's have a dop.

Lena registers Boesman's hard stare. She studies him in return.

You're the hell-in. Don't look at me *ou ding.* Blame the whiteman. Bulldozer! Ja! You were happy this morning. "Push it over my baas! *Dankie baas!* We're on our way!" It was funny hey Boesman! All the shanties flat. The poor people running around trying to save their things. You had a good laugh. And now? Here we sit. Just now it's dark, and Boesman's thinking about building another shanty. The world feels big when you sit like this. Now's the time to laugh. This is also funny. Look at us! Boesman and Lena with the sky for a roof again.

Pause . . . Boesman stares at her.

What are you waiting for?

BOESMAN *(shaking his head as he finally breaks the silence):* Jesus Lena! I'm telling you, the next time we walk . . .

LENA: Don't talk about that now man.

BOESMAN: The Next Time We Walk! . . .

LENA: Where?

BOESMAN: . . . I'll keep on walking. I'll walk and walk . . .

LENA: *Eina!*

BOESMAN: . . . until you're so bloody tired that when I stop you can't open your mouth!

Boesman insists that this very morning the white man did him a favor by pushing over his shanty and forcing him to move on. Lena felt otherwise: "It was too early in the morning to have your life kicked in again. Sitting there in the dust with the pieces . . . bare-assed!"

During the walk to Swartkops Lena kept looking around, hoping her dog would follow, but he did not. Today Lena felt very old, used up like a leaky pot that ought to be thrown away. And on the way to returning their collection of empty bottles to the store, Boesman had beaten Lena in public for dropping the empties and breaking three. Numbly, she followed Boesman here to the

Swartkops mud, where they will dig for worms and sell them as live bait to the baas.

Boesman begins to sort the contents of his bundle, while Lena reminds him they have been here to this place before, and it has never been good to them. Once, even, the river flooded them out. But *"Boesman turns away from her, dragging their one mattress to the spot where he will build the shelter. He then picks up the piece of corrugated iron and examines it, trying it out in various positions . . . as a roof, a wall, etc."*

It seems to Boesman that Lena has been talking continuously ever since their very first "walk" long ago from Coega to Veeplaas—and there have been many such migratory journeys since. Lena feels that many other places would have been better than this lonely one, with no people around, without "even a dog to look at us."

Lena begs again for a "dop" of wine to warm her, but Boesman ignores her plea. Lena busies herself with starting a fire, and remembers a time when a Boer ran them off his property at gun point: "When he showed us the bullets Boesman dropped his tin and went down that road like a rabbit . . . 'Don't shoot, baas!' Me too, but the other way. Where did I find him . . . looking at the mud, the hell-in because we had lost all our things again. Just our clothes, and each other. Never loose that. Run your legs off the other way but at the end of it Boesman is waiting. How the hell does that happen."

The process of remembering lightens Lena's mood, and she is actually humming as she goes about the little chores of laying out mugs and filling a pot with water. Boesman, collecting odds and ends like a sack, a few pieces of wood and a discarded automobile door for the shelter, suspects that Lena has been at the wine—but he finds it intact.

Boesman goes back to work building a shelter out of the bits and pieces of material, while Lena tries to remember the sequence in which they've traveled from place to place in their life together. Boesman mischievously sets out to confuse her, and finally does.

LENA: Veeplaas—Redhouse—Korsten? *(Pause.)* Where's Swartkops.
> *The sight of her vacant confusion is too much for Boesman. He has a good laugh, now thoroughly enjoying himself.*
To hell with it! I'm not listening to you. I'm here!
BOESMAN: Where? Veeplaas?
LENA *(closing her eyes):* I'm here. I know how I got here. Redhouse, then Swartkops . . . *(Pause. She has forgotten.)* Wait . . . ! Redhouse—Swartkops . . .
BOESMAN: Go on. But don't forget Bethelsdorp this time. You've been there too. And Missionvale. And Kleinskool.
LENA: Don't mix me up Boesman! *(Trying desperately to remember her sequence.)* Redhouse—Swartkops . . . then Veeplaas . . . then . . .
BOESMAN: It's wrong!
> *Pause. She looks at him desperately. He leaves his work on the shelter and goes to her.*

Yes! It's wrong! Now what are you going to do?

LENA *(she moves around helplessly, trying to orient herself physically):* It's mixed up again. I had it!

Lena is "lost" and begs Boesman to help her "find" herself, but he only mocks her, making her furiously angry. Some day she'll be so confused she'll wonder not only where but also *who* she is.

LENA: Mary. I want to be Mary. Who are you?
> *The laugh dies on Boesman's lips.*
That's what I ask next. Ja, you! Who's this man? And then I'm gone. Goodbye darling. I've had enough. S'truesgod, that day I'm gone.

BOESMAN: You mean that day you get a bloody good hiding.

LENA: *Aikona!* I'll go to the police.

BOESMAN: You tried that before and what happened? "She's my woman baas. Just warmed her up a little bit." "Take her . . ." finish *en klaar.* They know the way it is with our sort.

LENA: Not this time! My name is Mary remember. "Don't know this man baas." So where's your proof.

BOESMAN *(holding up a clenched fist):* Here!

LENA: Watch out! You'll get too far one day. Death penalty.

BOESMAN: For you? *(Derisive laughter.)* Not guilty and discharge.

LENA: Don't talk big. You're frightened of the rope. When you stop hitting it's not because you're tired or had enough. You're frightened! Ja.
> *Pause.*
Ja. That's when I feel it most. When you do it carefully. The last few . . . when you aim. I count them. One . . . another one . . . wait for the next one! He's only resting.
> *Pause.*
You're right Boesman. That's proof. When I feel it I'll know. I'm Lena.

BOESMAN *(emphatically):* And I'm Boesman.

LENA: Boesman and Lena.

BOESMAN: Yes! That's who that's what. When . . . where . . . why! All your bloody nonsense questions. That's the answer.

LENA: Boesman and Lena.

Boesman surveys his shelter—it will leak if it rains, he fears. Lena cries out for something better than this—remembers a better time than this, when they lived in a real room with a door. Now it is cold, and wet, and "never enough wine to make us sleep the whole night."

Lena makes as if to "walk," to leave this place, but stands still a few paces from the fire when she sees somebody else out there in the mud of the river. Yearning for another person to talk with besides Boesman who mocks her, Lena calls out to the stranger, beckoning him with "We got a fire!" *"A moment of mutual uncertainty at the approach of the stranger. Lena falls back to Boesman's side. He picks up a stick in readiness for trouble. They stand to-*

gether, waiting. An old African (whom they call a "Kaffer") appears slowly, hat on his head, the rest of him lost in the folds of a shabby old overcoat. He is an image of age and decrepitude . . . . . Lena almost turns away with disappointment. Boesman sees this and has a good laugh."

Stubbornly, Lena accepts the old man as "better than nothing" despite Boesman's mockery, and she goes to help him to the fire. Obviously, the Old African is travel-weary and not feeling very well. To Boesman's disgust, Lena invites the Old African to sit by the fire and refresh himself with a drink of water. Boesman snatches the water away, even though the Kaffer's "sort" had often given Boesman a drink on the road. Lena calls the old man "Outa" and reassures him that "It's a hard life for us brown people hey." Boesman is quick to correct her: "He's not brown people, he's black people," but Lena replies, "They got feelings too."

Lena is impatient for the "Outa" to speak and at last he does, in the Xhosa language—politely, friendly in manner, but of course totally and disappointingly (to Lena) unintelligible.

Lena begs Boesman for a dop, insisting that one of the bottles belongs to her, but Boesman merely becomes threatening. Boesman moves off in disgust, and Lena tells the Old African her name and fetches him some water to drink.

The Old African continues to speak to Lena in Xhosa, telling what is obviously a sad tale of wandering, lost, overcome by old age and fatigue. Lena can understand almost nothing of what the Old African is saying, but her need for a listener is so great that when he finishes she in turn hurries to tell *her* unhappy tale of how she befriended a dog in Korsten against Boesman's wishes, and how the dog vanished in the mix-up of their hurried departure this morning. The Old African, likewise, understands nothing of what Lena is telling him.

Lena tells the Old African how it was: "Outa know the empties. Brandy bottles, beer bottles, wine bottles. Any kind. Medicine. Tomato sauce. Sell them at the Bottle Exchange. We were doing good with the empties there in Korsten. Take your sack, knock on some back doors and it's full by no time. Whiteman's drinking himself to death. It was going easy for us man. Eating meat. Proper chops! Then this morning: Walk Hotnot! Just had time to grab our things. That's when I dropped the sack. Three bottles broken. I didn't even have on pants or a petticoat when we started walking . . ."

Lena continues to pour her complaints into the Old African's uncomprehending ear. The old man in his turn mumbles his unintelligible account of his own troubles, and Lena pretends that his mutterings are replies to her own conversation. Lena describes her relationship with Boesman: "He walks in front. I walk behind. It used to be side by side, with jokes." They have been walking a long time, and nowadays "something stays heavy" inside even when she puts her burden down at the end of the day.

Lena pretends that one of the Old African's murmurings is a question, which she answers: "One, Outa, that lived. For six months. The others were born dead." She remembers the intense pain of childbirth. The Old African, locked into his own despair, gets up as though to leave, but Lena's need to talk to someone is still so great that she holds him and sits him down again by the fire.

Boesman comes back and is annoyed that the Old African is still there. Lena tries to convince Boesman that the old man will buy them wine tomorrow, but Boesman doesn't believe it. He refuses to divide their supper with the old man (so Lena plans to give the visitor half of hers).

> *Without realizing what she is doing, Lena starts humming a little song as she works away at the fire. She realizes her mistake too late. Boesman is staring hard at her when she looks up.*

LENA *(desperately):* I'm not happy!

BOESMAN: You're up to something.

LENA: S'truesgod, I'm not happy.

BOESMAN: He must go.

LENA: Please Boesman!

BOESMAN: He's had his rest. Hey!

LENA: It's dark now.

BOESMAN: That's his troubles. Hey! *Hamba wena.*

LENA: He's not doing any harm.

BOESMAN: He'll bring the others. It's not far to their location from here.

LENA: Boesman! Just for once a favor. Let him stay.

BOESMAN: What's he to me?

LENA: For me, man. *(Pause.)* I want him.

BOESMAN: What for? What you up to Lena?

> *Pause. Lena can't answer his question.*

LENA *(impulsively):* You can have the wine. All of it. Next time as well.

> *She dives to the shelter, produces the two bottles of wine.*

There!

BOESMAN *(unbelievingly):* For that!

LENA: I want him.

BOESMAN: This is wine Lena. That's a Kaffer. He won't help you forget. You want to sit sober in this world? You know what it looks like then?

LENA: I want him.

BOESMAN *(shaking his head):* You off your mind tonight. *(To the Old African.)* You're an expensive old turd. Two bottles of wine! *Ek se.* Boesman has party tonight.

> *He tantalizes Lena by opening a bottle and passing it under her nose.*

Smell! Hotnot's forget-me-not. *(First mouthful.)* Away world, come brandy-wine!

LENA *(restraining the Old African):* No Outa. I've paid. You can stay the night with us . . . . .

Boesman refuses to permit the old man to share their shelter. Lena prepares to stay out in the cold with her guest, fetching one of the blankets, declaring angrily "I'd sit out there with a dog tonight!" Her strange determination is now finally disconcerting to Boesman; this stubborn mood of hers is new to him, and he doesn't know what to make of it. Lena goes to find some more wood for the fire.

> *Boesman, in front of his shelter with the two bottles of wine, watches her go. When she has disappeared he studies the old man. Takes a few more swallows, then gets up and moves a few steps in the direction that Lena left. Certain that she is not about he turns and goes back to the old man.*

BOESMAN (*standing over him*): Hond!

> *The Old African looks up at him. Boesman pulls the blanket away.*

I want two blankets tonight.

> *Still not satisfied, he sends the Old African sprawling with a shove. The old man crawls laboriously to his seat. Boesman watches him, then hears Lena returning. He throws back the blanket.*

If you tell her, I'll kill you. *Bulala wena!*

> *He returns to his shelter, sits down and continues drinking . . . . .*

LENA (*a few small pieces of wood is all she has found*): It's too dark now.

> *She goes to the fire. Their tea is now ready. She pours it into two mugs, taking one of them and the bread to Boesman. Then she joins the Old African with her share. She sits down beside him.*

As long as it doesn't rain it won't be so bad. The blanket will also help. Nights are long, but they don't last forever. This wind will also get tired.

> *Her mug of tea and bread are placed before them.*

It's a long time since we had somebody else with us. Sit close to the fire. That's it!

> *She throws on another piece of wood.*

It won't last long, but it's big enough. Not much to see. This is all. This is mine. Look at this mug Outa . . . old mug hey. Bitter tea, piece of bread. Bitter and brown. The bread should have bruises. It's my life.

> *Passing him the mug.*

There, don't waste time. It's still warm.

> *They drink and eat. Boesman is watching them from the shelter, his bread and tea untouched before him. (The printed version of the script calls for a curtain, the end of Act I and an intermission at this point. The 1970-71 New York production was presented in continuous action, without intermission.)*

An hour later, Lena and the Old African are still huddled together, seated on the box by the fire, while Boesman is on his second bottle of wine. *"Under the influence of the wine his characteristic violence is now heightened by a wild excitability. His bread and tea are still untouched on the ground."*

Boesman is ordering Lena to rehearse over and over again the humiliating phrase "Please, my baasie" to be used in begging sympathy from the white man, on occasions such as that very morning when the bulldozers came in to level the Korsten shacks for slum clearance. Lena had sat there crying (Boesman reminds her), while Boesman ran around laughing at the shanty dwellers scurrying about trying to save their belongings. He remembers how it was.

BOESMAN: . . . . . The women and children sitting there with their snot and tears. The pondoks falling. The men standing, looking, as the big yellow fucker pushed them over, and then staring at the pieces when they were the only things left standing. I saw all that! The whiteman stopped the bulldozer and smoked a cigarette. I saw that too. *"Ek se* my baas . . . !"* He threw me the stompie. *"Dankie baas."*

LENA: They made a big pile and burnt everything.

BOESMAN: Bomfire!

LENA: He helped drag what was left of the pondoks . . .

BOESMAN: Of course, full of disease. That one in the uniform told me. *"Dankie baas!"*

LENA: Just like that.

BOESMAN *(violently):* Yes! *"Dankie baas!"* You should have said it too, sitting there with your sad story. Whiteman was doing us a favor. You should have helped him. He wasn't just burning pondoks. They alone can't stink like that. Or burn like that. There was something else in that fire, something rotten. Us! Our sad stories, our smells, our world! And it burnt brother. It burnt. I watched that too. The end was a pile of ashes. And quiet. Then . . . Jesus! . . . then I went back to the place where our pondok had been. It was gone! You understand that? Gone! I wanted to call you and show you. There where we crawled in and out like baboons, where we used to sit like them and eat, our fingers in the pot, hiding away so that the others wouldn't see our food . . . I could stand there! There was room for me to stand straight. You know what that is? Listen now. I'm going to use a word. Freedom! Ja, I've heard them talk it. Freedom! That's what the whiteman gave us. I've got my feelings too sister. It was a big one I had when I stood there. That's why I laughed, why I was happy. When we picked up our things and started to walk I wanted to sing. It was freedom!

To Boesman, suddenly "The world was open this morning. It was big! All the roads . . ." But Lena kept trying to take away Boesman's feeling of freedom by trying to pin him down to a destination with questions about where they were going, attempts to narrow the choice. Finally Boesman was worn down. "I saw that piece of iron on the side of the road. I should have passed it. Gone on! Freedom's a long walk. But the sun was low. Our days are too short. Too late Boesman. Too late for it today. So I picked it up. Finish and *klaar.* Another pondok. *(Shouting violently.)* It's no use baas. Boesman's done it again. Bring your bulldozer tomorrow and push it over!"

The white man is wasting his time trying to "help," Boesman concludes.

BOESMAN: . . . . . Push this one over and I'll do it somewhere else. Make another hole in the ground, crawl into it and live my life crooked. One push. That's all we need. One push, into jail; one push, out of your job; one push and it's pieces. Must I tell you why? Listen! I'm thinking deep tonight. We're whiteman's rubbish. That's why he's so fed-up with us. He can't get rid of his rubbish. He throws it away, we pick it up. Wear it. Sleep in it. Eat it. We're made of it now. His rubbish is people.

LENA: Throw yourself away and leave us alone.

BOESMAN: It's been done. Why do you think we sit here like this? We've been thrown away. Rubbishes. Him too. They don't want him anymore. Useless. But there! You see what happens. Lena picks him up. Wraps him in a blanket. Gives him food.

Boesman still resents Lena's attachment to the Old African and still cannot see what she wants with him. Boesman's inability to understand Lena's need translates itself into anger, and when Lena begs for the uneaten piece of bread, Boesman hurls it out into the darkness. He tries to pretend that he has thrown Lena out of the coffin-like pondok, and Lena calmly reminds him that she spurns it of her own free will and has no desire to join Boesman inside.

Boesman disappears into his shelter. Lena urges the Old African: "Sit close. Ja! Hotnot and a Kaffer got no time for apartheid on a night like this." She suggests they think not about how they feel now, but of warmer times. Lena remembers parties and a time of dancing: "Just your feet on the earth and then stamp. Hit it hard! . . . . . Nothing fancy. We don't tickle it like the white people. Maybe it laughs for them. It's a hard mother to us."

Lena rises to her feet, sings, and begins to dance. Boesman is watching her from the shelter. Soon Lena is warm and sweating, and she returns to the blanket to share her warmth with the Old African.

As soon as they settle down, Boesman confesses frankly to Lena: *"I dropped the empties."* It was Boesman, not Lena, who was carrying the sack and dropped it. He lied to Lena and beat her for nothing. Lena fears Boesman is telling her this in order to hurt her again. She challenges him: "Why must you hurt me so much? What have I really done? Why didn't you hit yourself this morning? You broke the bottles. Or the whiteman that kicked us out? Why did you hit me?"

The question is too deep for Boesman to find the answer. He strikes his own palm with his fist, trying to find out why; perhaps he beats Lena because she is the only reality in his life; simply because he wants to feel her, touch her. The Old African is now slumped over, and Lena shakes him; she wants him to hear what Boesman is saying, even though obviously he cannot understand the words. She wants another living human being to hear and see the unfairness in Boesman's treatment of her; she urges Boesman to beat her again, to show the Kaffer.

Boesman's sharp reply to Lena's pleading is "Shit!" He explodes: "Shit! Small little word hey. Shit. But it fits. *(Parodying himself.)* 'Ja baas! Dankie baas!' Shit Boesman! And you? Don't ask me what you've done. Just look. You say you can see yourself. Take a good look tonight! Crying for a bottle, begging for bruises. Shit Lena! Boesman and Lena, shit! We're not people anymore. Freedom's not for us. We stood there under the sky . . . two crooked Hotnots. So they laughed. Shit, world! All there is to say. That's our word. After that our life is dumb. Like your womb. All that came out of it was silence. There should have been noise. You pushed out silence. And Boesman buried it. Took the spade the next morning and pushed our hope back into the dirt. Deep holes! When I filled them up I said it again: Shit. One day your turn. One day mine. Two more holes somewhere. The earth will puke when they push us in. And then it's finished. The end of Boesman and Lena. That's all it is, tonight or any other night. Two dead people living together. And you want him to look? To see? He must close his eyes . . . . ."

But the Old African can no longer feel either their misery or his own; he is dead (Lena informs Boesman), he has slipped away holding her hand. His companionship was a short-lived pleasure, like Boesman's bottle of wine.

To Lena's increasing displeasure, Boesman won't have anything to do with the body, though he warns Lena it is dangerous and should be disposed of somehow. Boesman is afraid "They" will ask questions, and Lena remarks sharply, "Why don't they ask some questions when we're alive?"

Nevertheless Boesman reminds Lena that he never touched the Old African, Lena is witness to that.

LENA: Teach me again Boesman. You really know how the whiteman likes to hear it. "He's jus' a Hotnot baas. Wasn't doing any harm" How's that? Will that make him feel sorry for you?
BOESMAN: Then the Kaffer came. And you called him to the fire.
LENA: *"Siestoggies my baas."*
BOESMAN: I didn't want him. I didn't touch him.
LENA: "Boesman didn't want him baas."
BOESMAN: I hate Kaffers.
LENA: "He hates Kaffers baas."
BOESMAN: NO! !
LENA: "He loves Kaffers baas."
BOESMAN: God Lena!
   He grabs a bottle and moves violently toward her. He stops himself in time. Lena has made no move to escape or protect herself.
LENA: Ja, got to be careful now. There's one already.
   Boesman is now very frightened. Lena watches him.
Whiteman's dog, his tale between his legs because the baas is going to be cross. Jesus! We crawl hey. You're right Boesman. And beg. "Give us a chance." *Siestog.* I'm sorry for you.

Lena taunts Boesman with the hope that maybe the Kaffer is still alive after all. Unable to ignore this possibility, Boesman goes to examine the corpse, tries to kick it violently into life, crying "Go die in your own world!" Boesman, losing control, falls to his knees and beats the unwanted body with his fists. Lena's comment is "So that's how you do it. I know what it feels like. Now I know what it looks like."

She continues to taunt Boesman: now there are fingerprints and bruises in evidence against him. They'll punish Boesman for something he didn't do, and maybe he'll understand how Lena feels for having been beaten for dropping the empties.

Boesman panics, prepares to flee; as Lena says, to "crawl around looking for a way out of your life." Lena tells him the word in her mouth is "No": she refuses to go with him this time. Here in the Swartkops mud, Lena will stop running. When Boesman, who is frantically packing his belongings, has gone, she will crawl into the shelter and go to sleep. To spite her, Boesman smashes the shelter. Defying Boesman, Lena challenges him to take everything they own and go—she pulls her blanket from the dead Kaffer and throws it at Boesman. There are too many bundles for Boesman to carry by himself, and still Lena hurls defiance at him.

LENA *(violently):* . . . . . What you waiting for? Can't we say goodbye? We'll have to do it one day. It's not forever. Come on. Let's say it now. Goodbye! Okay, now go. Walk. Go. Walk! !
> *Lena turns her back on him violently and walks away.*

Outa, why the hell you do it so soon. There's things I didn't tell you man. And now this as well. It's still happening! *(Softly.)* O my God. Can't throw yourself away before your time. Hey Outa. Even you had to wait for it.
> *She goes to Boesman.*

Give.
> *He passes over the bucket.*

Might be whiteman's rubbish, but I can still use it.
> *It goes on to her head.*

Where we going? Better be far. Coegakop. That's our farthest, That's where we started.

BOESMAN: Coega to Veeplaas.

LENA *(slowly loading up the rest of her share):* First walk. I always remember that one. It's the others.

BOESMAN *(as Lena loads):* Veeplaas to Redhouse. On Baas Robbie's place.

LENA: My God, old Baas Robbie.

BOESMAN: Redhouse to Missionvale . . . I worked on the saltpans . . . Missionvale to Bethelsdorp. Back again to Redhouse . . . that's where the child died. Then to Kleinskool. Kleinskool to Veeplaas. Veeplass to here. First time. After that Redhouse, Baas Robbie was dead, Bethelsdorp, Korsten, Veeplaas, back here the second time. Then Missionvale again, Veeplaas, Korsten, and then here, now.

LENA *(pause . . . she is loaded):* Is that the way it was? How I got here?

BOESMAN: Yes.

LENA: Truly?

BOESMAN: Yes.
> *Pause.*

LENA: It doesn't explain anything.

BOESMAN: I know.

LENA: Anyway, somebody saw a little bit. Dog and a deadman. *(They are ready to go.)* I'm alive Boesman. There's daylights left in me. You still got a chance. Don't lose it. Next time you want to kill me, do it. Really do it. When you hit, hit those lights out. Don't be too late. Do it yourself. Don't let the old bruises put the rope around your neck. Okay. But not so fast. It's dark.
> *They look around for the last time then turn and walk off into the darkness. Curtain.*

STEAMBATH

A Play in Two Acts

BY BRUCE JAY FRIEDMAN

Cast and credits appear on page 325

BRUCE JAY FRIEDMAN was born in the Bronx in 1930. His father, whose business was women's apparel, moonlighted as a piano player for silent films, and his aunt was assistant treasurer of the Broadhurst Theater, where young Friedman saw his first Broadway shows. He graduated in 1947 from DeWitt Clinton High School and in 1951 from the University of Missouri, where he was drama critic for the college newspaper. He served two years as a lieutenant in the Air Force and wrote a series of fables for the magazine Air Training *until these were suppressed because of their anti-establishment flavor.*

Friedman's first professional publication was the short story Wonderful Golden Rule Days *in* The New Yorker *in 1953. Other short Friedman pieces have appeared in* Playboy, Commentary, Mademoiselle *and other magazines and have been published in two collections:* Far From the City of Class *(1963) and* Black Angels *(1966). In 1954 Friedman joined the Magazine Management Company and remained there for 12 years, editing the publications* Man, Male *and* Man's World. *He is the author of three novels:* Stern *(1962),* A Mother's Kisses *(1964) and* The Dick *(1970).*

Friedman's first stage work of record was his adaptation of his own story 23 Pat O'Brien Movies *in an experimental production at The American Place Theater. He made his professional playwriting debut with* Scuba Duba *in 1967, a Best Play of its season. His effort to adapt his novel* A Mother's Kisses *for a musical closed out of town in 1968. Now, with* Steambath, *he has his second Best Play citation.*

Friedman is married, with three sons, and lives on Long Island.

Time: The present

Place: A steamroom

ACT I

SYNOPSIS: In the foreground of the steamroom at right is a pillar surrounded by benches, another one upstage center. Down center is an overhead shower. At left is an alcove with washbasin. The background of the room is shadowy, but doors are visible at left and right. *"Effect of steam is achieved by either steam or light or both. People speak, disappear in the haze, reappear. Characters are costumed in sheets or cloths or something in between. At the beginning of the action, a young man (35 to 45) enters and sits down next to an Oldtimer. He is ever so slightly puzzled by his surroundings but does his best to conceal this mild concern. He has a great deal of trouble when he makes contact with the hot seat."*

The Oldtimer reassures the young man—whose name is Tandy—that his rear end will become acclimatized in time. He goes on to the subject of heart attacks: the one thing to be said for them is, "They don't mark you on the outside. They leave you clean as a whistle. That's more than you can say for a gall bladder."

"An unattractive fellow" named Bieberman has been concealed behind the pillar and lets himself be noticed by spitting on the floor, an action which the Oldtimer finds disgusting.

OLDTIMER *(to Tandy):* What's your line, young fella?

TANDY: I just quit my job. I was teaching art appreciation over at the Police Academy.

OLDTIMER: That right. What the hell . . . I guess you got to do something. Police, eh? Ever notice how you never get any trouble from the good people?

TANDY: Well, that's for sure.

OLDTIMER: It's the bad ones you got to watch. You run the bad ones off the street that'll be the end of your crime. You got a son?

TANDY: No, I've got a little girl.

OLDTIMER: You got a son, I hope he's a drunk. That'll keep him off drugs. He starts in on that dope stuff you can kiss his ass goodbye. *(In reference to Bieberman.)* What's that guy doing now?

TANDY *(checking behind pillar):* Looks like he's eating an orange.

OLDTIMER: Yeah, but what's he *doing?*

TANDY *(checks again, gets hit by a fusillade of pits):* He's spitting out the pits.

OLDTIMER: Stupid mother. *(Shouting to Bieberman.)* Hey, knock it off, will you?

BIEBERMAN: Well, what am I supposed to do with them?

OLDTIMER: Hold them in your hand. Swallow them. Shove them up your ass, what do I care. Just don't spit them out. Didn't you ever hear of a person tripping on pits? *(To Tandy.)* They got some crowd in here. He's probably a fag, too.

TWO YOUNG MEN *(invisible, speaking in unison):* No, we're the fags.

OLDTIMER: I beg your pardon. *(More or less to himself.)* I knew there were fags in here.

The Oldtimer hankers for a nice cold beer. No sooner said than done—a bar boy, Gottlieb, enters with beers for Oldtimer and Tandy. Oldtimer is telling Tandy how he used to be a cab driver and wound up in a smash "with the car radio in my stomach," when a beautiful young blonde enters, wrapped in a sheet. *"Matter-of-factly she drops the sheet, steps beneath the shower and pulls the shower chain. Little cry of alarm when the water hits her, but she enjoys it. She puts the sheet back on and disappears in the haze."*

Tandy is amazed to see the naked blonde taking a shower, but Oldtimer accepts it nonchalantly. The Two Young Men come downstage doing a dance step in unison to show music from a cheap little tape-player, then go back to their seats ("This is some place," Tandy comments). Bieberman starts to gargle.

The blonde girl, whose name is Meredith, reappears, refreshed by her needle-point shower. She doesn't quite remember how she got here. The last thing she remembers is starting to buy a miniskirt at Paraphernalia. She is interrupted by the appearance of Bieberman on a ledge around the pillar above the benches. Bieberman *"speaks with a certain stopped-up anger"* about what these short skirts have meant to his generation, to a fellow like himself "who could sit through the same movie seven times, willing to sell himself into bondage on a farm in Mississippi if he could see just an eighth of an inch of Ann Rutherford's inner thigh. And then, there they are, out of the blue, those pitzel cocker skirts. And the girls wearing them, more beautiful than Ann Rutherford herself, are handing out massive looks at their thighs and crotches . . . . ."

Bieberman drops his sheet and, dressed in his shorts, starts to do exercises close to the others. Tandy orders him in his authoritative police-academy voice to move away. Resentfully, Bieberman obeys.

Tandy is usually shy with blondes and is amazed to find how easily he can talk with Meredith. But Meredith warns him that she doesn't want to be romantically involved. She has had enough of that recently—maybe Tandy should phone her around Labor Day, she might feel differently by then. Tandy agrees.

The Oldtimer is complaining about Bieberman again, when the lights darken and a screen carrying stock quotations descends from the ceiling. A Broker enters, sits down watching the screen and starts taking notes. He explains to Tandy that he has always recommended blue chips to his clients—"So what happens in the last five years? The good stuff lays there, shit goes right through the roof." Disgustedly, the Broker picks up his chair, and he and the screen disappear.

Tandy tells Meredith how strange-appearing are all the goings-on in this strange steamroom. He finds himself confiding to Meredith: "I'm doing fine. I got a divorce. I quit the Police Academy. I'm writing a novel about Charlemagne. And I just got involved in a charity. Helping brain-damaged welders. I was looking for a charity, and that's the one I picked . . . . ."

Tandy is telling Meredith about his ten-year-old daughter, and how he began to get close to her during a recent trip to Las Vegas, when Meredith interrupts.

MEREDITH: Listen, you don't think . . .

TANDY: What? What?

MEREDITH: All I can remember is that Sheila and I were buying skirts at Paraphernalia. Then we went back to our high-rise apartment on 84th Street, and, oh, yes, the Gristede's delivery boy was waiting behind the drapes, with a crazy look on his face, holding a blunt instrument . . .

TANDY: I was in my favorite restaurant, eating some Chinese food. I was just about to knock off a double order of Won Shih pancakes . . .

MEREDITH: You don't think?

TANDY: . . . We're dead? Is that what you were going to say? That's what I was going to say. That's what we are. The second I said it, I knew it. Bam! Dead! Just like that! Christ!

MEREDITH: I had it pictured an entirely different way.

TANDY: What's that?

MEREDITH: Being dead. I thought dying meant that you'd have to spend every day of your life at a different Holiday Inn. Then I decided it was seeing *So Proudly We Hail* with Veronica Lake over and over for the rest of time. In a place where there were no Mounds bars.

> *Voice is heard: "Cold drinks, popcorn, Raisinettes, Goobers. And no Mounds bars."*

TANDY: Don't pay any attention. Somebody's kidding around.

MEREDITH *(with real loss):* No Mounds bars.

TANDY: I don't know about you, but I'm not accepting this.

MEREDITH: What do you mean?

TANDY: I don't like the whole way it was done. Bam. Dead. Just like that? Just like you're a schmuck or something.

MEREDITH: What are you going to do?

TANDY: I'll do something. Don't worry. I'm a doer . . . . .

Meredith and Tandy agree, it's too soon for them to die, it's not fair (Meredith confides: "I just had my first orgasm"). Tandy disappears into the haze looking for some way out.

The Oldtimer and the Broker discuss weapons of death, while Bieberman trims his toenails. Tandy drifts back and confides his objections to the Oldtimer (he's right in the middle of a novel, he has a new girl friend, he hardly ever thinks about his wife Wendy any more) and tries to find out who's in charge around here. The Oldtimer tells him "There's a guy comes around" and promises to point him out.

Meredith is telling Tandy about how occasional nudity makes her feel tranquil, while a Puerto Rican attendant drifts into view, mopping up the steambath, singing and humming "Sorrento." The Oldtimer signals to Tandy that the attendant is the man in charge here.

> *Attendant now wheels out what appears to be a console with a screen. It is a very tacky-looking affair. The screen is visible to the Attendant but not to the audience. The console, from time to time, answers the Attendant with little blipping noises as though taking note of his instructions. In between sections of his monologue, The Puerto Rican does little snatches of "Sorrento" again.*

ATTENDANT *(leaning over console):* San Diego Freeway . . . All right, first thing, I want that Pontiac moving south past Hermosa Beach to crash into the light blue Eldorado coming the other way. Make it a head-on collision . . . the guy in the Chevy—his wife's got her ass out the window—it's the only way they get their kicks—they're going to jump the rail into the oncoming lane, and fuck up a liquor salesman in a tan Cougar. No survivors . . . All right, what's-his name, Perez, the Puerto Rican schmuck from the Bronx. The one who says, "My wife and I—we are married forty years. We are born on the same hill. There can be no trouble." He comes home tonight, I want her screwing her brother. Perez walks in, goes crazy, starts foaming at the mouth, the other tenants in the building have to tie him to a radiator . . . All right, the guy from St. Louis . . . bedspread salesman . . . adopted all those Korean kids. Him they pick up in the men's room of the Greyhound Bus Terminal, grabbing some truck driver's schvontz. They ask around, find out he's been doing it for years . . . The kids get shipped back to Korea. Now, here's one I like . . . the screenwriter flying out to Beverly Hills. Coming on with the broads. Here's what happens. Over Denver, a stewardess throws a dart in his eye. No doctor on board. He has to go all the way to Los Angeles like that. Pheww! . . . . .

After some more of the same, the Attendant picks up his mop and fades for a moment into the haze of steam. That Attendant is the boss, the Oldtimer assures Tandy. His name is Morty, or something that sounds like that in Spanish.

The Attendant comes back to the console and starts on "the other side of the coin."

ATTENDANT: . . . . . That Indian tribe outside of Caracas. Sick little guys, they ain't got a hundred bucks between 'em . . . Government doesn't give a shit. CBS moves in, shoots a jungle series there, throws a lot of money around . . . The old lady with the parakeet, flies out the window, flies back in . . . Wellesley girl, parents got a lot of dough—she's sitting on a ledge—35th floor of the Edison Hotel. A cop sprawls out after her, tells her she's a pain in the ass.

They go back in, watch a hockey game on TV . . . And clean up that garbage in the lobby . . . It's disgusting . . . That spade they beat up at Chicago Police headquarters. Got a landing strip for a head. All right, kill the cop who roughed him up—and then send the spade over to Copenhagen for a vacation. At least three months. I don't know who picks up the tab. He's got a cousin in the music business. Records for Decca . . . All right, that's enough good stuff.

VOICE: You need one more.

ATTENDANT: Christ, I'm exhausted. Uhh . . . Put bigger bath towels in all the rooms at the Tel Aviv Hilton Hotel.

VOICE: Terrific!

ATTENDANT: You kidding, buddy . . . *(Exits.)*

The Oldtimer tells Tandy he's convinced the Attendant is God. Tandy is determined to get out of here but doesn't dare to try the entrance door—he's sure it's locked, but if he finds out for certain he'll get claustrophobia.

There is a grated door on the opposite side of the room, and the Oldtimer explains that "You go through there" whenever the Attendant is pleased to send you. Once through there, there's no coming back.

Tandy reassures Meredith: he'll get them out of this somehow. Meredith worries that if they're really dead, then there is no way back, no more Mr. Skeffington (her cat), no more airline stewardesses for Tandy.

The Attendant returns and Tandy decides to confront him.

TANDY: . . . . . What's the deal around here? The Oldtimer says you're God.

ATTENDANT: Some people call me that.

TANDY: But that's ridiculous . . . a Puerto Rican . . .

ATTENDANT: The Puerto Ricans go back hundreds of years. Millions. There were Puerto Ricans in Greece, Rome. Diogenes—very big, very strong Puerto Rican. Too many people make fun of the Puerto Ricans. Very fine people. Lots of class. We got José Torres, Mario Procaccino . . .

TANDY: All right, I'll go along with you for a second. You're God. Why would you be sweeping up, a lowly job like that?

ATTENDANT: It's therapeutic. I like it. It's easy on the nerves.

TANDY: God . . . A Puerto Rican steambath attendant. That'll be the day.

ATTENDANT: Look, I'll tell you what, fella. You say I'm not God. All right. You got it. I'm not God. Fabulous. You got what you want. *(Pointing to Bieberman.)* He's God.

The Oldtimer refuses to believe this. Bieberman whines; the Two Young Men flutter. Tandy keeps after the Attendant.

TANDY: . . . God talking slang. How can I go along with that?

ATTENDANT: I talk any way I want, man. The Lord speaks in funny ways. Remember that. You want to discuss the relativity of mass, the Lorentz Transformation, galactic intelligence, I'll give you that, too. Just don't bug me. All right? Don't be no wise ass.

TANDY: That was more like it. You had me going there for a second. I respect anyone who really knows something, my work being as transitory as it is. It's when you talk dirty . . .

ATTENDANT: The way I talk, the way I talk . . . Don't you see that's just a little blink of an eye in terms of the universe, the job I got to do? The diameter of an electron is one ten-trillionth of an inch. And you're telling me I shouldn't talk dirty. Let me talk the way I want. Let me relax a little.

TANDY: I can't see it. You're not God.

ATTENDANT: You can't see it? Don't see it. I got things to do. *(Approaches console screen again.)* All right, give that girl on the bus a run on her body stocking. I want to close up that branch of Schrafft's . . . And send up a bacon-and-lettuce-and-tomato sandwich, hold the mayo. You burn the toast, I'll smite you down with my terrible swift sword. *(Leaves the console.)*

TANDY: I still don't buy it. That could be an ordinary TV screen. You could have been watching *Laugh-In.*

ATTENDANT: *Laugh-In? (Goes over to console.)* Cancel *Laugh-In.* You still want to fool around?

Tandy keeps on doubting the Attendant. Gottlieb arrives with the Attendant's sandwich. Tandy goads the Attendant into trying to demonstrate his divinity. He does a card trick, then causes a scarf to materialize—minor magic, Tandy has seen better on the Ed Sullivan Show. The Attendant picks a lock with his teeth, and still Tandy is not impressed: "I'm not moved. If you had made one interesting intellectual assault on my mind, maybe that would do it."

The Attendant tries a simple Latin phrase, then a complex philosophical concept; still Tandy is unmoved. The Attendant orders Gottlieb to bring him a huge whisky sour, in a glass taller than any person in the room. The Attendant drains off the monstrous drink through a straw. Tandy is impressed, but not yet convinced: "I'm still not buying it. The God routine."

ATTENDANT: You really making me work, boy. All right. I have but one choice, my son. *(Gestures.)* Shazam . . .
> *Stage, theater suddenly fill with deafening organ music, churchlike, ancient, soaring, almost unbearable. Theater then fills with angels or other miraculous and heavenly effects. Attendant stands majestically, his head crowned with celestial light. He ascends to highest tier in steambath. Music is deafening in its churchlike call to the divinity. Voice of Attendant, magnified a hundredfold, similar to that of Cecil B. DeMille, booms out.*

ATTENDANT'S VOICE:
ASCRIBE UNTO THE LORD
YE KINDREDS OF THE PEOPLES . . .
ASCRIBE UNTO THE LORD
GLORY AND STRENGTH . . .

ASCRIBE UNTO THE LORD
THE GLORY DUE UNTO HIS NAME
BRING AN OFFERING
AND COME UNTO HIS COURTS
OH, WORSHIP THE LORD
IN THE BEAUTY OF HOLINESS
TREMBLE BEFORE HIM
ALL THE EARTH . . .

> *One by one, the steambath people drop to their knees. Tandy looks*
> *around, observes that he is the only one standing. He shrugs, goes*
> *to one knee as the curtain descends.*

ACT II

Most of the steambath people are lying around, as though exhausted. The
Broker is skipping rope to keep in condition and reminiscing about his life.
The Oldtimer is quarreling with Bieberman, who is watching a 1940s movie
on TV and tells them all: "I suppose it never occurred to you that every
smile, every whisper, every puff of a cigarette taken by my generation was
inspired by the forties movie. That my generation wouldn't know how to mix
a drink, drive a car, kiss a girl, straighten a tie—if it weren't for Linda Darnell
and George Brent . . . That the sole reason for my generation's awkward
floundering in the darkness is that Zachary Scott is gone . . . and I assure you
that Dennis Hopper is no substitute."

Tandy reminisces about police work, Meredith about her unpaid Bloomingdale's bill. Tandy remembers his book on Charlemagne—he has work to
do, he must get out of here, and he goes looking for the Attendant.

Bieberman complains of pimples, and the Oldtimer advises him to cut down
on malteds.

BIEBERMAN: Malteds are the marijuana of my generation.

OLDTIMER: Your generation . . . what the hell generation is that?

BIEBERMAN: It went by very quickly . . . It was Dolf Camilli, Dane Clark,
Uncle Don, Ducky Medwick and out . . .

OLDTIMER: Sounds like a real bunch of winners.

BIEBERMAN: We produced Norman Podhoretz.

OLDTIMER: Congratulations . . . *(To the Broker.)* Who the fuck is Norman
Podhoretz?

BROKER: Probably some wealthy bastard who made it when you could keep
it.

Tandy comes back and confides to Meredith that he'd like her to be his girl
if they ever get out of this. Meanwhile, the Oldtimer is describing to the
Broker one of the many strange sights he has seen during his colorful career:
"Toughest son of a bitch I ever knew used to dress up like Carmen Miranda.

They found him floating five kilometers outside Hamburg Harbor . . . all those bananas bobbing in the water."

The Attendant comes in with Gottlieb and orders the group to sit, campfire-style. Gottlieb distributes Mounds candy bars to all. Tandy argues "I got to talk to you about getting out of here. I don't belong here, I don't need this," but the Attendant refuses to listen: "You know what I don't need? Right now? Aggravation."

Around this "campfire," it seems, they are all to tell their stories. The Broker goes first. After 20 years, he began to wonder why his partner was getting rich while he was having trouble making ends meet. The Broker started asking questions, and his partner dismissed him with a check for $800. The Broker went out to the golf course, where he died with his head thrown back in a grotesque laugh and the $800 check in his lap.

The Two Young Men hanged themselves for love of the same boy: "A swing dancer in the national company of *Zorbá* . . . . . we loved the way he moved . . . the rough carving of his arms . . . the way the veins were printed on them . . . . . Neither of us meant a thing to him."

The Attendant doesn't like "fag stories," and has already been irritated by Tandy's protestations, his "Charlemagne routine." He warns Tandy that he's going to do something bad to him, and Tandy is genuinely frightened.

TANDY *(looks at second door):* You're not going to put me in there, are you?

ATTENDANT: No. *(Points to Oldtimer.)* I'm putting him in there. *(To Tandy.)* You come in here . . . you're looking for fair, reasonable . . . Where'd you get that from? Old Man . . .

OLDTIMER *(rising):* My time, eh?

ATTENDANT: That's right, baby.

OLDTIMER: Well, that's okay. I done everything. I once had a pair of perfectly matched wooden-legged frauleins powder me up from head to toe and dress me up in silk drawers. I run up against a Greek sailor walking around for thirty years with a lump on his chest he took to be a natural growth. Turned out to be the unborn fetus of a twin brother he'd spent all his life hankering for. I seen most everything. I dipped my beak in Madrid, Spain; Calcutta, India; Leningrad, Russia, and I never once worried about them poisoning the water. I had myself the fifth-richest woman in Sydney, Australia, genuine duchess she was, all dressed up in a tiger suit; by the time I finished with her I had them stripes going the wrong way. I played a pretty good trumpet. I had to face the fact that I was no Harry James, but then again, Sir Harry couldn't go in there and break up a Polish wedding the way I could. I talked back to the biggest guys. Didn't bother me. I didn't care if it was me way down in the valley, hollering up at Mount Zion. I'd holler up some terrific retorts. You're not going to show me anything I haven't seen. I paid my dues. *(Starts to go.)* And I'll tell you something else. If there's anything in there kicks me, you watch and see if I don't bite.

> *He hitches himself up with great dignity and does a sailor's dance, then a proud old man's walk into the grated room.*

ATTENDANT: Old man had a lot of balls.

TANDY: Damn right. *(To Attendant.)* Listen, I was the wise guy. Why didn't you send me in there?

ATTENDANT: That's direct. I don't work that way. I always put a little spin on the ball . . . . .

The Attendant calls for another story, this time to be acted out rather than narrated. The scene is set for a longshoremen's saloon, with Gottlieb behind the bar talking to a customer. A couple comes into the bar, the man an almost total cripple in a wheel chair, neck brace, etc., the girl pretty and short-skirted.

The girl puts money in the juke box and begins to dance to the rock tune. The longshoreman at the bar approaches her and suggests that he'd be better company than the cripple. The cripple throws off his braces and gets out of his wheelchair, revealing himself as an able, well-muscled silver-belt karate (it turns out to be Bieberman). He knocks the longshoreman down. The Attendant is delighted with this story of how Bieberman and his girl would get their kicks and at the same time "smoke out society's predators" every Friday night. Bieberman wound up in the steambath (he tells the Attendant) because "An Arab at the 92d Street YMHA dropped a 200-pound barbell on my neck."

The Attendant has enjoyed the story, but now it's time for the whole group to go through the grated door, to make room for a new group coming in. The Broker goes through the door, then the Two Young Men. Bieberman is next, after making his farewells to Meredith: "Goodbye. My generation's out of style—I know that—but you'll never know the thrill of having belonged to it. *(Starting through the grated door.) John Hodiak*—hold on, I'll be right with you . . ."

The Attendant orders Meredith and Tandy, the last two left, through the door. Meredith hesitates and Tandy is adamant: "I'm not accepting this," this being cut off in the middle of a good Chinese dinner before he had even had a chance to sample the main course. Tandy tells the Attendant about his wife, Wendy; how she went off with a new-wave film maker, how her private parts were magnified on the screen in a huge closeup; how Tandy shrugged all this off, even went to see the movie. Tandy has been kind to his mother, he has quit his job at the Police Academy (one detective who has sworn to get him for this appears with gun in hand, but is quickly consigned to the grated door by the Attendant). For the first time, Tandy believes, his life is in order.

TANDY: . . . . . I'm closer than ever to my daughter. That trip to Vegas really brought us together. I'm doing work that I love. Warner Brothers saw the first hundred pages of my Charlemagne book and I understood they like it for Steve McQueen . . .

ATTENDANT: Twentieth is going to buy it . . . for Charlton Heston.

TANDY: Then you admit . . . you admit I'm getting out of here.

ATTENDANT: They're going to buy it from your estate.

TANDY: Look, I'm all clean and straight . . . . . I don't hate anybody. I love a lot of people. I'm at the Goddamned starting line. I'm ready to breathe clean air. I tore myself inside out to get to where I am—and I'm not taking up anybody's space. I'm ready to cook a little. Swing. What kind of fellow is that to snuff out?

ATTENDANT: A good fellow. But I'm snuffing him out anyway.

TANDY: Where's your compassion?

ATTENDANT: I do plenty of good things. Half the things I do are good, maybe even a little more, that's right, maybe even a little more. Nobody notices them. I never get any credit, but I do plenty of good things. I make trees, forests, soccer fields. I let hernias get better . . .

TANDY: But you'll wipe out a guy like me . . . and a lovely blonde girl like that . . .

MEREDITH: Oh, listen, the blonde part shouldn't enter into it, I can see that.

ATTENDANT: I let you you go, I got to let the next guy go. Pretty soon nobody's dead. You'd have people coming out of your ears. Have you seen Istanbul lately? Downtown Istanbul? Los Angeles?

Tandy offers to make a sacrifice, a burnt offering for the Attendant if he would like it. He tries anger, calling the Attendant names, but the Attendant merely mocks him for blasphemy. Tandy is unrepentant: "When I was in that Chinese restaurant . . . and I lost my breath, and I had no feelings, and I was numb and white, as white as a piece of typing paper, and I said over and over and over I don't want to die, I don't want to die, I don't want to die . . . and told you, in my way, how much I treasured every drop of life—you weren't impressed, you didn't hear a whisper of it."

On the contrary (the Attendant tells Tandy) he *did* hear him and supposed he might have an interesting story to tell—otherwise Tandy would have gone straight to the area behind the grated door. Only "neurotics, freaks . . . those with stories to tell" come to the steambath.

Tandy threatens the Attendant, then wrestles with Gottlieb and forces Gottlieb to reveal his master's weakness: the Attendant can't stand mirrors. Tandy uses Meredith's purse mirror to make the Attendant cringe, but he can't bring himself to follow through with this use of force. He puts the mirror away and lets Gottlieb go.

After Meredith goes through the grated door with an "Au revoir" to Tandy, the Attendant admits: "You got a lot of nice qualities . . . Too bad I'm filled up. I'd let you work around here for a while . . . Listen, what are you giving yourself such a hard time for . . . Suppose, for a second, I let you out of here . . . What would you do?"

Tandy reminds the Attendant of his exciting new life, his terrific new girl. If that is the case—Tandy asks himself—"How come I'm constantly chasing chicks all over the place?" Well—he admits—maybe his new girl *is* a bit dull, maybe he should look for a new one . . . he is always looking.

Tandy continues to explain to the Attendant why he absolutely, urgently *must* get back to his life. He has so many things to do, so many friends who "hang around this bar called The Quonset Hut, run by a dyke" (there is no need for the Attendant to interrupt Tandy, who is inevitably raising doubts about the worth and meaning of his life even as he tries to answer them).

TANDY: . . . . . These friends of mine are terrific people—they're a little screwed up in their personal lives—most of them have been divorced three or four times—but very often those are the best people, the ones who get divorced over and over . . . Anyway, I want to do a lot more of that, hanging around this dyke bar till five in the morning with my divorced friends, talking about Milton and the Brontë sisters . . . And I have to get back to my book. Now I know what you're going to say and I'm way ahead of you—that I have no real visceral interest in Charlemagne—that I just picked that subject because it has a prestige sound to it. Well, you're wrong. To me it's just a loosening-up process, a way of warming up the writing muscles so I can be ready for the real book I want to write on—Vasco da Gama and the Straits of Magellan.

Weak little laugh as though aware he's told a joke. No response from Attendant.

No, seriously . . . you have to get the muscles limber . . . What you're saying is if I really wanted to write I'd stop crapping around with Charlemagne . . . I see what you mean . . . You get more prestige from a truly observed book about . . . cheeseburgers than you can from a schlock Charlemagne book . . . Boy, you really nailed that one down . . . I'll tell you what, let me smoke a cigar, all right?

Takes one out; Attendant has sat down and begun to arrange the cards for a game of solitaire.

I get these from Switzerland from a guy who brings them in from Cuba. It costs you a little extra, but it's really worth it. They say you're supposed to stop smoking these when you get about half way down, but I don't know. Sometimes I think the last half of the cigar is the best part. I can tell a Havana cigar in one puff. It's not the tobacco so much as the rolling process they use. They have a secret rolling process that nobody's ever been able to pry away from the Cubans . . . If it kills me I got to get back and have some more weekends with my daughter. Those weekends are the most beautiful part of my life now. I mean there's no more hassle . . . no more crazy marriage in the background . . . It all gets telescoped down to just me and her, hanging around together.

Looks at Attendant for response, doesn't get one.

. . . So you're asking me how come I'm always going crazy thinking up places to take her . . . How come I'm always dragging her to puppet shows . . . Well, all I can say is that it's the city's fault . . . Where the hell are you supposed to take a kid in the city . . . If we were out on a farm, it'd be a different story . . . But I do see what you mean—Jesus, you really know how to zing it in there . . . what you're driving at is that I have to keep taking her places because I actually have nothing to say to her . . . Maybe I don't even like kids . . . She'd be better off staying home and hanging around with a pack of little girls . . .

Handling cigar.

A guy once told me the reason for the special flavor of these Havana cigars is that the tobacco is supposed to be rolled on the thighs of Cuban women . . . Jesus, wouldn't that be something . . . I got to get out of here . . . I got to get out of here . . . I got things to do.

Attendant continues his game of solitaire—the last sound heard is the flicking of the cards . . . Curtain.

CONDUCT UNBECOMING

A Play in Three Acts

BY BARRY ENGLAND

Cast and credits appear on page 290

BARRY ENGLAND is a British playwright born in 1934, educated at Down-side and experienced in the ways of Her Majesty's military, having served two years as a subaltern in the Far East. After shedding the uniform he spent 5 years as an actor before starting to write for the theater in 1960. Three of his plays—End of Conflict, The Big Contract *and* The Damn-Givers—*have been produced at the Belgrade Theater in Coventry. His television scripts have in-cluded* The Move After Checkmate, You'll Know Me by the Stars in My Eyes, An Experience of Evil *and* The Man Who Understood Women. *Mr. England is making his American theater debut with* Conduct Unbecoming, *his first international London-New York production and of course his first Best Play. In addition to his theater work, he is the author of a novel entitled* Fig-ures in a Landscape. *He is married, with one child, and lives in England.*

132

Time: The late 1800s

Place: India, the anteroom to the Officers' Mess of a British Army regiment in India

ACT I

Scene 1

SYNOPSIS: Two brand new British second lieutenants—Edward Millington and Arthur Drake—enter the lounge section of the Officers' Mess of the regiment to which they've been assigned.

There's no one else in the room this afternoon, and the two young men are free to examine the relics on display here, mementoes of the Regiment's distinguished history: medals, portraits of former officers, etc. The room is furnished as a club lounge. It opens onto a verandah upstage and into the rest of the building—dining area, card room, living quarters—by a short flight of stairs at right and a door leading into a hall at left.

Both Millington and Drake are sons of former officers, Drake's father a major and Millington's a general whose portrait hangs here in the Mess: "General Sir William Millington, V.C., Colonel of the Regiment, 1875-1881." Yet Millington's attitude toward the Regiment and its holy relics contains a faint distemper of flippancy, which Drake resents.

DRAKE: I think I should warn you, Millington, that while I might—through force of circumstances—tolerate your imbecilities throughout our voyage together, you will find they are not appreciated here.

MILLINGTON: Oh, but my dear fellow, we are not yet officially members of the Regiment. Won't you allow me a moment or two more of my native joie de vivre?

DRAKE: You realize, of course, that how you choose to behave will reflect on me?

MILLINGTON: Surely not?

DRAKE: There is no question of it. Unfortunately, we shall be judged together.

MILLINGTON: Oh, dear . . .

DRAKE: I should therefore tell you that I have every intention of making a success of my three months probationary period with this Regiment, and of joining it properly and fully at the end of that time.

MILLINGTON: That is kind of you, Arthur. There is, unhappily, a little matter that I should perhaps share with you.

DRAKE: What is that?

MILLINGTON: I have no intention whatever of surviving my three months probationary period. There is a ship, the *Doric Castle,* which sails for England in almost exactly three months to the day from now. I intend to be on her.

Pradah Singh, a stately, dignified Indian in his 60s, who served under General Millington and is now in charge of the Mess, enters. Millington yearns for a whisky and soda but is reminded by Drake that they must wait until they have presented themselves to the Adjutant and been properly introduced into the Mess. These formalities are part of Regimental tradition and must be observed.

Pradah Singh informs the young men that all the other officers are attending a polo match against the Seventh Lancers but should be returning shortly. The Junior Subaltern, Fothergill, enters and puts the two newcomers to a kind of test by offering them a drink. Millington is ready to accept, but Drake declines, and they get over this first hurdle.

Pradah Singh leaves the room. Millington, tired, sinks into a chair, then leaps out of it when he learns it is the Colonel's chair. Fothergill explains some of the protocol to Drake and Millington: "It's my job as Junior Subaltern to watch over you chaps for the next week or two. Make sure you understand what's what and so on. So let me remind you of one or two of the basic facts of life. *You* don't speak to anyone, of course. Nor will anyone speak to you. Except me. It's my job to speak to you. And you may speak to me. But never to a senior officer—unless addressed first—in which case you reply, 'Yes, sir.' Unless it is the Colonel, in which case you reply, 'Yes, Colonel.' We always call the Colonel, Colonel, in this Regiment . . . . . Now, when the Colonel arrives, we shall withdraw to a corner over there. At an appropriate moment, I shall strike the gong, announce Strangers in the Mess, and introduce each of you individually. No one will pay the least attention except the Colonel, who will say, 'Thank you, Mister Fothergill.' *You* will say nothing. We shall then wait for the Adjutant to join us, when you will present yourselves, and we shall withdraw to your quarters."

Fothergill explains further that a Mrs. Hasseltine will be in the Colonel's party, as well as the Colonel's lady. Mrs. Hasseltine is an officer's widow who is "not above—returning certain favors—particularly to younger officers" and Fothergill warns the young men to steer politely clear of her, leave her to the senior officers.

Fothergill informs the young men that the Regiment has won the polo match, thanks to two goals by Major Wimborne, the Regiment's third V.C. (Millington's father was its first).

Millington stares at a stained and torn scarlet tunic displayed on a dummy-like frame enshrined in a glass case. Deliberately, he affronts his listeners by calling it a "filthy, scruffy old tunic." This is slighting one of the Regiment's most sacred relics, the tunic worn by the fallen and revered Captain Scarlett at the battle of Ratjahpur (Fothergill informs Millington angrily).

They are silenced by the arrival of Pradah Singh and the Mess waiters, followed closely by Colonel Strang and his entourage.

The Colonel enters with Mrs. Marjorie Hasseltine, Mem Strang, Major Alastair Wimborne, V.C. (who is in polo gear with scarf), the Doctor, the Second in Command (Major Lionel Roach), the Adjutant (also in polo gear), Lt. Hart (in polo gear), 2d Lts. Winters, Boulton and Hutton.

MRS. HASSELTINE: I'm sure you are wrong, Colonel. I'll wager it is seven, not six. What do you say, Mem?

MEM: Oh, dear. I'm not very good at that sort of thing, I'm afraid. I'd have to look it up.

COLONEL: Lionel will know. Tell us, Lionel. How many matches are we up on the Lancers now?

ROACH: Seven, Colonel, counting today's.

MRS. HASSELTINE: There you are. What did I say?

WIMBORNE: We really will have to scratch that fixture soon, Colonel.

COLONEL: Oh, I don't think tradition is ever pointless, is it, Alastair?

WIMBORNE *(grins):* No, no, perhaps not.

DOCTOR: Besides, you enjoy whacking the pants off them, Alastair. You know damned well you do.

WIMBORNE: How right you are, Doctor.

MRS. HASSELTINE: He's a clever boy, isn't he Colonel, to have scored two such beautiful goals?

WIMBORNE: My dear Marge, I did it all for you!

COLONEL: He left it damned late in the day, I will say. What were you trying to do Alastair, throw a scare into us?

WIMBORNE: Thought I'd try to make the game more interesting for them, Colonel.

The Colonel leads them all toward the verandah upstage, but before they exit Fothergill taps the gong and performs his "Strangers in the Mess" ritual, introducing Drake and Millington. The Colonel looks the two young men over briefly, thanks Fothergill and goes outdoors without another word.

Mrs. Hasseltine can't resist making a comment about Millington's youthful appearance as she passes (she knew his father), and Millington commits the unpardonable crime of speaking, returning her compliment graciously. All but the Adjutant, Capt. Rupert Harper, ignore this gaffe, but it is the Adjutant's duty to administer a strong reprimand to Fothergill when the Colonel's party has left the room—as Junior Subaltern, Fothergill is responsible for the behavior of the newcomers, who now must proceed to the next step of the ritual and present themselves formally to the Adjutant.

DRAKE *(smart pace forward):* I have the honor to present myself, sir. Mister Drake, sir.

ADJUTANT *(looks him up and down):* . . . Thank you, Mister Drake.

MILLINGTON *(pace forward):* I, also, have the honor to present myself, sir.

ADJUTANT: Do you lack a name, sir?

MILLINGTON: Millington, sir.
>   *A silence.*
ADJUTANT: Come here, Mister Millington.
MILLINGTON: Sir.
>   *In silence Millington, subdued by this cutting, cold, quiet man, goes to stand before him. Pause.*
ADJUTANT: If I hear from you again, it will be for the last time. Do you understand me?
MILLINGTON: May I be allowed to say . . .
ADJUTANT: Be quiet! *(A cracked whip. A pause.)* Now. Have I succeeded in making my instructions plain?
MILLINGTON: Yes, sir.
ADJUTANT: Return to your place.
>   *Millington does so. Silence.*
If you find your duties too arduous, Mister Fothergill, I can arrange to have you relieved of them.
FOTHERGILL: . . . No, sir.
ADJUTANT: That is all.
>   *He goes. Junior Subaltern, Fothergill, rounds on Millington.*
FOTHERGILL: You bloody little fool! What the hell were you playing at? !
MILLINGTON: I'm sorry, my dear fellow . . .
FOTHERGILL: Be quiet! I told you to remain silent while there were senior officers in the Mess!

The Junior Subaltern threatens to have Millington thrown out of the Regiment if he persists in his misconduct. He directs Drake and Millington to their quarters, as the lights change to evening. *"Pradah Singh, magnificent in Mess dress, comes on—directs the Mess waiters, also in Mess kit, in straightening the furniture. Offstage: relatively distant hunting cries and shouting."*

Scene 2

That evening, the Second in Command and Junior Subaltern enter the Mess. They are in duty dress, with swords, and they order brandies. Roach is Officer of the Week and Fothergill Officer of the Day, so that they are on duty and not participating with the others in a traditional Mess Night contest whose laughter and hunting cries can be heard coming closer.

They discuss Millington, who let the Colonel's new string of ponies get loose the day before. Disciplining him, a general's son, for these and other lapses is bound to be an awkward business.

>   *Offstage: a sudden loud burst of shouting and laughter, very close. Then Lt. Hart runs in from stage right, dragging behind him what is in fact a stuffed boar on wheels or rollers, attached to a sort of metal broom handle by which he pulls it. He runs across and off left, shouting . . .*

HART: Oink, oink—chaaaaarrge!
> *Almost at once the pursuing body comes through after him, Wimborne and Adjutant in lead, closely followed by Colonel Strang, Lts. Hutton, Winters and Boulton—and the Doctor, trailing, out of condition. All are in Mess dress: Wimborne and Adjutant (like Hart) have discarded jackets. They carry drawn swords (senior officers) or lances. They charge across, off left.*

WIMBORNE: There he goes . . . !
HUTTON: This way, sir.
ADJUTANT: After the devil . . . !
BOULTON: Charge . . . !
COLONEL: Up the Regiment . . . !
DOCTOR *(puffing):* My word, Colonel, we'll have to find someone slower next time . . . ! *(He is the last off.)*

An injured officer, Lt. Truly, limps by, gamely taking part in "hunt." Roach confides to Fothergill that they are concerned about Millington, who seems to be mistake-prone. What's more, they have both noted that Millington drank rather too much at dinner and should be led to his quarters as soon and as quietly as possible.

> *Hart comes charging through again, dragging the boar, Adjutant, Wimborne and Winters close at his heels.*

WIMBORNE: Nearly got him . . . !
HART: Hell . . . !
> *Hart skids and falls. The others at once close round the boar, sinking swords and lances into its hind quarters.*

WIMBORNE: Aha—yes!
> *Sinks in sword.*

A point!
ADJUTANT *(stab):* A point!
WIMBORNE *(stabs again):* A veritable point!
WINTERS *(stabs):* Hooray!
> *The joke is evidently to stab the boar only in the hind quarters, this being the area presented in "flight." Drake and Millington have now appeared on the verandah, watching. Hart scrambles up as the others stab and stab again.*

Hart starts off again with the boar, but the Colonel and the Doctor are winded, and the "Mess Game" comes to an end for this evening, in an argument over how many points were scored. Hart protests that he fell down, and points shouldn't count when the runner is down. Asked for a ruling, the Second in Command decides: "Should the runner be incapacitated, there shall be allowed, during the period of his incapacitation, one valid point only."

Pradah Singh has served drinks all around, and Lt. Truly limps in, last in pursuit of the quarry. He is solicitously lifted into a chair by Wimborne.

"There is much warmth and affection in all this boisterousness. This is their world."

Drake and Millington, watching, are not quite of it yet. Millington is very drunk but holding himself well.

The time has come for one of the younger officers to entertain the others with a turn of some kind, and Wimborne secures the Colonel's permission to call on one of the newcomers. He selects Millington, who manages to place himself at attention before the Colonel and is perfectly prepared to sing a song. It is a French love song—which sends the listeners into paroxyms of heckling. But Millington pays no attention; he finishes his song in excellent, well-modulated voice. Everyone including the Colonel gives him a "Well done!" Millington, still at attention, requests the Colonel's permission to pass out and falls dead drunk at the Colonel's feet, much to the consternation of the Mess in general and the Adjutant in particular.

Millington is carried out, and Hart breaks the tension in the room by challenging the Colonel to a game of billiards. Lt. Truly asks permission to fall out—his leg is troubling him—and he too faints, from pain, before he can make his exit. Wimborne carries Truly out to his quarters, followed by the Doctor, who is told by the Colonel in a last-minute concession: "Perhaps you'd better take a look at the other young gentleman too."

Scene 3

The lights fade and change to the bright morning after. Millington staggers in and persuades Pradah Singh to serve him a restoring whisky. Drake joins him—they are to meet the Junior Subaltern here at 8 o'clock. Drake is completely fed up with Millington.

DRAKE: Why did you ever come here, Millington?

MILLINGTON *(smiles):* Oh, one cannot escape one's destiny, my dear fellow. One must go through the motions of failure.

DRAKE: Then, let me warn you, Millington. I have never in my life wanted anything but to be a part of this Regiment. I do not intend to have that ambition destroyed by you. If necessary, I shall resort to physical means to protect it. Do you understand me?

MILLINGTON *(astonished):* My dear fellow, you are never referring to fisticuffs, surely.

DRAKE: What do you think I am referring to, Mister Millington? Or do you imagine there is a particular dispensation that protects the sons of generals?

MILLINGTON: Of course I do not.

DRAKE: Do you not, Mister Millington?

MILLINGTON: Certainly not, Arthur ...

DRAKE: It has never entered your head that were you anyone but a general's son, you would be on a ship by now and bound for home?

MILLINGTON: That can't be true.

DRAKE *(turns away in disgust):* Of course it is.
  Pause. Millington shaken.
MILLINGTON: . . . My God, that's awful.
  DRAKE *(cruel, amused):* . . . It is also rather amusing, is it not, Mister Millington? Your plans to quit this Regiment may prove more sanguine than you had imagined.
  MILLINGTON *(stunned pain):* How much further have I got to go?

The Junior Subaltern enters the Mess, *"ablaze with rage."* He is furious at Millington's behavior and forces him to look outdoors at a structure which he describes as "a whipping-post . . . . . where they flogged sepoys in '57!"
  At the implied threat that he might be flogged for his sins, Millington smiles and chills his listeners with the remark, "The whip holds no terrors for me. No terrors at all."
  Nevertheless Fothergill warns Millington that the whip has been used on a difficult subaltern recently and might easily be used again. He instructs the two that one more offense on the part of either man will cause that man's service to be terminated. Millington is to cut down on his drinking. They are both to attend the ball tonight in Mess dress; meanwhile, they are to busy themselves cleaning out the stables. The lights fade to evening setting.

Scene 4

The ball is in progress, with waiters moving about with trays and music coming from just offstage at left. *"All officers, including Millington and Drake, wear full Mess dress—except the Second in Command, Officer of the Week, and Hart, Officer of the Day. Hart and senior officers wear swords; subalterns do not. The women are beautifully gowned."*
  Wimborne and subalterns are dancing attendance on Mrs. Hasseltine. The Colonel joins them, and then Mem Strang, who leads off all the officers, including her husband, to dance with the other ladies, whom they call "crows" in comparison to Mrs. Hasseltine. She is not alone for long. Millington enters and manages to consume three or four drinks off the tray of a passing waiter, before noticing that Mrs. Hasseltine is watching. Conversation between them begins on a plane of excessive politeness, with Millington edging warily toward familiarity and the lady holding him at arm's length. She warns him against drinking too much, and about making slighting remarks about his father, the General in the portrait.

MILLINGTON: . . . . . He was a perfect swine.
  MRS. HASSELTINE: That is not an attitude you will find appreciated here, Mister Millington. The General is revered in this Mess.
  MILLINGTON: It was not a pronouncement to the Mess, Mrs. Hasseltine, but an aside to you.
  MRS. HASSELTINE: Under the impression, apparently, that it would fall on sympathetic ears.
  MILLINGTON: My sole impression of you, Mrs. Hasseltine, is that you are a woman.

MRS. HASSELTINE: Don't be insolent, Mister Millington.

MILLINGTON: Forgive me. I had not thought the remark insolent. *(Sighs.)* Oh, dear. I so wanted to make a good impression. Clearly you must have taken to him.

MRS. HASSELTINE: I scarcely knew your father. He was a hard man. But never without cause.

MILLINGTON *(smiles):* I think you do him an injustice, Mrs. Hasseltine. I don't remember that he ever flogged me himself. We had an estates manager, Mister Radlett, who was adept at that particular function. A fine, free-flowing action.

MRS. HASSELTINE *(turns away):* . . . I doubt it was more than you deserved.

MILLINGTON: I wouldn't argue with you, ma'am. *(Chuckles.)* What is amusing is that they are proposing to repeat the dose here. Did you know? Out there, on that frame thing—strapping me up and walloping away.

MRS. HASSELTINE: . . . I should derive what amusement you can from it now, Mister Millington. They will certainly do it if you compel them to.

MILLINGTON: I'm sure of that, ma'am.

MRS. HASSELTINE: What they have done before, and recently, they will do again.

MILLINGTON: What has escaped me, thus far, is the identity of the victim of that last occasion.

MRS. HASSELTINE: It was Mister Truly.

MILLINGTON: Ah. He of the gammy leg. No wonder he is such an example to us all.

MRS. HASSELTINE: Let us hope he will prove an example to you, Mister Millington.

MILLINGTON: Let us hope so. He must have done something spectacularly wicked to have been accorded such a privilege.

MRS. HASSELTINE: He behaved stupidly towards me.

MILLINGTON *(quietly; inward):* Yes. Yes, I wondered about that. *(Looks up. Smiles.)* Dear me. It appears that I shall have to restrain myself.

Nevertheless Millington persists in conversation while the music softly plays "Plaisir d'Amour." At the approach of the Colonel and Wimborne along the verandah, Mrs. Hasseltine warns him: "Stay away from me."

Mrs. Hasseltine goes off to dance with Wimborne, and the Colonel seems almost embarrassed to be left to make conversation with Millington; yet their exchange is somehow amiable as well as formal. The Colonel offers Millington a cigar; Millington declines but is quick to light the Colonel's. The Colonel remembers Millington's father with admiration, which Millington echoes politely. Drake enters, and the Colonel, glad to escape from these embarrassing pleasantries, exists onto the verandah.

Drake suggests that perhaps it would be best for Millington to go to his quarters, but Millington runs out to dance.

Officers and lady guests cross the room in playful mimicry of the Game. Roach and Hart, Officers of the Week and Day, enter and prepare for their rounds of inspection, Roach orders Hart: "Come along, we'll begin at the east gate and work our way round through to the piquets." They depart via the verandah, as the music swells and the lights change to early morning.

Scene 5

It is 2 a.m.; the ball is nearly over; most of the guests have departed. Mem Strang and the Colonel, though weary, decide to have one last dance together. They are interrupted by screams and cries offstage. Mem Strang is already moving toward the sound, when *"Mrs. Hasseltine scrabbles on all fours onto verandah—moving at a terrifying pace—making mindless noises— hair dishevelled, dress torn . . . . ."*
Pradah Singh, Winter, Boulton, Drake all run to Mrs. Hasseltine's assistance, as she clings to Mem Strang in a state of terror. Hart, Wimborne, the Doctor and the Junior Subaltern run in, followed by the Adjutant and the Second in Command. Truly comes in as Wimborne lifts Mrs. Hasseltine to a chair and the Doctor bends over her.

DOCTOR *(crouches):* What on earth has happened, Mem?
MEM: She's been attacked, Doctor . . .
    Millington now appears on the empty verandah, rubbing his head behind the ear. He looks bemused, slightly drunk.
DOCTOR: Let me see, my dear . . . Let me just see . . .
WIMBORNE: Who by? That's what I want to know! Who did it? !
    Mrs. Hasseltine, looking about wildly, suddenly points at Millington.
MRS. HASSELTINE: It was him! It was him!
MILLINGTON *(vaguely):* What . . . ?
WIMBORNE *(makes for him):* My God, you little . . . !
COLONEL: Alastair!
    They freeze at his tone. He turns formally to the Second in Command.
Major Roach. This officer is under arrest.
ROACH: Mister Harper, detail two officers.
ADJUTANT: Sir. Mister Fothergill, Mister Hart.
    Hart and Junior Subaltern advance on Millington, who smiles. Curtain.

ACT II

Scene 1

The next morning, the younger officers—Fothergill, Hart, Winters, Boulton, Truly and Drake—are speculating on what will happen to Millington; a court martial, they guess.
The Adjutant enters and informs them that the matter is to be settled by

the rare procedure of a Subalterns Court Martial. Mrs. Hasseltine has agreed to this, so that knowledge and discussion of the incident can be kept in Regimental confidence.

Millington is brought in and the procedure explained to him by the Adjutant: "A Subalterns Court consists of five officers. One president and four members. There will also be one officer prosecuting, and one defending. Verdict will be by vote of the five. A Subalterns Court Martial has no official existence, gentlemen. It is outside the normal structure of discipline and command. Should a senior officer become officially aware of it, he would be obliged to end it. However, make no mistake. The powers of this court are summary and absolute. There is no appeal to higher authority. Do I make myself plain? . . . . . As to witnesses, you may, by tradition, require any officer of whatever rank to appear before you. You may also call civilian personnel. But should you choose to call a senior officer, gentlemen, his appearance before this court will in no sense affect his official knowledge of these proceedings, which do not exist. Do you understand me?"

Millington is amused at these contradictions. The Adjutant informs them all coldly that he will preside over the court, whose members will be Boulton, Hart, Winters and Truly. Fothergill is to prosecute, Drake will defend; Drake is reluctant to take on the assignment but must do his duty, since Millington indicates that he accepts the choice of counsel.

The court will convene at midnight tonight here in the Mess (Pradah Singh will be in attendance but must not be noticed) and for as many nights thereafter as necessary to complete the trial.

The Adjutant, along with Drake after sending Millington out under guard and the others off to their day's duty, consoles him: "I don't think you need to fear to find yourself guilty by association." Drake understands that by tradition he must defend Millington to the best of his ability.

ADJUTANT: . . . . . Any young subaltern would appreciate your dilemma. Though I don't think that, in this particular instance, you will need to embarrass yourself unduly. It is very much a fait accompli, is it not?

DRAKE: Still it is, of course, my duty to defend Mister Millington in the best manner that I can. I see that now, sir.

ADJUTANT: Naturally you will be required to find whatever you can to say in his favor.

DRAKE: No, I mean to say, it is a matter of honor, is it not, sir? The honor of the Regiment demands that Mister Millington be properly defended.

ADJUTANT: . . . As I say, it is necessary to go through the motions. But there. You are no fool, Mister Drake. You know what is required of you.

DRAKE: . . . To be fair, sir.

ADJUTANT: Just so. To be fair. To the Regiment. Good. Excellent. Carry on, Mister Drake.

The Adjutant leaves, and Millington comes in to consult with his defending counsel. Harshly, Drake makes it clear that he has no taste for this assignment, and that in spite of this Millington will probably get a fairer trial than he deserves.

Millington tells Drake his story of the incident. Being a bit drunk, always looking for an excuse to be discharged from the Regiment, and seeing Mrs. Hasseltine enter the Folly, he recognized a chance "to combine business with pleasure." He followed her and "Endeavored to touch her . . . . . to come to grips with her. Without, it must be admitted, any marked success."

Millington does not know how Mrs. Hasseltine came to be in the appalling condition of hysteria and torn dress. He remembers the events well enough to know that he did not leave her in that state. He is perfectly willing to plead guilty, though. Drake advises him that he cannot; he must plead not guilty to ensure a hearing.

DRAKE: You are very proud of yourself, aren't you Millington?

MILLINGTON: . . . It was necessary.

DRAKE: Necessary. To assault an older woman, simply in order to—

MILLINGTON: In heaven's name, anyone would think I'd raped the blasted female.

DRAKE: Didn't you?

MILLINGTON: My dear Arthur, I took hold of her arm, she pulled away, I took hold of it again—and wallop! She did me more damage than I her.

DRAKE: How so?

MILLINGTON: Well, look, my dear fellow. (Pulls forward right ear.) I've a gash that must be every bit of two inches long.

DRAKE: . . . That is the work of Mrs. Hasseltine?

MILLINGTON: It certainly isn't the work of myself.

DRAKE: How did she do it?

MILLINGTON: She hit me, Arthur.

DRAKE: With what?

MILLINGTON: I haven't the faintest idea. It felt at the time like the Cawnpore cannon. Laid me out cold.

Drake doesn't believe Millington and cannot defend him on the grounds that Millington in reality did nothing to the lady. Millington reminds Drake that the defense is *supposed* to fail—that's the way the Adjutant wants it. Drake replies angrily: "Well, you'll get a fair trial, Millington! I shall see to that! Much as I should prefer to prosecute you, I shall defend you to the utmost of my ability! For I, at least, have some conception of where my duty lies!"

The two young officers exit, the lights fade to night. Pradah Singh and the Waiters set up the room for the trial.

Scene 2

At midnight, a long table with five chairs upstage awaits the members of the court. The prosecution's table and chair is at right, the defense's at left and the witness chair at center.

Millington, relaxed, and Drake, tense, are the first to arrive; Pradah Singh shows them their places. Then come the members of the court, with Adjutant Harper as president, and the prosecutor, Fothergill.

Winters reads the charge: "That on the seventeenth instant, the accused officer, Second Lieutenant Millington, E., serving with this Regiment, did attack, wound and assault Mrs. Marjorie Hasseltine, then a guest of this Regiment, the widow of the late Major Robert Hasseltine, also of this Regiment. That in this, as in his prior actions, he has grossly insulted his brother officers, he has betrayed the trust reposed in him by his Colonel and his brother officers, he has brought the name of this Regiment into dishonor and disrepute, and has conducted himself in a manner unbecoming an officer and a gentleman."

Millington pleads "Indifferent" but Drake quickly interposes "Not guilty." The Adjutant warns Millington that if he does not hold his tongue he will be removed from the room and the proceedings continued in his absence.

The prosecution's first witness is the Doctor, who testifies that Mrs. Hasseltine was the victim of "a most gross and cowardly assault" on the evening in question; that she identified Millington as her attacker not only in the hysteria of the evening but calmly and in the presence of Major Wimborne after she had recovered her composure; and that Millington not only bears a scar from the encounter but freely admits that he was the attacker.

Cross-examining, Drake asks about the lady's injuries. The Doctor describes them as skinned and bruised wrists, arms, hands, legs, knees, and "otherwise cut about the body." The Adjutant forestalls Drake from questions about rape—Millington is charged with assault only, not rape, so that testimony along this line would be irrelevant.

DOCTOR: The shock to the nervous system—to the emotions of the patient —is extreme. You saw for yourself, Mister Drake. Mrs. Hasseltine was in a state of terror—bordering, in my opinion, on acute hysteria.

DRAKE: . . . . . I am not clear, Doctor . . . as to exactly why . . . Mrs. Hasseltine was so afraid.

DOCTOR: I cannot believe that is a serious comment, Mr. Drake.

DRAKE: I mean to say, Mister Millington is not a large man, sir. On the day that you examined us, you said that you would have to "put some meat on him."

ADJUTANT: We appear to have strayed yet again from the purpose of these proceedings, Mister Drake.

DRAKE: But it is surely relevant, Mister President, that Mister Millington is hardly capable of any . . . serious assault on Mrs. Hasseltine, particularly if he were affected by alcohol at the time . . .

Millington is attentive now.

DOCTOR: It is surely well known that a man may find many times his strength in a bottle?

DRAKE: But—Doctor . . .

ADJUTANT: Mister Drake. This court will not accept drunkenness as mitigation of any act on the part of Mister Millington.

Drake has one more question for the Doctor: "Would you not expect a woman of Mrs. Hasseltine's character to be able easily to deal with importunate advances?" The Adjutant chokes off the answer—the court has not been convened to investigate the character of Mrs. Hasseltine. Drake argues that Fothergill had warned them about her character their first day on the post, that it is relevant to the matter in hand, and that he must be allowed to explore this subject. The Adjutant will not permit it: "So far as this court is concerned, Mrs. Hasseltine is a woman of the highest character and probity."

Drake grasps at one last straw.

DRAKE: Well surely on the evidence, Mister Millington is made not stronger, but weaker by alcohol?

DOCTOR: Mr. Drake, since you persist in pursuing this matter, I am forced to tell you that in my opinion Mister Millington is on the point of becoming a complete and incurable drunkard. It is almost certain therefore that there would be periods when he would have no control whatsoever over his actions.

DRAKE (to Millington; stunned): . . . Is this true?

MILLINGTON: Don't sound so shocked, for Christ's sake.

There is a strange, taut, overstrung mixture of amusement, contempt—almost sub-hysteria in Millington at this point.

Millington ridicules Drake for trying to put up a real defense instead of merely going through the motions, as the Regiment wants him to. He seems to want to be thrown out of the court as he wants to be thrown out of the Regiment, and for once the Adjutant understands: "I have every sympathy with your point of view. You are entitled to rejoin your escort if you wish." Millington leaves the room after a parting shot at Drake: "What a bourgeois little creature you are, to be sure, Arthur."

Drake, who finds himself suddenly and unaccountably the object of general disapproval, has no further questions for the Doctor. Fothergill asks Drake to accept a written deposition in place of a personal appearance for the next witness, Mrs. Hasseltine. Drake needs time to consider this, so the Adjutant adjourns the court until the next evening, asking Drake to remain behind.

The Adjutant all but orders Drake to plead Millington guilty, as the defendant so clearly wishes, and get the whole affair over with. He also tells Drake to accept Mrs. Hasseltine's deposition, but Drake feels that the accused must be permitted to face his accuser.

The Adjutant hints that only through Mrs. Hasseltine's good will have they been able to avoid an open complaint and trial and full public disgrace of the Regiment; that in retribution the Regiment won't permit Millington to be discharged and go home but will keep him two, five, even ten years until he learns his lesson.

Drake asks to be relieved of this trial duty, but the Adjutant refuses. Just after he goes, an Indian woman, Lal, appears on the verandah and approaches

Drake to offer the cryptic advice: "Ask about the bleeding, sahib! And Mrs. Bandanai . . ."

Lal flees at the approach of Pradah Singh, who tells Drake that the Indian woman is the servant of Mrs. Hasseltine. Drake asks Pradah Singh to arrange a meeting with Mrs. Bandanai.

The lights fade, then come up with the stage still set for the court.

Scene 3

The next night, Millington comes in with the intention of changing his plea to guilty, but is genuinely shaken by Drake's news that his punishment would be to remain in the Regiment for two years or more, "learning his lesson," instead of being sent home.

The court enters, all its members clearly and visibly angry at Drake, who has insisted that Mrs. Hasseltine appear in person, not merely by deposition. She is called to testify at once, whether Drake is now ready to question her or not.

Mrs. Hasseltine enters and takes the witness chair. The prosecutor, Fothergill, elicits from her the testimony that on the night of the 17th she was attacked, Millington was her attacker, and she is sure of "both his identity and his intentions."

Much to the Adjutant's displeasure and Mrs. Hasseltine's inconvenience, Drake insists on his right to call another witness before questioning this one. Drake's chosen witness is the Second in Command, and the lady goes to wait outside while Roach comes in to testify.

Roach tells the court that he actually witnessed the incident while making his 2 a.m. tour of inspection as Officer of the Week.

ROACH: As I passed the Folly, I heard what sounded like some sort of altercation among the shrubbery and trees just there. I stopped. And then I heard Mister Millington's voice. I am not certain as to what he said, except that he appeared to be pleading with someone. But then I heard Mrs. Hasseltine—very sharply and clearly. She said: "I have already told you, Mister Millington, your—advances are not only . . . offensive to me, but pointless." Or words very much to that effect.

DRAKE: She must have sounded angry, sir.

ROACH: She did, indeed. Extremely.

DRAKE: And frightened?

ROACH: No. I would have said she sounded—in command of the situation, rather than afraid.

DRAKE: . . . I see. And then, sir?

ROACH: Well I immediately stepped in among the trees to put an end to this nonsense. But it was extremely dark in there, Mister Drake—in the end I could make them out only from their voices—and then against the paler color of the stonework.

DRAKE: They were fighting, sir?

ROACH: Mister Millington had hold of Mrs. Hasseltine's arm. But before

I was able to intervene, she had broken away from him—had ordered him to leave her alone—and had begun to walk angrily back through the trees towards the Mess.

DRAKE: To walk, sir?

ROACH: Yes.

DRAKE: Not to run?

ROACH: No, no. I could see her quite clearly. The lights of the Mess were directly beyond her, if you understand me. About thirty or forty yards away.

DRAKE: Still, she must have appeared extremely distressed.

ROACH: I should have said . . . angry, rather than distressed.

Immediately after this, there was quite a bit of commotion (Roach testifies), with officers running and finally Mrs. Hasseltine arriving at the mess "in an anguished condition. Extremely so. Far more than I should have imagined." Millington's behavior, while reprehensible (Roach insists) did not seem quite so shocking or aggressive.

In the Adjutant's judgment, Roach has "given an extremely detailed account of precisely the offense with which Mister Millington is charged." Roach testifies further that for all he knows, Millington may have been knocked down when Mrs. Hasseltine broke from him "with some force."

Drake dismisses Roach and recalls Mrs. Hasseltine to the witness chair. The Adjutant assures her that the Second in Command has just corroborated her story.

Under Drake's questioning, Mrs. Hasseltine explains that she sought a brief respite from the ball, a moment of solitude seated at a stone bench there on the grounds, when Millington approached her. At first she was not alarmed, but he persisted, "determinedly and viciously drunk," and "made it absolutely plain that he was determined to use me as a means of having himself dismissed from this Regiment."

Mrs. Hasseltine had no alternative (she testifies) but to ward off Millington even with fists and arms, perhaps striking him with her bag. Drake calls attention to the gash behind Millington's ear—no lady's fist or handbag could inflict such a wound. Drake tells the court that he has searched the grounds, and there is nothing anywhere around that the lady could have used to strike such a blow. The Adjutant insists that Millington could have stumbled against a tree or wall when the lady broke from him. For the moment Drake must accept this possible explanation of the gash, even though Millington, himself puzzled, insists aloud that she struck him.

Drake turns back to the witness.

DRAKE: . . . . . You then ran—screaming—a matter of forty yards or so to the Mess.

ADJUTANT: Mister Drake. We already have the evidence of the Second in Command that in the first instance—

DRAKE: Of course, Mister President. I am sorry. In the first instance you walked, ma'am.

Slight pause.

And then perhaps you ran? Perhaps you feared he might attack you again?

MRS. HASSELTINE: ... That thought did enter my mind, yes.

DRAKE: He didn't, of course, ma'am?

MRS. HASSELTINE: No, Mister Drake, he did not.

DRAKE: Then he must have attacked you with extreme severity on the first occasion. Exactly what did he do, ma'am?

MRS. HASSELTINE: Well, he ...

DRAKE: Did he take hold of your arm?

MRS. HASSELTINE: He did, yes.

DRAKE: And he pulled you about?

MRS. HASSELTINE: Yes.

DRAKE: And then, ma'am?

MRS. HASSELTINE: Well, he ...

DRAKE: Yes, ma'am?

MRS. HASSELTINE: ... Really, I cannot be expected to remember—

DRAKE: Well, did he perhaps attempt to place his hand on your bosom? Your dress was torn—

ADJUTANT: Mr. Drake—

MRS. HASSELTINE: He may have done, yes.

DRAKE: Well, did he, or didn't he, ma'am?

MRS. HASSELTINE: I can't remember, Mister Drake!

DRAKE: But this was a terrifying experience for you, Mrs. Hasseltine. You ran, screaming, all the way into the Mess!

MRS. HASSELTINE *(rises; blazing):* Exactly what are you implying?

ADJUTANT *(jumps up):* That is all, Mister Drake! Sit down!

DRAKE: I have only one more question for this—

ADJUTANT: No, Mister Drake! Be seated!

Pause.

DRAKE: Why are you lying, Mrs. Hasseltine?

ADJUTANT: Mister Drake!

MRS. HASSELTINE: How dare you! How dare you, Mister Drake!

ADJUTANT: Ma'am, I'm sorry. This—

MRS. HASSELTINE *(storming out):* I shall tolerate no more of this, Mister President! You may play your childish games in future without me!

She is gone. A shocked silence. Millington dazed, baffled. In silence the Adjutant comes round the table and down to Drake.

ADJUTANT: You have finished yourself here, Mister Drake. Do you hear me. You are finished here.

DRAKE *(sick at heart):* ... If what I have seen in this court room ... is typical of the honor of this Regiment ... then I shall be only too happy to depart.

ADJUTANT: And we shall be only too happy to accommodate you.

(Turns away.)

Now the rest of you, pay attention to me.

DRAKE: That woman is lying, Mister Harper.

ADJUTANT: Be silent, sir! *(Pause.)* This court will reconvene at midnight tomorrow, when this matter will be ended. You hear me? Mister Drake! Ended!

DRAKE *(pause; nods slowly):* . . . Yes, Mister President.

ADJUTANT: Very well. That is all.

> *He stalks out. Pause. The others leave . . . Drake is near to tears, but for him this is not possible. Millington has no way to express sympathy for this man. Pause.*

DRAKE: . . . I thought this was a regiment of honor.

MILLINGTON *(embarrassed):* So it is, my dear fellow. A regiment of the highest honor. As you yourself have made plain to me.

DRAKE: . . . It appears that I owe you an apology, Mister Millington.

Millington wonders why Mrs. Hasseltine should lie and repeats that she hit him extremely hard. He cautions Drake to do as the Adjutant wishes if he wants to remain with the Regiment.

MILLINGTON: You know, Arthur, if you . . . wish to remain here . . . you really will have to abandon this enterprise. It isn't too late.

DRAKE: I can survive without your sympathy, Millington. Yours least of all.

MILLINGTON: You disappoint me, Arthur. Is it just pride, then? Wounded pride?

DRAKE: . . . Let us call it principle. Why not? "Bourgeois" principle. But that, of course, is something you would not understand. *(Turns away.)*

MILLINGTON: No. That is true. I am told, though, that it is invincible.

DRAKE: Are you? Well. *(Turns; great pain.)* Then you have met . . . an invincible man, have you not?

MILLINGTON: . . . Goodnight, Arthur.

Millington departs, and Pradah Singh ushers into Drake's presence Mrs. Bandanai, extremely shy and retiring, not wishing to be involved. Under Drake's questioning, however, she divulges that she, too, was "attacked," about six months previously. As Pradah Singh interprets her story (Mrs. Bandanai speaks no English): "She was with an officer. She had been with him, lain with him, sahib . . . She was alone though, he had left the bungalow . . . . . She was naked, sahib, naked on the bed . . . . . There came another man, I think she said, another man in scarlet and gold . . . . . He made her get off the bed, sahib, he made her run about on her hands and knees . . . . . She had to make noises, noises like a . . . he had a sword . . . . . It is the Game, sahib, as they play it in the Mess. Sticking the pig. With a sword. ᵀrom behind. As it runs . . ."

Drake, shocked, demands to know who could have done such a thing. Mrs. Bandanai identifies her attacker as "Captain Scarlett"—the dead hero, Captain Scarlett, whose tunic is preserved in the glass case in the Mess. Mrs. Bandanai runs off, as Drake wonders "What's happening . . . ?"

ACT III

Scene 1

The next midnight, the trial is preparing to resume. Drake brings in a paper-wrapped package and places it on the defense table, where Millington is waiting. Drake assures the accused that he knows he was telling the truth.

DRAKE: You may have been stupid, but you were not vicious.

MILLINGTON: No . . . Besides, I rather like her, as a matter of fact . . .

DRAKE: . . . Look here. I want you to trust me, Millington. Tonight's proceedings will not be pleasant, but you must remain silent whatever happens.

MILLINGTON *(awkwardly):* That is what I wanted to speak to you about . . .

DRAKE: . . . What?

MILLINGTON *(awkward):* Look here, Arthur, I went riding this morning . . .

DRAKE: I'm afraid I don't—

MILLINGTON: No, no, let me finish, please . . . I received this note from the Colonel. Yes. "The Colonel presents his compliments to Mister Millington, and wonders whether Mister Millington might care to exercise the Colonel's string again. The Colonel would of course be grateful if Mister Millington would endeavor to maintain contact with the Colonel's animals on this occasion." I like horses, Arthur . . .

Pause.

DRAKE: Millington . . .

MILLINGTON: It is in one, do you see, Arthur? One is not to escape. I felt this morning, as you must . . . that one is . . . intended for a particular place.

Drake looks away.

So you see, Arthur, you are . . . destroying yourself here for no reason . . . I . . .

DRAKE: You are not to concern yourself with me.

MILLINGTON: But I do, Arthur, I do . . . I know what this place means to you.

DRAKE: No. No. I do not expect to remain here.

The court convenes. Drake intends to recall the Doctor, and the Adjutant reminds him that the whole matter is to be settled this night, regardless.

Drake accepts written depositions from the Colonel, Wimborne and two representatives of the Lancers, so the prosecution has no further witnesses (Drake sets these depositions to one side, without reading them). Fothergill rests the prosecution's case.

Drake calls the Doctor and wants to know: "Why did you not tell us that she (Mrs. Hasseltine) had been attacked with a sword?" Millington and the court are mystified by this line of inquiry; Millington, being a subaltern, wore no sword that night. The Doctor doubts Drake can prove that a sword was used, but Drake persists: Didn't the Doctor also examine Mrs. Bandanai recently, and wasn't she also suffering from sword wounds? The Doctor admits that it is possible, yes.

Drake reminds the doctor of the Regimental Game, played in the Mess with a dummy but having originated in the field where, as Drake puts it, "To penetrate the anus of a living animal with steel . . . . is a revolting game."

Drake then suggests to the Doctor that someone played the Game with Mrs. Bandanai forced into the role of the pig. The Doctor is shocked—such a thought has never occurred to him—but he admits that Mrs. Bandanai's wounds might be consistent with this "horrible" explanation.

Drake produces in evidence from his paper-wrapped package the dress worn by Mrs. Hasseltine that fateful evening (she had given it to be destroyed by an Indian woman who had decided to preserve it). He demonstrates to the witness and to the court a rip in it corresponding to a wound on Mrs. Hasseltine's thigh: "It has absolutely straight, uniform sides, has it not? Is it not a cut—such as might be made by a blade in piercing the material?"

Millington rises to protest aloud that he didn't attack the lady with a sword —but no one is saying he did, and besides, he had not yet joined the Regiment when Mrs. Bandanai was attacked six months ago. And now that the facts have been pointed out to him, the Doctor is forced to admit that it is at least possible that the injuries and the incidents were connected, caused by the same person.

Drake declares to the court his belief that there were two attacks on Mrs. Hasseltine that evening, the inept one by Millington and the injurious one by some person who knocked Millington on the head with his sword pommel and then wounded the lady with the point. When Drake begins a line of questioning designed to disclose who the guilty person really was ("How did Mrs. Bandanai come to the hospital, Doctor? Was she brought? . . . By whom? An officer of this regiment?"), the Doctor refuses to answer any more questions and leaves the room.

The Adjutant—now shaken with doubt and puzzlement—permits Drake to recall the Second in Command. Drake wants Roach to review some events of Regimental history, to describe in detail how the hero Captain John Scarlett died.

ROACH: Well . . . John Scarlett, Major Wimborne and I were subalterns together. At the battle of Ratjahpur, John and I were taken prisoner. When he heard about it, Major Wimborne got together a team of volunteers to attempt a rescue. He didn't know that they were holding John and me separately, some two or three hundred yards apart. As it happened, he came to the place they were holding me first, and we were able to break out of the rebel position. But when we went down the line to rescue John, we were too late. He was already dead.

DRAKE: How exactly had he died, sir?

ROACH: He was flayed, Mister Drake, flayed alive.

DRAKE: I see . . .

ROACH: Not a particularly . . . agreeable spectacle.

DRAKE: . . . But he was recognizable, sir?

ROACH: Well . . . the face was terribly distorted, of course. Flaying involves the . . . removal of the skin, as you probably know.

DRAKE: Yes, sir.

ROACH: Then, too, the body had been mutilated. The eyes and tongue had been put out . . . the sex removed.

DRAKE: But it had been . . . Captain John Scarlett?

ROACH: Oh yes. There's no question of that whatever.

Drake turns to another subject: the night of the attack on Mrs. Hasseltine. After the lady turned away from Millington to return to the Mess, and before she screamed, (Drake wants to know) what happened? Roach testifies that as far as he knows, nothing happened. He had turned away to inspect the perimeter piquet and only turned back when the lady screamed. He remembers that Wimborne, Boulton and Winters ran past him. In addition, Roach remembers that when he first saw the couple "I had a curious impression that . . . that I was not alone. That I was being . . . watched by someone else . . ."

Drake informs Roach that they have pretty well established that Mrs. Hasseltine was attacked a second time that evening by someone whose identity is unknown. Roach, terribly distressed at this information, wants to warn the Colonel at once, but at this moment the Colonel enters the Mess.

The Colonel is gravely disturbed at the turning the trial has taken and feels that loyalty to the Regiment has been breached. He dismisses all the officers except Harper and Drake, and it is against the latter that he launches his anger.

COLONEL: . . . . . You have been permitted to come to a regiment of the very highest honor and integrity, Mr. Drake. A regiment whose history and traditions stretch far back into the past—far beyond the life span of any single man . . . And you have chosen to repay this privilege—with an insult so . . . intolerable, so . . . wounding—

DRAKE: Permission to speak, Colonel—

COLONEL: No, sir! You have nothing to say to me. I am barely able to bring myself to speak to you . . .

DRAKE: But these are facts, Colonel, which I can prove to be true.

COLONEL: You cannot prove an impossibility.

DRAKE: I'm sorry, Colonel, but—

COLONEL: No, sir! There is—no officer in this Regiment—capable of . . . such an act.

> *The Colonel is struggling to reject something which strikes at the basic premise of his whole life.*

ADJUTANT: Colonel . . .

COLONEL: No, sir!

DRAKE: I beg you to ask the Adjutant, Colonel—

COLONEL: I am no better pleased with the Adjutant than I am with yourself in this affair.

ADJUTANT: With your permission, Colonel.

COLONEL: Well?

ADJUTANT: I know that I am justly rebuked . . .

COLONEL: You are, sir.

ADJUTANT: But I cannot in honor say other than that I believe Mister Drake to be right in this affair.

> *Pause. Colonel is shocked.*

The Colonel does not wish to review such facts as torn dresses and sword thrusts; but in his heart he knows that Mrs. Bandanai was attacked and that this truth was hidden from him, even though he insists that "We do not—lie to one another in this Mess! Gentlemen do not question the honor of other gentlemen, Mister Drake!"

Drake warns the Colonel that an assailant who has already struck twice in such fashion will undoubtedly attack again. Drake tells his Colonel that he can prove it was a Regimental officer by continuing the trial and re-calling Mrs. Hasseltine to the witness chair. Drake stakes his own honor on this: "I can best serve you and this Regiment by examining the matter here—where I alone shall suffer if I am mistaken—rather than in the public forum to which you would be compelled, Colonel."

Harper also pledges his honor, and the Colonel reluctantly agrees to let the trial continue the following night—and he himself will be present. When the Colonel has gone, Drake thanks the Adjutant for his support. The Adjutant replies as he leaves: "It is necessary, at all times, to support the honor of the Regiment."

Drake is staring back and forth between Captain Scarlett's stained tunic in the glass case and Mrs. Hasseltine's torn dress, as the lights go down and then up again to bridge 24 hours.

Scene 2

The next night at almost midnight, Roach is confiding to Wimborne that he fears injury to the Regiment out of this affair, and he feels some responsibility for not having dealt with the matter the evening it happened. Wimborne reassures him, and as Roach leaves Mrs. Hasseltine appears on the verandah. She tells Wimborne that she has been called again as a witness and warns him "They must know."

WIMBORNE: Listen to me! Nobody knows anything! Nobody will discover anything! Just so long as you remain silent.

> *Crosses away from her. Pause.*

MRS. HASSELTINE: I don't know that I am any longer prepared to.

WIMBORNE: What the hell does that mean?

MRS. HASSELTINE: I have been humiliated once because of you, Alastair. I do not intend to be humiliated again!

WIMBORNE: Listen to me! You are the last person here who can afford to tell the truth! Remember that!

MRS. HASSELTNE: Oh! What does that mean?

WIMBORNE: You owe us everything, Marge! Your house, your servants, your land; everything. Without this Regiment, you are nothing.

MRS. HASSELTINE: . . . I see. Thank you for reminding me of my place, in this community.

The others, including the Colonel, enter for tonight's session of the Subalterns Court. Again, Drake carries his wrapped package. Mrs. Hasseltine is called to the witness chair, and after reminding her of her previous testimony Drake places his package on the floor and slowly draws Mrs. Hasseltine's torn dress from it, the dress which she wore on the night in question and had asked an Indian woman to burn.

Drake forces Mrs. Hasseltine's attention to the tunic in the glass case and indicates that he knows the truth about what happened that evening. "Were you attacked by Captain Scarlett?" Drake asks Mrs. Hasseltine, and to the Colonel's consternation the lady admits "Yes, I was."

Drake further elicits from Mrs. Hasseltine the testimony that Millington is "The only gentle man I have met in all my years with this Regiment" and she has no charge or complaint against him of any kind.

DRAKE: Thank you, ma'am. I must now ask you about the night of the seventeenth . . .

MRS. HASSELTINE: . . . He came—so suddenly. Out of the darkness. My name. And then . . . No face. The lights on the Plain. No face . . .
Absolutely still, calm.

DRAKE: . . . He had a sword?

MRS. HASSELTINE: I tried to run. But I fell. He . . . He cut me. And then . . . he said . . .

DRAKE: . . . What did he say, ma'am?

MRS. HASSELTINE: He laughed and said . . . "A point, Marge. A veritable point . . ."
She covers her face with one hand—not weeping. The Colonel lowers his head.

DRAKE: I'm sorry to persist in these questions, ma'am. But you have only to tell us who he was . . .

MRS. HASSELTINE: I don't know who he was . . .

DRAKE: But you must, ma'am . . .

MRS. HASSELTINE: I don't, Mr. Drake . . .

DRAKE: Then why did you accuse Mister Millington, ma'am?

MRS. HASSELTINE: . . . I had to do something.

DRAKE: Why, Mrs. Hasseltine? Unless you recognized your attacker and knew that you could never accuse that man?

MRS. HASSELTINE: I only knew . . .

DRAKE: What Major Wimborne chose to tell you?

MRS. HASSELTINE: I have nothing to say. Nothing!

DRAKE: But . . . his voice, ma'am. You must have recognized his voice.

MRS. HASSELTINE: It was the voice of John Scarlett . . .

DRAKE: But—

MRS. HASSELTINE *(terrible amused weariness):* Don't you understand, Mister Drake? It doesn't matter which one of these men it was. They are all the same. Stupid, cruel men, who treat—pigs and women—as though they were . . . objects . . .

COLONEL *(rises):* Mrs. Hasseltine, you are overwrought.

MRS. HASSELTINE *(rises):* Colonel. Do you not yet know what you are sire to? They are all John Scarlett. Every one of them.

COLONEL: That will be all, ma'am.

MRS. HASSELTINE: Yes. *(Nods.)* Oh, yes.

> *Crosses to exit.*

It has taken me too long to accept what I have always known. You are scum.

> *She goes. Silence.*

COLONEL: Mister Drake. Explain.

DRAKE: Colonel, there is an officer in this Regiment who dresses in the uniform worn by this Regiment until shortly after the Mutiny; and in that fashion attacks women.

The Colonel argues that no one was dressed in that way the night of the ball. Drake explains that perhaps the tunic isn't always essential to the impersonation of Captain Scarlett.

Major Wimborne is called in to testify. He is in an angry mood, but Drake questions him coldly about Mrs. Bandanai. Wimborne admits that he is the officer who brought her to the "wog" orderlies in the hospital. She had spent the evening in Wimborne's bungalow and was attacked when Wimborne, as Officer of the Week, absented himself briefly to inspect the piquets. Wimborne didn't consider this attack on an Indian woman important enough to be worth the trouble it might cause by reporting it, so he didn't.

Wimborne can hardly believe that the attack on Mrs. Hasseltine was of the same nature, or that it could have had anything to do with Captain Scarlett ("I brought in his remains myself"). Drake tells Wimborne that the likeliest suspect would be the Regiment's champion sportsman, the acknowledged champion at the Game—Wimborne himself. But Wimborne has an alibi—he has many witnesses, including Fothergill, to the fact that he was dancing at the time Mrs. Hasseltine was assaulted. Drake is stunned, his whole case awry.

DRAKE *(quietly; to Wimborne):* You know, sir.

WIMBORNE: What . . . ?

DRAKE: You know who Captain Scarlett is.

WIMBORNE: He's dead.

DRAKE: Sir, if you do nothing, this man will attack again.

WIMBORNE *(slightest hesitation):* Then I must remember to stand with my back to the wall, mustn't I?

DRAKE: Sir!

WIMBORNE *(rises; turns away):* I cannot help you, Mister Drake.

Drake recalls the Second in Command to question him about the vague presence he sensed the night of the attack on Mrs. Hasseltine. He describes the scene for Roach, trying to recreate it in the officer's mind and jog his memory. But it is no use—Roach cannot remember any concrete details. They are so near and yet so far.

Disappointed, with a sense of failure, Drake concludes his case. The Colonel reassures Drake that he has done well and takes charge, directing the Subalterns Court to proceed with its verdict on Millington which is of course "not guilty."

The Colonel tells Millington, "You have been unjustly treated by this Regiment. You have yourself behaved with some stupidity. I trust we may see a new beginning." The Adjutant congratulates Millington, who turns to Drake and thanks him for his "bourgeois principles." Millington goes off with the other subalterns to celebrate, a brother-in-arms at last.

The Adjutant confesses to the Colonel that "I would that we had done less well" and exits. Drake, too, is unhappy about the outcome, and he has tendered his resignation to the Colonel because "I find that I cannot . . . put my honor onto a regiment. Or onto a man. It is what I am . . . what I do." The Colonel accepts Drake's resignation with sincere regret.

Wimborne comes in and apologizes to the Colonel for concealing the truth from him.

WIMBORNE: I couldn't tell you, Ben. You would have been obliged to take official action. The Regiment could never have survived the scandal. What we have hidden, has been hidden too long.

COLONEL: . . . I want the matter ended now.

WIMBORNE: Very well. Then leave it to me. It is a matter of honor. It will be settled in the traditional manner.

Pause.

COLONEL: . . . A matter of honor.

WIMBORNE: It is not as you think, Ben.

COLONEL: Oh, yes. I am the Regiment. What I have allowed to happen, is what I am.

Slight pause.

It is as well my time here is nearly done. You will not again speak to me of honor.

He exits.

Wimborne studies the tunic for a moment, as the room grows darker, and there is *"the sound of hunting cries, laughter—but strange, not real, distant, as though remembered . . ."*

Wimborne orders Pradah Singh to turn out all the lamps except one on the table, upon which Wimborne places a revolver which he has carefully loaded. He sends Pradah Singh away and informs Drake that he is finally going to get his wish to see Captain Scarlett. When Wimborne turns down the last lamp, Scarlett will appear: "We talk together, Mister Drake. He likes to have someone to talk to."

Wimborne turns down the last lamp, leaving only moonlight to illuminate the verandah and the Mess.

WIMBORNE: You think this is just a matter of honor, don't you?

DRAKE: ... Isn't it?

WIMBORNE: No, Mister Drake, it is not. It is a matter of comradeship, friendship. Now you wait in there. You can watch, if wish. But you will not intervene. Do you understand me?

DRAKE: But sir ... !

WIMBORNE: Be quiet! Look, just do as you're told!

> *A voice beyond the moonlight. One we have not heard. Captain Scarlett.*

SCARLETT: Alastair! Are you there, you old rogue? !

WIMBORNE: Get in there—quickly!

DRAKE: But ... !

WIMBORNE (*pushing him*): Get in there!

> *Drake is forced just inside card room doorway. Wimborne crosses to sit by table with lamp and gun. Silence. Intense moonlight. An approach. Booted feet on the verandah. A commanding, faceless figure steps into view. The bright moonlight, coming from behind, hides his face. The voice is amused, harsh.*

SCARLETT (*entering*): Alastair, are you there?

WIMBORNE: I'm here, John.

SCARLETT: Well, turn up the lamp, you silly bugger.

> *Wimborne turns up lamp. Scarlett has the face—but only the face—of Lionel Roach.*

That's better. Now we can see what we're doing.

> *Scarlett crosses to showcase, opens it to take out and put on uniform jacket.*

WIMBORNE: You won't be needing the jacket tonight, John. You won't be going anywhere tonight.

SCARLETT: Why not? Because of that little swine Lionel Roach? That was a close call when he started talking about the man he almost saw. He damned nearly did see me too, the little runt. Damned nearly gave me away.

WIMBORNE: The little runt, as you called him, never found it necessary to attack women.

SCARLETT: Oh go on, Alastair. Bit of sport! Right in your country, that is.

WIMBORNE: No, John.

SCARLETT (*fiercely*): Well no matter! I'm getting stronger, Alastair ... I've almost taken over from the little swine once for all ...

WIMBORNE: That's why we must be rid of you now.

SCARLETT: What ... ?

> *Wimborne fires. The case shatters. The dummy plunges out. Scar-*

lett jerks as though shocked, puts hand to head in confusion, becomes Roach again, looks at Wimborne, recognizes him.

ROACH *(puzzled):* Alastair?

WIMBORNE: Lionel . . . look . . .

He points to the showcase. Roach turns slowly, looks at dummy, stares as though at his own dead body.

ROACH: No! No!

Tears jacket from himself, throws it away, covers eyes.

Oh God! I saw him! *(Stares at Wimborne.)* Alastair, I saw him!

WIMBORNE *(moves center to join Roach):* I know.

Roach sits.

ROACH: . . . It was me.

WIMBORNE: It was Scarlett.

ROACH: Oh God, it was me.

WIMBORNE: . . . You've done too much damage—I can no longer protect you . . . Do you understand?

Wimborne puts gun on table beside Roach. Long pause. Roach looks at gun.

ROACH: I understand. *(Pause.)* You will tell the Colonel that—Captain Scarlett—is dead.

Wimborne turns down the lamp and goes. There is a shot in the darkness. Curtain.

SLEUTH

A Play in Two Acts

BY ANTHONY SHAFFER

Cast and credits appear on page 299

ANTHONY SHAFFER was born in England, at Liverpool, in 1926, the twin brother of Peter Shaffer (also a playwright, who has won three Best Plays citations for Five Finger Exercise, The Royal Hunt of the Sun *and* Black Comedy). *Anthony came down from Cambridge in 1950—while at the university he edited its magazine,* Granta. *The twins collaborated on three mystery novels, the first,* How Doth the Little Crocodile? *under the pseudonym "Peter Anthony" and the other two under their full names. In 1951 Peter went to America to seek his fortune, while Anthony became in turn a barrister, an advertising man and a television writer and producer of commercials and documentaries.*

Pursuing his own writing career while his brother became a world-renowed playwright, Anthony turned from TV writing to the legitimate stage. Sleuth, *his theater debut, is a trans-Atlantic success. Anthony is also the author of several screen plays including the one for his brother's* Black Comedy *and an Antarctic story entitled* Fourbush and the Penguins.

Anthony Shaffer is married to Carolyn Soley, a former model. They have two daughters and live in England, dividing their time between London and Somerset.

Time: The present

Place: Andrew Wyke's country home in Wiltshire, England

ACT I

SNYOPSIS: On a summer evening, Andrew Wyke is seated at his desk in the center of his Norman manor house's large living room. A staircase winds out of the room to a minstrels' gallery on which are placed a wardrobe, grandfather clock and bureau. A basket hamper stands in the corridor leading to the other part of the house. There are games of all kinds—cards, dice, checkers, etc.—scattered around the room, and *"Sitting by the window, under the gallery, is a life-sized figure of a Laughing Sailor."*

As the clock strikes eight, Wyke is just finishing typing the last page of his latest mystery novel. Wyke is *"a strongly built, tall, fleshy man of 57, gone slightly to seed. His fair hair carries on it the suspicion that chemical aid has been invoked to keep the grey at bay. His face, sourly amused and shadowed with evaded self-knowledge, is beginning to reflect the absence of constant, arduous employment. He wears a smoking jacket and black tie."*

Wyke reads over the page he has just written and is rather self-satisfied with his fictional detective's—Inspector Merridew's—solution of the case. The doorbell rings offstage—it is Milo Tindle, the tenant of an estate cottage, and Wyke goes to the door and brings him back into the room. Tindle is *"about 35, slim, dark-haired and of medium height. He has a sharp, sallow face alive with a faintly Mediterranean wariness. Everything about him is neat, from his exactly parted hair to the squared-off white handkerchief in the breast pocket of his blue mohair suit."*

The men exchange courtesies and Andrew Wyke pours a drink for his guest Milo Tindle and raises the subject of detective stories, which he calls "the normal recreation of noble minds." He harks back to the golden age of this literary form "When every cabinet minister had a thriller by his bedside and all the detectives were titled."

ANDREW: . . . . . You know, even in these days I still set my own work among the gentry. And a great number of people enjoy it, in spite of the Welfare State.

MILO: I'm surprised they haven't done any of your stuff on television.

ANDREW: Oh, God forbid.

MILO: Well, they're always doing crime stories.

ANDREW: What— you mean those ghastly things where the police race around in cars and call all the suspects chummy?

MILO: Yes. That's the kind of thing.

ANDREW: Oh no. That's not my line of country at all. That is detective fact, not detective fiction.

MILO: And of course as such is of much less interest to noble minds.

ANDREW: Yes, yes, you've put it in a nutshell, my dear Milo, if I may so address you?

MILO: Of course.

ANDREW: Thank you, we need to be friendly. Now do sit down and let me get you another drink. I'm one up on you already.

Milo starts to sit in chair below staircase. Andrew moves to drinks table.

I understand you want to marry my wife.

A pause. Milo is disconcerted by the directness of the question.

You'll forgive me raising the matter, but as Marguerite is away for a few days, she's up in the North you know, visiting some relatives . . .

MILO: Is she?

ANDREW: Yes, so I thought it an appropriate time for a little chat.

MILO: Yes.

ANDREW: Well, is it true?

MILO: Well . . . Well, yes, with your permission of course.

Andrew behaves as though he were his wife's parent rather than her husband, asking Milo questions about his background and prospects. Milo is the son of an English farmer's daughter and a half-Italian, half-Jewish father. His original family name of Tindolini has been changed to Tindle, and he is in the travel business in Dulwich.

Milo admits frankly that he loves Andrew's wife Marguerite, that he has rented the cottage in order to be near her, and that he resents Andrew's frequent sarcastic references to her.

MILO: If you don't love Marguerite, you don't have to abuse her.

ANDREW: Never speak ill of the deadly, eh?

MILO: Now look here . . .

ANDREW: If I choose to say that my wife converses like a child of six, cooks like a Brightlingsea landlady, and makes love like a coelacanth, I shall.

MILO: That's just about enough . . .

ANDREW: And I certainly don't need her lover's permission to do so either. In fact, the only thing I need to know from you is, can you afford to take her off my hands?

MILO: Afford to . . .

ANDREW: Afford to support her in the style to which she wasn't accustomed before she met me, but now is.

MILO *(gestures around the room):* She won't need all this when we're married. It'll be a different life—a life of love and simplicity. Now go ahead —sneer at that. It's almost a national sport in this country—sneering at love.

ANDREW: I don't have to sneer at it. I simply don't believe you. For Marguerite, love is the fawning of a willing lap dog, and simplicity a square cut ten-carat diamond from Van Cleef and Arpels.

Milo is on the edge of anger, but Andrew jokes him out of it. Milo admits that he's somewhat pressed for funds at the moment, but he will manage. Milo in his turn taunts Andrew about "Tẽa, the Finnish lady who runs the sauna bath at Swindon."

ANDREW *(mock mystical):* Tẽa is a Karelian goddess. Her mother was Ilma, supreme divinity of the air; her father was Jumala, the great Creator. Her golden hair smells of pine, and her cobalt eyes are the secret forest pools of Finlandia.

MILO: I hear she's a scrubbed blonde with all the sex appeal of chilled Lysol.

ANDREW *(with dignity):* There are those who believe that cleanliness is next to sexiness. And if I were you, I wouldn't pay much attention to what Marguerite says. You can take it from me that Tẽa's an engaging little trollop, and she suits me mightily. Mind you, she takes a bit of keeping up with; it's a good thing I'm pretty much of an Olympic sexual athlete.

MILO: I suppose these days you're concentrating on the sprints rather than the long distance stuff.

ANDREW: Not so, dear boy. *(He sits.)* I'm in the pink of condition. I could copulate for England at any distance.

MILO: Well, they do say in Olympic circles, that the point is to take part, rather than to win, so I suppose there's hope for us all. Are you going to marry her?

ANDREW: Marry a goddess? I wouldn't presume. I might get turned into a birch tree for my audacity. Oh, no. I simply want to live with her.

And he and Tẽa, Andrew continues, are being annoyed by detectives Milo and Marguerite have hired to watch them. Milo admits that the detectives are "an insurance policy against you changing your mind about divorcing Marguerite."

Andrew wants a divorce, he assures Milo, but he wants to guarantee a permanent separation—he doesn't want Marguerite back on his hands after a couple of weeks. Marguerite, he insists, will not live on love alone; she requires liberal charge accounts, and on this subject Andrew has a proposition for Milo. As a hedge against devaluation, Andrew has invested some 135,000 pounds in jewelry for his wife. It is kept, not at the bank, but in a safe under the stairs of this house. Andrew has sent the servants away for the weekend and proposes that Milo steal the jewels. Andrew will see that a certain Amsterdam fence gives Milo at least 90,000 pounds for the loot, Andrew will collect the insurance, and they can all live happily ever after.

Milo's first reaction is: "A scummy little plot to defraud the insurance company"—but he keeps on listening to Andrew. The police are not stupid as in detective novels (Andrew admits), and they must rig the crime very carefully. Milo suspects that Andrew is really plotting to turn him into the police, as a husband's revenge, but Andrew convinces him that he doesn't want Marguerite back.

Milo finally agrees: "All right. I'll do it." Andrew starts to sketch out an

elaborate plan as though he were arranaging the events in a detective novel.
The first step is to choose a disguise from Andrew's hamper full of costumes.

MILO: . . . . . Haven't you just got an old pair of wellies, a raincoat, and a
sock that I can pull over my head?
ANDREW: Old pair of wellies and a sock? How dreary! That's the whole
trouble with crime today. No imagination. I mean, you tell me, does your
heart beat any faster when you hear that a truck load of cigarettes has been
knocked off in the Walworth Road?
MILO: Not particularly.
ANDREW: Well of course not. Or that a ninety-three-year-old night watchman has had his silly interfering old skull split open with a lead pipe?
MILO: Of course not.
ANDREW: Well, then, what's the matter with you? Where's your spunk? Let's
give our crime the true sparkle of the thirties, a little amateur aristocratic
quirkiness. Think of all that wonderful material. There's the ice dagger, the
poison that leaves no trace, the Regie cigarette stubbed in the ash tray, charred
violet notepaper in the grate, Dusenberg tire marks in the driveway, the gramo-
phone record simulating conversation, the clutching hand from behind the
arras, sinister Orientals, twin brothers from Australia—"Hi there, cobber, hi
there, blue"—where were you on the night of the thirteenth? I swear I didn't
do it, Inspector, I'm innocent, I tell you, innocent . . .
MILO: God, you've gone off like a firecracker!
ANDREW: And why not? We're on the brink of a great crime. Don't you
feel the need to give your old arch-enemy Inspector Plodder of the Yard a
run for his money? And you're the star, you're the who-what-dun-it!

They settle on a Joey-the-clown costume for Milo, who strips to his under-
wear and puts on the costume, complete with heavy boots. Andrew throws
Milo's clothes into the wardrobe upstairs and returns to give him the bag of
burglar's tools he will require for breaking in through the living room window,
and for opening the safe.
At Andrew's direction, Milo goes outside, places a ladder against the window and breaks into the room at gallery level. Under Andrew's orders, Milo
jimmies a bureau drawer and leaves a conspicuous mess signifying a burglar's
purposeful search.
Downstairs, Andrew blows the safe door open with a small charge of
gelignite. Milo joins him, takes the jewel box and jimmies it open. Admiring
the rubies, Milo puts the jewels in his pocket while Andrew sets about staging the next step: a struggle between homeowner and burglar. Andrew must
be supposed to have seen the thief at close quarters so that he can identify
him—misleadingly—to whatever Inspector Plodder shows up to investigate
the case.
Milo and Andrew stage a struggle in which Andrew cuffs Milo somewhat
too vigorously. But next the script might call for Milo to knock Andrew out
with a glancing blow—from a poker, say. Andrew considers, then rejects this

possibility. Instead, Milo will tie Andrew up. Andrew gets his revolver and explains: "Hearing a noise and fearing burglars, I took my revolver and went to investigate. You attacked me. In the struggle it went off, blowing to smithereens several priceless heirlooms. Being an old fraidy cat householder, I allowed brutish you to take possession of it. You then held it on me while you tied me up. Right?"

A shot must be fired, so Andrew raises the pistol and demolishes a Staffordshire mug (the bullet passing very close to Milo's head). Next, Andrew shatters a Dresden figurine on the banister rail, then presses a button on his desk which animates the Laughing Sailor to mechanical mirth. But instead of echoing the laugh, Andrew abruptly changes his mood.

ANDREW: There's an open season on some creatures all the year round.
    He turns the gun on Milo.
Seducers and wife stealers for example.
    MILO *(nervous):* Only in Italian opera, surely.
    ANDREW *(hard):* You should know. It's your country of origin, is it not?
    MILO: No, I was actually born here in England.
    ANDREW: Were you now. Dear old cradle-of-the-parliamentary-system-who-screws-my-wife-merits-a-large-pink-gin-England?
    MILO: Sense-of-humor-fair-trial-England, I mean.
    ANDREW: That's the way a foreigner talks. In private, he thinks, filthy wet country, ugly red cold men who don't know how to treat women.
    MILO: What's brought all this on? What are you doing with that gun?
    ANDREW: Pretty obviously pointing it at you.
    MILO: For God's sake, why?
    ANDREW *(slowly, Italian accent):* Because I'm going to kill you.
    MILO: You're going to . . . *(Laughs nervously.)* Oh Jesus! I suppose this is some sort of game.
    ANDREW: Yes. We've been playing it all evening. It's called "You're going to die and no one will suspect murder."

Andrew the game-player has framed his wife's lover for burglary and set him up for being shot while committing the crime. Even Marguerite will be persauded that Milo only loved her for her jewels.

Andrew offers Milo a "sporting chance:" make a run for it. Milo tries but stumbles in his oversized clown boots.

Andrew continues to behave as though he were writing a detective story, trying to choose whether to shoot the quaking Milo or knife him or smash in his skull with a golf club. Andrew decides on the bullet.

    Andrew forces Milo to mount the stairs by shoving the gun in his back. Milo gives a sudden spasmodic shudder.
    ANDREW: Did you know that Charles I put on two shirts the morning of his execution? "If I tremble with cold," he said, "my enemies will say it was from

fear; I will not expose myself to such reproaches." You must also attempt dignity as you mount the steps to the scaffold.

Milo demurs and sinks to his knees near the top step.

MILO *(terrified and pleading):* But why, Andrew? Why?

ANDREW: Don't snivel. You can't think it'll gain you mercy.

MILO: I must know why!

ANDREW: I'm amazed you have to ask. But since you do, it's perfectly simple. I hate you. I hate your smarmy, good-looking Latin face and your easy manner. I'll bet you're easy in a ski lodge, and easy on a yacht, and easy on a beach. I'll bet you a pound to a penny, that you wear a gold charm round your neck, and that your chest is hairy and in summer matted with sun oil. I hate you because you are a mock humble, jeweled, shot cufflinked sponger, a world is my oyster-er, a seducer of silly women, and a king among marshmallow snakes. I hate you because you are a culling spick. A wop—a not one-of-me. Come, little man, did you really believe I would give up my wife and jewels to you? That I would make myself *that* ridiculous.

MILO: Why not? You're not in love with her.

ANDREW: She's mine whether I love her or not. I found her, I've kept her. I am familiar with her. And once, she was in love with me.

MILO: And now she's in love with me, and the dog in the manger won't let go.

He tries to attack Andrew.

The mad dog in the manger who should be put down for everyone's sake.

ANDREW *(deadly):* And you are a young man, dressed as a clown, about to be murdered. Put the mask on, Milo.

A pause.

MILO: No, please.

Andrew reaches up and lifts the clown mask off the banister where Milo has previously hung it.

ANDREW: Put it on!

Milo takes the mask and fumbles it onto his face.

Excellent. Farewell, Punchinello!

Andrew lifts the pistol to Milo's head, Milo is shaking with fear.

MILO *(high falsetto):* Please . . .

Andrew slowly pulls the trigger. Milo falls backwards down the stairs and lies still. Andrew walks past him, pausing to peer closely to see whether there is any sign of life. He lifts the lolling head and lets it thump back, carelessly, onto the stairs. Satisfied that he has done his work well, he straightens up, and smiles to himself.

ANDREW: Game and set, I believe.

Curtain.

ACT II

Two days later in the same room, Andrew is eating caviar and drinking champagne and listening to Beethoven's Seventh. He has just finished talking to his servants on the phone—urging them to return the next day—when the doorbell rings. Andrew goes to answer it and finds on his doorstep Inspector Doppler of the Wiltshire County Constabulary: *"a heavily built, tallish man of about 50. His hair is balding, and he wears cheap, round spectacles on his fleshy nose, above a greying moustache. His clothes—dark rumpled suit, under a half-open light-colored mackintosh—occasion no surprise, nor does his pork-pie hat."*

Andrew makes Inspector Doppler welcome. The policeman has no scruples against drinking on duty, so Andrew obliges him with a brandy. Doppler has come to see Andrew about Milo Tindle, a young tenant of a nearby cottage who hasn't been seen since last Friday.

The policeman has been informed by the barman at the local pub that Milo said he was on his way to see Andrew on Friday night; and another passing witness has testified to a struggle taking place in this house that evening, with shots fired.

To Andrew's discomfiture, the Inspector produces a note found in Milo's cottage, reading: "Urgent we talk. Come Friday night eight o'clock. Wyke." Again, Inspector Doppler asks for an explanation. They were playing a game, Andrew declares.

ANDREW: Tindle arrived at eight and left about an hour and a half later. I haven't seen him since.

DOPPLER: And nor has anyone else, sir.

ANDREW: This is absurd. Are you suggesting that I killed Tindle?

DOPPLER: Killed Tindle, sir? I never mentioned kill.

ANDREW: Oh really! You can't pull that old one on me. *(Mimicking Inspector's voice.)* Garotted, sir? Might I ask how you knew that her ladyship was garotted? *(Normal voice.)* Surely *you* told me so, Inspector. *(Inspector's voice.)* No, sir. I never mentioned it.

DOPPLER: I'm sorry you find us so comic, sir. On the whole what we do is necessary.

ANDREW: "You're just doing your job," that's the overworked phrase, isn't it?

DOPPLER: Possibly, sir. Your wife and Mr. Tindle have been associating closely for some time.

ANDREW: Oh, so you know about that, do you? I suppose you can't keep anything quiet in a small village.

DOPPLER: Perfectly true, sir.

Andrew serves Doppler another brandy and makes his statement. Tindle was having an affair with his wife, and Andrew resented it. His view of the whole matter is expressed in the observation: "Sex is the game with marriage the penalty"—still, he disliked the idea of another man intruding into his marriage, and he thought he would teach Tindle a lesson. Andrew prepared an "initiation" in the manner of the old secret societies, a humiliation for his wife's lover. He set up the fake theft and then confronted the "burglar" with a pistol.

"It was electrifying!" exclaims Andrew for Doppler's benefit. "He swallowed my story hook, line and sinker. He fell on his knees, and pleaded for his life, but I was implacable. I put the gun against his head and shot him with a *blank* cartridge. He fainted dead away. It was most gratifying."

After Tindle regained consciousness (Andrew tells the Inspector) a glass or two of brandy put him right and he went on his way. Andrew boasts that he was "upholding the sanctity of marriage," revenging himself by playing a cat-and-mouse game with his rival. To Doppler, however, the "game" has a whiff of illegal torture about it. Doppler persists in believing that murder may have been done. He begins a search of the room and soon finds the bullet holes.

DOPPLER: I understood you to say, sir, that you used a blank.

ANDREW: Two live bullets to set up the trick. One blank to complete it. I had to persuade Tindle I was in earnest. After all, there's really no point in playing a game unless you play it to the hilt.

DOPPLER: I see, sir. One blank. I'd like you to show me where Mr. Tindle was when you killed him.

ANDREW: Pretended to kill him, you mean.

DOPPLER: Quite so, sir. Show me, please, exactly where he was when the bullet hit him.

ANDREW: You do realize, of course, there wasn't a real bullet.

DOPPLER *(skeptically):* Very well, sir. Show me where he was when the blank cartridge was fired.

Andrew mounts the stairs, followed by the Inspector.

ANDREW: He was standing, kneeling, crouching about here. He fainted and fell down the stairs. Bang!

DOPPLER *(passes Andrew):* I see. About here you say, sir?

ANDREW: Towards me. Come on. Come on. Stop.

DOPPLER: Were you close to Mr. Tindle when you fired the gun?

ANDREW: Very. I was standing over him, in fact, with the gun pressed against his head. The actual feel of the gun coupled with the noise of the explosion was what did the trick.

Doppler scrutinizes the staircase.

Could I interest you in a magnifying glass?

Doppler bends down to examine the staircase, then the banisters. Suddenly he rubs a finger on them, and straightens up, wiping them on his handkerchief.

DOPPLER: Joke blood, sir?

ANDREW *(nervous):* I'm not quite sure I follow, Inspector.

DOPPLER: This here on the banisters. It's dried blood.

ANDREW: Blood? Where?

DOPPLER: Here in the angle of the banister—

Warily Andrew crosses to the stairs. He examines the banisters and slowly straightens up. His expression is confused and fearful.

Andrew calls Doppler's attention to the evidence—the footprints in the flower bed, the hole in the window, etc.—which substantiate his story of a "game" that ended short of murder.

Doppler looks out the window and calls Andrew's attention to a mound of fresh earth in the garden—Andrew professes to know nothing about it and challenges the police to dig it up. Doppler assures Andrew that they will.

Continuing his search, Doppler finds Milo's clothes in the wardrobe and wonders whether Milo walked home naked after his humiliation on Friday night. In great distress, Andrew declares he knows nothing about how the clothes got there—Milo changed out of the clown suit back into his clothes before he went home.

Doppler now propounds his theory of the case: "I think you started this as a game, exactly as you say you did, in order to play a diabolical trick on Mr. Tindle, but that it went wrong. Your third shot was not a blank as you had supposed, but was in fact a live bullet which killed Mr. Tindle stone dead, spattering his blood on the banisters in the process. When you realized what you'd done, you panicked and simply buried him in the garden. It was silly of you not to wash the blood properly off the banisters and burn his clothes, though."

Andrew shouts denial; Doppler reassures him that the police will be satisfied with a charge of manslaughter. Doppler tries to place Andrew under arrest, and Andrew resists frantically.

DOPPLER: . . . . . Come on, sir. Don't despair. At the most you'll only get seven years.

ANDREW *(horrified):* Seven years!

DOPPLER: Seven years to regret playing silly games that go wrong.

ANDREW *(bitterly):* It didn't go wrong. It went absolutely right. You've trapped me somehow.

DOPPLER: Yes, sir. You see, we real-life detectives aren't as stupid as we are sometimes portrayed by writers like yourself. We may not have our pipes, or orchid houses, our shovel hats or deer-stalkers, but we tend to be reasonably effective for all that.

ANDREW: Who the hell are you?

DOPPLER: Detective Inspector Doppler, sir, spelled as in C. Doppler, 1803-1853, whose principle it was that when the source of any wave movement is approached, the frequency appears greater than it would to an observer moving away. It is also not unconnected with Doppler meaning double in German—hence Doppleganger or double image. And of course, for those whose minds run to these things, it is virtually an anagram of the word Plodder. Inspector Plodder becomes Inspector Doppler, if you see what I mean, sir!

ANDREW *(a shriek):* Milo!

MILO *(normal voice):* The same.

Milo peels off his disguise which apart from elaborate face and hair make-up—wig, false nose, glasses, cheek padding and moustache—also includes a great deal of body padding, and elevator shoes, which have had the effect of making him taller than Andrew, where in reality he is a fraction shorter.

ANDREW: You shit!

MILO: Just so.

ANDREW: You platinum-plated, copper-bottomed, dyed-in-the-wool, all-time knock-down drag-out, champion bastard. Milo!

MILO: Thanks.

ANDREW: You weasel! You cozening coypu!

MILO: Obliged.

Furious, shaken, completely taken in, Andrew nevertheless can't help admiring the skill with which Milo played his game. He prepares a drink while Milo goes to wash off his disguise.

Andrew tries to pretend that his own frantic behavior was a performance, too. Milo comments as he returns to the room: "Undignified—if it was a performance." Milo explains how he did it: he entered the house the day before when Andrew went to Salisbury to put the jewels in the bank, giving Milo the opportunity to plant the clothes in the wardrobe and pig's blood on the stairs.

Coldly, Milo congratulates Andrew on the success of his game two days previously. Milo is not angry because "anger is a meaningless word in this context."

Andrew identifies Milo as a fellow games-player, which he defines for Milo: "He's the complete man—a man of reason and imagination, of potent passions and bright fancies. He's joyous and unrepenting. His weapons are the openness of a child and the cunning of a pike and with them he faces out the black terrors of life . . . . . I've turned my whole life into one great work of happy invention."

Milo insists he is *not* in reality a games-player, he merely wanted to revenge himself upon Andrew in kind.

ANDREW: And is honor satisfied? Is it one set all?

MILO *(hard)*: By no means. Your game was superior to mine. I merely teased you for a few minutes with the thought of prison. *(Low.)* You virtually terrified me to death.

ANDREW: My dear fellow . . .

MILO *(slowly, thinking it out)*: And that changes you profoundly. Once you've given yourself to death, actually faced the fact that the coat sleeve button, the banister, the nail on your fourth finger are the last things you're going to see ever—and then *heard* the sound of your own death—things cannot be the same again. I feel I've been tempered by madness. I stand outside and see myself for the first time without responsibility.

ANDREW *(nervous):* That's shock, my dear chap. It'll pass. Here, have another drink.

> *Andrew reaches for the glass. Milo jerks away. He is in great distress.*

How cold you are. Milo, my dear fellow, I didn't realize how absolutely cold . . .

MILO: So that my only duty is to even our score. That's imperative. As you would put it, "I'm three games up in the second set, having lost the first six-love." That's right, isn't it? That's about how you see it? I should hate to cheat.

ANDREW: You're being too modest, Milo. In my scoring it's one set all.

But Milo is deadly serious about going on with the "game." In order to make the next move (he informs Andrew), he has already killed someone, actually committed murder. He has raped and strangled Andrew's mistress Tēa right here in this room, when she happened to come by while Andrew was in Salisbury and Milo was planning his Doppler scene.

Andrew is first shocked, then incredulous. Milo insists: he strangled Tēa, then buried her in the garden where the earth is freshly turned. Later, though, Milo moved the body because just framing Andrew for his mistress's murder would be too easy, not really playing the game.

No, the game begins in earnest right now, Milo warns Andrew. He has tipped off the local police authority, Detective Sergeant Tarrant ("a *real* policeman"), that Andrew is ambitious to commit and get away with a real-life murder, with Tēa as his victim.

Andrew, still partly disbelieving, calls his mistress on the phone and is dismayed by what Tēa's flat-mate has to tell him. Andrew puts down the phone and takes a drink straight from the bottle.

MILO: I told you. I killed her yesterday. Now, sweat for your life. You have a little over eight minutes before the law arrives. It's your giant brain against their plodding ones. Concealed in this room are two incriminating clues. And as a final expression of your contempt for the police, you hid the murder weapon itself. Do you follow me so far?

ANDREW *(admiringly):* You bastard!

MILO: No judgments please. Three objects. Those you don't find, be sure the police will. I should add that they're all in plain view, though I have somewhat camouflaged them to make the whole thing more fun. The first object is a crystal bracelet.

ANDREW: Not . . .

MILO: Yes, I tore it off her wrist . . . off you go. It's inscribed "From Andrew to Tēa, a propitiary offering to a Karelian goddess.

ANDREW: All right! All right! I know how it's inscribed.

> *He takes off his jacket and starts his search.*

While Andrew searches, Milo goads him with hints, clues, riddles. He taunts Andrew to anger by slighting his fictional detective creation, the great

Inspector Merridew. Now thoroughly convinced that he is playing for his life, Andrew searches more anxiously, more urgently, until finally he spies the bracelet submerged in the ornamental tank.

From Milo's riddling clue, Andrew guesses that the second object he must find is a shoe—one of Tēa's shoes, Milo tells him, matching the one still worn by the corpse. As Andrew searches diligently for it, Milo observes that he seems more excited by the game than grieving for his murdered mistress.

Andrew finds the shoe at last, and Milo taunts him with a Latin clue to the nature and whereabouts of the third incriminating object, the "weapon" with which Milo strangled Tēa. Milo offers a strong hint that the sought-after object is a stocking. He goes to the hallway for a moment, then returns.

MILO: Yes, Andrew, it's the police. They're coming up the drive.
ANDREW *(desperate):* Keep them out! Give me one more minute!
MILO: A glimpse of stocking, remember.
        Milo exits to hallway.
(Offstage.) Good evening, Detective Sergeant Tarrant.
TARRANT *(offstage):* Yes sir. This is Constable Higgs.
MILO *(off):* Good evening, Constable.
HIGGS *(off):* Good evening, sir.

Making one last strenuous effort, Andrew finds the stocking in the grandfather clock just as Milo in the hallway is inviting the policemen to hang up their coats. Andrew throws the stocking into the fire and turns to face the police.

MILO *(off):* Come in, gentlemen. May I introduce Mr. Andrew Wyke. Andrew, may I introduce Detective Sergeant Tarrant and Constable Higgs.
ANDREW *(calls):* Come in, gentlemen, come in.
        A pause. No one enters.
MILO *(off):* Or perhaps I should say, Inspector Plodder and Constable Freshface. Thank you, sergeant. We won't be needing you after all.
TARRANT: That's all right, sir. Better to be safe than sorry, that's what I say, good night, sir.
MILO *(own voice):* Good night, Sergeant. Good night, Constable. Good night, sir.
        Milo returns from hallway. Andrew sinks on the settee, shattered.
Aren't you going to ask about Tēa? She did call here yesterday looking for you when I was here setting the Doppler scene. I told her about the trick you had played on me with the gun. She wasn't a bit surprised. She knows only too well the kind of games you play—the kind of humiliation you enjoy inflicting on people. I said I wanted to play a game to get even with you, and I asked her to help me. I asked her to lend me a stocking, a shoe and a bracelet. She collaborated with enthusiasm. So did her flat-mate, Joyce. Would you like to telephone her, she'll talk to you now? Of course you don't really have much to say to her, do you? She's not really your mistress. She told me you and

she hadn't slept together for over a year. She told me you were practically impotent—not at all, in fact, the selector's choice for the next Olympics.

Andrew hides his head as Milo starts up the stairs.

ANDREW: Where are you going?

MILO: To collect Marguerite's fur coat.

ANDREW: She's not coming back?

MILO: No. Among other things she said she was fed up with living in Hamleys.

ANDREW: Hamleys?

MILO: It's a toy shop in Regent Street.

ANDREW: Milo.

MILO: Yes?

ANDREW: Don't go. Don't waste it all on Marguerite. She doesn't appreciate you like I do. You and I are evenly matched. We know what it is to play a game and that's so rare. Two people coming together who have the courage to spend the little time of light between the eternal darkness—joking.

MILO: Do you mean live here?

ANDREW: Yes.

MILO *(scornfully):* Is it legal in private between two consenting game-players?

ANDREW: Please . . . I just want someone to play with.

MILO: No.

ANDREW: Please.

MILO: No. Most people want someone to *live* with. But you have no life to give anyone—only the tricks and the shadows of long ago. Take a look at yourself, Andrew, and ask yourself a few simple questions about your attachment to the English detective story. Perhaps you might come to realize that the only place you can inhabit is a dead world—a country house world where peers and colonels die in their studies; where butlers steal the port, and pert parlormaids cringe, weeping malapropisms behind green baize doors. It's a world of coldness and class hatred, and two-dimensional characters who are not expected to communicate; it's a world where only the amateurs win, and where foreigners are automatically figures of fun. To be *puzzled* is all. Forgive me for taking Marguerite to a life where people try to *understand.* To put it shortly, the detective story is the normal recreation of snobbish, outdated, life-hating, ignoble minds. I'll get that fur coat now. I presume it *is* Marguerite's, unless, that is, you've taken to transvestism as a substitute for non-performance.

Milo disappears into the bedroom. Andrew sits on below, crushed and humiliated . . . . .

In the midst of his defeat, it occurs to Andrew that perhaps he can make the burglar game work again, shoot Milo while he is carrying the coat and explain to the real police that he mistook Milo for a burglar. Andrew gets his revolver from the desk and hides it behind his back while Milo returns with the coat and packs it into a suitcase.

Andrew threatens Milo with the gun, but Milo defies him. Milo has been to the real police (he insists) and told them everything, so Andrew could no longer deceive the law with any pretense that he shot Milo by mistake.

If this is true—Andrew wants to know—why haven't the police been around to question him about the incident two days ago? Milo doesn't know the answer, perhaps the police are still planning to call on Andrew. But Andrew doesn't believe that Milo has *really* been to the police, *really* told them everything, even though Milo invites Andrew to call the real Inspector Tarrant on the phone and check. Andrew has been fooled twice before and refuses to believe Milo's story now.

ANDREW: I shall shoot you, Milo. You come here and ask my permission to steal away my wife, you pry into my manhood, you lecture me on dead worlds and ignoble minds, and you mock Merridew. Well, they're all real bullets this time.

MILO: I'm going home now.

Milo starts to leave, Andrew fires. Milo drops in pain, fatally shot. Andrew kneels and holds his head up.

ANDREW: You're a bad liar, Milo, and in the final analysis, an uninventive games-player. Can you hear me? Then listen to this, NEVER play the same game three times running.

There is the sound of a car approaching and pulling to a halt. A flashing blue police car light shines through the window. The door bell rings. There is a loud knocking on the door. Painfully Milo lifts his head from the floor, he laughs.

MILO: Game, set and match!

His laugh becomes a cough. Blood trickles from his mouth. He grimaces in surprise at the pain and dies. The knocking on the door is repeated more loudly. Andrew staggers to his desk and accidentally presses the button on it. This sets off the sailor who laughs ironically. The knocking becomes more insistent. Andrew leans weakly against the pillar. He shouts in anguish as the curtain falls.

THE TRIAL OF THE CATONSVILLE NINE

A Play in One Act

BY DANIEL BERRIGAN, S.J.

TEXT PREPARED FOR THE NEW YORK PRODUCTION
BY SAUL LEVITT

Cast and credits appear on page 343

DANIEL BERRIGAN was born in Minnesota and grew up in Syracuse, N.Y.
He began his Jesuit training in 1939 and in 1952, after 13 years of study, he
entered the priesthood. He served for a time in France and later was active in
community work in New York City, particularly in black and Puerto Rican
neighborhoods. He returned to Syracuse as a professor at Le Moyne College,
where he acquired a growing reputation as an advocate of liturgical modern-
ism and as a supporter of the civil rights movement.

In 1963 Father Berrigan was reassigned to France, then journeyed to Hun-
gary, Russia and Czechoslovakia. Upon his return to the United States he sup-
ported many anti-war activities and traveled to Hanoi (after an assigned so-
journ in Latin America) to arrange the release of three American pilots.

This long road of peace activism lead Father Berrigan at last to Catons-
ville, Md. in May 1968, and into the events of this play including trial, con-
viction and sentence. After all appeals failed, Father Berrigan went under-

ground in April 1970, was found and captured on Block Island, R.I. by Federal agents four months later and was sent to serve his term in Federal prison in Danbury, Conn.

Father Berrigan is the author of many published works of poetry, of which Time Without Number *won the Lamont Poetry Award in 1957 and* False Gods, Real Men *was nominated for a National Book Award in 1969. His others included* They Call Us Dead Men, No One Walks Waters, Consequences, Truth and . . . *and* Love, Love at the End, No Bars to Manhood, Trial Poems *(illustrated by a co-defendant, Thomas Lewis) and* The Trial of the Catonsville Nine *in book form. In play form, it is Father Berrigan's first work for the professional theater.*

SAUL LEVITT was born in Hartford, Conn. March 3, 1913; his father was a hatmaker. He studied at Morris High School in the Bronx and the College of the City of New York. After World War II, in which he served in the Air Force, he pursued a writing career as a magazine contributor, novelist, TV and screen play author and playwright. For Broadway he wrote The Andersonville Trial *(1959, a Best Play of its season). The Trial of the Catonsville Nine, which opened off Broadway and transferred to Broadway at season's end, is Levitt's first New York play since then, his second Best Play in a row. He is married and lives in New York City.*

Time: October 7, 1968

Place: The United States District Court for the District of Maryland in Baltimore

SYNOPSIS: Daniel Berrigan is standing at a reading desk which resembles a pulpit. The other eight defendants in the trial which is about to take place are silhouetted behind him.

DANIEL BERRIGAN: On a June morning, I lay before the altar in the chapel —to be ordained a priest—and the voice of Cardinal Cushing shook the house like a great war horse. His hands lay on my head like a stone. I remember a kind of desolation, the cold of the floor on which I stretched like a corpse, while the invocation of the saints went over me like a tide, a death. Would these bones live? I arose to my feet and went out into the sunshine and gave my blessing to those who had borne with me, who had waited for me. A most unfinished man! What would it mean to be a Catholic? Who would be my teacher? It was, finally, the world, the world we breathe in, the only stage of redemption, the men and women who toil in it, sin in it, suffer and die in it. Apart from them, as I came to know, the priesthood was a pallid, vacuumatic enclosure, a sheepfold for sheep.

Discards the reading desk.

Priests? Why priests kept their peace muttered the Mass sidestepped
queasily the public horror made Jesus mild as milk a temple eunuch
I don't want to miss the action but
I must tell you my brother Phil and
I were in jail at the same
time last year He for that little
business of pouring blood on draft records
and I for marching on the Pentagon Those
prison blue jeans and denim shirts! It's a
clerical attire I highly recommend for a
new church. As Camus said—*(Laughs.)*
I love to talk to people but I've got to
get to a burning *Oremus pro fratribus*
in periculo

Defendants begin pantomiming the burning of draft files.

Imagine nine felonious Catholics
jerky harried as Keystone Cops
running out of a building bearing
baskets heaped with trash
dumping them out
setting them alight dancing like dervishes around the fire
the TV cameras ground it out
those four or five minutes when our past
went up in flames
whirling like ashes down a parking lot
then sober as the flames died we joined hands
praying Our Father who are in heaven
The film impounded rests in peace
in FBI archives

TAPE RECORDER: Criminal Action Number 28111, the United States of
America against Daniel Berrigan . . . How do you plead?

DANIEL BERRIGAN: Not guilty.

TAPE: Philip Berrigan?

PHILIP BERRIGAN: Not guilty.

TAPE: David Darst?

DAVID DARST: Not guilty.

TAPE: John Hogan?

JOHN HOGAN: Not guilty.

TAPE: Thomas Lewis?

THOMAS LEWIS: Not guilty.

TAPE: Marjorie Melville?

MARJORIE MELVILLE: Not guilty.

TAPE: Thomas Melville?

THOMAS MELVILLE: Not guilty.

TAPE: George Mische?

GEORGE MISCHE: Not guilty.
TAPE: Mary Moylan?
MARY MOYLAN: Not guilty.
> Gavel.
JUDGE: The court will come to order. The jury panel will take their places.

Now the courtroom scene is established: judge, jury, counsel, marshals, witnesses. The Judge explains to the jury that this is an action of the United States against the nine defendants for seizing and burning some records of the local draft board at Catonsville, Md.

A prosecution witness tells how the intruders came into the draft board offices and quietly but firmly emptied the 1-A classification files into a trash burner and took them outside to be incinerated. This caused the draft board staff many hours of extra work to get the system going again. Under cross-examination, the witness testifies to the non-violent manner, even the politeness, of the intruders.

The Defense postulates: "We agree with the government that the defendants did participate in the burning of the records." David Darst, one of the defendants, explains that they used napalm home-made from a Green Beret handbook's formula to burn the files.

Under defense questioning, the defendants identify themselves. Mary Moylan is a Baltimore newspaper reporter's daughter, active in Catholic lay organizations. Thomas Melville is a former priest who met his wife Marjorie, a former Maryknoll nun, while working in Guatemala. John Hogan is a former Maryknoll brother who worked with the Melvilles. David Darst was a summa cum laude student, a candidate for Harvard Divinity School. George Mische came from a working class family with a strong ethic of helping those less fortunate than themselves. Thomas Lewis is an artist who teaches in the ghetto. Then it is the Berrigan brothers' turn.

DANIEL BERRIGAN: Phil was the first priest in the country to be tried for a political crime and be convicted. I have always thought my brother to be one of the most fearless of men. If you think this is bias, well, others have thought so too.

PHILIP BERRIGAN:
> All of us (there were six brothers) were born
> in Minnesota
> My father was railroading out there
> and he married my mother who was a German immigrant
> Minnesota was still pioneer country
> We lived on the Iron Range
> It was a struggle
> to survive the bitter winters
> We were poor
> I remember the Depression years very well
> I think this is true of my brother Dan as well

I remember my mother putting up people from the road
there were many men traveling the roads then
who were impoverished and desperate
Even though we did not have too much to eat
she would never refuse them
DANIEL BERRIGAN:
We were obsessed by poverty
I remember my mother being sick with TB
hospitalized for over a year
and my Aunt Maggie my father's spinster sister
keeping house for us She starved us:
bread and butter sandwiches molasses cookies
What a scene I know that made revolutionaries out of us
Every Sunday we'd go to see Mom at the hospital
and she'd look at those six pale thin little faces
and cry out in sorrow
The doctors were pessimistic about my mother
surviving but she recovered out of
sheer will power in order to get the witch
out of the house

The brothers continue to recite their memories of the past. They attended parochial school. Philip served in World War II as an "enthusiastic participant," he admits, in contrast to his present convictions. Daniel was sequestered in the seminary during that wartime period.

Philip Berrigan chose the Society of St. Joseph, dedicated to the service of the American black, as the order in which he would study for the priesthood. The Prosecution complains that the brothers' testimony is rambling off the point of this trial, and the Judge is inclined to agree. But Philip insists that his empathy for the black condition is relevant to the present matter: "I see that racial situation as leading me straight to the pouring of blood on draft records," and then on to the fire of Catonsville.

The defendants rise to explain themselves and the motives for their actions. First of the nine are Mary Moylan and George Mische (see photo and text, opposite page).

MARY MOYLAN (*left, played by Nancy Malone*): Of all that happened to me in Africa the instance which is most indelibly printed on my mind was the bombing by American planes. I came home to Washington, D.C. and had to deal with the scene there: the insanity and the brutality of the cops and the type of life that was led by most of the citizens of that city—seventy per cent black. Nobody believed that cops were ever brutal; all black people just happened to be lippy and they needed to get a slap in the face once in a while . . . . .

GEORGE MISCHE (*right, played by Richard Jordan*):

I went down to Yucatan
down to Central America
for the Alliance for Progress
going with the idea
that the Latins would be
waiting at the boat to greet me
because I was an American
This is the naivete we have I
                      guess
until we arrive overseas
We were not only not welcome
we had bricks thrown at us
This confused me but

after I became involved
I started to understand
why bricks were thrown at us
We were working in two countries
where revolutions had taken place
I should not say "revolution"
I should say "coup d'etat"
military overthrow of governments
Two democratically elected
                      governments
were overthrown by the military
with Pentagon support . . . . .

PHOTOS BY VAN WILLIAMS

THOMAS MELVILLE (*at witness stand, played by Joe Ponazecki*):
I went to Guatemala
                in August of 1957
I was not there very long
when I felt I was getting
a little ahead of myself
The material circumstances
                of the people—
I hesitate to use the
                word "poverty"
they were living in
                utter misery . . . . .
The United States Government
identifies its interests
in Guatemala with
the Guatemalan two per cent
who control the country
So if the peasant movement
does not conduct itself
according to their wishes
that is to say
if such a movement is not
                completely ineffectual
they start screaming
"They are communists!"
And begin executing
                these people

JUDGE (*at top, played by William Schallert*): You mean to say that the United States Government is executing Guatemalans?

THOMAS MELVILLE: Yes, your Honor . . . . .

MARJORIE MELVILLE (*at witness stand, played by Gwen Arner*):
. . . . . in Guatemala it was really
a shock to me to realize
                my country
was not exactly the great
                ideal I had
always pictured
It might sound silly
but I think it was a little
                bit like
a child's discovery
That Santa Claus does not exist

DAVID DARST (*right, at witness stand, played by Leon Russom*): I will try to say it clearly, your Honor. Two years ago I was teaching high school for the first time. Many of the boys were facing imminent induction. I began to feel it was my duty to cry out. One of the things I did was to send back my own draft card to my board. But they gave me a clerical deferment, and then drafted me as a Christian Brother. I thought well, good, I will refuse this and thus perhaps raise a cry. But only my friends knew about this. Thus it was not a cry. Later on I was prosecuted for this failure to report for induction and a trial was set, but the government somewhat mysteriously and, I feel, somewhat cowardly, dropped the charges just before the trial was to begin—

THOMAS LEWIS (*left, played by Sam Waterston*):
At Catonsville
we used a contemporary symbol napalm
which has been used in South America
as well as Vietnam The United States
                       makes it
It is part of our foreign aid
At Catonsville we used this symbol
to destroy records
which are potential death certificates
they stand for the death of men
they represent men who are put
                  in the situation
where they have to kill
But beyond this
napalm manufactured in the United States
is part of our foreign aid

(*continued on the next page*)

THOMAS LEWIS (*continued from preceding page*):

We supply weaponry
to more than 80 countries
           We have troops
in more than 40 countries
              These troops
are backed up with our weaponry
The fact is
The American system can flourish

only if we expand our economy . . . . .
The young men
whose files we destroyed
have not been drafted
              may not be drafted
may not be sent to Vietnam
             for cannon fodder . . . . .

JUDGE: If these men were not sent, other people would have been sent, who would not otherwise have been sent, would they not?

THOMAS LEWIS:

. . . . . You are accepting the fact
that if these men were not sent
other men will be sent
You are not even asking
              what can be done
to stop the insane killing—

You are accepting this insane
             killing your Honor
as in Nazi Germany
people accepted the massacre
of other people
This is insane and I protest this

JOHN HOGAN (*left, played by Barton Heyman*):

If there were a group of children
walking along the street
returning home from school
and a car
came down the street
out of control even though
there was a driver in that car
if I could divert the car
from crashing into those children
I would feel an obligation
to turn the car from its path
And I know too that
if I were driving that car
I would hope and pray to God
that somebody would smash the car
so that I might not destroy
             those children . . . . .
I just want
to let people live
That is all

PHILIP BERRIGAN (*at witness stand, played by Michael Kane*):

We do not consider ourselves
as having committed a crime . . . . .
Our intention was to destroy the files
but our motive
was to illustrate genocide in Vietnam
and corruption at home
The real isue is: how can men
                    serve love and war?
The fact is they can't
Most Americans have great difficulty
seeing the I the self.
as being the we humanity . . . . .
We think we can rape a people
and have them love us . . . . .
We cannot fight the abstraction
                    of communism
by killing the people who believe in it
We cannot talk peace while our deeds
give the lie to our words
We can't have it both ways
The point at issue for us personally
when we went to Catonsville
was not leniency or punishment
not being a danger to the community
or a benefit to it
but what it means to be
                    a democratic man
and a Christian man
America can treat us as it wills
If it can find justice for us
and for the growing numbers
who refuse complicity in *its* crime
then it will show a stamina
in accord with its national creed
If it cannot
then its cup of violence will fill up
and up
finally to brim over

DANIEL BERRIGAN (*played by Ed Flanders, above at witness stand in scene in-cluding Defense, played by David Spielberg at left, and Prosecution, played by Davis Roberts at right; and in closeup in photo below right*):

I was the last of the nine
who agreed to go to Catonsville
I sat up with Philip through a long night
resisting (*Pause.*)
Suddenly I saw
my sweet skin was hiding behind others

(*Daniel Berrigan testifies about his association with the French worker priests in 1952; about his first Mass in English in 1961; about exposure to apartheid in South Africa in 1964; about his growing opposition to the Vietnam war and being "exiled" by his Jesuit superiors to Latin America in 1965; and about his trip to Hanoi in 1968 to bring home three captured American airmen.*)

DEFENSE: And was there anything else that determined you to act at Catons-ville?

DANIEL BERRIGAN:

Another event   in the spring of 1968
The self-immolation   This boy had come to
of a high school student   a point of despair
in Syracuse New York   about the war He had gone

into the Catholic cathedral
drenched himself with kerosine
and immolated himself in the street
He was still living a month later
when I visited him in the hospital
I smelled the odor of burning flesh
and understood anew what I had
          seen in Vietnam
The boy was dying in torment
his body like a piece of meat
upon a grill
He died shortly thereafter
I felt that my senses
     had been invaded in a new way
I understood again
the power of death in the modern world
This boy's death
was being multiplied
a thousandfold
in the land of Burning Children
So I went to Catonsville and
         burned some papers
because the burning of children
   is inhuman and unbearable . . . . .
My intention on that day
was

to save the innocent
from death by fire
Yes I poured napalm
on behalf of the prosecutor's
           and the judge's
and the jury's children
        and grandchildren . . . . .
I was trying to be concrete
about death because death
is a concrete fact
as I have throughout my life
tried to be concrete
about the existence of God
Who is not an abstraction
but is someone before me
for Whom I am responsible . . . . .
May I say your Honor
that if my religious belief
         is not accepted
as a substantial part of my action
then the action is eviscerated
of all meaning and I should be
committed for insanity . . . . .
Our apologies good friends
for the fracture of good order
        the burning of paper
instead of children . . . . .
We say: killing is disorder
life and gentleness and community
        and unselfishness
is the only order we recognize
For the sake of that order
we risk our liberty our good name . . . . .
Christ is not forsaken
In a time of death some men
the resisters those who work hardily
        for social change
preach and embrace the truth
In the jaws of death
they proclaim their love
        of the brethren
We think of such men
in the world in our nation
        in the churches
and the stone in our breast
        is dissolved
and we take heart once more

PROSECUTION: . . . . . I want it clearly understood that the government is not about to put itself in the position —has not heretofore and is not now—of conducting its policies at the end of a string tied to the consciences of these nine defendants. This trial does not include the issues of the Vietnam conflict . . . . . this prosecution is the government's response, the people's response, to what the defendants did. And what they did was to take government property and throw flammable material on it and burn it beyond recognition. And that is what this case is about . . . . . It is your sworn duty to assert, by finding the defendants guilty, that our problems will not be solved, but will be increased beyond imagining, by people who deliberately violate the law under which we all live . . . . .

DEFENSE: . . . . . The trial of Socrates was not merely a question of a man sowing confusion and distrust among the youth of Athens; the trial of Jesus could not be reduced to one of conspiracy against the Empire. In a parallel way, there are overriding issues at stake in this case . . . . .

JUDGE: (*above, left*): . . . . . The jury may not decide this case on the basis of conscience. The jury will decide this case solely on the basis of the facts presented in this courtroom by both sides. (*Continued on the opposite page*)

The Judge warns the jury not to be influenced by sympathy, but to decide the case according to the letter of the law, and the jury files out. With the jury absent, the Judge grants the defendants' request to "speak out in open court." They discuss the case with the Judge, who tells them: "I am not questioning the morality of what you did. But people who violate the law in order to make a point must expect to be punished."

Daniel Berrigan complains that this makes the legal process a mere "autopsy," without moral passion. The Judge emphasizes the strength of the legal tradition, including the Constitution; Daniel wonders why it isn't possible to include conscience in the considerations of the law, so as to keep it a living tradition.

JUDGE: Well, I think there are two answers to that. You speak to me as a man and as a judge. As a man, I would be a very funny sort if I were not moved by your sincerity on the stand, and by your views. I agree with you completely, as a person. We can never accomplish what we would like to accomplish, or give a better life to people, if we are going to keep on spending so much money for war. But it is very unfortunate, the issue of the war cannot be presented as sharply as you would like. The basic principle of our law is that we do things in an orderly fashion. People cannot take the law into their own hands.

DAVID DARST: Your Honor, does that include the President of the United States?

JUDGE: Of course, the President must obey the law.

THOMAS LEWIS: He hasn't.

JUDGE: Well, if the President has not obeyed the law, there is very little that can be done . . .

GEORGE MISCHE: And that is one of the things this trial is all about.

JUDGE: . . . except not to reelect him.

George Mische goes on to suggest that the whole question of the legality of the Vietnam war be raised in a brief by a peace organization at this trial, and sent to the Supreme Court if necessary, to be decided once and for all. The Judge advises them that in order to raise this ultimate legal question they have to create a case, they have to break the law first (but the Catonsville case does not suit this grand purpose legally).

Daniel Berrigan interrupts the continuing colloquy between defendants and judge with, "We welcome the rigors of this court. Our intention in appearing here after Catonsville was to be useful to the poor of the world, to the black people of the world and of our own country, and to those in our prisons who have no voice. We do not wish that primary blade of intention to be honed down to no edge at all by a gentlemen's agreement, whereby you agree with us and we with you. We do not agree with you, and we thank you."

The defendants receive permission to recite the Lord's Prayer. Following it, the tape recording is heard once again as the jury's verdict is announced: all defendants are guilty as charged.

Daniel Berrigan makes the final comment: "We would simply like to thank the Court and the Prosecution. We agree that this is the greatest day of our lives." *(Curtain.)*

HOME

A Play in Two Acts

BY DAVID STOREY

Cast and credits appear on page 299

DAVID STOREY was born in 1934 in Wakefield, Yorkshire, the son of a British coal miner. He was educated at Wakefield Grammar School, and he showed such promise as an athlete that at 17 he was signed to a 15-year contract with Leeds Rugby League Club. But soon afterward he won a scholarship to the Slade School of Art in London and accepted it, paying back to the rugby group most of his signing bonus. He exhibited paintings in London with other Yorkshire artists and still paints in his spare time, but he finally decided that writing was to be his chosen medium of expression.

Storey worked as a secondary school teacher in London's East End while writing seven novels which failed to satisfy even himself ("I was getting a bit wild, before I started getting on," he confided to an interviewer recently). His eighth, This Sporting Life, *was published in 1960 and made into a movie in 1963 by Lindsay Anderson, who has also directed Storey's recent plays. His next two novels,* Flight Into Camden *(1961) and* Radcliffe *(1963) were well received.*

Eight years after he first wrote it, Storey's first play, The Restoration of Arnold Middleton, *was produced in London by the Royal Court in 1967 and transferred to the West End for an extended run. His other London productions were* In Celebration *(1969),* The Contractor *(1970) and* Home *(1971), which also represented its author's American stage debut in November, 1971 and won him this Best Play citation and the New York Drama Critics Circle Award for the best play of the 1970-71 season.*

Storey is now at work on another novel. He lives in the Hampstead section of London with his wife and four children.

Time: The present

Place: A terrace

ACT I

Scene 1

SYNOPSIS: On a terrace of some form of institution—a sanatarium or asylum or home for the elderly and/or mentally disturbed—is *"a round metalwork table, set slightly off-center, and two metalwork chairs."* The time is before lunch.

> *Harry comes on. He wears a hat which he takes off and puts on the table beside him, along with a pair of well-used leather gloves and a folded newspaper. Jack comes on, carrying a cane.*

JACK: Harry!

HARRY: Jack.

JACK: Been here long?

HARRY: No. No.

JACK: Mind?

HARRY: Not at all.

> *Jack sits down.*

JACK: Nice to see the sun again.

HARRY: Very.

JACK: Been laid up for a few days.

HARRY: Oh dear.

JACK: Chill. In bed.

HARRY: Oh, dear. Still . . . Appreciate the comforts.

JACK: What? . . . You're right. Still . . . Nice to be out.

HARRY: 'Tis.

Jack and Harry are both elderly, gray-haired, well-spoken, alike in most respects including the irritating habit of leaving thoughts unfinished in mid-sentence, or introducing a new subject without warning. Their thoughts and reactions are predictable but not always rational or clear.

Jack glances at Harry's newspaper; they frown over the news, but from some half-forgotten source of memory there sputters in them the spirit of "Not to grumble."

Harry diverts Jack's attention to the changing shape of the clouds going by overhead; then, just as he has Jack's focus shifted, he brings him back to the newspaper, apparently to some story of manipulation of the human mind which alarms them both.

Jack has brought a plastic mackintosh in case the weather changes. Flickering in his mind is some recollection of a recent shock; and some recollection

RALPH RICHARDSON AND JOHN GIELGUD IN "HOME"

of a frail and delicate wife who, "Two years ago . . ." But Jack cannot remember or doesn't say exactly what happened two years ago.

They see a man named Saxton and feel threatened in some vague way. Jack
remembers an uncle who bred horses. Then:

HARRY: Clouds.
JACK: I'd say so.
HARRY: *My* wife was coming up this morning.
JACK: Really?
HARRY: Slight headache. Thought might be better . . .
JACK: Indoors. Well. Best make sure.
HARRY: When I was in the army . . .
JACK: Really? What regiment?
HARRY: Fusiliers.
JACK: Really? How extraordinary.
HARRY: You?

JACK: No. No. A cousin.
HARRY: Well . . .
JACK: Different time of course.
HARRY: Ah.
JACK: Used to bring his rifle . . . No. That was Arthur. Got them muddled.
HARRY: Still.
JACK: Never leaves you.
HARRY: No. No.
JACK: In good stead.
HARRY: Oh, yes.
JACK: All your life.
HARRY: Oh, yes.
JACK: I was—for a very short while—in the Royal Air Force.
HARRY: Really?
JACK: Nothing to boast about.
HARRY: Oh, now. Flying.
JACK: On the ground.
HARRY: Chrysanthemums is my wife's hobby.
JACK: Really.

The exchange continues in this vein, as though the words and phrases arising in the minds of these two old men were only those which were the deepest ingrained by cliched over-use in some past existence; the ideas and their connective tissue of thoughts have crumbled, and only the words remain.

They see Saxton coming by again, and Jack recalls that they had a boy of that name at his school. Jack also recalls an early ambition to become a priest; Harry wanted to become a dancer. They remember some of their friends' nicknames at their two schools, and Harry remarks: "The past. It conjures up some images . . . You wonder how there was ever time for it all." Jack's reply is, "Time . . . Oh . . . Don't mention it."

A friend of Jack's used to exercise in order to stay healthy but was killed in the war. Harry saw some fighting. Jack's father-in-law was in the army all his life and managed to acclimatize himself to the tropics, with all the diseases.

JACK: At times one's glad simply to live on an island.
HARRY: Yes.
JACK: Strange that.
HARRY: Yes.
JACK: Without the sea—all around—civilization would never have been the same.
HARRY: Oh, no.
JACK: The ideals of life, liberty, freedom, could never have been the same —democracy—well, if we'd been living on the continent, for example.
HARRY: Absolutely.

Jack notices Harry's gloves because he has a pair almost exactly like them. Harry got the gloves as a present from his wife at Christmas (a holiday whose spirit, they agree, has been destroyed by materialism).

One December Harry knocked down a careless pedestrian with his car. Jack understands: he had a cousin who fell off a cliff. Harry once fell off a cliff, too—but there was someone there to catch him. Jack once had a boat, and this reminds them of their island greats—Drake, Nelson, Beatty, Raleigh.

Harry wonders why so much dust seems to collect in this spot, and in the next breath he wonders whether Jack ever became a priest. No, Jack couldn't resolve the difficulties.

JACK: The how's and the wherefor's I could understand. How we came to be, and His presence, lurking everywhere, you know. But as to the "why" . . . I never could understand. Seemed a terrible waste of time to me.

HARRY: Oh yes.

JACK: Thought it better to leave it to those who didn't mind.

HARRY: Ah, yes.

JACK: I suppose the same was true about dancing.

HARRY: Oh, yes. I remember turning up for instance, to my first class, only to discover that all the rest of them were girls.

JACK: Really?

HARRY: Well . . . there are men dancers, I know. Still . . . took up football after that.

JACK: To professional standard, I imagine.

HARRY: Oh, no. Just the odd kick around. Joined a team that played in the park on Sunday mornings.

JACK: The athletic life has many attractions.

HARRY: It has. It has.

JACK: How long have you been here, then?

HARRY: Oh, a couple of er (sic).

JACK: Strange—meeting the other day.

HARRY: Yes.

JACK: On the way back, thought to myself, "what a chance encounter."

HARRY: Yes.

JACK: So rare, these days, to meet someone to whom one can actually talk.

HARRY: I know what you mean.

JACK: One works. One looks around. One meets people. But very little communication actually takes place.

HARRY: Very.

JACK: None at all in most cases!

HARRY: Oh, absolutely.

JACK: The agonies and frustrations. I can assure you. In the end one gives up in absolute despair.

They see someone else walk by but cannot settle on the name. They consider the eccentricities of others: married couples who show affection in public are headed for divorce; Harry's father, out of superstition, would never turn out a light. Harry was the youngest of three children; Jack, a strong advocate of family life, was one of seven. Jack remembers an aunt who lived near Gloucester, which reminds him that the Vale of Evesham, according to local legend, was the Garden of Eden. This theological subject triggers some deep response in Jack, who begins to lecture knowledgeably on the probability of this legend being true. Eden (he explains to Harry) would abound in lush growth and animals. "There is ample evidence," Jack continues, "to suggest that during the period in question equatorial conditions prevailed in the very region in which we are now sitting . . . . . Discoveries have been made that would indicate that lions and tigers, elephants, wolves, rhinoceros, and so forth, actually inhabited these parts . . . . . In those circumstances, it wouldn't be unreasonable to suppose that the Vale of Evesham was such a place itself. The very cradle, as it were, of . . ."

Jack is interrupted by Harry, who wants to examine Jack's cane because its quality is unusually high. They discuss the merits of mustaches, and of travel. Learning to fight with bayonets and even with bombs in the Air Force has its character-building merits (they decide). The next war may be a catastrophe in which their island itself will sink. Jack observes, "While we're sitting here waititng to be buried . . . . . We'll end up being drowned."

They see a Mrs. Washington going by—a distant relative, says Jack. Jack takes out a coin and three cards, does simple tricks which mystify Harry. They watch someone named Jennings stroll by (Jack isn't fond of him). One good thing about the war was the camaraderie, Jack noticed, and "No sooner was the fighting over than back it came. Backbiting. Complaints. Getting what you can. I sometimess think if the war had been prolonged another thirty years we'd have all felt the benefit."

Jack tells Harry he has two children, a boy and a girl, both married now.

JACK: Daughter's married to a salesman. Refrigerators: he sells appliances of that nature.
HARRY: Oh. Opposite to me.
JACK: Yes?
HARRY: Heating engineer.
JACK: Really. I'd never have guessed. How extraordinary.
HARRY: And yourself?
JACK: Oh, I've tinkered with one or two things.
HARRY: Ah, yes.
JACK: What I like about my present job is the scope that it leaves you for initiative.
HARRY: Rather. Same with mine.
JACK: Distribution of foodstuffs in a wholesale store.
HARRY: Really.
JACK: Thinking out new ideas. Constant speculation.

Jam sells better in cardboard containers than in glass jars, Jack informs Harry. He also wonders why he's never met Harry's wife: Harry and his wife, it seems, are separated.

They remember that it will soon be time for lunch, and they haven't had their walk. Carefully they pick up their articles—gloves, newspaper, folded mackintosh—and stroll off.

Scene 2

Into the same setting come Kathleen and Marjorie. *"Kathleen carries a bag; she limps. Marjorie carries a bag and an umbrella."* They are about of an age with Jack and Harry, but somewhat less polished. They, too, notice the clouds and pessimistically assume that it is going to rain, Kathleen punctuating her speech with the frequent exclamation "Cor . . . blimey!" Jack and Harry pass upstage, on their constitutional.

Kathleen and Marjorie discuss the lunch menus ("it's going to be sprouts today") and Kathleen's aching feet in ill-fitting shoes: "Took me laced ones, haven't they? Only ones that fitted. Thought I'd hang myself, didn't they? Only five inches long."

At the last place Marjorie lived, they let her paint on the walls, but her fellow-inmates indulged in strange practises. Jack and Harry stroll by again, as Marjorie discusses her teeth: "All went rotten when I had my little girl. There she is, waitress at the seaside."

KATHLEEN: . . . . . Tried catching a serious disease.

MARJORIE: When was that?

KATHLEEN: Only had me in two days, Said, nothing the matter with you, my girl.

MARJORIE: Don't believe you.

KATHLEEN: Next thing: got home: smashed everything in sight.

MARJORIE: No?

KATHLEEN: Winders. Cooker . . . Nearly broke me back . . . thought I'd save the telly. Still owed eighteen months. Thought: "Everything or nothing, girl . . ."

MARJORIE: Rotten programs.

KATHLEEN: . . . Didn't half give it a good old conk.

MARJORIE: There's one thing. You get a good night's sleep.

KATHLEEN: Like being with a steam engine, where I come from. Cor blimey, that much whistling and groaning; think you're going to take off.

MARJORIE: More like a boa-constrictor, ask me. Here . . . Started crying everywhere I went . . . Started off on Christmas Eve.

KATHLEEN: S'happy time, Christmas.

MARJORIE: Didn't stop till Boxing Day.

KATHLEEN: . . . If He ever comes again I hope He comes on Whit Tuesday. For me that's the best time of the year.

Whit Tuesday is Kathleen's lucky day; Marjorie's lucky days are certain special Fridays. They notice other people around them: a man watching them through binoculars, a woman with dyed hair who claims to have acted in blue movies, etc.

Jack and Harry stroll in and address the ladies.

JACK: Good-day, ladies.
KATHLEEN: Good-day yourself, your lordships.
JACK: Oh, now. I wouldn't go as far as that.
HARRY: No. No. Still a bit of the common touch.
JACK: Least, so I'd hope.
HARRY: Oh, yes.
MARJORIE: And how have you been keeping, professor?
JACK: Professor? I can see we're a little elevated today.
MARJORIE: Don't know about elevated. But *we're* sitting down.
KATHLEEN: Been standing up, we have, for hours.
HARRY: Hours?
MARJORIE: When you were sitting down.
JACK: Oh dear . . . I wasn't aware . . .
KATHLEEN: 'Coure you were. My bleedin' feet. Just look at them.
MARJORIE: Pull your skirt down, girl.
KATHLEEN: Oh, Gawd . . .

They continue in this vein. The men tell the women a little about them-selves, and Kathleen responds again and again with an astonished "Oooh!"

They get to talking about treacle, and where it comes from—the mysterious East perhaps. They discuss a fellow-inmate, a woman with an embarrassing disfigurement to her nose, caused by an attack by her husband. Jack would like to sit, but there aren't enough chairs; in fact, there are only these two chairs and the one table for one or two thousand people, as Marjorie tells it, plus some benches that are uncomfortable.

The previous evening they all attended a lecture entitled "Up the Amazon" and they particularly noticed a man in a loincloth who exposed himself by chance, for a fleeting instant. This leads Marjorie to ask Jack, "Were you the feller they caught climbing out of a window here last week?" Jack's reaction is on the order of "Who, me?" but he doesn't answer the question directly.

Kathleen has the impression that Jack is or was a doctor, but Jack sets her straight: he once started studying medicine, but his family couldn't afford for him to continue.

Harry, it seems, has been asking to be let out in order to attend to some problems, but he managed to straighten things out by mail. Marjorie specu-lates on how she would handle Harry if she were married to him. Harry craves forbearance.

HARRY: We all have our little foibles, our little feelings.
JACK: Oh, indeed.

HARRY: Hardly be human without.

JACK: Oh, no.

HARRY: The essence of true friendship, in my view, is to make allowances for one another's little lapses.

MARJORIE: Heard all about your little lapses, haven't we?

KATHLEEN: Ooooooooh!

JACK: All have our little falls from grace.

MARJORIE: Burn down the whole bleedin' building, he will. Given up smoking because they won't let him have any matches.

KATHLEEN: Oooh!

JACK: The rumors that drift around a place like this . . . hardly worth the trouble . . .

HARRY: Absolutely.

JACK: If one believed everything one heard . . .

HARRY: Oh, yes.

JACK: I was remarking to my friend earlier this morning: if one can't enjoy life as it takes one, what's the point of living it at all? One can't, after all, spend the whole of one's life inside a shell.

HARRY: Oh, no.

MARJORIE: Know what he'd spend it inside if he had half a chance.

KATHLEEN: Oooooh!

MARJORIE: Tell my husband of you, I shall.

KATHLEEN: Bus-driver.

JACK: Really? I've taken a life-long interest in public transport.

Marjorie's mind runs along its single track of sexual insinuation, and again she cautions Kathleen to pull her skirt down. For a moment Jack remembers the good old days when "one stood for a lady as a matter of course." Marjorie suggests the possibility that Jack might miss lunch, and this upsets Jack in a mild way—he starts to weep. He explains his distress: if they don't get on the lunch line early, they'll get a cold plate. Kathleen agrees—they ought to go—but Marjorie suspects Jack is only trying to trick her into vacating her chair so he can have it.

Kathleen asks for Harry's arm; gallantly, he offers it. Jack and Marjorie exchange courtesies, and they prepare to go in to lunch.

HARRY: Ready? . . . All aboard then are we?

MARJORIE: Well, then. All right . . .

JACK: Right then . . . Dining-hall—here we come!

HARRY: Sausages today, if I'm not mistaken.

KATHLEEN: Ooooh!

MARJORIE: Corned beef hash.

KATHLEEN: Ooooh!

JACK: One as good as another, I always say.

KATHLEEN: Oooooh!

HARRY: Turned out better.

JACK: Turned out better.
HARRY: Altogether.
JACK: Altogether.
HARRY: Well, then. Here we go.
    They go. Curtain.

ACT II

After lunch, a youth named Alfred is struggling with the table on the same spot. Marjorie comes on and warns him to be careful with the table, but Alfred seems only barely to understand her. He speaks almost exclusively in monosyllables.

Marjorie is looking for Kathleen, whom she expects will join her after a session of "Remedials," such as basket-weaving. She goes off and Alfred continues lifting furniture. He is carrying one of the chairs when he walks off.

Kathleen limps on, accompanied by Harry, who is carrying a wicker chair. They are disturbed to see that even with the chair they brought with them, there are still only two chairs.

Kathleen sits in the remaining metal chair and lets Harry know they all have heard about his "Making up things." Harry's reply is, "What's life for if you can't . . ." He flutters his fingers, and Kathleen imitates the action.

HARRY: . . . . . After all, one looks around: what does one see?
KATHLEEN: Gawd . . .
HARRY: A little this. A little that.
KATHLEEN: Here. Everything you know is little.
HARRY: Well . . . I er . . . Yes . . . No great role for this actor, I'm afraid. A little stage, a tiny part.
KATHLEEN: You an actor then?
HARRY: Well, I did, as a matter of fact, at one time . . . actually, a little . . .
KATHLEEN: Here, little again. You notice?
HARRY: Oh . . . You're right.
KATHLEEN: What parts you play then?
HARRY: Well, as a matter of fact . . . not your Hamlets, of course, your Ophelias: more the little bystander who passes by the . . .
KATHLEEN: Here. Little.
HARRY: Oh . . . yes!
KATHLEEN: Play anything romantic?
HARRY: Oh, romance, now, was . . . never very far away.

Kathleen vaguely remembers that she had a chance for romance, once, right here in the institution . . . but she is distracted by worry about what will happen when Jack and Marjorie return from remedials and find that, even if they are bringing a chair, there will still be only three.

Kathleen wants Harry to tell her: was Jack put in here for pursuing little girls? Harry hints there may have been "proclivities." It doesn't matter much what Harry says, though, because Kathleen can scarcely understand him. She complains again of her uncomfortable shoes with no laces (and they took away her belt, too, for fear she'd strangle herself; a belt that helped her show off her figure to better advantage).

Kathleen tells Harry about her husband. He is employed by a corporation as a clean-up man—"Smells awful, he does." Then she starts to fret again.

KATHLEEN: It's going to be tea-time before they get here.
HARRY *(examines watch):* No, no. Still a little time.
KATHLEEN: Your wife alive?
HARRY: Er.
KATHLEEN: Separated?
HARRY: Well, I . . .
KATHLEEN: Unsympathetic.
HARRY: Yes?
KATHLEEN: Your wife.
HARRY: Well . . . One can ask too much these days, I believe, of er.
KATHLEEN: Met once a fortnight wouldn't be any divorce. Ridiculous, living together. S'not human.
HARRY: No . . .
KATHLEEN: Like animals . . . Even they run off when they're not feeling like it.
HARRY: Oh, yes.
KATHLEEN: Not natural . . . One man. One woman. Who's He think He is?
    Harry looks round.
No . . . Him. *(Kathleen points up.)*
HARRY: Oh, yes . . .
KATHLEEN: Made Him a bachelor. Cor blimey: no wife for Him.
HARRY: No.
KATHLEEN: Saved somebody the trouble.
HARRY: Yes.
KATHLEEN: Does it all by telepathy.

A man shouldn't marry till he's 40, Kathleen states firmly, as Alfred returns with the other chair. Kathleen tells Harry that Alfred is a would-be wrestler who has something wrong with his brain (as Alfred exits again, still carrying the chair). Kathleen disconcerts Harry by asking him what he plans to do after he leaves this place; he cannot answer. Kathleen understands his depression; she once tried to kill herself by putting her head in the gas oven, but was saved by the milkman's arrival. Kathleen gives Harry her hand to hold, to comfort him. As Alfred glides by again with his chair, Kathleen confides to Harry that she wants to grow old, she wants to die and get out of being a woman.

Jack and Marjorie enter; he too is carrying a wicker chair. Kathleen sits, and Marjorie sits, and of course there is an Alphonse-Gaston routine between

Harry and Jack as to who will sit in the one remaining chair. They decide to take turns, and Jack sits first.

Marjorie harps on Kathleen's weakness: "Men all the time . . . . . Can't let no tradesman near the house." Kathleen, irritated, reproaches Marjorie with *her* weakness: "Can't go down the street without her trousers wetting." The men ignore this quarrel and talk about sports; but Kathleen walks off in a huff, taking Harry with her.

Marjorie goes on about Kathleen even after she's left, and Jack finally manages to change the subject with "One of the advantages of a late lunch, of course, is that it leaves a shorter space to tea."

Marjorie still wonders why Jack is a patient here.

JACK: Oh . . . Little . . .
MARJORIE: Girl?
JACK: Girl?
MARJORIE: Girls.
JACK: Girls?
MARJORIE: In the street.
JACK: Really?
MARJORIE: Here . . . What you in for?
JACK: A wholly voluntary basis, I assure you.
MARJORIE: Wife put you away?
JACK: Oh, no. No, no. Just a moment . . . needed . . . Thought I might . . .
MARJORIE: Ever been in the padded whatsit?
JACK: Don't believe . . .

Marjorie confides to Jack that she's been there and finds it restful. She has been to this place twice before, though Kathleen doesn't know it. Marjorie is "one of the regulars" and considers herself "good as cured."

Marjorie questions Jack about his wife, about going home, and soon Jack is weeping again. Marjorie advises Jack to stay here for good, make this place his permanent home.

Alfred comes in again, still carrying the chair. Alfred admires Jack's cane, then asks both Jack and Marjorie quite casually if they would care to fight. They decline.

MARJORIE: What you in for?
ALFRED: In what?
MARJORIE: Thinks he's at home, he does. Doesn't know his own strength, do you?
ALFRED: No.
MARJORIE: Took a bit of his brain, haven't they?
ALFRED: Yeh.
MARJORIE: Feel better?
ALFRED: Yeh.

Marjorie pretends that she is going to fight Alfred, and the poor youth backs off. Alfred (Marjorie informs Jack) was an apprentice painter who painted "rude letters" in the road in the center of town, and it took weeks to clean them off.

Jack tries to tell a story about another of his many cousins, but Marjorie implies that he is making things up, cousins and all, and warns Alfred: "Wanna watch him. Trained as a doctor he has."

Marjorie wants to know what Alfred painted in the road, and when Alfred refuses to tell her she gets angry and threatens to "knock your head off." Alfred stands his ground sullenly, twirling the chair. Jack gets up to leave, when Harry and Kathleen return—they've been to the canteen, they explain, in response to Marjorie's usual insinuation about where they've been and what doing.

Marjorie orders Alfred to put down his chair. Alfred obeys, and the two couples sit. Alfred hangs around—"Waiting to be born, he is," Marjorie comments.

MARJORIE *(to Alfred):* What you want?
ALFRED: Nothing.
KATHLEEN: Give you nothing if you come here . . . What you staring at?
ALFRED: Nothing.
MARJORIE: Taken off a bit of his brain they have.
KATHLEEN *(to Alfred):* Where they put it then?
MARJORIE: Thrown it in the dustbin.
KATHLEEN: Could have done with that. Didn't cut a bit of something else off, did they.
MARJORIE: You know what your trouble is, my girl.
JACK: Time for tea I shouldn't wonder.
    Stands.
HARRY: Yes. Well . . . let me see. Very nearly.
JACK: Stretch the old legs . . .
HARRY: Oh, yes.
MARJORIE: Not your legs need stretching ask me.
JACK: Ah, well . . . trim.

Kathleen is telling them all that she heard in the office that Marjorie has been classed as a "Persistent Offender," when Harry starts to weep, for no apparent reason. Marjorie urges Jack to help his friend, but Jack explains that Harry will be all right in a minute, "Comes and goes."

Marjorie decides that it's time for Kathleen and herself to be on their way. They depart without much ceremony, wrangling as usual, Marjorie assisting the limping Kathleen. Alfred lifts the table in a demonstration of strength and then walks off.

The two men begin discussing the weather; then Jack talks of tolerating other people's foibles, telling Harry about a relative who wore dark glasses only at night. Alfred returns, carries off one of the metal chairs. Jack remembers another relative who served on a corvette, and this reminds him of the sea.

JACK: At no point is one more than seventy-five miles from the sea.
HARRY: Really.
JACK: That is the nature of this little island.
HARRY: Extraordinary when you think.
JACK: When you think what came from it.
HARRY: Oh, yes.
JACK: Radar.
HARRY: Oh, yes.
JACK: Jet propulsion.
HARRY: My word.
JACK: Television.
HARRY: Oh . . .
JACK: Steam engine.
HARRY: Goodness.
JACK: Empire the like of which no one has ever seen.
HARRY: No. My word.
JACK: Light of the world.
HARRY: Oh, yes.
JACK: Penicillin.
HARRY: Penicillin.
JACK: Darwin.
HARRY: Darwin.
JACK: Newton.
HARRY: Newton.
JACK: Milton.
HARRY: My word.

All this and Raleigh too, sprung from "This little island." Harry remarks "Shan't see its like" and "The sun has set," and Jack replies, "Couple of hours . . ."

Harry comments that the place they are in is so large and populous that you never meet the same people twice. Even so, there isn't room for all the people who want to get in, not enough money to take care of all. Jack calls to witness that there is only one table and two chairs provided for two thousand people here, "While overhead . . ." They both look up as though to see how money is being spent on skyborne ventures.

Alfred comes back, lifts a chair, then goes. The two men comment on clouds, flowers, shadows. Jack takes out his deck of cards and goes through the motions of a trick or two, then puts them away.

HARRY: Amazing thing, of course, is the er.
JACK: Oh, yes.
HARRY: Still prevails.

JACK: Oh, my goodness.

HARRY: Hendriks I find is a . . .

JACK: Oh, yes.

HARRY: Moustache . . . Eyebrows.

JACK: Divorced.

HARRY: Oh, yes,

JACK: Moral fibre. Set to a task, never complete it. Find some way to back out.

HARRY: Oh, yes.

JACK: The sea is an extraordinary . . .

HARRY: Oh, yes.

JACK: Cousin of mine . . .

HARRY: See the church.

JACK: Shouldn't wonder He's disappointed.

HARRY: Oh, yes.

JACK: Heartbreak.

HARRY: Oh, yes.

JACK: Same mistake . . . Won't make it twice.

HARRY: Oh, no.

JACK: Once over. Never again.

> *Alfred has come on.*

ALFRED: You finished?

JACK: Well, I . . . er . . .

ALFRED: Take 'em back.

JACK: Oh, well. That's very . . .

> *Alfred grasps the two wicker chairs, picks up both. Takes them off.*

What I . . . er . . . yes.

> *Curtain.*

THE GINGERBREAD LADY

A Play in Three Acts

BY NEIL SIMON

Cast and credits appear on page 300

NEIL SIMON was born in the Bronx, N.Y. on July 4, 1927. He attended New York University and the University of Denver. His first theatrical work consisted of sketches for camp shows at Tamiment, Pa., in collaboration with his brother Danny. He became a TV writer, supplying a good deal of material to Sid Caesar and Phil Silvers.

On Broadway, Simon contributed sketches to Catch a Star *(1955) and* New Faces of 1956. *His first Broadway play was* Come Blow Your Horn *(1961), followed by the book for the musical* Little Me *(1962). His comedy* Barefoot in the Park *(1963) was selected as a Best Play of its season, as was* The Odd Couple *(1965). Neither of these had closed when the musical* Sweet Charity, *for which Simon wrote the book, came along early in 1966; and none of the three had closed when Simon's* The Star-Spangled Girl *opened the following season in December 1966—so that Simon had the phenomenal total of four hit shows running simultaneously on Broadway during the season of 1966-67. When the last of the four closed the following summer, Simon's hits had played a total of 3,367 performances over four theater seasons.*

Simon immediately began on another stack of Broadway hits. His Plaza Suite *(1968) was named a Best Play of its year; his book for the musical* Promises, Promises *(1969) was another smash, and last season's* Last of the Red Hot Lovers *became his fourth Best Play and the third in still another group of Simon shows in grand simultaneous display on Broadway. The* Gingerbread Lady *is—let's see, now—Simon's eighth straight success and fifth Best Play.* Plaza Suite *closed before* Gingerbread *opened, so this season Simon has a stack of only three—a paltry three shows running on Broadway at the same time.*

Simon lives in the New York City area where he can keep an eye on all this action (he owns the Eugene O'Neill Theater, too). He is married, with two daughters.

Time: The present

Place: A brownstone apartment in the West Seventies

ACT I

SYNOPSIS: On a late afternoon in November, James Perry comes into the living room of Evy Meara's apartment to put a vase of cut flowers on the coffee table. The room is large, high-ceilinged, with somewhat battered furniture including a piano at right covered with theatrical photographs, a sofa at center and a theatrical poster on the wall at center. The windows are at right, and doors lead to a bedroom at right, the hall at center and the kitchen at left.

James (Jimmy) Perry is *"in his early forties, portly and probably homosexual. Probably but not obviously. He wears slacks with a dark blue turtleneck sweater."* He is waiting for someone, but when the doorbell rings he is cautious about opening the door until he's sure it's the grocery delivery man —Spanish, about 20, carrying two bags. The delivery man has been instructed to collect cash for the food, not charge it, and Jimmy manages to come up with the right sum from his various pockets (though he is out of a job and obviously short of cash). The man departs, with an arrogant gesture of contempt for Jimmy.

The phone rings—it's the phone company asking why their bill hasn't been paid. Jimmy explains that Evy Meara has "been away sick for the past ten weeks . . . But you're not going to cut it off, are you, she'll pay it as soon as she gets home . . . Fourth notice already, my goodness . . . But you must realize she's good for it, I mean this is Evelyn Meara, the singer . . . . ."

The doorbell rings; this time it's Toby Landau, *"a very pretty woman in her early 40s, but you'd never believe it."* She looks much younger and obviously spends a lot of time caring for her appearance. Toby is wearing a tailored suit and carrying a suitcase—she has just brought Evy back from Long Island in a taxi.

JIMMY: Where is she? *(He looks out the door.)* Evy? Where's Evy?

TOBY: She's saying hello to a neighbor . . . I thought you were going to clean the apartment. Didn't you say you would clean the apartment for Evy?

JIMMY: I tried rearranging the furniture, but it always came out like a bus terminal in Passaic. Where is she? Is she all right?

TOBY: Yes, but you're going to be shocked when you see her. She lost forty-two pounds.

JIMMY: Oh, my God.

TOBY: I will tell you right here and now that a rest home for drunks is the most depressing place in the world.

JIMMY: I never thought she'd last it out. I'm so nervous. What do I say to her? How do I act in front of her?

TOBY: You hug her and love her and above all, you must trust her.

JIMMY: I'll kill her if she ever takes another drink . . . Where the hell is she?

EVY *(offstage):* I'm out in the hall. Are you ready?

JIMMY: Ready.

Evy enters, in mink coat and carrying books.

EVY: All right, say it, I'm gorgeous, right?

JIMMY: Oh, my God, I don't believe it. Who is she? Who is this beautiful woman?

EVY: It better be me or I'm out twenty-seven hundred bucks.

JIMMY: Am I allowed to hug you?

EVY: You're allowed.

Jimmy rushes into her arms and hugs her.

Evy is an attractive woman, about the same age as Toby, now looking her best and hardly showing signs of damage, a great improvement over Jimmy's most recent memory of her as "That fat lady who used to drink a lot and use foul language."

Evy looks around, happy to be home again, looking over the furniture, remembering that she once threw some of it out of the window. She has been given some mild tranquillizers to help her sleep; otherwise she seems to be fine. But Jimmy insists on being nervously worried about her. To humor him, Evy agrees to let him make her a sandwich and a pot of coffee. He goes off into the kitchen.

TOBY *(looking at herself in the mirror):* And what can I do, Evy?

EVY: You can stop looking at yourself and give me a cigarette.

TOBY: You *are* nervous, aren't you?

EVY: I hated that place so much I used to save up matches planning to burn it down. It was a God damn prison. And then when it came time to leave I was afraid to go . . . I suddenly felt comfortable there . . . Can I have my cigarette, please?

TOBY: That's almost a whole pack since we left the hospital. Are you sure they said it's all right to smoke?

EVY: Once you pay your bill and check out, they don't care if you get knocked up by a dwarf.

Takes cigarette and smokes.

I thought I'd have a million things to do once I got home. I'm here six minutes, I'm bored to death.

MAUREEN STAPLETON, BETSY VON FURSTENBURG AND MICHAEL LOMBARD IN
"THE GINGERBREAD LADY"

TOBY: You've got to give yourself time, Evy. And then you're going to start
your life all over again and you're going to grow up to be a beautiful wonderful person like me.

EVY: What's that? What's that crap you're putting on your face?

TOBY: It's a special crap that protects the skin. Have you noticed you've
never seen pores on me. As long as you've known me, have you ever seen a
single pore on my face?

EVY: I've never even seen your face . . . Who are you anyway?

TOBY: A woman can never be too pretty. It's her feminine obligation. I
love my looks, don't you?

EVY: You're gorgeous. If you went bald and lost your teeth, you'd still be
cute looking. Leave yourself alone.

TOBY: I can't. Isn't it terrible? I'm obsessed.

EVY: You remind me of the psycho in the room next to me. She used to shampoo her eyelashes every night. Thought all the doctors were in love with her. An eighty-seven-year-old virgin screwball.

TOBY: What a sweet story. You just going to sit there forever? Aren't you going to unpack or something?

EVY: Unpack what? A pair of pajamas and a bottle of mineral oil? Besides, I'm never going in that bedroom again. I ruined half my life in there, the next half I'm playing it safe.

Toby would prefer to stay and keep Evy company during her first night back home, but she is expected by Martin, her husband, at a business dinner. Jimmy can't stay either—he has an audition which, as an out-of-work actor, he can't afford to miss.

Toby suggests that Evy might phone her daughter Polly, but Evy feels it's too soon for that.

EVY: I'm not ready to see my daughter yet, thank you. What I'd really like to do is move the hell out of this dump.

TOBY: Then why don't you move?

EVY: Because, dumb dumb, I still pay a hundred and twenty dollars for three and a half rooms. It's on a sublet from Mary Todd Lincoln.

TOBY: You can borrow from Marty and me until you go back to work again.

EVY: Work? Singing in clubs? The last job I had was two years ago in Pittsburgh. I broke the house record. Fell off the stool seventeen times in one show.

TOBY: That's old news, I don't want to hear about it.

EVY: I shared a dressing room with a female impersonator who had the hots for me. I think we made it but I forget which way.

Toby departs, after extracting a promise from Evy that she "will now be a good girl. Forever and ever." Jimmy brings the coffee and entertains Evy with shop talk about the theater, telling her about his first naked role, confessing "What kills me is that I'm so good." Evy stares out the window while Jimmy daydreams out loud: "I won't get this job tonight. They'll turn me down. I'm auditioning for some nineteen-year-old putz producer who has seventy-five thousand dollars and a drama degree from Oklahoma A & M . . . First time he walked into the theater he fell off the stage, broke two ribs . . . some chance an intelligent actor has today . . . Oh God, I want to be a star so bad. Not a little star. I want to be a big star with three agents and two lawyers and a business manager and a press agent and then I'd fire all of them and get new ones because I'm such a big star. And I'd make everyone pay for the twenty-two years I poured into this business. I wouldn't do benefits, I wouldn't give money to charity. I would become one of the great shit-heels of all time. Isn't that a wonderful dream, Evy?"

But Evy is thinking only of cigarettes at this moment, and Jimmy gives her the remnants of his crumpled pack. She is obviously on edge, and Jimmy knows why.

JIMMY: Why don't you ask me, Evy? Why don't you get it over with and *ask me?* . . . No, I have not seen him or spoken to him, all right?

EVY *(Pause . . . nods):* All right.

JIMMY: I'm lying. I saw him at the bar in Downey's last week. I don't think he's doing well because he had one beer and ate all the pretzels in the dish . . .

EVY: Was he alone?

JIMMY: Yes. I know because when he left I watched him through the window hoping he'd get hit by the Eighth Avenue bus . . . What else do you want to know?

EVY: Nothing. I was curious, not interested.

JIMMY: Oh really? Is that why you keep staring out the window? Is that why you won't go into the bedroom? What are you afraid of, you'll see his lousy ghost sitting on the john doing the Times crossword puzzle? . . . Go on. Go in the bedroom and get it over with, for crise sakes.

Evy takes his advice and goes into the bedroom—but no ghosts after all. The doorbell rings. It is the delivery man, who had forgotten to bring the Coca-Cola and ginger ale. Again he demands cash, but when Jimmy goes to get it Evy steps into view and works her charms on the twenty-year-old until he agrees to let her charge the soda and departs with the very obvious implication "I come again—you take care of me another time—you know what I mean?"

Jimmy cautions Evy not to get herself in hot water again, and Evy protests that she has no designs on the delivery man (and warmly appreciates Jimmy's concern about her).

EVY: Why don't you marry me?

JIMMY: Because you're a drunken nymphomaniac and I'm a homosexual. We'd have trouble getting our kids into a good school.

EVY: Give me a kiss.

> *He kisses her lightly.*

Come on. Give me a real kiss. Who the hell's gonna know?

> *He kisses her with feeling.*

JIMMY: God will punish us for the terrible thing we're doing.

EVY: Don't get depressed but you get me very excited.

JIMMY: I don't have to stay and listen to this kind of talk.

> *Breaks away from her.*

I've got to go. If you promise to behave yourself, I may be nice to you when I'm a star.

EVY: We could live together in Canada. They don't do sex in Canada.

Jimmy really must go for his audition, and he leaves Evy alone in the apartment. Evy tells herself out loud not to panic and makes herself face the fact that she is now alone. She punches up pillows and fingers the piano, then goes to the phone to call her daughter. But then there is the sound of a key in the lock. The door opens, and standing there is her daughter Polly, *"17, pretty, with long straight hair and no pretensions. She wears blue jeans, a sweater and a jacket."* She is carrying a suitcase and means to stay.

Mother and daughter rush into each other's arms. Polly came as soon as she could get out of school (she explains). Evy, tears in her eyes, is overjoyed to see Polly, but she is cautious about letting her move in to the apartment for more than a night or two. Polly may not be allowed to live here—her father decides where Polly is to live (Evy remembers her ex-husband as a man who spits his sibilants, and his new wife Felicia as a teeth-clicker).

Polly reassures her that she has her father's permission to move in with her mother.

POLLY: We've been talking about it for months. He knows how hard you've been trying, he spoke to your doctor, he knows you're all right . . . And he thinks that you need me now.

EVY: *Now* I need you? Where does he think I've been the last seven years, Guatemala?

POLLY: He knows where you've been.

EVY: And what about you? Is this what you really want?

POLLY: I've been packed for three years. Every June I put in bigger sizes.

EVY: You wanna hear something. My whole body is shaking. I'm scared stiff. I wouldn't know the first thing about taking care of you.

POLLY: I'm seventeen years old. How hard could it be?

EVY: I'll level with you, it's not the best thing I do. I was feeling very motherly one time, I bought a couple of turtles, two for eighty-five cents, Irving and Sam. I fed them once, in the morning they were floating on their backs. I don't think I could go through that again.

POLLY: I'm a terrific swimmer.

EVY: Jesus, the one thing I hoped I wouldn't have is a dumb daughter. What kind of influence would I be on you. I talk filthy. I have always talked filthy. I'm a congenital filthy talker.

POLLY: Son of a bitch.

EVY: I don't think that's funny.

POLLY: Well, I just got here, give me a chance.

Polly remembers a gingerbread house and lady her mother gave her for Christmas when she was nine; Polly cherished it. She remembers the good times and bad; she has seen her mother drunk ("Mostly I hated it but once or twice you sure were cute") and she remembers Lou Tanner who once lived with Evy.

Evy insists on Polly knowing about her promiscuity ("I sure know true love when I see it. It's wherever I happen to look"). She confesses to her daughter that she loved the eight months with Lou Tanner, "that guitar player," who walked out on her one night for "an eighteen year old Indian hippie." Evy continues: "I sat at that window for six weeks waiting and hoping while I ran through two liquor stores in this neighborhood alone . . . Finally Toby came

in one day and found me face down in the bathtub . . . I woke up in a sanatarium in Long Island, and the rest isn't very interesting unless you like stories
about human torture . . . But I went through it and I'm here. And I figure,
pussycat, that I have only one more chance at this human being business . . .
and if I blow it this time, they'll probably bury me in some distillery in
Kentucky . . . And if this is the kind of person you'd like to live with, God has
cursed me with one of the all-time great schmucks for a daughter."

Polly insists that she wants to stay, and Evy makes plans for a new life—
they will spruce up the place, she will get a job. Evy goes into the bedroom
and Polly to the kitchen, just as the doorbell rings. Polly opens the door, and
*"Lou Tanner stands there. He is in his mid-30s, with scruffy, unmanageable
hair, a full, bushy mustache, a dirty turtleneck sweater and light tan desert
boots, very worn. He is, despite his appearance, attractive."*

Lou greets Polly awkwardly, as Evy comes out of the bedroom. Polly leaves
them alone. Lou notices how well Evy looks, and Evy notices how bedraggled
Lou appears; his "Indian" girl has left him (he tells her) and he is staying in a
friend's apartment.

Lou tries to pick up where they left off, but to Evy he seems "one priceless, unbelievable bastard" for walking in on her like this at a moment when
her nerves are stretched tight. She wants no part of him.

EVY: Lou, I'm forty-three years old and I'm trying to be a grown up lady.
The doctors told me I'm not allowed to drink any more or have affairs with
thirty-three-year-old guitar players . . . I thank you for this visit. Now go
home, find someone your own age and light up some Astro-Turf or whatever
you're smoking these days.

LOU *(smiles):* If nothing else, Evy, you have a way with a phrase. I used
to quote you. Word for word. Of course this dumb little Indian chick never
saw the humor. We communicated in other ways. But whenever I needed a
good honest laugh, I had to quote you, Ev. You weren't in the room, but you
were there, you know what I mean?

EVY: It's an image I think I'll cherish forever . . . Listen, Polly is here and
I think we ought to cut this short.

LOU: I want to come back, Ev.
        There is a pause.
. . . Today, tomorrow, next week . . . but I want to come back.

EVY: I see! . . . Would that be with or without meals?

LOU: Maybe with a little humility. I'll scrape up whatever I can.

Still, Evy brushes him off. She asks him a casual question about his work,
not really caring about the answer, and Lou reproaches her: Evy cared about
him all right, but not about his songs. In fact, she disliked them. Evy admits
she never expressed her real opinion because "I had enough trouble getting
affection from you without giving bad reviews," and Evy always craved
affection.

Lou admits that at least while he was living with Evy he functioned as a music writer, good or bad, and he hopes to function again: "Christ, Evy, you want me to say it, I'll say it. I need you very badly." He tries to persuade her.

LOU: . . . . . There's still a whole life to get through Evy . . . I'm not coming in here offering you any phony promises. Sure, in six weeks I may find another cute assed little chick, and in eight weeks they might find you under the piano with a case of Thunderbird wine. Then again, maybe not. Together, Evy, we don't add up to one strong person. I just think together, we have a better chance.

EVY: What I need now is a relative, not a relationship. And I have one in there unpacking.

LOU: Who are you kidding?

EVY: She'll be here in the morning. That's good enough for me.

LOU: The mornings have never been your problem.

EVY: We were just going to have dinner. I'd ask you to stay but it's just the immediate family.

LOU: Well, it was kind of a slow afternoon, I just thought I'd ask . . . I'm really glad to see you in good shape, Ev . . . Take care of yourself.

EVY: That's the general idea.

LOU (at the door): You still have ten seconds to change your mind.

He waits. No reply.

My, how time flies.

He opens the door, about to go.

EVY: Lou!

He stops, turns.

. . . Will you call me some time? Just to say hello?

LOU (looks at her): Probably not.

He turns, goes, closes door behind him. Evy stands there a moment . . . The bedroom door opens, Polly comes out.

POLLY: . . . I didn't hear a word . . . But can I say something?

EVY: Only if it'll make me laugh . . . Are you unpacked yet?

POLLY: It would take me two minutes to put it all back.

EVY: If you're unpacked, then wash your hands, set the table and light the stove. It's dinner time.

POLLY (brightly): O.K., Evy.

EVY: And none of the Evy crap . . . I'm your mother. I want a little respect for crise sakes!

Evy starts to remove tablecloth from table as Polly, beaming, exits into kitchen. Curtain.

ACT II

Three weeks later, at about 9 p.m., Evy hasn't come home for dinner and Polly is worried, phoning the bars. But soon Evy comes in, carrying packages, bubbling over about the day's adventures: lunching with a friend, being ogled by an 86-year-old admirer. Polly's concern shows in the way she questions her mother; she reminds her mother that she hardly ever eats, that she stays up all night smoking and watching TV. Reflexively, Evy bridles at Polly's overprotectiveness—but she doesn't want to offend her daughter, to fail at this business of being a mother, so she promises to take better care of herself and live a more regular life.

Evy can hardly wait to tell Polly how she happened to meet a friend whose husband owns four restaurants. One of them, in Garden City, has an opening for a hostess at $190 a week.

EVY: . . . . . So I played it very cool, and nonchalantly got down on my knees, kissed her shoes, licked her ankles and carried her packages out the store.

POLLY: A hostess in a restaurant? Is that what you want to do?

EVY: No, what I *want* to do is be a masseur at the New York Athletic Club but there are no openings . . . Can I finish my story?

POLLY: Why don't you finish your story?

EVY: Thank you, I'll finish my story . . . So we go around the corner to Schrafft's and she buys me a sherry and we sit there chatting like a couple of Scarsdale debutantes—me, the former lush, and her, a chippy married to Joe Bananas . . . and she writes down the address and I have to be—

Consults scrap of paper in her pocket.

—at the Blue Cockatoo Restaurant in Garden City at ten o'clock tomorrow morning where Lucky Luciano's nephew will interview me. All this in one day, *plus* getting my knees rubbed by an eighty-six-year-old degenerate on the crosstown bus . . . And you're going to sit there and tell me there's no God . . .

She looks at Polly expectantly, hoping Polly will be as exuberant and enthusiastic about her prospects as she is. But Polly just glares at her.

What's the matter?

POLLY: . . . You had a glass of sherry?

EVY *(turns away):* Oh, Christ.

POLLY: Why did you have a glass of sherry?

EVY: Because the waitress put it down in front of me.

POLLY: They don't put it down in front of you unless you order it. I don't understand you.

EVY: I don't understand *you.* I rush home happy, excited, bubbling with good news and who do I find when I get here, a seventeen-year-old cop! I am not loaded, I am not smashed, I am thrilled to death because I spent a whole day out of this house and I came home alive and noticed and even wanted.

POLLY: Do you need a drink to feel that?

EVY: I was tense, I was afraid of blowing the job. So I had one stinking little drink. Did you ever have a cocktail in Schrafft's? Half of it is painted on the glass.

The offer of the job made Evy feel wanted. Polly does not quite understand and, not understanding, decides to mute her criticism of her mother.
And Evy has just about decided *not* to take the job anyway—but it felt good
to be asked.

Evy has brought home some champagne ("All I'm doing is pouring") for
a party to celebrate Toby's birthday. Before the guests arrive, Polly takes the
opportunity to tell Evy they have a lunch date at Rumpelmayer's the next day
with her father, who wants to see how they are getting along. Polly tells her
mother not to worry and exits to get dressed for the party.

The doorbell rings—it's Jimmy. He enters the apartment without a word
and sits without taking his coat off. His leg is shaking in an uncontrollable
spasm; obviously he is in a state of extreme tension. He finally explodes: he
has been fired from the cast of the off-Broadway show by the 19-year-old
producer, his part has been given to someone else, "Three nights before the
opening. My name was in the Sunday *Times* ad. I've got eighteen relatives from
Paterson, New Jersey coming to the opening. Six of them already sent me
telegrams . . . My Aunt Rosario sent me a Candygram, I already ate the God
damned candy."

Evy tries to comfort Jimmy: the show will probably be a flop. But Jimmy
is humiliated to the point of utter despair. When Evy tries to take off his coat
Jimmy merely buries his face in his hands, weeping. He continues sobbing, in
an orgy of self-pity, doubting he'll ever make it as an actor. Evy sends out her
own signal of alarm: "You want to destroy me? You want to tear my guts
out? You know I can't handle it."

Nevertheless Jimmy keeps on begging for reassurance.

JIMMY: Evy, you've seen me on the stage, you know I can be good. Was I
good, Evy? Tell me, I really have to know.

EVY: You're the best. There's no one better. You ring a doorbell, the
house comes down . . . Let me get you a driink. You'll feel much better if you
have a drink.

JIMMY: I'm not Olivier. I never said I was Olivier, did I?

EVY: I don't even like Olivier. I can't understand him half the time.

JIMMY (*as Evy goes into the kitchen*): Remember *Mister Roberts* at Bucks
County? Or *Born Yesterday* in Westport? I never heard laughs like that in my
life . . . Did you? The truth! Did you?

EVY (*offstage*): I have never heard laughs like that in my life.

JIMMY: In my life, I never heard laughs like that . . . And I don't have to
get laughs all the time. My God, the things I've done . . . *Phaedra, Mother
Courage, Rhinoceros, The Balcony, Detective Story* . . . Jesus, remember
Detective Story? The second hood? I was incredible.

EVY (*offstage*): You were brilliant.

We hear a cork pop from champagne bottle.

JIMMY: When did you see me in *Detective Story?* I did that in Columbus,
Ohio.

EVY *(comes out with champagne bottle and two glasses):* You were so brilliant I didn't have to see it.

She hands Jimmy a glass. He takes it without being aware he has it.

JIMMY: I played the Dauphin in *Saint Joan* at the Cleveland Auditorium three years before that nineteen-year-old rich Oklahoma idiot schmuck was born.

Evy pours champagne into his glass, then hers.

EVY: Forget it. He's not worth it.

JIMMY: I actually pleaded with him. I humiliated myself in front of the entire cast. I had no shame. No shame, Evy. *(He drinks.)* Opening night my mother will throw herself in front of a rented limousine.

EVY: That's the best thing that could happen to *your* mother.

She sips a little champagne.

JIMMY: I don't wish anybody in the world harm. I don't curse anybody. I want everybody to live their lives healthy and without pain . . . but I pray that little bastard gets a Baby Ruth stuck in his throat and chokes him on the spot.

He drinks more champagne. Evy pours more into his glass. Jimmy suddenly watches her and realizes what's happening.

. . . Oh, my God, what am I doing? I'm sitting here drinking with you. Are you crazy? Are you out of your mind? Put that glass down.

He reaches for it but she pulls it away.

EVY: I'm not drinking, I'm sipping.

JIMMY: You've already sipped a whole glass. Give it to me.

EVY: You think I'm going to stand here and watch you have a breakdown on ginger ale. I need help too.

Evy finishes the glass, excusing herself by explaining that she simply panicked at the sight of Jimmy's unhappiness. When the doorbell rings, Evy reminds Jimmy quickly that she doesn't want anyone else to know that she drank the champagne.

It is Toby on the doorstep, looking pretty as usual—but alone, without her husband Marty. Toby announces that her husband is not coming to her birthday party. He is going to leave her. He wants a divorce. Trying to conceal a tearful outburst, Toby quickly disappears into the kitchen. Jimmy and Evy are stunned. Jimmy reacts first, running into the kitchen after Toby. Evy's reaction is to pour another glass of champagne and gulp it, putting the empty glass down before Polly emerges from the bedroom.

Toby and Jimmy come back from the kitchen, and Polly sees that there is a tense situation. Toby greets Polly, then asks her for a few moments to talk with her mother. Polly politely withdraws to the bedroom once again.

Toby unburdens herself: her husband wants a divorce. Before she can go on she feels the need of a drink, and Jimmy quickly pours her a glass of champagne. Then Toby continues. "Martin—has grown accustomed to my face. *(She is visibly wounded but is trying hard not to show the hurt.)* . . . Accustomed to my touch, accustomed to my voice . . . and I think he's a little

bored with my hair. *(She looks at them, forces a smile, sips a little wine.)* . . .
He's devoted to me . . . He is respectful of me . . . He is indebted to me . . .
but he's having a lot of trouble sleeping with me. For some inexplicable reason . . . 'inexplicable' is his word . . . he has had no desire to make sexual
advances towards me . . . He makes them, but there's no desire . . . It's as
though someone were in back of him 'pushing' . . . He is not tired . . . he is
not overworked . . . he is not distracted . . . He is simply—'Turned off.' That's
my word."

Toby's desperation is quiet where Jimmy's was voluble, but it is deeply felt,
too. Calmly, Toby recalls all the conquests of her youth after being recognized
as the prettiest girl at the University of Michigan: a halfback, a book publisher, a symphony conductor, a member of the British royal household, a Senator—"and that son-of-a-bitch four-hundred-dollar-a-week television salesman
tells me *he isn't interested . . . . .*"

Evy herself is almost desperate with the need to help Toby in some way,
but all she can do is pour Toby another glass of champagne, while Toby continues to protest. Only the year before Toby had an affair with a young man
in Los Angeles and was asked for proof of her age in a cocktail lounge. She
is obsessed with the conviction that men are attracted to women by their
physical beauty, and she has spared no effort to enhance hers for her husband:
special creams, baths, attention to every part of the body, even a Japanese foot
man from White Plains.

TOBY: . . . . . But I've never done it for me. None of it . . . It's what
Martin wanted when he came into his house at night, what all men want . . .
Femininity and beauty . . . But Evy—if it no longer interests Martin . . . then
I assure you . . . somewhere . . . soon, someplace, someone else will be very
. . . very . . . very . . . interested!
            Her voice has trailed off almost becoming inaudible at the end . . .
            There is a long, desperate silence in the room . . .
    EVY *(finally):* For purely medicinal purposes, I'm having a drink.
            She starts for the bottle.
    JIMMY *(warning):* Evy!
    EVY: I'm only a hundred and thirty pounds but if you try and stop me, I'll
kill you . . . *One* drink, for Christ's sakes.
    JIMMY: You *had* one drink.
    EVY: For *your* story. Now I need one for hers.
            She pours into glass.
    TOBY *(looks up as if in the room for the first time):* What's the matter?
What's going on?
    EVY: *Nothing's* going on but it's going to start right now . . . We've *all*
had a few minor setbacks, but it's a birthday party . . . and I don't give a shit
if the room is on fire, we're going to start having some fun.
            She drinks her glass of champagne quickly, then looks at bottle
            and holds it up.
We need a new bottle. *(Calls out.)* Polly! Fun and games.

Polly comes out, ready for a party, noticing that something is wrong with Evy, who goes to the kitchen to open another bottle. It dawns on Toby that maybe she shouldn't have put the extra strain on Evy, burdening her with her troubles. Toby tries to reassure Evy when she comes back into the room with the new bottle of wine, but it's too late now. Evy is under the influence, losing her inhibitions, letting all her feelings show, swinging wildly with aggressive sarcasm at all except her daughter.

Polly takes this situation in stride, enduring even her mother's exaggerated sentimentality. "Do you know what it is to have a daughter worried about you?" Evy asks no one in particular, "It is the single greatest pleasure in the world."

Toby and Jimmy too are worried about Evy and are in no mood for a party, but Evy insists on forcing the gayety. She demands a toast from Jimmy who delivers a limp one in honor of Toby's birthday. Evy waxes sentimental about Toby's friendship but manages to spill a glass of wine all over her (Evy has consumed most of the second bottle of champagne herself and is pretty far gone now.)

Toby leaves—she can't bear to stay there and watch Evy destroying herself, even though she knows her own trouble triggered Evy's relapse. Polly continues to watch the situation coolly, an observer. Jimmy tries to get the bottle away from Evy, then decides it's too late. He too leaves angrily: " . . . . . you just drank yourself out of a couple of friends. I don't want to see you any more, Evy. I swear to God, I am through. Finished forever, I've *had* it . . . Goodbye, Polly, I'm sorry."

Jimmy avoids a kiss from Evy and departs, even though Evy calls after him begging him to stay. Evy tries to compose herself in front of her daughter.

EVY: . . . . . You're mad at me. I don't know what I did, but you're mad at me, right?

POLLY: I'm not mad at you, Mother.

EVY: What then? You're ashamed? Ashamed of your sweet little old mother because she had two tiny glasses of domestic wine?

POLLY: I'm not ashamed.

EVY: *Then what are you?*

POLLY: I'm sorry . . . I'm just plain sorry.
She looks at Evy, then slowly goes into bedroom and closes the door behind her. Evy stands there.

EVY *(loudly):* Sorry for what? For me? Well, don't be sorry for me because I don't need your God damned teenage pity . . . I'm terrific baby, haven't you noticed? Cost me twenty-seven hundred bucks and I'm skinny and terrific and I can have any dirty old man in the neighborhood . . . *(Suddenly softening.)* Oh, Jesus, Polly, I'm sorry . . .
Crosses to bedroom door.
Polly, don't be mad . . . Come on out, we'll have our own private party . . . Look! Look, I'm gonna put on some music.
She crosses to record player.

I've just had a request to play one of my old numbers.
> *She takes out her album.*

Come listen to mother sing when she was a big star, darling.
> *Puts record on machine.*

Well, not exactly a big star . . . But I once had a sandwich named after me at the Stage Delicatessen . . .
> *The music starts . . . We hear Evy singing . . . She stands there listening, drinking from wine glass.*

. . . That's not bad, is it? . . . It's not bad . . . It's not *thrilling* but it's not bad . . . *(She sings along, looks around room.)* This is about the same size audiences I used to get . . .
> *She crosses to bedroom door.*

Polly, please come out . . . I don't want to listen to me all by myself . . . Polly? *(No answer. She looks at the phone.)* I am *not* going to listen all by myself . . .
> *She crosses to phone . . . Takes a deep breath and dials.*

(Into phone.) . . . Hello? Lou? . . . You alone? . . . Guess who wants to come over to your place?
> *Curtain.*

ACT III

The following morning, Saturday, at 11 o'clock, Polly and Toby (dressed in polo coat over her pajamas) are sitting, waiting, telling each other they're not worried about Evy. Polly is angry that Evy has stayed out all night without a word to anyone, and she vows that "The minute I hear she's all right I'm not going to forgive her." Polly starts to cry and exits to the bedroom.

Evy comes into her apartment stealthily, hiding her face. When she finally turns to face Toby, Toby sees that Evy has a black eye. Evy explains "I didn't get beaten, Toby, just punched. One clean, little punch, I never even felt it," but she despairs of explaining her all-night absence and her black eye to Polly. To Toby, Evy admits that she spent the night with Lou Tanner.

EVY: He plays requests, I was lonesome.

TOBY: Why did you start drinking yesterday? Everything was going so good for you. Why, Evy?

EVY: What did you want, a nice, simple answer? When I was six years old my father didn't take me to the circus . . . How the hell do I know why I do anything.

TOBY: Didn't you learn anything in ten weeks at the hospital?

EVY: The doctor tried to explain but I was too busy making a pass at him . . . If I knew, Toby, would it make any difference?

TOBY: It would help.

EVY: If you haven't eaten in three months you don't want a description of food, you want a little hot something in the plate.

TOBY: And did you get your fill last night, Evy? Did you get your little hot something in the plate?

EVY: No, but we negotiated for a while . . .

TOBY: With someone like that? A deadbeat musician who doesn't give a damn about hitting some drunken woman.

EVY: You just don't get hit like that, you gotta ask for it . . . I happened to make a bad choice. I broke his guitar. I smashed it against the refrigerator, handed him the pieces and said, "Now you can look for work you're equipped to do." I thought it was cute, the man has no sense of humor.

At least Lou didn't just walk away in indifference the way Marty did (Evy reminds Toby): "If you powdered Marty once in a while instead of your face, you'd be wearing *his* pajamas now instead of yours." Toby admits she is afraid to have Martin look too closely at her without all the makeup. She and Evy and Jimmy (Toby goes on) are three flawed creatures too weak to stand alone, needing to hold each other up. But Polly is another matter, Polly loves her mother, and Toby advises Evy: "Either get a book on how to be a mature, responsible person . . . or get her out of here before you destroy her chance to become one."

Evy appreciates this advice and puts her arms around Toby, who still needs all the reassurances she can get. Evy advises Toby to go home, wash her face and bring Marty a TV dinner—what has she got to loose? Toby leaves, but not before advising Evy not to tell Polly all the truth, protect her a little. Evy agrees: "I'll say I was walking along West End Avenue and was hit by the Eastern Airlines shuttle to Boston."

Polly comes in, sees the black eye, and mother and daughter fall into each other's arms. Polly confesses that she herself has been up all night and tried a drink to ease the strain of worrying about Evy, but didn't like it, and doesn't ever want to try another. Polly also reminds Evy of their lunch date with Polly's father (he is coming alone, without his new wife Felicia), but Evy declares she can't go to Rumpelmayers and meet her former husband, sporting this black eye. In addition (she admits) she has a hangover and a case of the shakes.

Polly agrees to postpone the lunch date and tries to encourage her mother: "Okay, you had a little setback . . . onwards and upwards." But Evy has no confidence that she can make progress, or that she can qualify as a fit mother for Polly. Last night wasn't her only backslide since leaving the hospital (Evy confesses). "Before last night there was an occasional beer on a wet, lonely afternoon, a couple of glasses of wine on a sunny, lonely afternoon . . . and once, after a really rotten Swedish movie, a double vodka."

But Polly is all forgiveness and encouragement; whatever her mother's failings, she urges her to try again—and again. Evy suggests that Polly go home for two weeks while she straightens herself out, but Polly knows this would be a form of surrender for Evy. Polly refuses to leave, and she gets angry at Evy's continuing despair.

POLLY (angrily): Is it such a God damned big deal to need somebody? If you can need a bottle of scotch or a Lou Tanner, why can't you need me?

EVY: I do need you, baby. I just don't want to use you. Like the rest of the company around here . . . In a few weeks you'll know the regular routine . . . You'll get a two-hour storm warning then wait in your bedroom until all the bottles are empty and all the glasses are smashed and in the mornings there'll be a lot of Alka Seltzers and black coffee and crying and forgiving and promises and we'll live happily ever after for two more weeks. And in a year or so you won't even mind it . . . Like Jimmy and Toby . . . But they have nothing better to do with their lives. You're only seventeen.

POLLY: They're just friends, I'm your daughter.

EVY: You get my point?

POLLY: No . . . what *is* it, Evy? Am I getting kicked out because you're afraid I'm going to grow up to be a crutch instead of a person? Or do you just want to be left alone so there's no one here to lock up the liquor cabinet?

EVY: You're going to be late for Rumpelmayers.

POLLY: *Screw* Rumpelmayers.

EVY *(looks at Polly and smiles):* . . . My, my . . . Look how quickly you can learn if you pay attention.

POLLY: I'm sorry.

EVY: Go on. Please, Polly. Go now.

POLLY: Don't I get to argue my side?

EVY: Not today. Mother is hung over.

Reluctantly, Polly leaves the apartment. The phone and doorbell ring, but Evy ignores them; she takes a pint bottle from her coat pocket and pours a drink. On the other side of the door is Jimmy. He knows she's there—he met Polly on the stairs—and demands to be let in. When Evy still ignores him, Jimmy breaks the door down and falls into the room.

Seeing the black eye and the drink in Evy's hand, Jimmy is angry—angry at Lou for hitting her, angry at Evy for letting herself go. Finally he calms down and turns to comforting her. They've been through this kind of thing before, they can get through it again.

Evy remembers the scene in *Great Expectations* in which the old lady lived in a shuttered house surrounded by the rotting mementoes of her wedding, which never took place because her groom jilted her at the last moment—Evy remembers thinking the old lady wasn't so insane after all. Jimmy urges her to get some rest, goes around turning off the lights. But as soon as Jimmy leaves, Evy gets up, pours herself another drink and puts on the record of her song.

Polly comes back, ostensibly because she's forgotten her wallet. She begins turning on the lights one by one, destroying the *Great Expectations* mood (and noticing the half-empty liquor bottle), commenting, "Why don't you get some bats and owls in here? Fly around the room on a broomstick. Crazy old spook mother."

Evy tells Polly to go away and leave her alone, but Polly has no intention of obeying. She challenges her mother: Evy wants her to get out because she is afraid of Polly. Unlike Jimmy who merely does anything Evy asks, Polly makes demands on her mother—demands that she *act,* do something, anything, only take positive action. Evy threatens to tell Polly's father about what she has become after only three weeks at her mother's.

POLLY (yells): *Then tell him!* Tell him what I've become after three weeks. You want things to tell him about, Evy?
          Picks up liquor glass.
Here!
          She hurls it against the book case, smashing it to pieces.
All right? Now come to Rumpelmayers and tell him . . . Only please don't sit in the dark for the rest of your life.
               Polly has burst into tears. She kneels, crying . . . Evy finds it dif-
               ficult to go to her . . . Then it's quiet.
EVY: . . . Couldn't he have picked a nice out-of-the-way restaurant in Nebraska?
POLLY (turns around hopefully): You mean you've changed your mind?
EVY: I didn't change anything.
POLLY: All right, don't change your mind. Just change your dress. You can change your mind on the way over.
EVY (looks to heaven): She's *his* daughter. I have too much class for a daughter like this.
POLLY: Listen, how about if I don't come back as a daughter? I could be a house guest. I'll just stay till I'm thirty-five, then get out, I promise.
EVY: Didn't we just settle all that?
POLLY: You and your daughter settled all that. I'm a stranger. Why don't you show me the rest of the apartment?
EVY (again up to heaven): Who is she? Who sent this monster to torment me?
POLLY: Felicia. She can't stand any of us.
          Polly has clearly won. Evy wilts, opens her arms and Polly runs in.
EVY: Oh, God, I'm not strong enough to resist you . . . I suppose I'll be speaking at your school next week.
POLLY: We've got fifteen minutes. What can we do with your face in fifteen minutes?
EVY: Christ, I don't know. There's a one-hour cleaner around the corner.
POLLY: You've known Toby Landau for twelve years and you never heard of makeup? Come on, sit down.
EVY: We'll never get away with it.
POLLY: Yes you will.
          She takes a compact from her purse.
EVY: I'll get twenty years for impersonating a mother.
POLLY: Good. We'll share a cell together.
EVY: The hell we will. I'm forty-three years old. Someday I'm getting my own place.
          Polly starts to apply makeup under eye.
POLLY: Now remember. Once we get there, don't be nervous. Just be cool and nonchalant.

EVY: What if I do something stupid like eat the ice cream with a fork?

POLLY: Then I'll eat mine with a fork. He'll look at us, think *he's* wrong, and eat *his* with a fork . . . Try not to move.

EVY: Who would believe this? A middle-aged drunk with a black eye is worried about impressing a forty-seven-year-old spitter.

POLLY: All right, I'm through.

EVY: How does it look?

POLLY: Much better.

EVY *(picks up mirror and looks at herself):* It's *not* better. It looks like I was punched in the eye and someone put makeup on it.

POLLY: If we don't get away with it, we'll tell him the truth. He's a terrific person, Evy. He'll understand the truth.

EVY: About Lou Tanner?

POLLY: No. The Eastern Airlines shuttle to Boston. Come on. Let's get a decent dress on you. You look like you're collecting for UNICEF.

EVY: Polly.

POLLY: What?

EVY: When I grow up, I want to be just like you.

    Curtain.

THE HOUSE OF BLUE LEAVES

A Play in Two Acts

BY JOHN GUARE

MUSIC AND LYRICS BY JOHN GUARE

Cast and credits appear on page 344

JOHN GUARE was born Feb. 5, 1938 in New York City. His father was a Wall Streeter and his uncle is Billy Grady, the erstwhile M-G-M casting director. Guare attended Roman Catholic schools and graduated from Georgetown in 1960. He received his M.F.A. in 1963 from the Yale School of Drama, where his one-acter Did You Write Your Name on the Snow? *was produced.*

Guare has been working on The House of Blue Leaves *since 1966 and had done a draft of it when his* The Loveliest Afternoon of the Year *and* A Day of Surprises *were done at Caffee Cino. His professional playwriting debut took place in 1968 with* Muzeeka *which played on an off-Broadway double bill for 36 performances and won its author an Obie Award (it had previously been produced at the Mark Taper Forum in Los Angeles). The following season, Guare's* Cop-Out, *a program of two one-acters, was produced on Broadway for 8 performances, enough to bring him the "Most Promising Playwright" citation in* Variety's *poll of New York drama critics.*

This season that promise has been amply fulfilled with The House of Blue Leaves, *Guare's first full-length play, named here as a Best Play and by the New York Drama Critics Circle as the best American play of 1970-71. Guare, single, lives in Greenwich Village and is now working on a new full-length play.*

The following synopsis of The House of Blue Leaves *was prepared by Jeff Sweet in collaboration with the* Best Plays *editor.*

Time: October 4, 1965

Place: Sunnyside, Queens, New York City

PROLOGUE

The stage of the El Dorado Bar & Grill

SYNOPSIS: Artie Shaughnessy, a 45-year-old zookeeper with dreams of show biz glory, sits down behind an upright piano, fumbling with the sheet music and beer he has brought out with him. The house lights are still up. Artie addresses the audience nervously: "I wrote all these songs. These are my songs. Words and the music. Could I have some quiet please?"

Artie plunges into a jaunty rendition of an original called "Back Together Again." It is not a smashing success. Artie calls to the man running lights, "A spotlight on me? You promised me a spotlight. I got a ballad I'm singing and you promised me a blue spotlight." His ballad, "I'm Looking for Something," also fails to connect. Artie turns to the audience again.

ARTIE: Could you please take your seats and listen? I'm going to sing you a song I wrote at work today and I hope you like it as much as I do. *(Plays and sings:)*
> Where is the devil in Evelyn?
> What's it doing in Angela's eyes?
> Evelyn is heavenly
> Angela's in a devil's disguise.
> I know about the Sin in Cynthia
> And the Hell in Helen of Troy
> But where is the devil in Evelyn
> What's it doing in Angela's eyes?
> Oh boy!
> What's it doing in Angela's eyes?
>> *He leaps up from the piano with his sheet music and beer, bows to the audience. Waits for applause. Bows. Waits. Looks. He runs off stage. House lights go down.*

ACT I

Later that night, Artie is sleeping in the living room of his shabby Queens apartment. Tacked to the walls are pictures of movie stars and jungle animals. A piano upstage center is littered with sheet music and manuscript paper, and behind it is the room's window, giving onto a fire escape and barred with a metal grill such as jewelers use on their shop doors. There is a Pullman kitchen at right, and there are three doors into this room: to the bedroom upstage right, to the hall at left of the window and to another bedroom down left.

Artie is lying asleep on a sofa in the center of this room, *"zipped tightly into a sleeping bag, snoring fitfully."* In between snores he mumbles, "Pope Ronnie. Pope Ronnie. Pope Ronald the first. Pope Ronald."

Ronnie clambers off the fire-escape and through the window upstage. He is not the Pope. He is an 18-year-old private with a service haircut modelled after Yul Brynner, wearing *"big glasses . . . a heavy Army overcoat and under that a suit of Army fatigue clothes."* He is Artie's son. He manages to extract the keys from his father's trousers draped near the window and opens the jeweler's bar door that blocks his way into the room. Replacing the pants, he tiptoes to the kitchen and raids the ice box for milk and bread.

His rummaging is interrupted by someone's insistent knocking and buzzing at the front door. He dashes across the stage and through the door of his bedroom, downstage left. The noise awakens Artie, who unpeels the sleeping bag, and runs to undo the six bolts on the inside of the front door, as the person outside inserts a key and rattles the knob. The door opened, Artie dives into his sleeping bag again.

His visitor is Bunny Flingus, *"a pretty, pink, electric woman in her 40s. She wears a fur collar and plastic booties"* and is carrying two cameras and binoculars. She is *"freezing, uncomfortable and furious,"* and she starts to yell at Artie, "You know what your trouble is? You got no sense of history." The Pope is scheduled to ride down Queens Boulevard that morning, and already it is crowded with cripples, nuns and thousands of others. "I haven't seen so many people Artie, so excited since the premiere of *Cleopatra*. It's that big." But Artie refuses to budge, even though Miss Henshaw is saving choice places for them.

Suspecting there is something behind his bitterness, Bunny quickly pries out of him the story of his disaster at the El Dorado Bar Amateur Night. She is outraged at the audience's treatment of him, but her faith in his music remains unshaken. She spotted "Mairzy Doats," "Old Black Magic" and "I Could've Danced All Night" as classics right off, and she knows "Where Is the Devil in Evelyn" is destined for similar glory. "I didn't work in Macy's music department for nix."

A *"sick woman in a nightgown"* enters from the door upstage right. Unnoticed, she stands there watching as Bunny continues to urge Artie to see the Pope with her! "And when he passes by in his limousine, I'll call out Your Holiness, marry us—the hell with peace to the world—bring peace to us. And he won't hear me because bands will be playing and the whole city yelling, but he'll see me because I been eyed by the best of them, and he'll nod and I'll grab your hand and say marry us, Pope, and he'll wave his holy hand and all the emeralds and rubies on his fingers will send Yes beams."

This will be a new beginning for them, says Bunny. After that they will go to California and Artie's old friend, Billy Einhorn, the big-shot moviemaker, will use Shaughnessy songs in his films. The sick woman retreats to her room as Artie, getting out of his sleeping bag, tries to bargain with Bunny: "I'll come if—"

Bunny knows what that "if" is—Artie wants her to cook for him. He has put together a scrapbook of pictures of all the delectable dishes she has told him she knows how to cook. Now he wants the real thing. "I'm not asking for a ten-course dinner," he pleads. All he wants is breakfast. But Bunny refuses. She will not cook for him until they are married. She is "not that kind of a girl."

BUNNY: . . . I'll sleep with you any time you want. Anywhere. In two months I've known you, did I refuse you once? Not once! You want me to climb in the bag with you now? Unzip it—go on—unzip it—Give your fingers a smack and I'm flat on my back. I'll sew those words into a sampler for you in our new home in California. We'll hang it right by the front door. Because, Artie, I'm a rotten lay and I know it and you know it and everybody knows it—
ARTIE: What do you mean? Everybody knows it—
BUNNY: I'm not good in bed. It's no insult. I took that sex test in the *Reader's Digest* two weeks ago and I scored twelve. Twelve, Artie! I ran out of that dentist office with tears gushing out of my face. But I face up to the truth about myself. So if I cooked for you now and said I won't sleep with you till we're married, you'd look forward to sleeping with me so much that by the time we did get to that motel near Hollywood, I'd be such a disappointment, you'd never forgive me. My cooking is the only thing I got to lure you on with and hold you with. Artie, we got to keep some magic for the honeymoon. It's my first honeymoon and I want it to be so good, I'm aiming for two million calories. I want to cook for you so bad I walk by the A & P, I get all hot jabs of chili powder inside my thighs . . . but I can't till we get those tickets to California safe in my purse, till Billy knows we're coming, till I got that ring right on my cooking finger . . . Don't tempt me . . . I love you . . .
ARTIE (Beaten): Two eggs easy over?

Sitting dressed in his wrinkled green zookeeper's uniform, Artie is down in the dumps. As Bunny sympathizes, the sick woman calls out from her room, "Is it light? Is it daytime already?", producing a change in Bunny's attitude.

BUNNY: I'll pour your cornflakes.
ARTIE (Nervous): You better leave.
BUNNY (Standing her ground): A nice bowlful?
ARTIE: I don't want her to know yet.
BUNNY: It'll be like a coming attraction.
ARTIE: You're a tease, Bunny, and that's the worst thing to be.

Artie pushes Bunny into the kitchen to hide as Bananas enters from her room. "Bananas" is Artie's wife's nickname. *"She's lived in her nightgown for the last six months. She's in her early 40s and has been crying for as long as she's had her nightgown on. She walks uncertainly as if hidden barriers lay scattered in her path."* Seeing him dressed, Bananas asks him if he has gotten an emergency call from the zoo. He tells her he hasn't, and she suddenly turns on him.

BANANAS: Are you leaving to get away from me? Tell me? The truth? You hate me. You hate my looks—my face—my clothes—you hate me. You wish I was fatter so there'd be more of me to hate. You hate me. Don't say that! You love me. I know you love me. You love me. Well, I don't love you. How does that grab you?
> *She is shaking violently. Artie takes pills from the piano and holds her and forces the pills in her mouth. He's accepted this as one of the natural facts of his life. There is no violence in the action. Her body shakes. The spasms stop. She's quiet for a long time. He walks over to the kitchen. Bunny kisses his hand's palm.*

Bananas complains that Artie never lets her emotions come out. "If I laugh, you give me a pill. If I cry, you give me a pill." Artie threatens to give her more. It is a threat he doesn't like making. To stop him, Bananas forces a smile and assures him, "I'm a peaceful forest . . . All the wild animals have gone back into hiding. But once—once let me have an emotion? Let the animals come out? I don't like being still, Artie. It makes me afraid . . ."

Artie explains that the Pope is coming to talk to the U.N. about Vietnam; maybe he'll end the war before Ronnie has to go there. Bananas remembers that Ronnie has been away from home and in the army three weeks now, and she wonders: "How can twenty-one days be a hundred years?"

Artie turns to the audience and tells us that Bananas really doesn't grasp what is going on, that the Pope is going to stop the war and Ronnie will be home soon.

Bananas tells Artie she couldn't go out to see the Pope because her fingernails are all different lengths. She is convinced that they are growing at different speeds. "I can feel them growing . . . they're connected to my veins and heart and pulling my insides out my fingers." Seeing she is getting hysterical, Artie forces more pills down her throat, and she is quiet once more. Artie looks at her with hate in his eyes: "The Pope takes one look at you standing on Queens Boulevard, he'll make the biggest U-turn you ever saw right back to Rome."

Artie tells Bananas of his dream—Ronnie was Pope, and after stopping the war in Vietnam, he had Artie canonized and put in charge of all the hymns for the Church. How did Bananas figure into the glory? She didn't. Seeing her, Ronnie slammed the door of his limousine in her face and sped away.

Bananas spots Bunny's fur coat, and when Artie's back is turned, throws it out the front door. Artie goes to the piano and improvises a song about the Pope's arrival. ("It really was comical/The Pope wore a yarmulke.") Bananas heads for the kitchen and Bunny, who has been eating the cornflakes, tries to hide. Artie intercepts Bananas and tells her he will get her food for her.

Artie prepares some food for his wife while Bunny, still in concealment, whispers that Artie is to hurry—Mrs. Henshaw is waiting, saving places for them. Bananas gets down on all fours, pretending to be a dog, one of her favorite games.

> *She sits up on her haunches and puts her hands palm downwards under her chin.*

BANANAS: Hello, Artie!

ARTIE: You're going to eat like a human being.

BANANAS: Woof? Woof?

ARTIE: Work all day in a zoo. Come home to a zoo.

> *He takes a deep breath. He throws her the food. She catches it in her mouth. She rolls on her back.*

BANANAS: I like being animals. You know why? I never heard of a famous animal. Oh, a couple of Lassies—an occasional Trigger—but, by and large, animals weren't meant to be famous.

> *Artie storms into the kitchen.*

What a work of art is a dog. How noble in its thought—how gentle in its dignity—

> *Artie buries his head against the ice box.*

BANANAS *(smiling out front):* Hello. I haven't had a chance to welcome you. This is my home and I'm your hostess, and I should welcome you. I wanted to say Hello and I'm glad you could come. I was very sick a few months ago. I tried to slash my wrists with spoons. But I'm better now and glad to see people. In the house. I couldn't go out. Not yet. Hello.

> *She walks the length of the stage, smiling at the audience, at us. She has a beautiful smile. Bunny comes out of the kitchen down to the edge of the stage.*

BUNNY *(to us):* You know what my wish is? The priest told us last Sunday to make a wish when the Pope rides by. When the Pope rides by, the wish in my heart is gonna knock the Pope's eyes out. It is braided in tall letters, all *my* veins and arteries and aortas are braided into the wish that she dies pretty soon.

> *She goes back to the kitchen.*

Bananas puts a red mask on, sneaks up behind Bunny and scares the living daylights out of her. Bunny is furious. She refuses to take abuse from "a sick person . . . . . I don't like to be degraded. A sick person has fumes in their head—you release poison fumes and it makes me sick—dizzy—like riding the back of a bus. No wonder Negroes are fighting so hard to be freed, riding in the back of busses all those years. I'm amazed they even got enough strength to stand up straight."

Bunny discovers her fur is missing and turns on Bananas once again— "What did you do with my coat, Looney Tunes?" Artie finds it and returns it to Bunny. Bunny decides to force the issue of an immediate Mexican divorce.

Artie will handle the situation (he tells Bunny). He informs Bananas that he and Bunny are planning to get married.

ARTIE: I didn't tell you this, Bunny. Last week, I rode out to Long Island.
To Bananas, taking her hand.
You need help. We—*I* found a nice hosp . . . By the sea . . . by the beautiful sea . . . it's an old estate and you can walk from the train station and it
was raining and the roads aren't paved so it's muddy, but by the road where
you turn into the estate, there was a tree with blue leaves in the rain—I
walked under it to get out of the rain and also because I had never seen a tree
with blue leaves and I walked under the tree and all the leaves flew away in
one big round bunch—just lifted up leaving a bare tree. Woosh . . . it was
birds. Not blue leaves, but birds, waiting to go to Florida or California . . .
and all the birds flew to another tree a couple of hundred feet off and that bare
tree blossomed—snap! like that—with all these blue very quiet leaves . . .
You'll like the place, Bananas. I talked to the doctor. He had a mustache. You
like mustaches. And the Blue Cross will handle a lot of it, so we won't have
to worry about expense . . . you'll like the place . . . A lot of famous people
have had crackdowns there, so you'll be running in good company.

BANANAS: Shock treatments?

ARTIE: No. No shock treatments.

BANANAS: You swear?

BUNNY: If she needs them, she'll get them.

ARTIE: I'm handling this my way.

BUNNY: I'm sick of you kowtowing to her. Those poison fumes that come
out of her head make me dizzy—suffering—look at her—what does she know
about suffering . . .

BANANAS: Did you read in the paper about the bull in Madrid who fought
so well they didn't let him die. They healed him, let him rest before they put
him back in the ring, again and again and again. I don't like the shock treatments, Artie. At least the concentration camps—I was reading about them,
Artie—they put the people in the ovens and never took them out—but the
shock treatments—they put you in the oven and then they take you out and
then they put you in and then they take you out . . .

Bunny describes a story she read in *Modern Screen* called "Sandra Dee's
Night of Hell." It seems Miss Dee couldn't find her hair curlers the night before her first picture was to start. Too proud to ask her mother's help to find
them, she was in mental anguish until Annette Funicello came by and gave
her friend "the hair curlers out of her very own hair." Bananas, Bunny insists,
doesn't know what it is to really suffer. "You're a nobody and you suffer like
a nobody." And Artie explains himself further: "I feel I only got about this
much life left in me, Bananas. I got to use it. These are my peak years. I got
to take this chance. You stay in your room. You're crying. All the time.
Ronnie's gone now. This is not a creative atmosphere . . . Bananas, I'm too
old to be a young talent."

Bunny tells Artie he should admit that he didn't have the courage to act
until he met her. Artie says that is ridiculous. Him not have courage? "I walk
right into the cage! . . . I got panthers licking out of my hands like goddamn

pussycats . . ." Bunny says that if he weren't afraid he would have called his Hollywood friend Billy Einhorn long ago. Meanwhile, Bananas is wondering what it would be like to "jump out right in front of the Pope's car," imagining that he would "take me in his arms and bless me."

Bunny challenges Artie to call Billy right that very moment. But it's too late, Artie protests. Bunny says, "If you can't call your best friends in the middle of the night, then who can you call—" Bananas offers to get Billy on the phone for him. After all, she says, "he was always my much better friend than yours, Artie." No, says Artie, Billy and he were always the closest. Hadn't they grown up together, gone to school together?

Bunny continues to urge Artie to call Billy. If he does, she says, in a couple years he's a cinch to win the Oscar for Best Song. Excited, Artie picks up the phone. He has the number memorized, and in a few moments he has Billy Einhorn on the line: "Billy, it's Artie Shaughnessy. Artie. No, New York! Did I wake you up! Can you hear me! Billy, hello! I got to tell you something— first of all, I got to tell you how bad I feel about Georgina dying—the good die young—what can I say—and second, since you you old bum never come back to your old stomping grounds—your happy hunting grounds, I'm thinking of coming out to see you . . . I know you can fix up a tour of the studios and that'd be great . . . and you can get us hotel reservations—that's just fine . . . But, Billy, I'm thinking I got to get away—not just a vacation—but make a change, get a break if you know what I'm getting at . . . Bananas is fine. She's right here. We were just thinking about you—NO, IT'S NOT FINE. Billy, this sounds cruel to say, but Bananas is as dead for me as Georgina is for you."

Artie tells Billy about how he met Bunny—by accident they were both in the same steam room. They couldn't see each other, and Bunny started talking about food. The cataloguing of her favorite dishes so aroused him that he "kind of raped her." Anyway, Artie says, he's looking forward to the three of them—Artie and Billy and Bunny—getting together in California soon.

ARTIE: . . . . . I'm a new man, Billy—a new man—and I got to make a start before it's too late and I'm calling you, crawling on my hands and knees —no, not like that, I'm standing up straight and talking to my best buddy and saying Can I come see you and bring Bunny and talk over old times . . . I'll pay my own way. I'm not asking you for nothing. Just your friendship. I think about you so much and I read about you in the columns and *Conduct of Life* is playing at the Museum of Modern Art next week and I get nervous calling you and that Doris Day pic—well, Bunny and I fell out of our loge seats—no, Bananas couldn't see it—she don't go out of the house much . . . I get nervous about calling you because, well, you know, and I'm not asking for any Auld Lang Syne treatment, but it must be kind of lonely with Georgina gone and we sent five dollars into the Damon Runyon Cancer Fund like Walter Winchell said to do and we're gonna send more and it must be kind of lonely and the three of us—Bunny and you and me—could have some laughs. What do you say? You write me and let me know your schedule and we can come any time. But soon. Okay, buddy? Okay? No, this is my call. I'm paying for this call so you don't have to worry—talking to you I get all opened up. You still drinking rye? Jack Daniels! Set out the glasses—open the bottle— No, I'll bring the bottle—we'll see you soon. Good night, Billy.

The call is over.

Soon, Billy. Soon. Soon.

He hangs up.

Bunny and Artie are elated—Artie is so happy he even takes the trouble to inform Bananas that Billy asked about her. Bunny's way of expressing her joy is, "Oh, Christ, the dinners I'm going to cook for you." She exits to take her place to see the Pope.

Artie stays behind to take a shower (he is soaked with sweat from the excitement of his phone call). He sings and jumps up and down on the floor in defiance of Bananas's worries about disturbing the people downstairs. He bangs the piano as a symphony for "the people upstairs," and Bananas reminds him that there is only the roof upstairs. Artie in his turn reminds Bananas that she should know all there is to know about roofs—one time, Bananas disappeared for 24 hours and Artie found her standing on the edge of a snow-covered roof, dressed only in her nightgown.

BANANAS: Can I have my song?

ARTIE: You're tone-deaf.

Hits two bad notes on the piano.

Like that.

BANANAS: So I won't sing it . . . My troubles all began a year ago—two years ago today—two days ago today? Today.

Artie plays the "Anniversary Waltz."

We used to have a beautiful old green Buick. The Green Latrine! . . . I'm not allowed to drive it any more . . . But when I could drive it . . . the last time I drove it, I drove into Manhattan.

Artie plays "In My Merry Oldsmobile."

And I drive down Broadway—to the Crossroads of the World.

Artie plays "Forty-second Street."

I see a scene that you wouldn't see in your wildest dreams. Forty-second Street. Broadway. Four corners, Four people. One on each corner. All waving for taxis. Cardinal Spellman. Jackie Kennedy. Bob Hope, President Johnson. All carrying suitcases. Taxi! Taxi! I stop in the middle of the street—the middle of Broadway and I get out of my Green Latrine and yell Get in. I'm a gypsy. A gypsy cab. Get in. I'll take you where you want to go. Don't you all know each other? Get in? Get in! . . . . .

In her irrational fantasy, Bananas tried to push them all into the car, with disastrous results: suitcases opening and spilling out; confusion; blows exchanged; crying, laughing, screaming.

BANANAS: . . . . . And then the Green Latrine blew four flat tires and sinks and I run to protect the car and four cabs appear and all my friends run into four different cabs. And cars are honking at me to move. I push the car over the bridge back to Queens. You're asleep. I turn on Johnny Carson to get my mind off and there's Cardinal Spellman and Bob Hope whose nose is still bleeding and they tell the story of what happened to them and everybody laughs. Thirty million people watch Johnny Carson and they all laugh. At me. At me. I'm nobody. I knew all those people better than me. You. Ronnie. I know everything about them. Why can't they love me. And then it began to snow and I went up on the roof . . .

ARTIE (after a long pause): Come see the Pope. Pray. Miracles happen. He'll bless you. Reader's Digest has an article this month on how prayer answers things. Pray? Kneel down in the street? The Pope can cure you. The Reader's Digest don't afford to crap around.

BANANAS: My fingernails are all different lengths. Everybody'd laugh . . .

But Bananas is beginning to think that maybe with gloves on she *could* go to see the Pope. Artie turns on the TV to watch the Pope's arrival at the airport. He begs the Pope's TV image to make Bananas better, urges Bananas to lean forward and kiss the Pope's image on the screen.

Artie continues to hug the TV set, while Bananas goes into the bedroom and Bunny bursts in through the front door, bubbling over with the excitement of the Pope's arrival in New York. She is sporting a large "I Love Paul" button and explains that it is left over from the Beatles' last visit.

> *Bananas comes out of the bedroom, a coat over her nightgown, a hat cocked on her head, two different shoes, one higher than the other. She is smiling. She is pulling on gloves. Bunny gapes. Band music plays joyously in the distance. Artie goes to Bananas and takes her arm.*

BUNNY: Now wait one minute, Miss Henshaw is going to be mighty pissed off.

ARTIE: Just for today.

BANANAS: Hold me tight . . .

ARTIE (grabbing his coat): Over the threshold . . .

> *They go out.*

BUNNY: Artie, are you dressed warm? Are you dressed warm? Your music! You forgot your music! You gotta get it blessed by the Pope! !

> *Bananas appears in the doorway and grabs the music from Bunny.*

BANANAS (sings):

It really was comical
The Pope wore a yarmulke
The day that the Pope came to New York.

BUNNY: You witch! You'll be in Bellevue tonight with enough shock treatments they can plug Times Square into your ear. I didn't work for Con Edison for nothing!

> *She storms out after them, slams the door behind her. The bedroom door Ronnie went into at the beginning of the act opens. Ronnie*

comes out carrying a large box. He comes downstage and stares at us. Curtain.

ACT II

Scene 1

Ronnie, 17, tall and skinny with a G.I. haircut, is standing in the same position, staring, as the curtain rises. Finally he takes two hand grenades out of his pockets and wires them to his father's alarm clock, then setting it at a special time, as he speaks to us *"with deep, suffocated, religious fervor. His eyes bulge with a strange mixture of terrifying innocence and diabolism."*

Ronnie tells us that when he was 12 years old, his father's friend Billy was casting a film version of *Huckleberry Finn,* and everywhere Billy went he was hounded by little boys who would pop out of the woodwork chirping, "Hello, I'm Huckleberry Finn." Billy called Artie to ask if he could use the apartment as a hide-out. Ronnie asked at school who Huckleberry Finn was and was told, "The ideal American boy." And at that moment Ronnie knew Billy would take one look at him and whisk him out to California with him that very day. It was fate. Inevitable. He didn't tell his parents about this, because "I didn't want tears from them—only trails of envy . . . I went to my room and packed my bag and waited." Billy arrived and he and Artie and Bananas kissed and shook hands and cried and slapped backs. Then Artie called out to Ronnie to come out of his room and join them.

RONNIE: I picked up my bag and said Goodbye to myself in the mirror. Came out. Billy there. Smiling. It suddenly dawned on me. You had to do things to get parts. I began dancing. And singing. Immediately. Things I have never done in my life—before or since. I stood on my head and skipped and whirled—spectacular leaps in the air so I could see veins in the ceiling—ran up and down the keys of the piano and sang and began laughing and crying soft and loud to show off all my emotions. And I heard music and drums that I couldn't even keep up with. And then cut off all my emotions just like that. Instantly. And took a deep bow like the Dying Swan I saw on Ed Sullivan. I picked up my suitcase and waited by the door. Billy turned to my parents, whose jaws were down to about there, and Billy said, "You never told me you had a mentally retarded child." . . . . . I picked up my bag and went into my room and shut the door and never came out the whole time he was here.

Now, six years later, everybody—Artie, Billy, his sergeant—laughs at Ronnie. They won't be laughing long. "By tonight, I'll be on headlines all over the world. Cover of *Time. Life.* TV specials." He tells us we can laugh, too. He doesn't care. "I'll show you all. I'll be too big for any of you." Hearing the door being unlocked, Ronnie disappears into his room.

It is Artie. Bunny has insisted he return to bring more of his music for the

Pope to bless. He is interrupted by the arrival of a beautiful girl carrying flowers and liquor. She gazes around his apartment, admiringly. Artie recognizes her. She is Corrinna Stroller, a movie star who made one film for Billy and then suddenly retired. It was Billy's suggestion that she drop by on the way to the airport. Artie rushes out to get Bunny and Bananas.

> *Corrinna is alone. There is a high, loud whine. Her hands go to her ears. The whine becomes very electronic. The sound is almost painful. She pulls a hearing aid from each ear. The sound suddenly stops. She reaches under her dress and removes a receiver that the aids are wired to.*

CORRINNA *(to us):* Don't tell—please? I don't want them to know I'm deaf. I don't want them to think Billy's going around with some deaf girl. There was an accident on a set—a set of Billy's . . . I can hear with my transistors.
> *She shows them to us.*
I want them to know me first. So please, don't tell. Please.

Bunny rushes in with Artie. She tells Corrinna that her one movie, *Warmonger*, "is permanently enshrined in the Loew's of my heart." Why didn't she make more movies? Corrinna, who can't hear a thing with her hearing aid disconnected, answers, smiling, "I just dropped in to say hi—"

Bunny tells Artie this is his big chance. She pushes him behind a piano, saying, "You get your ass on those tunes while the Pope's blessing is still hot on them. Artie, the Pope looked right at me! We're in solid." She offers Corrinna celery and shows her the sheet music.

In the middle of Artie's rendition of "Back Together Again," the sudden appearance of three nuns at the window startles Corrinna and she drops her transistors. As Corrinna searches for them, the nuns explain they have come "all the way from Ridgewood" to see the Pope and were accidentally locked out on the roof. After they plead with him, Artie agrees to allow them to watch the Pope on television. They complain because Artie doesn't have a color set and the beers he gives them aren't imported.

Bananas finally arrives. When Bunny disappeared, she got lost. "I had to ask directions how to get back." She sees the nuns.

BANANAS: Artie, did you bring work home from the office?

ARTIE: They're nuns, Bananas, nuns.

HEAD NUN: We got locked out on the upstairs roof. Hi!

BANANAS: Hi!

ARTIE: This is Corrinna Stroller, Billy's girl friend. Corrinna, this is Bananas.

THE NUNS: Corrinna Stroller! The movie star!

BANANAS: Hello, Billy's girl friend. God, Billy's girl friends always make me feel so shabby!

BUNNY *(to Corrinna):* Arthur believes in keeping family skeletons out in the open like pets. Heel, Bananas, heel!

LITTLE NUN *(running to Corrinna's side . . .):* I saw *The Sound of Music* thirty-one times. It changed my entire life.
CORRINNA: Unitarian.

Artie tries to continue the audition, but what with the nuns taking pictures of each other with the televised images of Jackie Kennedy and Mayor Lindsay and Bananas burning herself while trying to cook Brillo pads for their guests (she thinks they're hamburgers), he doesn't get very far. He tells the nuns they will have to take the TV set into the next room, Ronnie's bedroom. The Second Nun tells him: "Go on with what you're doing. Don't bother about us. We're nothing. We've just given up our lives praying for you. I'm going to start picking who I pray for."
Bunny tells Bananas to put salt and vinegar on her burn. The Head Nun reports the presence of an altar boy in Ronnie's room and retreats into it. Bananas disappears into her room and Bunny turns to Corrinna saying, "Sometimes I think the whole world has gone cuckoo, don't you?" Corrinna smiles and replies, "For two days." The Little Nun dashes into Ronnie's room with a jar of peanut butter from the kitchen as Artie, having relocated the set, runs out of Ronnie's bedroom to tell them the news that his son Ronnie is in there, dressing as an altar boy—Ronnie has been selected from the soldiers at Fort Dix to be the Pope's altar boy in a Yankee Stadium ceremony. Artie doesn't want Bananas to see Ronnie, fears she would come apart at the sight of him.
Artie sits down at the piano and finally manages to finish one of his songs, while Bananas wanders back into the living room and watches. Bunny applauds the end of the song and Corrinna, observing Bunny, imitates her act of applauding.

ARTIE *(happy now):* What should I play next?
BUNNY: Oh God, how do you pick a branch from a whole redwood forest?
BANANAS *(licking her hands):* "*I Love You So I Keep Dreaming.*"
BUNNY *(picks up the phone but doesn't dial):* Come and get her!
BANANAS: Play "I Love You So I Keep Dreaming."
ARTIE *(pleased):* You really remember that?
BANANAS: How could I forget it . . .
BUNNY: I'm not used to being Queen of the Outsiders. What song is this?
ARTIE: I almost forgot it. It must have been like Number One that I ever wrote. The one that showed me I should go on.
BUNNY: Well, let me hear it.
ARTIE: You really surprise me, Bananas. Sometimes I miss you so much . . .
BUNNY *(a warning):* Arthur, I still haven't forgiven you for this morning.
ARTIE *(sings):*
    I love you so I keep dreaming
    Of all the lovely times we shared . . .
BUNNY: Heaven. That is unadulterated heaven.
BANANAS: Now play "White Christmas."

BUNNY: Shocks for sure.

BANANAS *(slams the piano):* Play "White Christmas?"

ARTIE *(to Corrinna):* She's . . . not feeling too . . . hot . . .

BUNNY *(to Corrinna):* In case you haven't noticed . . .

ARTIE: She keeps crawling under the weather . . .

A run on the piano.

BANANAS: "White Christmas"? ? ? ? ? ? ?

Artie groans; plays and sings "White Christmas."

BUNNY *(to Corrinna):* It really burns me up all these years the Telephone Hour doing salutes to fakers like Richard Rodgers. Just listen to that. Blaaaagh.

Artie stops playing.

BANANAS: Don't you hear it?

Artie plays "White Christmas" again. He plays his song. They are the same tune.

ARTIE: Oh God. Oh God.

BANANAS *(sings desperately):* "I love you so I keep dreaming"—Are you tone deaf? Can't you hear it?

She slams the keys on the piano. He bangs the lid shut. She yells. She licks her fingers to get the pain off them.

Artie, furious at Bananas, decides to commit her to the institution right then and there. He picks up the phone. Now Bananas, really frightened, clings to Corrinna, begging her help in the name of Billy Einhorn, who always liked Bananas. Trying to show them all that she will be quiet and take her pills, Bananas picks up Corrinna's vial of transistors and swallows them. Corrinna has no idea of what has been going on, but she has seen this and knows that her transistors are now irrecoverably lost.

Artie reaches the sanatarium and arranges to have them come to pick up Bananas, who runs into her room. Bunny goes out to pack her suitcase—now that Bananas is finally out of the way she has $1,000 saved up to pay their fare to Hollywood with Corrinna. Artie goes off to pack his own suitcase, as the nuns enter from Ronnie's room.

Corrinna tells the nuns she is on her way to Australia for a major ear operation. Billy is going with her, they are to be married and spend "two fabulous years" in Australia making a movie, *Kangaroo.* The nuns pray for Corrinna, as Ronnie comes out of his room. Artie also enters, with suitcase half packed. He has heard the part about Australia and wonders how this might affect his own plans.

Ronnie tries to make contact with Artie to say goodbye, but Artie is preoccupied with his own concerns.

RONNIE: Pop, I'm going to blow up the Pope.

ARTIE: See how nice you look with your hair all cut—

The nuns have finished singing "Ave Maria" and take flash pictures of themselves posing with Corrinna.

RONNIE: Pop, I'm going to blow up the Pope and when *Time* interviews me tonight, I won't even mention you. I'll say I was an orphan.

ARTIE: Ronnie, why didn't you write and let me know you were coming home. I might've been in California—it's great to see you—

Running to the front door, Corrinna turns and asks if anyone wants her two tickets to the Pope's mass at Yankee Stadium. Beating the nuns to the draw, Ronnie grabs the tickets, retrieves his *"gift-wrapped bomb"* and dashes into his room, followed by the irate sisters.

An M.P. enters, looking for Ronnie. Hearing the commotion in the next room, the M.P. rushes in, followed by an outraged Artie, who is almost knocked over by the Little Nun. She has grabbed the tickets. Everyone piles out of Ronnie's room, and, ultimately, the M.P. arrests Ronnie for being A.W.O.L. The Head and Second Nuns now have the tickets. "Good luck with your ear operation," says the Second Nun, and the two sisters exit.

Ronnie, under arrest, tosses his gift-wrapped bomb to Corrinna, who can hardly wait to open it as she departs toward the elevator where the two nuns are waiting.

An attendant from the sanatarium arrives to pick up Bananas. Artie runs into the bedroom to fetch her, but at this precise moment Bunny dances in announcing herself as "Mrs. Arthur M. Shaughnessy." This is the person the attendant has been told to pick up, so he immediately slips a straitjacket over Bunny.

Artie comes into the room, sees Bunny being dragged into the hall and makes a move to save her.

> *Ronnie pulls Artie from the door as there is a terrible explosion. Pictures fly off the wall. Smoke pours in from the hall.*

BUNNY *(Entering through the smoke):* Artie? Where's Corrinna? Where's Corrinna?

ARTIE: Corrinna?

> *Artie runs out into the hall with Bunny. The lights dim as Ronnie and the M.P. grapple in slow motion, the Little Nun trying to pull the M.P. off Ronnie. Bananas comes downstage into the light. An unattached vacuum hose is wrapped around her shoulders. She cleans the floor with the metallic end of the hose. She smiles at us.*

BANANAS *(To us):* My house is a mess . . . Let me straighten up . . . I can do that . . . *(Sings as she vacuums.)* "I love you so I keep dream . . ."

> *Closes her eyes.*

Artie, you could salvage that song. You really could.

> *Curtain*

Scene 2

The curtain is down at the beginning of the scene and we hear the voice of the Pope, broadcasting from Yankee Stadium, talking about the noblest and most characteristic traits of Americans, describing them as "a people basing its conception of life on spiritual values, on a religious sense, on freedom, on loyalty, on work, on the respect of duty, on family affection, on generosity and courage—"

As if to answer this description, the curtain goes up on Artie's living room. It is *"vaguely picked up"* but, what with the miscellaneous junk piled in the corners and pictures hanging crooked on the wall, it is hardly back to normal. Artie is watching the Pope on television. Another man is sitting in front of the set in an easy chair, letting out heartbreaking sobs. Artie turns off the set and introduces his companion to us: "This is the one. The only. You guessed it: This is Billy. He got here just before the eleven o'clock news. He had to identify Corrinna's body, so he's a little upset. You forgive him, okay?"

Artie tries to make Billy look at things on the bright side. After all, Corrinna's death was instantaneous, painless. Billy finds little solace in these thoughts: "My future is all ashes, Artie. In the morning, I'll fly back with Corrinna's body, fly back to L.A. and stay there. I can't work. Not for a long, long time, if ever again. I was supposed to go to Australia but no . . . all ashes . . ."

Artie tells Billy he must not give up. He encourages Billy to make his next picture a musical, underscoring his point with a bit of "Back Together Again," on the piano.

Bananas enters *"dressed in clothes that must have been very stylish and elegant 10 years earlier."* Billy sees her and gasps, "Georgina!" But he quickly realizes it is not his late wife's ghost but Bananas wearing a dress Georgina had given her.

BANANAS: I put it on to make you happy, Billy.
        Billy is crying again.
ARTIE: Easy, Billy, easy . . .
BANANAS: It's a shame it's 1965. I'm like the best-dressed woman of 1954.
BILLY *(starting to laugh and cheer up):* You got the best of them all, Artie. Hello, Bananas!
BANANAS: Sometimes I curse you for giving me that name, Billy.
BILLY: A little Italian girl. What else was I going to call her?
        The Little Nun rushes in from the bedroom.
LITTLE NUN: Mr. Shaughnessy! Quick—the bathtub—the shower—the hot water is steaming—running over—I can't turn it—there's nothing to turn—
        Artie runs into the bedroom. The Little Nun looks at Billy. Billy smiles at her. The Little Nun runs into the bedroom.
BANANAS: I did it to burn her.
BILLY: Burn who?
BANANAS: Burn her downstairs. Have the hot water run through the ceiling and give her blisters. He won't like her so much when she's covered with blisters. Hot water can do that. It's one of the nicest properties of hot water.
BILLY: Burn who? ? ?
BANANAS: Kate Smith! !

Artie races back in, looking for a wrench, trying to put a good face on the situation for Billy's sake, starts reminiscing about the good old days when they went together to such places as Leon and Eddie's and the Village Barn (meanwhile desperately trying to find a wrench to turn off the water). Artie runs into the bedroom and the Little Nun comes back to the living room.

LITTLE NUN: Mr. Einhorn?

BILLY: Hello?

LITTLE NUN: I was an usher before I went in and your name always meant quality.
> She runs into the bedroom.

BILLY: Why—Thank you . . .

BANANAS: Help me, Billy? They're coming again to make me leave. Let me stay here? They'll listen to you. You see, they give me pills so I won't feel anything. Now I don't mind not feeling anything so long as I can remember feeling. You see? And this apartment, you see, here, right here, I stand in this corner and I remember laughing so hard. Doubled up. At something Ronnie did. Artie said. And I stand over here where I used to iron. When I could iron, I'd iron right here, and even then, the buttons, say, on button-down shirts could make me sob, cry . . . and that window, I'd stand right here and mix me a Rye-and-Ginger-Pick-Me-Up and watch the lights go on in the Empire State Building and feel so tender . . . unprotected . . . I don't mind not feeling so long as I can be in a place I remember feeling. You get me? You get me? Don't look at me dead. I'm no Georgina. I'm no Corrinna. Help me? Help Ronnie?

BILLY: Ronnie's in jail.

BANANAS: I don't mind the bars. But he can't take them. He's not strong like his mom. Come closer to me? Don't let them hear. Oh, you kept your mustache. Nothing's changed. (She sings.) "Should auld acquaintance be forgot . . ."
> Artie comes out of the bedroom, soaking wet.

ARTIE: Come on, where is it?
> He reaches behind Bananas's back and pulls the silver faucet handle from her clenched fist.

Billy, you see the wall I'm climbing.
> He goes back into the bedroom with it. The Little Nun looks out into the living room.

LITTLE NUN (to Billy): We never got introduced.

BILLY: Do I know you?
> Bananas goes into the corner by the window.

LITTLE NUN (coming into the room): No, but my two friends died with your friend today.

BILLY: I'm very sorry for you.

LITTLE NUN: No, it's all right. All they ever wanted to do was die and go to heaven and meet Jesus. The convent was very depressing. Pray a while. Scream a while. Well, they got their wish, so I'm happy.

BILLY: If your friends died with my friend, then that makes us—oh, God! Bananas! That makes us all friends! You friends and me friends and we're all friends!

Again, Bananas pleads with Billy to help Ronnie and hands him the phone. Billy calls his friend General Revere in the Pentagon and tells him about Ronnie being in the Ft. Dix brig for going A.W.O.L. to see the Pope (of course no one knows he made the bomb or what he meant to do with it). The General fixes it so that Ronnie can see the Pope any time he wants—he'll be stationed in Rome with NATO after serving a nominal two weeks in jail.

Meanwhile, Bunny has come back looking *"swell and great and all the Webster Dictionary synonyms for terrific,"* carrying a casserole of veal and oranges and an umbrella, complaining about the water coming through her ceiling. Being introduced to Billy Einhorn makes Bunny forget all that, though, and she is so impressed with Billy she even invites him to join her and Artie in a snack.

Bunny tries to console Billy for the loss of Corrinna: "I hope when I go I got two sisters of charity with me. I don't know what your persuasion is God-wise, but your friend Corrinna, whether she likes it or not, is right up there in heaven tonight." Billy is strangely consolable: "Corrinna. How easily deaf becomes dead. It was her sickness that held us together." Billy envies Artie his health, his wife and son.

Artie plays Billy a cheering chorus of "Where Is the Devil in Evelyn," and all at once Billy jumps to his feet, a new man, looking into the future. Now he has an extra ticket to Australia . . . Artie would love to go, but Billy's invitation is not for him. Billy addresses himself to Bunny: "Cook for me a while? Stay with me a while? . . . . . Someone who listens. That's what I need." Bunny needs time to consider deserting Artie and accepting Billy's offer of an exciting new life, new place names like Hawaii, Samoa, Melbourne.

The Little Nun comes in dressed not in her habit but in one of Bananas's dresses. Billy proposes that the Little Nun take over Bunny's apartment and stay here and take care of Bananas—he begs Artie not to send Bananas away and presses hundred-dollar bills on the Little Nun to persuade her to stay.

The phone rings. It's the zoo, for Artie—the animals are all giving birth. Artie tries to fend off this new crisis: "Look, this is what you have to do. Heat the water. Lock the male elephants out. They get testy. The leopardess tends to eat her children. Watch her careful . . ."

Bunny comes downstage to tell us directly how the Pope has granted her wish for a miraculous new life. She has decided to go with Billy, to be the best of companions for him, and she hands the Little Nun the keys to her apartment.

Artie puts down the phone. He must go to the zoo at once, and weakly he invites Billy and Bunny to accompany him to watch new life entering the world. But Billy and Bunny have other plans. In final desperation Artie pounds the piano and reminds his friend, "I write songs, Bill." Billy sits down beside Artie.

BILLY: Artie, can I tell you a secret?
> *Artie stops playing.*

Do you know who I make my pictures for? Money? No. Prestige? No. I make them for you.

ARTIE: Me?

BILLY: I sit on the set and before every scene I say, Would this make Artie laugh? Would this make Artie cry?

ARTIE: I could come on the set and tell you personal . . .

BILLY: Oh no, Artie. If I ever thought you and Bananas weren't here in Sunnyside, seeing my work, loving my work, I could never work again. You're my touch with reality.
> *He goes to Bananas.*

Bananas, do you know what the greatest talent in the world is? To be an audience. Anybody can create. But to be an audience . . . Be an audience . . .

Artie desperately starts banging away a song at the piano, as Billy and Bunny start to leave.

BUNNY: Artie, I mean this in the best possible sense: You've been a wonderful neighbor.

BILLY *(to Artie):* I just saved your life.
> *They exit: Artie plays "Where Is the Devil in Evelyn" hysterically, then runs out after them. He shouts.*

ARTIE: Bill! Bill! I'm too old to be a young talent! ! !
> *The Little Nun comes downstage; she speaks to us:*

LITTLE NUN: Life is this orchard and we walk beneath it and apples and grapes and cherries and mangoes all tumble down on us. Ask and You Shall Receive. I didn't even ask and look how much I have. Thank you. Thank you all.
> *She kisses the television.*

A shrine . . . I wanted to be a Bride of Christ but I guess now I'm a young divorcee. I'll go downstairs and call up the convent. Goodbye. Thank you.
> *She wrings out her wet habit, then throws it up in the air and runs out. Artie returns.*

BANANAS: I don't blame you for that lady, Artie. I really don't. But I'm going to be good to you now. Cooking. I didn't know you liked cooking. All these years and I didn't know you liked cooking. See, you can live with a person . . . Oh God, Artie, it's like we're finally alone for the first time in our life. Like it's taken us eighteen years to get from the church to the hotel room and we're finally alone. I promise you I'll be different. I promise you . . .
> *She sits on her haunches like a little dog smiling for food as she did in Act I.*

Hello, Artie. *(She barks. She sings:)*
> Back together again
> Back together again
> Since we split up

The skies we lit up
Looked all bit up
Like Fido chewed them
But they're
Back together again
You can say you knew us when . . .

> *Artie strangles her. She smiles radiantly at him. He squeezes the breath out of her throat. She falls. The stage begins to change. Blue leaves begin to filter all over the room until it looks like Artie is standing in a forest of leaves that are blue. A blue spotlight appears downstage and he steps into it. He is very happy and smiles at us.*

ARTIE: Hello. My name is Artie Shaughnessy and I'd like to thank you for that blue spot and to sing you some songs from the pen of. *(He sings:)*

I'm here with bells on
Ringing out how I feel
I'll ring
I'll roar
I'll sing
Encore!
I'm here with bells on
Ring! Ring! Ring!

> *Blackout. Curtain*

THE PHILANTHROPIST

A Comedy in Two Acts

BY CHRISTOPHER HAMPTON

Cast and credits appear on page 308

CHRISTOPHER HAMPTON was born in the Azores, at Fayal, in 1946 and was educated at Alexandria in Egypt (where he wrote a play at age 9) and later at New College, Oxford. He was still in college in 1966 when his play When Did You Last See My Mother? *was produced in London at the Royal Court and later transferred to the Comedy Theater. At this time Hampton was only 20 and reportedly the youngest playwright ever produced in the West End. His script was brought to New York by the Young People's Repertory Theater, playing off Broadway at the Sheridan Square Playhouse for 11 performances beginning January 4, 1967.*

After his graduation from Oxford in 1968, Hampton joined the Royal Court Theater as a resident dramatist. London soon saw his second play, Total Eclipse, *about the lives of Rimbaud and Verlaine. His adaptation of* Uncle Vanya *was produced at the Royal Court last season, which also saw his version of* Hedda Gabler *produced by the Festival Theater at Stratford, Ontario.*

Hampton's Ibsen adaptations provided the material for his Broadway playwriting debut this season with A Doll's House *and* Hedda Gabler *in repertory beginning January 13, 1971 and starring Claire Bloom in both revivals (see their entries in the "Plays Produced on Broadway" section of this volume). His* The Philanthropist *soon followed, opening on Broadway March 15, 1971 fresh from its successful Royal Court production in London this very season.*

235

Time: The near future

Place: A university town

ACT I

Scene 1

SYNOPSIS: Philip and Donald—faculty members—are seated in Philip's living room listening to a student, John, read the last scene of a play he has written. This is *"the room of a bachelor don, comfortable but not well furnished, ordered but not tidy,"* furnished with sofa, armchair, table, etc., with doors at either side leading to bedroom and kitchen and another door upstage left leading to the hall. Ivied walls are visible through a large, high window at left.

As he reads, John holds a revolver which he uses to pantomime the suicide which is the last act of his play. He finishes reading, then looks up expectantly, wanting to know what his listeners thought of his work. Philip says "Very good" almost automatically and then goes to mix a drink. Donald has reservations about the play—he liked parts of it, not other parts. He was confused by a window cleaner who kept appearing, and John explains that this character was meant to symbolize Man. Philip simply took this character literally, as a window cleaner.

Donald really didn't care for either the beginning or the ending of the play. Philip liked the beginning, though he doesn't feel qualified to comment.

JOHN: You do lecture in English don't you?

PHILIP: Yes, but in philology, not literature.

JOHN: Philology? Don't you find that incredibly tedious?

PHILIP: No, it's exactly the right subject for me. I'm fascinated by words.

JOHN: Individual rather than consecutive.

PHILIP: Yes. My only advice to writers is "make the real shapes."

JOHN: Pardon?

PHILIP: It's an anagram of "Shakespeare" and "Hamlet."

DON: He's obsessed by anagrams.

JOHN *(coldly)*: Really. *(Pause.)* What's your objection to the end of the play?

DON: It just doesn't convince me. It seems artificial. Do you really think he'd commit suicide in front of them like that?

JOHN: Yes. Why not?

DON: It doesn't seem to tie in with his character as we've seen it in the rest of the play.

PHILIP: I don't know. I liked it.

JOHN: You don't have to say that, you know. I'd much prefer to have honest criticism than your, if you don't mind me saying so, rather negative re-marks.

PHILIP: Please take no notice of what I say. I always like things. I get pleasure from the words that are used, whatever the subject is. I've enjoyed every book I've ever read for one reason or another. That's why I can't teach literature. I have no critical faculties. I think there's always something good to be found in the product of another man's mind. Even if the man is, by all objective standards, a complete fool. So you see I'd like a play however terrible it was.

JOHN: So you think my play is terrible.

PHILIP: I didn't say that, I . . .

JOHN: I'm not an idiot, you know, I can take a hint.

PHILIP: Please don't get angry.

But John is furious at Philip, even though Philip protests that he likes the play and tries to soothe its author. John turns again to Don for comment.

DON: I was just wondering whether the suicide is altogether justified.

JOHN: Oh, I think so. Given the kind of man he is. I think it could be quite powerful. I think perhaps he might put the revolver in his mouth. Then, if the back wall of the set was whitewashed, they could use some quaint device to cover it with great gobs of brain and bright blood at the vital moment. And just the two of them sitting there gaping. That would be wonderful.

>*To illustrate, John puts the revolver into his mouth and presses the trigger. Loud explosion. By some quaint device, gobs of brain and bright blood appear on the whitewashed wall. Philip and Don sit gaping. Long silence.*

DON: Jesus.

>*John slumps to the ground. Philip rushes abruptly from the stage. Don gropes shakily for the telephone and begins to dial. Blackout.*

Scene 2

A few days later, Philip is setting a dinner table for six. Don comes in, offers to help, then pours himself a drink. Philip is still brooding about the in-cident of John's suicide (of which all traces have been cleaned up). Don con-fides that John's play was really no good at all.

DON: . . . . . The ideas were there, but not the technique, it was far too cerebral.

PHILIP: Under the circumstances, I think that's an uniquely unfortunate adjective.

DON: What? Oh, oh yes. *(He laughs.)* Anyway, I see you've managed to get him off the wall.

PHILIP: Don.

DON: Sorry.
>*Silence.*

PHILIP: Celia wasn't very sympathetic either. The first thing she said when I rang her up and told her about it was: "I'm not surprised, he's always been ludicrously absent-minded."

DON: Did she?

PHILIP: Yes.

DON: Come to think of it, absent-minded's even more unfortunate than cerebral. *(He laughs, recovers, shakes his head.)* No, it was a terrible thing to happen, really. *(He tries to look solemn but is suddenly overcome by helpless laughter.)* Sorry.

Celia, Philip's fiancee, comes in from the kitchen where she has been preparing the dinner. Philip recites the guest list and Don makes appropriate comments: a girl named Liz ("Good"), a fellow-philologist named Araminta ("The quickest drawers in the faculty") and a visiting novelist named Braham Head ("Incredible prick. He's one of those writers who've been forced to abandon the left wing for tax reasons"). He also abandoned his family and was divorced by his wife.

Brooding, Don changes the subject. He informs Philip (who hasn't been listening to the radio all day) that an insane fanatic has entered the House of Commons and let loose with a submachine gun, murdering the Prime Minister and much of the Cabinet. Philip is appalled to hear this, but his attention is immediately distracted by Celia, who is looking for lemons to season the dish she's preparing. Don has some lemons in his room, and Celia goes off to get them.

DON: When is it you're getting married?

PHILIP: I, er, not sure really. Probably some time in the vacation.

DON: Are you looking forward to it?

PHILIP: Well, yes I think so. Why?

DON: Just wondered.
>*Silence.*

PHILIP: You don't really think it's a good idea, do you?

DON: I don't know, Philip.

PHILIP: I mean, you don't really like her, do you?

DON: It's not that I don't like her, that's not it at all. She's very amusing and intelligent and attractive—it's just I sometimes wonder whether she's your kind of person.

PHILIP: What do you mean? You mean I'm not amusing and intelligent and attractive.

DON: Of course not. But you're rather . . . serious, aren't you?

PHILIP: I suppose so.

DON: And Celia isn't. In fact, she's rather frivolous.

PHILIP: But I like that.

DON: Oh, I'm sure you do. Sure you do. But it may cause you some trouble.

Don suggests that Liz is very fond of Philip and would marry him if he asked her. Don is not suggesting that Philip should marry Liz instead of Celia, but . . .

Celia comes back, makes herself a drink and sinks into a chair.

CELIA: . . . . . I can't bear cooking: and I cook. I can't bear working: and I work. *(She smiles.)* And I can't bear Philip: and I'm marrying him.

PHILIP: It's all part of one basic condition.

CELIA: What?

PHILIP: You can't bear being a woman: and you are.

CELIA *(bristles):* What do you mean?

PHILIP: It was a joke.

CELIA: Not a very funny joke.

PHILIP: It was about as funny as yours.

CELIA: Mine?

PHILIP: Yes, when you said you couldn't bear me and you were marrying me.

CELIA: You think that was a joke?

PHILIP: I . . .

CELIA *(laughing):* Your trouble is you have no sense of humor.
     Philip is bested.

PHILIP: Sorry.

Braham Head knocks and enters. *"He is a tall, good-looking man, fashionably and expensively dressed."* He has brought Celia a "flower"—a cauliflower in a paper bag. Celia takes this somewhat dubious present to the kitchen as Braham watches her go and comments, "Lovely girl."

Philip makes a drink for Braham and offers him a cigarette. Philip gets tangled in an explanation of why he himself decided to give up smoking, balancing nervousness from not smoking against nervousness about getting cancer. Celia comes back into the room and accuses Philip of "burbling," and Philip agrees that he isn't expressing himself very well.

Braham advises Philip simply to have a cigarette, as the scene blacks out.

Scene 3

After dinner, the guests are relaxing over brandy and coffee. *"Araminta, a rather large girl with a dramatically low-cut dress, sits on the floor drinking creme de menthe. Liz, a quiet, reserved girl (she does not in fact speak during the course of the scene) is dressed more soberly, and sits watching, smiling to herself from time to time."* Braham leads the conversation with a reminiscence of an old priest's clandestine and somewhat perverted sexual exploits.

The talk turns to the assassination of the Ministers. Braham judges that the killing and its aftermath (the Minister of Sport, someone named Edith, is to be sent for by the Queen and asked to form a Government as the senior surviving Minister) represent a kind of decadence which may be better for the country in the long run that the starry-eyed pursuit of Socialism, which Braham terms "as much use . . . as a pogo stick to a paraplegic." Braham was once an ardent left-winger but came to realize his true role in life.

BRAHAM: . . . . . I was just one little person in this enormous bloody world. God, in his infinite wisdom, had given me the ability to create essentially frivolous entertainments, which were enjoyed by enough essentially frivolous people for me to be able to amble comfortably through life. Naturally, it distresses me that people are wasting their energies killing each other all over the world, and of course I'm sorry thousands of Indians starve to death every year, but I mean that's their problem, isn't it, if they will go in for all this injudicious fucking. I actually used to think that in some obscure way it was my fault.

DON: You've got over that now, have you?

BRAHAM: Well, I have, yes. Nowadays if I get one of those things through my letter-box telling me I can feed an entire village for a week for the price of a prawn cocktail, I tear it up, throw it in my waste-paper basket, go out to my favorite restaurant and order a prawn cocktail.

DON: And do you find that amusing?

BRAHAM: Oh, come now, the next thing you're going to say is what if everybody was like me. Fortunately for the world and even more fortunately for me, not everybody is. Look, if I actually get a concrete chance to help people, then I do.

ARAMINTA: Yes, I saw that TV appeal you did a few weeks ago.

DON: What was that for?

BRAHAM: Twenty-five guineas.

DON: I meant, on behalf of whom.

BRAHAM: I know you did.

DON: Well?

BRAHAM (playing up): Oh, I don't know, it was an appeal on behalf of spavined children. Or something equally sordid.

DON: And did it raise much money?

BRAHAM: Enough to cover my fee.

Don finds this attitude "disgusting." The others don't, which encourages Braham to expand on the subject of his success. As long as he can supply what the public wants, he gets rich, fairly, and once in a while maybe he can contribute a real insight in his writing. And, Braham adds, ". . . . . there's no point in feeling guilty about these things, there's only two alternatives, keep it or give it all away, and that's a very interesting proposition, as the rich man said to Christ, but don't call me, I'll call you."

Braham goes on to compare his kind of writing to the act of masturbation; he is an enthusiastic advocate of this activity.

Don tells a story about a pupil of his named Boot who became so depressed over the state of the world that he laid in a huge amount of supplies and went to bed and stayed there for six weeks. At the end of this time he decided to set fire to his room, and did—and was then committed to an asylum. This reminds Braham of literary critics, and he changes the subject abruptly to tell of a recent correspondence with one.

Celia tells Braham that Don is the only one of her teachers who hasn't made a pass at her (except Philip, of course, but Philip is not one of her teachers). She describes the awkward amorous techniques of a couple of gropers named Burrows and Johnson, then goes on to one named Noakes.

CELIA *(to Braham):* Noakes, I must tell you, is not one of the world's ten best. In fact, he looks as if he's escaped off the side of Notre Dame. His face is enormous. And he sweats profusely, which makes him a very . . . shiny man. Ice-hockey matches could be played on his forehead. He's also kind of Neanderthal, I mean his knuckles scrape along the pavement as he walks. He's a college politician, which means his tongue is long enough to reach places other people don't even know exist. I tell you, at college meetings, or cocktail parties, he lurches from one important man to another, leaving a trail like a slug. Fortunately, his flattery is so grotesquely and transparently insincere, only about three-quarters of the old cretins are taken in by it. I must say, though, his grope was a great deal more thorough than Johnson's. Fortunately, his palms are so slimy, he wasn't able to get a proper purchase, as they say. But it was very nasty. He is, in every sense, oleaginous.

ARAMINTA: I think he's rather sweet.

CELIA: *Chacun à son goût.*

ARAMINTA: What do you mean?

CELIA *(feigning innocence):* Nothing.

BRAHAM: He certainly sounds extraordinarily repulsive.

ARAMINTA: I think she's exaggerating.

BRAHAM: No, no, he sounds very familiar to me. *(To Philip.)* What do you think about all this?

PHILIP: What?

BRAHAM: All your colleagues leching after your fiancee.

PHILIP: Oh, well, I think it's quite understandable. I don't really mind.

BRAHAM: Don't you? I'm sure I would.

PHILIP: I don't know, you know . . .

BRAHAM: How come you don't teach her? Is there some fifteenth-century statute against seeing your betrothed in school hours?

PHILIP: No, the thing is, I teach philology which is sort of optional, and old texts and things like that, which she doesn't do because she's a graduate.

BRAHAM: Philology?

PHILIP: Yes.

BRAHAM: My God, I thought that went out years ago.

PHILIP: No.

BRAHAM: I seem to remember it as the only subject which cunningly combined the boredom of the science faculties with the uselessness of the arts faculties.

PHILIP: Well . . .

BRAHAM: The worst of both cultures.
PHILIP: Most people seem to think that way. But I . . . find it interesting.

Philip is fascinated with "Words as objects . . . . . structural linguistics." He notices how people use and abuse words; for example, he has noticed that Braham has a habit of picking up and re-using the exceptionally colorful phrases of others, and of over-using the word "actually." Braham is nettled; the others are somewhat embarrassed. Celia tries to smooth over the situation by explaining about Philip: "He's just obsessed with the way people talk, that's all. Sometimes I think he's more interested in that than in what they actually say."

Celia has also used the word "actually," and Braham takes this as a sign that they are each other's kind of person. Don mentions Philip's extraordinary skill at working out anagrams in his head. Braham challenges Philip to do his stuff and gives him "La Comédie Française" to work on. Philip sinks deep into thought while Braham makes rude comments about the French theater troupe's ability.

When two minutes are up, Philip comes up with the anagram of "La Comédie Française," as follows: " 'A defence o' racialism.' It doesn't quite work. There's an f missing. But it's the best I can do." Don's admiration of Philip is genuine; Braham's is grudging and sour.

The brandy bottle is handed around, and Braham tells them of the novel he's writing about a social worker who decides to become a merchant banker, a cynical reversal of the usual revelation theme. Then it is time for Braham to depart. Insistently, he maneuvers the situation so that he is to take Celia home in his two-seater, while Don drives Liz home. Celia tries to signal to Philip that she does *not* want to be driven home by Braham, she wants to remain here with Philip, but Philip thinks she merely wants to stay in order to help clean up; he thinks he's doing Celia a favor by insisting she leave now, with Braham.

Braham and Celia depart, as do Don and Liz, but Araminta insists on remaining behind to help with the clearing away. Philip sinks into the sofa, exhausted from the effort of the party, while Araminta makes a few half-hearted gestures of cleaning up. Then she comes over to Philip, massaging his temples (thereby making him even more tense), sits on his lap and finally kisses him.

ARAMINTA: Shall we go to bed?
        Brief silence.
PHILIP: I'll . . . . just go and get my coat.
        Araminta stares at him for a moment in blank incomprehension, then realizes what he means. She stands up.
ARAMINTA: I meant together.
PHILIP: Oh, I wasn't quite sure.
        Panic overcomes him. He looks at his watch, stares fixedly at it for a moment.

ARAMINTA: Well?

PHILIP: Well . . .

ARAMINTA: Don't be too enthusiastic.

PHILIP: It's just . . . it's just . . .

ARAMINTA: What?

PHILIP *(clutching at a straw):* I haven't any, haven't got any . . .

ARAMINTA: Not necessary.

PHILIP: Oh.

ARAMINTA: If you don't want to, just say so—

PHILIP: No, no, I do, I do.

ARAMINTA: —and I'll go home—

PHILIP: No.

ARAMINTA: —it's not a matter of life or death to me, you know.
Philip stands up.

PHILIP: I know, I'm sorry, it just took me a bit by surprise, that's all.
He kisses her.

ARAMINTA: Didn't look like a very pleasant surprise.

PHILIP: Please.
He kisses her again.
It's just that I'm shy, that's all.

ARAMINTA: I know. I love shy men.

PHILIP: All right now?

ARAMINTA: Yes.
They embrace.
Is that the bedroom, through there?

PHILIP: Yes.
She moves across to it, turns at the door.

ARAMINTA: Don't be long.
Philip smiles weakly at her, as she exits, then sinks down on to the sofa again. A moment later he gets up, moves over to the table, takes a cigarette from the cigarette-box, and puts it in his mouth, where it hangs limply for a moment. Then he returns it to the box, sighs deeply.

PHILIP: God help us all.
He exits wearily and reluctantly into the bedroom. Curtain.

ACT II

Scene 4

The next morning Araminta is seated on the sofa with coffee and cigarette, dressed in pajamas, reading the newspaper, when Celia walks in and takes in the scene. After a moment or two of shock, she asks for Philip and is told he's in the bath.

CELIA: I never thought you'd manage to add Philip to your collection.

ARAMINTA: What do you mean?

CELIA: You know, I sometimes think, although I can never quite bring myself to accept it, that you really are as thick as you pretend to be.

ARAMINTA: You're very offensive, this morning.

CELIA: I'm very offended. I don't know why you couldn't have left him alone. Do you write all their names up in a Book of Remembrance, or something? Do you give every hundreth one a pair of gold cuff-links with some discreetly erotic motif? Are you thinking of turning professional?

  Silence.

ARAMINTA: Would you care for some coffee?

CELIA: No, I would not.

ARAMINTA: Don't be like that.

CELIA: Why not?

ARAMINTA: It wasn't serious.

Araminta hints that nothing happened between her and Philip, and the whole futile experience has left her mildly dissatisfied. "And where did you spend last night?" she asks Celia. Celia stalks out, angry.

Philip comes in and apologizes for his performance—or lack of it—the evening before. It was the first time he'd ever been invited point-blank like that, and it put him off.

Araminta dismisses the incident as a case of "First-night nerves," urges Philip not to worry. She explains her own feelings: "I like being with people. And if you're with them you might as well do it as not." Her uncle raped her when she was 12, which has sort of taken the romance out of sex for her; she's never really been in love. "I did have an affair with a gypsy when I was about fifteen. I used to climb out of the window every night and cycle about three miles to meet him. He never used to say very much. I was terrified of him. It went on for about a month, then he moved on, and I remember being very sad. But I don't know that I was in love with him."

Araminta often brings out the worst in men, but she keeps after them because they relieve her loneliness. Araminta takes Philip's hand and indicates they might try again. After a moment of indecision, Philip says no.

PHILIP: . . . . . I think I'd better explain.

ARAMINTA: There's no point in explaining, love, you either want to or you don't.

PHILIP: No, I mean about last night.

ARAMINTA: I've told you . . .

PHILIP: I know it was my fault, I was very weak-minded.

ARAMINTA: Weak-minded, was it?

PHILIP: I should never have agreed, I knew it would be a disaster.

ARAMINTA: Well, I could see you were thrown by the directness of my approach.

PHILIP: It wasn't that, it was just, I didn't really want to.

ARAMINTA: I know, it's funny how important fidelity is to some people. I mean, it's something that never occurs to me.

PHILIP: It wasn't that, the truth is, I don't really find you attractive.

Silence.

ARAMINTA: I see.

PHILIP: No, don't be upset, it's my fault, my taste has always been terribly limited.

ARAMINTA *(upset):* I'm not upset.

PHILIP: No . . .

ARAMINTA: I don't know why you should think that.

PHILIP: It's just . . .

ARAMINTA: I mean, I don't exactly find you irresistible.

Growing more and more furious, a woman scorned, Araminta stalks into the bedroom to get dressed. She comes back and informs Philip of Celia's visit this morning, of Celia's anger. Philip can't understand at first why Celia should be angry; then he begins to comprehend how Celia might react to Araminta's presence in her fiance's apartment. Philip groans; Araminta, by now becoming sorry for him, departs.

Philip picks up the phone and dials—no answer. *"He wanders back to the table, sits down, picks up a bowl of cornflakes and starts eating. Blackout."*

Scene 5

Later that day, Philip is working at his desk when Celia walks in. Celia tells him, "I just came back to tell you I wasn't coming back." She is truly angry.

CELIA: It's so insulting, Philip. I mean you deliberately got rid of me.

PHILIP: What do you mean?

CELIA: Well, I did ask you to let me stay.

PHILIP: You didn't.

CELIA: Of course I did. I couldn't have made it much clearer if I'd started unbuttoning myself.

PHILIP: But I thought you just wanted to help with the washing-up.

CELIA: You amaze me. You really do.

PHILIP: Christ, I wish you had stayed.

CELIA: Why?

PHILIP: I didn't realize you wanted to stay the night. Oh, God, I wish you had.

Silence.

CELIA: You're being cunning.

PHILIP: I'm not.

CELIA: Don't. It's most unlike you.

PHILIP: I'm not.

CELIA: Look.

PHILIP: What?

CELIA: If you didn't let me stay because you thought I wanted to do the washing-up. why did you let her stay when you thought she wanted to do the washing-up?

PHILIP: She insisted.

CELIA: And more to the point, why did you let her stay when you realized she didn't want to do the washing-up?

PHILIP: She insisted.

CELIA: And you gave in.

PHILIP: Yes.

CELIA: Well, why?

PHILIP: Because I didn't want to hurt her feelings.

CELIA: What about my feelings?

PHILIP: You weren't there.

Celia is increasingly irritated at Philip's bland, emotionless explanations— he just sits there "like a pudding, wobbling gently." Celia would rather Philip became angry, or apologetic, but no, he prefers to tell her the plain facts and let her decide what she will. He explains the evening's fiasco to Celia, who comments "Sounds to me like a triumph of emotional incompetence."

Philip insists on being reasonable; he has decided he wants to marry Celia, it is up to her now to make up her mind whether she wants to marry him. His cool, chess-like rationality defeats Celia's purpose. She complains, "You never understand what I'm trying to say," and Philip replies calmly, "Maybe not, but I think I usually understand what you *do* say."

What Celia is trying to say is that she was only using the Araminta incident as an excuse to break off their engagement. It is what happened to *her* last night, not Philip's little adventure, that has made Celia think perhaps safe, admiring Philip isn't the right man for her after all. Celia informs Philip that she spent last night with Braham at his hotel.

PHILIP: But . . . why?

CELIA: I don't know, he went on at me. And I finally thought oh well, why not, I was still very angry about your not letting me stay. I don't know why. I felt dreadful this morning. He kept saying that creative artists had a much more consuming sexual urge than ordinary people. He told me that's why Bach had thirty children.

PHILIP: And were you convinced by this argument?

CELIA: No.

PHILIP: But you still . . . ?

CELIA: Yes.

PHILIP: Why? I don't see why.

CELIA: Well, he's so confident and self-assured, I don't know why. I just suddenly felt like it, don't go on about it.

PHILIP: And is that what you want?

CELIA: I don't know, I suppose so. Not him, I don't mean him, he's awful, but something like that.

Celia was put off by Braham this morning, partly by remarks Braham made about Philip. Celia found herself defending Philip, in spite of everything. Philip can't understand why Braham hates him; he holds no grudge against Braham, even now.

Braham, it seems, was particularly upset this morning because the papers are full of the murder of a literary personality. Some lunatic has sworn to kill the country's 25 most eminent authors, and—insult too grave to be borne —Braham isn't included among the intended victims. But Braham pretended to believe that he is one of the threatened ones, and he refused to leave his hotel room, forcing Celia to walk home by herself.

Philip asks to let bygones be bygones, but Celia fears that Philip isn't assertive enough to make her happy. Celia admits that those stories she told about professors making advances to her were all invented, "more interesting than the truth." Philip promises to pretend to be firm, but Celia will not accept this kind of deceit. Philip admits quite frankly that he's always been a failure with women and describes to Celia how his first love failed because he happened to remark to her that he was a virgin at the time, and she didn't want to be used as a "guinea pig." Philip tells Celia: "You think I'm being sentimental and self-pitying just because I say I'm a failure with women. But I'm not. I'm just telling the simple truth, which is that I've never managed to give a woman satisfaction. I hoped to. I hoped to with you. Given a bit of time."

Celia wonders why, with his comfortable bachelor existence, Philip ever wanted to get married. Philip admits to a growing consciousness of his aloneness. He is growing more and more melancholy, he sees life as a great traffic circle with all connecting roads marked one way in the wrong direction, so that there is no exit and the traffic merely keeps on moving around and around. As he sees it, Philip lives his life in a sort of perpetual terror: "I mean that the basic feature of my character is an anxiety to please people and to do what they want, which leads to, that is, which amounts to a passion, and which is, in fact, so advanced that I can only describe it as . . . terror."

Philip launches into another story illustrating his character to Celia; a story about a hunchback beggar in Hong Kong, where Philip once taught. He fell into the habit of giving this beggar some money every day, and the beggar would clean Philip's car.

PHILIP: . . . . . I used to keep a cache of small change handy to pay him, but one day, for some reason, I found I had none left, in fact, as I was leaving the building I found I had nothing smaller than a ten-dollar note, which was obviously, I thought to myself, far too much to give him. So, on this particular day I walked hurriedly past on the other side of the street, hoping he wouldn't see me, and crossed into the car-park as quickly as I could. But I'd just got into the car and put the key in the ignition, when I saw him hobbling towards the entrance of the car-park on his crutches at great speed, stopping occasionally to wave his duster at me. No, I thought, I can't face this, so I started up, and put my foot down, and raced out of the car-park. Now, I don't know about this, I mean, I'm sure I wasn't anywhere near him, but for some reason he panicked, an^c tried to jump backwards—and I just had this appalling glimpse of his crutches going up in the air as he overbalanced and fell on to his back. Needness to say, I didn't stop. After that, whenever he saw me coming, he used to get up, move down the road a bit and go indoors. I hoped I'd be able to make it up with him, but I never got a chance, he never, he never let me get near him again. No wonder they want our blood.

CELIA: Why are you telling me all this?

PHILIP: All what?

CELIA: All these stories. I can't ever remember you talking as much as this.

PHILIP: I don't want you to go.

Silence.

CELIA: My problem is, all the men I fall in love with turn out to be such terrible people.

PHILIP: Oh. Do you think so?

CELIA: Not you, I don't mean you. That's what I'm trying to say. I was never really in love with you because you weren't firm enough. I don't think I'm capable of loving anyone as weak as you.

PHILIP: Do you prefer to be bullied then?

CELIA: I prefer to know where I stand.

Silence.

PHILIP: Can't we . . . isn't there . . . ?

CELIA: I don't think so.

PHILIP: Are you sure?

CELIA: Yes. Yes, now I've made up my mind, I honestly don't know what it is I ever saw in you.

PHILIP: Oh, well. Oh, well, then.

CELIA: No, don't misunderstand me. I'll always like you. I'll always be fond of you. It's just that we're not compatible.

PHILIP: So you already said. I still can't see it myself, but I suppose I shall just have to take your word for it.

CELIA: Now I think it would be best if I went. *(She gets up.)*

PHILIP: Don't.

CELIA: Yes.

PHILIP: Please.

CELIA: I think it would be best.

PHILIP: Stay and talk to me. I feel a bit suicidal.

CELIA: Oh, don't exaggerate.

PHILIP: Well, you know. Stay and talk for a bit.

CELIA: Look, what have we got to talk about now? What could we possibly talk about?

PHILIP: Anything.

Celia bursts into tears. Philip is amazed, he takes her in his arms and she sobs uncontrollably for a minute, then slowly recovers.

CELIA: Sorry.

PHILIP: Are you all right love?

CELIA: Yes. All right now.

PHILIP: What's the matter?

CELIA: What do you think?

PHILIP: But I mean . . . I mean, it's your decision.

CELIA: What difference does that make?

PHILIP: All right now, are you?

CELIA: Yes, thanks.

PHILIP: Would you like a glass of water or anything?

CELIA: No, no. I really must go now. Goodbye.

PHILIP: Goodbye.

He takes her face in his hands and kisses her on the eyes and on the mouth.

What now? Death, hell, destruction, suicide, or will he come through smiling?

CELIA: Yes.

PHILIP: When will I see you again?

CELIA: Not for a bit. Not until we've got over it.

PHILIP: Soon.

CELIA: I expect so. *(She moves quickly to the door.)* Goodbye. *(Exits.)*

PHILIP: Goodbye, love.

He stands for a moment in the center of the stage, disconsolate. Then he sits at his desk, picks up a book, and reads. He breaks off for a moment and stares into the distance, then returns to his book. He makes a note. Blackout.

Scene 6

A few hours later, that evening, Philip is trying very hard to write a letter. He looks off into space, finally calls Don on the telephone and asks him to come over, he needs advice. A few moments later Don enters, sinks into a chair and is served a Scotch. Philip recapitulates the Celia-Araminta-Braham situation and tells Don of his broken engagement. Don remarks: "I always divide people into two groups. Those who live by what they know to be a lie, and those who live by what they believe, falsely, to be the truth. And having decided that Celia belonged to the first group and you to the second, I concluded that you weren't compatible, and that furthermore was what attracted you to one another."

Philip does not quite understand. Don, trying to illustrate, falls into talking about himself; how he is trying to develop laziness as a fine art, seeming to work hard as a teacher but in reality making almost no effort at all.

Philip repeats to Don some of what he told Celia about his need to get married simply to relieve his loneliness. Philip has remembered what Don said about silent Liz being right for him, and he is now trying to compose a letter to Liz, inviting her to something or other like lunch.

But Philip is too late. Liz is in Don's room right now, and Don has "rather fallen for her." Philip is thrown by this turn of events, and he asks Don to leave him alone; finally orders him "Will you please get out!"

Don exits uncertainly. Philip sits for a moment. Then he drains his drink, gets up, moves to his desk, crumples up the letter and throws it into the wastepaper basket. Next he moves back to the table, takes a cigarette from the cigarette-box and puts it in his mouth. Pause. Then he returns to the desk, opens the drawer and takes out a small pistol. He considers it for a moment, then puts it down on the desk. He lifts the telephone and dials two figures.

PHILIP: Hello, Don? . . . I'm sorry about all that . . . yes, I just, you know, well, I am sorry anyway . . . What? . . . Now? All right, if you're sure that's all right . . . are you sure? . . . Yes, I am quite hungry . . . well, that's very kind . . . yes, I'm all right, now . . . no, don't let's get sentimental about it . . . well anyway, I'm about to do something terrible . . . you'll see in a minute . . . I forgot to tell you, I thought of a new anagram today . . . "imagine the theater as real" . . . "imagine the theater as real" . . . it's an anagram for "I hate thee, sterile anagram" . . . Yes, I thought so too . . . all right, then . . . yes . . . yes . . . see you both in a minute.

He hangs up, pauses a moment, then picks up the pistol. He turns it toward him and pulls the trigger. A small flame springs from the hammer. Philip lights his cigarette from it, inhales deeply, pockets the pistol and leaves the stage. Curtain.

FOLLIES

A Musical in One Act

BOOK BY JAMES GOLDMAN

MUSIC AND LYRICS BY STEPHEN SONDHEIM

Cast and credits appear on page 310

JAMES GOLDMAN (book) was born in Chicago in 1927. He attended the University of Chicago as an undergraduate and Columbia as a graduate student in musicology until his studies there were interrupted by the Korean War. Following two years' military service, he began working toward the new goal of becoming a playwright. He made it to Broadway in 1961 with the comedy Blood, Sweat and Stanley Poole *and in 1962 with the book for* A Family Affair, *both written in collaboration with his brother William. A play written on his own,* They Might Be Giants, *was staged in London in 1961 by Joan Littlewood and is currently in release in a screen version.*

James Goldman's first Broadway script written alone was The Lion in Winter, *which was named a Best Play of the 1965-66 season, so that* Follies *is his second Best Play in a row.* The Lion in Winter *subsequently became an Academy Award-winning motion picture. He is also the author of the screen play for* Nicholas and Alexandra *and of a novel,* Waldorf. *He lives in New York City with his wife Marie and two children.*

STEPHEN SONDHEIM (music, lyrics) was born March 22, 1930 in New York City. At Williams College he won the Hutchinson Prize for musical composition, and after graduating B.A. he studied theory and composition with Milton Babbitt. He wrote scripts for the Topper *TV series and the incidental music for the Broadway productions of* Girls of Summer *(1956) and* Invitation to a March *(1961).*

It was as a lyricist that he first commanded major attention with West Side Story *(1957). He wrote both the music and lyrics for* A Funny Thing Happened on the Way to the Forum *(1962),* Anyone Can Whistle *(1964) and last season's* Company, *which won him his first Best Play citation and New York Drama Critics Circle Award for best musical. With* Follies *he has repeated in both categories. His other credits include the lyrics for* Gypsy *(1959) and* Do I Hear a Waltz? *(1965), as well as many brain-twisting word puzzles published in* New York Magazine *in the recent past.*

Time: Tonight

Place: A party on the stage of the Weismann Theater

SYNOPSIS: The scene is a partially demolished theater, a rubble of cracked plaster ornaments and a maze of wreckers' scaffolding, its roof partly open to the sky. *"The curtain rises to the sound of pastiche music as if recorded years ago: tinny, scratchy, full of ghosts."*

Sally Durant Plummer arrives onstage and is greeted by a major domo and handed a sash by a passing waitress. She is a former showgirl (the sash bears the date of the *Follies* in which she appeared), now a middle-aged matron but still pert and pretty and happy to be here, the first guest at a party to be held in this forbidding but nostalgic setting.

This is to be an evening of reunion and reminiscence, and deep in the shadow corners of the abandoned stage the past almost seems to come to life. In fact it actually does, right before our eyes, in the form of memory-figures dressed in black and white, moving among or in unison with the guests, unseen by them but visible to us. The memory-people are all young—they are the party guests as they were 20 years before, starring in the annual editions of the Weismann *Follies* on this very stage.

Sally goes off as Ben Stone (distinguished looking, but a bit seedy) and his wife Phyllis (still extremely handsome) enter and look around. Ben approves of the theater's crumbling appearance.

BEN: . . . . . It's the way nostalgia ought to look. I sometimes wonder why our memories don't go the way these walls have gone. Our bodies do: our plaster flakes away and yet the fool things we remember stay as fresh as paint. I can remember you . . . *(He smiles.)*
PHYLLIS: Oh? What was I like?

FIFI D'ORSAY, ETHEL SHUTTA, ALEXIS SMITH, DOROTHY COLLINS, MARY MC-
CARTY AND YVONNE DE CARLO IN "FOLLIES"

BEN: That was a long time ago. What kind of loving wife are you to drag
me here?

PHYLLIS: I think you wanted me to drag you.

BEN: Any bets?

PHYLLIS: I wanted to come back, Ben. One last look at where it all began.
I've been devoting my attention to beginnings lately. I wanted something
when I came here thirty years ago but I forgot to write it down and God
knows what it was.

BEN: Well, I'm glad you're glad to be here: that makes one of us.

She laughs lightly, smiling as she crosses.

PHYLLIS: I love the way you hate it when I'm happy and you're not.

Buddy Plummer, Sally's husband, enters. *"He can't stop smiling and he
can't stop talking and he can't hold still."* He's cracking jokes nervously,
looking for Sally.

Dmitri Weismann, the former impresario of the *Follies* and host of this
party appears in the spotlight. He explains: "Every year, between the wars, I
staged a *Follies* in this theater. Since then, this house has been a home to
ballet, rep, movies, blue movies and now, in a final burst of glory, it's to be a

parking lot." Meanwhile, they are here for a party with refreshments, a band and "the inevitable Roscoe, here as always to bring on the Weismann Girls."

Roscoe is a white-haired tenor in white tie and tails who appears at the top of a stairway and sings for the showgirls' entrance as he always did.

> ROSCOE *(sings):*
> Hats off!
> Here they come, those
> Beautiful girls.
> That's what
> You've been waiting for.
>
> Nature never fashioned
> A flower so fair,
> No rose can compare—
> Nothing respectable
> Half so delectable.
>
> Cheer them
> In their glory,
> Diamonds and pearls,
>
> Dazzling jewels by the score.
>
> This is what beauty can be:
> Beauty celestial—the best, you'll agree.
> All for you,
> These beautiful girls! . . . . .

The ladies have formed a line across the stage, each wearing her *Follies*-year sash, and as the song finally ends the line breaks up into party guests greeting and chatting. Buddy comes up to his wife Sally to greet her. There is an awkwardness between them, and Buddy reminds her: "You're my girl, honey; just remember that."

Max and Stella Deems, another guest couple, are telling Weismann how they switched from show biz to storekeeping and love it. A matronly guest named Hattie Walker is getting an autograph from Ben for her grandson; Ben, it seems, is a famous diplomat, now president of a foundation. He charms Hattie by remembering how she appeared onstage "in a white dress cut to here. I didn't hear a note you sang." Solange Lafitte, French and fifty-ish, drifts by and tells Weismann about her perfume business. Sally greets Weismann, who doesn't remember her.

Phyllis and Sally come upon each other in the midst of the party. On stage with them, the memory-figures of Young Phyllis and Young Sally are *Follies* girls hurrying to get ready for their chorus call, helping each other into costume, giggling, throwing their arms around each other, acting out the memory of 20 years ago.

The grown women greet each other, Phyllis coolly, Sally bubbling over:

"Just look at you. I want to hug you but I can't. You're like a queen, like Jackie Kennedy or something." (The memory-figures fade.)

Sally is now a Phoenix housewife who bleaches her hair and is thrilled to recall the days when she and Phyllis shared an apartment on Third Avenue. Sally married Buddy, and Phyllis married Ben.

The focus of the party shifts to Hattie Walker reminiscing about her five husbands, "crazy boys," then to Ben and Buddy, who are seated on the rubble to one side and *have drinks in their hands and seem casual and friendly.*

BUDDY: Sure, I think about the past. A lot, I guess. Don't you?

BEN: There's not much to think about.

BUDDY: I haven't read your book on Wilson yet. Sally bought a copy, though. We keep it on the coffee table.

BEN: Just the place.

BUDDY: I always knew you'd make it big.

BEN: I had a lot of luck. (*He doesn't mean a word of it.*)

BUDDY: How's life with you and Phyllis?

BEN: She's an extraordinary woman, endlessly exciting.

Young Buddy and Young Ben appear, memory-figures walking on their way to law school class. Young Buddy tells his friend he has a great blind date for him that evening—a lonely girl named Phyllis. Then the memory-figures disappear, and grown-up Buddy is telling Ben about his married life with Sally: "I come home and I'm welcome. I see Sally and I'm glad to see her. No big deal, no fireworks—I'm sentimental on my second drink."

Both men claim that they've given up playing around. Buddy admits he'd have made a poor lawyer even if he'd made it through law school as Ben did.

The attention shifts to Vincent and Vanessa, former ballroom dancers (and accompanied by their dancing memory-figures) who now have an Arthur Murray franchise; then to Heidi Schiller, for whom Franz Lehar once wrote a waltz; then to Carlotta, a full-blown rose perhaps past her prime but still beautiful, once a showgirl, telling Ben that she now has her own TV series.

Sally comes on and sees Ben. The sight of him after all these years flusters her.

SALLY (*sings*):
. . . . . No, don't look at me—
Please, not just yet.
Why am I here? This is crazy!
No, don't look at me—
I know that face,
You're trying to place
The name.
Say something, Ben,
Anything!
No, don't talk to me . . .

Ben, I forget:
What were we like? It's so hazy!
Look at these people,
Aren't they eerie?
Look at this party,
Isn't it dreary?
I'm so glad I came!

Ben is happy to see Sally, who almost feels 19 again at the sight of him. They go in search of a drink.

The focus shifts to Carlotta, who is describing her love life; then to Phyllis and Buddy reminiscing about the past, watching Ben and Sally dancing. Buddy is in the oil business now. He remembers how it was in the old days, Ben and Buddy sitting by the call board waiting for Sally and Phyllis to go out on a double date. Phyllis wants to forget the past, but Ben and Sally join them, and Buddy's reminiscence takes the form of a song.

BUDDY *(sings):*
    Waiting around for the girls upstairs
    After the curtain came down,
    Money in my pocket to spend,
    "Honey, could you maybe get a friend for my friend?"
BEN:
    Hearing the sound of the girls above,
    Dressing to go on the town . . .
BUDDY:
    Clicking heels on steel and cement . . .
BEN:
    Picking up the giggles floating down through the vent . . .
BEN & BUDDY:
    Goddamnedest hours that I ever spent
    Were waiting for the girls
    Upstairs.

In their song, the boys remember how it was: the final curtain, all the girls backstage running to their dressing rooms. Phyllis and Sally remember how it was too.

PHYLLIS *(sings):*
    Waiting around for the boys downstairs,
    Stalling as long as we dare.
    Which dress from my wardrobe of two?
    (One of them was borrowed and the other was blue.)
SALLY:
    Holding our ground for the boys below,
    Fussing around with our hair . . .

PHYLLIS:
   Giggling, wriggling out of our tights . . .
   Chattering and clattering down all of those flights—
SALLY & PHYLLIS:
   God, I'd forgotten there ever were nights
   Of waiting for the boys
   Downstairs.

Young Sally, Young Phyllis, Young Ben and Young Buddy come in and take up the song, acting out how it was when the girls would finally come down and they would decide where they were going to spend the evening. The girls hold out for a "ritzy" place called Tony's, where there's dancing. The memory figures fade, leaving their middle-aged counterparts shaken by the memory.

PHYLLIS, SALLY, BEN & BUDDY (sing):
   Waiting around for the girls upstairs—
   Thank you but never again.
   Life was fun but oh, so intense,
   Everything was possible and nothing made sense

   Back there when one of the major events
   Was waiting for the girls,
   Waiting for the girls . . . . .
   Waiting for the girls
   Upstairs.

The focus shifts to three more guests—Willy Wheeler, Emily and Theodore Whitman. With Weismann and a group of ladies, they are posing for a photographer. "They look back on their life here and see it as a golden time," Weismann comments, adding that in those days he could have any of them for the asking. The Whitmans sing one of their old numbers about being cozy together with rain going "plunk-a-plink" on the roof. Then Solange Lafitte takes the spotlight for her solo. It celebrates Paris as the world capital of love. Then it is Hattie Walker's turn; she remembers the deep yearning to make it on Broadway.

HATTIE WALKER (sings):
   . . . . . Say, Mr. Producer,
   I'm talking to you, sir:
   I don't need a lot,
   Only what I got,
   Plus a tube of greasepaint and a follow-spot!

   I'm a Broadway baby,
   Slaving at a five-and-ten,
   Dreaming of the great day when
   I'll be in a show.

Broadway baby,
Making rounds all afternoon,
Eating at a greasy spoon
To save on my dough.

At
My tiny flat
There's just my cat,
A bed and a chair.
Still,
I'll stick it till
I'm on a bill
All over Times Square!
I'm just a
Broadway baby . . . . .

The number ends in a medley of Hattie's, Solange's and the Whitmans' songs. The focus shifts to Ben and Sally. Sally is admiring, and Ben deprecating, Ben's glamorous life. Find out what you want to do and do it, Ben philosophizes. He sings to her that life gives you only one chance, one choice: "The road you didn't take/Hardly comes to mind/Does it?" Behind the song, Young Buddy loans Young Ben his car for a date with Phyllis. Ben continues convincing himself in song that the choices he didn't make will be forgotten, will not come back in memory to haunt him with might-have-been.

BEN *(sings):*
. . . . . The books I'll never read
Wouldn't change a thing,
Would they?
The girls I'll never know
I'm too tired for.
The lives I'll never lead
Couldn't make me sing,
Could they? Could they? Could they? . . . . .

The roads you never take
Go through rocky ground,
Don't they?
The choices that you make
Aren't all that grim.
The worlds you never see
Still will be around,
Won't they?
The Ben I'll never be,
Who remembers him?
> *The number ends as Ben stares into space. Buddy and Phyllis appear upstage, look down on Ben and Sally.*

SALLY: *I* remember him. I even think I loved him once.

She takes Ben by the hand, moves with him to join the dancing.

BUDDY *(looking at them):* They make a lovely couple. What's wrong with me tonight?

PHYLLIS: You got the shakes?

BUDDY *(drinking):* Not me, I'm on the wagon. You got any kids, Phyl?

PHYLLIS: None at all. Ben put it off and then it was too late.

BUDDY: We've got two. Tom and Tim. Sally picked the names out. They're in San Francisco now and she gets lonely for them so she calls them on the phone and fights. She's fought with everyone she knows. It's crazy. Phyl, all I want is Sally back the way she used to be. I want the girl I married.

PHYLLIS *(wryly):* That's impossible but never mind.

BUDDY: I told her not to come tonight. She's forty-nine, Phyl, and she ran away from home to be with Ben.

PHYLLIS: Oh, that's absurd.

BUDDY: It's happening again, just like I knew it would.

PHYLLIS: What is?

BUDDY: She's still in love with Ben.

PHYLLIS: I used to wonder but I never knew for sure. Times change. It might have mattered once.

The memory-figures of Young Phyllis and Young Ben materialize to relive the moment when they became engaged. Then they fade, and Phyllis reassures Buddy that life is a bargain to be struck, a selection of colors, a deliberate work of art. She remembers an affair she had with an ardent and devoted young lover: "I thought it answered everything, but these things pass and I have thirty thousand dollars worths of Georgian silver in my dining room."

Buddy is unable to crack Phyllis's veneer of ice. A Vincent and Vanessa dance number takes over the stage, and following it Sally and Ben are having a talk—or rather, Sally is telling Ben about her life and Ben is half-listening. What makes her life fun (Sally would like to believe) is her husband Buddy. She sings about Buddy's devotion to her, but her memory-figure acts out a scene with Young Ben, who is still "playing around" with Young Sally, though he has given a ring and his promise to Young Phyllis.

Grown-up Sally remembers that she couldn't resist Young Ben—she couldn't help herself. Then she continues her song about Buddy to grown-up Ben.

SALLY *(sings):*
 In Buddy's eyes
 I'm young, I'm beautiful.
 In Buddy's eyes,
 I can't get older.
 I'm still the princess,
 Still the prize.
 In Buddy's eyes,

I'm young, I'm beautiful.
In Buddy's arms,
On Buddy's shoulder,
I won't get older . . . . .

Sally and Ben start to dance, but Phyllis interrupts them and takes Sally over to a corner for a chat. Phyllis questions Sally about Ben, but Sally avoids answering her questions directly.

Stella Deems and three of the other girls join Phyllis and Sally for a song-and-dance number. The six ex-Follies girls have a little trouble getting through the dance motions, but Stella belts out a song, as though asking her mirror, "Who's that woman?"

STELLA *(sings):*
 . . . . . Who's that woman?
I know I know that woman,
So clever but ever so sad.
Love, she said, was a fad.
The kind of love that she couldn't make fun of
She'd have none of.
Who's that woman?
That cheery, weary woman
Who's dressing for yet one more spree.
Each day I see her pass
In my looking glass—
Lord, Lord, Lord, that woman is me . . . . .

After the number, Buddy corrals Sally, congratulating her, telling her that her performing is still fabulous. Phyllis joins Ben and has to prod him for a compliment.

The focus alternates between the Stones and the Plummers. Buddy begs Sally to leave the party and come home with him, back to Phoenix; he promises to arrange it so that he won't have to travel so much, he'll be home more. Phyllis startles Ben by kissing him—but his astonishment is the only response she gets from him. Buddy reminds Sally that "We had it once." Phyllis reproaches Ben: "My God, we haven't had an honest talk since '41."

And to the Plummers as—
BUDDY: What do you want from me? It doesn't matter what I do. It's never good enough. I come home feeling great and touch you and you look at me like I'd been living in some sewer.
SALLY: Haven't you? You've always got a woman some place. Oh, I know. You leave things in your pockets so I'll know.
BUDDY: She lives in Dallas, and her name is—
SALLY: I don't want to hear it.
BUDDY: Margie. Margie, that's her name. She works at Neiman's and she's

got a little house. It's quiet there. She gives me books to read each time and when I'm there we talk for hours. And she cooks for me and sews my buttons on and when we go to bed, it's like she thought I was some kind of miracle. She's twenty-nine and pretty and you know what my luck is?

Sally has had enough and starts to go.

My luck is I love you.

He turns and strides away as Phyllis speaks.

PHYLLIS *(to Ben):* When did you love me last? Was it ten years ago or never? Do you ever contemplate divorce? Or suicide? Why don't you play around? Or do you? Have you cried much lately? Are you ever savaged by regret? Does one day more with me seem insupportable? Or are you dead?

BEN: I have my moments.

PHYLLIS: Tell me one.

BEN: I used to wish that life were work and sleep and nothing else, that I could go from bed to desk to bed again; and now I look at what I do and find it meaningless.

PHYLLIS: You cleft my heart.

BEN: I cleave it. Cleft is past.

PHYLLIS: Damn right. You don't much cleave it any more. The way I wanted you. I'd come home with my panties wringing wet. You're shocked. Why? Is my language getting bad? It used to be, before you taught me everything I know. What was I? Just some chorus girl who lost it in a rumble seat. Don't you remember? You were there. Son of a bitch, I'm going to cry.

She bites her lip. There are no tears.

BEN: You wore a gray dress and the zipper stuck and all you did was sob about your mother and how she'd feel if she knew. You were terrific. See that waitress over there? I've been wanting to make her all night.

Phyllis feels she still has a chance to enjoy life, she is not too old yet. She demands to know where Ben stands, and Ben tells her: "Yes to all your questions. Yes, I loved you once and yes, I play around and yes, I have regrets and God, yes, one more day with you—"

Ben strides away as Phyllis reaches for a drink and also for the handsome waiter carrying it.

Carlotta comes on to sing her former *Follies* number about a durable and gallant woman who has seen just about everything and has managed somehow to survive.

CARLOTTA *(sings):*
. . . . . I've been through Gandhi,
Windsor and Wally's affair,
And I'm here.
Amos 'n' Andy,
Mahjongg and platinum hair,
And I'm here.

I got through *Abie's*
Irish Rose,
Five Dionne babies,
Major Bowes,
Had heebie-jeebies
For Beebe's
Bathysphere.
I've lived through Brenda Frazier
And I'm here.
I've gotten through Herbert and J. Edgar Hoover,
Gee, that was fun and a half.
When you've been through Herbert and J. Edgar Hoover,
Anything else is a laugh . . . . .

I've run the gamut,
A to Z.
Three cheers and dammit,
C'est la vie.
I got through all of last year,
And I'm here.
Lord knows, at least I've been there,
And I'm here!
Look who's here!
I'm still here!

As Carlotta finishes her song, Ben is confiding to Sally his wife Phyllis is "untouchable." Their memory-figures sit with their arms fondly around each other, as Ben tells Sally that just that afternoon he made love to a girl—and then, afterward, began to weep. Young Sally, who it seems is grown-up Ben's dream girl, joins Sally in reassuring Ben that it isn't too late to find happiness. Young and grown-up Sally reach out their hands, and Ben takes Young Sally's hand and sings his song of wishing. Grown-up Sally reacts as though the song were being sung to her. She begs Ben to kiss her. Their illusion of paradise once lost and now regainable is perfect.

    The music soars joyously.
BEN & SALLY *(sing):*
Too many mornings
Wasted in pretending I reach for you.
How many mornings
Are there still to come?
How much time can we hope that there will be?
Not much time, but it's time enough for me,
If there's time to look up and see
Sally standing at the door,
Sally moving to the bed,

Sally resting in my arms,
With your head against my head.

Buddy enters on an upper level; he doesn't see Ben and Sally but he can imagine what they are up to and is muttering to himself about it. Young Sally and Young Ben drift off. Grown-up Ben kisses Sally passionately and declares himself to her: he wants her, they must go away together. Sally agrees, but there is one things she'd like to confirm before they leave.

SALLY: We're getting married, aren't we?
> *Ben stops, looks at her frozen. Young Ben and Young Sally reappear. He wears a sailor suit. She wears a street coat. They are walking down a street.*
BUDDY: What do I see in her for God's sake?
SALLY: I mean, this time you're going to marry me, aren't you?
> YOUNG SALLY: You love me, Ben.
SALLY: You love me, Ben. That's what people do when they're in love. They get married.
> YOUNG SALLY: Why not get married now?
BEN: Oh my God, what am I doing?
> YOUNG BEN: There's lots of time for that.
SALLY: Sally wants another kiss, please.
> YOUNG SALLY: What if there's not?
BEN: I must be insane.
SALLY: We'll be so happy, we'll be—
> YOUNG SALLY: What if you don't come back?
> YOUNG BEN: Don't worry, lawyers don't get shot.
> YOUNG SALLY: What if there's someone else? Ben, marry me.
BEN: Sally, listen.
SALLY: I'll make you the best wife.
> YOUNG BEN: Sure, sure.
> YOUNG SALLY: Now. If you really love me.
> YOUNG BEN *(irritation rising):* Love you, yes I love you.
> YOUNG SALLY: Then why not?

Neither Young Ben nor grown-up Ben can find an answer to Sally's question "Why not?" They extricate themselves, Young Ben abruptly and old Ben with a polite evasion. Sally speaks her belief that it's going to turn out all right, no matter what. She moves off in company with her memory-figure of Young Sally.

Buddy, alone, bursts into an angry song about the Right Girl.

BUDDY *(sings):*
    . . . . . Hey, Margie, I'm back, babe.
    Come help me unpack, babe.
    Hey Margie, hey, bright girl,
    I'm home . . . . .

    Des Moines was rotten and the deal fell through.
    I pushed, babe.
    I'm bushed, babe.
    I needed you to tell my troubles to—
    The heck, babe—
    Let's neck, babe . . . . .

    The right girl—
    She sees you're nothing and thinks you're king,
    She knows you got other songs to sing.
    You still could be—hell, well anything,
    When you got—yeah!
    The right girl . . . . .

Buddy finishes his song and talks out loud as though to Sally. He is sick of her moods. Sally appears above him, listens, then tells him Ben has asked her to marry him. Buddy doubts it and is furious: "I've spent my whole life making things the way you want them and no matter what we do or where we go or what we've got, it isn't what you want. It used to drive me nuts. Not any more. So you wake up hung over or you wake up in the funny farm, it's all the God damn same to me."

Ben strides off, leaving Sally starry-eyed with the conviction that "I'm getting married and I'm going to live forever with the man I love." But meanwhile Ben (as the focus shifts) has attached himself to Carlotta. He begs Carlotta to take him home with her and soothe his loneliness. But Carlotta has other romantic commitments—besides, she knows that this mood of Ben's will pass.

A spotlight catches Heidi Schiller alone, in a wheel chair, dreaming of romance. The reverie becomes a song, an exaggerated operetta love lyric, with her young memory-figure joining her for a duet.

HEIDI SCHILLER *(sings):*
    One more kiss before we part,
    One more kiss and—farewell,
    Never shall we meet again,
    Just a kiss and then
    We break the spell.

    One more kiss to melt the heart,
    One more glimpse of the past,
HEIDI & YOUNG HEIDI:
    One more souvenir of bliss

Knowing well that this
One must be the last.

Dreams are a sweet mistake.
All dreamers must awake . . . . .

The focus shifts from the Heidis to Phyllis, who is toying with the handsome waiter. She asks him rhetorical questions about love and sex but establishes no satisfactory rapport with him.

The waiter leaves and Ben appears. Phyllis doesn't want to continue their relationship another day, and Ben agrees: he wants a divorce.

Phyllis taunts Ben with visions of a honeymoon with Sally, and Ben admits: "I'm not in love with Sally. Hell, I never was." On the contrary, he now sees, his trouble is that he's never known what love is and hopes desperately that some one will show him before it's too late.

Phyllis echoes Ben: "You haven't got a clue what love is. Hell, you've had it all your life. I should have left you years ago," but Phyllis didn't because she thought Ben needed her. Now she finally sees the light.

PHYLLIS *(sings):*
     . . . . . Could I leave you
And your shelves of the world's best books
And the evenings of martyred looks,
Cryptic sighs,
Sullen glares from those injured eyes?
Leave the quips with a sting, jokes with a sneer,
Passionless lovemaking once a year? . . . . .

Could I live through the pain
On a terrace in Spain?
Would it pass? It would pass.
Could I bury my rage
With a boy half your age
In the grass? Bet your ass.
But I've done that already—or didn't you know, love?
Tell me, how could I leave when I left long ago, love?

Could I leave you?
No, the point is, could you leave me?
Well, I guess you could leave me the house,
Leave me the flat,
Leave me the Braques and Chagalls and all that.
You could
Leave me the stocks for sentiment's sake
And ninety per cent of the money you make . . . . .
Leave you? Leave you?
How could I leave you?

Sweetheart, I have to confess:
Could I leave you?
Yes.
Will I leave you?
Will *I* leave *you?*
Guess!

The stage is empty; just the two of them. The lights are strange.
BEN *(looking at his hands):* They won't stop shaking.

As he jams them in his pockets, Young Ben appears upstage and speaks to an enraptured Young Phyllis.

YOUNG BEN: You'll make a good wife, Phyl.

YOUNG PHYLLIS: I'll try. Oh, Ben, I'll try so hard. I'll study and I'll read—I'm not much now, I know that—

PHYLLIS: I tried so hard. I studied and I read—I thought I wasn't much: I was terrific—*(Turning to Young Phyllis.)* What happened to you, Phyl?

YOUNG PHYLLIS: I love you, Ben.

BEN *(to Young Ben):* She did—and what did you give her?

YOUNG BEN: Some day, I'll have the biggest Goddamn limousine.

BEN *(to Young Ben, with loathing):* You were so smart.

PHYLLIS *(to Young Phyllis):* Where did you go?

YOUNG PHYLLIS: We've got each other, Ben. What difference does it make?

BEN *(to Young Ben):* You had it all and you threw it away.

The memory-figures freeze as Buddy storms into the scene. He is furious at Ben for playing around with Sally (and at the same time Young Ben is reassuring Young Buddy that there's nothing between him and Young Sally).

Sally comes on, still dreaming that Ben is going to carry her off. The crosscurrents among the four grown-ups and the four memory-figures begin to run in all directions. Their individual reproaches and deceits are expressed to each other singly at first; then in pairs, then *"Each of them turns on his past self with mounting rage, as if they meant to do physical violence to the memories."* Finally all eight of the characters are reproaching and threatening, all talking at once—*"It's senseless now, completely unintelligible and rather frightening . . . . . The madness of the confrontation rises. At its peak, just as there seems to be no possible way out, drums start to roll, trumpeters in medieval costumes emerge from the shadows, heavenly music is heard, flying down come drop after drop, all valentines and lace and, as the lights rise to bright gold, dancers, young and beautiful, all dressed like Dresden dolls and cavaliers, appear. Ben, Phyllis, Buddy and Sally, eyes wild and half demented, stand in the midst of it all, taking their first look at 'Loveland' ".*

The saccharine setting of "Loveland" has now been superimposed on the crumbling theater, obscuring it completely. Rosy romantic dreams come true in "Loveland," and therefore are exposed for the fraudulent self-deceptions they really are. The Folly of Love, the Folly of Youth in general are revealed here, as well as the individual Follies of Ben, Phyllis, Buddy and Sally, as setpieces in an old-fashioned revue: as overblown valentines, exaggerated to the point of irony.

The chorus's song sets the mood.

CHORUS *(sings):*
    Time stops, hearts are young,
    Only serenades are sung
    In Loveland
    Where everybody lives to love.

    Raindrops never rain,
    Every road is lover's lane
    In Loveland
    Where everybody loves to live.

    See that sunny sun and honeymoon,
    There where seven hundred days hath June.

    Sweetheart, take my hand,
    Let us find that wondrous land
    Called Loveland, Loveland, Loveland . . .

Elaborately costumed showgirls come mincing forth, escorted by bewigged and powdered young men. They are dressed as the spirits (and by implication the Follies) of various forms of love.

The Folly of Youth is expressed in the optimism of a song by Young Ben and Young Phyllis called "You're Gonna Love Tomorrow": "We're in this thing together/Arent'cha glad?/Each day from now will be/The best day you ever had." Then it is Young Sally and Young Buddy's turn for pink-cheeked optimism:

YOUNG BUDDY *(sings):*
    I've some traits, I warn you, to which you'll have objections.
YOUNG SALLY:
    I, too, have a cornucopia of imperfections.
    I may burn the toast.
YOUNG BUDDY:
    Oh, well, I may make a rotten host.
YOUNG SALLY:
    Do tell.
YOUNG BUDDY & YOUNG SALLY:
    But no matter what goes wrong,
    Love will see us through
    Till something better comes along . . . . .

The four memory-figures join voices for a finale of their youthful Folly, then it is grown-up Buddy's turn to act out his Folly. He comes on strong, like a vaudeville song and dance man.

BUDDY *(sings):*
I've got those
"God-why-don't-you-love-me-oh-you-do-I'll-see-you-later"
Blues,
That
"Long-as-you-ignore-me-you're-the-only-thing-that-matters"
Feeling,
That
"If-I'm-good-enough-for-you-you're-not-good-enough-
And-thank-you-for-the-present-but-what's-wrong-with-it?" stuff,
Those
"Don't-come-any-closer-'cause-you-know-how-much-I-love-you"
Feelings,
Those
"Tell-me-that-you-love-me-oh-you-did-I-gotta-run-now"
Blues.

Buddy imagines himself in a scene with Margie—she expresses her adoration, and he runs away. But Sally (Buddy's Folly concludes) loves someone else, so of course Buddy is crazy about her.

Sally's Folly is a torch song, yearning for something she dreams of, reaching for an illusion: "I dim the lights/And think about you/Spend sleepless nights/To think about you/You said you loved me/Or were you just being kind?/Or am I losing my mind?"

Phyllis takes the spotlight, now dressed in an uncharacteristically short-skirted, flamboyant costume; no longer the U.N. matron, she is now the *Follies* girl, and her Folly is a story about two contrary women named Lucy and Jessie. Lucy is young and pure, Jessie is middle-aged and well established, and each wishes she had the other's advantages.

PHYLLIS *(sings):*
Lucy is juicy
But terribly drab.
Jessie is dressy
But cold as a slab.
Lucy wants to be dressy
Jessie wants to be juicy,
Lucy wants to be Jessie,
And Jessie Lucy. You see,
Jessie is racy
But hard as a rock.
Lucy is lacy

But dull as a smock.
Jessie wants to be lacy,
Lucy wants to be Jessie.
That's the sorrowful precis.
It's very messy . . . . .

Juicy Lucy,
Dressy Jessie,
Tell them that they ought to get together quick
'Cause getting it together is the whole trick.

Finally it is Ben's turn. In his Folly, Ben struts at the center of a chorus line of girls, dressed in top hat, white tie and tails and twirling a cane nonchalantly, riding high, with a philosophy of "Live, Laugh, Love," and never mind ideals or ambitions.

BEN *(sings):*
. . . . . Me, I like to love,
Me, I like to . . .
    He forgets his lyric, calls for it from the conductor.
Some break their asses
Passing their bar exams,
Lay out their lives
Like lines on a graph . . .
One day they're diplomats—
Well, bully and congrats!
Me, I like to love me . . .
    In the midst of "Live, Laugh, Love" Ben suddenly goes dry. The
    chorus girls backing him keep dancing. Ben tries to start, gets out
    a bar or two, then loses his way again. His desperation grows.
    Nothing comes. He looks around for help, chokes down the rising
    panic, makes one last try that fails, and—
(Speaks.) Me, I like—me, I love—me. I don't love me!

Ben struggles against the thought that he loves himself only. Desperately, he tries to justify himself and his life to the showgirls. *"He catches sight of a fragment of the party, high up on a downstage platform,"* and the Loveland valentine settings begin to disappear. The ruined stage and the party emerge. It is a chaotic nightmare to Ben, with the showgirls still in line and dancing. The party people are all there, but they can't see Ben as he goes from one group to another trying to explain himself and his treatment of Sally: "She said she'd kill herself. I didn't think she meant it." Finally he calls Phyllis's name. The party chaos begins to fade. The lights come up on a stage that is deserted except for Phyllis rushing to Ben's side and Buddy crouching by Sally, trying to bring her out of a daze. The growing light of dawn is visible through the hole in the theater's roof.

SALLY (*voice dead, eyes straight ahead*): I left the dishes in the sink, I left them there, I was in such a hurry and there is no Ben for me, not ever, any place.

BUDDY: There never was and that's the truth.

Helping her to rise.

Come on. I'll take you home.

SALLY: I can't stand up.

BUDDY: I'll help you.

SALLY: I should have died the first time.

BUDDY: Cut that out.

SALLY: I should have been dead all these years.

BUDDY: Don't talk that way. You've got a lot to live for: friends, a home, some money—Go on, say it after me, out loud. You say it. Friends . . .

SALLY: Friends . . .

BUDDY: Home . . .

SALLY: Home . . .

BUDDY: We're gonna go and get some rest . . . And then we're gonna make plans for tomorrow.

SALLY: For tomorrow . . .

She pauses, looks up at the morning light. There is no hope at all. Oh dear God, it is tomorrow.

They go off.

BEN: I've lost my jacket.

Phyllis picks it up.

There has to be a way . . . I won't face one more morning feeling— (*Impatiently.*) Despair: I'm sick to Goddam death of it.

PHYLLIS (*with a flash of white hot anger*): Amen. It's easy, life is empty; there is no hope. Hope doesn't grow on trees; we make our own and I am here to tell you it's the hardest thing we'll ever do.

BEN: I've always been afraid of you. You see straight through me and I've always thought, "It isn't possible; it can't be me she loves."

PHYLLIS (*still hot with the intensity of what she feels*): Well, think again. Come on. We're going home.

BEN: You're really something, aren't you?

PHYLLIS (*as they join hands and move upstage*): Bet your ass.

Their memories take the stage.

YOUNG BUDDY (*sings*):

Hey, up there!

YOUNG BEN:

Way up there!

YOUNG BEN & YOUNG BUDDY:

Whaddaya say, up there.

YOUNG SALLY (*speaks*): Hi . . .

YOUNG BEN: Girls . . .

YOUNG PHYLLIS: Ben . . .

YOUNG BUDDY: Sally . . .

Curtain.

A GRAPHIC GLANCE

LOUIS NYE AND MAUREEN O'SULLIVAN
IN THE REVIVAL OF "CHARLEY'S AUNT"

HAL LINDEN (TOP), PAUL HECHT (LEFT), CHRIS SARANDON, ALLAN GRUET,
TIMOTHY JEROME AND DAVID GARFIELD IN "THE ROTHSCHILDS"

JOAN COPELAND, MARILYN COOPER, HARRY GOZ, MADELINE KAHN,
MICHAEL KARMS, TRICIA O'NEIL, WALTER WILLISON
AND DANNY KAYE IN "TWO BY TWO"

RUBY KEELER IN THE REVIVAL OF "NO, NO, NANETTE"

TOM ALDREDGE, JEANNE HEPPLE, BERNICE MASSI,
RICHARD MULLIGAN, PHIL SILVERS AND SANDY DENNIS
IN "HOW THE OTHER HALF LOVES"

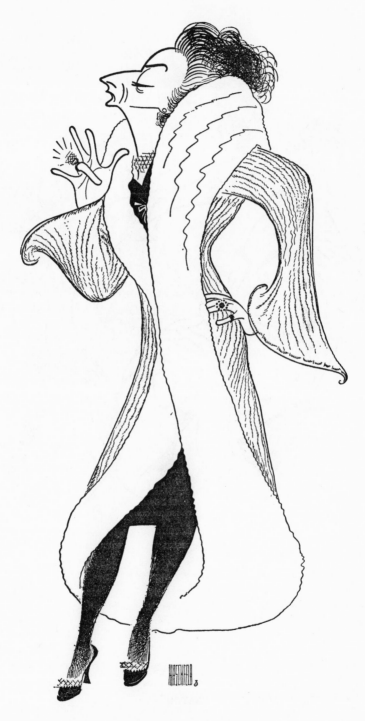

MILDRED NATWICK IN "70, GIRLS, 70"

WILL GEER AND PATRICK MAGEE IN "SCRATCH"

CLIFF GORMAN IN THE TITLE ROLE OF "LENNY"

ON SEPTEMBER 9, 1970 "HELLO, DOLLY!" BECAME THE LONGEST RUNNING MUSICAL IN BROADWAY HISTORY. PICTURED BELOW ARE PRODUCER DAVID MERRICK AND THREE OF THE ACTRESSES WHO PLAYED THE TITLE ROLE ON BROADWAY: CAROL CHANNING, PEARL BAILEY AND ETHEL MERMAN.

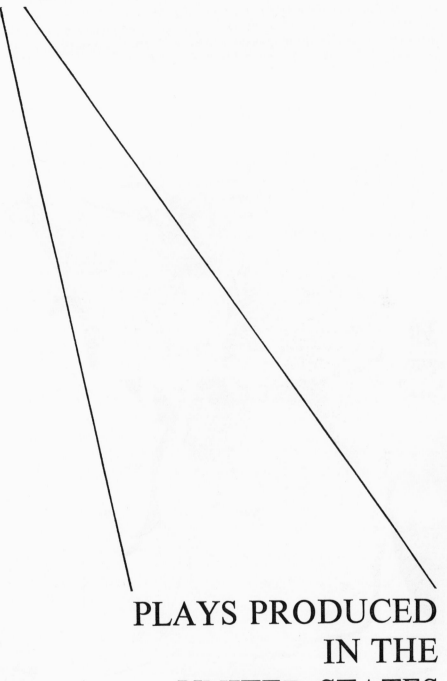

PLAYS PRODUCED
IN THE
UNITED STATES

PLAYS PRODUCED ON BROADWAY

Figures in parentheses following a play's title indicate number of performances. The figures are acquired directly from the production office in each case and do not include previews or extra non-profit performances.

Plays marked with an asterisk (*) were still running on June 1, 1971. Their number of performances is figured from opening night through May 31, 1971.

Beginning with this volume, shows presented under the new "Limited Gross Broadway Theater Agreement" are listed as Broadway productions, with a notation (Limited Broadway) following the name of the theater in each such listing.

In a listing of a show's numbers—dances, sketches, musical scenes, etc.— the titles of songs are identified by their appearance in quotation marks (").

HOLDOVERS FROM PREVIOUS SEASONS

Plays which were running on June 1, 1970 are listed below. More detailed information about them appears in previous *Best Plays* volumes of appropriate years. Important cast changes are recorded in a section of this volume.

Hello, Dolly! (2,844). Musical suggested by Thornton Wilder's *The Matchmaker;* book by Michael Stewart; music and lyrics by Jerry Herman. Opened January 16, 1964. (Closed December 27, 1970 matinee)

* Fiddler on the Roof (2,788). Musical based on Sholom Aleichem's stories; book by Joseph Stein; music by Jerry Bock; lyrics by Sheldon Harnick. Opened September 22, 1964.

* Man of La Mancha (2,297). Musical suggested by the life and works of Miguel de Cervantes y Saavedra; book by Dale Wasserman; music by Mitch Leigh; lyrics by Joe Darion. Opened November 22, 1965.

Plaza Suite (1,097). Program of three one-act plays by Neil Simon. Opened February 14, 1968. (Closed October 3, 1970)

* Hair (1,294). Musical with book and lyrics by Gerome Ragni and James Rado; music by Galt MacDermot. Opened April 29, 1968.

* Promises, Promises (1,038). Musical based on the screen play *The Apartment* by Billy Wilder and I.A.L. Diamond; book by Neil Simon; music by Burt Bacharach; lyrics by Hal David. Opened December 1, 1968.

Forty Carats (780). By Jay Allen; adapted from a play by Pierre Barillet and Jean-Pierre Gredy. Opened December 26, 1968. (Closed November 7, 1970)

* **1776** (920). Musical based on a conception of Sherman Edwards; book by Peter Stone; music and lyrics by Sherman Edwards. Opened March 16, 1969.

* **Oh! Calcutta!** (812). Musical revue devised by Kenneth Tynan; with contributions by Samuel Beckett, Jules Feiffer, Dan Greenburg, John Lennon, Jacques Levy, Leonard Melfi, David Newman and Robert Benton, Sam Shepard, Clovis Trouille, Kenneth Tynan and Sherman Yellen; music and lyrics by The Open Window. Opened June 17, 1969 (originally classified off Broadway but classified Limited Broadway when that designation was established; moved to Belasco Theater February 26, 1971 after 704 performances at the Eden theater through February 21, 1971)

* **Butterflies Are Free** (665). By Leonard Gershe. Opened October 21, 1969.

The Repertory Theater of Lincoln Center. Schedule of four plays (see entry in 1969-70 *Best Plays* volume) concluded with **Beggar on Horseback** (52). Revival of the play by George S. Kaufman and Marc Connelly. Opened May 14, 1970. (Closed June 27, 1970)

Coco (332). Musical with book and lyrics by Alan Jay Lerner; music by Andre Previn. Opened December 18, 1969. (Closed October 3, 1970)

* **Last of the Red Hot Lovers** (595). By Neil Simon. Opened December 28, 1969.

Child's Play (342). By Robert Marasco. Opened February 17, 1970. (Closed December 12, 1970)

* **Purlie** (504). Musical based on the play *Purlie Victorious* by Ossie Davis; book by Ossie Davis, Philip Rose and Peter Udell; music by Gary Geld; lyrics by Peter Udell. Opened March 15, 1970.

* **Applause** (489). Musical based on the film *All About Eve* and the original story by Mary Orr; book by Betty Comden and Adolph Green; music by Charles Strouse; lyrics by Lee Adams. Opened March 30, 1970.

Borstal Boy (143). By Brenden Behan; adapted for the stage by Frank McMahon. Opened March 31, 1970. (Closed August 1, 1970)

The Boy Friend (119). Musical revival with book, music and lyrics by Sandy Wilson. Opened April 14, 1970. (Closed July 18, 1970).

* **Company** (459). Musical with book by George Furth; music and lyrics by Stephen Sondheim. Opened April 26, 1970.

PLAYS PRODUCED JUNE 1, 1970—MAY 31, 1971

Charley's Aunt (9). Revival of the play by Brandon Thomas. Produced by Jay H. Fuchs and Jerry Schlossberg in association with John Murray at the Brooks Atkinson Theater. Opened July 4, 1970. (Closed July 11, 1970)

Jack Chesney ....Michael Goodwin	Col. Sir Francis Chesney ......Martyn Green
Brassett ....Melville Cooper	Stephen Spettigue ....Eric Berry
Charles Wykeham ....Rex Thompson	Brassett's Assistant ....Bruce Blaine
Lord Fancourt Babberley ....Louis Nye	Donna Lucia
Amy Spettigue ....Lynn Milgrim	d'Alvadorez ....Maureen O'Sullivan
Kitty Verdun ....Andra Akers	Ela Delahay ....Elizabeth Swain

Directed by Harold Stone; scenery, Robert T. Williams; costumes, Richard Anderson; lighting, F. Mitchell Dana; production stage manager, Elissa Lane; stage manager, Bruce Blaine; press, Marvin Kohn.

Charley's Aunt was first produced in New York 10/2/93 and has been revived many times since, most successfully 10/17/40 at the Cort Theater for 233 performances starring José Ferrer. Cy Feuer and Ernest H. Martin produced the musical version *Where's Charley?* at the St. James Theater 10/11/48 for 792 performances. Its most recent New York revival was at New York City Center 12/22/53 for 15 performances.

Othello (16). Revival of the play by William Shakespeare. Produced by Stratford, Connecticut's American Shakespeare Festival Theater at the ANTA Theater. Opened September 14, 1970. (Closed September 26, 1970)

Roderigo ....John Tillinger	1st Messenger ....Gary Poe
Iago ....Lee Richardson	2d Messenger ....Paul Corum
Brabantio ....Josef Sommer	Desdemona ....Roberta Maxwell
Othello ....Moses Gunn	Montano ....James Cromwell
Cassio ....Peter Thompson	1st Cypriot Soldier ....Tim Riley
Duke of Venice ....Wyman Pendleton	2d Cypriot Soldier ....John Ventantonio
1st Senator ....Bernard Frawley	3d Cypriot Soldier ....Josef Warik
Lodovico ....Danny Davis	Emilia ....Jan Miner
2d Senator ....Ken Parker	Bianca ....Maureen Anderman
Senators ....Tom Tarpey, Robert Blumenfeld	

Officers, Attendants, Venetians, Cypriots: Eugene Brezany, Patricia Callahan, Gary Copeland, Jack Heifner, Ron Lohse, Edwin McDonough, Lizbeth Mackay, William Schory, Mark Niedzialkowski, Joseph Remmes, John Ogden, Mary Ellen Ray, Ralph Redpath, Paul Shutt, Garland Wright, Mary Wright.

Principal understudies: Mr. Richardson—Josef Sommer; Mr. Thompson—John Ventantonio; Miss Miner—Mary Ellen Ray; Mr. Tillinger—Josef Warik; Mr. Sommer—Bernard Frawley; Mr. Pendleton—Ken Parker.

Directed by Michael Kahn; scenery, Karl Eigsti; costumes, Jane Greenwood; lighting, John Gleason; music composed and directed by Conrad Susa; duels, Christopher Tanner; executive producer, Joseph Verner Reed; managing producer, Berenice Weiler; director of educational projects, Mary Hunter Wolf; artistic director, Michael Kahn; production stage manager, Lo Hardin; stage manager, Nikos Kafkalis; press, Reginald Denenholz, Ellen Levene.

Othello was last produced in New York 10/12/64 by Circle in the Square, in the New York Shakespeare Festival Central Park production brought indoors. Recent Broadway productions have included the New York City Center Theater Company's, starring William Marshall, 9/7/55 for 15 performances and the Theater Guild's, starring Paul Robeson, 10/19/43 for 280 performances and 5/22/45 for 24 performances.

Bob and Ray the Two and Only (158). Two-man program written and performed by Bob Elliott and Ray Goulding. Produced by Joseph I. and Johnna Levine in association with Hy Saporta at the John Golden Theater. Opened September 24, 1970. (Closed February 13, 1971)

Directed by Joseph Hardy; scenery, William Ritman; lighting, Thomas Skelton; associate producer, Ben Gerard; production stage manager, D.W. Koehler; press, Harvey B. Sabinson, Lee Solters, Leo Stern.

Program of comedy interviews and sketches including many of the following Bob-and-Ray characterizations: Jacobus Pike, Captain Larson, Wally Ballou, David & Linda Lovely, Mary Backstayge, Ricky L. Lewellyn, Leonard Bonfiglio, Barry Campbell, Kent Lyle Birdley, Matt Neffer, Webley Webster, Fielding Backstayge, T. Wilson Messy, Fahnstock P. Bodry, Uncle Eugene, T. Wilson Messy Jr., Tex Blaisdell, O. Leo Lahey, Thomas E. Röte, Word Carr, Wolfman, Gregg Marlowe, Dean Archer Armstead, Mr. Trace, Clyde L. "Hap" Whartney, Mister

Science, Arthur Schermerhorn, Komodo Dragon Expert, Dr. Muu, Good Professor Groggins, Steve Bosco, McBeebee Twins, Gabe Preston, Clifford Fleming, Charles (poet), Jack Headstrong, Mary McGoon, Van Tassel Sturdley, Calvin Hoogavin, Chester Hasbrouck Frisbie, Natalie Attired.

Opium (8). Play adapted by Roc Brynner from Jean Cocteau's *Opium—Journal of a Cure*. Produced by Preston Fischer and Norman Kean, by arrangement with Marc Princi, Ltd. at the Edison Theater (Limited Broadway). Opened October 5, 1970. (Closed October 10, 1970)

Performed by Roc Brynner; conceived and directed by Ranald Graham; scenery, Roger Cheveley; costumes, Mr. Fish; lighting, Lloyd Burlingame; production stage manager, R. Derek Swire; press, Harvey B. Sabinson, Marilynn LeVine.

One-character play in which the drug becomes the second character, dramatized from Jean Cocteau's diaries about withdrawal from addiction.

Conduct Unbecoming (144). By Barry England. Produced by Donald Albery and Roger L. Stevens at the Ethel Barrymore Theater. Opened October 12, 1970. (Closed February 14, 1971)

2d Lt. Edward Millington .....Jeremy Clyde	2d Lt. John Truly ....Nicholas Hammond
2d Lt. Arthur Drake ....Paul Jones	2d Lt. Simon Boulton ....Robert Murch
Colonel Strang ....Michael Barrington	2d Lt. Edward Winters ....Noel Craig
Major Lionel Roach ......Michael Bradshaw	2d Lt. Frank Hutton ....Edwin Owens
Major Alastair	Pradah Singh ....Ronald Drake
Wimbourne, V.C. ....Paul Harding	Mess Head Waiter ....Thomas Cover
Lt. Col. Maurice Pratt ....Robert Hewitt	Mrs. Marjorie Hasseltine ..Elizabeth Shepherd
Capt. Rupert Harper ......Donald Pickering	Mem Strang ....Sylvia O'Brien
Lt. Richard Fothergill ......Richard Lupino	Mrs. Bandanai ....Madhur Jaffrey
Lt. Frank Hart ....Richard Clarke	Lal ....Pandora Bronson Lupino

Ladies at the Ball: Vanya Franck, Pandora Bronson Lupino, Jean Hogan. Waiters: James Tripp, Dan Hamilton, James Leggi.

Standbys: Mr. Clyde—Rex Thompson; Mr. Jones—Nicholas Hammond. Understudies: Mr. Pickering—Richard Clarke; Misses Shepherd, O'Brien—Vanya Franck; Messrs. Harding, Drake —Edwin Owens; Mr. Hewitt—Howard Fischer; Mr. Bradshaw—Ronald Drake; Miss Jaffrey— Pandora Bronson Lupino.

Directed by Val May; designed by Finlay James; associate producer, Nobuko Morros; technical director, Ian B. Albery; production supervisor, Paul Morrison; production stage manager, Frederic de Wilde; stage manager, Howard Fischer; press, Harvey B. Sabinson, Lee Solters, Ted Goldsmith.

Time: The late 1800s. Place: India, the anteroom to the officers' mess of a regiment in the Indian Army. The play was divided into three acts.

Mysterious evil and violence threatens the honor of the officer corps of one of Her Majesty's proudest regiments. A foreign play previously produced in London.

A Best Play; see page 132

* The Rothschilds (256). Musical based on *The Rothschilds* by Frederic Morton; book by Sherman Yellen; music by Jerry Bock; lyrics by Sheldon Harnick. Produced by Lester Osterman in the Hillard Elkins production at the Lunt-Fontanne Theater. Opened October 19, 1970.

Prince William; Joseph Fouche;	1st Vendor ....Thomas Trelfa
Herries; Metternich ....Keen Curtis	2d Vendor ....Kenneth Bridges
Guard; Banker ....Roger Hamilton	3d Vendor ....Jon Peck
Mayer Rothschild ....Hal Linden	General; Skeptic ....Paul Tracey
1st Urchin; Young Nathan	Budurus ....Leo Leyden
Rothschild ....Michael Maitland	1st Banker ....Elliott Savage
2d Urchin ....Kim Michels	2d Banker ....Carl Nicholas
3d Urchin; Young Solomon	Young Amshel Rothschild .....Lee Franklin
Rothschild ....Robby Benson	Young Jacob Rothschild .....Mitchell Spera
Gutele (Mama) Rothschild ....Leila Martin	Blum ....Howard Honig

Mrs. Kaufman ....Nina Dova	Jacob Rothschild ....Chris Sarandon
Mrs. Segal ....Peggy Cooper	Nathan Rothschild ....Paul Hecht
Peasant ....Christopher Chadman	Kalman Rothschild ....Allan Gruet
Amshel Rothschild ....Timothy Jerome	Hannah Cohen ....Jill Clayburgh
Solomon Rothschild ....David Garfield	

Members of Hessian Court, People of Frankfurt Ghetto, Members of Austrian Court, Grenadiers, Couriers, Crowned Heads of Europe, Banker-Brokers: Rick Atwell, Steve Bookvor, Kenneth Bridges, Henry Brunges, Chris Chadman, Peggy Cooper, Patrick Cummings, Nina Dova, Vicki Frederick, Penny Guerard, Roger Hamilton, Ann Hodges, Howard Honig, Del Lewis, John Mineo, Carl Nicholas, Jon Peck, Ted Pejovich, Denise Pence, Jean Richards, Elliott Savage, Wilfred Schuman, Lani Sundsten, Paul Tracey, Thomas Trelfa.

Principal Understudies: Mr. Linden—Howard Honig; Mr. Hecht—Chris Sarandon; Miss Martin—Nina Dova; Mr. Curtis—Roger Hamilton; Miss Clayburgh—Jean Richards.

Directed and choreographed by Michael Kidd; scenery and costumes, John Bury; lighting, Richard Pilbrow; orchestrations, Don Walker; musical direction and vocal arrangements, Milton Greene; dance music arrangements, Clay Fullum; production supervision, Michael Thoma; associate producers, Richard Horner, Emanuel Azenberg, Robert Malina, George Platt; production stage manager, Charles Gray; stage manager, John Actman; press, Samuel J. Friedman, Louise Weiner Ment.

Time: The 19th Century. Place: Frankfort, London, Aix-la-Chapelle and elsewhere in Europe.

Musical based on Frederic Morton's account of the noted banking family's efforts in progress from the ghetto to the stock exchanges and courts of Europe.

Sidney Ben-Zali replaced Timothy Jerome 4/20/71. Caroline McWilliams replaced Jill Clayburgh 2/28/71.

ACT I

Prologue: "Pleasure and Privilege" ....Prince William
"One Room"...Mayer, Mama
"He Tossed a Coin"...Mayer, Vendors, Ensemble
"Sons" ....Mayer, Mama, Young Amshel, Young Solomon, Young Nathan, Young Jacob
"Everything" ....Nathan, Mama, Solomon, Kalman, Amshel, Jacob
"Rothschild and Sons" ....Meyer, Nathan, Solomon, Kalman, Amshel, Jacob
"Allons" ....Fouche, Male Ensemble
"Rothschild and Sons" (Reprise) ....Mayer, Nathan, Solomon, Kalman, Amshel, Jacob
"Sons" (Reprise) ....Mama, Mayer

ACT II

Hymn: "Give England Strength" ....Herries, Male Ensemble
"This Amazing London Town" ....Nathan
"They Say" ....Skeptic, Male Ensemble
"I'm in Love! I'm in Love!" ....Nathan
"I'm in Love! I'm in Love!" (Reprise) ....Hannah
"In My Own Lifetime" ....Mayer
"Have You Ever Seen a Prettier Little Congress?" ....Metternich
"Stability" ....Metternich, Ensemble
"Bonds" ....Nathan, Solomon, Kalman, Amshel, Jacob, Metternich, Ensemble

Gandhi (1). By Gurney Campbell. Produced by Roy N. Nevans and Albert J. Schiff at the Playhouse Theater (Limited Broadway). Opened and closed at the evening performance, October 20, 1970.

The Antagonist ....David Selby	Mirabehn ....Dina Poisner
Sarolini ....Estelle Omens	Maharajah ....Rik Colitti
Mahadev ....Leroy Lessane	Father Nehru ....Lawrence Stern
Mohandas K. Gandhi .....Jack MacGowran	Jinnah Sahib ....Jack Axelrod
Kasturbai Gandhi ....Betty Miller	Jawaharlal Nehru ....Vic Mohica
Viceroy ....Thomas B. Markus	Webb Miller ....Tom Coble
Kallenbach ....Martin Meyers	Sushila ....Donna Pizzi
Patel ....Louis Guss	Chief Inspector ....Kenneth Marsolais

Maun ....Cathryn Roskam   Hindu Youth ....Frank Liu
Metab ....Shelly Desai   The Maulvi ....Joseph C. Davies

Directed by Jose Quintero; scenery, Ming Cho Lee; costumes, Jane Greenwood; lighting, Roger Morgan; production stage manager, Iris O'Connor; press, Bill Doll.
Story of Mahatma Gandhi's life and struggles for Indian independence.

* **Paul Sills' Story Theater.** Repertory of two programs. **Story Theater** (218). Adapted by Paul Sills. Opened October 26, 1970; see note. **Ovid's Metamorphoses** (26). Created by Paul Sills; adapted and translated by Arnold Weinstein; lyrics by Arnold Weinstein. Opened April 22, 1971. Produced by Zev Bufman at the Ambassador Theater.

STORY THEATER

"A Lot Can Happen in a Day" composed and sung by Hamid Hamilton Camp
The Little Peasant
  Little Peasant ....Hamid Hamilton Camp
  Peasant's Wife ....Melinda Dillon
  Cowherd ....Paul Sand
  Judge ....Peter Bonerz
  Farmer's Wife ....Valerie Harper
  Parson ....Richard Libertini
  Farmer ....Richard Schaal
  Rich Peasants ....Melinda Dillon, Mary Frann, Paul Sand, Valerie Harper
The Bremen Town Musicians
  Ass ....Richard Schaal
  Hound ....Paul Sand
  Cat ....Peter Bonerz
  Cock ....Richard Libertini
  Robbers ....Valerie Harper, Hamid Hamilton Camp
Is He Fat
  Man #1 ....Hamid Hamilton Camp
  Man #2 ....Richard Schaal
  Sexton ....Richard Libertini
  Parson ....Peter Bonerz
The Robber Bridegroom
  Miller ....Richard Schaal
  Daughter ....Melinda Dillon
  Robber Bridegroom ....Paul Sand
  Old Woman ....Valerie Harper
  Maiden ....Mary Frann
  Robbers ....Peter Bonerz, Richard Schaal, Richard Libertini
  "I'll Be Your Baby Tonight" by Bob Dylan, sung by Hamid Hamilton Camp
Henny Penny
  Henny Penny ....Valerie Harper
  Cocky Locky ....Richard Schaal
  Ducky Daddles ....Hamid Hamilton Camp
  Goosey Poosey ....Melinda Dillon
  Turkey Lurkey ....Paul Sand
  Foxy Woxy ....Richard Libertini
  "Fixin' to Die Rag" by Joe McDonald, sung by Lewis Ross
"About Time" composed and sung by Hamid Hamilton Camp
The Master Thief
  Old Man; Parson ....Richard Schaal
  Wife ....Melinda Dillon
  Master Thief ....Peter Bonerz
  Count ....Richard Libertini
  Soldiers ....Hamid Hamilton Camp, Paul Sand, Richard Schaal
  Countess ....Valerie Harper
  Clerk ....Paul Sand

"Dear Landlord" by Bob Dylan, sung by Hamid Hamilton Camp
Venus and the Cat
  Man ....Richard Schaal
  Cat ....Mary Frann
  Venus ....Valerie Harper
The Fisherman and His Wife
  Narrator ....Hamid Hamilton Camp
  Fisherman ....Richard Libertini
  Flounder ....Peter Bonerz
  Wife ....Melinda Dillon
Two Crows
  Crow #1 ....Peter Bonerz
  Crow #2 ....Hamid Hamilton Camp
The Golden Goose
  Mother; Eldest Daughter ....Valerie Harper
  Simpleton ....Paul Sand
  Eldest Son; Peasant ....Richard Schaal
  Little Gray Man; King ....Hamid Hamilton Camp
  Second Son; Parson ....Richard Libertini
  Second Daughter ....Mary Frann
  Sexton ....Peter Bonerz
  Princess ....Melinda Dillon
  "Here Comes the Sun" composed by George Harrison, sung by Lewis Ross

Alternates: Lewis Arquette, Molly McKasson. Music performed by The True Brethren.
Directed by Paul Sills; scenery and projections, Michael Devine; costumes, Stephanie Kline; lighting, H.R. Poindexter; production stage manager, Don Winton; presented with the help and cooperation of City Center of Music and Drama, Inc., The Shubert Organization and the Theater Development Fund, as originally presented at the Mark Taper Forum by the Center Theater Group of Los Angeles, Gordon Davidson artistic director; press, John Springer Associates, Howard Haines.
Selected Grimm Brothers fairy tales staged as stories told with some theatrical adaptation and occasional music, presented in two parts. Previously presented at the Mark Taper Forum, Los Angeles, and elsewhere.
Linda Lavin replaced Valerie Harper 11/10/70. Valerie Harper replaced Linda Lavin 3/3/71.

OVID'S METAMORPHOSES

Lewis Arquette	Valerie Harper
Regina Baff	Paula Kelly
Charles Bartlett	Richard Libertini
Hamid Hamilton Camp	Paul Sand
Melinda Dillon	Richard Schaal
MacIntyre Dixon	Avery Schreiber
Mary Frann	Penny White

Directed by Paul Sills; music composed and performed by The True Brethren; scenery, James Trittipo; costumes, Noel Taylor; lighting, H.R. Poindexter; production stage manager, Martin Gold.
Love stories and mythical romances from the works of Ovid, presented in story, mime, dance and song.
ACT I—The Creation, Io, Europa, Vulcan and Venus and Mars, Phaethon, Callisto. ACT II —Picus and Canens, Procris and Cephalus, Pygmalion, Peleus and Thetis, Baucis and Philemon.
NOTE: *Story Theater* opened first and ran by itself during most of the season. It was joined in repertory by *Ovid's Metamorphoses* in April.

Light, Lively and Yiddish (88). Musical in the Yiddish language with text and lyrics by A. Shulman and Wolf and Sylvia Younin; music by Eli Rubinstein; adaptation by Ben Bonus; additional texts by M. Gershenson, Ch. N. Bialik, Ch. Cheffer, Mina Bern. Produced by Sol Dickstein at the Belasco Theater. Opened October 27, 1970. (Closed January 10, 1971)

English Narrator	David Ellin	Sosye	Miriam Kressyn
Zelde	Mina Bern	Nokhem	Seymour Rexite
Rag Seller	Leon Liebgold	Kvas Seller	David Carey
Dumpling Woman;		Gitele	Diane Cypkin
Innkeeper	Reizl Bozyk	Hershele	Ben Bonus
Bagel Woman	Lili Liliana	Kalmen	Leon Liebgold

Dancers: Marcia Brooks, Helen Butleroff, Jack Dyville, Harry Endicott, Robyn Kessler, Tony Masullo, Maggie Masullo, Eileen McCabe. Joseph Tripolino.

Directed by Mina Bern; musical staging and choreography, Felix Fibich; scenery, Josef Ijaky; costumes, Sylvia Friedlander; musical conductor, Renee Solomon; production stage manager, Bernard Sauer; press, Max Eisen, Milly Schoenbaum.

Place: Act I: The shtetl, the little village; Act II: New York City and Tel Aviv, Israel.

Jewish life in a small Eastern European village contrasted with life in big American and Israeli cities, in Yiddish with English narration.

MUSICAL NUMBERS—Act I: "A Yarid" (A Fair), "Yiddish," "Shver Tsu Zain a Yidene" (It's Hard To Be a Jewish Woman), "Dus Hut Mir Kainer Nit Gezugt" (Nobody Told Me This), "Tsen Azeyger" (Ten O'Clock), "Tfile Tsu Got" (Prayer to God), "Vu Iz Yoysher?" (Where is Justice?), "A Freilekhs" "A Joyful Song." Act II: "Light Lively and Yiddish" (arrangement of Yiddish folk music), "Khavertes" (Girl Friends), "Tsu Mayn Dor" (The Song of My Generation), "Israel," "A Shukh Putser" (Shoe Shine Boy), "A Briv" (A Letter), "S'vet Kumen Der Tog" (The Day Will Come).

Not Now, Darling (21). By Ray Cooney and John Chapman. Produced by James Nederlander and George M. Steinbrenner III by arrangement with Michael Codron at the Brooks Atkinson Theater. Opened October 29, 1970. (Closed November 15, 1970)

Miss Whittington	Marilyn Hengst	Janie McMichael	Roni Dengel
Arnold Crouch	Norman Wisdom	Mr. Frencham	Claude Horton
Miss Tipdale	Joan Bassie	Sue Lawson	Ardyth Kaiser
Mrs. Frencham	Jean Cameron	Maude Bodley	M'el Dowd
Gilbert Bodley	Rex Garner	Mr. Lawson	Curt Dawson
Harry McMichael	Ed Zimmermann		

Understudies: Messrs. Wisdom, Garner, Horton, Zimmermann, Dawson—Hugh Alexander; Misses Bassie, Dowd, Cameron—Elizabeth Owens; Misses Kaiser, Hengst—Pamela Gruen.

Directed by George Abbott; designed by Lloyd Burlingame; associate producers, Sheldon B. Guren, Edward Ginsberg; production stage manager, Ben Janney; press, Sol Jacobson, Lewis Harmon.

Time: The present. Place: The fourth-floor salon of Bodley, Bodley and Crouch, an exclusive London firm of furriers. Act I: Noon on a day late in September. Act II: Immediately following.

Comedy, a day of sex intrigue in the lives of two playful furriers and several wives and husbands. A foreign play previously produced in London.

The President's Daughter (72). Musical partly in the Yiddish language with book by H. Kalmanov; music by Murray Rumshinsky; lyrics by Jacob Jacobs. Produced by Jacob Jacobs at the Billy Rose Theater. Opened November 3, 1970. (Closed January 3, 1971)

Frances	Michele Burke	Nathan	Jacob Jacobs
Esther	Charlotte Cooper	Sam Golden	George Guidall
Yanek	Jack Rechtzeit	Reb Yosel	Jaime Lewin
Minke	Diana Goldberg	Bertha	Thelma Mintz
Freidel	Chayele Rosenthal	Miriam	Rachela Relis

Directed by Jacob Jacobs; dances staged by Henrietta Jacobson; design, Barry Arnold; stage manager, Mordecai Yachson; press, Joseph Burstin, William Mercur.

Time: The present, within a period of several weeks. Place: Sam Golden's Flatbush home.

Yiddish-American family comedy with light romantic complications; a compendium of sketches, songs and dances.

Prologue: "Women's Liberation" ....Minke, Bertha, Esther, Miriam

ACT I

"The President's Daughter" ....Freidel
"I Have What You Want!" ....Minke, Nathan
"A Lesson in Yiddish" ....Yanek
"Everything Is Possible in Life" ....Freidel, Sam Golden
"Welcome, Mr. Golden!" ....Freidel, Nathan, Minke, Esther, Reb Yosel, Frances

ACT II

"Stiochket" ....Yanek
"Without a Mother" ....Freidel
"Love at Golden Years" ....Miriam, Reb
"If Only I Could Be a Kid Again" ....Freidel
"An Old Man Shouldn't Be Born" ....Nathan
"We Two" ....Minke, Yanek
"What More Do I Need?" ....Sam
"What Would You Do?" ....Freidel, Nathan

Emlyn Williams as Charles Dickens (5). One-man performance by Emlyn Williams of scenes from the novels and stories. Produced by S. Hurok at Alice Tully Hall. Opened November 3, 1970. (Closed November 7, 1970)

Production supervisor and lighting consultant, Robert Crawley; press, Martin Feinstein.
Dramatic reading of excerpts from Dickens, much of it off the beaten track of the more familiar characters.

Orlando Furioso (32). Theater-in-the-surround spectacle in the Italian language; based on the poem by Ludovico Ariosto; adapted by Eduardo Sanguineti. Produced by Dick Feldman and Joseph Wishy in association with Doyle Dane Bernbach in a production of Teatro Libero di Roma at the Bryant Park Bubble Theater. Opened November 4, 1970. (Closed November 29, 1970)

Olimpia ....Adriana Asti
Bireno; Agramante ....Marco Berneck
Sprite Messenger;
  Orrilo; Dwarf ....Nino Bignamini
Doralice;
Damsel of Ebuda ....Elettra Bisetti
Dardinello ....Paolo Bonetti
Gabrina ....Liu Bosiso
Host; Saracen; Cairo Plebian;
  Queen's Dwarf ....Gaetano Campisi
Melissa ....Pina Cei
Ebuda Citizen; Rodomonte's Dwarf;
  Saracen ....Francesco Censi
Cimosco's Daughter; Fiammetta;
  Outraged Damsel ....Marina Coffa
Ebuda Citizen; Saracen ..Vittorio De Bisogno
Ruggiero ....Luigi Diberti
Astolfo ....Antonio Fattorini
Zerbino ....Giorgio Favretto
Sacripante; Rodomonte ....Spiros Focas
Isabella ....Paola Gassmann, Daniela Nobili
Ferrau; Cimosco; Mandricardo;
  Charlemagne ....Cesare Gelli
Marfisa; Fiordispina ..Maria Grazia Grassini
Pinabello's Damsel;
  Iocondo's Wife ....Veronica Lazar

Host's Son; Cairo Plebian;
  Ricciardetto ....Giorgio Maich
Malandrini Chief; Caligorante;
  Gradasso ....Pino Manzari
Medoro ....Marzio Margine
Homicidal Female;
  Longobard Queen .....Loredana Martinez
Grifone;
  Handsome Morando ......Luigi Masironi
Aquilante; Adonio ...Michelangelo Masironi
Saracen; Greek;
  Messenger ....Gino Milli
Orlando; Sacripante;
  Rodomonte ....Carlo Montagna
Rinaldo ....Sergio Micolai
Bradamante ....Anna Nogara
Atlante; Anselmo ....Enrico Ostermann
Arbante; Errand Boy;
  Iocondo ....Michele Placido
Horseback Messenger;
  Astrologer ....Giancarlo Prati
Old Dutchman;
  Bishop of Paris ....Armando Pugliese
Hermit; Ebuda Pirate ....Aldo Puglisi
Pinabello;
  Gentleman of Cup ....Enzo Robutti

Queen of Homicidal	Cloridano; Rodomonte ......Gabriele Tozzi
Females ....Anna Teresa Rossini	Alcina; Serpent Woman;
Filandro; Saracen ......Benedetto Simonelli	Homicidal Female ......Barbara Valmorin
Angelica; Lady of Cup ......Paola Tanziani	

Directed by Luca Ronconi; produced by Paolo Radaelli; scenery, Uberto Bertacca; costumes, Elena Mannini; lighting consultant, Imero Fiorentino; assistants to the director, Piero Baldini, Giorgia Ferrara, Pino Manzari, Armando Pugliese; presented in cooperation with the office of Mayor John V. Lindsay and the Parks Recreational and Cultural Affairs Administration, August Heckscher administrator, Dore Schary commissioner; stage manager, Gianni De Benedictis; press, Lee Solters, Harvey B. Sabinson, Marilynn LeVine.

Ariosto's 16th Century poem about the struggle between Christians and Saracens adapted for the stage as an action and adventure fantasy with extravagant effects on a broad canvas, staged in 12 scenes in the round. A foreign play previously produced in Spoleto, Milan, Amsterdam and Edinburgh.

* The Repertory Theater of Lincoln Center. Schedule of four revivals. **The Good Woman of Setzuan** (46). By Bertolt Brecht; new translation by Ralph Manheim. Opened November 5, 1970. (Closed December 13, 1970) **The Playboy of the Western World** (52). By John Millington Synge. Opened January 7, 1971. (Closed February 20, 1971) **An Enemy of the People** (54). By Henrik Ibsen; adapted by Arthur Miller. Opened March 11, 1971. (Closed April 25, 1971) ***Antigone** (22). By Sophocles; English version by Dudley Fitts and Robert Fitzgerald. Opened May 13, 1971. Produced by The Repertory Theater of Lincoln Center, under the direction of Jules Irving, at the Vivian Beaumont Theater.

THE GOOD WOMAN OF SETZUAN

Wang	......................Lou Gilbert	Brother	....................Dan Sullivan
1st God	......................Philip Bosco	Sister-in-Law	.............Elizabeth Huddle
2d God	......................Sydney Walker	Mrs. Mi Tzu	..............Frances Foster
3d God	..........................Ray Fry	Boy	..................Kenneth H. Maxwell
Gentleman; Priest	............Jack Harrold	Grandfather	...............Herbert Foster
Gentleman; Waiter	............Luis Avalos	Niece	......................Tandy Cronyn
Shen Teh	................Colleen Dewhurst	Policeman	.................Joseph Mascolo
Mrs. Shin	................Elizabeth Wilson	Carpet Dealer's Wife	...........Anne Ives
Husband	...................Maury Cooper	Yang Sun	................David Birney
Wife	.....................Eda Reiss Merin	Old Prostitute	.............Florence Tarlow
Nephew	....................Robert Phelan	Mr. Shu Fu	................Stephen Elliott
Unemployed Man	...........Robert Levine	Carpet Dealer	...........Eugene R. Wood
Lin To	....................Michael Levin	Mrs. Tang	...........Priscilla Pointer

Townspeople: James Cook, Susan Sharkey. Children: Toby Obayashi, Rico Williams, Rebecca Symonds.

Principal understudies: Miss Dewhurst—Elizabeth Huddle; Messrs. Gilbert, Sullivan—Luis Avalos; Messrs. Bosco, Walker—Michael Levin; Mr. Fry—Herbert Foster; Misses Wilson, Pointer—Florence Tarlow.

Directed by Robert Symonds; scenery, Douglas W. Schmidt; lighting, John Gleason; costumes, Carrie Fishbein Robbins; music, Herbert Pilhofer; songs, Herbert Pilhofer, John Lewin; vocal director, Roland Gagnon; production stage manager, Barbara-Mae Phillips; stage managers, Paul Bengston, Patrick Horrigan; press, Susan Bloch, William Schelble.

Place: The capital of Setzuan, a half-Europeanized city. The play was presented in two parts.

Brecht's *The Good Woman of Setzuan* was first produced in New York by the Phoenix Theater 12/18/56 for 24 performances. It was revived off Broadway by the Institute for Advanced Studies in the Theater Arts 3/10/63 for 12 performances. Both of these productions were of the Eric Bentley adaptation.

THE PLAYBOY OF THE WESTERN WORLD

Pegeen Mike	................Martha Henry	Michael James Flaherty	.....Sydney Walker
Shawn Keogh	.............James Blendick	Philly Cullen	....................Ray Fry

Jimmy Farrell ....Philip Bosco	Honor Blake ....Tandy Cronyn
Christy Mahon ....David Birney	Sara Tansey ....Elizabeth Huddle
Widow Quin ....Frances Sternhagen	Old Mahon ....Stephen Elliott
Susan Brady ....Susan Sharkey	Bellman ....Herbert Foster

Townspeople: James Cook, Maury Cooper, Peter Nyberg, Dan Sullivan, Macon McCalman.
Principal understudies: Mr. Birney—James Cook; Miss Henry—Tandy Cronyn; Miss Stern-
hagen—Elizabeth Huddle.
Directed by John Hirsch; music by John Duffy based on traditional Irish folk songs; scenery
and costumes, Douglas W. Schmidt; lighting, John Gleason; production stage manager, Frank
Bayer; stage manager, Patrick Horrigan.
Place: A village on a wild coast of Mayo. Act I: An evening in autumn. Act II: The fol-
lowing day. Act III: The same. The play was presented in two parts, with an intermission following Act II.
Synge's *The Playboy of the Western World* was first presented in New York by the visiting
Irish Players in the fall of 1911. Its last Broadway revival was by Theater Incorporated 10/26/46
for 81 performances, and it was staged off Broadway the season of 1957-58. This production
commemorated the 100th anniversary of Synge's birth.
Herbert Foster replaced Ray Fry and Dan Sullivan replaced Herbert Foster 1/30/71.

AN ENEMY OF THE PEOPLE

Morten Kiil ....Sydney Walker	(Morten) ....Michael Meyers, Timmy Ousey
Billing ....James Blendick	(Ejlif) .....Michael Meyers, Barry Symonds
Mrs. Stockmann ....Barbara Cason	Capt. Horster ....Don Plumley
Peter Stockmann ....Philip Bosco	Petra ....Tandy Cronyn
Hovstad ....David Birney	Aslaksen ....Conrad Bain
Dr. Stockmann ....Stephen Elliott	Drunk ....Macon McCalman

(Parentheses indicate roles in which the actors alternated)

Townspeople: Esther Benson, Robert Benson, Joseph Boley, Richard Bowler, James Cook,
Blaine Cordner, Ronald Frazier, Robert Levine, David Little, Michael Miller, Susan Sharkey,
George Van Den Houten.
Principal understudies: Mr. Elliott—Macon McCalman; Mr. Bosco—George Van Den Hou-
ten; Miss Cason—Esther Benson; Mr. Birney—David Little; Mr. Walker—Richard Bowler;
Miss Cronyn—Susan Sharkey.
Directed by Jules Irving; scenery, Douglas W. Schmidt; lighting, John Gleason; costumes,
Carrie Fishbein Robbins; production stage manager, Barbara-Mae Phillips; stage manager,
Robert Benson.
Arthur Miller's adaptation of Ibsen's *An Enemy of the People* was first produced on Broad-
way 12/28/50 for 36 performances. It was revived off Broadway during the 1958-59 season
and by the Equity Library Theater in the 1967-68 season.

ANTIGONE

Antigone ....Martha Henry	Haimon ....David Birney
Ismene ....Tandy Cronyn	Teiresias ....Sydney Walker
Choragos ....Charles Cioffi	Boy ....Timmy Ousey
Female Chorus Leader ....Pauline Flanagan	Messenger ....John Harkins
Creon ....Philip Bosco	Eurydice ....Dimitra Arliss
Sentry ....James Blendick	

Chorus: Diana Kirkwood, David Little, Myra Rubin, George Van Den Houten. Guards: Rob-
ert Legionaire, Frank T. Wells.
Principal Understudies: Misses Henry, Flanagan—Myra Rubin; Mr. Bosco—George Van Den
Houten; Mr Cioffi—Macon McCalman; Chorus—Frank T. Wells; Mr. Walker—Ray Fry; Mr.
Birney—Robert Phalen; Miss Cronyn—Diana Kirkwood.
Directed by John Hirsch; scenery, Douglas W. Schmidt; lighting, John Gleason; costumes,
Jane Greenwood; music, Lukas Foss; production stage manager, Barbara-Mae Phillips; stage
manager, Jean-Daniel Noland.
Prologue: Antigone, Ismene. Parados: Chorus. Scene 1: Creon, Sentry, Chorus. Ode 1:
Chorus. Scene 2: Sentry, Creon, Antigone, Ismene, Chorus. Ode 2: Chorus. Scene 3: Haimon,
Creon, Chorus. Ode 3: Chorus. Scene 4: Antigone, Creon, Chorus. Ode 4: Chorus. Scene 5:

Teiresias, Creon, Chorus. Paean: Chorus. Exodos: Messenger, Creon, Eurydice, Chorus. The play was presented without intermission.
Presentations of the Sophocles play on New York stages have included the 1969 Living Theater version of the Bertolt Brecht adaptation and a revival of this Fitts-Fitzgerald version off Broadway 1/14/67 for 4 performances.
Ray Fry replaced James Blendick 5/18/71.

Hay Fever (24). Revival of the play by Noel Coward. Produced by Leonard Sillman at the Helen Hayes Theater. Opened November 9, 1970. (Closed November 28, 1970)

Sorel Bliss	Roberta Maxwell	Sandy Tyrell	John Tillinger
Simon Bliss	Sam Waterston	Myra Arundel	Marian Mercer
Clara	Sudie Bond	Richard Greatham	Michael McGuire
Judith Bliss	Shirley Booth	Jackie Coryton	Carole Shelley
David Bliss	John Williams		

Standbys: Misses Booth, Mercer, Bond—Carol Teitel; Misses Shelley, Maxwell—Kendall March; Messrs. Williams, McGuire—Richard Woods; Messrs. Waterston, Tillinger—Joseph Hindy.
Directed by Arvin Brown; scenery and lighting, Ben Edwards; costumes, Jane Greenwood; associate producers, Zenon R. Mocarski Inc., Brandon Maggart, James Catusi; production stage manager, Mortimer Halpern; stage manager, Dean McIlnay; press, Howard Atlee, David Roggensack.
Time: The present. Place: The Blisses' country home at Cookham, in June.
Hay Fever was first produced in London in 1925 and in New York 10/5/25. It was revived on Broadway 12/29/31 for 95 performances. Laurence Olivier's National Theater revived it in London in the 1969-70 season with Celia Johnson in the leading role.

* Two by Two (231). Musical based on the play *The Flowering Peach* by Clifford Odets; book by Peter Stone; music by Richard Rodgers; lyrics by Martin Charnin. Produced by Richard Rodgers at the Imperial Theater. Opened Noverber 10, 1970.

Noah	Danny Kaye	Leah	Marilyn Cooper
Esther	Joan Copeland	Ham	Michael Karm
Japheth	Walter Willison	Rachel	Tricia O'Neil
Shem	Harry Goz	Goldie	Madeline Kahn

Standbys: Mr. Kaye—Harry Goz; Messrs. Karm, Willison—Jess Richards; Mr. Goz—Stephen Pearlman; Misses Copeland, Cooper—Janet McCall; Misses Kahn, O'Neil—Caryl Jeanne Tenney.
Conceived and directed by Joe Layton; musical direction, Jay Blackton; scenery, David Hays; costumes, Fred Voelpel; lighting, John Gleason; orchestrations, Eddie Sauter; dance and vocal arrangements, Trude Rittmann; projections designed by Cris Alexander; production stage manager, Harry Young; stage manager, Phil King; press, Frank Goodman, Les Schecter.
The story of Noah, the Flood and the Ark adapted from Clifford Odets's play depicting Noah and his brood in the character of a nice Jewish family.

ACT I

"Why Me?" ....Noah
"Put Him Away" ....Shem, Ham, Leah
The Gitka's Song ....The Gitka
"Something, Somewhere" ....Japheth, Family
"You Have Got to Have a Rudder on the Ark" ....Noah, Shem, Ham, Japheth
"Something Doesn't Happen" ....Rachel, Esther
"An Old Man" ....Esther
"Ninety Again!" ....Noah
"Two by Two" ....Noah, Family
"I Do Not Know a Day I Did Not Love You" ....Japheth
"Something, Somewhere" (Reprise) ....Noah

ACT II

"When It Dries" ....Noah, Family
"Two by Two" (Reprise) ....Noah, Esther
"You" ....Noah
"The Golden Ram" ....Goldie
"Poppa Knows Best" ....Noah, Japheth
"I Do Not Know a Day I Did Not Love You" (Reprise) ....Rachel, Japheth
"As Far as I'm Concerned" ....Shem, Leah
"Hey, Girlie" ....Noah
"The Covenant" ....Noah

* **Sleuth** (229). By Anthony Shaffer. Produced by Helen Bonfils, Morton Gottlieb and Michael White at The Music Box. Opened November 12, 1970.

Andrew Wyke ....Anthony Quayle   Milo Tindle ....Keith Baxter

(Philip Farrar, Harold K. Newman and Roger Purnell and their understudies Henry Raymond and John Stephen were listed in the Broadway program for the roles of Inspector Doppler, Detective Sergeant Tarrant and Police Constable Higgs in order to sustain the audience's mystification. They are fictitious names.)

Standbys: Mr. Quayle—Michael Allinson; Mr. Baxter—Victor Arnold.
Directed by Clifford Williams; designed by Carl Toms; lighting, William Ritman; production stage manager, Warren Crane; stage manager, John Stephen; press, Dorothy Ross, Herb Striesfield.
Time: The present. Place: Andrew Wyke's country home in Wiltshire. Act I: A summer evening. Act II: Two days later.
Cat-and-mouse games of life and death played between a resentful husband and his wife's lover, in a mystery thriller. A foreign play previously produced in London.
A Best Play; see page 159

Les Blancs (40). By Lorraine Hansberry; final text adapted by Robert Nemiroff. Produced by Konrad Matthaei at the Longacre Theater. Opened November 15, 1970. (Closed December 19, 1970)

Warrior ....Charles Moore	3d African ....William Ware
Witch Doctor ....Joan Derby	Dr. Willy Dekoven ..Humbert Allen Astredo
Drummers ....Ladji Camara, Charles Payne	Maj. George Rice ....Ralph Purdum
Dr. Marta Gotterling ....Marie Andrews	1st Soldier ....Garry Mitchell
1st African ....Dennis Tate	2d Soldier ....Gwyllum Evans
2d African ....George Fairley	Madame Neilsen ....Lili Darvas
African Child ....Gregory Beyer	Eric ....Harold Scott
Peter ....Clebert Ford	Tshembe Matoseh ....James Earl Jones
Charlie Morris ....Cameron Mitchell	Abioseh Matoseh ....Earle Hyman

Understudies: Mr. Jones—Earle Hyman; Messrs. Cameron Mitchell, Purdum—Garry Mitchell; Mr. Hyman—Clebert Ford; Mr. Allen—Gwyllum Evans; Mr. Scott—Dennis Tate; Mr. Ford—George Fairley; Messrs. Tate, Fairley, Ware—Charles Briggs; Messrs. Camara, Payne—Butch Jackson.
Directed by John Berry; scenery, Peter Larkin; costumes, Jane Greenwood; lighting, Neil Peter Jampolis; ritual, Louis Johnson; sound, Jack Shearing; script associate, Charlotte Zaltzberg; production stage manager, Martin Gold; stage manager, Charles Briggs; press, Max Eisen, Warren Pincus.
Time: Yesterday, today, tomorrow—but not very long after that. Place: In and about a Mission compound and the Matoseh hut in Africa. The play was presented without intermission.
Europeanized African returns to his native village for his father's funeral in an atmosphere of racial violence; is torn between his two cultures.

Home (110). By David Storey. Produced by Alexander H. Cohen in the The Royal Court Theater Production at the Morosco Theater. Opened November 17, 1970. (Closed February 20, 1971)

Harry ....John Gielgud	Kathleen ....Mona Washbourne
Jack ....Ralph Richardson	Alfred ....Graham Weston
Marjorie ....Dandy Nichols	

Standbys: Miss Washbourne—Stellar Bennett; Miss Nichols—Lucy Landau; Mr. Weston—Andrew Johns.

Directed by Lindsay Anderson; designed by Jocelyn Herbert; lighting, Jules Fisher; music, Alan Price; associate producer, Clinton Wilder; production associates, Hildy Parks, Roy A. Somlyo; production supervisor, Jerry Adler; stage manager, Robert L. Borod; press, James D. Proctor, Richard Hummler.

Time: The present. Act I: Before lunch. Act II: After lunch.

An orchestration of despair, frustration and the sense of oncoming oblivion in character studies of elderly inmates in an asylum for the mentally ill. A foreign play previously produced in London.

Jessica Tandy replaced Dandy Nichols 1/11/71.

A best play; see page 181

The Castro Complex (7). By Mel Arrighi. Produced by Jeff Britton at the Stairway Theater (Limited Broadway). Opened November 18, 1970. (Closed November 22, 1970)

Betsy Kress	Marian Hailey	Paco Montoya	Raul Julia
Hadley Marcus	Terry Kiser		

Directed by James Burrows; scenery, Kurt Lundell; lighting, Roger Morgan; costumes, John J. Whitmore; associate producer, Sidney Annis; assistant to the producer, Erlinda Zetlin; production stage manager, Gail Hubbard; press, David Powers.

Time: The present. Place: The attic apartment of Betsy Kress in New York City. The play was presented in three acts.

Comedy, woman persuades her fiance to dress up and behave like Fidel Castro—on whom she has a crush—prior to making love to her.

The Candyapple (1). By John Grissmer. Produced by William F. DeSeta at the Edison Theater (Limited Broadway). Opened and closed at the evening performance, November 23, 1970.

Foster Fine	Raymond Singer	Connie Antonelli	Joy Garrett
Frank McGrath	Ray Edelstein	Larry McGrath	Arlen Dean Snyder
Jim Ferndock	Noel Conlon	Tom McGrath	John Beal
Joanie Klinger	Irene Bunde		

Directed by Stuart Bishop; scenery and lighting, David R. Ballou; costumes, Sara Brook; production stage manager, Robert Burgos; press, Bill Doll.

Comedy about attitudes toward Roman Catholicism among a father and two sons, on the eve of one son's marriage.

Foreplay (38). By Robert M. Lane. Produced by Sweet Alice Ltd. at the Bijou Theater (Limited Broadway). Opened December 11, 1970. (Closed January 10, 1971)

Walter	Donn Whyte	Alice	Tara Tyson
Neil	Sam Stoneburner	Rich	Alan Castner

Directed by Nicholas Rock; scenery and lighting, Leo B. Meyer; production stage manager, Clint Jakeman; press, Betty Lee Hunt Associates, Henry Luhrman, Harriett Trachtenberg.

Time: The present. Place: A Central Park West apartment somewhere in the 80s. Act I, Scene 1: 6 p.m. Saturday. Scene 2: Two hours later. Act II, Scene 1: Later Saturday night. Scene 2: Sunday morning.

First steps in a false heterosexual's release from wife and family into homosexual life.

The Gingerbread Lady (193). By Neil Simon. Produced by Saint-Subber at the Plymouth Theater. Opened December 13, 1970. (Closed May 29, 1971)

Jimmy Perry	Michael Lombard	Evy Meara	Maureen Stapleton
Manuel	Alex Colon	Polly Meara	Ayn Ruymen
Toby Landau	Betsy von Furstenberg	Lou Tanner	Charles Siebert

Standbys: Misses Stapleton, von Furstenberg—Jan Farrand; Mr. Lombard—Ken Kimmins; Mr. Siebert—Don Billett; Miss Ruymen—Eda Zahl; Mr. Colon—Hector Troy.

Directed by Robert Moore; scenery, David Hays; costumes, Frank Thompson; lighting, Martin Aronstein; stage manager, George Rondo; press, Harvey B. Sabinson, Lee Solters, Cheryl Sue Dolby.

Time: The present. Place: A brownstone apartment in the West Seventies. Act I: Mid-November, late afternoon. Act II: Three weeks later, about 9 p.m. Act III: The following morning.

Pop singer fights alcoholism with a little help—and sometimes a little hindrance—from her friends.

A Best Play; see page 196

* **The Me Nobody Knows** (396). Musical with book by Stephen M. Joseph; edited from the book *The Me Nobody Knows* and adapted by Robert H. Livingston and Herb Schapiro; music by Gary William Friedman; lyrics by Will Holt; original idea by Herb Schapiro. Produced by Jeff Britton in association with Sagittarius Productions, Inc. at the Helen Hayes Theater. Opened December 18, 1970; transferred from off Broadway.

Rhoda	Melanie Henderson	Melba	Gerri Dean
Lillian	Laura Michaels	Donald	Paul Mace
Carlos	Jose Fernandez	Lloyd	Northern J. Calloway
Lillie Mae	Irene Cara	Clorox	Carl Thoma
Benjamin	Douglas Grant	William	Kevin Lindsay
Catherine	Beverly Ann Bremers	Nell	Hattie Winston

Directed by Robert H. Livingston; musical members staged by Patricia Birch; musical direction, Edward Strauss; scenery and lighting, Clarke Dunham; costumes, Patricia Quinn Stuart; media design and photography, Stan Goldberg and Mopsy; additional lyrics, Herb Schapiro; arrangements and orchestrations, Gary William Friedman; assistant to producer, Erlinda Zetlin; production stage manager, Martha Knight; press, Samuel J. Friedman, Louise Weiner Ment.

This musical study of underprivileged New York City children ran for 208 performances 5/18/70 to 11/15/70 in this same production off Broadway before being transferred to Broadway.

The list of musical numbers in *The Me Nobody Knows* appears on page 369 of the *1969-70* Best Plays volume.

A Place Without Doors (30). By Marguerite Duras; translated by Barbara Bray. Produced by Edge Productions at the Stairway Theater (Limited Broadway). Opened December 22, 1970. (Closed January 16, 1971)

The Questioner	Alvin Epstein	Claire Lannes	Mildred Dunnock
Pierre Lannes	Richard A. Dysart		

Directed by Brian Murray; scenery, John Conklin; lighting, Ronald Wallace; production stage manager, Mitch Erickson; press, Betty Lee Hunt Associates, Henry Luhrman, Harriett Trachtenberg.

The play was presented in two acts.

An interrogation-in-depth of first a husband and then his wife, who has murdered their housekeeper. A foreign play previously produced in Paris as *L'Amante Anglaise* and in the American premiere of its English version at the Long Wharf Theater, New Haven, Conn. *L'Amante Anglaise* was produced off Broadway later in the 1970-71 season, in French (see its entry in the "Plays Produced off Broadway" section of this volume).

Happy Birthday, Wanda June (143). By Kurt Vonnegut Jr. Produced by Lester M. Goldsmith at the Edison Theater (Limited Broadway). Opened December 22, 1970; transferred from off Broadway. (Closed March 14, 1971 matinee)

Penelope Ryan	Marsha Mason	Herb Shuttle	Nicolas Coster
Harold Ryan	Kevin McCarthy	Wanda June	Ariane Munker
Dr. Norbert Woodly	Keith Charles	Siegfried von Konigswald	Louis Turenne
Looseleaf Harper	William Hickey	Mildred	Pamela Saunders
Paul Ryan	Steven Paul		

Understudies: Mr. McCarthy—Louis Turenne; Mr. Paul—Jeffrey Edmund; Miss Munker—Ellen Dano; Misses Mason, Saunders—Dianne Wiest; Messrs. Charles, Coster, Turenne, Hickey—Jess Osuna.

Directed by Michael J. Kane; restaged at the Edison Theater by Paul John Austin; scenery, Ed Wittstein; lighting, David F. Segal; costumes, Joseph G. Aulisi; sound, Gary Harris; associate producer, Walter Rosen Scholz; production stage manager, Paul John Austin; press, Betty Lee Hunt Associates, Henry Luhrman, Harriett Trachtenberg.

Time: The present. Place: The Ryan apartment in a large city. The play was presented in three parts.

This production of *Happy Birthday, Wanda June* opened off Broadway 10/7/70 at the Theater de Lys and played 47 performances through 11/15/70 before being transferred to a Limited Broadway situation (see its entry in the "Plays Produced Off Broadway" section of this volume). It played 96 more performances uptown.

Lovely Ladies, Kind Gentlemen (16). Musical based on Vern J. Sneider's book *The Teahouse of the August Moon* and the play by John Patrick; book by John Patrick; music and lyrics by Stan Freeman and Franklin Underwood. Produced by Herman Levin at the Majestic Theater. Opened December 28, 1970. (Closed January 9, 1971)

Sakini ....Kenneth Nelson	Mr. Hokaida ....Big Lee
Missionary; Logan ....David Steele	Lotus Blossom ....Eleanor Calbes
Col. Wainwright Purdy III .....David Burns	Capt. McLean ....Remak Ramsay
Sgt. Gregovich ....Lou Wills	Miller ....Jim Weston
Capt. Fisby ....Ron Husmann	O'Malley ....Stephen Bolster
Old Lady ....Sachi Shimizu	Cabot ....Stuart Craig Wood
The Daughter ....Tisa Chang	Stock ....James B. Spann
Lady Astor ....Herself	Lipshitz ....Kirk Norman
Ancient Man; Mr. Keora ......Sab Shimono	Swenson ....James Hobson
Mr. Seiko ....Alvin Lum	Cardone ....Dennis Roth
Miss Higa Jiga ....Lori Chinn	Mancini ....Richard Nieves
Mr. Oshira ....David Thomas	Colombo ....Charlie J. Rodriguez

Children: June Angela, Gene Profanato, Dana Shimizu. Okinawans and Americans: Barbara Coggin, Catherine Dando, Joan Nelson, Sumiko, Tisa Chang, Lori Chinn, Christi Curtis, Marjory Edson, Rosalie King, Sylvia Nolan, Jo Ann Ogawa, Sachi Shimizu, Susan Sigrist, Stephen Bolster, James Hobson, Alvin Lum, Richard Nieves, Kirk Norman, Charlie J. Rodriguez, Dennis Roth, Sab Shimono, James B. Spann, David Steele, Jim Weston, Stuart Craig Wood, Henry Boyer, Paul Charles, Charlie Goeddertz, J.J. Jepson, Tim Ramirez, Steven Ross, Joe Milan, Ken Urmston.

Principal understudies: Mr. Nelson—J.J. Jepson; Mr. Husmann—Stephen Bolster; Mr. Burns—David Thomas; Miss Calbes—Sumiko.

Directed by Lawrence Kasha; dances and musical numbers staged by Marc Breaux; musical direction and choral arrangements, Theodore Saidenberg; scenery, Oliver Smith; costumes, Freddy Wittop; lighting, Thomas Skelton; orchestrations, Philip J. Lang; dance arrangements, Al Mello; associate choreographer, Gary Menteer; production stage manager, Phil Friedman; stage manager, Richard Hughes; press, Martin Shwartz.

Time: A few months in the year 1946. Place: The island of Okinawa.

Lovely Ladies, Kind Gentlemen is a comic view of the American occupation of Okinawa after World War II, based on *The Teahouse of the August Moon*, which was originally produced on Broadway 10/15/53 for 1,027 performances and was named a Best Play of its year.

ACT I

"With a Snap of My Finger" ....Sakini, Okinawans, G.I.s
"Right Hand Man" ....Purdy, Sakini, Fisby, G.I.s
"Find Your Own Cricket" ....Sakini, Oshira, Higa Jiga, Villagers
"One Side of the World" ....Sakini
"Geisha" ....Lotus Blossom
"You Say—They Say" ....Sakini, Villagers
"This Time" ....Fisby
"Simple Word" ....Lotus Blossom
"Garden Guaracha" ....McLean
"It's Good Enough for Lady Astor" ....Fisby, McLean, Sakini, Villagers

ACT II

"Chaya" ....Sakini, Villagers
"Call Me Back" ....Fisby, McLean, Sakini
"Lovely Ladies, Kind Gentlemen" ....Sakini
"You've Broken a Fine Woman's Heart" ....Col. Purdy
"One More for the Last One" ....Sakini, Gregovich, G.I.s, Villagers

Soon (3). Musical based on an original story by Joseph Martinez Kookoolis and Scott Fagan; adapted by Martin Duberman; music by Joseph Martinez Kookoolis and Scott Fagan; lyrics by Scott Fagan. Produced by Bruce W. Stark and Sagittarius Productions, Inc. at the Ritz Theater (Limited Broadway). Opened January 12, 1971. (Closed January 13, 1971)

Kelly	Barry Bostwick	Faith	Leata Galloway
Annie	Marta Heflin	Charity	Vicki Sue Robinson
Wilson Wilson	Dennis Belline	Rita	Pamela Pentony
Neil	Joseph Campbell Butler	Sharon	Nell Carter
Michael	Richard Gere	Songwriter	Tony Middleton
Henry	Peter Allen	Psychedelic Necktie	Pendleton Brown
Groupies:			
Hope	Marion Ramsey		

Henry's Friends: Singer Williams, Michael Jason, John C. Nelson. Record Company Executives: Del Hinkley, Angus Cairns, Larry Spinelli, Paul Eichel. Pit-Shit (sic): Tim Case, drums; John Trivers, fender bass, guitar; Richard Apuzzo, guitar, acoustic guitar; Adam Ippolito, organ, tuba; Louis St. Louis, piano, electric piano.

Understudies: Messrs. Bostwick, Gere—Michael Jason; Messrs. Butler, Belline, Brown—John C. Nelson; Messrs. Hinkley, Cairns, Spinelli, Eichel—Pendleton Brown.

Additional staging, Gerald Freedman; choreography, Fred Benjamin; musical direction, Louis St. Louis; scenery, Kert Lundell; costumes, David Chapman; lighting, Jules Fisher; orchestrations, Howard Wyeth, Jon Huston; vocal arrangements, Louis St. Louis, Jacqueline Penn; audio design, Jack Shearing; production stage manager, Alan Hall; stage manager, Mary Porter Hall; press, Seymour Krawitz, Patricia McLean Krawitz.

Self-styled "rock opera" about a group of young musicians coming to New York, achieving popular success and suffering from it.

ACT I, Part One: On the road—Prologue ("Let the World Begin Again"). Scene 1: The country ("In Your Hands," "I See the Light/Gentle Sighs"). Scene 2: Coming to the city ("Roll Out the Morning"). ACT I, Part Two: The city—Scene 3: The city ("Everybody's Running"). Scene 4: Henry's office ("Henry Is Where It's At"). Scene 5: The club ("Music, Music," "Glad to Know Ya," "Rita Cheeta"). Scene 6: Around the city ("Henry's Dream Theme," "To Touch the Sky"). Scene 7: The offices of the music industry (The chase: "Everybody's Running," "Marketing, Marketing," "Sweet Henry Loves You," "One More Time," "Straight," "Wait").

ACT II—Scene 1: A series of recording sessions ("Faces, Names and Places," "Annie's Thing," "Doing the High," "Soon"). Scene 2: City downs ("Country Store Living," "What's Gonna Happen to Me," "On the Charts," "Molecules," "So Much That I Know," "Child of Sympathy," "Frustration"). Scene 3: On the tour ("Doing the High," "It Won't Be Long").

* Two by Ibsen. Repertory of two revivals by Henrik Ibsen; new adaptations by Christopher Hampton. ***A Doll's House** (89). Opened January 13, 1971. *** Hedda Gabler** (46). Opened February 17, 1971. Produced by Hillard Elkins at the Playhouse Theater (Limited Broadway).

PERFORMER	"A DOLL'S HOUSE"	"HEDDA GABLER"
Claire Bloom	Nora	Hedda Gabler
Patricia Elliott	Mrs. Linde	Mrs. Elvsted
Robert Gerringer	Nils Krogstad	Judge Brack
Donald Madden	Torvald Helmer	Eilert Lovborg
Eda Reiss Merin	Helene	Berte
Roy Shuman	Dr. Rank	George Tesman
Kate Wilkinson	Anne-Marie	Aunt Julia

Standbys: Mr. Madden (*A Doll's House*)—Gil Rogers; Mr. Madden (*Hedda Gabler*)—Simm Landres. Understudies: Miss Bloom—Patricia Elliott; Misses Wilkinson, Merin, Elliott—Dorothy Lyman; Mr. Shuman—Gil Rogers; Mr. Gerringer (*A Doll's House*)—Simm Landres; Mr. Gerringer (*Hedda Gabler*)—Gil Rogers.

BOTH PLAYS—Directed by Patrick Garland: scenery, costumes, lighting, John Bury; production supervision, Michael Thoma; associate producer, George Platt; press, Samuel J. Friedman, Shirley Herz.

The play was presented in three acts. *A Doll's House* was entitled *A Doll's Home* when first presented in New York 12/21/89. Its most recent professional revival was off Broadway by David Ross 2/2/63 for 66 performances. It was last revived on Broadway in the Thornton Wilder version, with Ruth Gordon as Nora, 12/27/37 for 144 performances.

The play was presented in two parts. *Hedda Gabler* was most recently revived off Broadway last season by The Opposites Company 1/16/70 for 81 performances and by David Ross 11/9/60 for 340 performances. It was last performed on Broadway by Eva Le Galienne in her own translation, 2/24/48 for 15 performances.

Hamlet (2). Revival of the play by William Shakespeare for a limited engagement. Produced by Paul Gregory, in association with the American Conservatory Theater, by arrangement with the Carnegie Hall Corporation, at Carnegie Hall. Opened January 14, 1971 (Closed January 15, 1971)

Hamlet ....Judith Anderson	Marcellus; Gravedigger;
Claudius; Ghost ....Laurence Hugo	Player King ....Leon Charles
Polonius ....Don McHenry	Rosencrantz ....Rick Poe
Gertrude ....Ludi Claire	Guildenstern ....Robert Ground
Laertes ....Philip Kerr	Horatio ....Stephen D. Newman
Ophelia ....Jeanne Bartlett	Lady; Player Queen ....Ruth Hunt
	Lord; Player Murderer ......Charles Dillon

Directed by William Ball; scenery and costumes, Robert Fletcher; lighting, Jules Fisher; associate director, Eugene Barcone; sound, Parker Young; press, Anne Mulhall, Marjorie Young.

This version of *Hamlet* was presented somewhat like a reading, with mimed props. Recent New York production of the play included the Roundabout Repertory and Oxford-Cambridge versions this season off Broadway and Nicol Williamson's Hamlet 5/1/69 for 50 Broadway performances.

Ari (19). Musical with book and lyrics by Leon Uris based on his novel *Exodus;* music by Walt Smith. Produced by Ken Gaston and Leonard Goldberg in association with Henry Stern at the Mark Hellinger Theater. Opened January 15, 1971. (Closed January 30, 1971)

Joab ....Joseph Della Sorte	Kitty Fremont ....Constance Towers
Zev ....Mark Zeller	Dov ....John Savage
David ....Martin Ross	Karen ....Jacqueline Mayro
Mandria, the Greek .........C.K. Alexander	Benjy ....Roger Morgan
Gen. Sutherland ....Jack Gwillim	Armeteau ....Alexander Orfaly
Maj. Caldwell ....Jamie Ross	Friend of Armeteau ....Edward Becker
Ari Ben Canaan ....David Cryer	Capt. Henley ....Casper Roos
Mark Parker ....Norwood Smith	

Refugee Children: Tracey Eman, Kelley Boa, Mona Daleo, Toni Lund, Lynn Reynolds, Timmy Ousey, Todd Jones, Johnny Welch, Tony Dean.

Refugees and British Soldiers—Dancers: Bryant Baker, Bjarne Buchtrup, Ron Crofoot, Richard Dodd, Pi Douglass, Richard Maxon, Ronn Steinman, Carol Estey, Reggie Israel, Karen L. Jablons, Joanna Mendl, Gayle Pines, Deborah Strauss.

Refugees and British Soldiers—Singers: Edward Becker, Ted Bloecher, Bennett Hill, Henry Lawrence, Art Matthews, Casper Roos, D. Brian Wallach, Bonnie Marcus, Patricia Noal, Susan Schevers, Suzanne Horn.

Standby: Miss Towers—Rita Gardner. Understudies: Mr. Cryer—Norwood Smith; Miss Mayro—Patricia Noal, Bonnie Marcus; Mr. Morgan—Timmy Ousey; Mr. Savage—Ronn Steinman; Mr. Orfaly—Henry Lawrence; Mr. Gwillim—Casper Roos; Messrs. Ross, Roos—Art Matthews.

Directed by Lucia Victor; choreography, Talley Beatty; vocal arrangements & musical direction, Stanley Lebowsky; scenery, Robert Randolph; costumes, Sara Brook; lighting, Nananne Porcher; orchestrations, Philip J. Lang; dance & incidental music arrangements, Peter Howard; additional music, William Fisher; associate producers, Ronald Reckseit, Lisa Lipsky; production stage manager, Wade Miller; stage manager, Jack Timmers; press, David Lipsky.

Time: 1947. Place: The island of Cyprus.

Jewish refugees confront British authorities in a valiant effort to reach their new homeland, Israel.

ACT I

"Children's Lament" ....Children
Scene 1: Beach near Famagusta, Cyprus, at night
   "Yerushaliam" ....Ari
   "The Saga of the Haganah" ....David, Zev, Joab, Mandria
Scene 2: Mandria's house, immediately thereafter
   "The Saga of the Haganah" (Reprise) ....Mandria
Scene 3: A waterfront cafe, the next night
   "Give Me One Good Reason" ....Kitty
Scene 4: Detention camp, children's compound, the following afternoon
   "Dov's Nightmare" ....Dov, Victims of Holocaust
   "Karen's Lullaby" ....Karen
Scene 5: A waterfront cafe, quayside, Larnaca, a few days later
   "Aphrodite" ....Mandria, Armeteau
Scene 6: Detention camp, children's compound, the following week
   "My Galilee" ....Ari, Palestinians
Scene 7: A military camp, a week later
   "The Lord Helps Those Who Help Themselves" ....David, Palestinians
Scene 8: Detention camp, a few days later
   "The Alphabet Song"; Tactics ....Karen, Children
Scene 9: The dispensary
   "Give Me One Good Reason" (Reprise) ....Kitty
Scene 10: Mandria's house, a few days after; British H.Q. the same day; Mandria's house, the following afternoon
   "My Brother's Keeper" ....Ari

ACT II

Scene 1: A hidden cove, the next morning
   "The Exodus" ....David, Ensemble
Scene 2: Gen. Sutherland's quarters, noon
   "He'll Never Be Mine" ....Kitty
Scene 3: Detention camp, 2 p.m.
   "One Flag" ....Karen, Children
Scene 4: Military camp, 5 p.m.
   "The Lord Helps Those Who Help Themselves (Reprise) ....Mandria
Scene 5: Dockside, Kyrenia, 6 p.m.
Scene 6: Parker's hotel room, immediately thereafter
Scene 7: Aboard the Exodus, Kyrenia Harbor, 80th hour of hunger strike through 120th hour
   "I See What I Choose to See" ....Karen, Dov
   Hora-Galilee (Dance) ....Karen, Dov, Children, Palestinians
   "Ari's Promise" ....Ari
Scene 8: Dockside, Kyrenia, immediately thereafter
Finale
   "Ari's Promise" (Reprise) ....Company
   "The Exodus" (Reprise) ....Company

* No, No, Nanette (153). Musical revival with book by Otto Harbach and Frank Mandel; music by Vincent Youmans; lyrics by Irving Caesar and Otto Harbach. Produced by Pyxidium Ltd. at the Forty-Sixth Street Theater. Opened January 19, 1971.

Pauline	Patsy Kelly	Tom Trainor	Roger Rathburn
Lucille Early	Helen Gallagher	Nanette	Susan Watson
Sue Smith	Ruby Keeler	Flora Latham	K.C. Townsend
Jimmy Smith	Jack Gilford	Betty Brown	Loni Zoe Ackerman
Billy Early	Bobby Van	Winnie Winslow	Pat Lysinger

Nanette's Friends: Bob Becker, John Beecher, Joretta Bohannon, Roger Braun, Marcia Brushingham, Kenneth Carr, Jennie Chandler, Kathy Conry, Christine Cox, Kevin Daly, Ed Dixon, Ellen Elias, Mercedes Ellington, Jon Engstrom, Marian Haraldson, Gregg Harlan, Jamie Haskins, Gwen Hillier, Sayra Hummel, Scott Hunter, Dottie Lester, Cheryl Locke, Joanne Lotsko, Mary Ann Niles, Kate O'Brady, Sue Ohman, Jill Owens, Ken Ploss, John Roach, Linda Rose, Ron Schwinn, Sonja Stuart, Monica Tiller, Pat Trott, Phyllis Wallach.

Standbys: Miss Keeler—Betty Wragge; Mr. Gilford—Ted Tiller; Miss Kelly—Dorothy Claire. Understudies: Mr. Van—Roger Braun; Miss Gallagher—Pat Lysinger; Miss Watson—Kathy Conry; Mr. Rathburn—Kenneth Carr; Miss Ackerman—Linda Rose; Miss Townsend—Dottie Lester; Miss Lysinger—Gwen Hillier.

Production supervised by Busby Berkeley; adapted and directed by Burt Shevelove; dances and musical numbers staged by Donald Saddler; musical direction and vocal arrangements, Buster Davis; design, Raoul Pene du Bois; lighting, Jules Fisher; orchestrations, Ralph Burns; dance music arrangements and incidental music, Luther Henderson; tap supervisors, Mary Ann Niles, Ted Cappy; sound, Jack Shearing; production manager, May Muth; stage manager, Robert Schear; press, Merle Debuskey, M.J. Boyer.

Time: A weekend in early summer, 1925. Act I: The home of James Smith, New York City. Act II: The garden of Chickadee Cottage, Atlantic City. Act III: The living room at Chickadee Cottage.

No, No, Nanette was first produced on Broadway 9/16/25 for 321 performances, at which time its title appeared as No! No! Nanette! It was based on Frank Mandel's three-act farce My Lady Friends (1923), in turn based on the novel, Oh, James, though these sources have never appeared in the billing.

Sandra O'Neill replaced K.C. Townsend 3/17/71.

ACT I

"Too Many Rings Around Rosie" .... Lucille, Boys, Girls
"I've Confessed to the Breeze" .... Nanette, Tom
"Call of the Sea" .... Billy, Girls
"I Want to Be Happy" .... Jimmy, Nanette, Sue, Boys, Girls
"No, No, Nanette" .... Nanette, Tom
Finaletto Act I .... Nanette, Boys, Girls

ACT II

"Peach on the Beach" .... Nanette, Boys, Girls
"Tea for Two" .... Nanette, Tom, Boys, Girls
"You Can Dance With Any Girl" .... Lucille, Billy
Finaletto Act II .... Entire Company

ACT III

"Telephone Girlie" .... Billy, Betty, Flora, Winnie
"Where-Has-My-Hubby-Gone Blues" .... Lucille, Boys
"Waiting for You" .... Nanette, Tom
"Take a Little One-Step" .... Sue, Billy, Lucille, Pauline, Boys, Girls
Finale .... Entire Company

A Midsummer Night's Dream (62). Revival of the play by William Shakespeare. Produced by David Merrick Arts Foundation in the Royal Shakespeare Company Stratford-Upon-Avon production at the Billy Rose Theater. Opened January 20, 1971. (Closed March 13, 1971)

Theseus; Oberon	Alan Howard	Hermia	Mary Rutherford
Hippolyta; Titania	Sara Kestelman	Lysander	Terence Taplin
Philostrate; Puck	John Kane	Helena	Frances de la Tour
Egeus; Quince	Philip Locke	Demetrius	Ben Kingsley
Bottom	David Waller	Fairies:	
Flute	Glynne Lewis	Cobweb	Hugh Keays Byrne
Starveling	Phillip Manikum	Moth	Ralph Cotterill
Snout	Patrick Stewart	Peaseblossom	Celia Quicke
Snug	Barry Stanton	Mustardseed	John York

Directed by Peter Brook; scenery and costumes, Sally Jacobs; music, Richard Peaslee, with the actors and Felix Mendelssohn; lighting, Lloyd Burlingame; presented with the cooperation of the Billy Rose Foundation and by arrangement with the governors of the Royal Shakespeare Theater; production supervisor, Samuel Liff; general stage manager, Roger Howells; stage manager, Roger Gregory; press, Lee Solters, Harvey B. Sabinson, Leo Stern.

The play was presented in two parts. *A Midsummer Night's Dream* was last revived off Broadway 6/29/67 at the Theater de Lys for 28 performances. It was last produced on Broadway by the Old Vic 9/21/54 for 29 performances. This production played an additional engagement of 16 performances at the Brooklyn Academy of Music beginning 3/16/71, following the end of its limited engagement at the Billy Rose.

Four on a Garden (57). Program of four one-act plays by Abe Burrows: *House of Dunkelmayer, Betty, Toreador* and *The Swingers*. Produced by David Merrick at the Broadhurst Theater. Opened January 30, 1971. (Closed March 20, 1971)

PERFORMER	"HOUSE OF DUNKELMAYER"	"BETTY"	"TOREADOR"	"THE SWINGERS"
Sid Caesar	Max	Bob	The Painter	Mr. Lewis
Carol Channing	Mrs. Dunkelmayer	Betty	Irene	Mrs. Wexel
Mary Hamill	Helga			
George S. Irving	TV Repairman	Real Estate Agent		
Tom Lee Jones	Delivery Man	Joel	Joel	
Christine Lavren		Jessica		

Understudies: Messrs. Irving, Jones—Lee Ames; Miss Lavren—Mary Hamill; Miss Hamill—Christine Lavren.

Directed by Abe Burrows; scenery, Oliver Smith; costumes, William McHone; lighting, Martin Aronstein; associate producer, Samuel Liff; production stage manager, Jeff Chambers; stage manager, Lee Ames; press, Harvey B. Sabinson, Lee Solters, Sandra Manley.

Time: The present. Place: A four-room cooperative brownstone apartment in Manhattan. In this production, the program was presented without intermission.

Four comedy playlets credited to Abe Burrows; a tryout version under this title was reportedly based on work of Pierre Barillet and Jean Pierre Gredy. *House of Dunkelmayer* is about a rich delicatessen owner's widow who has an eye for handsome young waiters. *Betty* is a reminiscence of a wild Fire Island summer long ago. *Toreador* is an encounter between a nervous, inhibited woman and an obliging house painter. *The Swingers* are two old folks who have just met at a dance hall and are going to try to have one more romantic evening. The apartment setting remains the same, but the characters are different in each playlet.

The School for Wives (120). Revival of the play by Molière; new English verse translation by Richard Wilbur. Produced by Phoenix Theater, T. Edward Hambledon managing director, at the Lyceum Theater. Opened February 16, 1971. (Closed May 29, 1971)

Crysalde	Paul Ballantyne	Horace	David Dukes
Arnolphe	Brian Bedford	Notary	George Pentecost
Alain	James Greene	Enrique	Mario Siletti
Georgette	Peggy Pope	Oronte	Gordon Gould
Agnes	Joan van Ark		

Understudies: Mr. Bedford—George Pentecost; Misses van Ark, Pope—Brooke Harrow; Messrs. Dukes, Siletti, Gould, Pentecost—Anthony Manionis; Mr. Ballantyne—Gordon Gould; Mr. Greene—Mario Siletti.

Directed by Stephen Porter; scenery and lighting, James Tilton; costumes, Nancy Potts; music, Conrad Susa; production stage manager, Bob Beard; press, Sol Jacobson, Lewis Harmon, Ruth D. Smuckler.

Time: 1662. Place: A street in front of Arnolphe's house. The play was presented in two acts.

The School for Wives was first presented on Broadway 3/18/51, in French, for 22 performances with Louis Jouvet in the role of Arnolphe. It was produced in musical version as *The Amorous Flea* off Broadway 2/17/64 for 93 performances. This is its first Broadway presentation in English translation.

Maria Tucci replaced Joan van Ark 5/10/71.

And Miss Reardon Drinks a Little (108). By Paul Zindel. Produced by James B. McKenzie, Spofford J. Beadle, Seth L. Schapiro, Kenneth Waissman and Maxine Fox at the Morosco Theater. Opened February 25, 1971. (Closed May 29, 1971)

Catherine Reardon	Estelle Parsons	Anna Reardon	Julie Harris
Mrs. Pentrano	Virginia Payne	Fleur Stein	Rae Allen
Delivery Boy	Paul Lieber	Bob Stein	Bill Macy
Ceil Adams	Nancy Marchand		

Directed by Melvin Bernhardt; scenery, Fred Voelpel; lighting, Martin Aronstein; costumes, Sara Brook; produced in association with Gordon Crowe; stage manager, James Haire; press, Harvey B. Sabinson, Lee Solters, Sandra Manley.

Time: The present. Place: The Reardon sisters' apartment. The play was presented in three acts.

The neuroses of three middle-aged school teachers—two spinsters, one married—are exposed in various incidents of attrition.

Abelard & Heloise (53). By Ronald Millar; inspired by *Peter Abelard* by Helen Waddell and the letters of Heloise and Abelard. Produced by Elliot Martin, James Nederlander and George M. Steinbrenner III by arrangement with John Gale at the Brooks Atkinson Theater. Opened March 10, 1971. (Closed April 24, 1971)

Peter Abelard	Keith Michell	Fulbert	Barnard Hughes
Heloise	Diana Rigg	Belle Alys; Sister Laura	Barbara Lester
Alain	Dirk Benedict	Abbess of Argenteuil	Jacqueline Brookes
Gerard	Ron Hale	Sister Godric	Beulah Garrick
Philippe	Barney McFadden	Sister Constance	Jennifer Moore
Bernard	John Tremaine	Mariella	Samantha Doane
Robert de Montboissier	Peter Coffield	Gisela	Nora Coppola
Guibert	Robert H. Rovin	Alberic of Rheims	Byron Webster
Gilles de Vannes	Ronald Radd	Denise	DeAnn Mears
Jehan	Christopher Pennock	Hugh	Kelly Fitzpatrick

Standby: Miss Rigg—DeAnn Mears. Principal understudies: Mr. Michell—Barney McFadden; Mr. Coffield—Dirk Benedict; Mr. Hughes—Kelly Fitzpatrick; Mr. Radd—Byron Webster; Miss Garrick—Barbara Lester; Miss Lester—Samantha Doane.

Directed by Robin Phillips; scenery, Christopher Morley; costumes, Daphne Dare; lighting, H.R. Poindexter; production stage manager, Norman A. Grogan; stage manager, Dom Salinaro; press, Mary Bryant, Stanley F. Kaminsky, Sadie Stein.

Time: The first half of the 12th century. Place: France. The play was presented in two acts.

Drama based on the famous love story of Heloise, a young girl, and her tutor Abelard, who was a churchman and had taken a vow of celibacy. A foreign play previously produced in London, and at the Ahmanson Theater, Los Angeles.

The Philanthropist (72). By Christopher Hampton. Produced by David Merrick in association with Byron Goldman and Michael Codron in association with the Royal Court Theater at the Ethel Barrymore Theater. Opened March 15, 1971. (Closed May 15, 1971)

Philip	Alec McCowen	John	Paul Corum
Donald	Ed Zimmermann	Celia	Jane Asher

Braham ....Victor Spinetti   Liz ....Carolyn Lagerfelt
Araminta ....Penelope Wilton

Standby: Messrs. Spinetti, Zimmermann—Albert Stratton. Understudy: Miss Asher—Carolyn Lagerfelt.
Directed by Robert Kidd; scenery, John Gunter; lighting, Lloyd Burlingame; costumes, Sara Brook; associate producer, Samuel Liff; stage manager, Mitchell Erickson; press, Harvey B. Sabinson, Lee Solters, Leo Stern.
Time: The near future. Place: A university town. The play was presented in two acts.
Varicolored comedy, deepest black to most sentimental rose, about the love life of a shy professor. A foreign play previously produced in London.
A Best Play; see page 235

Father's Day (1). By Oliver Hailey. Produced by Joseph Kipness and Lawrence Kasha at the John Golden Theater. Opened and closed at the evening performance, March 16, 1971)

Louise ....Brenda Vaccaro   Harold ....Ken Kercheval
Estelle ....Jennifer Salt   Richard ....Donald Moffat
Marian ....Marian Seldes   Tom ....Biff McGuire

Directed by Donald Moffat; scenery and lighting, Jo Mielziner; costumes, Ann Roth; production associate, Phyllis Dukore; production stage manager, Phil Friedman; stage manager, Gene Tyburn; press, Bill Doll & Co., Dick Williams, Virginia Holden, Susan L. Schulman.
Time: Father's Day 1971. Place: Manhattan. The play was presented in two parts.
Three divorcees compare notes on their plight and invite their ex-husbands to a cocktail party.

National Theaters of Japan (3). Schedule of three programs of Noh (Komparu School) and Kyogen (Izumi School) theater in the Japanese language in an engagement limited to one performance each. **Kirokuda** (The Half Delivered Gift—Kyogen) and **Funa-Benkei** (Benkei in the Boat—Noh). March 24, 1971. **Boshibari** (Tied to a Stick—Kyogen) and **Aoi-No-Ue** (Lady Aoi-Noh). March 25, 1971. **Shidohogaku** (Shidohogaku the Horse—Kyogen) and **Sumidagawa** (The River Sumida—Noh). March 26, 1971. Produced by The Carnegie Hall Corporation and Pacific World Artists, Inc. under the sponsorship of the Foreign Ministry of Japan, K.B.S. and the Asahi Shimbun at Carnegie Hall.

KYOGEN

PERFORMER	KIROKUDA	BOSHIBARI	SHIDOHOGAKU
Manzo Nomura	Tarokaja	Master	Tarokaja
Mannosuke Nomura	Master	Jirokaja	Horse
Mansaku Nomura	Tea Shop Owner	Tarokaja	Master
Matasaburo Nomura	Uncle		Uncle

NOH

PERFORMER	FUNA-BENKEI	AOI-NO-UE	SUMIDAGAWA
Kan Hosho	Benkei	Kohijiri	Ferryman
Nobutaka Komparu	Lady Shizuka; Ghost		
Yasuaki Komparu	Hogan		
Kazuya Kudo	Retainer	Courtier	
Mansaku Nomura	Chief Boatman		
Matasaburo Nomura		Messenger	Mother
Kintaro Sakurama		Princess Rokujo	
Keisuke Suzuki		Teruhi	

Masters of chorus, Kintaro Sakurama, Yoshimi Moriya; staff members, Yasuhiro Kakigahara, Sumiko Sakurama; musicians, Asataro Fujita, Junzo Miyamasu, Soichiro Kawamura, Shinichi Uno.

Kyogen is a satirical form of Japanese theater emphasizing the farcical side of life. Noh is a form which relies heavily upon song and dance.

All Over (42). By Edward Albee. Produced by Theater 1971 (Richard Barr, Charles Woodward, Edward Albee) at the Martin Beck Theater. Opened March 28, 1971. (Closed May 1, 1971)

The Wife	Jessica Tandy	The Best Friend	George Voskovec
The Daughter	Madeleine Sherwood	The Nurse	Betty Field
The Mistress	Colleen Dewhurst	Newspapermen	John Gerstad,
The Doctor	Neil Fitzgerald		Charles Kindl, Allen Williams
The Son	James Ray		

Standbys: Misses Dewhurst, Sherwood—Frances Sternhagen; Misses Tandy, Field—Carolyn Coates; Messrs. Voskovec, Fitzgerald—Wyman Pendleton; Mr. Ray—John Gerstad.
Directed by John Gielgud; scenery and costumes, Rouben Ter-Arutunian; lighting, Richard Nelson; production stage manager, Bruce A. Hoover; stage manager, Charles Kindl; press, Betty Lee Hunt Associates, Henry Luhrman, Harriett Trachtenberg, Maria Pucci.
The play was presented in two parts.
Family quarrels and resentments flare among those assembled and waiting at the bedside of a dying man.

* How the Other Half Loves (73). By Alan Ayckbourn. Produced by Michael Myerberg, Peter Bridge and Eddie Kulukundis in association with Lawrence Shubert Lawrence at the Royale Theater. Opened March 29, 1971.

Fiona Foster	Bernice Massi	Bob Phillips	Richard Mulligan
Teresa Phillips	Sandy Dennis	William Detweiler	Tom Aldredge
Frank Foster	Phil Silvers	Mary Detweiler	Jeanne Hepple

Standby: Miss Dennis—Monica Moran.
Directed by Gene Saks; design, David Mitchell; lighting, Peggy Clark; costumes, Winn Morton; production stage manager, Mortimer Halpern; stage manager, Wayne Carson; press, Lee Solters, Harvey B. Sabinson, Leo Stern.
Time: The present. Place: The living rooms of the Fosters and the Phillipses. Act I, Scene 1: Thursday morning. Scene 2: Thursday AND Friday night. Act II, Scene 1: Saturday morning. Scene 2: Sunday morning.
Farce of marital infidelity, with a space-time gimmick. the same living-room set is used by two couples simultaneously, seen by the audience but unaware of each others' presence. A foreign play previously produced in London.

* Follies (66). Musical with book by James Goldman; music and lyrics by Stephen Sondheim. Produced by Harold Prince in association with Ruth Mitchell at the Winter Garden. Opened April 4, 1971.

Major-Domo	Dick Latessa	Theodore Whitman	Charles Welch
Sally Durant Plummer	Dorothy Collins	Vincent	Victor Griffin
Young Sally	Marti Rolph	Vanessa	Jayne Turner
Christine Crane	Ethel Barrymore Colt	Young Vincent	Michael Misita
Willy Wheeler	Fred Kelly	Young Vanessa	Graciela Daniele
Stella Deems	Mary McCarty	Solange LaFitte	Fifi D'Orsay
Max Deems	John J. Martin	Carlotta Campion	Yvonne De Carlo
Heidi Schiller	Justine Johnston	Phyllis Rogers Stone	Alexis Smith
Chauffeur	John Grigas	Benjamin Stone	John McMartin
Meredith Lane	Sheila Smith	Young Phyllis	Virginia Sandifur
Chet Richards	Peter Walker	Young Ben	Kurt Peterson
Roscoe	Michael Bartlett	Buddy Plummer	Gene Nelson
Deedee West	Helon Blount	Young Buddy	Harvey Evans
Sandra Donovan	Sonja Levkova	Dimitri Weismann	Arnold Moss
Hattie Walker	Ethel Shutta	Kevin	Ralph Nelson
Young Hattie	Mary Jane Houdina	Young Heidi	Victoria Mallory
Emily Whitman	Marcie Stringer		

Party Musicians: Taft Jordan, Aaron Bell, Charles Spies, Robert Curtis. Showgirls: Suzanne Briggs, Trudy Carson, Kathie Dalton, Ursula Maschmeyer, Linda Perkins, Margot Travers. Singers and Dancers: Graciela Daniele, Mary Jane Houdina, Rita O'Connor, Julie Pars, Suzanne Rogers, Roy Barry, Steve Boockvor, Michael Misita, Joseph Nelson, Ralph Nelson, Ken Urmston, Donald Weissmuller.

Standbys: Misses Smith, De Carlo, D'Orsay—Sheila Smith; Mr. Moss—Edwin Steffe.

Understudies: Gene Nelson—Dick Latessa; Misses Collins, Johnston—Ethel Barrymore Colt; Mr. McMartin—Peter Walker; Misses Colt, Shutta, McCarty—Helon Blount; Messrs. Steffe, Welch, Latessa—Fred Kelly; Mr. Griffin—Donald Weissmuller; Miss Turner—Sonja Levkova.

Directed by Harold Prince and Michael Bennett; choreography, Michael Bennett; musical direction, Harold Hastings; scenery, Boris Aronson; costumes, Florence Klotz; lighting, Tharon Musser; orchestrations, Jonathan Tunick; dance music arrangements, John Berkman; production stage manager, Fritz Holt; stage manager, George Martin; press, Mary Bryant, Stanley F. Kaminsky, Sadie Stein.

Time: Tonight. Place: At a party on the stage of the Weismann Theater. The play was presented without intermission.

Reunion of Follies girls on the stage of a crumbling theater causes the leading characters to examine themselves and their lives—what they think they want and what they really want, who they think they are and who they really are—with pretenses ironically stripped away in a final "Loveland" sequence.

A Best Play; see page 251

MUSICAL NUMBERS

"Beautiful Girls" ....Roscoe, Company
"Don't Look at Me" ....Sally, Ben
"Waiting for the Girls Upstairs" ....Buddy, Ben, Phyllis, Sally, Young Buddy, Young Ben, Young Phyllis, Young Sally
"Rain on the Roof" ....The Whitmans
"Ah, Paris!" ....Solange
"Broadway Baby" ....Hattie
"The Road You Didn't Take" ....Ben
"Bolero d'Amour" ....Vincent, Vanessa
"In Buddy's Eyes" ....Sally
"Who's That Woman?" ....Stella, Company
"I'm Still Here" ....Carlotta
"Too Many Mornings" ....Ben, Sally
"The Right Girl" ....Buddy
"One More Kiss" ....Heidi, Young Heidi
"Could I Leave You?" ....Phyllis

Loveland

1—The Folly of Love
"Loveland" ....Ensemble
(The Spirit of First Love—Kathie Dalton; The Spirit of Young Love—Margot Travers; The Spirit of True Love—Suzanne Briggs; The Spirit of Pure Love—Trudy Carson; The Spirit of Romantic Love—Linda Perkins; The Spirit of Eternal Love—Ursula Maschmeyer)
2—The Folly of Youth (Scene: A bower in Loveland)
"You're Gonna Love Tomorrow" ....Ben, Phyllis
"Love Will See Us Through" ....Buddy, Sally
3—Buddy's Folly (Scene: A thoroughfare in Loveland)
"The God-Why-Don't-You-Love-Me Blues" ....Buddy
(With Suzanne Rogers, Rita O'Connor)
4—Sally's Folly (Scene: A boudoir in Loveland)
"Losing My Mind" ....Sally
5—Phyllis's Folly (Scene: A honky-tonk in Loveland)
"The Story of Lucy and Jessie" ....Phyllis, Dancing Ensemble
6—Ben's Folly (Scene: A supper club in Loveland)
"Live, Laugh, Love" ....Ben, Dancing Ensemble

Johnny Johnson (1). Musical revival with book and lyrics by Paul Green; music by Kurt Weill. Produced by Timothy Gray and Robert Fletcher in association with

Midge La Guardia at the Edison Theater (Limited Broadway). Opened and closed at the evening performance, April 11, 1971.

Johnny Johnson ....Ralph Williams
Minny Belle Tompkins ....Alice Cannon
Mayor; Pvt. Fairfax; Amer. Cmdr.;
  Brother Thomas ....Paul Michael
Miz Smith; French Nurse ....June Helmers
Photographer; Sniper ....Bob Lydiard
Messenger; How-
  ington Jr. ....Christopher Klein
Grandpa Joe; Pvt. Goldberger; Chief;
  Dr. Mahodan ....James Billings
Howington; Pvt. Harwood ...Gordon Minard
Aggie; Sister; Miss Newro ...Charlotte Jones
Capt. Valentine ....Norman Chase

Dr. McBray; Pvt. O'Day; Scottish Col.;
  German Priest; Secretary .Wayne Sherwood
Pvt. Jessell; Pvt. Svenson; Orderly;
  British Cmdr.; Lieutenant; M.P.;
  Brother George ....Clay Johns
Recruiting Sgt.; Cpl. George; Belgian
  Maj. Gen.; Captain;
  Dr. Frewd ....Alexander Orfaly
Goddess of Liberty ....Nadine Lewis
Eng. Sgt.; Doctor; French Maj. Gen.;
  Amer. Priest;
  Brother William ....Norman Riggins

Wounded French Soldiers: Wayne Sherwood, Clay Johns, Alexander Orfaly, James Billings, Paul Michael. Villagers: Entire Company.

Directed by José Quintero; choreography, Bertram Ross; musical direction, Joseph Klein; scenery, Peter Harvey; costumes, Robert Fletcher; lighting, Roger Morgan; orchestrations, Kurt Weill; production stage manager, Jamie Howard; press, Howard Atlee, David Roggensack, Irene Gandy.

Johnny Johnson was first presented on Broadway by the Group Theater 11/19/36 for 68 performances and was named a Best Play of its year. It was revived off Broadway in the seasons of 1940-41 and 1956-57.

ACT I

Introduction ....Orchestra
"Over in Europe" ....Mayor
"Democracy's Call" ....Minny Belle, Mayor, Company
"Up Chuckamauga Hill" ....Grandpa Joe
"Johnny's Melody" ....Johnny
"Aggie's Song" ....Aggie
"Oh Heart of Love" ....Minny Belle
"Farewell, Goodbye" ....Minny Belle
"The Sergeant's Chant" ....Recruiting Sgt.
"Valentine's Tango" ....Capt. Valentine
"You're in the Army Now" (Interlude) ....Orchestra
"Johnny's Oath" ....Orchestra
"Song of the Goddess" ....Goddess of Liberty
"Song of the Wounded Frenchmen" and "Tea Song"
"Cowboy Song" ....Pvt. Harwood
"Johnny's Dream" ....Minny Belle
"Song of the Guns"
"Music of the Striken Redeemer" ....Orchestra

ACT II

"Army Song" (Entr'act)
"Mon Ami My Friend" ....French Nurse
"Allied High Command," "The Laughing Generals" and "The Battle"
"Prayer: In Times of War and Tumults" ....American & German Priests
"No Man's Land" ....Orchestra
"Song of the Goddess" (Reprise) ....Goddess of Liberty
"The Psychiatry Song" ....Dr. Mahodan
"Hymn to Peace" ....Asylum Inmates
"Johnny Johnson's Song" and "How Sweetly Friendship Binds"
"Oh Heart of Love" (Reprise) ....Minny Belle
"Johnny's Melody" (Finale) ....Johnny

70, Girls, 70 (36). Musical with book by Fred Ebb and Norman L. Martin; adaptation by Joseph Masteroff; music by John Kander; lyrics by Fred Ebb. Produced by Arthur Whitelaw in association with Seth Harrison at the Broadhurst Theater. Opened April 15, 1971. (Closed May 15, 1971)

Thomas Anderson	Lucie Lancaster
Tommy Breslin	Marjorie Leach
Hans Conried	Abby Lewis
Robert G. Dare	Steve Mills
Sally De May	Mildred Natwick
Joey Faye	Naomi Price
Dorothea Freitag	Lillian Roth
Ruth Gillette	Goldye Shaw
Lloyd Harris	Beau Tilden
Lillian Hayman	Bobbi Tremain
Henrietta Jacobson	Jay Velie
Gil Lamb	Coley Worth

Standbys: Misses Natwick, Roth—Nancy Andrews; Miss Freitag—Karen Gustafson. Principal understudies: Mr. Conried—Coley Worth; Mr. Lamb—Joey Faye; Miss Hayman—Naomi Price; Miss Lancaster— Abby Lewis; Miss Shaw—Henrietta Jacobson; Mr. Faye—Robert G. Dare.

Directed by Paul Aaron; dances and musical numbers staged by Onna White; entire production supervised by Stanley Prager; musical direction and vocal arrangements, Oscar Kosarin; scenery and lighting, Robert Randolph; costumes, Jane Greenwood; orchestrations, Don Walker; dance music, Dorothea Freitag; assistant musical director, Karen Gustafson; associate choreographer, Martin Allen; production stage manager, Edwin P. Aldridge; stage manager, Victor Straus; press, Max Eisen, Warren Pincus.

Story parallels the movie *Make Mine Mink;* a group of elderly adventurers in a West Side New York old folks' home organize themselves into a gang of thieves to steal from the haves and distribute their loot to the have-nots.

ACT I

Prologue
"Old Folks" ....Company
Scene 1: The Cornucopia Tea Room
"Home" ....Mildred Natwick, Lillian Roth, Lucie Lancaster, Gil Lamb,
Hans Conried, Lillian Hayman, Goldye Shaw
Scene 2: The Broadhurst Theater
"Broadway My Street" ..Misses Hayman, Shaw; Thomas Anderson, Joey Faye, Lloyd Harris,
Henrietta Jacobson, Beau Tilden, Bobbi Tremain, Jay Velie, Coley Worth
Scene 3: Ida's room
Scene 4: The Broadhurst Theater
"The Caper" ....Conried
Scene 5: Sadie's Fur Salon
Scene 6: The Broadhurst Theater
"Coffee in a Cardboard Cup" ....Misses Hayman, Shaw
Scene 7: Lobby of the Sussex Arms
"You and I, Love" ....Steve Mills, Abby Lewis, Anderson, Harris, Velie,
Worth, Ruth Gillette, Miss Tremain
"Do We?" ....Miss Lancaster, Lamb
"Hit It, Lorraine" ....Misses Natwick, Roth, Lancaster, Dorothea Freitag, Conried
Scene 8: The Broadhurst Theater
Scene 9: Bloomingdale's
"See the Light" ....Miss Roth, Faye, Worth, Anderson, Velie

ACT II

Entr'Acte ....Miss Gillette, Faye, Harris, Velie
Scene 1: The Broadhurst Theater
"Boom Ditty Boom" ....Misses Natwick, Roth, Hayman, Lancaster, Shaw,
Messrs. Conried, Lamb

Scene 2: Arctic Cold Storage Co.
"Believe" ....Misses Hayman, Natwick, Roth, Lancaster, Shaw; Messrs. Conried, Lamb
Scene 3: The Broadhurst Theater
"Go Visit" ....Breslin, Miss Jacobson
Scene 4: Lobby of the Sussex Arms
"70, Girls, 70" ....Company
Scene 5: The Broadhurst Theater
"The Elephant Song" ....Misses Natwick, Hayman, Shaw
Scene 6: The Coliseum
Scene 7: The Broadhurst Theater
Scene 8: A Chapel
"Yes" ....Miss Natwick, Company

Frank Merriwell, or Honor Challenged (1). Musical with book by Skip Redwine, Larry Frank and Heywood Gould; music and lyrics by Skip Redwine and Larry Frank. Produced by Sandy Farber and Stanley Barnett in association with Nate Friedman at the Longacre Theater. Opened and closed at the evening performance, April 24, 1971.

Clyde	J.J. Jepson	Mrs. Snodd	Liz Sheridan
Ned	Larry Ross	Esther Carmichael	Jennifer Williams
Hugh	Walter Bobbie	Bart Hodge	Peter Shawn
Belinda Bell Snodd	Neva Small	Tad Jones	Gary Keith Steven
Snella Jean	Lori Cesar	Frank Merriwell	Larry Ellis
Una Marie	Ellie Smith	Inza Burrage	Linda Donovan
Professor Burrage	Thomas Ruisinger	Manuel	Bill Hinnant

Directed and choreographed by Neal Kenyon; musical direction and vocal arrangements, Jack Lee; scenery, Tom John; costumes, Frank Thompson; lighting, John Gleason; orchestrations, Arnold Goland; conducting and dance arrangements, Jack Holmes; associate producer, Aaron Ziegelman; assistant choreographer, Bonnie Ano; production stage manager, Don Lamb; stage manager, James Bernardi; press, Seymour Krawitz, Martin Shwartz, Patricia McLean Krawitz.

Story of an American college hero circa 1896, based on *Frank Merriwell's School Days* by Burt L. Standish (Gilbert Patten) whose series of Frank Merriwell novels and short stories about a high-minded and heroic young man were read by millions.

PART I

Chapter I: The Blow of a Coward—Fardale train station
"There's no School Like Our School" ....Students, Local Girls
"Howdy, Mr. Sunshine" ....Frank, Tad
Chapter 2: Death at the Picnic—Picnic grounds
"Prim and Proper" ....Students, Local Girls
"Inza" ....Frank
Chapter 3: Explosion in Tunnel G—Fardale caves
Chapter 4: War!—Mrs. Snodd's Boarding House
"Look for the Happiness Ahead" ....Frank, All
Chapter 5: The Spanish Spy—Professor's laboratory
Chapter 6: By Fair Means or Foul—Mrs. Snodd's Boarding House
"I'd Be Crazy to Be Crazy Over You" ....Belinda Belle, Bart
Chapter 7: Terror at the Junction—Picnic grounds
"Now It's Fall" ....Students
"The Fallin'-Out-of-Love Rag" ....Belinda, Students, Local Girls, Frank

PART II

Chapter 1: A Hatred Grows—Picnic grounds
"Frank, Frank, Frank" ....All
Chapter 2: Waterloo—On the campus
"In Real Life" ....Frank
"The Broadway of My Heart" ....Professor, Mrs. Snodd

Chapter 3: Into the Enemy's Hands—Picnic grounds
"Winter's Here" ....Students
"The Pure in Heart" ....Frank, All
"I Must Be Crazy" (Reprise) ....Belinda
"Don't Turn His Picture to the Wall" ....Tad, Students, Local Girls
Chapter 4: Frank Is Missing—Burrage front porch
Chapter 5: Death by Dynamite—Fardale caves
"Manuel Your Friend" ....Manuel
"The Pure in Heart" (Reprise) ....Frank, All
"Look for the Happiness Ahead" (Reprise) ....Finale

Dance of Death (5). Revival of the play by August Strindberg; adapted by Paul Avila Mayer. Produced by Leo Kerz, Allan Pepper and Stanley Snadowsky at the Ritz Theater. Opened April 28, 1971. (Closed May 1, 1971)

Edgar	Rip Torn	Kurt	Michael Strong
Alice	Viveca Lindfors	Lieutenant	Robert O'Herron

Directed by Alfred Ryder; scenery and lighting, Leo Kerz; costumes, Marjorie Slaiman; technical director, James Hamilton; produced in association with Portales Productions, Inc.; production stage manager, William Dodds; stage manager, Robert O'Herron; press, David Lipsky, Joel Dein.

Strindberg's play *The Dance of Death* (the title commonly carries the definite article) was last revived 9/13/60 for 13 productions off Broadway, in an adaptation by John Bowman who directed and co-produced.

Earl of Ruston (5). Musical with book and lyrics by C.C. Courtney and Ragan Courtney; music by Peter Link. Produced by David Black at the Billy Rose Theater. Opened May 5, 1971. (Closed May 8, 1971)

Earl	C.C. Courtney, Ragan Courtney	Rhythm Guitar	Chip McDonald
Leda Pearl Crump	Jean Waldo Beck	Doctor; Drums	Bobby Thomas
Leecy R. Woods Moore	Herself	Ernestine	Lynda Lawley
Sherriff; Bass Guitar	Leon Medica	Mary Lee Woods	Bonnie Guidry
Mr. Turner; Lead Guitar	Bootsie Normand	Piano	John Bergeron
Rev. Reynolds;			

Standby: Messrs. Courtney—Terry Mace.

Directed by C.C. Courtney; music played by Goatleg; production designed by Neil Peter Jampolis; production manager, Martin Herzer; stage manager, Alvarez Kelly; press, Betty Lee Hunt associates, Henry Luhrman.

Country rock musical based on the true story of the Courtneys' cousin Earl Woods, an eccentric who lived some of his life in mental institutions and died young. The musical was presented without intermission.

MUSICAL NUMBERS: "Just Your Old Friend," "Earl Is Crazy," "Guitar Song," "Easy to Be Lonely," "Standing," "Der Blues—Traditional," "Probably" (music by C.C. and Ragan Courtney), "Mama, Earl Done Ate the Tooth Paste Again" (music by C.C. Courtney), "Silvers Theme," "Mama, Mama, Mama," "I've Been Sent Back to the First Grade" (music by C.C. Courtney), "The Revival," "My Name is Leda Pearl" (music by C.C. Courtney), "Insane Poontang" (music by C.C. and Ragan Courtney), "You Still Love Me" (music by C.C. Courtney), "Earl Was Ahead."

Scratch (4). By Archibald MacLeish; suggested by Steven Vincent Benet's short story *The Devil and Daniel Webster*. Produced by Stuart Ostrow at the St. James Theater. Opened May 6, 1971. (Closed May 8, 1971)

Jabez Stone	Will Mackenzie	Susan	Joanne Nail
Daniel Webster	Patrick Magee	Porter Wright	Rex Robbins
Scratch	Will Geer	Seth Peterson	Roy Poole
Forbes	Daniel Keyes	Judge Hathorne	Thomas Barbour
Mrs. Forbes	Mary Loane		

Farm Hands and Jury: Robert Baines, Philip Carling, Dominic Chianese, John Coe, William Francis, Walter Gorney, Richard Hamilton, Peter Harris, Dino Laudicina, Garnett Smith.

Principal understudies: Mr. Mackenzie—Rex Robbins; Mr. Poole—Daniel Keyes; Farm Hands and Jury—Peter Blaxill.

Directed by Peter H. Hunt; scenery, John Conklin; costumes, Patricia Zipprodt; lighting, Feder; production stage manager, Mark Healy; press, Harvey B. Sabinson, Lee Solters, Cheryl Sue Dolby.

Time: 1850. Place: New England. Scene 1 (following Prologue): The kitchen of Daniel Webster's farmhouse at Marshfield, Mass., dawn of a day in late July. Scene 2: The elms outside Webster's farm house, high noon of the same day. Scene 3: The bar-way of a field in Jabez Stone's farm at Cross Corners, N.H., sunset of the same day. Scene 4: Interior of Jabez Stone's barn at Cross Corners, night, the same day. The play was presented in two parts with intermission following Scene 3.

Struggle between the Devil and Daniel Webster for the soul of a New Hampshire farmer at a mock trial, with overtones of the modern political problem of preserving individual liberty and at the same time preserving the Union.

* **Lenny** (5). By Julian Barry; music by Tom O'Horgan; based on the life and words of Lenny Bruce. Produced by Jules Fisher, Marvin Worth and Michael Butler at the Brooks Atkinson Theater. Opened May 26, 1971.

Lenny Bruce ....Cliff Gorman
Judges; Sherman Hart; General; Vampire
Priest; Plainclothesman; Mr. Wollenstein;
Photographer ....Joe Silver
Sally; Primitive Mother; Gypsy Woman;
Phone Operator ....Erica Yohn
Rusty ....Jane House
Arty; Igor; Hitler; Southern Gentleman;
Photographer ....Johnny Armen
Juan; Primitive Drummer; Snoopy;
Cop ....Marker Bloomst
Trumpet; Sailor;
Nod Out ....Vaughn De Forest
Mema; Stripper; Sister Theophane;
Lucille; R.C. Lady; Matron;
Southern Lady ....Jeannette Ertelt
Bass; *Life* Reporter; Cop .....Ernie Furtado

Trombone; Nod Out ....John Gordon
Ernie; Kiki; Student;
Interviewer ....Paul Lieber
Piano; D.A.; Old Leper; Lenny's Lawyer;
Eichman ....Warren Meyers
Reeds; Sailor; Nod Out ....Ron Odrich
Primitive Daughter; Girl in Wheel Chair;
Little Girl at Pool ....Jody Oliver
Stripper; Singer; Mrs. Hart; Secretary; Girl
Without I.D. Card ....Melody Santangelo
Drums; Cop ....Bill Smith
Clubowner; Primitive Father; Lenny's
Father; Ike; Blah, blah Judge; D.A.;
Photographer ....Robert Weil
Cop; Witch Doctor; Chinese Waiter; Sophie
Tucker; Bishop ....James Wigfall

Primitives, Lepers, Puppets, Acolytes, Jurors, Night Club Audiences, Stoned People, etc., played by the Company.

Principal Understudies: Mr. Gorman—Johnny Armen; Mr. Silver—Robert Weil; Misses Yohn, Santangelo—Jeannette Ertelt; Misses House, Ertelt—Melody Santangelo; Mr. Armen—Paul Lieber; Messrs. Weil, Wigfall—Warren Meyers.

Directed by Tom O'Horgan; scenery, Robin Wagner; lighting, Jules Fisher; costumes, Randy Barcelo; production manager, Richard Scanga; stage manager, Galen McKinley; press, Gifford/Wallace Inc.

Dramatization of episodes of marriage, obscenity trials, etc. in Lenny Bruce's life, especially a reenactment of many of his night club routines satirizing hypocrisy, religious dogma, false modesty, etc., partly based on the book *The Essential Lenny Bruce*.

PLAYS WHICH CLOSED
PRIOR TO BROADWAY OPENING

Plays which were organized in New York for Broadway presentation, but which closed during their tryout performances, are listed below.

Prettybelle. Musical based on the novel *Prettybelle* by Jean Arnold; book and lyrics by Bob Merrill; music by Jule Styne. Produced by Alexander H. Cohen in a Gower

Champion production in a pre-Broadway tryout at the Shubert Theater in Boston.
Opened February 1, 1971. (Closed March 6, 1971)

Henry Baines ....William Larsen
Sybil Mae Asch ......Barbara Ann Walters
Prettybelle Sweet ....Angela Lansbury
Nurse; 1st GoGo Girl;
    Baby Doll ....Susan Plantt
Nurse; 2d GoGo Girl;
    Waitress ....Linda Lubera
Doctor Dimmer;
    Magistrate ....Richard Kuss
Mayor; Pool Hall Mexican; Sheriff;
    1st TV Interviewer ....Chad Block
Mother Sweet ....Charlotte Rae
Lovey Sweet ....Renee Lippin
John Sweet ....Dean Crane Jr.
Ray Schaeffer ....Jon Cypher
Willy Thomas ....Joe Morton
Cully Hart ....Igors Gavon

Huey Lipscomb;
    Sheriff ....Robert Karl
Bubba Rawlings ....Jan Leighton
Boy Scout ....Brian Hall
Folksinger ....Michael Jason
Leroy Sweet ....Mark Dawson
3d GoGo Girl; Marie;
    Waitress ....Christine Cooper
Bouncer; Japanese Gardens Waiter; Sheriff;
    2d TV Interviewer ....Joe Milan
Mason Miller ....Peter Lombard
Jesus ....Bert Michaels
Motel Clerk ....George Blackwell
Juan Lopez ....Bobby Lee
Bud Michaels ....Sean Walsh
Rose Anson ....Maggie Task
Pickett Webster ....Howard Porter

Directed by Gower Champion; musical direction and incidental music arrangement, Peter
Howard; scenery, Oliver Smith; costumes, Ann Roth; lighting, Nananne Porcher; orchestra-
tions, Elliot Lawrence, Jack Cortner; associate producer, Hildy Parks; production supervisor,
Jerry Adler; production stage manager, Marnel Sumner; stage manager, Edward Julien; press,
James D. Proctor, Bob Ullman, Richard Hummler.

A Southern widow, upon finding that her husband was a bigot, sets out to right the wrongs
done to her community.

ACT I

Scene 1: Newspaper office
 "Piciyumi Gazette" ....Prettybelle, Baines, Sybil Mae
 "Manic Depressives" ....Prettybelle
Scene 2: Cemetery
 "Policeman's Hymn" ....Police Band
 "Prettybelle" ....Folksinger
Scene 3: New Orleans
 "You Ain't Hurtin' Your Ole Lady None" ....Leroy, Ray, Cully, Bubba, Huey
Scene 4: Go-Go-Dive
Scene 5: The living room
 "To a Small Degree" ....Prettybelle
 "Back From the Great Beyond" ....Leroy
Scene 6: Poolroom
Scene 7: Mason Miller's office
 "How Could I know What Was Goin' On?" ....Prettybelle
Scene 8: The kitchen
 "I Never Did Imagine" ....Prettybelle, Jesus
Scene 9: The nightmare
 "New Orleans Poon" ....Mother Sweet
Scene 10: The Japanese Gardens
 "In the Japanese Gardens" ....Prettybelle
 "An Individual Thing" ....Mason
Scene 11: On the way home
 "I Met a Man" ....Prettybelle
 "Prettybelle" (Reprise) ....Folksinger

ACT II

Scene 1: Newspaper office
Scene 2: The No-Tell Motel
 "The No-Tell Motel" ....Prettybelle, Company
Scene 3: The living room

Scene 4: Lapeer Street
"I'm in a Tree" ....Prettybelle
Scene 5: The living room
"When I'm Drunk" ....Prettybelle
"Give Me a Share in America" ....Willy
Scene 6: Newspaper office
"Prettybelle" (Reprise; finale) ....Prettybelle, Folksinger

Lolita, My Love. Musical based on the novel *Lolita* by Vladimir Nabokov; book and lyrics by Alan Jay Lerner; music by John Barry. Produced by Norman Twain in a pre-Broadway tryout at the Shubert Theater in Philadelphia February 15, 1971 (closed for additional rehearsals). Reopened at the Shubert Theater in Boston March 18, 1971. (Closed March 27, 1971)

Claire Quilty	Leonard Frey	1st Bellboy	John Mineo
Vivian Darkbloom	Velerie Camille	2d Bellboy	Irwin Pearl
Humbert Humbert	John Neville	Miss Amy Pratt	Gretel Cummings
Charlotte Haze	Dorothy Louden	Miss Cormorant	Jacque Dean
Lolita	Denise Nickerson	Mona Dahl	Jill Streisant
Rev. Dr. Neiling	Josh Wheeler	Max Brogan	Neil McNelis
Young Man	Lance Westergard	Bill Crest	Daniel Walsh
Neighbor	David Thomas	Patrolman Power	Adam Petroski
Mr. Bliss; Dick Schiller	John Witham	Patrolman Steel	Frank Bouley

Singing Ensemble: Frank Bouley, Jacqueline Britt, Walter P. Brown, Rhoda Butler, Jacque Dean, Lynn East, Linda Ellis, Robert Hultman, Jacqueline Johnson, Neil McNelis, Irwin Pearl, Adam Petroski, Meg Scanlan, Fran Stevens, David Thomas, Trudy Wallace, Daniel Walsh, John Wheeler, John Witham.

Dancing Ensemble: Velerie Camille, Carol Conte, Larry Grenier, Mickey Gunnerson, Carolin Kirsch, John Mineo, Jo Anne Ogawa, Pamela Peadon, Don Percassi, Rosalin Ricci, Patrick Spohn, Jill Streisant, Lance Westergard, Lee Wilson.

Directed by Noel Willman; choreography, Dan Siretta; musical direction and vocal arrangements, Herbert Grossman; scenery, Ming Cho Lee; costumes, Jose Varona; lighting, Jules Fisher; orchestrations, Eddie Sauter; dance arrangements, John Morris; audio, Jack Shearing; associate producer, Stone Widney; production associate, Larry Coleman; stage manager, Steve Zweigbaum; press, Frank Goodman, Les Schecter.

Act I, Scene 1: Casa Q, Elphinstone, Arizona, lately. Scene 2: The home of Mrs. Charlotte Haze, Ramsdale, Vt., three years earlier. Scene 3: Humbert's bedroom, one week later. Scene 4: The Haze back yard, one week later. Scene 5: Humbert's bedroom, ten days later. Scene 6: The back yard, one week later. Scene 7: The Haze-Humbert living room, three weeks later. Scene 8: The living room, two days later.

Act 2, Scene 1: The lobby of the Bed-D-By Motel, Mohawk Valley, the following day. Scene 2: Room 342 in the Bed-D-By Motel, immediately following. Scene 3: The park at Beardsley, Ohio, the following spring. Scene 4: The Humbert living room, Beardsley, four weeks later. Scene 5: From Ohio to Arizona. Scene 6: The park at Beardsley, lately. Scene 7: Mulligan's Trailer Camp, Kansas City, two days later.

Musical stage version of Nabokov's novel about a middle-aged man's infatuation with a "nymphet."

ACT I

"If It Ain't Fun" ....Quilty, Friends
"I Found You at Last" ....Humbert
"The Same Old Song" ....Charlotte, Lolita
"Saturday" ....Lolita
"In the Broken Promise Land of Fifteen" ....Humbert
"The Same Old Song" (Reprise) ....Charlotte, Lolita, Humbert
"Dante, Petrarch and Poe" ....Humbert, Quilty, Charlotte, Guests
"Sur les Quais" ....Charlotte
"Charlotte's Letter" ....Humbert, Charlotte, Choir
"Farewell, Little Dream" ....Humbert
Finale

ACT II

"At the Bed-D-By Motel" ....Mr. Bliss, Quilty, Conventioneers
"Tell Me. Tell Me" ....Humbert
"Buckin' for Beardsley" ....Humbert
"Beardsley School for Girls" ....Students
"I Always Believe Me" ....Students
"Farewell, Little Dream" (Reprise) ....Quilty
"All You Can Do Is Tell Me You Love Me" ....Humbert
"How Far Is It to the Next Town" ....Lolita
"How Far Is It to the Next Town" (Reprise) ....Humbert
"How Far Is It to the Next Town" (Reprise) ....Humbert, Lolita, Ensemble
"Lolita" ....Humbert
Finale ....Humbert

PLAYS PRODUCED
OFF BROADWAY

Some distinctions between off-Broadway and Broadway productions at one end of the scale and off-off-Broadway productions at the other end were beginning to blur in the New York theater of the 1970s. For the purposes of this *Best Plays* listing, the term "off Broadway" signifies a show other than a Broadway or Limited Broadway show which opened for general audiences in a Manhattan theater during the time period covered by this volume and 1) employed an Equity cast, 2) planned a regular schedule of 7 or 8 performances a week and 3) offered itself to public comment by critics at opening performances. Occasional exceptions are made to include visiting troupes and also to include a few non-qualifying productions which readers might expect to find in this list because they appear under the off-Broadway heading in other major sources of record. Such exceptions are always labeled "off off Broadway" in the entry's notes.

Figures in parentheses following a play's title indicate number of performances. These figures are acquired directly from the production office in each case and do not include previews or extra non-profit performances.

Plays marked with an asterisk (*) were still running on June 1, 1971. Their number of performances is figured from opening night through May 31, 1971.

In a listing of a show's numbers—dances, sketches, musical scenes, etc.— the titles of songs are identified by their appearance in quotation marks (").

Most entries of off-Broadway productions that ran fewer than 20 performances are somewhat abbreviated.

HOLDOVERS FROM PREVIOUS SEASONS

Plays which were running on June 1, 1970 are listed below. More detailed information about them appears in previous *Best Plays* volumes of appropriate years. Important cast changes are recorded in a section of this volume.

* The Fantasticks (4,605; longest continuous run of record in the American theater). Musical suggested by the play *Les Romantiques* by Edmond Rostand; book and lyrics by Tom Jones; music by Harvey Schmidt. Opened May 3, 1960.

You're a Good Man Charlie Brown (1,597). Musical based on the comic strip "Peanuts" by Charles M. Schulz; book, music and lyrics by Clark Gesner. Opened March 7, 1967. (Closed February 14, 1971)

* Jacques Brel Is Alive and Well and Living in Paris (1,391). Cabaret revue with music by Jacques Brel; production conception, English lyrics, additional material by Eric Blau and Mort Shuman; based on lyrics and commentary by Jacques Brel. Opened January 22, 1968.

The Boys in the Band (1,000). By Mart Crowley. Opened April 15, 1968. (Closed September 6, 1970)

Adaptation by Elaine May and **Next** by Terrence McNally (707). Opened February 10, 1969. (Closed October 18, 1970)

Oh! Calcutta! (704). Opened June 17, 1969. (Closed off Broadway February 21, 1971 and moved to the Belasco Theater; see its entry in the "Plays Produced on Broadway" section of this volume)

No Place to Be Somebody (312). Revival of the play by Charles Gordone. Opened January 20, 1970 following original off-Broadway run of 252 performances and special Broadway engagement of 16 performances; see entries in previous *Best Plays* volumes. (Closed October 18, 1970)

The Last Sweet Days of Isaac (485). Musical with book and lyrics by Gretchen Cryer; music by Nancy Ford. Opened January 26, 1970. (Closed May 2, 1971)

Joy (208). Musical revue by Oscar Brown Jr. Opened January 27, 1970. (Closed July 26, 1970).

Dark of the Moon (86). Revival of the play by Howard Richardson and William Berney. Opened April 3, 1970. (Closed June 14, 1970)

* The Effect of Gamma Rays on Man-in-the-Moon Marigolds (421). By Paul Zindel. Opened April 7, 1970.

New York Shakespeare Festival Public Theater. Indoor schedule of three musicals (see entry in 1969-70 *Best Plays* volume) concluded with **Mod Donna** (56). Musical with book and lyrics by Myrna Lamb, music by Susan Hulsman Bingham. Opened April 24, 1970. (Closed June 7, 1970)

The American Place Theater. Schedule of four programs (see entry in 1969-70 *Best Plays* volume) concluded with **The Pig Pen** (46). By Ed Bullins. Opened April 29, 1970. (Closed June 6, 1970)

What the Butler Saw (224). By Joe Orton. Opened May 4, 1970. (Closed November 15, 1970)

Colette (101). By Elinor Jones; adapted from *Earthly Paradise,* the Robert Phelps collection of Colette's autobiographical writings; original music by Harvey Schmidt; lyrics by Tom Jones. Opened May 6, 1970. (Closed August 2, 1970; reopened October 14, 1970—see entry in the "Plays Produced off Broadway" section of this volume)

Room Service (71). Revival of the play by John Murray and Allen Boretz. Opened May 12, 1970. (Closed July 11, 1970)

Slow Dance on the Killing Ground (36). Revival of the play by William Hanley. Opened May 13, 1970. (Closed June 14, 1970)

The Me Nobody Knows (208). Musical with book by Stephen M. Joseph; edited from the book *The Me Nobody Knows;* music by Gary William Friedman; lyrics by Will Holt; original idea by Herb Schapiro. Opened May 18, 1970. (Closed November 15, 1970 and reopened on Broadway; see its entry in the "Plays Produced on Broadway" section of this volume)

The Negro Ensemble Company. Schedule of three programs (see entry in 1969-70 *Best Plays* volume) concluded with **Akokawe** (44). Dramatized presentation of traditional and modern African writings selected by Afolabi Ajayi. Opened May 19, 1970. (Closed June 28, 1970)

Chicago 70 (24). Play improvised by the Toronto Workshop Company; based on transcripts of the Chicago 8 conspiracy trial and *Alice's Adventures in Wonderland* by Lewis Carroll; Imperialist Units (interpolations) by Brent Larson. Opened May 25, 1970. (Closed June 14, 1970)

The Open Theater. Repertory of two new plays and one revival. **Terminal** (9). Collective work created by The Open Theater Ensemble; text by Susan Yankowitz. Opened May 26, 1970. **The Serpent: A Ceremony** (3). Created by the Open Theater Ensemble; words and structure by Jean-Claude van Itallie. Opened May 29, 1970. **Endgame** (6). Revival of the play by Samuel Beckett. Opened May 30, 1970. (Repertory closed June 14, 1970)

Awake and Sing! (41) Revival of the play by Clifford Odets. Opened May 27, 1970. (Closed June 28, 1970)

Repertory Theater of Lincoln Center. Schedule of four programs (see entry in 1969-70 *Best Plays* volume) concluded with **Amphitryon** (28). By Peter Hacks; translated from the German by Ralph Manheim. Opened May 28, 1970. (Closed June 20, 1970)

PLAYS PRODUCED JUNE 1, 1970—MAY 31, 1971

The Nuns (1). By Eduardo Manet; adapted by Don Parker and Paul Verdier. Produced by Don Parker in association with Stanley J. Hatoff, production associate Sandra Berke, in a Westgate Production at the Cherry Lane Theater. Opened and closed at the evening performance, June 1, 1970.

Directed by Paul Verdier; scenery, Peter Harvey; costumes, Rita Riggs; lighting, F. Mitchell Dana; production stage manager, Elissa Lane; press, Betty Lee Hunt, Henry Luhrman. With Sydney Walker, Roy R. Scheider, Robert Brink, Maxine Herman.

Symbolical drama of three nuns in hiding during a 1791 revolution in Haiti. A foreign (Cuban) play previously produced in Paris and elsewhere.

Whispers on the Wind (15). Musical with book and lyrics by John B. Kuntz; music by Lor Crane. Produced by Bruce W. Paltrow and Mitchell Fink, by special arrangement with Lucille Lortel Productions, Inc., at Theater de Lys. Opened June 3, 1970. (Closed June 14, 1970)

Directed by Burt Brinckerhoff; musical director, Jack Holmes; scenery and lighting, David F. Segal; costumes, Joseph G. Aulisi; orchestrations and musical supervision, Arthur Rubinstein; musical consultant, Wally Harper; production stage manager, Iris O'Connor; press, Max Eisen. With David Cryer, Nancy Dussault, Patrick Fox, R.G. Brown, Mary Louise Wilson.

Folk rock musical biography of young Middle Westerner who succeeds in New York.

The Cage (126). By Rick Cluchey. Produced by David Carroll in the Barbwire Theater Production at the Playhouse Theater. Opened June 18, 1970. (Closed October 11, 1970)

Hatchet	Rick Cluchey	Jive	Randolph Dobbs
Al	Robert Poole	Guard Captain	Henry Everhart
Doc	Ernie Allen	Guard Lieutenant	Gene Ackley

Directed by Kenneth Kitch; scenery and lighting, Jonathan Stuart; production manager, Jonathan Stuart; press, Robert Ganshaw, John Prescott.

Drama of a young man's effort to accommodate himself to prison life, written by a parolee from a life sentence at San Quentin and acted by former inmates.

Boesman and Lena (205). By Athol Fugard. Produced by Circle in the Square, Theodore Mann and Paul Libin in association with John Berry, at Circle in the Square. Opened June 22, 1970. (Closed January 24, 1971)

Boesman	James Earl Jones	Old African	Zakes Mokae
Lena	Ruby Dee		

Directed by John Berry; scenery, Karl Eigsti; costumes, Margie Goldsmith; lighting, David F. Segal; production stage manager, Jan Moerel; press, Merle Debuskey, M.J. Boyer.

Time: The present. Place: The mud flats of the river Swartkops, South Africa, between the cities of Redhouse, Coegakop, Veeplaas, Missionvale, Kleinskool, Bethelsdorp, Swartkops and Korsten. The play was presented without intermission.

An itinerant black couple living surrounded by whites' cast-off junk strives for meaning and dignity in their existence. A foreign play previously produced in South Africa.

Zakes Mokae replaced James Earl Jones in the role of Boesman and Paul Benjamin replaced Zakes Mokae 10/6/70.

A Best Play; see page 107

New York Shakespeare Festival. Summer repertory of three outdoor revivals of plays by William Shakespeare under the series title "The Wars of the Roses." **The Chronicles of King Henry VI, Part 1** (18). Adapted from *Henry VI, Part 1* and *Henry VI, Part 2*. Opened June 23, 1970; see note. **The Chronicles of King Henry VI, Part 2** (17). Adapted from *Henry VI, Part 2* and *Henry VI, Part 3*. Opened June 24, 1970; see note. **Richard III** (20). Opened June 25; see note. Produced by New York Shakespeare Festival, Joseph Papp producer, Bernard Gersten associate producer, in cooperation with the City of New York, Hon. John V. Lindsay Mayor, Hon. August Heckscher Commissioner of Parks, at the Delacorte Theater in Central Park. (Repertory closed August 22, 1970)

PERFORMER	"CHRONICLES, PART 1"	"CHRONICLES, PART 2"	"RICHARD III"
David Aaron	Gunner's Son; 1st Prentice	Edmund Plantagenet	Prince of Wales
Gregory Abels	Somerset	Somerset; Oxford	Oxford
John Allee	York Messenger; Townsman	1st Gentleman; Messenger; Nobleman; Henry Richmond	1st Messenger
Rocky Anderson	1st Warder	Cade Rebel; Hugh Mortimer; Stanley; 1st Warwick Messenger	Blunt
Frank Borgman	Woodville; Sheriff	Clifford; Rivers	Rivers
Christopher Burgess	Fiend		
Robert Burr	Talbot		
Robert Benson Ross Burr			Duke of York
David Byrd	Bedford	Say; Hastings	Hastings

PERFORMER	"CHRONICLES, PART 1"	"CHRONICLES, PART 2"	"RICHARD III"
Brian Calloway	Talbot Messenger	2d Gentleman; Henry Messenger	2d Messenger
John Carpenter	Exeter	Exeter	Stanley
Barbara Caruso	Margaret	Margaret	Margaret
Gretchen Corbett	Joan La Pucelle		
Ronny Cox	Vernon; 1st Neighbor	Bevis; Sinkloe; Montague	Grey
John W. Davis	French Sgt.; Simpcox	Whitmore; Norfolk	Norfolk; Vaughan
James De Marse	1st Gloucester Man	1st Rebel; Tutor; 2d Watchman; Messenger	Ely Messenger
Charles Durning	Mayor of London	Cade	
Dan Durning	Hume	Clerk; Lewis XI; Mayor of York	Ely
Sarah Jane Eigerman	Fiend		
Patricia Falkenhain	Dame Eleanor		
Robert Gerringer	Humphrey	Humphrey; Montgomery	Buckingham
Howard Green	Buckingham	Buckingham; Brackenbury	Bra(c)kenbury
Mervyn Haines Jr.	Lawyer; Armorer	Dick	Ratcliff
Albert Hall	Talbot's Capt.; Stanley	Master; York Messenger	3d Messenger
Betty Henritze	Margaret Jourdain	Duchess of York	Duchess of York
Jeanne Hepple		Lady Grey (Queen Elizabeth)	Lady Grey (Queen Elizabeth)
Patrick Hines	Beaufort	Beaufort	
David Hooks	Warwick	Warwick	
James Keach	English Soldier; Beadle	Michael; 1st Watchman	Berkley
Nicholas Kepros	King Henry VI	King Henry VI	Henry VI Ghost
Kevin Kline		Huntsman; Soldier	Tressel
John LaGioia	Lord Salisbury; 2d Neighbor	Sea Capt.; Young Clifford	Surrey
Christopher Leahy	French Sentinel; Peter	Son That Has Killed His Father; 2d Messenger	Page
Donald Madden		Richard of Gloucester	Richard III
Susan McArthur			Lady Anne
Mike Moran	Basset; 3d Neighbor; 2d Petitioner	Holland; Humphrey (Keeper)	Scrivener
Fred Morsell	2d Gloucester Man; Legate; Post	Messengers to King, Warwick	
Moses		Huntsman's Dog	
William Myers	Earl of Salisbury	Earl of Salisbury	
Alexander Panas	Reignier	2d Murderer; Northumberland	Tyrell
Stuart Pankin	2d Warder; Southwell	Wm. Stafford; John Mortimer	Hastings Messenger; Herbert
Don Perkins	Dauphin	Smith; Young Somerset	Lovel
Jeff Peters	Porter; Mayor St. Albans; Master Gunner	Westmoreland; Humphrey Stafford	1st Citizen
Albert Quinton	Servingman; Shepherd; 1st Petitioner	Mate; Father That Has Killed His Son	Mayor of London
Peter Reznikoff	Countess Messenger	2d Rebel	Dorset
Leon Russom	Young Talbot	Prince of Wales	1st Murderer; Ghost of Prince Edward
Jack Ryland	De La Pole	De La Pole	Catesby
Tom Sawyer	Orleans	Edward IV	Edward IV
David Snell	Lucy; Bolingbroke	Iden	Richmond

PERFORMER	"CHRONICLES, PART 1"	"CHRONICLES, PART 2"	"RICHARD III"
Drew Snyder	Alencon	Clarence	Clarence
Paul Sparer	Richard Plantagenet	Richard Plantagenet	
George Spelvin	Gov. of Paris; 2d Prentice	1st Murderer; Gov. of Paris	2d Murderer
Anne Thompson	Wife to Simpcox	Bona	
Sasha von Scherler	Countess of Auvergne		
Sally Westerman	Fiend		Mistress Shore

Ensemble: JoAnne Astrow, Rennie Elmar, John Ferraro, David Guzman, Michael Hayes, Mark Robinson, Mark Russel, Kathy Sillaway, Stephen Snow, Rafael Triana, Erik White. Musicians: Donald Marcone, Allan J. Dean, Richard San Filippo.

ALL PLAYS: Directed by Stuart Vaughan; scenery, Ming Cho Lee; lighting, Martin Aronstein; costumes, Theoni V. Aldredge; music, John Corigliano; fights, James Sloyan; *Henry VI, Part 2* choreography, Diane Adler; production stage manager, R. Derek Swire; press, Merle Debuskey, Faith Geer.

Time: 15th Century. Place: France and England. The plays were presented one each evening in rotation, except that on 6/27/70 all three were given in a 12-hour, dusk-to-dawn continuous presentation, and on 7/25/70 the two parts of *The Chronicles of King Henry VI* were given in a continuous presentation.

The last New York production of *Richard III* was at the City Center 12/9/53 for 15 performances, with José Ferrer in the title role. The first professional New York production of record of *Henry VI* was the interpolation of four scenes into John Barrymore's *Richard III* 3/6/20. An excerpt from Part 3 was included in John Gielgud's program of Shakespeare selections *Ages of Man* in the seasons of 1958-59 and 1962-63, and excerpts were included in the off-Broadway production *The White Rose and the Red* 3/16/64 for 31 performances.

NOTE: In this volume, production companies like the New York Shakespeare Festival are exceptions to our rule of counting the number of performances from the date of the press coverage, because the press opening night often takes place late in the play's run of public performances. In these cases, therefore, we count the first public performance, not the press date, as opening night. Press date for *The Chronicles of King Henry VI, Part 1* was 6/30/70, for *Part 2* was 7/1/70, for *Richard III* was 7/2/70.

* **The Dirtiest Show in Town** (383). By Tom Eyen. Produced by Jeff Barry Enterprises, Inc., Ellen Stewart-Bruce Mailman, in association with the Theater of the Eye Repertory Company, 1970, at the Astor Place Theater. Opened June 27, 1970.

Blonde	Madeleine le Roux	Lawrence	Bradford Riley
Brunette	Jennifer Mitchell	Blonde Bird-Watcher	Robert Schrock
Jet Black	Sommer Sally	Second Sergeant	Arthur Morey
Redhead	Elsa Tresko	Jiffy Mover	R.A. Dow
Jonathan	Paul Matthew Eckhart	Stoned Angel	Ellen Gurin
Cyril	Jeffrey Herman		

Directed by Tom Eyen; music, Jeff Barry; scenery, T.E. Mason; costumes, Victor Bijou; lighting, Steve Whitson; production stage manager, Bonnie Gable; press, Saul Richman.

Series of sketches and vignettes of modern experience, from sex to environmental problems. The play was presented without intermission. It was previously produced at the Cafe La Mama.

Steambath (128). By Bruce Jay Friedman. Produced by Ivor David Balding at the Truck and Warehouse Theater. Opened June 30, 1970. (Closed October 18, 1970)

Old Timer	Conrad Bain	Broker	Mitchell Jason
Tandy	Anthony Perkins	Attendant	Hector Elizondo
Bieberman	Marvin Lichterman	Longshoreman	Jack Knight
Young Man	Jere Admire	Young Girl	Eileen Dietz
Young Man	Teno Pollick	Flanders	Alfred Hinckley
Gottlieb	Gabor Morea	2d Longshoreman	William Walsh
Meredith	Annie Rachel		

Directed by Anthony Perkins; scenery, David Mitchell; costumes, Joseph G. Aulisi; lighting, Jules Fisher; special visual effects, Marvin Torfield; choreography, Grover Dale; associate producer, Richard Scanga; stage manager, Robert Pitman; press, Shirley Herz, Mary Thomas.

Time: The present. Place: A steam room. The play was divided into two acts.

The steambath setting turns out to be a waiting room for troubled souls of the dead, supervised by an inscrutible Puerto Rican attendant, who is God.

A Best Play; see page 119

Sambo (22). Outdoor revival of the musical with words by Ron Steward; music by Ron Steward and Neal Tate. Produced by the New York Shakespeare Festival Mobile Theater, Joseph Papp producer, Bernard Gersten associate producer, at parks and playgrounds in the five boroughs of New York City. Opened July 14, 1970. (Closed August 8, 1970)

Sambo	Ron Steward	Miss Sally Muffat	Jane Stuart
Bo Peep	Veronica Redd	Tiger Lady	Sandi Morris
Jack Horney	George Turner	Tiger Man	Joe Darby
Untogether Cinderella	Judy White		

Musicians: Margaret Harris piano, Fred Waifs drums, Ted Dunbar guitar, Reggie Johnson bass, Hal Vick saxophone and flute, Woody Shaw trumpet.

Directed by Michael Schultz; choreography, Tommy Jonsen; scenery, Ming Cho Lee; costumes, Milo Morrow; lighting, Lawrence Metzler; musical direction, Margaret Harris; stage manager, Ken Glickfield; press, Merle Debuskey, Faith Geer.

Sambo was originally produced last season in New York Shakespeare's schedule of indoor programs, 12/12/69 for 37 performances.

Golden Bat (152). Musical in the Japanese language with book and lyrics by Yutaka Higashi; music by Itsuro Shimoda. Produced by Kermit Bloomgarden and Arthur Cantor at the Sheridan Square Playhouse. Opened July 21, 1970. (Closed November 29, 1970)

Jun Arakawa	Setsuko Nakagawa
Sakae Kato	Kyoichi Nagakura
Yukiko Kobayashi	Shoichi Saito
Yoshie Matsuno	Yasunori Saito
Noboru Mine	Kenkichi Sato
Reiko Nagai	Sansho Shinsui

Directed by Yutaka Higashi; musical director, Itsuro Shimoda; scenery, Kenkichi Sato; costumes, Kiyoko Chiba; lighting, Barry Arnold; musical arrangements, Yoko Shimoda; special asst. to director, Kazuko Oshima; English language coach, Jennifer Merin; stage managers, Mitsuko Yamada, Karen de Francis; press, Arthur Cantor Associates, Tom Sergott, Jay Smith.

Potpourri of sketches, songs and dances in a Japanese rock musical. A foreign play previously produced in Japan and at the Cafe La Mama by The Tokyo Kid Brothers, a Japanese theater group.

Scene 1, Japan: Introduction—Yukiko Kobayashi; "America, America"—Setsuko Nakagawa (Extra, Extra), Kenkichi Sato (American Flag); "Goeika" (song of invocation and supplication); "Ba-Ba-Ba" (song for fun); Home—Setsuko Nakagawa; I Like Girls—Noburu Mine.

Scene 2, The Pacific: Western Movies—Yasunori Saito; Soliloquy (Look Over There)—Yasunori Saito; "North-Northwest."

Scene 3, American Rock: "American Rock;" Encountering America (vaudeville interlude)—Narrator, Reiko Nagai, Visitors, Jun Arakawa, Shoichi Saito, Setsuko, Nakagawa; Strike! America—Kyoichi Nagakura; "Rock, Crane's Town;" Looking Over My Life—Shoichi Saito (background music "Indus River"); "Peace;" "I Like" and "Love! Love! Love!"; "For Whom" —Troupe; "Mawari Toro" (Revolving Lantern)—Sakae Kato; Kids' World (Temari)—Yukiko Kobayashi (background song, Warabe-Uta); Soliloquy-Yukiko Kobayashi; Hana Wa (songs of flowers); "Namu Amida Butsu"—Sansho Shinsui, Yoshie Matsuno; "Medeta, Medeta" (festival song)—Kenkichi Sato; Japanese Lesson—Kenkichi Sato.

Scene 4, Matsuri: "Matsuri"—Yukiko Kobayashi; "Okage, Okage!"; Affirmation of Life—Sakae Kato; "Hana, Yuki, Kaze" (Flower, Snow, Wind); Final Declaration—Reiko Nagai.

The Emerald Slippers (10). By Jose Alcarez. Produced by Henry P. Testa at the Gramercy Arts Theater. Opened September 1, 1970. (Closed September 7, 1970)

Directed by Jose Alcarez; scenery, Leo K. Cohen; costumes, Sandra Takahashi; lighting, Louis Rios; choreography, Tony Anton; production stage manager, William Bowen; press, Betty Lee Hunt, Henry Luhrman. With Rob Sadang, Nessa Lynn Segal, Bruno Fleao, Inez Yvette Perez, Donald J. Scotti, Frederick Tuso, Alfred Lozito, Paul Kanluk.
Oriental fantasy, multiple romances in simplistic style.

Three by Ferlinghetti (8). Program of three one-act plays by Lawrence Ferlinghetti: *Three Thousand Red Ants, The Alligation* and *The Victims of Amnesia.* Produced by Winters/Rosen Productions in association with Elliott Taibenslag at the Jan Hus Theater. Opened September 22, 1970. (Closed September 27, 1970)

Directed by William E. Hunt; scenery, Sandi Marks; costumes, Deborah Foster; lighting, Ray McCutcheon; sound, Hamilton O'Hara; production stage manager, Virginia Friedman; press, Sol Jacobson, Lewis Harmon. With Martha Greenhouse, Roger Morden, Charles Gregory.
Three Thousand Red Ants is a metaphor of a sinking marriage and sinking yacht. *The Alligation* is about a pet alligator who desires his freedom. *The Victims of Amnesia* is a collection of symbols in an incident of a woman checking into a strange hotel to give birth to babies. Previously produced off off Broadway at the Cubiculo.

Dames at Sea (170). Cabaret revival of the musical with book and lyrics by George Haimsohn and Robin Miller; music by Jim Wise. Produced by Jordan Hott and Jack Millstein, associate producer Robert S. Mankin, at the Plaza 9 Music Hall. Opened September 23, 1970. (Closed January 31, 1971)

Mona Kent	Jane Sell	Ruby	Leland Palmer
Joan	Carol Morely	Dick	Kurt Peterson
Hennessey; The Captain	Raymond Thorne	Lucky	Voight Kempson

Directed and choreographed by Neal Lenyon; scenery and costumes, Peter Harvey; lighting, Chenault Spence; musical direction, Richard Demone; production manager, John Lamb; press, Saul Richman.
Dames at Sea was produced off Broadway 12/20/68 for 575 performances. Listing of scenes and musical numbers appears on page 442 of the 1968-69 *Best Plays* volume.

Children in the Rain (1). By Dennis McIntyre. Produced by James Clifford Productions at the Cherry Lane Theater. Opened and closed at the evening performance October 2, 1970.

Directed by Frank R. Giordano; scenery and assistant director, Patrick Donovan; stage manager, John Van Domlin; press, Sol Jacobson, Lewis Harmon, Stanley F. Kaminsky. With Elizabeth Harryman, Lane Smith, Frank R. Giordano.
Three on a drug trip.

* **New York Shakespeare Festival Public Theater.** Schedule of ten programs. **The Happiness Cage** (32). By Dennis J. Reardon. Opened October 4, 1970. (Closed November 1, 1970) **Trelawny of the "Wells"** (48). Revival of the play by Arthur Wing Pinero. Opened October 11, 1970. (Closed January 10, 1971) **Jack Mac-Gowran in the Works of Samuel Beckett** (67). One-man show performed and adapted by Jack MacGowran with the advice and approval of Samuel Beckett. Opened November 19, 1970. (Closed January 25, 1971) **Subject to Fits** (127). By Robert Montgomery; a "response" to Dostoevsky's *The Idiot.* Opened February 14, 1971. (Closed May 30, 1971) **Slag** (32). By David Hare. Opened February 21, 1971. (Closed March 21, 1971) **Here Are Ladies** (67). One-woman show from the works of Irish writers, performed by Siobhan McKenna. Opened February 22, 1971. (Closed May 9, 1971) **Blood** (14). Musical conceived by Doug Dyer. Opened March 7, 1971. (Closed March 21, 1971) **Underground** (38). Program of two one-act plays: *Jazznite* by Walter Jones and *The Life and Times of J. Walter*

Smintheus by Edgar White. Opened April 18, 1971. (Closed May 16, 1971) **Candide** (14). Adaptation of Voltaire's *Candide* by the Organic Theater Company. Opened April 14, 1971. (Closed April 25, 1971) * **The Basic Training of Pavlo Hummel** (14). By David Rabe. Opened May 20, 1971. Produced by New York Shakespeare Festival Public Theater, Joseph Papp producer, Bernard Gersten associate producer, at the Public Theater (see note).

THE HAPPINESS CAGE

Reese	Lewis J. Stadlen	General	Paul Sparer
Orderly	Charles Durning	Aide	George Loros
Miles	Ronny Cox	Nurse	Pamela Grey
Rhodes	James De Marse	Assistant	Jason Miller
Dr. Freytag	Henderson Forsythe	Anna Ames	Bette Henritze

Visitors: John Benson, Walter De Lano, Alice Merton Benson. Ladies & Gentlemen of the Press: Alice Merton Benson, John Benson, Walter De Lano, James De Marse, Jason Miller.

Directed by Tom Aldredge; scenery, Marjorie Kellogg; costumes, Theoni V. Aldredge; lighting, Martin Aronstein; music, Ronny Cox; assistant director, Steven Shaw; stage manager, Jane Neufeld; press, Merle Debuskey, Faith Geer.

Time: The present. Place: A Veteran's Administration hospital. Scene 1: The Rats. Scene 2: Requiescat in Pace. (Intermission) Scene 3: The Button. Scene 4: Cerebella. Scene 5: The Cage.

Wounded and sick veterans are guinea pigs in a fantastic, mysterious medical experiment in the nature of human happiness.

TRELAWNY OF THE "WELLS"

James Telfer	Frederic Warriner	Theater	Douglas Hayle, Arlene Nadel, Con Roche
Augustus Colpoys	Geoff Garland		
Ferdinand Gadd	Michael Wager	Sir William Gower	George Bartenieff
Tom Wrench	Robert Ronan	Arthur Gower	Dean Santoro
Mrs. Telfer	Elaine Eldridge	Clara de Foenix	Jane Kapral
Avonia Bunn	Sasha von Scherler	Mrs. Mossop	Jean Bruno
Rose Trelawny	Nancy Dussault	Ablett	Dan Durning
Imogen Parrott	Valerie French	Charles	Grant Code
O'Dwyer; Capt. de Foenix	Gene Nye	Sarah	Arlene Nadel
Members of Pantheon			

Directed by Robert Ronan; scenery, David Mitchell; costumes, Theoni V. Aldredge; lighting, Martin Aronstein; stage manager, Dean Compton.

Pinero's play about life in the London theater at the turn of the century was first produced in New York 11/22/98 for 131 performances. It was revived last season off off Broadway by The Other Stage. It was last done on Broadway 1/31/27 for 56 performances.

JACK MacGOWRAN IN THE WORKS OF SAMUEL BECKETT

Scenery, Ming Cho Lee; costumes, Theoni V. Aldredge; lighting, Martin Aronstein; stage manager, Andrew Mihok.

The program included selections from *Embers, Molloy, Echo's Bones* and *Cascando* (from *Poems in English*), *Waiting for Godot, From an Abandoned Work, Watt, Words and Music, Krapp's Last Tape, Endgame, The Unnamable, Malone Dies.* It was presented in two parts.

SUBJECT TO FITS

Prince Myshkin	Andy Robinson	Ganya Ivoglin	James DeMarse
Paryfon Rogozhin	Jason Miller	General Ivoglin	Albert Quinton
Lebedev	John Mahon	Ippolit Ivoglin	Jim Borrelli
Madame Yepanchin	Jean David	Natasha Fillipovna	Sharon Laughlin
Aglaya Yepanchin	Katharine Dunfee		

Musicians: Ken Guilmartin organ and conductor, Ruben Rivera cello, Todd Roberto bass.

Directed by A.J. Antoon; scenery, Leo Yoshimura; costumes, Theoni V. Aldredge; lighting, Ian Calderon; stage manager, Ken Glickfeld.

The play was presented in two parts.
Episodic projection of *The Idiot* characters and relationships in new fanciful forms—in the words of the author "smacking of *The Idiot*, dreaming of *The Idiot* but mostly taking off from where *The Idiot* drove it."
John Glover replaced Andy Robinson and Walter McGinn replaced Jason Miller 4/20/71.

SLAG

Joanne ....Roberta Maxwell   Ann ....Kathryn Walker
Elise ....Margo Ann Berdeshevsky

Brackenhurst Girls: Gina Rose Horowitz, Rose Marie Smith.
Directed by Roger Hendricks Simon; scenery, Daisy Page Pickman; costumes, Milo Morrow; lighting, Robert Kellogg; stage manager, John Beven.
Time: The present. Place: A private girls' school. Scene 1: Common room, summer. Scene 2: Cricket pitch, summer. Scene 3: Bathroom, summer. Scene 4: Common room, same day. Scene 5: Bedroom, autumn. Scene 6: Common room, January. The play was presented in two parts with an intermission between Scenes 4 and 5.
Sexual and other neuroses of three teachers hanging on in a school that is in the last stages of failure. A foreign play previously produced in London by the Royal Court and in New York in the Public Theater's Other Stage experimental program.

HERE ARE LADIES

Directed by Sean Kenney; scenery, Sean Kenney; music, Sean O'Riada.
Siobhan McKenna impersonated a series of women characters from Irish literature. A foreign play previously produced in London. The program included selections from the works of James Joyce, George Bernard Shaw, Sean O'Casey, William Butler Yeats, John Millington Synge and Samuel Beckett.

BLOOD

Alex Ander   Horald Griffiths
Roberta Baum   Elizabeth Howard
Alexandra Borrie   Maggie Hyatt
Mary Boylan   Madge Sinclair
Christopher Cox   Joyce Stanton
Margaret Dorn   Jack Starkey
Doug Dyer   Linda Swenson
William Ellington   Jim Turner
Patrick Fox

Directed by Doug Dyer; design, Doug Dyer; costumes, Theoni V. Aldredge; lighting, Keith Nelson; movement, Cora Cahan; musical supervision, John Morris; musical director, Patrick Fox; music and lyrics, a collaboration of the *Blood* company; electric bass, Herb Bushler; associate producer, Bernard Gersten; stage manager, Dean Compton.
Folk rock musical with a story about a returning Viet Nam veteran, loosely based on the *Oresteia*.
MUSICAL NUMBERS—"Baby Rue," "High Lonesome," "Hard Time War Time," "Hear the Guns," "Lullaby," "Snake," "Cold Steel," "Every Father," "I Had a Son," "There You Go Again," "Father, Father," "Gas Can," "Dance of Murder," "Nobody's Fault," "I Dreamt About My Home," "Madness Murder," "Whistles," "I Woke up Today," "Prophesy," "Four Thousand Years," "Walk on Home," "Heebie-Jeebie Furies," "Don't Call Us," "Before You Knew I Love You," "Destruction," "Rhythms," "Monkey in a Tree," "Minute by Minute," "Love Came to Me," "New Snow," "Just a Little Bit," "Hail to the Blood."

CANDIDE

Amy Benesch   Carolyn Gordon
Simone Deely   Gerald Kirschbaum
Bob Engel   Cecil O'Neal

Directed by Stuart Gordon; music composed and played by Jonathan Pearthree.
A version of the Voltaire satire improvised by the actors, the Organic Theater Company of Chicago, and then frozen for this production.

THE LIFE AND TIMES OF J. WALTER SMINTHEUS

J. Walter Smintheus ....Dennis Tate	Dr. Comma ....John McCants Trotter
Edward; Manager ....Edward Seamon	Margie ....Robin Braxton
Robert ....Walter Jones	Walter ....MacArthur Flack
Joyce ....Noorma Darden	Bob Kaufman; Paul ....John Gallagher

JAZZNITE

Leola ....Robin Braxton	Baylock ....Walter Cotton
Dudder ....Demond Wilson	Heavy ....MacArthur Flack
Slick ....Lennal Wainwright	Barbara ....Noorma Darden
Eligah ....Sam Singleton	

Directed by Walter Jones; scenery, Leo Yoshimura; costumes, Theoni V. Aldredge; lighting, Ian Calderon; stage manager, John Beven.

The Life and Times of J. Walter Smintheus is about the mental disintegration of a black intellectual who can make nothing out of any part of his life. It was previously produced in the ANTA Matinee Series. *Jazznite* is about an intellectual who brings back to the ghetto the knowledge derived from his contact with the white man's world.

THE BASIC TRAINING OF PAVLO HUMMEL

Pavlo Hummel ....William Atherton	Hinkle ....Edward Herrmann
Yen; Zung ....Victoria Racimo	Kress ....Earl Hindman
Ardell ....Albert Hall	Pierce ....Robert Lehman
1st Sgt. Tower ....Joe Fields	Hendrix ....D. Franklyn Lenthall
The Company	Mickey ....Frederick Coffin
Capt. Saunders ....Edward Cannan	Mrs. Hummel ....Sloane Shelton
Cpl. Ferrara ....Anthony R. Charnota	Sgt. Brisbey ....Lee Wallace
Parker ....Peter Cameron	Cpl. Jones ....Garrett Morris
Burns ....Stephen Clarke	Mamasan ....Christal Kim
Ryan ....John Walter Davis	Sgt. Wall ....John Benson
Hall ....Bob Delegall	Parham ....Bob Delegall
Grennel ....Tom Harris	Linh; Farmer ....Hoshin Seki

Directed by Jeff Bleckner; scenery, David Mitchell; costumes, Theoni V. Aldredge; lighting, Martin Aronstein; stage manager, Dean Compton.

Time: 1965-1967. Place: The United States Army. The play was presented in two parts.

One soldier's rocky road through basic training and fighting in Vietnam, to death in a Saigon fragging incident.

NOTE: In Joseph Papp's Public Theater there are many separate auditoriums. *The Happiness Cage, Jack MacGowran in the Works of Samuel Beckett, Here Are Ladies* and *The Basic Training of Pavlo Hummel* played the Estelle R. Newman Theater. *Trelawny of the "Wells", Subject to Fits* and *Slag* played the Florence S. Anspacher Theater. *Blood* played Martinson Hall, *Underground* played the Other Stage and *Candide* played the South Hall.

Happy Birthday, Wanda June (47). By Kurt Vonnegut Jr. Produced by Lester M. Goldsmith at the Theater de Lys. Opened October 7, 1970. (Closed November 15, 1970; see note)

Penelope Ryan ....Marsha Mason	Harold Ryan ....Kevin McCarthy
Looseleaf Harper ....William Hickey	Wanda June ....Ariane Munker
Paul Ryan ....Steven Paul	Siegfried von Konigswald .....Louis Turenne
Dr. Norbert Woodly ....Keith Charles	Mildred ....Pamela Saunders
Herb Shuttle ....Nicolas Coster	

Directed by Michael J. Kane; scenery, Ed Wittstein; lighting, David F. Segal; costumes, Joseph G. Aulisi; sound, Gary Harris; associate producer, Walter Rosen Scholz; presented by special arrangement with Lucille Lortel Productions, Inc.; production stage manager, Paul John Austin; press, Ben Washer.

Time: The present. Place: The Ryan apartment in a large city. The play was presented in two parts.

Re-working of the story of Ulysses's homecoming with modern characters, in order to expose outworn concepts of heroism and virility.

NOTE: Closed 11/15/70 by the Equity strike off Broadway, *Happy Birthday, Wanda June* moved to a Limited Broadway house for a continued engagement. See its entry in the "Plays Produced on Broadway" section of this volume.

Alice in Wonderland (119). Adapted from the writings of Lewis Carroll by the Manhattan Project. Produced by Lyn Austin and Oliver Smith in the Manhattan Project (An N.Y.U.S.O.A. Theater Company) production at The Extension. Opened October 8, 1970. (Closed May 1, 1971)

Gerry Bamman	Jerry Mayer
Tom Costello	Angela Pietropinto
Saskia Noordhoek Hegt	Larry Pine

Directed by André Gregory; designers, Eugene Lee, Franne Newman; translator, Kenneth Cavander; presented in association with Extension Inc.; stage manager, John P. Holms; press, Alan Eichler.

Alice and its author viewed in a theatrical form which is part comedy and part psychological terror tale, developed by this off-off-Broadway company.

Colette (7). Return engagement of the play by Elinor Jones; adapted from *Earthly Paradise*, the Robert Phelps collection of Colette's autobiographical writings; original music by Harvey Schmidt; lyrics by Tom Jones. Produced by Cheryl Crawford in association with Mary W. John at the Ellen Stewart Theater. Opened October 14, 1970. (Closed October 18, 1970)

Colette	Fenella Fielding	Daniele; Polaire; Ida; Amalia; Valentine;	
Sido	Ruth Nelson	Marguerite; Reporter	Janet Dowd
Willy	Albert Stratton	Leo; Jacques; Pierre; Jean;	
Captain; Max; George Wague;		Henri; Maurice	Michael Goodwin
Reporter	Erik Rhodes	Pianist	Elman Anderson

Directed by Gerald Freedman; scenery, David Mitchell; costumes, Theoni V. Aldredge; lighting, Roger Morgan; production stage manager, Gail Bell; press, David Powers.

This production of *Colette* opened 5/6/70 and played 101 performances in its original run.

My House Is Your House (1). By Lee Loeb and Sam Ross. Produced by John J. Nestor in association with Wolf William Moss at the Players Theater. Opened and closed at the evening performance October 15, 1970.

Directed by William Tegroe; scenery and lighting, Robert Engstrom; costumes, Leila Larmon; production stage manager, Elissa Lane; press, David Lipsky, Lisa Lipsky. With Don Bishop, Jenny O'Hara, Don Fellows, Frank Moon, Milo Boulton, Anita Stewart, Jan McElhaney, Harry Eno, June Graham.

Comedy, a district attorney inherits a bordello.

The American Place Theater. Schedule of three programs. Sunday Dinner (41). By Joyce Carol Oates. Opened October 16, 1970; see note. (Closed November 25, 1970) The Carpenters (39). By Steven Tesich. Opened December 10, 1970; see note. (Closed January 16, 1971) Pinkville (42). By George Tabori. Opened February 22, 1971; see note. (Closed April 3, 1971) Back Bog Beast Bait by Sam Shepard opened April 29, 1971 as a work-in-progress not submitted for review. Produced by The American Place Theater, Wynn Handman director, at St. Clement's Church.

SUNDAY DINNER

Estella	Jacqueline Brookes	Jack	Jerome Dempsey
Mary	Lois Smith	Leroy	Martin Shakar
Jake	Brooks Morton	Census Taker	Patrick McVey

Directed by Curt Dempster; scenery, Kert Lundell; costumes, Willa Kim; lighting, Roger Morgan; music composed by Kirk Nurock; production stage manager, David Sell; stage manager, Grania Hoskins; press, Howard Atlee, David Roggensack.

Time: The present. Place: A family home. The play was presented without intermission.

Symbolical drama of a seemingly normal family whose actual or potential record of evil is exposed by the visit of a mysterious blind census-taker.

THE CARPENTERS

Father	Vincent Gardenia	Sissy	Laura Esterman
Mother	Alice Drummond	Mark	Glenn Walken
Waldo	John Korkes		

Directed by Eugene Lesser; scenery, Kert Lundell; costumes, Jeanne Button; lighting, William Mintzer; sound, James Reichert; production stage manager, Peter B. Mumford; stage manager, Grania Hoskins.

Time: The present. The play was presented without intermission.

Symbolical ruination of a family man's life, as all he worked hard for is slipping away, including his wife and children who turn against him.

PINKVILLE

Jerry the Naz	Michael Douglas	Suck Ass	Art Evans
The Honeychild	Milton Earl Forrest	Acting Jack	Constantine Katsanos
Consequently Joe	Raúl Juliá	The Captain	Lane Smith
The Jock	Bob Lesser	Papasan	Dimo Condos
TwoTon Tessie	James Tolkan	The Girl	Barbara Tai Sing

Pianist conductor, Bob Norden. Drummer, David Frost.

Directed by Martin Fried; music composed and directed by Stanley Walden; production design and lighting, Wolfgang Roth; costumes, Ruth Morley; movement, Anna Sokolow; electronic music, Jacob Druckman; production stage manager, Peter B. Mumford; stage manager, Kenneth Cox.

The play was presented without intermission.

Drama of mens' brutalization by military training and war.

NOTE: In this volume, the programs of off-Broadway subscription companies like The American Place Theater are sometimes exceptions to our rule of counting the number of performances from the date of the press coverage. When the press opening night takes place late in the play's run of paid public performances (after previews) for the subscription audience, we count the first subscription performance, not the press date, as opening night. Press date for *Sunday Dinner* was 11/2/70; for *The Carpenters* 12/21/70; for *Pinkville*, 3/17/71.

Bil Baird Marionettes. Schedule of three marionette programs. **The Whistling Wizard and the Sultan of Tuffet,** revival with book by Alan Stern, songs by Bil Baird and Alan Stern, and **A Pageant of Puppet Variety** (33). Opened October 17, 1970. (Closed November 29, 1970) **Ali Baba and the 40 Thieves,** book by Alan Stern, songs by George Kleinsinger, Bil Baird and Joe Darion, and **Holiday on Strings,** created and designed by Bil Baird. Opened December 26, 1970. (Closed March 21, 1971) **Winnie the Pooh,** revival based on the book by A.A. Milne, adapted by A.J. Russell, music by Jack Brooks, lyrics by A.A. Milne and Jack Brooks, and **Bil Baird's Variety** (48). Opened March 27, 1971. (Closed May 16, 1971) Produced by the American Puppet Arts Council, Arthur Cantor executive director, in the Bil Baird's Marionettes production at the Bil Baird Theater.

PERFORMER	"WHISTLING WIZARD & SULTAN OF TUFFET"	"ALI BABA & THE 40 THIEVES"	"WINNIE THE POOH"
Cary Antebi	Pasha	(Danhasch)	
Bil Baird	Dooley; Casbah	(Danhasch); (Cassim)	Eeyore; Owl
Peter Baird	Birds & Animals	Robber	Roo

PERFORMER	"WHISTLING WIZARD & SULTAN OF TUFFET"	"ALI BABA & THE 40 THIEVES	"WINNIE THE POOH"
Pady Blackwood	Dragon	Zsa-Zsa	Kanga; Rabbit
David Canaan	Sasha; Akimbo	Selim	Tigger
Olga Felgemacher	Peekaboo; J.P.	Morgiana; Mrs. Ali	Christopher Robin
Carl Harms	Prod. Manager	Prod. Manager	Prod. Manager
Simon Sisters			Mice
Frank Sullivan	Ali Booby; Turtle	Ali Baba	Winnie-the-Pooh
Byron Whiting	Heathcliff	Mahmoud; (Cassim)	Piglet

(Parentheses indicate roles in which the actors alternated)

ALL PROGRAMS: Artistic associate, Frank Sullivan; *The Whistling Wizard, Ali Baba, Holiday on Strings* and *Winnie the Pooh* directed by Gordon Hunt; musical direction, Alvy West; press, Joel Wyman.

THE WHISTLING WIZARD AND THE SULTAN OF TUFFET—Musical arrangements, Alvy West. Place: The country of Tuffet and the Land of Beyond. First produced 12/20/69 for 167 performances in a program with *A Pageant of Puppet Variety.*

A PAGEANT OF PUPPET VARIETY—Demonstration of the art of the marionette theater presented on many Bil Baird programs since its first production of record 4/19/57.

ALI BABA AND THE 40 THIEVES—Special musical arrangements, George Kleinsinger; thieves, animals & assorted characters portrayed by members of the company. Place: The land of Persia. Spectacle with story about a wife-dominated Ali Baba aided by a slave girl to out-wit a band of thieves.

HOLIDAY ON STRINGS—Billed as "a story of how Christmas and the winter holidays belong to everyone all over the world," with demonstrations of marionette techniques.

WINNIE THE POOH—Musical arrangements, Alvy West. Place: In and around the 100 Acre Wood. This marionette version of the Milne stories was first produced 11/23/67 for 185 performances and has been performed in the Baird repertory every season since.

The Roundabout Repertory Company. Schedule of five programs. **Hamlet** (37). Revival of the play by William Shakespeare. Opened October 18, 1970. (Closed November 29, 1970) **Tug of War** (13). By Alan Rossett. Opened December 23, 1970. (Closed January 3, 1971) **Uncle Vanya** (50). Revival of the play by Anton Chekhov; adapted by Gene Feist. Opened January 24, 1971. (Closed March 14, 1971; see note) **Chas. Abbott & Son** (24). By Lewis S. Salsburg. Opened March 12, 1971. (Closed April 4, 1971) **She Stoops to Conquer** (36). Revival of the Play by Oliver Goldsmith. Opened April 25, 1971. (Closed May 30, 1971) Produced by The Roundabout Repertory Company, Gene Feist producing director, at the Roundabout Theater.

HAMLET

Hamlet	Art Burns	Laertes; Player Queen	Thomas McCann
Gertrude	Philip Campanella	Guildenstern; Marcellus	John Guerrasio
Claudius; Ghost	Sterling Jensen	Rosencrantz; Francisco	Stephen Greenstein
Horatio; Player King	Bruce M. Kornbluth	Bernardo; Priest	
Polonius; Gravedigger	Fred Stuthman	Gonzago	Lyle Lorentz
Ophelia	Louis G. Trapani	Osric; Gentleman	Robert Marinaccio

Directed by Gene Feist; original score, Philip Campanella; scenery, Holmes Easley; costumes, Mimi Maxmen; lighting, Loran Bruns; production stage manager, Michael Fields; press, William Campbell.

All the roles in this *Hamlet,* including those of Gertrude and Ophelia, were played by male actors. The play was presented in two parts.

TUG OF WAR

Mopsy	Carole Martin	Carol	Ann Sachs
Peter	Philip Campanella	Fred	Manuel Santiago
Liliane	Jacqueline Bertrand	Robert	Jack Axelrod

Directed by William Campbell; scenery, Michael Fields; costumes, Mary Etta Lang; lighting, Robert Murphy; music, Philip Campanella; production stage manager, Michael Fields.

Time: Late afternoon and evening in summer. Place: A country home. The play was presented in two parts.

Six people strip away each other's defenses.

UNCLE VANYA

Prof. Serebryakov	Thayer David	Michael Astrov	Winston May
Helena	Elizabeth Owens	Telyegin	Fred Stuthman
Sonya	Julie Garfield	Marina	Joni Ruth White
Marya Voynitsky	Ann Kingsley	Laborer	Lyle Lorentz
Vanya	Sterling Jensen		

Directed by Gene Feist; score, Philip Campanella; scenery, Holmes Easley; costumes, Mimi Maxmen; lighting, Robert Murphy; production stage manager, Michael Fields.

The last professional New York production of this Chekhov play was David Ross's off Broadway during the season of 1955-56.

NOTE: *Uncle Vanya* played its final 8 performances at the Cherry Lane Theater 3/8/71-3/14/71.

CHAS. ABBOTT & SON

Danny O'Boyle	Lyle J. Lorentz	Eleanor Wagner	Nancy Reardon
Ann Honeywell	Alice Drummond	Jacob Morris	Philip Campanella
Charles Abbott	Fred Stuthman	Sylvia Abbott	Babette New
Byron Abbott	Robert G. Murch	Mark Gilbert	Norman Lind

Directed by Gene Feist; scenery, Holmes Easley; costumes, Gilson Sarmento; lighting, Robert Murphy; musical supervision, Philip Campanella; production stage manager, Michael Fields.

Time: October, 1928. Place: The offices of the furniture factory of Chas. Abbott & Son. Act I, Scene 1: Sunday morning. Scene 2: Three days later. Act II, Scene 1: The next morning. Scene 2: The following day. Act III: Four weeks later.

Generation gap widening between father and son in a small Pennsylvania town on the eve of the Depression.

SHE STOOPS TO CONQUER

Mrs. Hardcastle	Jane Connell	Hardcastle	Fred Stuthman
Miss Hardcastle	Nancy Reardon	Hastings	Tom V. V. Tammi
Miss Neville	Arlene Nadel	Tony Lumpkin	Louis G. Trapani
Pimple	Judith Sullivan	Diggory	Philip Campanella
Sir Charles Marlowe	Lyle J. Lorentz	Roger	Roger Cunningham
Young Marlowe	Robert G. Murch		

Directed by Gene Feist; original score by Philip Campanella; scenery Holmes Easley; costumes, Mimi Maxmen; lighting, Robert Murphy; assistant director, Paul Bennett; production stage manager, Michael Fields.

The play was presented in two parts. The Goldsmith comedy's most recent New York professional revival of record was by Theater Incorporated (T. Edward Hambleton and Norris Houghton) 11/1/60 for 31 performances, returning 1/3/61 for 16 additional performances.

To Be or Not to Be—What Kind of a Question Is That? (23). Musical revue by H. Ritterman and Zvi Reisel; music by Eli Rubinstein; lyrics by Max Meszel. Produced by Henry Goldgran and Arthur V. Briskin at the Barbizon Plaza Theater. Opened October 19, 1970. (Closed November 15, 1970)

James Brochu	Denise Lor
Moti Giladi	Sarah Rubine
Shmulik Goldstein	Yoel Sharr
Evelyn Kingsley	Mark Stuart

Directed by Marvin Gordon; musical direction, Eli Rubinstein, lighting, Sally Small; art consultant, Ami Shamir; production coordinator, Larry Whiteley; stage manager, Patricia Smisko; press, Max Eisen.

Topical revue about life in Israel.

PART I: "Beyachad"—Entire company; About Israel—Moti Giladi; My Son the Kibutsnik—James Brochu, Denise Lor, Giladi; "The Wolf and the Lamb"—Brochu; "Vanya"—Sarah Rubine (Egypt), Brochu (Russia); El-Al (A Nudnik)—Evelyn Kingsley, Shmulik Goldstein, Brochu; "I'm in Love With a Flyer"—Miss Kingsley; Inflight Nudniks—Miss Lor; "Tilibim"—Giladi; "Tel-Aviv I Love You"—Misses Kingsley, Runine; "Chasidik"—Mark Stuart, Company.

PART II: "Chiribim"—Yoel Sharr, Company; Interview With a Maid—Misses Kingsley, Lor; Prisoner of War—Sharr, Giladi; "Letter From My Son"—Miss Lor; "Haifa Melody"—Giladi; Burglar—Miss Rubine, Goldstein, Sharr; "The Eighth Day"—Stuart; Party—Entire Company.

Theater of the Balustrade (7). Czechoslovakian mime program. Produced by Hunter College Concert Bureau at the Hunter College Playhouse. Opened October 19, 1970. (Closed October 24, 1970)

Josef Faita	Ivan Lukes
Ladislav Fialka	Rudolf Papezik
Lucie Hoffmeisterova	Olga Przygrodska
Jiri Kaftan	Bozena Vechetova
Ludmilla Kovarova	Richard Weber
Zdenka Kratochvilova	

Directed by Ladislav Fialka; stage manager, Joe Londin.

Czechoslovakian mime production in the form of a comedy in 12 scenes entitled *Button, Button*. A foreign play previously produced in Prague (the company's home base), Edinburgh and elsewhere.

Sensations (16). Musical suggested by William Shakespeare's *Romeo and Juliet;* book and lyrics by Paul Zakrzweski; music by Wally Harper. Produced by John Bowab and Charles Celian at Theater Four. Opened October 25, 1970. (Closed November 8, 1970)

Directed by Jerry Dodge; designed by William & Jean Eckart; costumes, Jeanne Button; lighting, Beverly Emmons; musical direction, Jack Lee; orchestrations, Bill Brohn; stage manager, Barbara Wood; press, Saul Richman. With Paulette Attie, Arthur Bartow, Judy Gibson, Joe Maisell, Ron Martin, James Ray, Marie Santell, John Savage, Bruce Scott.

Rock music and modern problems like drugs and violence superimposed on Shakespeare's love story.

The Immaculate Misconception (1). By W. Randolph Galvin. Produced by W. Randolph Galvin at the Cherry Lane Theater. Opened and closed at the evening performance, October 27, 1970.

Directed by William E. Kinzer; scenery, William E. Kinzer and W. Randolph Galvin; costumes, Mary Lou Harvey; lighting, Lee Goldman; press, Betty Lee Hunt, Henry Luhrman. With Frank Borgman, Herb Buck, James Glenn, William Kelsey, Gwenn Mitchell, Mary McGregor, John Swearingen, Tony Thomas.

Comedy with a plot concerning artificial insemination.

Score (23). By Jerry Douglas. Produced by Michael Harvey at the Martinique Theater. Opened October 28, 1970. (Closed November 15, 1970)

Elvira	Claire Wilbur	Eddie	Ben Wilson
Jack	Michael Beirne	Mike	Sylvester E. Stallone
Betsy	Lynn Swan		

Directed by Jerry Douglas; scenery, T.E. Mason; lighting, Candace Kling; stage manager, Mark Healy; press, Alan Eichler, Stanley F. Kaminsky.

Male and female homosexual games, often played naked.

A Dream Out of Time (49). By Irv Bauer. Produced by Harvey and Clara Klingeman at the Promenade Theater. Opened November 8, 1970. (Closed January 24, 1971).

Mike	James J. Sloyan	Cybil	Zina Jasper
Laura	Patsy Sabline	Blanche	Ruth Manning
Hanna	Clara Heller	Josh	Gary Tigerman
Aaron	Sam Levene	Raymond	John Towey
Morris	Philip Bruns		

Directed by Paul Aaron; scenery and lighting, David F. Segal; costumes, Joseph G. Aulisi; dance movement, Kathryn Posin; original music, Kirk Nurock; sound, Maury Benkoil; production stage manager, Martin Herzer; press, Max Eisen, Warren Pincus.

Time: The present. Place: In reality and dreams. Act I: Deck of an ocean liner one night before docking in New York, then the Gordon apartment on the upper West Side two days later. Act II: Pieces from Mike's life and dream during the next month. Act III: The Gordon apartment, a Thursday evening one month later.

Two generations of a Jewish family suffering the modern emotional and social distortions of American life.

* **Touch** (264). Musical with book by Kenn Long and Amy Saltz; music by Kenn Long and Jim Crozier; lyrics by Kenn Long. Produced by Edith O'Hara in association with Robert S. Weinstein and The Two Arts Playhouse, Inc., in The Plowright Players production, at the Village Arena Theater. Opened November 8, 1970.

Awol	Norman Jacob	Mark	Peter J. Mitchell
Guiness	Barbara Ellis	Patti	Susan Rosenblum
Wyan	Kenn Long	Susan April	Ava Rosenblum
Melissa	Phyllis Gibbs	Alex	Dwight Jayne
Roland	Gerard S. Doff		

And Eileen Gottermeyer, David J. Stoudnour, Cherie McDonald, Gary Graham. Musicians: David J. Rodman, Fredrick L. Ebner, Andrew I. Schwartz.

Directed by Amy Saltz; musical direction, David J. Rodman; scenery, Robert U. Taylor; lighting, Charles Lewis; stage manager, David Stoudnour; press, Saul Richman.

Episodes of life among companionship-seeking youth in modern communes.

ACT I

"Declaration" ....Company
"Windchild" ....Company
    (music and lyrics by Gary Graham)
"City Song" ....Susan April (and Miss McDonald)
"Sitting in the Park" ....Roland, Wyan
"I Don't Care" ....Melissa, Company
"Goodbyes" ....Awol
"Come to the Road" ....Wyan, Susan April, Company
"Reaching, Touching" ....Guiness, Awol, Company

ACT II

"Guiness, Woman" ....Awol
"Susan's Song" ....Susan April
"Maxine!" ....Wyan, Roland, Commune
"Quiet Country" ....Roland, Wyan, Company
"Tripping" ....Patti, Commune
"Garden Song" ....Commune
"Watching" ....Melissa
"Hasseltown" ....Company
"Confrontation Song" ....Commune
"Alphagenesis" ....Company

Saved (29). By Edward Bond. Produced by the Chelsea Theater Center of Brooklyn, Robert Kalfin artistic director, Michael David executive director, at the Cherry Lane Theater. Opened November 13, 1970; see note. (Closed December 6, 1970)

Pam	Dorrie Kavanaugh	Mike	Richard Cox
Len	James Woods	Colin	Tom Leopold
Fred	Kevin Conway	Mary	Margaret Braidwood
Pete	Stefan Hartman	Harry	Donald Ewer
Barry	Donald Warfield	Liz	Lynn Ann Leveridge

Directed by Alan Schneider; designed by Eugene Lee and Franne Newman; lighting, Roger Morgan; production stage manager, David Eidenberg; press, Harvey B. Sabinson, Marilynn LeVine.

Place: South London—a living room, a park, a bedroom, a cell, a cafe. The play was presented in two parts.

Degradation and violence, including the stoning to death of a baby, in a tragic treatment of the dark side of human nature. A foreign play previously produced in London and in New Haven, Conn.

NOTE: This production of *Saved* was performed 10/28/70 to 11/7/70 at the Brooklyn Academy of Music before moving to the Cherry Lane Theater.

Die Brücke (The Bridge). German theater ensemble for overseas in a schedule of two programs in the German language. **Amphitryon** (8). Adapted from the Molière play by Heinrich von Kleist. Opened November 17, 1970. (Closed November 22, 1970). **Die Kurve** (The Curve) by Tankred Dorst and **Die Kleinbürgerhochzeit** (The Wedding Feast) by Bertolt Brecht (10). Program of two one-act plays. Opened November 24, 1970. (Closed December 2, 1970) Produced by the Goethe Institute of Munich and Gert von Gontard at the Barbizon Plaza Theater.

PERFORMER	"AMPHITRYON"	"DIE KLEINBURGER-HOCHZEIT"	"DIE KURVE"
Dieter Brammer	Mercury	Father	Kriegbaum
Gisela Dreyer	Alkmene		
Ursula Erber		Bride's Sister	
Heini Göbel	Sosias	Mother	
Michael Hoffmann	Colonel	Young Man	
Claudia Lobe		Bride	
Inge Rassaerts	Charis	Wife	
Christian Rode	Amphitryon	Bridegroom's Friend	
Erich Schellow	Jupiter		
Heinz Schubert		Husband	Anton
Joost Siedhoff	Argatiphontidas	Bridegroom	Rudolf

BOTH PROGRAMS—Makeup and wigs, Ursula Esch; technical director, Thomas Siedhoff; assistant, Heinz Grape; press, Nat Dorfman, Irvin Dorfman.

AMPHITRYON—Directed by Dieter Munck; scenery, Christian Bussmann.

Molière's *Amphitryon* was last produced in New York last season by the Comédie Française in the French language, 2/3/70 for 6 performances.

DIE KURVE and DIE KLEINBURGERHOCHZEIT—Directed by Otto Tausig; scenery, Hansheinrich Palitzsch.

Die Kurve is an absurdist comedy about two men contemplating a curve in the road, the site of 24 fatal accidents. *Die Kleinbürgerhochzeit* is Brecht's farcical treatment of a bourgeois wedding feast, written when he was 20.

* The Negro Ensemble Company. Schedule of four programs. **Ododo** (Truth) (48). Musical play by Joseph A. Walker; music by Dorothy A. Dinroe. Opened November 17, 1970; see note. (Closed December 27, 1970) **Perry's Mission** by Clarence Young III and **Rosalee Pritchett** by Carlton and Barbara Molette (44). Program of two one-act plays. Opened January 12, 1971; see note. (Closed February 21, 1971) **The Dream on Monkey Mountain** (48). By Derek Walcott. Opened March 9, 1971; see note. (Closed April 18, 1971) *** Ride a Black Horse** (7). By John Scott. Opened May 25, 1971. Produced by The Negro Ensemble Company, Douglas Turner Ward artistic director, Robert Hooks executive director, Frederick Garrett administrative director, at St. Marks Playhouse.

ODODO

Ray Aranha	Jack Landron
Ethel Ayler	Garrett Morris
Marilyn B. Coleman	Roxie Roker
Deloris Gaskins	Garrett Saunders
Tonice Gwathney	Charles Weldon
Robert Jackson	Anita Wilson

Musicians: Chuck Fowler, pianist; Eustis Guillemet, bass; Dennis Heaven, guitarist; Andre Strombert, drummer.

Directed by Joseph A. Walker; musical direction, Dorothy A. Dinroe; choreography, Syvilla Fort, Joseph A. Walker; scenery, Edward Burbridge; lighting, Ernest Baxter; costumes, Dorothy A. Dinroe, Monica Myrie; stage manager, Buddy Butler; press, Howard Atlee, David Roggensack.

Act I, Scene 1: Conjuration of the original people. Scene 2: Africa re-experienced; Scene 3: Prisoners of war. Scene 4: Victory and death. Scene 5: Reconstruction blues. Act II, Scene 1: Slapping palms and checking out Harlem. Scene 2: Harlem's black women. Scene 3: Harlem's black men. Scene 4: Checking out the illusions. Scene 5: Black magnificence. Scene 6: Our children know. Scene 7: A hard look at us. Scene 8: What we need. Scene 9: The return of the original people.

Ododo, a Yoruba word for "truth," is a series of episodes, historical and contemporary, in a militant, angry representation of the black struggle, with a musical background.

PERRY'S MISSION

Lester (Bobo) Johnson	Adolph Caesar	Boosie Taylor	Win Wilford
Susie Collett	Katherine McGrath	Pooky Fields	Charles Grant
Henry Jorden	Charles Weldon	A Black Man	David Downing
Charles Stripling	William Jay	Jouba (Rockfist) Spinter	Arthur French
Bob Hinton	Jeff David	Bus Driver	Harold Triggs

ROSALEE PRITCHETT

Rosalee (Rose) Pritchett	Frances Foster	Robert Barron	Adolph Caesar
Doretha Ellen		Augustin (Gus) Lowe	Arthur French
(Dorry Sanders	Roxie Roker	Donald King	William Jay
Maybelle (Belle) Johnson	Esther Rolle	Wilbur Wittmer	David Downing
Dolly Mae (Doll) Anderson	Clarice Taylor	Thelma Franklin	Anita Wilson

BOTH PLAYS—Scenery, Edward Burbridge; lighting, Ernest Baxter; costumes, Monica Myrie.

PERRY'S MISSION—Directed by Douglas Turner Ward; assistant director, Afolabi Ajayi.
Time: The present. Place: A bar in the black section of a city. White and black characters—a cross-section of materialists, militants, etc.—in opposition which finally leads to a violent clash.

ROSALEE PRITCHETT—Directed by Shauneille Perry.
Time: The present. Place: A city in the deep South. Snobbish upper-class blacks ignore the revolutionary riot which seethes outside their doors.

THE DREAM ON MONKEY MOUNTAIN

Tigre	Lawrence Cook	Moustique	Antonio Fargas
Souris	Afolabi Ajayi	Basil	Robert Jackson
Cpl. Lestrade	Ron O'Neal	Market Wife	Esther Rolle
Makak	Roscoe Lee Browne	Market Inspector Pamphilion	David Downing
The Apparition	Margret Spear		

Village Women, Wives of Makak: Esther Bailey, Charliese Drakeford, Freda Teresa Vanterpool, Anita Wilson, Alma Woolsey. Village Men, Warriors: K. Lawrence Dunham, Laijba Durr, Noel Hall, Alexander O. Sallid.

Directed by Michael A. Schultz; choreography, Mary Barnett; scenery, Edward Burbridge; costumes, Lewis Brown; lighting, Ernest Baxter, Oyamo; production stage manager, Nate Barnett; assistant to director, L. Lawrence Dunham.

Time: The present. Place: A West Indian island. Prologue: Quatre Chemin Jail. Part I: Makak's hut, a country road, a village market. Part II: The cell, the forest, apotheosis. Epilogue: Quatre Chemin Jail.

An old man thrown in jail for drunkenness dreams of his past and of his future. A foreign play previously produced in Trinidad and in the United States at the Eugene O'Neill Memorial Foundation and the Mark Taper Forum, Los Angeles.

RIDE A BLACK HORSE

Carl Blanks	Graham Brown	Junior Bonner	David Downing
Bob	Madison Arnold	Alfred	Charles Grant
Edie	Marilyn Chris	Rudy	Charles Weldon
Harold	Adolph Caesar	Sharon	Deloris Gaskins
Max	William Countryman	Sandy	Barbara Clarke
Lloyd	Bill Cobbs	Harley	Jay Montgomery
Faye	Esther Rolle		

Directed by Douglas Turner Ward; scenery, Edward Burbridge; costumes, Monica Myrie; lighting, Ernest Baxter; sound, Charles Vincent; production stage manager, David Hanigan; press, Howard Atlee, David Roggensack, Irene Gandy.

Time: Now . . . before and after. Place: In the mind of the city and in the city of the mind. The play was presented in two acts.

Black liberal intellectual (a college professor) vs. the policies and philosophies of the ghetto. Previously produced as a work-in-progress at the Eugene O'Neill Foundation, Waterford, Conn.

NOTE: In this volume, the programs of off-Broadway subscription companies like The Negro Ensemble Company are sometimes exceptions to our rule of counting the number of performances from the date of the press coverage. When the press opening night takes place late in the play's run of paid public performances (after previews) for the subscription audience, we count the first subscription performance, not the press date, as opening night. Press date for *Ododo* was 11/24/70, for *Perry's Mission* and *Rosalee Pritchett* 1/21/71, for *The Dream on Monkey Mountain* 3/14/71.

Commune (64). Play compiled and arranged from various sources and group improvisations by The Performance Group. Produced by The Performance Group at the Performing Garage. Opened December 17, 1970. (Closed April 11, 1971)

David Angel	Stephen Borst	Spalding	Spalding Gray
Lara	Patricia Bower	Fearless Jim	James Griffiths
Mischa	Mik Cribben	Clementine	Joan MacIntosh
Jason	Jayme Daniel	Bruce	Bruce White
Susan Belinda Moonshine	Patric Epstein		

Directed by Richard Schechner; dramaturg, Lado Kralj; environmentalist, Jerry Rojo; technical director, Jerry Powell; stage manager, Elizabeth Lecompte; press, Catherine Farinon.

Scenes: A Day at the Ranch, Discovery and Exploration, The Belly of the Whale, Possibilities.

Hodge-podge of theatrical comments on the life and events of the day including the Sharon Tate murders, in a shapeless "non-literary" theater presentation devised by Richard Schechner's off-off-Broadway Performance Group.

Hamlet (7). Revival of the play by William Shakespeare. Produced by the Hunter College Concert Bureau in the Oxford and Cambridge Shakespeare Company production at Hunter College Playhouse. Opened December 26, 1970. (Closed January 3, 1971)

Claudius	Jonathan James-Moore	Priest; Player Queen	James Barraclough
Hamlet	Hugh Thomas	Marcellus; Lucianus	Adrian Webster
Polonius	Mike Baker	Barnardo	Richard Willey
Horatio	James Harris	Reynaldo	Stephen Wright
Laertes	Keith Kirby	Ghost; Fortinbras;	
Rosencrantz	Charles Sturridge	Player King	Andrew Hilton
Guildenstern	Gal Hawkesworth	Gertrude	Christabel Gairdner
Osric	John Madden	Ophelia	Claire Howard

Lords: Richard Willey, Stephen Wright, Ladies-in-Waiting: Gaynor Arnold, Sue Urwin.

Directed by Jonathan Miller; scenery, Bernard Culshaw; lighting, David Hersey; fight directed by William Hobbs; assistant director, Nicholas Arnold; stage manager, Jeremy Dain.

The touring Oxford-Cambridge college production of Hamlet, in a limited New York engagement at Hunter College.

One Night Stands of a Noisy Passenger (7). Program of three one-act plays by Shelley Winters: *The Noisy Passenger, Un Passage* and *Last Stand*. Produced by Howard Otway, Susan Richardson and Lawrence Goosen at the Actors Playhouse. Opened December 30, 1970. (Closed January 3, 1971)

Directed by Patricia Carmichael; scenery, Peter Harvey; costumes, Joseph G. Aulisi; lighting, Roger Morgan; production stage manager, Barbara Tuttle; press, Alan Eichler. With Richard Lynch, Sally Kirkland, Elizabeth Franz, Sam Schacht, Diane Ladd, Robert DeNiro.

Playlets about three sets of lovers. The first in *The Noisy Passenger* is a Marxist virgin and a young actor in 1940; the second in *Un Passage* is a movie star and a movie director called to Washington to testify in the McCarthy era, 1953; the third in *Last Stand* is an aging Academy Award-winning actress and a flower child in present-day Hollywood.

Stag Movie (88). Musical with book and lyrics by David Newburge; music by Jacques Urbont. Produced by Robert L. Steele at the Gate Theater. Opened January 3, 1971. (Closed March 21, 1971)

Mike Rosenthal	Hy Anzell	Cookie Kovac	Adrienne Barbeau
Marty Strauss	Stan Wiest	Arthur Jensen	Moose Matthews
Tanya Taranovna	Renata Mannhardt	Cop	Josip Elic
Tommy Tucker	Tod Miller	Maid	Shirl Bernheim
Rip Cord	Brad Sullivan		

Directed by Bernard Barrow; dances and musical numbers staged by Doug Rogers; musical direction and arrangements, Jacques Urbont; scenery and lighting, David Chapman; costumes, David Toser; music supervision, Len Berge; associate producer, Charles Prentiss; production stage manager, Charles Roden; press, Sol Jacobson, Lewis Harmon.

Time: The present. Place: A motel room near Kennedy Airport. The play was presented without intermission.

Naked actors and sex scenes in a tale of filming a blue movie in a motel room.

Gene Gebauer replaced Brad Sullivan 3/2/71.

MUSICAL NUMBERS

"Stag Movie"	Marty, Mike
"Looking at the Sun"	Rip
"I Want More Out of Life Than This"	Cookie, Rip
"Grocery Boy"	Tommy
"Splendor in the Grass"	Tommy, Cookie
"Splendor in the Grass" Ballet	Tommy, Cookie
"It's So Good"	Cookie, Tommy
"Get in Line"	Maid
"Try a Trio"	Rip, Cookie, Tommy
"Get Your Rocks off Rock"	Rip, Cookie, Tommy
"We Came Together"	Rip, Cookie, Tommy
Finale—Bows	Company

Macbeth (132). Revival of the play by William Shakespeare. Produced by Cora Gay Carr and Jerry Schlossberg at the Mercer-O'Casey Theater. Opened Monday, January 4, 1971. (Closed May 9, 1971)

Macbeth	David H. Leary	Ross	David Snell
1st Witch	Anne Ashcraft	Fleance	Tony Battelle
2d Witch; Gentlewoman	Sheila Coonan	Banquo	Rob Evan Collins
3d Witch; Macduff's Son	David Aaron	Macduff	Richard Greene
Duncan; Porter; Doctor	Peter Murphy	Lady Macbeth	Lynn Milgrim
Malcolm	Dalton Cathey	Macbeth's Servant	Jared Davis
Lennox	Devin Scott	Lady Macduff	Gwen Saska

Conceived and directed by Dino DeFilippi; lighting, Richard Nelson; scenery and costumes, David Chapman; production stage manager, Barbara Tuttle; press, Michael Alpert.

The play was presented in two parts, divided into three major sequences—I: Obtaining the crown, II: Defending the crown, III: Losing the crown.

The events of the play are staged as though seen in Macbeth's mind's eye, with a "stand-in" sometimes taking part in events on his behalf. *Macbeth* was staged as a collage last season off off Broadway by Richard Schechner's Performance Group. Its most recent straight productions were by IASTA for 12 performances 4/26/64 and by Joseph Papp at the Heckscher Theater 11/15/62 for 116 performances.

Earthlight (56). By Allan Mann and the Earthlight Ensemble; with music written and performed by Pure Love and Pleasure. Produced by Garrick Productions at the Garrick Theater. Opened January 17, 1971. (Closed March 21, 1971)

The Earthlight Ensemble:
 Wendy Blakely
 Sheila Rachel Cohen
 Ellyn Diskin
 Doug Fowley
 Tylar Gustavson
Pure Love and Pleasure:
 John Allair, organ
 Bob Bohanna, guitar
 Jacque Forman, drums

Barbara Pieters
Rick Pieters
Jane Richardson
Greg Stone
Richard Williams

Rob Moitaza, bass
Dave McAnally, vocalist
Pegge May, vocalist

Directed by Allan Mann; sounds, Stan Goldstein; lighting, Jim Gaine; scenery, Ron Tannis; additional choreography, Peggy Chiereska; press, Saul Richman, Myrna Post, Leslie Coven.

The play was presented without intermission. A collection of about two dozen topical vignettes, with a rock score.

The Shrinking Bride (1). By Jonathan Levy; music by William Bolcom; lyrics by Jonathan Levy. Produced by Tony Capodilupo and John Fink at the Mercury Theater. Opened and closed at the evening performance, January 17, 1971.

Directed by Marvin Gordon; scenery, T.E. Mason; costumes, Joseph G. Aulisi; lighting, Molly Friedel; press, Michael Alpert. With Joe Silver, Jack Somack, Diane Simkin, Donald Symington, Danny DeVito.

A "comedy with songs" about a self-made Jewish millionaire in his castle on the Hudson River.

In New England Winter (8). By Ed Bullins. Produced by the New Federal Theater, Woodie King Jr. and Dick Williams directors, at the Henry Street Playhouse. Opened January 26, 1971. (Closed January 31, 1971)

Directed by Dick Williams; scenery, Pedro Lujan; lighting, Buddy; production stage manager, Harry Grier; press, Howard Atlee, David Roggensack. With Norman Bush, Gloria Edwards, Mel Winkler, Tony Major, J. Herbert Kerr Jr., Darryl W. Lee, Donna O. Black, Garrett Morris.

Second in a planned 20-play cycle (first was entitled *In the Wine Time*) about the life of black people in the industrial areas of northern and western United States.

* Waiting for Godot (136). Revival of the play by Samuel Beckett. Produced by Edgar Lansbury, Mark Wright and Joseph Beruh in association with Stuart Duncan and H.B. Lutz at the Sheridan Square Playhouse. Opened February 3, 1971.

Estragon (Gogo)	Paul B. Price	Pozzo	Edward Winter
Vladimir (Didi)	Henderson Forsythe	A Boy	David Jay
Lucky	Anthony Holland		

Directed by Alan Schneider; designed by William Ritman; production stage manager, Gigi Cascio; produced in association with Alanjean Productions, Inc.; press, Max Eisen, Warren Pincus, Jeanne Merrick.

Waiting for Godot was first produced in New York by Michael Myerberg at the John Golden Theater 4/19/56 for 59 performances. It was revived by Mr. Myerberg 1/21/57 for 6 performances; by the San Francisco Actors Workshop off Broadway in the 1958-59 season, en route to the Brussels Worlds Fair; and in French as *En Attendant Godot* by Le Tréteau de Paris off Broadway 4/22/68 for 11 performances.

Oliver Clark replaced Paul B. Price 4/6/71. Jordan Charney replaced Henderson Forsythe 5/4/71. Larry Bryggman replaced Edward Winter 5/11/71.

The Repertory Theater of Lincoln Center. Schedule of five programs. **The Birthday Party** (39). Revival of the play by Harold Pinter. Opened February 5, 1971. (Closed March 14, 1971). **Landscape** and **Silence** (6). Program of two one-act revivals by Harold Pinter. Opened February 9, 1971 and played in repertory with *The Birthday Party*. (Closed February 19, 1971) **Scenes From American Life** (30). By A.R. Gurney Jr. Opened March 25, 1971. (Closed April 18, 1971) **Pictures in the Hallway** (20). Revival of the play by Sean O'Casey adapted by Paul Shyre. Opened April 29, 1971. (Closed May 15, 1971) And *Play Strindberg* by Friedrich Duerrenmatt, suggested by August Strindberg's *Dance of Death,* scheduled to open June 3, 1971. Produced by The Repertory Theater of Lincoln Center under the direction of Jules Irving at the Forum Theater.

THE BIRTHDAY PARTY

Petey	Ray Fry	Lulu	Lee Lawson
Meg	Betty Field	Goldberg	Robert Symonds
Stanley	Robert Phalen	McCann	John Harkins

Directed by Jules Irving; scenery, Marsha Louis Eck; lighting, John Gleason; costumes, Joseph G. Aulisi; production stage manager, Paul Bengston; stage manager, Barbara-Mae Phillips; press, Susan Bloch, William Schelble.

The Birthday Party was first produced on Broadway 10/3/67 for 126 performances. This is its first professional New York revival.

LANDSCAPE

Duff	Robert Symonds	Beth	Betty Field

SILENCE

Ellen	Barbara Tarbuck	Bates	Robert Phalen
Rumsey	Robert Symonds		

Directed by Jules Irving, based on the original Forum production by Peter Gill; scenery, Douglas W. Schmidt, based on designs by John Gunter; costumes by Douglas W. Schmidt, based on designs by Deirdre Clancy; lighting, John Gleason; production stage manager, Paul Bengston; stage manager, Barbara-Mae Phillips.

Pinter's one-actors had their New York premiere last season at the Forum Theater, 4/2/70 for 53 performances. On this program *Silence* was given first, then *Landscape,* then *Silence* was repeated.

SCENES FROM AMERICAN LIFE

James Broderick
Herbert Foster
Martha Henry
Elizabeth Huddle

Lee Lawson
Priscilla Pointer
Robert Symonds
Christopher Walken

David Frishberg, piano

Directed by Dan Sullivan; scenery and lighting, John Scheffler; costumes, James Berton Harris; production stage manager, Paul Bengston; stage manager, Jean-Daniel Noland. The play was presented in two acts.

Thirty-six vignettes of American life from the Depression into the 1980s, when the computers and authoritarians have taken over.

PICTURES IN THE HALLWAY

Mrs. Casside ....Aline MacMahon
Johnny Casside ....Stephen McHattie
Alice Boyd ....Helena Carroll

Mr. Anthony ....Michael McGuire
Uncle Tom ....Dermot McNamara
Narrator ....Paul Shyre

Directed by Paul Shyre; scenery and costumes, Douglas W. Schmidt; lighting, John Gleason; production stage manager, Paul Bengston.

O'Casey's second of six autobiographical volumes, in a stage adaptation which was first produced on Broadway 9/16/56 for 19 performances and has been revived often since that time.

Cooler Near the Lake (26). New edition of the Second City cabaret revue, with skits based on improvisations by the performers. Produced by Plaza 9 Music Hall in the Second City production at Plaza 9. Opened February 7, 1971. (Closed February 28, 1971)

David Blum
Brian Doyle-Murray
Jim Fisher
Roberta Maguire

Judy Morgan
Joseph O'Flaherty
Dan Ziskie

Directed and produced by Barnard Sahlins; music by Fred Kaz; choreography, Mel Spinney; piano interludes, Baldwin Bergersen; associate producer, Joyce Sloane; stage manager, Sandy Martin; press, Saul Richman.

Topical revue satirizing TV, politics, etc., in material developed from improvisations by members of this Chicago troupe. Sessions of new improvisation were held following performances on Tuesday, Wednesday and Thursday evenings. The production was presented in two acts.

Istanboul (8). By Rochelle Owens. Produced by Robert Weinstein in association with Trendsetter Enterprises, Ltd. at the Actors Playhouse. Opened February 8, 1971. (Closed February 13, 1971)

Directed by Robert Weinstein; scenery, Robert U. Taylor; costumes, Mylo Quam; lighting, John Dodd; music composed and performed by George Mgrdichian; additional music and sound, David Walker; movement consultant, Louis Johnson; production stage manager, Jon Froscher; press, Saul Richman. With Despo, Peter Carew, Marilyn Sokol, Irene Cooper, Conard Fowkes, Sarina C. Grant, Joseph Hunter, Gayla Osbourne.

Lustful and other adventures of Norman knights in Constantinople in the 15th century.

The Trial of the Catonsville Nine (130; see note). By Daniel Berrigan, S.J.; text prepared for New York production by Saul Levitt. Produced by the Phoenix Theater, T. Edward Hambleton managing director, and Leland Hayward, in cooperation with and at the Good Shepherd Faith Church. Opened February 7, 1971. (Closed May 30, 1971)

Daniel Berrigan	Ed Flanders	George Mische	Richard Jordan
Philip Berrigan	Michael Kane	Mary Moylan	Nancy Malone
David Darst	Leon Russom	Defense	David Spielberg
John Hogan	Barton Heyman	Judge	William Schallert
Thomas Lewis	Sam Waterston	Witness	Mary Jackson
Marjorie Melville	Gwen Arner	Prosecution	Davis Roberts
Thomas Melville	Joe Ponazecki		

Marshals: Peter Gorwin, James O'Connell, Harry Spillman.

Directed by Gordon Davidson; scenery, Peter Wexler; costumes, Albert Wolsky; lighting, Tharon Musser; production stage manager, Daniel Freudenberger; press, Sol Jacobson, Lewis Harmon, Ruth D. Smuckler.

Time: Monday, October 7, 1968. Place: United States District Court for the District of Maryland. The play was presented without intermission.

Edited transcript of the trial of the Berrigan brothers and seven others for the anti-war demonstration of burning draft records 5/17/68 at Catonsville, Md. The nine were found guilty and sentenced to 2, 3 and 3½ year terms. Previously produced by the Center Theater Group of Los Angeles at the Mark Taper Forum.

Ronnie Claire Edwards replaced Nancy Malone 4/6/71. Michael Moriarty replaced Richard Jordan 4/20/71. Colgate Salisbury replaced Ed Flanders and Mason Adams replaced William Schallert 5/4/71.

NOTE: *The Trial of the Catonsville Nine* closed off Broadway 5/30/71 after 130 performances and moved to the Lyceum Theater on Broadway to continue its run 6/2/71.

A Best Play; see page 174

* The House of Blue Leaves (126). By John Guare. Produced by Warren Lyons and Betty Ann Besch at the Truck and Warehouse Theater. Opened February 10, 1971.

Artie Shaughnessy	Harold Gould	2d Nun	Kay Michaels
Ronnie Shaughnessy	William Atherton	Little Nun	Alix Elias
Bunny Flingus	Anne Meara	M.P.	Thomas F. Flynn
Bananas Shaughnessy	Katherine Helmond	The White Man	Bruce Cobb
Corinna Stroller	Margaret Linn	Billy Einhorn	Frank Converse
Head Nun	Rita Karin		

Directed by Mel Shapiro; original songs by John Guare; scenery, Karl Eigsti; costumes, Jane Greenwood; lighting, John Tedesco; production stage manager, Carl Hunt; press, Merle Debuskey, Faith Geer.

Time: 1965. Place: New York City. Prologue: The El Dorado Bar and Grill. Act I: An apartment in Sunnyside, Queens, on October 4, 1965. Act II, Scene 1: Immediately following. Scene 2: That evening.

The Pope's visit to New York touches off all the latent neuroses among the family and friends of a middle-aged zookeeper who longs for a chance to write songs for the movies; the tone is mostly comic, mostly black.

Jeremiah Sullivan replaced Frank Converse and Glenn Walken replaced William Atherton 4/20/71.

A Best Play; see page 215

Acrobats and **Line** (32). Program of two one-act plays by Israel Horovitz. Produced by the New Comedy Theater (Jerry Schlossberg, James Hammerstein, Israel Horovitz, Albert Poland) at the Theater de Lys. Opened February 15, 1971. (Closed March 14, 1971)

ACROBATS

Man	Danny duVal	Edna	Trina duVal

LINE

Fleming	John Randolph	Dolan	John Cazale
Stephen	Richard Dreyfuss	Arnall	Barnard Hughes
Molly	Ann Wedgeworth		

Directed by James Hammerstein; design, Neil Peter Jampolis; additional staging, Grover Dale; production stage manager, Robert Vandergriff; press, Samuel J. Friedman, Louise Weiner Ment.

Both plays—Time: The present. Place: The present.

Acrobats is a comic quarrel between a husband-and-wife team of acrobats during a performance. *Line* is about the human being's, particularly the artist's, drive to excel. It has been previously produced in various experimental versions at Cafe La Mama, Stowe, Vt., Paramus, N.J. and the Mark Taper Forum in Los Angeles.

Do It Again! (14). Musical revue with music by George Gershwin; lyrics by Ira Gershwin; conceived by Bert Convy. Produced by Jay H. Fuchs and Stuart Duncan at the Promenade Theater. Opened February 18, 1971. (Closed February 28, 1971)

Directed by Bert Convy; musical supervision, William Cox; lighting, Roger Morgan; scenic consultant, Barry Arnold; press, Marvin Kohn. With Margaret Whiting, Clifton Davis, Robin Benson, Susan Long, Marion Ramsey.

Described as a "Gershwin Musicade," a cabaret-style collection of songs by the Gershwins.

Things That Almost Happen (6). Program of three one-act plays by Claude McNeal: *Morton: The Patient, The Courtship of Kevin and Roxanne* and *Dominic's Lover* based on Robert Browning's *Porphyria's Lover*. Produced by Jules and Gila Zalon at the Provincetown Playhouse. Opened February 18, 1971. (Closed February 21, 1971)

Directed by Claude McNeal; scenery, Tim Wilson; lighting, Paul T. Holland; production stage manager, Robert W. Perkins; press, Howard Atlee, David Roggensack. With Sam Coppola, Richard Lynch, Karen Rosenblatt, Patrick McDermott.

Morton: The Patient is a session between analyst and psychotic patient. *The Courtship of Kevin and Roxanne* is about lovers arguing whether or not to indulge in sex. *Dominic's Lover* is about a princess playing games with two lovers.

AC/DC (28). By Heathcote Williams. Produced by the Chelsea Theater Center of Brooklyn, Robert Kalfin artistic director, Michael David executive director, at the Brooklyn Academy of Music. Opened February 23, 1971. (Closed March 21, 1971)

Gary	James Cromwell	Maurice	Edward Zang
Melody	Jillian Lindig	Perowne	Stefan Gierasch
Sadie	Susan Batson	Pixie Bosanquet	Margaret Braidwood

Directed by John Hirsch; scenery, John Scheffler; video by Video Free America; lighting, Burl Hash; stage manager, Judi Fisher; press, Ron Christopher.

Off-off-Broadway performance group's production of a play in which pin-ball machines, TV sets and other electronic equipment are symbols of the hallucinations of this freaked-out generation. A foreign play previously produced in London at the Royal Court.

The Survival of St. Joan (17). Musical with book and lyrics by James Lineberger; music by Hank and Gary Ruffin. Produced by Haila Stoddard and Neal Du Brock at the Phyllis Anderson Theater. Opened February 28, 1971. (Closed March 14, 1971)

Directed by Chuck Gnys; scenery and costumes, Peter Harvey; lighting, Thomas Skelton; musical supervisor, Stephen Schwartz; production stage manager, Sean Gillespie; press, Betty Lee Hunt, Henry Luhrman. With F. Murray Abraham, Gary Allan, Lenny Baker, Ronald Bishop, Richard Bright, Gretchen Corbett, Elizabeth Eis, Judith Granite, Peter Lazer, Anthony Marciona, Patricia O'Connell, Janet Sarno, Tom Sawyer, Matthew Tobin, Willie Rook, Bill Braden and the Smoke Rise vocal-instrumental group.

Described as a "medieval rock opera" (in which none of the characters sings) imagining what might have happened if Joan of Arc had been set free instead of executed.

Tarot (38). Musical pantomime conceived by Rubber Duck (Joe McCord); music by Tom Constanten and Touchstone. Produced by Richard Fields, William W. Rippner associate producer, at Circle in the Square. Opened March 4, 1971; see note. (Closed April 4, 1971)

Hanged Man; Justice ......Edward Barton	Old Fool; Mystic Carpenter ...Renos Mandis
Frog; Tree; Page of Wands ....Cassia Besson	The Fool ....Joe McCord
Eternity; Maiden ....Cynthia Briggs	Turtle; Death;
Thief; Moon; Judgment ....Maxine Herman	Philosopher ....John Proctor Parriott
White Magician;	Black Magician; Greed;
Mystic Farmer ....John Kuhner	Devil ....Frederick Rivera

Touchstone (rock combo): Jim Byers classic guitar, Tom Constanten electric piano, Paul Dresher electric guitar, flute, sitar, steel pedal, Art Fayer electric violin, Gary Hirsh percussion, Wes Steele bass guitar, cello.

Directed by Robert Kalfin; scenery and costumes, Stephen Hendrickson; lighting, Burl Hash; production stage manager, Jan Moerel; press, Robert Ganshaw, Fred Weterick.

Symbolic adventures of a Fool among characters representing various cards in the Tarot deck, in the form of a rock-mime musical (no singing or talking).

NOTE: This production of *Tarot* originated off off Broadway in the schedule of Chelsea Theater Center at the Brooklyn Academy of music, opening 12/11/71, before being transferred to off Broadway, with some changes.

Look Where I'm At (5). Musical based on Thorne Smith's *Rain in the Doorway;* book by James Leasor and Gib Dennigan; lyrics by Frank Stanton and Murray Semos. Produced by Jean Merie Lee at Theater Four. Opened March 5, 1971. (Closed March 7, 1971)

Directed by Wakefield Poole; dances, Wakefield Poole; scenery and lighting, Robert Guerra; costumes, Rosemary Heyer; arrangements, Sid Ramin; musical director, Jack Lee; press, Bill Doll. With Ron Husmann, Sherri Spillane, Mary Bracken Phillips, Arthur Bartown, Martin Ross, Jennifer Williams.

About a man in the middle, equally disenchanted with hippies and hard hats.

A Day in the Life of Just About Everyone (8). Musical with book, lyrics and music by Earl Wilson Jr.; additional dialogue by Michael Sawyer. Produced by Robert Shelley, associate producers Lawrence Simon and Midge LaGuardia, at the Bijou Theater. Opened March 9, 1971. (Closed March 14, 1971)

Directed by Tom Panko; musical direction, Elman Anderson; scenery and lighting, Andrew Greenhut; costumes, Miles White; orchestrations and vocal arrangements, Don Pippin; production stage manager, Joseph Olney; press, David Lipsky. With Earl Wilson Jr., June Gable, Daniel Fortus, Dickie Evans, DeMarest Grey, Bennett Kinsey.

Examination of one man's life in the present era.

King Heroin (30). By Al Fann. Produced by Al Fann Theatrical Ensemble at St. Philip's Community Theater. Opened March 17, 1971. (Closed April 11, 1971)

Bessie ....Barbara Fann	Mable; Nurse's Aid ....Vernee Watson
Doctor; Bartender ....Victor Mims	Lt. Hendrix;
Mrs. Johnson; Barfly .....Marilyn Thomas	Voice of King Heroin ....Al Fann
Court Clerk; Lucky ....Joe Johnson,	1st Woman; Secretary; Booster;
Adam Wade	Social Worker ....Susan Singleton
1st Child ....Melanie Fann	2d Woman; Mrs. Grey ....Nathylin Flowers
2d Child ....Tracy Fann	Reeta Johnson ....Reeta White
Shelley ....Shelley Fann	Adam; Waiter; Murphy;
Mark ....Alfred Little	Perfume Hustler ....Adam Wade
Candy; Nurse ....Candy Mobley	James "Mad Daddy"
Benny the Cat ....Tim Pelt	McDonald ....William Pelt
Crap Shooter; Gary ....Gary Harris	Socialite ....La-Vern Fields
Addict; Sylvester C. Fenton;	Adrian; Harlem Belle ....Adrian James
Weasel ....Duke Sparks	

Directed by Al Fann; scenery and costumes, Al Fann; production stage manager, Tim Pelt; stage manager, Victor Mims; press, Joe Johnson, Robert Ganshaw.

Drama of drug addiction in Harlem written partly as a reaction to the death of Walter Vandermeer, a 12-year-old schoolboy, and presented under the auspices of the St. Philips Community Service Council, in this off-off-Broadway production in Harlem.

* One Flew Over the Cuckoo's Nest (79). Revival of the play by Dale Wasserman. Produced by Sankowich/Golyn Productions at the Mercer-Hansberry Theater. Opened March 23, 1971.

Chief Bromden ....William Burns	Frank Scanlon ....Edwin Cooper
Aide Williams ....William Paterson Jr.	Anthony Martini ....Danny De Vito
Aide Washington .....John Henry Redwood	Ruckly ....Joseph Napoli
Nurse Ratched ....Janet Ward	Randle Patrick McMurphy ..William Devane
Nurse Flinn ....Eve Packer	Dr. Spivey ....Jack Aaron
Dale Harding ....James J. Sloyan	Aide Turkle ....Jeffrey Miller
Billy Bibbitt ....Lawrie Driscoll	Candy ....Louie Piday
Charles Atkins	Technician ....Kelly Monaghan
Cheswick III ....William Duff-Griffin	Sandy ....Sydney Andreani

Voices: John Garber, Doug Armand, Joseph Napoli, Danny Rich, Marc Nelsen, Teddi Kern, James Barnett, John Blakeley, Lee D. Sankowich.

Directed by Lee D. Sankowich; designed by Neil Peter Jampolis; produced by Rudi Golyn; production superviser, Harvey Medlinsky; stage manager, Daniel Hild; press, Seymour Krawitz, Patricia McLean Krawitz.

Place: A ward in a state mental hospital. The play was presented in two acts.

A partial rewrite by Dale Wasserman of his play adapted from a Ken Kesey novel, about the systematic destruction of a patient by the cruelty of the authorities of a mental institution. The play was previously produced on Broadway 11/13/63 for 82 performances with Kirk Douglas in the leading role of McMurphy.

* The Proposition (99). Improvisational revue conceived by Allan Albert. Produced by Manon Enterprises Ltd. and Propositions, Inc. at the Gramercy Arts Theater. Opened March 24, 1971.

Actors:
Jane Curtin	Paul Kreppel
Munson Hicks	Josh Mostel
Judy Kahan	Karen Welles

Musicians:
Tanny Troob, piano	Gualberto Pillich, bass

Directed by Allan Albert.

Revue improvised entirely from suggestions supplied by the audience at each performance, tending to be topical and comic. Previously produced in Boston.

The Red White and Black (1). Musical with book and lyrics by Eric Bentley; music by Brad Burg. Produced by Donald Goldman at the Players Theater. Opened and closed at the evening performance, March 30, 1971.

Production conceived by John Dillon; directed by Eric Bentley; musical direction and arrangements, Brad Burg; scenery, Bill Mikeulewicz; lighting, Robert Engstrom; costumes, Margaret Tobin; production stage manager, Rick Rotante; press, Saul Richman. With Pamela Adams, Sofia Adoniadis, Antonio Azito, Rob Farkas, Phil Patterson, Marilyn Sokol, Bill Sweeney and The History of Russia (rock group).

Topical political satire with a left-of-center stance. Previously produced at Cafe La Mama.

Behold! Cometh the Vanderkellans (23). By William Wellington Mackey. Produced by Woodie King Associates in association with Russell Price and Ida Epps, by special arrangement with Lucille Lortel Productions, Inc. at the Theater de Lys. Opened March 31, 1971. (Closed April 18, 1971)

Dr. Vanderkellan ....Graham Brown   Gregory Vanderkellan ....Carl Byrd
Mrs. Vanderkellan ....Frances Foster   Luiz Vanderkellan ....Robert Christian
Desiree Vanderkellan ....Roxie Roker

Directed by Edmund Cambridge; scenery, George Corrin; costumes, Audrey Smaltz; lighting, Roger Morgan; sound, Gary Harris; production stage manager, Steven Holmes; press, Howard Atlee.
Black college president and his well-to-do family face revolt among the black students on their campus.

The Olathe Response (6). By Jack Marshall. Produced by Rene Enriquez and Jack Marshall at the Actors Playhouse. Opened April 5, 1971. (Closed April 10, 1971)

Directed by Rene Enriquez; scenery, Jim Hardy; costumes, Alexis Blassini; special music composed by Joe Cain; press, Betty Lee Hunt. With Joe Santos, Ann Whiteside, Peter Burnell.
Nymphomaniac and homosexual fight over a young man whom they have captured.

Six (8). Musical revue with book, music and lyrics by Charles Strouse. Produced by Slade Brown at the Cricket Playhouse. Opened April 12, 1971. (Closed April 18, 1971)

Directed by Peter Coe; musical direction, Wally Harper; associate musical director, Rod Derefinko; scenery, Richard Nelson; press, Samuel J. Friedman, Shirley Herz. With Johanna Albrecht, Lee Beery, Alvin Ing, Gail Nelson, Gilbert Price, Hal Watters.
Topical revue with contemporary political, sociological and ecological subjects.

L'Amante Anglaise (14). Play in the French language by Marguerite Duras. Produced by Le Tréteau de Paris, Jean de Rigault executive producer, at the Barbizon Plaza Theater. Opened April 14, 1971. (Closed April 24, 1971)

Claire Lannes ....Madeleine Renaud   L'Interrogateur ....Michael Lonsdale
Pierre Lannes ....Claude Dauphin

Directed by Claude Régy; recorded announcement, François Perier; production stage manager, Francis Charles; press, Arthur Cantor, Joel Wyman.
The play was presented without intermission. Study of a murderess, previously produced in English translation this season under the title *A Place Without Doors* (see its entry in the "Plays Produced on Broadway" section of this volume).

Kiss Now (4). Musical with book and lyrics by Maxine Klein; music by William S. Fischer. Produced by John Ramsey, William Formaad and Milan Stitt at the Martinique Theater. Opened April 20, 1971. (Closed April 23, 1971)

Conceived and directed by Maxine Klein; musical direction and vocal arrangements, Herbert Kaplan; orchestrations, Bill Brohn; choreography, Sandra Caprin; scenery and lighting, Richard Devin; costumes, Nancy Adzima; assistant to the producers, Barbara Wood; press, Howard Atlee, David Roggensack. With Lloyd Bremseth, Sandra Caprin, Nancy Denning, Louise Hoven, Irving A. Lee, Susan McAneny, Lyle Pearsons, Eddie Silas.
Episodic variations on the word "kiss."

* Long Day's Journey Into Night (35). Revival of the play by Eugene O'Neill. Produced by Edgar Lansbury, Jay H. Fuchs, Stuart Duncan and Joseph Beruh at the Promenade Theater. Opened April 21, 1971.

James Tyrone ....Robert Ryan   Edmund Tyrone ....James Naughton
Mary Cavan Tyrone ....Geraldine Fitzgerald   Cathleen ....Paddy Croft
James Tyrone Jr. ....Stacy Keach

Directed by Arvin Brown; scenery, Elmon Webb, Virginia Dancy; costumes, Whitney Blausen; lighting, Ronald Wallace; production stage manager, Gail Bell; press, Max Eisen, Warren Pincus.
Long Day's Journey Into Night was first produced on Broadway 11/7/56 for 390 performances, a Best Play and a Critics and Pulitzer Prize winner. Its most recent New York revival was by the Royal Dramatic Theater of Sweden, 5/15/62 for 2 performances.
John Atkins replaced Stacy Keach 5/25/71.

The Ballad of Johnny Pot (16). Musical with book and lyrics by Carolyn Richter; music by Clinton Ballard. Produced by Wyler Productions and Bob McDevitt at Theater Four. Opened April 26, 1971. (Closed May 9, 1971)

Directed by Joshua Shelley; musical direction and dance arrangements, Harrison Fisher; music performed by Bandana; scenery and lighting, Lloyd Burlingame; costumes, Alvin Colt; orchestrations, William Goldstein; choreography, Jay Norman; stage manager, Paul W. Stetz; press, Betty Lee Hunt, Henry Luhrman. With John Bennett Perry, Betty Buckley, Ben Bryant, Jim Weston, Peter Jason, Colin Garrey, Leroy Lessane.

About a hippie Johnny Appleseed who plants marijuana all over the place.

And Whose Little Boy Are You? (1). By Rod Parker. Produced by Haap Productions Company at the McAlpin Rooftop Theater. Opened and closed at the evening performance May 3, 1971.

Directed by Sherwood Arthur; scenery and costumes, Charles Rosen; lighting, Robert Guerra; stage manager, Robert W. Perkins; press, Seymour Krawitz. With Richard Dreyfuss, Will Hussung, Stratton Walling, Joe Jamrog, Henry Calvert, Loretta Fury, Kathryn Grody, Marty Greene, Martin Shakar, Grant Code, Philip Huston, Rudolph Weiss.

Woman claims that God is the father of her child conceived out of wedlock.

* Godspell (16). Musical based on the Gospel according to St. Matthew; conceived by John-Michael Tebelak; music and lyrics by Stephen Schwartz. Produced by Edgar Lansbury, Stuart Duncan, Joseph Beruh, associate producer Charles Haid, at the Cherry Lane Theater. Opened May 17, 1971.

Lamar Alford	Sonia Manzano
Peggy Gordon	Gilmer McCormick
David Haskell	Jeffrey Mylett
Joanne Jonas	Stephen Nathan
Robin Lamont	Herb Simon

Musicians: Steve Reinhardt keyboard, Jesse Cutler bass and guitar, Richard Labonti bass and guitar, Ricky Shutter percussion.

Directed by John-Michael Tebelak; lighting, Lowell B. Achziger; costumes, Susan Tzu; stage manager, Nina Faso; press, Gifford/Wallace.

The story of Jesus Christ told simplistically, in a semi-rock musical. Previously produced at the Cafe La Mama. The play was presented in two parts.

MUSICAL NUMBERS—"Tower of Babble," "Prepare Ye the Way of the Lord," "Save the People," "Day by Day," "Learn Your Lessons Well," "Bless the Lord," "All for the Best," "All Good Gifts," "Light of the World," "Turn Back, O Man," "Alas for You," "By My Side" (music by Peggy Gordon, lyrics by Jay Hamburger), "We Beseech Thee," "On the Willows," Finale.

* The Homecoming (16). Revival of the play by Harold Pinter. Produced by Joel W. Schenker at the Bijou Theater. Opened May 18, 1971.

Max	Eric Berry	Joey	Danny Sewell
Lenny	Tony Tanner	Teddy	Lawrence Keith
Sam	Norman Barrs	Ruth	Janice Rule

Directed by Jerry Adler; scenery and lighting, Dahl Delu; press, Sol Jacobson, Lewis Harmon.

The Homecoming, originally produced in London, was first produced on Broadway 1/5/67 for 324 performances. It was named a Best Play of its season and was voted the best play of the season by the New York Drama Critics Circle.

Any Resemblance to Persons Living or Dead . . . (8). By Elliott Caplin. Produced by Lou-Na-Poseidon Ltd. by arrangement with Robert L. Steele at the Gate Theater. Opened May 24, 1971. (Closed May 30, 1971)

Directed by Loukas Skipitaris; music by Saul Honigman; scenery, Donald Padgett; costumes, David Toser; lighting, Richard Nelson; production stage manager, Smith Lawrence; press,

Robert Ganshaw. With Marc Alaimo, John Call, Joanne Dusseau, Frank Freda, Charles Hudson, Fred Morsell, Ted Thurston, Matthew Tobin, Ruth Warrick.
Comic allegory, a man strives to become God.

Woyzeck (8). Revival of the play by Georg Buchner; translated by Henry J. Schmidt; additional adaptation for this production by Richard Reich. Produced by Robert Weinstein in association with Two Arts Playhouse at the Fortune Theater. Opened May 25, 1971. (Closed May 30, 1971)

Directed by Robert Weinstein; scenery, Bob Olson; costumes, Daniel Michaelson; lighting, Jon Brittain; production stage manager, Robert O'Rourke; press, Saul Richman. With Curt Karibalis, Kenneth W. Lowry, Julienne Marshall, Dorin McGough and the Actors' Group.
New version of the Buchner scenes about a man's murder of his mistress.

Some Additional Productions
And Off Off Broadway

This selected listing of off-off-Broadway and other experimental New York productions was compiled by Robert Schroeder (see his report on the 1970-71 off-off-Broadway scene in "The Season in New York" section of this volume). Leading producing groups are identified in alphabetical order in bold face type; their special characteristics are identified, and examples of their outstanding 1970-71 programs are listed. In most cases these are works-in-progress with changing scripts and casts, seldom with a premiere or engagement of record.

ADAL Theater (Agrupacion de Arte Latinamericano). In an end-stage loft, well-equipped technically, this group is performing Latin-American plays in Spanish. The weekend performances are publicized in the Spanish-language press. Admission is charged. This season's plays included:

THE TOOTHBRUSH by Chilean playwright Jorge Diaz, directed by Max Ferra. THE INVADERS by Chilean playwright Egon Wolff, directed by Max Ferra. THE CRIMINALS by the Cuban Jose Triana, directed by Magaly Alabaus and Manuel Martin.

Afro-American Studio. Seating about 50 in a loft over a fraternal organization building, and using minimal equipment, this troupe specializes in dramas of interest to the Harlem community. Actors are usually non-Equity, and shows run several weekends. Performances are not advertised, but a mailing list is circulated. Admission is charged. This season's presentations included:

EL HAJJ MALIK by N. R. Davidson, directed by Ernie McClintock.

Al Fann Theatrical Ensemble. Made up of youths recruited from the Harlem streets over the past five years, this troupe has been built by founder-director Al Fann into a touring unit presenting annual productions in various New York locations, and on wide-ranging road trips. This year's show also was presented on Teleprompter Cable TV in uptown Manhattan. When the show was running at St. Philip's Community Theater on West 133d St., the troupe ran buses from Columbus Circle, midtown, with the kids entertaining enroute. The production this season:

KING HEROIN by Al Fann, directed by the author (see its entry in this volume's "Plays Produced Off Broadway" listing).

American Center for Stanislavski Theater Art. Sonia Moore's school for acting, set hard into the Stanislavski tradition, plays several productions a year in an end-stage loft seating about 50. Productions are advertised, and admission is charged. This year's work included:

DESIRE UNDER THE ELMS by Eugene O'Neill, directed by Sonia Moore. BIRD-BATH by Leonard Melfi, directed by Sonia Moore. THE CHERRY ORCHARD by An-ton Chekhov, directed by Sonia Moore, in a new translation by Irene Moore and Sonia Moore.

American Place Theater Workshop. In addition to its schedule of Equity-cast, subscription-audience regular presentations, the American Place Theater conducts season-long workshop activity, including short runs on the main stage between major productions. Workshop presentations this season included:

BIGFOOT by Ronald Tavel, directed by Mr. Tavel.

The American Theater Club. In an end-stage loft, this group specializes in the early American drama, although some new dramas are included. Shows run three or four weekends, before some 40 spectators. Performers generally are Equity, playing under showcase provisions. Facilities are minimal. Performances are advertised, and admission is charged. The shows this season included:

THE GLADIATOR by Robert Montgomery Bird, directed by Ellis Santone. THE PATRIOTS, ETC. by Robert Munford, directed by Richard Kuss. ROCKET TO THE MOON by Clifford Odets, directed by Ellis Santone. HE AND SHE by Rachel Crothers, directed by Ellis Santone.

ANTA Matinee Theater Series. Nominally sponsored by the American National Theater and Academy, and actually impresarioed by Lucille Lortel, and presented in Miss Lortel's proscenium Theater de Lys, this annual series plays Monday nights and Tuesday afternoons on the set of the show playing the de Lys Tuesday evening through Sunday. Productions are advertised, and the series' mailing list is kept advised. Admission is charged, and subscription sales are sought. This season's shows:

THE LIFE AND TIMES OF J. WALTER SMINTHEUS by Edgar White, directed by Alice Spivak. A PASSAGE TO E. M. FORSTER, a play based on the works of Forster "compiled" by William Roerick and Thomas Coley, directed by Roerick. THE PERFECT MATCH written and directed by William Derringer, and SLOW MEMORIES by Barry Litvack, directed by Joseph Cali. HERITAGE written and directed by P. J. Barry.

The Assembly. This new operation in Greenwich Village presents a wide range of plays from the theater's literature, as well as new offerings. The full schedule is regularly advertised, and admission is charged. This year's presentations included:

'TIS A PITY SHE'S A WHORE by John Ford, directed by Terry Walker. THE OUTHOUSE by Dennis Spedelieri and Kirk Lovell, directed by Bill Lentsch and Leanna Lenhardt. CREDITORS by August Strindberg, director not credited. UP EAST AND WAY DOWN WEST by Robert Clapsadle, and THE BRIDE COMES TO YELLOW SKY adapted by Frank Crocitto from Stephen Crane, director not credited. TWO FROM ULYSSES by F. V. Hunt, directed by Shelly Warwick. THE GINGER MAN by J. P. Donleavy, directed by Terry Walker. DYLAN by Sidney Michaels, directed by June Rovenger. ANNA CHRISTIE by Eugene O'Neill, directed by Terry Walker.

Byrd Hoffman School of Byrds. This troupe, in its third season under the direction of Robert Wilson, creates a production a year, utilizing literally scores of actors, dancers, musicians, etc. Showings are two or three times a season at the Brooklyn Academy of Music. Performances are advertised, and admission is charged: This year's extravaganza:

DEAFMAN GLANCE, a troupe conception inspired and directed by Robert Wilson, with a cast of 60, not counting the nine apes, four turtles, and seven babies, but including the pregnant women. The set: a forest of white ladies.

Circle Theater Company. In its upper-Broadway loft, this troupe carries forward the work of a number of the originators of off off Broadway. The shows are advertised, admission is charged, and the playing area is almost infinitely variable. Technical facilities are good to average. This season's work included:

SEXTET (YES) by Lanford Wilson, directed by Marshall W. Mason. THE GHOST SONATA by August Strindberg, directed by Rob Thirkield. PRINCESS IVONA by Witold Gombrowicz, directed by Joe Jacobs.

CSC Repertory. This troupe presents season-long repertory performances of established plays, or adaptations of well-known literary works, and endeavors to build a subscription audience. Its 75-seat store-front theater in Greenwich Village is rudimentary, but the approach to the work is serious. Performances are advertised, and admission is charged. This year's repertory has included:

MAN AND SUPERMAN by George Bernard Shaw, directed by Christopher Martin, performed with the *Don Juan in Hell* sequence. HAMLET by William Shakespeare, directed by Christopher Martin assisted by Frank Dwyer. This was the three and one-half hour uncut version. MOBY DICK based on the novel by Herman Melville, adapted and directed by Christopher Martin. ROSEN-CRANTZ & GUILDENSTERN ARE DEAD by Tom Stoppard, directed by Frank Dwyer. TWELFTH NIGHT by William Shakespeare, directed by Harris Laskawy, music arranged by Paul E. Doniger. UNCLE VANYA by Anton Chekhov, translated by Constance Garnett, directed by Christopher Martin, music composed by Paul E. Doniger. PERICLES, PRINCE OF TYRE by William Shakespeare, directed by Christopher Martin.

The Cubiculo. Philip Meister conducts an experimental theater associated with his Equity troupe known as The National Shakespeare Company. Seating about 50 in a well-equipped theater, the Cubiculo advertises and charges admission. Productions this season included:

GEORGIE-PORGIE by George Birimisa, directed by Ron Link. CLEARING HOUSE by Donald Kvares, directed by Frank Errante. RELATIONS by Lynne Honickman, directed by Philip Meister. THE PLAYBOY OF SEVILLE by Tirso de Molina, adapted by Mandel and Schizzano, directed by Clinton Atkinson. MRS. DALLY HAS A LOVER in a new version by William Hanley, directed by Paulette Attie. BRAND by Henrik Ibsen, directed by Alan Fox, in the Michael Meyer translation. THE CAGE by Mario Fratti, directed by Robert Geary. THE FRIDAY BENCH by Mario Fratti, and THEY CAME by Bonnie Beardsley, both directed by Harry F. Thompson. EXPERIMENTS WITH THE GREAT GOD BROWN staged by Steve Sunshine, no author credit other than a recognition of Eugene O'Neill as springboard. SHE STOOPS TO CONQUER by Oliver Goldsmith, directed by Edward Greer. A BAG OF FLIES by Venable Herndon, directed by Bob Sickinger. THE SWEETSHOPPE MYRIAM and KLARA, two plays by Ivan Klima, translated by Ruth Willard, directed by Pirie MacDonald.

The Dove Company. Harold Herbstman's long-established group performs new and old plays in repertory in a church auditorium. Performances are advertised, and donations are accepted. 500 could be seated, but rarely are. Technical equipment is minimal; the church is everywhere. This season included:

ASSES by Wilson Lehr, directed by Ray Hagan. BEAD-TANGLE a revue in one act, and A BAD PLACE TO GET YOUR HEAD by Robert Patrick, directed by Denny Leone. DISCOVER AMERICA by Jeannine O'Reilly, directed by Eric Conklin. STRANGULA-TION by Donald Kvares, directed by Harold Herbstman. A PHOENIX TOO FREQUENT by Christopher Fry, directed by Kathleen Huber. HOW HE LIED TO HER HUSBAND by George Bernard Shaw, directed by Harold Herbstman.

Dramatis Personae. Now the oldest of Manhattan's porno palaces, this theater has —again—gone the competition one step farther. You can catch the show in street clothes, or in "Contemplation Robes" (you guessed it—you can see right through them), or nude. This season's offering:

THE V.I.P. (VERY IMPORTANT PHAL-
LUS) by Stanley Seidman, directed by Steven
Baker.

Equity Library Theater. As a means of displaying new talent among its membership, Actors Equity Association produces a season-long series of revivals at the Master Theater, a 300-seat house just off upper Broadway. The stage is proscenium and the equipment professional-level. Admission is on a donation basis. Performances usually are not advertised, but a mailing list is circulated. This season was made up of:

BEN BAGLEY'S SHOESTRING REVUES, a compendium based on the revues produced by Ben Bagley, directed and choreographed by Miriam Fond, with special dances choreographed by Bick Goss. JOHNNY NO-TRUMP by Mary Mercier, directed by Chuck Vincent. (Miss Mercier revised and updated her script for this production.) GREENWIL-LOW, a musical with music and lyrics by Frank Loesser, book by Lesser Samuels and Frank Loesser, based on the novel by B. J. Chute, choreography by Deborah Jowitt, directed by Clinton Atkinson. PRESENT LAUGHTER by Noel Coward, directed by

Raphael Kelly. HÉLOISE by James Forsyth, directed by S. Darrell Calvin. RUDDIGORE by W. S. Gilbert and Arthur Sullivan, directed by Lewis Pierce, choreographed by Joan Ashlyn. THE FALSE CONFESSIONS by Pierre de Marivaux, English version by W. S. Merwin, directed by Kent Paul. NOW IS THE TIME FOR ALL GOOD MEN, a musical with book and lyrics by Gretchen Cryer, music by Nancy Ford, directed by Ronald Roston, choreography by Judy Blackstone. (Like *Johnny No-Trump*, a revised and updated script by the original authors).

Equity Theater Informals. In addition to its productions at the Master Theater, Equity presents "informals" in the auditorium of the Library & Museum of the Performing Arts at Lincoln Center. Admission is free. The Equity Library Theater mailing list receives notices, and the presentations are publicized in the New York Public Library bulletins. Shows this season included:

A MUSICAL TIMEPIECE, by Alan Foster Friedman, directed by Allen R. Belknap. SMALLER THAN LIFE by and with Dorothy Vann and Jim Evering, directed by Leland Ball. SKYE, a musical with book and

lyrics by Avery Corman and Dan Rustin, music by Ben Finn, directed by James Curtan. SHOE STORE by Shirley Rhodes, directed by Joe Silver.

The Greenwich Mews Spanish Theater. In a facility long associated with the process of presenting works of minority groups to the New York public, this troupe presents theatrical works from the Spanish-language literature in alternate English and Spanish versions. The proscenium house seats about 200, performances are advertised, and admission is charged. Among this season's presentations:

YERMA by Federico Garcia Lorca, in an English version by James Graham-Lujan and Richard L. O'Connell, directed by Rene Buch.

YERMA in the original Spanish of Federico Garcia Lorca, directed by Rene Buch.

The Judson Poets' Theater. Still in the throes of far-reaching changes in its program, personnel and outlook, this progenitor of off off Broadway is today relatively quiescent in terms of production activity. Shows, when given, are either in the choir loft or the sanctuary of the striking, Stanford White-designed Judson Memorial Church. Performances are advertised, and admission is charged. Presentations this season included:

DRACULA SABBAT by Leon Katz, directed by Lawrence Kornfeld, music by John Herbert McDowell, based on the novel *Dracula* by Bram Stoker. THE JOURNEY OF SNOW WHITE, libretto and music by Al Carmines, staging and movement by Gus Solomons Jr. THREE ONE-ACT PLAYS WITH SONGS by Lyon Phelps, no director credit.

La Mama Experimental Theater Club. With the passing of Joe Cino, Ellen Stewart's La Mama became the mama of all the theaters that make up today's off off Broadway. Two theaters, one above the other, comprise La Mama's well-equipped facility, and Miss Stewart herself lives, literally, atop it all. The theaters seat about 150 apiece, but must run alternately, because sound carries too readily from one to the other. Contrary to earlier practise, La Mama now has a resident artistic director, Wilford Leach, and organizes many of its own shows, although quite a number are still packages imported after outside preparation. Shows usually play Wednesday through Sunday for two weekends. Notices of performances appear in the *Village Voice*, and while the fiction of "members only" continues, anyone with a phone reservation and the price in hand gets admitted. Presentations this season included:

A LIBERATED WOMAN by Barry Reckord, directed by the author, presented by the Jamaican National Theater Trust. GERTRUDE, text by Wilford Leach, music by Ben Johnston, orchestration and musical direction by James Cuomo, directed by Wilford Leach and John Braswell. REAL REEL by Frederic Baal, directed by Jean-Pol Farbus and Frederic Flamand, of the Théâtre Laboratoire Vicinal of Belgium. THE RED WHITE AND BLACK, a "patriotic demonstration" by Eric Bentley, music by Brad Burg, directed by John Dillon. (later restaged commercially off Broadway). THE CENCI by Antonin Artaud, translated by Simon Watson, directed by Martin Brenzell, music by David Walker. THE RED HORSE ANIMATION, music by Philip Glass, text and direction by Lee Breuer, a special presentation by a resident La Mama troupe, the Mabou Mines, at the Guggenheim Museum. CONEY ISLAND PLAY, a "Kabuki-vaudeville musical" written by Y. Higashi and the Tokyo Kid Brothers company, music by I. Shimoda, directed by Y. Higashi. STREET SOUNDS by Ed Bullins, directed by Hugh Gittens. KAAKA-MAKA-

AKOO by Tone Brulin and the Otrabanda Company of Curacao, directed by Tone Brulin. SAVAGE, conceived and directed by Maxine Klein, electronic music prepared by William S. Fischer, played by a troupe from Boston University. CARMILLA, derived from a story by S. LeFanu by Wilford Leach, music by Ben Johnston, staged by Wilford Leach and John Braswell. CORRINS FOR BUTTERFLIES, adapted by Aart from *The Butterfly Dream*, an ancient Chinese drama, directed by Juan Carlos Uviedo. DREAM OF DENANAG by Fred Curchack, directed by Joel Zwick, performed by the resident La Mama Plexus company. PORK by Andy Warhol, directed by Anthony J. Ingrassia. THE REFRIGERATORS by Mario Fratti, directed by Russell Treyz, music and lyrics by William Goldstein and Edward Kleban. EARLY MORNING by Edward Bond, staged by Melvin Bernhardt. A DOG'S LOVE, music by John Herbert McDowell, libretto by Michael Smith. THE TRAGEDY OF HOMER STILLS, written and directed by Tony Barsha.

The Loft Theater. Lyn Austin operates this off-off-Broadway showcase to check out possible commercial ventures. An end-stage, with good equipment, and seating about 100, the Loft functions irregularly, but when they do a show, they do it well. Admission may or may not be charged, and the showings are advertised. This season's presentations included:

TWO FROM LOST AND FOUND by John Ford Noonan, directed by Michael Cannon. NIGHTPIECE by Wolfgang Hildesheimer, directed by Bill Pardue. HEAVY DUTY

RADIO THEATER by David Dozer, directed by Joshua White. SOAP by Lawrence Osgood, directed by Ann McIntosh, with music by Steve Lawrence.

National Black Theater. Organized to evolve a uniquely American Negro theatrical expression from black roots—not from white—this troupe is in its second season of perfecting its accurately-titled *Ritual*. Its performers, some 30 in number, are not "actors", they are "liberators"; its theater in Harlem is a "temple". The production:

RITUAL, conceived and evolved by the ensemble, directed by Barbara Ann Teer.

New Federal Theater. The beautiful theater known most recently as the Henry Street Playhouse, dark to drama for several seasons, has reopened as the home of the New Federal Theater, a group planning to present a repertory of plays of particular interest to black audiences. The house seats several hundred and is very well equipped (until recently, it doubled as the home of Alwin Nikolais' spectrally-lighted and electronically-assisted dance presentations). The initial season's productions included:

IN NEW ENGLAND WINTER by Ed Bullins, directed by Dick Williams (see its entry in this volume's "Plays Produced off Broadway" listing).

The New Lafayette Theater. In a well-equipped, modern theater building seating several hundred in various stage-audience relationships, this troupe specializes in presentations of special interest to its Harlem community. Admission is charged, and advertising and publicity is limited to black-oriented periodicals. This season's work included:

THE FABULOUS MISS MARIE by Ed Bullins, directed by Robert Macbeth.

New York Theater Ensemble. This end-stage loft seats about 50, utilizes minimal equipment, advertises, and charges admission. Productions this season included:

CHE GUEVARA by Mario Fratti, directed by the author. BAD HABITS OF '71 by Frank Lee Wilde, directed by Vincent Van. SINGIN' HARE KRISHNA and SNOWS OF SPRING by Guy Gauthier, directed by Fred-erick Bailey. GRADUATION by Jeff Hochhauser, music by Rosemary Gimpel, directed by Jerry Grant. SHEILA by Anthony J. Ingrassio, directed by Robert Elston.

New York Theater of the Americas. This Lincoln Center-area theater specializes in presenting English translations of Spanish-language scripts, although Spanish performances are given on occasion. The extensive schedule is advertised, and admission is charged. This season's productions included:

EL MATADOR by Ricardo Castillo, music by Dan Padnos, directed by Castillo and Linda Pack. DIRTY FERDIE COMES CLEAN by Michael Groob, music by Paul Morse, directed by Shelly Kurz (children's theater). TALES TO BE TOLD by Oswaldo Dragun, translated by Ricardo Matamoros, directed by Miguel Ponce. THREE GROTESQUES by Rafael Bunuel, directed by Ricardo Castillo, Miguel Ponce, and the author. JOURNEY TO BAHIA by Alfredo Dias Gomes, adapted and translated by Stanley Richards.

The Old Reliable Free Theater. This back-room-of-a-bar end-stage house far, far, into the letter-Avenued section of the Lower East Side has recently formed an alliance with the remnants of Columbia University's decimated theater arts department. While not all of The Old Reliable's dramas are Columbia-inspired, a majority are. Performances in the minimally-equipped, quite small theater are advertised, and no admission is charged. Shows this season included:

THE HEAVEN MOTHER by Roma Greth, directed by the author. WUZIZ by Donald Kvares, with music written and arranged by Elise Bretton, lyrics by the author and composer, choreography by Tom Roberts, directed by the author. WHO'S HUNGRY by Edward Belling, directed by the author. REVEREND FERDINAND AND BESSIE MAE by Nat White and 3,000 RED ANTS by Lawrence Ferlinghetti, director uncredited. THE ACADEMY by Mario Fratti, no director credited. CONCERNING THE EFFECTS OF METHYL-CHLORIDE and RAINBOWS FOR SALE by John Ford Noonan, no director credited.

The Open Theater. This highly publicized group-mime, image theater troupe has reduced its membership to six and supplements its college tour performances with a relatively few New York appearances, normally in spaces other than its own rehearsal facility. Most of this season has been spent in the preparation of a new work concerned with human changes, or "mutations" (its two most recent pieces had to do with birth and death). There have been some tour and New York appearances in last season's major production:

TERMINAL, created by The Open Theater Ensemble, under the direction of Joseph Chaikin and Roberta Sklar, texts by Susan Yankowitz, with the participation of Mark Kaminski, Nancy Martin, and Sam Shepard, writers, and Dick Peaslee and Stanley Walden, composers (The production being played this season has been reworked for the reduced number of players—six rather than last season's 18).

The Other Stage. Joseph Papp's Public Theater enterprises are so prolific and occur in so many contexts that classification is difficult. The Public Theater (The New York Shakespeare Festival's fall, winter, and spring activity in the former Astor Library building) currently presents programs on six stages, as well as in odd hallways and corners. When programs are not eight-time-a-week Equity-cast productions with an admission charge, they tend to be free-admission shows, advertised in the *Times* and the *Village Voice*. Regardless of the area at the Public Theater— non-admission-charge productions are frequently referred to as Other Stage presentations whether or not they use the stage usually called the Other Stage—technical facilities are excellent. Like La Mama, its chief "competitor" in the off-off-Broadway arena, the Public Theater brings in some packages (more than formerly) and mounts some of the shows with its own "house" talent. Works shown this season included:

HERO by Israel Horovitz, performed by a company of Amherst students under the direction of David Rimmer. UNDERGROUND: THE LIFE AND TIMES OF J. WALTER SMINTHEUS, by Edgar White and JAZZ-NITE by Walter Jones, both plays directed by Walter Jones, performed by the Cornbread Players (the version of "Smintheus" given here was re-written following the earlier presentation of the play in the ANTA Matinee Series; see entry on *Underground* in the "Plays Produced off Broadway" section of this volume). THE GREY LADY CANTATA by Peter Schumann, performed by his Bread and Puppet Theater troupe. CANDIDE, a company-developed piece under the direction of Stuart Gordon, by the Organic Theater Company of Chicago (see its entry in the "Plays Produced off Broadway" section of this volume). SLAG by David Hare, directed by Roger Hendricks Simon (see its entry in the "Plays Produced off Broadway" section of this volume). WILLIE by Joe Ponzi, directed by Richard Jordan. SUBJECT TO FITS by Robert Montgomery, directed by A. J. Antoon (transferred later to an 8-time-a-week Equity-contract run in the Public Theater's Anspacher Theater; see its entry in the "Plays Produced off Broadway" section of this volume).

The Playbox. This small, corner-stage, 35-seat Village spot has been the home of off-off-Broadway theater for many seasons, under various managements. Technical facilities are minimal—everything is minimal—but the show does go on. Performances are advertised, admission is charged, and this season's presentations included:

JUDGEMENT DAY and COUNT THAT DAY LOST by Stewart Benedict and LUNCH BREAK by Michael Wolfe, directed by the authors. THE GIRL WITH A RING ON HER NOSE, THE OTHER ONE, THE FRIDAY BENCH and THE ACADEMY, four plays by Mario Fratti, directed by Frank Biancamano and Kent Wood. CELEBRATE ME by Gloria Gonzalez and Edna Schappert, directed by William E. Hunt. LISTEN SEAN TO THE SILHOUETTES OF RAINDROPS written and directed by John Hartnett. A VOICE TO CALL YOUR OWN by Clayelle Dalferes, directed by Dan Rosenwein. INJUN by Guy Gauthier, directed by Jack Sims, and THE GREEN MAN AND RED LADY IN THE RED AND GREEN by Guy Gauthier, directed by Ron Mullen. HAPPY, written and directed by William Kushner.

The Ridiculous Theatrical Company. Currently the most active of the several surviving offshoots of the late off-off-Broadway Theater of the Ridiculous, this troupe concentrates its ridicule upon the aspects of Charles Ludlam, who is playwright, director, and star performer. The showings are presented in various theaters, more often than not at the Gotham Art on West 43d Street. This season's works:

BLUEBEARD by Charles Ludlam, directed by Charles Ludlam, starring Charles Ludlam. THE GRAND TAROT by Charles Ludlam, directed by Charles Ludlam, starring Charles Ludlam.

St. Clement's Space. In the basement of the same church that houses the American Place Theater, but under other auspices, a series of productions is presented each season. The space is unstructured, the facilities minimal. Productions are not usually advertised, and admission may or may not be charged. Shows this season included:

A KNACK WITH HORSES and HERE BE DRAGONS, a twin bill by David Ward, staged by Russell Treyz. WHITSUNTIDE by Tom LaBar, directed by Russell Treyz. INVINCIBLE! by Daniel Curley, directed by Jacque Lynn Colton, music by John Herbert McDowell. ORIGINAL CHILD BOMB, by Thomas Merton, directed by Bill Tchakirides.

Soul and Latin Theater. Playing at the Theater Arts Center in what is popularly known as East Harlem, or Spanish Harlem, this troupe specializes in English-language productions having appeal to a Puerto Rican extraction audience. The auditorium, seating several hundred on folding chairs, and insufficiently sound-proofed to ward off the sounds of the streets, is a proper *mise en scene*. Presentations this season included:

WALLS, improvisational play by the company, directed by Clay Stevenson. THE BLOCK, improvisational play by the company, no director credited. WALLS OF THE GHETTO by Tony Vozzo, no director credited.

Theater Erotica. A new and innovative addition to off off Broadway's purveyors of pornography, this second-story mid-town showspot features continuous performances, noon 'till midnight. This season's production:

SEXUAL PRACTISES IN HEAVEN, no author credit, no director credit, performers performing anonymously, and barely.

Theater Genesis. In an end-stage loft above St. Mark's Church in the Bowery, this old-time off-off-Broadway group has, like its counterpart the Judson Poets' Theater, presented seminal experimental productions. Also like Judson, it has simmered 'way down. Among this season's few productions, played in a house seating about 100 and well-equipped technically, advertised and played to a donation-paying audience, were:

MAD DOG BLUES by Sam Shepard, directed by Robert Glaudini, songs and lyrics by O-lan (Mrs. Sam Shepard), Robin Remailly and Sam Shepard. LESSON IN DEAD LANGUAGE by Adrienne Kennedy, no director credited. GRAND MAL CRICK by Walter Hadler, directed by Hadler and Ralph Cook.

The Unit Theater. A new enterprise, this theater is adaptable to almost any mode of presentaion. Performances are advertised and admission is charged. This season included:

THE BITCH OF WAVERLY PLACE by Arthur Sainer, directed by the author, and THE DUMBWAITER by Harold Pinter, directed by David Shumaker. THREE . . . WITH WOMEN IN MIND, three one-act plays, JEFF CHANDLER by David Shumaker, HOW A NICE GIRL NAMED JANET CONTRACTED SYPHILIS by David Shumaker and I HEAR IT KISSING ME LADIES by Arthur Sainer, all directed by David Shumaker.

Urban Arts Corps. Vinnette Carroll's new training center for "new black actors and new black audiences"—her description—is midway between Bedford-Stuyvesant and Harlem in the Village. Premiere season productions included:

MOON ON A RAINBOW SHAWL by Errol John, directed by Vinnette Carroll, with music by Micki Grant (Miss Carroll had played in the original New York production). BURY THE DEAD by Irwin Shaw and LADIES IN WAITING by Peter de Anda, both directed by Vinnette Carroll. DON'T BOTHER ME, I CAN'T COPE, a musical revue by, and directed by, Vinnette Carroll.

Workshop of the Players' Art. One of the veterans of off off Broadway, taking into account its antecedants in a direct line of descent, WPA continues, in its new storefront Bowery home, to provide a full season of new plays and classics in a small, flexible theater seating perhaps 65, with reasonably good facilities. Performances are advertised, and admission is charged. This season included:

THE OTHER SIDE OF THE YEAR by Roma Greth, directed by Oscar Dole, and DINNER FOR ONE by Joseph Renard, directed by Joseph Pichette. FREAK IN, a revue by Robert Patrick, directed by the author. THE ADDING MACHINE by Elmer Rice, directed by Dick Gaffield. THE BUSINESS OF GOOD GOVERNMENT by John Arden, directed by Michael Feingold. MAYHEM AT MAYHEW by David S. Meranze and Marc Alan Zagoren, directed by Harry Or- zello. AS YOU LIKE IT by William Shakespeare, directed by Neil Flanagan. THE CONFESSION by Sarah Bernhardt, directed by Martin L. H. Reymert. THE CORRUPTERS by Gertrude Samuels, directed by Dick Gaffield. GUM by Walter Corwin, directed by Daniel P. Dietrich, and THE CLEANING SOLUTION by Delos Brown, directed by Fran Lohman. A MAN'S A MAN by Bertold Brecht, in the English version by Eric Bentley, directed by R. Mack Miller.

CAST REPLACEMENTS AND TOURING COMPANIES

Compiled by Stanley Green

The following is a list of the more important cast replacements in productions which opened in previous years, but were still playing in New York during a substantial part of the 1970-71 season; or were still on a first class tour; or opened in 1970-71 and sent out a first class touring company in the same season.

This record spans three seasons. Pre-1970-71 replacements in the few shows which have run longer than that—which opened before June 1, 1968—will be found in the cast-replacement sections of previous *Best Plays* volumes.

The name of each major role is listed in *italics* beneath the title of the play in the first column. In the second column directly opposite appears the name of the actor who created the role in the original New York production (whose opening date appears in *italics* at the top of the column). Immediately beneath the original actor's name are the names of subsequent replacements, together with the date of replacement when available.

The third column gives information about first-class touring companies, including London companies (produced under the auspices of their original Broadway managements). When there is more than one roadshow company, #1, #2, #3, etc., appear before the name of the performer who created the role in each company (and the city and date of each company's first performance appears in *italics* at the top of the column). Their subsequent replacements are also listed beneath their names, with dates when available.

A note on bus-truck touring companies appears at the end of this section.

ADAPTATION/NEXT

#1 Boston 9/16/69
#2 Los Angeles 10/23/69
New York 2/10/69   *#3 Chicago 2/27/70*

ADAPTATION

Games Master	Graham Jarvis	#1 Bill Story
	Dick Yarmy 9/22/69	#2 Graham Jarvis
	Philip R. Allen 4/27/70	#3 William Wise

Players (male)	Paul Dooley	#1 Don Billett
	Marvin Lichterman 8/25/69	#2 Bob Barend
	Richard Ramos 10/26/69	#3 Joe Greco

Players (female)	Carol Morley	#1 Stockard Channing
	Stockard Channing 3/21/70	#2 Rose Arrick
	Orie Seron 7/6/70	#3 Fawne Harriman
	Grace Kimmins 9/7/70	

Contestants	Gabriel Dell	#1 Philip R. Allen
	R.G. Brown 7/7/69	#2 Gabriel Dell
	Mark Gordon 11/1/69	#3 Spencer Milligan
	Dick Yarmy 4/27/70	
	Kenneth Kimmins 6/15/70	
	William Wise 7/6/70	

NEXT

Marion Cheever	James Coco	#1 William Young
	Dick Van Patten 9/22/69	#2 James Coco
	William Hickey 11/1/69	#3 Mike Nussbaum
	Oliver Clark 9/19/70	

Sgt. Thech	Elaine Shore	#1 Joan Tolentino
	Patricia Fay 4/20/70	#2 Elaine Shore
		#3 Karen Woodward

APPLAUSE

New York 3/30/70

| *Margo Channing* | Lauren Bacall |

| *Bill Sampson* | Len Cariou |
| | Keith Charles 5/3/71 |

Eve Harrington	Penny Fuller
	Patti Davis 4/16/71
	Penny Fuller 5/3/71

| *Howard Benedict* | Robert Mandan |
| | Lawrence Weber 4/19/71 |

| *Karen Richards* | Ann Williams |
| | Gwyda Donhowe 8/24/70 |

| *Bonnie* | Bonnie Franklin |
| | Carol Petrie 4/29/71 |

BORSTAL BOY

New York 3/31/70

Young Behan Frank Grimes
George Connolly 7/28/70

Brendan Behan Niall Toibin

THE BOYS IN THE BAND (see also previous *Best Plays* volumes)

New York 4/15/68

Michael Kenneth Nelson
Philip Cusack 6/11/70

Donald Frederick Combs
Phillip Clark 6/30/70

Emory Cliff Gorman
Joseph Palmieri 6/30/70
George Monk 8/4/70

Bernard Reuben Greene
Lisle Watson 8/4/70

Cowboy Robert La Tourneaux
Ted LePlat 8/5/70

Alan Peter White
Don Fenwick 6/30/70

Harold Leonard Frey
Gerald Taupier 6/30/70

BUTTERFLIES ARE FREE

	New York 10/21/69	#1 *Los Angeles 5/19/70* #2 *London 11/4/70*

Don Baker	Keir Dullea
	Kipp Osborne 10/13/70
		#1 Wendell Burton
		  Kipp Osborne 9/70
		  David Huffman 10/12/70
		#2 Keir Dullea

Mrs. Baker	Eileen Heckart Patricia Wheel 9/28/70 Rosemary Murphy 10/13/70	#1 Eve Arden Gloria Swanson 10/12/70 #2 Eileen Heckart
Jill Tanner	Blythe Danner Kathleen Miller 8/31/70	#1 Ellen Endicott-Jones Christina Callahan 10/12/70 #2 Barbara Ferris

COCO

	'ew York 12/18/69	*Cleveland 1/11/71*
Coco Chanel	Katharine Hepburn Danielle Darrieux 8/3/70	Katharine Hepburn
Louis Greff	George Rose	George Rose
Noelle	Gale Dixon Suzanne Rogers 9/28/70	Lana Shaw Gale Dixon 4/5/71
Georges	David Holliday	Don Chastain
Sebastian Baye	Rene Auberjonois	David Davis

COLETTE

New York 5/6/70

Colette   Zoe Caldwell
            Fenella Fielding 10/14/70

Sido   Mildred Dunnock
            Ruth Nelson 6/30/70

COMPANY

	New York 4/26/70	*Los Angeles 5/20/71*
Robert	Dean Jones Larry Kert 5/29/70	George Chakiris
Joanne	Elaine Stritch Jane Russell 5/13/71	Elaine Stritch
Sarah	Barbara Barrie	Marti Stevens
Harry	Charles Kimbrough Lee Goodman 3/29/71 Kenneth Kimmins 5/13/71	Charles Braswell
Susan	Merle Louise Alice Cannon 10/5/70 Charlotte Frazier 3/29/71	Milly Ericson
Peter	John Cunningham Kenneth Cory 4/26/71	Gary Krawford
Jenny	Teri Ralston Jane A. Johnston 5/13/71	Teri Ralston
David	George Coe Charles Braswell 3/29/71 George Wallace 5/13/71	Lee Goodman
Amy	Beth Howland Marian Hailey 5/13/71	Beth Howland
Paul	Steve Elmore	Del Hinkley
Larry	Charles Braswell Stanley Grover 3/29/71	Robert Goss
Marta	Pamela Myers Annie McGreevey 5/13/71	Pamela Myers
Kathy	Donna McKechnie Brenda Thomson 5/13/71	Donna McKechnie
April	Susan Browning	Bobbi Jordan

THE EFFECT OF GAMMA RAYS ON MAN-IN-THE-MOON MARIGOLDS

	New York 4/7/70	*Boston 4/20/71*
Beatrice	Sada Thompson Cathryn Damon 2/16/71	Eileen Heckart
Tillie	Pamela Payton-Wright Swoosie Kurtz 2/16/71	Marcia Jean Kurtz

THE FANTASTICKS (see also previous *Best Plays* volumes)

New York 5/3/60

Luisa   Rita Gardner
                          Virginia Gregory 7/27/70

Matt   Kenneth Nelson
                          Jimmy Dodge 9/20/70

FIDDLER ON THE ROOF (see also previous *Best Plays* volumes)

New York 9/22/64

Tevye   Zero Mostel
                          Jerry Jarrett 10/12/70
                          Paul Lipson 10/19/70

Golde   Maria Karnilova
                          Mimi Randolph 8/3/70
                          Peg Murray 9/14/70
                          Laura Stuart 12/21/70
                          Peg Murray 2/1/71

Tzeitel   Joanna Merlin
                          Mimi Turque 11/9/70

Perchik   Bert Convy
                          Michael Zaslow 4/71

Hodel   Julia Migenes
                          Susan Hufford 11/2/70

FORTY CARATS (see also previous *Best Plays* volumes)

New York 12/26/68

Ann Stanley   Julie Harris
                          Iva Withers 6/11/70
                          Zsa Zsa Gabor 7/6/70

Maude Hayes   Glenda Farrell
                          Lilia Skala 7/6/70

HAIR (see also previous *Best Plays* volumes)

N.Y. B'way 4/29/68

Berger   Gerome Ragni
                          Larry Marshall
                          Red Sheppard 12/17/70
                          Oatis Stephens 2/71
                          Allan Nicholls 4/71

Claude   James Rado
                          Robin McNamara 4/71

Sheila   Lynn Kellogg
                          Heather MacRae 6/70
                          Victoria Medlin 8/70
                          Marta Heflin 3/71

I NEVER SANG FOR MY FATHER

	New York 1/25/68	London 5/28/70
Tom Garrison	Alan Webb	Raymond Massey
Margaret Garrison	Lillian Gish	Catherine Lacey
Gene Garrison	Hal Holbrook	George Baker
Alice	Teresa Wright	Dorothy Bromley

JACQUES BREL IS ALIVE AND WELL AND LIVING IN PARIS (see also previous *Best Plays* volumes)

New York: 1/22/68

Replacements & alternates	Howard Ross 6/16/70
	Joy Franz 6/23/70
	Henrietta Valor 6/23/70
	Michael Vita 6/23/70
	Barbara Gutterman 11/24/70
	George Lee Andrews 12/26/70
	Ben Bryant 1/9/71
	Fran Uditsky 5/4/71

LAST OF THE RED HOT LOVERS

	New York 12/28/69	Washington 9/28/70

Barney Cashman	James Coco
	    A. Larry Haines 7/6/70
	    James Coco 7/20/70
		Jack Weston
		    Ken McMillan 3/29/71
		    Jack Weston 4/26/71

Elaine Navazio	Linda Lavin
	    Rita Moreno 7/27/70
	    Cathryn Damon 11/9/70
	    Rita Moreno 11/16/70
		Rosemary Prinz

Bobbi Michele	Marcia Rodd Barbara Sharma 3/8/71	Ginger Flick
Jeanette Fisher	Doris Roberts	Marge Redmond

MAN OF LA MANCHA (see also previous *Best Plays* volumes)

New York 11/22/65

Don Quixote (Cervantes)	Richard Kiley
	    Gideon Singer 9/18/70
	    David Atkinson 4/2/71

Aldonza	Joan Diener
	    Emily Yancy 1/21/71
	    Dell Brownlee 1/21/71
	        (matinees only)

Sancho Panza	Irving Jacobson Rudy Tronto 11/13/70

Innkeeper	Ray Middleton
	    Jack Dabdoub 10/5/70
	    Ray Middleton 10/19/70

Padre   Robert Rounseville
                               Ralph Farnsworth 7/6/70
                               Robert Rounseville 7/20/70

PLAY IT AGAIN, SAM

		#1 London 9/9/69
	New York 2/12/69	*#2 Chicago 9/15/70*
Allan Felix	Woody Allen	#1 Dudley Moore
	Bob Denver 1/12/70	#2 Red Buttons
Dick Christie *	Anthony Roberts	#1 Terence Edmond
	Lawrence Pressman 8/69	#2 William Bogert
Linda Christie *	Diane Keaton	#1 Lorna Heilbron
	Sheila Sullivan 1/12/70	#2 Deborah Deeble

* In London, characters were known as Brian and Sally Morris

PROMISES, PROMISES (see also previous *Best Plays* volumes)

	New York 12/1/68	*San Diego 4/23/70*
Chuck Baxter	Jerry Orbach	Anthony Roberts
	Gene Rupert 8/3/70	Anthony Teague 10/70
	Jerry Orbach 8/17/70	
	Anthony Roberts 10/26/70	
	Gene Rupert 4/12/71	
Fran Kubelik	Jill O'Hara	Melissa Hart
	Patti Davis 8/17/70	
	Jill O'Hara 8/31/70	
	Jenny O'Hara 12/7/70	
J.D. Sheldrake	Edward Winter	Bob Holiday
	James Congdon 12/7/70	
Mary MacDougall	Marian Mercer	Kelly Britt
	Mary Louise Wilson 7/20/70	

PURLIE

	New York 3/15/70
Purlie	Cleavon Little
Lutiebelle	Melba Moore
	Patti Jo 3/30/71
Missy	Novella Nelson
	Carol Jean Lewis 3/30/71

ROOM SERVICE

	New York 5/12/70
Gordon	Ron Leibman
	Dick Shawn 7/6/70

1776

	#1 San Francisco 4/23/70
New York 3/16/69	*#2 London 6/16/70*

John Adams	William Daniels John Cunningham 5/4/71	#1 Patrick Bedford #2 Lewis Flander
Benjamin Franklin	Howard Da Silva	#1 Rex Everhart #2 Ronald Radd
John Dickinson	Paul Hecht David Ford 7/70	#1 George Hearn #2 Bernard Lloyd
Edward Rutledge	Clifford David David Cryer 5/30/69 John Cullum 5/19/70	#1 Jack Blackton Michael Davis 11/16/70 #2 David Kernan
Stephen Hopkins	Roy Poole Edmund Lyndeck 1/70	#1 Truman Gaige #2 Tony Steedman
Thomas Jefferson	Ken Howard John Fink 5/30/69 Jon Cypher 9/16/69 Peter Lombard 11/24/69	#1 Jon Cypher George Backman 11/16/70 #2 John Quentin
Abigail Adams	Virginia Vestoff Ellen Hanley 12/69 Virginia Vestoff 2/16/70	#1 Barbara Lang #2 Vivienne Ross
Richard Henry Lee	Ronald Holgate Gary Oakes 2/9/71 Ronald Holgate 5/11/71	#1 Gary Oakes Virgil Curry 12/7/70 #2 David Morton
Martha Jefferson	Betty Buckley Mary Bracken Phillips 8/28/69 Betty Buckley 10/5/70 Pamela Hall 4/13/71	#1 Pamela Hall Kristen Banfield 10/26/70 #2 Cheryl Kennedy

WHAT THE BUTLER SAW

New York 5/4/70

Dr. Prentice	Laurence Luckinbill Thomas Connolly 7/12/70
Mrs. Prentice	Jan Farrand Elaine Hyman 9/70

BUS-TRUCK TOURS

These are touring productions designed for maximum mobility and ease of handling in one-night and split-week stands (with occasional engagements of a week or more). Among Broadway shows on tour in the season of 1970-71 were the following bus-truck troupes:

Forty Carats with Barbara Britton, 136 performances in 81 cities, 11/9/70-4/6/71
George M! with Tony Tanner, 175 performances in 92 cities, 9/25/70-3/28/71
Plaza Suite with Larry Parks and Betty Garrett, 182 performances in 92 cities, 10/16/70-4/25/71
Zorbá with Vivian Blaine and Michael Kermoyan, 217 performances in 118 cities, 9/11/70-5/18/71
1776 with Don Perkins, Paul Tripp and Patrick Hines, 217 performances in 128 cities, 9/18/70-5/14/71
Hadrian VII with Theo Barnes, 70 performances in 42 cities, 1/14/71-3/28/71
Your Own Thing, 49 performances in 49 cities (did not play continuous performances), 10/3/70-4/28/71
Will Rogers's U.S.A. with James Whitmore, 168 performances in 79 cities, 10/8/70-2/27/71
Fiddler on the Roof with Bob Carroll (continuing from 12/27/69), 416 performances in 52 cities, 6/1/70-5/31/71 (continuing)
You're a Good Man Charlie Brown, 202 performances in 113 cities, 9/21/70-5/17/71

FACTS AND
FIGURES

LONG RUNS ON BROADWAY

The following shows have run 500 or more continuous performances in a single production, usually the first, not including previews or extra non-profit performances, allowing for vacation layoffs and special one-booking engagements, but not including return engagements after a show has gone on tour. Where there are title similarities, the production is identified as follows: (p) straight play version, (m) musical version, (r) revival.

THROUGH MAY 31, 1971

(PLAYS MARKED WITH ASTERISK WERE STILL PLAYING JUNE 1, 1971)

Plays	Number Performances	Plays	Number Performances
Life With Father	3,224	The Music Man	1,375
Tobacco Road	3,182	Funny Girl	1,348
Hello, Dolly! †	2,844	Angel Street	1,295
*Fiddler on the Roof	2,788	*Hair	1,294
Abie's Irish Rose	2,327	Lightnin'	1,291
*Man of La Mancha	2,297	The King and I	1,246
Oklahoma!	2,212	Cactus Flower	1,234
South Pacific †	1,925	Guys and Dolls	1,200
Harvey	1,775	Cabaret	1,165
Born Yesterday	1,642	Mister Roberts	1,157
Mary, Mary	1,572	Annie Get Your Gun	1,147
The Voice of the Turtle	1,557	The Seven Year Itch	1,141
Barefoot in the Park	1,530	Pins and Needles	1,108
Mame (m)	1,508	Plaza Suite	1,097
Arsenic and Old Lace	1,444	Kiss Me, Kate	1,070
The Sound of Music	1,443	The Pajama Game	1,063
How To Succeed in Business Without Really Trying	1,417	*Promises, Promises	1,038
Hellzapoppin	1,404	The Teahouse of the August Moon	1,027

† Both *South Pacific* and *Hello, Dolly!*—and probably many other shows over the years—interrupted their runs for special one-booking engagements outside New York City. *South Pacific's* run was originally recorded as 1,925 performances but was cut back starting with the 1960-61 *Best Plays* volume to the 1,694 performances it played prior to just such a special booking. In the opinion of the present editor *South Pacific's* record should show the full 1,925 performances, which are restored in this volume's long-run list.

Plays	Number Performances	Plays	Number Performances
Damn Yankees	1,019	Finian's Rainbow	725
Never Too Late	1,007	Claudia	722
Any Wednesday	982	The Gold Diggers	720
A Funny Thing Happened on the Way to the Forum	964	Carnival	719
The Odd Couple	964	The Diary of Anne Frank	717
Anna Lucasta	957	I Remember Mama	714
Kiss and Tell	956	Tea and Sympathy	712
The Moon Is Blue	924	Junior Miss	710
Bells Are Ringing	924	Seventh Heaven	704
*1776	920	Gypsy (m)	702
Luv	901	The Miracle Worker	700
Can-Can	892	Cat on a Hot Tin Roof	694
Carousel	890	Li'l Abner	693
Hats Off to Ice	889	Peg o' My Heart	692
Fanny	888	The Children's Hour	691
Follow the Girls	882	Dead End	687
Camelot	873	The Lion and the Mouse	686
The Bat	867	White Cargo	686
My Sister Eileen	864	Dear Ruth	683
Song of Norway	860	East Is West	680
A Streetcar Named Desire	855	Come Blow Your Horn	677
Comedy in Music	849	The Most Happy Fella	676
You Can't Take It With You	837	The Doughgirls	671
La Plume de Ma Tante	835	The Impossible Years	670
Three Men on a Horse	835	Irene	670
The Subject Was Roses	832	Boy Meets Girl	669
*Oh! Calcutta! †	812	Beyond the Fringe	667
Inherit the Wind	806	*Butterflies Are Free	665
No Time for Sergeants	796	Who's Afraid of Virginia Woolf?	664
Fiorello!	795	Blithe Spirit	657
Where's Charley?	792	A Trip to Chinatown	657
The Ladder	789	The Women	657
Forty Carats	780	Bloomer Girl	654
Oliver	774	The Fifth Season	654
State of the Union	765	Rain	648
The First Year	760	Witness for the Prosecution	645
You Know I Can't Hear You When the Water's Running	755	Call Me Madam	644
Two for the Seesaw	750	Janie	642
Death of a Salesman	742	The Green Pastures	640
Sons o' Fun	742	Auntie Mame (p)	639
Gentlemen Prefer Blondes	740	A Man for All Seasons	637
The Man Who Came to Dinner	739	The Fourposter	632
Call Me Mister	734	The Tenth Man	623
West Side Story	732	Is Zat So?	618
High Button Shoes	727	Anniversary Waltz	615
		The Happy Time (p)	614
		Separate Rooms	613

† First 704 performances were played off Broadway.

Plays	Number Performances	Plays	Number Performances
Affairs of State	610	Floradora	553
Star and Garter	609	Ziegfeld Follies (1943)	553
The Student Prince	608	Dial "M" for Murder	552
Sweet Charity	608	Good News	551
Bye Bye Birdie	607	Let's Face It	547
Broadway	603	Milk and Honey	543
Adonis	603	Within the Law	541
Street Scene (p)	601	The Music Master	540
Kiki	600	Pal Joey (r)	540
Flower Drum Song	600	What Makes Sammy Run?	540
Don't Drink the Water	598	What a Life	538
Wish You Were Here	598	The Unsinkable Molly Brown	532
A Society Circus	596	The Red Mill (r)	531
*Last of the Red Hot Lovers	595	A Raisin in the Sun	530
Blossom Time	592	The Solid Gold Cadillac	526
The Two Mrs. Carrolls	585	Irma La Douce	524
Kismet	583	The Boomerang	522
Detective Story	581	Rosalinda	521
Brigadoon	581	The Best Man	520
No Strings	580	Chauve-Souris	520
Brother Rat	577	Blackbirds of 1928	518
Show Boat	572	Sunny	517
The Show-Off	571	Victoria Regina	517
Sally	570	Half a Sixpence	511
Golden Boy (m)	568	The Vagabond King	511
One Touch of Venus	567	The New Moon	509
Happy Birthday	564	The World of Suzie Wong	508
Look Homeward, Angel	564	*Purlie	504
The Glass Menagerie	561	Shuffle Along	504
I Do! I Do!	560	Up in Central Park	504
Wonderful Town	559	Carmen Jones	503
Rose Marie	557	The Member of the Wedding	501
Strictly Dishonorable	557	Panama Hattie	501
A Majority of One	556	Personal Appearance	501
The Great White Hope	556	Bird in Hand	500
Toys in the Attic	556	Room Service	500
Sunrise at Campobello	556	Sailor, Beware!	500
Jamaica	555	Tomorrow the World	500
Stop the World—I Want to Get Off	555		

LONG RUNS OFF BROADWAY

Plays	Number Performances	Plays	Number Performances
*The Fantasticks	4,220	You're a Good Man Charlie Brown	1,597
The Threepenny Opera	2,611		

Plays	Number Performances	Plays	Number Performances
The Blacks	1,408	The Balcony	672
*Jacques Brel Is Alive and Well and Living in Paris	1,391	America Hurrah	634
		Hogan's Goat	607
Little Mary Sunshine	1,143	The Trojan Women (r)	600
The Boys in the Band	1,000	Krapp's Last Tape and	
Your Own Thing	933	The Zoo Story	582
Curley McDimple	931	The Dumbwaiter and	
Leave It to Jane (r)	928	The Collection	578
The Mad Show	871	Dames at Sea	575
A View From the Bridge (r)	780	The Crucible (r)	571
The Boy Friend (r)	763	The Iceman Cometh (r)	565
The Pocket Watch	725	The Hostage (r)	545
The Connection	722	Six Characters in Search of an	
Adaptation and Next	707	Author (r)	529
Oh! Calcutta! †	704	Happy Ending and Day of	
Scuba Duba	692	Absence	504
The Knack	685	The Boys From Syracuse (r)	500

DRAMA CRITICS CIRCLE VOTING, 1970-71

The New York Drama Critics Circle voted *Home* the best play of the season on the second ballot by a plurality of 24 points in weighted voting, after no play won a majority of first choices expressed in the mandatory first ballot. Other best-play points on the weighted ballot (counting 3 for each critic's first choice, 2 for his second and 1 for his third) were distributed as follows: *The House of Blue Leaves* 23, *The Philanthropist* 18, *All Over* 13, *The Trial of the Catonsville Nine* 12, *Subject to Fits* 10, *Sleuth* 5, *Alice in Wonderland* 3, *Father's Day* 3, *A Place Without Doors* 2, *Les Blancs* 2, *Story Theater* 2, *Steambath* 1, *The Fabulous Miss Marie* 1, *The Gingerbread Lady* 1.

Having named a foreign play as best, the critics decided to vote on a best American play. By the same weighted scoring method as above after the first ballot, *The House of Blue Leaves* won with a plurality of 28 points. Other points in the category of best American play were distributed as follows: *The Trial of the Catonsville Nine* 19, *All Over* 16, *Les Blancs* 11, *Subject to Fits* 11, *Steambath* 6, *Alice in Wonderland* 5, *Father's Day* 5, *The Fabulous Miss Marie* 4, *Story Theater* 2, *The Happiness Cage* 2, *Happy Birthday, Wanda June* 1, *The Gingerbread Lady* 1, *In New England Winter* 1, *The Carpenters* 1, *Scratch* 1.

The critics voted *Follies* the best musical of the season by a simple majority on the first ballot of 11 first-choice votes (those of Brendan Gill, Martin Gottfried, Henry Hewes, Ted Kalem, Jack Kroll, John Lahr, Leo Mishkin, George Oppenheimer, Marilyn Stasio, Douglas Watt and Richard Watts Jr.). *The Me Nobody Knows* received 5 first-choice votes (those of Clive Barnes, Harold Clurman, Edward S. Hipp, Emory Lewis and John Simon). *No, No, Nanette* received 1 (Wil-

† After 704 off-Broadway performances, moved to Broadway to continue its run.

liam H. Glover) and *Two by Two* 1 (Walter Kerr). Hobe Morrison and William Raidy abstained on this ballot for best musical.

Here's the way the Circle members' votes were distributed on the weighted second ballots for best play and best American play (first-ballot choices are indicated by first choices in this list):

SECOND BALLOT FOR BEST PLAY

Critic	1st Choice (3 pts.)	2d Choice (2 pts.)	3d Choice (1 pt.)
Clive Barnes *Times*	All Over	Alice in Wonderland	Subject to Fits
Harold Clurman *The Nation*	All Over	Home	The House of Blue Leaves
Brendan Gill *New Yorker*	Home	Blue Leaves	Steambath
William H. Glover AP	All Over	The Trial of the Catonsville Nine	Home
Martin Gottfried *Women's Wear Daily*	Subject to Fits	Home	The Fabulous Miss Marie
Henry Hewes *Saturday Review*	Blue Leaves	A Place Without Doors	The Philanthropist
Edward S. Hipp *Newark News*	All Over	Home	The Philanthropist
Ted Kalem *Time*	Home	Father's Day	Alice in Wonderland
Walter Kerr *Times*	Blue Leaves	The Philanthropist	Home
Jack Kroll *Newsweek*	Subject to Fits	The Philanthropist	Catonsville
John Lahr *Village Voice*	Blue Leaves	Catonsville	Subject to Fits
Emory Lewis *Bergen Record*	Blue Leaves	Catonsville	Story Theater
Leo Mishkin *Morning Telegraph*	Blue Leaves	The Philanthropist	Story Theater
Hobe Morrison *Variety*	Sleuth	Home	The Gingerbread Lady
George Oppenheimer *Newsday*	Home	The Philanthropist	All Over
William Raidy Newhouse Papers	Catonsville	The Philanthropist	Subject to Fits
John Simon *New York*	The Philanthropist	Catonsville	Home
Marilyn Stasio *Cue*	Home	Blue Leaves	Subject to Fits
Douglas Watt *Daily News*	Blue Leaves	Sleuth	Father's Day
Richard Watts Jr. *Post*	The Philanthropist	Les Blancs	Home

SECOND BALLOT FOR BEST AMERICAN PLAY

Critic	1st Choice (3 pts.)	2d Choice (2 pts.)	3d Choice (1 pt.)
Clive Barnes	All Over	Alice in Wonderland	Subject to Fits
Harold Clurman	The Trial of the Catonsville Nine	The House of Blue Leaves	Les Blancs
Brendan Gill	Blue Leaves	Steambath	All Over
William H. Glover	All Over	Catonsville	Happy Birthday, Wanda June
Martin Gottfried	Subject to Fits	The Fabulous Miss Marie	Catonsville

Henry Hewes	Blue Leaves	Les Blancs	All Over
Edward S. Hipp	All Over	Catonsville	The Gingerbread Lady
Ted Kalem	Father's Day	Alice in Wonderland	Blue Leaves
Walter Kerr	Blue Leaves	Les Blancs	Steambath
Jack Kroll	Subject to Fits	Catonsville	In New England Winter
John Lahr	Blue Leaves	Miss Marie	Alice in Wonderland
Emory Lewis	Blue Leaves	Catonsville	Subject to Fits
Leo Mishkin	Blue Leaves	Story Theater	Les Blancs
Hobe Morrison	Abstain		
George Oppenheimer	All Over	Les Blancs	Steambath
William Raidy	Catonsville	All Over	Subject to Fits
John Simon	Catonsville	The Happiness Cage	The Carpenters
Marilyn Stasio	Blue Leaves	Subject to Fits	Catonsville
Douglas Watt	Blue Leaves	Father's Day	Scratch
Richard Watts Jr.	Les Blancs	Steambath	Blue Leaves

Choices of some other critics:

Critic	Best Play	Best Musical
Judith Crist "Today"	Blue Leaves	Follies
*Edwin Newman WNBC-TV	Home	Story Theater
*Ted Hoffman Critic-at-large	Blue Leaves	Abstain
Norman Nadel Scripps-Howard	All Over	Follies
Tom Prideaux Life	Blue Leaves	Follies
Leonard Harris WCBS-TV	Home	Follies

NEW YORK DRAMA CRITICS CIRCLE AWARDS

Listed below are the New York Drama Critics Circle Awards from 1935-36 through 1970-71, classified as follows: (1) Best American Play, (2) Best Foreign Play, (3) Best Musical, (4) Best, regardless of category.

1935-36—(1) Winterset
1936-37—(1) High Tor
1937-38—(1) Of Mice and Men, (2) Shadow and Substance
1938-39—(1) No award, (2) The White Steed
1939-40—(1) The Time of Your Life
1940-41—(1) Watch on the Rhine, (2) The Corn Is Green
1941-42—(1) No award, (2) Blithe Spirit
1942-43—(1) The Patriots
1943-44—(2) Jacobowsky and the Colonel
1944-45—(1) The Glass Menagerie
1945-46—(3) Carousel
1946-47—(1) All My Sons, (2) No Exit, (3) Brigadoon
1947-48—(1) A Streetcar Named Desire, (2) The Winslow Boy
1948-49—(1) Death of a Salesman, (2) The Madwoman of Chaillot, (3) South Pacific

1949-50—(1) The Member of the Wedding, (2) The Cocktail Party, (3) The Consul
1950-51—(1) Darkness at Noon, (2) The Lady's Not for Burning, (3) Guys and Dolls
1951-52—(1) I Am a Camera, (2) Venus Observed, (3) Pal Joey (Special citation to Don Juan in Hell)
1952-53—(1) Picnic, (2) The Love of Four Colonels, (3) Wonderful Town
1953-54—(1) Teahouse of the August Moon, (2) Ondine, (3) The Golden Apple
1954-55—(1) Cat on a Hot Tin Roof, (2) Witness for the Prosecution, (3) The Saint of Bleecker Street
1955-56—(1) The Diary of Anne Frank, (2) Tiger at the Gates, (3) My Fair Lady

* Indicates critic has not seen all this season's shows

1956-57—(1) Long Day's Journey Into Night, (2) The Waltz of the Toreadors, (3) The Most Happy Fella

1957-58—(1) Look Homeward, Angel, (2) Look Back in Anger, (3) The Music Man

1958-59—(1) A Raisin in the Sun, (2) The Visit, (3) La Plume de Ma Tante

1959-60—(1) Toys in the Attic, (2) Five Finger Exercise, (3) Fiorello!

1960-61—(1) All the Way Home, (2) A Taste of Honey, (3) Carnival

1961-62—(1) The Night of the Iguana, (2) A Man for All Seasons, (3) How to Succeed in Business Without Really Trying

1962-63—(4) Who's Afraid of Virginia Woolf? (Special citation to Beyond the Fringe)

1963-64—(4) Luther, (3) Hello, Dolly! (Special citation to The Trojan Women)

1964-65—(4) The Subject Was Roses, (3) Fiddler on the Roof

1965-66—(4) The Persecution and Assassination of Marat as Performed by the Inmates of the Asylum of Charenton Under the Direction of the Marquis de Sade, (3) Man of La Mancha

1966-67—(4) The Homecoming, (3) Cabaret

1967-68—(4) Rosencrantz and Guildenstern Are Dead, (3) Your Own Thing

1968-69—(4) The Great White Hope, (3) 1776

1969-70—(4) Borstal Boy, (1) The Effect of Gamma Rays on Man-in-the-Moon Marigolds, (3) Company

1970-71—(4) Home, (1) The House of Blue Leaves, (3) Follies

PULITZER PRIZE WINNERS, 1917-18 TO 1970-71

1917-18—Why Marry?, by Jesse Lynch Williams

1918-19—No award

1919-20—Beyond the Horizon, by Eugene O'Neill

1920-21—Miss Lulu Bett, by Zona Gale

1921-22—Anna Christie, by Eugene O'Neill

1922-23—Icebound, by Owen Davis

1923-24—Hell-Bent fer Heaven, by Hatcher Hughes

1924-25—They Knew What They Wanted, by Sidney Howard

1925-26—Craig's Wife, by George Kelly

1926-27—In Abraham's Bosom, by Paul Green

1927-28—Strange Interlude, by Eugene O'Neill

1928-29—Street Scene, by Elmer Rice

1929-30—The Green Pastures, by Marc Connelly

1930-31—Alison's House, by Susan Glaspell

1931-32—Of Thee I Sing, by George S. Kaufman, Morrie Ryskind, Ira and George Gershwin

1932-33—Both Your Houses, by Maxwell Anderson

1933-34—Men in White, by Sidney Kingsley

1934-35—The Old Maid, by Zoë Akins

1935-36—Idiot's Delight, by Robert E. Sherwood

1936-37—You Can't Take It With You, by Moss Hart and George S. Kaufman

1937-38—Our Town, by Thornton Wilder

1938-39—Abe Lincoln in Illinois, by Robert E. Sherwood

1939-40—The Time of Your Life, by William Saroyan

1940-41—There Shall Be No Night, by Robert E. Sherwood

1941-42—No award

1942-43—The Skin of Our Teeth, by Thornton Wilder

1943-44—No award

1944-45—Harvey, by Mary Chase

1945-46—State of the Union, by Howard Lindsay and Russel Crouse

1946-47—No award.

1947-48—A Streetcar Named Desire, by Tennessee Williams

1948-49—Death of a Salesman, by Arthur Miller

1949-50—South Pacific, by Richard Rodgers, Oscar Hammerstein II and Joshua Logan

1950-51—No award

1951-52—The Shrike, by Joseph Kramm

1952-53—Picnic, by William Inge

1953-54—The Teahouse of the August Moon, by John Patrick

1954-55—Cat on a Hot Tin Roof, by Tennessee Williams

1955-56—The Diary of Anne Frank, by Frances Goodrich and Albert Hackett

1956-57—Long Day's Journey Into Night, by Eugene O'Neill

1957-58—Look Homeward, Angel, by Ketti Frings

1958-59—J. B., by Archibald MacLeish

1959-60—Fiorello!, by Jerome Weidman, George Abbott, Sheldon Harnick and Jerry Bock

1960-61—All the Way Home, by Tad Mosel

1961-62—How to Succeed in Business Without Really Trying, by Abe Burrows, Willie Gilbert, Jack Weinstock and Frank Loesser

1962-63—No award

1963-64—No award

1964-65—The Subject Was Roses, by Frank D. Gilroy

1965-66—No award

1966-67—A Delicate Balance, by Edward Albee

1967-68—No award

1968-69—The Great White Hope, by Howard Sackler

1969-70—No Place to Be Somebody, by Charles Gordone

1970-71—The Effect of Gamma Rays on Man-in-the-Moon Marigolds, by Paul Zindel

ADDITIONAL PRIZES AND AWARDS, 1970-71

The following is a list of major prizes and awards for theatrical achievement. In all cases the names of winners—persons, productions or organizations—appear in **bold face type.**

MARGO JONES AWARD (for encouraging production of new playwrights). **Joseph Papp** of the New York Shakespeare Festival.

JOSEPH MAHARAM FOUNDATION AWARDS (for design by Americans). Musical scene design, **Boris Aronson** for *Follies.* Straight play scene design, **Peter Larkin** for *Les Blancs.* Costume design, **Raoul Pene du Bois** for *No, No, Nanette.* Special citation to **Clarke Dunham** for his settings for *The Me Nobody Knows.*

VERNON RICE AWARDS (for outstanding contribution to the off-Broadway theater). **Arvin Brown** (director) and **Paddy Croft, Geraldine Fitzgerald, James Naughton, Robert Ryan** and **Stacy Keach** (cast) of *Long Day's Journey Into Night.*

GEORGE JEAN NATHAN AWARD (for criticism). **John Simon.**

CLARENCE DERWENT AWARDS (for best male and female non-featured performances). **James Wood** in *Saved.* **Katherine Helmond** in *The House of Blue Leaves.*

GEORGE FREEDLEY MEMORIAL AWARD. **Brooks Atkinson** for *Broadway.*

SAM S. SHUBERT AWARD (for outstanding service to the American Theater). **Danny Kaye.**

OUTER CIRCLE AWARDS (voted by critics of out-of-town periodicals, for distinctive achievement in the New York theater). Outstanding productions: *Follies, A Midsummer Night's Dream, No, No, Nanette.* Outstanding achievements: **Joseph Papp** of the New York Shakespeare Festival, **Paul Sills** of *Story Theater,* the **Phoenix Theater.** Other citations: **John Guare** for *The House of Blue Leaves,* **Claire Bloom** in *Hedda Gabler,* **Anthony Quayle** and **Keith Baxter** in *Sleuth.*

VILLAGE VOICE OFF-BROADWAY (OBIE) AWARDS (for off-Broadway excellence, selected by a committee of judges whose members were Edith Oliver, Harold Clurman and John Lahr). Best play, *The House of Blue Leaves.* Best actress, **Ruby Dee** in *Boesman and Lena.* Best actor, **Jack MacGowran** in *MacGowran in the Works of Samuel Beckett.* Distinguished direction, **John Berry** for *Boesman and Lena,* **John Hirsch** for *AC/DC,* **Gordon Davidson** for *The Trial of the Catonsville Nine,* **Larry Kornfeld** for *Dracula Sabbat,* **Jeff Bleckner** for *The Basic Training of Pavlo Hummel.* Distinguished playwriting: **Ed Bullins** for *The Fabulous Miss Marie* and *In New England Winter,* **David Rabe** for *Pavlo Hummel.* Distinguished production: *The Trial of the Catonsville Nine.* Distinguished foreign plays: *Boesman and Lena* by Athol Fugard, *AC/DC* by Heathcote Williams, *The Dream on Monkey Mountain* by Derek Walcott. Distinguished performances: **Susan Batson** in *AC/DC,* **Hector Elizondo** in *Steambath,* **Joan MacIntosh** in *Commune,* **William Schallert** in *Catonsville,* **Margaret Braidwood** and **James Woods** in *Saved,* **Stacy Keach** in *Long Day's Journey*

Into Night, **Sonny Jim** in *The Fabulous Miss Marie*, **Harris Laskawy** in *Uncle Vanya*. Consistent excellence of performance: **Kirk Kirksey**. Best scenery, **John Scheffler** for AC/DC. Special citation: *Orlando Furioso*.

STRAW HAT AWARDS (for excellence in the American summer theater during 1970). **Mickey Rooney** in *George M!*. **Kay Medford** in *Light Up the Sky*. **Charles Forsythe** for *Boeing, Boeing* direction. **Charles Benson** in *The Price* (best supporting actor). **Audra Lindley** and **Kathleen Miller** in *A Chic Life* (best supporting actresses). Special Straw Hat achievement award for "a graduate of summer theater who has advanced to distinction in the performing arts" to **Henry Fonda**.

THEATER WORLD AWARDS (for promising new acting talent): **Julie Garfield, Martha Henry, Tricia O'Neil, Ayn Ruymen, Jennifer Salt, Joan Van Ark, Clifton Davis, Michael Douglas, James Naughton, Kipp Osborne, Roger Rathburn, Walter Willison**.

BROADWAY ASSOCIATION AWARD (1970's "man of the year"). **David Merrick**.

GEORGE DEVINE AWARDS (for the finest achievements in drama in the London Theater). *AC/DC* by Heathcote Williams and *The Foursome* by Edward Whitehead.

ANNUAL *VARIETY* POLL OF LONDON THEATER CRITICS (bests of the 1969-70 season in London, published during 1970-71). New British play, *The Contractor* and *The National Health* (tie). New British musical, no choice. New foreign play, *Tiny Alice*. New foreign musical, *Promises, Promises*. Male leading performances, **Leonard Rossiter** in *Arturo Ui* (straight play), **Anthony Roberts** in *Promises, Promises* (musical). Female leading performances, **Maggie Smith** in *The Beaux Stratagem* (straight play), **Carol Channing** in *Carol Channing and Stout Hearted Men* (musical). Male supporting performances, **David Waller** in *Much Ado About Nothing, Troilus and Cressida* and *Landscape* (straight plays), **Jack Kruschen** in *Promises, Promises* and **Denis Quilley** in *Sing a Rude Song* (musicals; tie). Female supporting performances, **Anna Calder Marshall** in *Uncle Vanya* (straight play), no choice for musical. Most promising new actor, **Alan Howard** in *Troilus and Cressida, Hamlet* and *The Revenger's Tragedy* and **Paul Jones** in *Conduct Unbecoming* (tie). Most promising new actress, **Pauline Collins** in *Night Chased Woman, Happy Apple* and *Come as You Are*. Decor, **Piero Gherardi** for *The White Devil* and **Ralph Koltai** for *Back to Methuselah* (tie). Director, **Lindsay Anderson** for *The Contractor*. Most promising playwright, **Anthony Shaffer** for *Sleuth*.

THE DRAMA DESK AWARDS

The Drama Desk Awards for the bests of the season are voted by the editors, critics and reporters who are members of Drama Desk, a New York organization of theater journalists. Selections are made from a long list of nominees covering outstanding Broadway, off-Broadway and even some off-off-Broadway contributions. Voters are asked to check only those candidates whose work they actually saw, and awards are made on the basis, not of number of votes alone, but of percentage of votes of those who saw the show.

Winners of Drama Desk Awards for 1970-71 are listed below, in the order of percentages received. The actual percentage figure is given for those who scored highest in each category. No percentage figure is given for most promising director and most promising scene and costume designers because these were chosen by a committee of Drama Desk.

OUTSTANDING PERFORMANCES. **Ralph Richardson** (75.5 per cent) and **John Gielgud** (71.4 per cent) in *Home*, **Cliff Gorman** in *Lenny*, **Claire Bloom** in *A Doll's House* and *Hedda Gabler*, **Jack MacGowran** in *MacGowran in the Works of Beckett*, **Ruby Dee** in *Boesman and Lena*, **Brian Bedford** in *The* *School for Wives*, **Alec McCowen** in *The Philanthropist*, **Siobhan McKenna** in *Here Are Ladies*, **Marian Seldes** in *Father's Day*, **Madeleine Renaud** in *L'Amante Anglaise*, **Alexis Smith** in *Follies*, **Mildred Dunnock** in *A Place Without Doors*, **Anthony Quayle** in *Sleuth*, **Helen Gallagher** in *No, No, Na-*

nette, **Keith Baxter** in *Sleuth,* **James Earl Jones** in *Les Blancs,* **Colleen Dewhurst** in *All Over,* **Maureen Stapleton** in *The Gingerbread Lady,* **Paul Sand** in *Story Theater* and *Metamorphoses,* **Roberta Maxwell** in *Slag.*

OUTSTANDING DIRECTORS. **Peter Brook** for *A Midsummer Night's Dream* (68.4 per cent), **Harold Prince** and **Michael Bennett** for *Follies,* **Paul Sills** for *Story Theater* and *Metamorphoses,* **Robert Wilson** for *Deafman Glance,* **Andre Gregory** for *Alice in Wonderland,* **Tom O'Horgan** for *Lenny.*

OUTSTANDING SCENE DESIGNERS. **Boris Aronson** for *Follies* (82.5 per cent), **Sally Jacobs** for *A Midsummer Night's Dream,* **Robin Wagner** for *Lenny.*

COSTUME DESIGNERS. **Florence Klotz** for *Follies,* **Raoul Pene du Bois** for *No, No, Nanette.*

CHOREOGRAPHERS. **Michael Bennett** for *Follies* (47.6 per cent), **Donald Saddler** for *No, No, Nanette.*

COMPOSER. **Stephen Sondheim** for *Follies* (76.2 per cent)

LYRICIST. **Stephen Sondheim** for *Follies* (85.9 per cent)

MUSICAL BOOK. **Burt Shevelove** for adaptation of *No, No, Nanette* (34 per cent)

MOST PROMISING PLAYWRIGHTS. **Kurt Vonnegut Jr.** for *Happy Birthday, Wanda June* (57.4 per cent), **David Rabe** for *The Basic Training of Pavlo Hummel,* **Robert Montgomery** for *Subject to Fits,* **A.R. Gurney Jr.** for *Scenes From American Life.*

MOST PROMISING COMPOSERS: **Stephen Schwartz** for *Godspell* (64 per cent), **Itsuro Shimoda** for *Golden Bat.*

MOST PROMISING LYRICISTS: **Stephen Schwartz** for *Godspell* (63 per cent), **Yutaka Higashi** for *Golden Bat.*

MOST PROMISING DIRECTORS. **Jeff Bleckner** for *The Basic Training of Pavlo Hummel,* **John-Michael Tebelak** for *Godspell,* **Russell Treyz** for *Whitsuntide.*

MOST PROMISING SCENE DESIGNERS. **Eugene Lee** and **Franne Newman** for *Alice in Wonderland.*

MOST PROMISING COSTUME DESIGNER. **Susan Tzu** for *Godspell.*

THE TONY AWARDS

The Antoinette Perry (Tony) Awards are voted by members of the League of New York Theaters, the governing bodies of the Dramatists Guild, Actors Equity, the American Theater Wing, the Society of Stage Directors and Choreographers, the United Scenic Artists Union and the first and second night press, from a list of three or four nominees in each category. Nominations are made by a committee serving at the invitation of the League of New York Theaters, which is in charge of Tony Awards procedure. The personnel of the nominating committee changes every year. The 1970-71 committee was composed of Harold Clurman, Judith Crist, Martha Deane, Radie Harris, Edward Kook, Stuart Little, George Oppenheimer, Isabelle Stevenson and Richard Watts Jr. Their list of nominees follows, with winners listed in **bold face type.**

BEST PLAY. *Home* by David Storey, produced by Alexander H. Cohen. **Sleuth** by Anthony Shaffer, produced by Helen Bonfils, Morton Gottlieb and Michael White. *Story Theater* by Paul Sills, produced by Zev Bufman. *The Philanthropist* by Christopher Hampton, produced by David Merrick and Byron Goldman.

BEST MUSICAL. **Company,** produced by Harold Prince. *The Me Nobody Knows,* produced by Jeff Britton. *The Rothschilds,* produced by Lester Osterman and Hillard Elkins.

ACTOR, STRAIGHT PLAY. **Brian Bedford** in *The School for Wives,* John Gielgud and Ralph Richardson in *Home,* Alec McCowen in *The Philanthropist.*

ACTRESS, STRAIGHT PLAY. Estelle Parsons in *And Miss Reardon Drinks a Little,*

Diana Rigg in *Abelard & Heloise*, Marian Seldes in *Father's Day*, **Maureen Stapleton** in *The Gingerbread Lady*.

ACTOR, MUSICAL. **David Burns** in *Lovely Ladies, Kind Gentlemen*, Larry Kert in *Company*, **Hal Linden** in *The Rothschilds*, Bobby Van in *No, No, Nanette*.

ACTRESS, MUSICAL. Susan Browning and Elaine Stritch in *Company*, Sandy Duncan in *The Boy Friend*, **Helen Gallagher** in *No, No, Nanette*.

SUPPORTING ACTOR, STRAIGHT PLAY. Donald Pickering in *Conduct Unbecoming*, Ronald Radd in *Abelard & Heloise*, **Paul Sand** in *Story Theater*, Ed Zimmerman in *The Philanthropist*.

SUPPORTING ACTRESS, STRAIGHT PLAY. **Rae Allen** in *And Miss Reardon Drinks a Little*, Lili Darvas in *Les Blancs*, Joan Van Ark in *The School for Wives*, Mona Washbourne in *Home*.

SUPPORTING ACTOR, MUSICAL. **Keene Curtis** in *The Rothschilds*, Charles Kimbrough in *Company*, Walter Willison in *Two by Two*.

SUPPORTING ACTRESS, MUSICAL. Barbara Barrie and Pamela Myers in *Company*, **Patsy Kelly** in *No, No, Nanette*.

DIRECTOR, STRAIGHT PLAY. Lindsay Anderson for *Home*, **Peter Brook** for *A Midsummer Night's Dream*, Stephen Porter for *The School for Wives*, Clifford Williams for *Sleuth*.

DIRECTOR, MUSICAL. **Michael Kidd** for *The Rothschilds*, Robert Livingston for *The Me Nobody Knows*, Harold Prince for *Company*, Burt Shevelove for *No, No, Nanette*.

SCENE DESIGNER. **Boris Aronson** for *Company*, John Bury for *The Rothschilds*, Sally Jacobs for *A Midsummer Night's Dream*, Jo Mielziner for *Father's Day*.

COSTUME DESIGNER. **Raoul Pene du Bois** for *No, No, Nanette*, Jane Greenwood for *Hay Fever* and *Les Blancs*, Freddy Wittop for *Lovely Ladies, Kind Gentlemen*.

LIGHTING DESIGNER. Robert Ornbo for *Company*, **R.H. Poindexter** for *Story Theater*, William Ritman for *Sleuth*.

CHOREOGRAPHER. **Michael Bennett** for *Company*, Michael Kidd for *The Rothschilds*, Donald Saddler for *No, No, Nanette*.

MUSICAL BOOK. **George Furth** for *Company*, Robert Livingston and Herb Schapiro for *The Me Nobody Knows*, Sherman Yellen for *The Rothschilds*.

MUSICAL SCORE. Jerry Bock for *The Rothschilds*, Gary William Friedman for *The Me Nobody Knows*, **Stephen Sondheim** for *Company*.

LYRICS. Sheldon Harnick for *The Rothschilds*, Will Holt for *The Me Nobody Knows*, **Stephen Sondheim** for *Company*.

SPECIAL AWARDS. **Elliot Norton, Ingram Ash, John W. Kluge, Roger L. Stevens.**

VARIETY'S POLL OF NEW YORK DRAMA CRITICS

1970-71 BROADWAY SEASON

Each year, representative New York drama critics are polled by *Variety* to learn their choices for Broadway's bests other than best play and musical. In 1970-71, 22 critics participated: Clive Barnes, Martin Bookspan, Harold Clurman, Jack Gaver, William H. Glover, Leonard Harris, Henry Hewes, Ted Kalem, Walter Kerr, Alvin Klein, Stuart Klein, John Lahr, Emory Lewis, Leo Mishkin, Norman Nadel, Edwin Newman, George Oppenheimer, Leonard Probst, John Simon, Marilyn Stasio, Peggy Stockton and Douglas Watt. Names of those cited in the various categories appear below, together with the number of critics' votes received (in parentheses). Winners are listed in **bold face type.**

MALE LEAD, STRAIGHT PLAY. **Ralph Richardson (6½)** and John Gielgud (3½) in *Home*, Cliff Gorman in *Lenny* (6), Brian Bedford in *The School for Wives* (2), James Earl Jones in *Les Blancs* (2), Anthony Quayle in *Sleuth* (2).

FEMALE LEAD, STRAIGHT PLAY. **Maureen Stapleton** in *The Gingerbread Lady* (10), Marian Seldes in *Father's Day* (5), Estelle Parsons (3) and Julie Harris (1) in *And Miss Reardon Drinks a Little*, Claire Bloom in *A Doll's House* and *Hedda Gabler* (1), Jessica Tandy in *All Over* (1), Joan Van Ark in *The School for Wives* (1).

MALE LEAD, MUSICAL. **Hal Linden** in *The Rothschilds* (9½), Danny Kaye in *Two by Two* (5), David Burns in *Lovely Ladies, Kind Gentlemen* (1½), Jack Gilford (1) and Bobby Van (1) in *No, No, Nanette*, Cliff Gorman in *Lenny* (1), Paul Sand in *Story Theater* (1), No Choice (2).

FEMALE LEAD, MUSICAL. **Alexis Smith** (15) and Dorothy Collins (1) in *Follies*, Helen Gallagher in *No, No, Nanette* (4), Mildred Natwick in *70, Girls, 70* (1).

ACTOR, SUPPORTING ROLE. **Paul Sand** (4½) and Hamid Hamilton Camp (1) in *Story Theater* and *Metamorphoses*, Keene Curtis in *The Rothschilds* (3), Keith Baxter in *Sleuth* (3), David Burns in *Lovely Ladies, Kind Gentlemen* (1), Peter Coffield in *Abelard & Heloise* (1), Neil Fitzgerald in *All Over* (1), Will Geer in *Scratch* (1), Bill Macy in *And Miss Reardon Drinks a Little* (1), Donald Moffat in *Father's Day* (1), Donald Pickering in *Conduct Unbecoming* (1), Victor Spinetti (1) and Ed Zimmermann (1) in *The Philanthropist*, David Waller in *A Midsummer Night's Dream* (½), No choice (1).

ACTRESS, SUPPORTING ROLE. **Mona Washbourne** (4½) and Dandy Nichols (½) in *Home*, Rae Allen (4) and Estelle Parsons (1) in *And Miss Reardon Drinks a Little*, Helen Gallagher (4) and Patsy Kelly (1) in *No, No, Nanette*, Lili Darvas in *Les Blancs* (2), Martha Henry in *Playboy of the Western World* (1), Henrietta Jackson in *70, Girls, 70* (1), Paula Kelly in *Story Theater* and *Metamorphoses* (1), Tricia O'Neil in *Two by Two* (1), Marian Seldes in *Father's Day* (1).

MOST PROMISING NEW BROADWAY ACTOR. Cliff Gorman in *Lenny* (6), Humbert Allen Astredo in *Les Blancs* (1), Charles Bartlett in *Metamorphoses* (1), Keith Baxter in *Sleuth* (1), Jeremy Clyde in *Conduct Unbecoming* (1), Ray Goulding in *Bob and Ray —The Two and Only* (1), Bill Hinnant in *Frank Merriwell* (1), **No choice** (9).

MOST PROMISING NEW BROADWAY ACTRESS. Jane Asher in *The Philanthropist* (3), Tricia O'Neil in *Two by Two* (3), Alexis Smith in *Follies* (3), Frances de la Tour (2) and Sara Kestelman (1) in *A Midsummer Night's Dream*, Joan Van Ark in *The School for Wives* (2), Martha Henry in *Playboy of the Western World* (1), Ayn Ruymen in *The Gingerbread Lady* (1), **No choice** (6).

BEST DIRECTOR. **Peter Brook** for *A Midsummer Night's Dream* (9), Harold Prince (3½) and Michael Bennett (1½) for *Follies*, Lindsay Anderson for *Home* (2), John Berry for *Les Blancs* (1), Tom O'Horgan for *Lenny* (1), Gene Saks for *How the Other Half Loves* (1), Burt Shevelove for *No, No, Nanette* (1), Paul Sills for *Story Theater* (1), No choice (1).

SET DESIGNER. **Boris Aronson** for *Follies* (13), Sally Jacobs for *A Midsummer Night's Dream* (4), Robin Wagner for *Lenny* (2), Jocelyn Herbert for *Home* (1), Peter Larkin for *Les Blancs* (1), No choice (1).

COSTUME DESIGNER. **Florence Klotz** for *Follies* (15), Raoul Pene du Bois for *No, No, Nanette* (5), Randy Barcelo for *Lenny* (1), No choice (1).

COMPOSER. **Stephen Sondheim** for *Follies* (15), John Kander for *70, Girls, 70* (2), Richard Rodgers for *Two by Two* (2), Gary William Friedman for *The Me Nobody Knows* (1), Vincent Youmans for *No, No, Nanette* (1), No choice (1).

LYRICIST. **Stephen Sondheim** for *Follies* (21), Fred Ebb for *70, Girls, 70* (1).

MOST PROMISING NEW PLAYWRIGHT. **Christopher Hampton** for *The Philanthropist* (6), David Storey for *Home* (4), Paul Zindel for *And Miss Reardon Drinks a Little* (3), Julian Barry for *Lenny* (1), A.R. Gurney Jr. for *Scenes From American Life* (1), Oliver Hailey for *Father's Day* (1), Anthony Shaffer for *Sleuth* (1), Paul Sills for *Story Theater* (1), No choice (4).

OUTSTANDING BROADWAY PRODUCER. **Harold Prince** for *Follies* (12), Zev Bufman for *Story Theater* (2), David Merrick for *The Philanthropist* and *A Midsummer Night's Dream* (1), Cyma Rubin and Harry Rigby for *No, No, Nanette* (1), No choice (6).

1969-1970 OFF-BROADWAY SEASON

Last year, representative New York drama critics were polled by *Variety* to learn their choices for bests other than best play or musical off Broadway, for the first time, in the same way they have been polled by *Variety* for many years on their choices of Broadway bests. Results of this balloting on the 1969-70 off-Broadway season were published in midsummer 1970, too late for inclusion in the 1969-70 *Best Plays* volume, so for the record we list them here. Twenty critics participated: Clive Barnes, Ethel Colby, Harold Clurman, Jack Gaver, William H. Glover, Martin Gottfried, Henry Hewes, Ted Kalem, Walter Kerr, Alvin Klein, Stuart Klein, John Lahr, Leo Mishkin, Norman Nadel, Edwin Newman, John O'Connor, Edith Oliver, George Oppenheimer, Marilyn Stasio and Peggy Stockton. Names of those cited in the various categories appear below, together with the number of critics' votes received (in parentheses). Winners are listed in **bold face type.**

MALE LEAD, STRAIGHT PLAY. **Ryszard Cieslak** in *The Constant Prince* (4), Stephen Elliot in *A Whistle in the Dark* (2), Ron Leibman in *Transfers* (2), Laurence Luckinbill in *The Memory Bank* (2), Christopher Walken in *Lemon Sky* (2), Tony Lo Bianco in *Nature of the Crime* (1½), Peter Bonerz in *The White House Murder Case* (1), Harold Gould in *The Increased Difficulty of Concentration* (1), Kevin O'Connor in *Dear Janet Rosenberg, Dear Mr. Kooning* (1), Ron O'Neal in *No Place to Be Somebody* (1), Charles Ludlam in *Bluebeard* (½), No choice (2).

FEMALE LEAD, STRAIGHT PLAY. **Sada Thompson** in *The Effect of Gamma Rays on Man-in-the-Moon Marigolds* (13), Zoe Caldwell in *Colette* (6).

MALE LEAD, MUSICAL. **Austin Pendleton** in *The Last Sweet Days of Isaac* (9), Donny Burks in *Billy Noname* (2), Northern J. Calloway in *The Me Nobody Knows* (1), Ron Seward in *Sambo* (1), any male performer in *The Me Nobody Knows* (1), No choice (6).

FEMALE LEAD, MUSICAL. **Fredricka Weber** in *The Last Sweet Days of Isaac* (8), Hattie Winston in *The Me Nobody Knows* (3), Jean Pace in *Joy* (2), Beverly Ann Bremers in *The Me Nobody Knows* (1), Madeline Kahn in *Promenade* (1), any female performer in *The Me Nobody Knows* (1), No choice (5).

SUPPORTING ACTOR. Paul Benedict and Anthony Holland in *The White House Murder Case* (3 each), Barry Bostwick in *Colette* (1), Stephen Elliot and Don Plumley in *A Whistle in the Dark* (1 each), Joseph Maher in *The Local Stigmatic* (1), John Mahon in *Nobody Hears a Broken Drum* (1), Jeremiah Sullivan in *A Scent of Flowers* (1), Alan Weeks in *Billy Noname* (1), Billy Dee Williams in *Slow Dance on the Killing Ground* (1), No choice (6).

SUPPORTING ACTRESS. **Pamela Payton-Wright** in *The Effect of Gamma Rays on Man-in-the-Moon Marigolds* (8), Roberta Maxwell in *A Whistle in the Dark* (3), Mildred Dunnock in *Colette* (2), Rue McLanahan in *Who's Happy Now?* (2), Patricia Roe in *Transfers* (2), Hattie Winston in *The Me Nobody Knows* (2), Rosalind Cash of the Negro Ensemble Company (1).

MOST PROMISING NEW OFF-BROADWAY ACTOR. Ryszard Cieslak in *The Constant Prince* (2), Beeson Carroll in *The Unseen Hand* (1), Jose Fernandez in *The Me Nobody Knows* (1), Donald Griffith in *Contributions* (1), Ron O'Neal in *No Place to Be Somebody* (1), J.A. Preston in *The Persians* (1), Jeremy Stockwell in *Fortune and Men's Eyes* (1), Kristoffer Tabori in *How Much, How Much?* (1), Alan Weeks in *Billy Noname* (1), No choice (10).

MOST PROMISING NEW OFF-BROADWAY ACTRESS. Gerri Dean in *The Me Nobody Knows* (3), Katharine Houghton in *A Scent of Flowers* (3), Catherine Burns in *Dear Janet Rosenberg, Dear Mr. Kooning* (2), Madeline Miller in *Slow Dance on the Killing Ground* (2), Roberta Maxwell in *A Whistle in the Dark* (1), Pamela Payton-Wright in *The Effect of Gamma Rays on Man-in-the-Moon Marigolds* (1), No choice (8).

DIRECTOR. **Alan Arkin** for *The White House Murder Case* (6), Melvin Bernhardt for *The Effect of Gamma Rays on Man-in-the-Moon Marigolds* (5), Jerzy Grotowski for *The Constant Prince* (1), Joseph Chaikin for *The Serpent* (1), Andre Gregory for *Alice in Wonderland* (1), Robert H. Livingston for *The Me Nobody Knows* (1), Brian Murray for *A Scent of Flowers* (1), Andrei Serban for *Ubu* (1), No choice (1).

SCENE DESIGNER. **Fred Voelpel** for *The Effect of Gamma Rays on Man-in-the-Moon Marigolds* (8), Ed Wittstein for *The Last Sweet Days of Isaac* (4), Clarke Dunham for

The Me Nobody Knows (2), Eugene Lee for Slave Ship (1), David Mitchell for Colette (1), Jerry Rojo for Makbeth (1), No choice (3).

COSTUME DESIGNER. Theoni V. Aldredge for Colette (4), Sara Brook for The Effect of Gamma Rays on Man-in-the-Moon Marigolds (2), Joseph Aulisi for Seven Days of Mourning (1), Patricia Quinn Curtis for The Me Nobody Knows (1), Gloria Gresham for Show Me Where the Good Times Are (1), Willa Kim for Promenade (1), Jean Pace for Joy (1), Peter Schumann for Bread and Puppet Theater, No choice (9).

COMPOSER. Kurt Weill for Mahagonny (4), Nancy Ford for The Last Sweet Days of Isaac (3), Gary William Friedman for The Me Nobody Knows (3), Peter Link and C.C. Courtney for Salvation (2), Oscar Brown Jr, for Joy (1), Harvey Schmidt for Colette (1), Stanley Silverman for Elephant Steps (1), No choice (5).

LYRICIST. Gretchen Cryer for The Last Sweet Days of Isaac (7), Bertolt Brecht for Mahagonny (3), Will Holt for The Me No-

body Knows (2), Peter Link and C.C. Courtney for Salvation (1), Tom Jones for Colette (1), Ron Seward for Sambo (1), No choice (5).

MOST PROMISING PLAYWRIGHT. Paul Zindel for The Effect of Gamma Rays on Man-in-the-Moon Marigolds (11), Conrad Bromberg for Transfers (1), Charles Gordone for No Place to Be Somebody (1), Thomas Murphy for A Whistle in the Dark (1), Charles Russell for Five on the Black Hand Side (1), Jeff Wanshel for The Disintegration of James Cherry (1), Susan Yankowitz for Terminal (1), No choice (3).

OUTSTANDING OFF-BROADWAY PRODUCER. Ellen Stewart of Cafe La Mama (4), Joseph Papp of New York Shakespeare Festival (3), Orin Lehman for The Effect of Gamma Rays on Man-in-the-Moon Marigolds (2), Haila Stoddard, Mark Wright and Duane Wilder for The Last Sweet Days of Isaac (2), Jeff Britton for The Me Nobody Knows (1), Joseph Chaikin of The Open Theater (1), Cheryl Crawford for Colette (1), Ted Mann of Circle in the Square (1), No choice (5).

1970-71 OFF-BROADWAY SEASON

This year for the second time, representative New York drama critics were polled by *Variety* to learn their choices for bests other than best play or musical off Broadway. 21 critics participated: Clive Barnes, Martin Bookspan, Harold Clurman, James Davis, Jack Gaver, William H. Glover, Henry Hewes, Ted Kalem, Walter Kerr, Alvin Klein, Stuart Klein, John Lahr, Emory Lewis, Leo Mishkin, Edwin Newman, Edith Oliver, George Oppenheimer, Leonard Probst, John Simon, Marilyn Stasio and Peggy Stockton. Names of those cited in the various categories appear below, together with the number of critics' votes received (in parentheses). Winners are listed in **bold face type.**

MALE LEAD, STRAIGHT PLAY. **Jack MacGowran** in MacGowran in the Works of Beckett (7), Harold Gould in The House of Blue Leaves (4), Robert Ryan in Long Day's Journey Into Night (4), William Devane in One Flew Over the Cuckoo's Nest (3), Richard Dreyfuss in Line (1), Ed Flanders in The Trial of the Catonsville Nine (1), James Woods in Saved (1).

FEMALE LEAD, STRAIGHT PLAY. **Geraldine Fitzgerald** in Long Day's Journey Into Night (6½), Claire Bloom in A Doll's House and Hedda Gabler (4), Ruby Dee in Boesman and Lena (3), Mildred Dunnock in A Place Without Doors (3), Siobhan McKenna in Here Are Ladies (1½), Susan Batson in AC/DC (1), Rosalind Cash in Charlie Was Here and Now He's Gone (1), Madeleine Renaud in L'Amante Anglaise (1).

MALE LEAD, MUSICAL. Stephen Nathan in Godspell (6), Shoichi Saito in Golden Bat (2), Bill Hinnant in Frank Merriwell (1), Gilbert Price in Six (1), No choice (11).

FEMALE LEAD, MUSICAL. Judy Gibson in Sensations (1), Madeleine le Roux in The Dirtiest Show in Town (1), Mary Bracken Phillips in Look Where I'm At (1), No choice (17).

BEST SUPPORTING ACTOR. **Stacy Keach** (5) and James Naughton (2) in Long Day's Journey Into Night, Hector Elizondo in Steambath (3), Conrad Bain in Play Strindberg (1), Ronny Cox in The Happiness Cage (1), Joe Fields (1) and Lee Wallace (½) in The Basic Training of Pavlo Hummel, Robert Guillaume in Charlie Was Here and Now He's Gone (1), John Harkins in The Birthday

Party (1), Jerry Mayer in *Alice in Wonderland* (1), Shoichi Saito in *Golden Bat* (1), Sydney Walker in *Antigone* (1), James Woods in *Saved* (1), William Atherton in *The House of Blue Leaves* (½), David Margulies in *The Last Analysis* (½), Roy Shuman in *A Doll's House* (½).

BEST SUPPORTING ACTRESS. **Katherine Helmond** (7) and Anne Meara (1) in *The House of Blue Leaves*, Sasha von Scherler in *Trelawny of the "Wells"* (3), Roberta Maxwell in *Slag* (2), Robin Braxton in *Jazznite* (1), Patricia Elliott in *A Doll's House* (1), Geraldine Fitzgerald in *Long Day's Journey Into Night* (1), Martha Henry in *Scenes From American Life* (1), Janice Rule in *The Homecoming* (1), Ann Wedgeworth in *Line* (1), No choice (2).

MOST PROMISING NEW OFF-BROADWAY ACTOR. **James Naughton** in *Long Day's Journey Into Night* (6), Johnny Bottoms in *Dance Wi' Me* (2), Larry Pine (2) and Jerry Mayer (1) in *Alice in Wonderland*, Ronny Cox in *The Happiness Cage* (1), Joe Fields in *The Basic Training of Pavlo Hummel* (1), Andy Robinson in *Subject to Fits* (1), Shoichi Saito in *Golden Bat* (1), William Schallert in *The Trial of the Catonsville Nine* (1), Drew Snyder in *The Wars of the Roses* (1), No choice (4).

MOST PROMISING NEW OFF-BROADWAY ACTRESS. Julie Garfield in *Uncle Vanya* (2), Judy Allen in *Dance Wi' Me* (1), Katherine Helmond (1) and Anne Meara (1) in *The House of Blue Leaves*, Judy Kahan (1) in *Proposition*, Paula Kelly in *Metamorphoses* (1), Kishasha in *Black Girl* (1), Sonia Manzano (1) and Gilmer McCormick (1) in *Godspell*, Marsha Mason in *Happy Birthday, Wanda June* (1), **No choice** (10).

BEST DIRECTOR. **Arvin Brown** for *Long Day's Journey Into Night* (5), Jeff Bleckner for *The Basic Training of Pavlo Hummel* (4), Andre Gregory for *Alice in Wonderland* (4), A.J. Antoon for *Subject to Fits* (1), Gordon Davidson for *The Trial of the Catonsville Nine* (1), James Hammerstein for *Line* (1), Robert Ronan for *Trelawny of the "Wells"* (1), Mel Shapiro for *The House of Blue Leaves* (1), Paul Sills for *Story Theater* (1),

Dan Sullivan for *Play Strindberg* (1), Robert Wilson for *Deafman Glance* (1).

SET DESIGNER. **Ming Che Lee** for *MacGowran in the Works of Beckett* (4), Karl Eigsti for *The House of Blue Leaves* (2), David Mitchell for *Steambath* and *Trelawny of the "Wells"* (2), Lowell B. Achziger for *Godspell* (1), Uberto Bertacca for *Orlando Furioso* (1), Edward Burbridge for *Ride a Black Horse* (1), John Bury for *A Doll's House* and *Hedda Gabler* (1), David Chapman for *Charlie Was Here and Now He's Gone* (1), Eugene Lee and Franne Newman for *Alice in Wonderland* (1), Kert Lundell for *The Carpenters* (1), John Scheffler for *AC/DC*, Ed Wittstein for *Happy Birthday, Wanda June* (1), **No choice** (4).

COSTUME DESIGNER. Susan Tsu for *Godspell* (4), Theoni V. Aldredge for *Trelawny of the "Wells"* (3), Eugene Lee and Franne Newman for *Alice in Wonderland* (2), Joseph G. Aulisi for *Happy Birthday, Wanda June* (1), Margaret S. Hall for *Deafman Glance* (1), Neil Peter Jampolis for *One Flew Over the Cuckoo's Nest* (1), **No choice** (9).

COMPOSER. Stephen Schwartz for *Godspell* (7), Tom Constanten for *Tarot* (2), Ituro Shimoda for *Golden Bat* (1), **No choice** (11).

LYRICIST. Stephen Schwartz for *Godspell* (6), Yutaka Higashi for *Golden Bat* (2), **No choice** (12).

MOST PROMISING PLAYWRIGHT. **David Rabe** for *The Basic Training of Pavlo Hummel* (10), A.R. Gurney Jr. for *Scenes From American Life* (2), Kurt Vonnegut Jr. for *Happy Birthday, Wanda June* (2), Robert Montgomery for *Subject to Fits* (1), Joyce Carol Oates for *Sunday Dinner* (1), Dennis Turner for *Charlie Was Here and Now He's Gone* (1), David Hare for *Slag* (½), Dennis J. Reardon for *The Happiness Cage* (½), No choice (3).

OUTSTANDING OFF-BROADWAY PRODUCER. **Joseph Papp** of N.Y. Shakespeare Festival (9), T. Edward Hambleton of Phoenix Theater (3), Chelsea Theater Center of Brooklyn (1), Negro Ensemble Company (1), No choice (7).

1970-71 PUBLICATION
OF RECENTLY-PRODUCED PLAYS

After Haggerty. David Mercer. Methuen.
Big Mother and Other Plays. Charles Dizenzo. Grove.
Black Quartet, A. Introduced by Clayton Riley. New American Library. (Paperback.) Includes

Prayer Meeting or The First Militant Minister by Ben Caldwell, *The Warning—A Theme for Linda* by Ronald Milner, *The Gentleman Caller* by Ed Bullins, *Great Goodness of Life (A Coon Show)* by LeRoi Jones.
Butterflies Are Free. Leonard Gershe. Random House.
Child's Play. Robert Marasco. Random House.
Contractor, The. David Storey, J. Cape.
Counting Sheep. Includes full text of *Sheep on the Runway.* Art Buchwald. Putnam.
Duplex, The. Ed Bullins. Morrow.
H. Charles Wood. Methuen.
Inquest. Donald Freed. Hill and Wang.
Last of the Red Hot Lovers. Neil Simon. Random House.
Lemon Sky. Lanford Wilson. Hill and Wang.
Memory Bank, The. Martin Duberman. Dial Press.
Mod Donna and Sckylon Z. Myrna Lamb. Pathfinder Press.
Night Thoreau Spent in Jail, The. Jerome Lawrence and Robert E. Lee. Hill and Wang.
Operation Sidewinder. Sam Shepard. Bobbs-Merrill.
Revenge. Howard Brenton. Methuen. (Paperback.)
Shango de Ima: A Yoruba Mystery Play. Pepe Carril. Doubleday. (Paperback.)
Showcase I. John Lahr. (Paperback.)
Sleuth. Anthony Shaffer. Dodd, Mead.
Steambath. Bruce Jay Friedman. A. Knopf.
Trial of the Catonsville Nine, The. Daniel Berrigan. Beacon Press. (Paperback.)
Underground: Four Plays. *Fun in Lethe, The Burghers of Calais, The Mummer's Play, The Wonderful Years.* Edgar White. Morrow.
Vatzlav. Slawomir Mrozek. Grove Press.

A SELECTED LIST OF OTHER PLAYS PUBLISHED IN 1970-71

Bertolt Brecht: Collected Plays. Vol. I. Edited by Ralph Manheim and John Willett. Pantheon.
Best Mystery and Suspense Plays of the Modern Theater. Stanley Richards, editor. Dodd, Mead.
Best Plays of the Sixties. Stanley Richards, editor. Doubleday.
Best Short Plays of 1970. Stanley Richards, editor. Chilton.
Blind Beauty, The. Boris Pasternak. Harcourt, Brace.
Borage Pigeon Affair, The. James Saunders. Andre Deutsch.
Camino Real. Tennessee Williams. New Directions. Third Revision. (Paperback.)
Christopher Fry: Plays. *The Boy With a Cart, The Firstborn, Venus Observed.* Oxford. (Paperback.)
Complete Plays and Selected Poems by Charles Dickens. Six plays: *The Strange Gentleman, The Village Coquettes, Is She His Wife?, The Lamplighter, Mr. Nightingale's Diary, No Thoroughfare.* Vision Press.
Dragon Country. Tennessee Williams. *In the Bar of a Tokyo Hotel, I Rise in Flame, Cried the Phoenix, I Can't Imagine Tomorrow, The Frosted Glass Coffin, A Perfect Analysis Given by a Parrot, The Mutilated, Confessional, The Gnadiges Fraulein.* New Directions.
Great Playwrights, The. Compiled by Eric Bentley *Prometheus Bound* by Aeschylus, *King Oedipus* and *Antigone* by Sophocles, *The Bacchae* by Euripides, *Troilus and Cressida* and *King Lear* by Shakespeare, *Volpone* by Ben Jonson; *Fuente Ovejuna* by Lope de Vega, *Life Is a Dream* by Calderon de la Barca, *Don Juan* and *The Misanthrope* by Molière, *Phaedra* by Racine, *Prince Frederick of Homburg* by Heinrich von Kleist, *The Wild Duck* and *Rosmersholm* by Henrik Ibsen, *Miss Julie* by August Strindberg, *The Importance of Being Earnest* by Oscar Wilde, *Three Sisters* by Anton Chekhov, *Saint Joan* and *Major Barbara* by George Bernard Shaw, *The Playboy of the Western World* by John Millington Synge, *Right You Are* and *Six Characters in Search of an Author* by Luigi Pirandello, *Mother Courage* and *The Caucasian Chalk Circle* by Bertolt Brecht. Two-volume set. Doubleday.
Hypocrite, The. Robert McLellan. Calder and Boyers.
Marriage. N. V. Gogal. Manchester University Press.
New Short Plays: 2. *Rites* by Maureen Duffy, *Lovers* by Carey Harrison, *Futz* by Rochelle Owens. Methuen. (Paperback.)
Oxford Shakespeare Concordances. Dr. T. H. Howard-Hill, editor. Separate volume for each of the following plays: *All's Well That Ends Well, As You Like It, The Merchant of Venice, Twelfth Night, The Winter's Tale.* Oxford.
People Are Living There. Athol Fugard. Oxford.
Pirandello's One-Act Plays. Translated by William Murray. *The Vise, The Doctor's Duty, The License, At the Exit, The Festival of Our Lord of the Ship, Sicilian Limes, The Jar, Chee-*

Chee, The Imbecile, I'm Dreaming, But Am I?, The Other Son, Bellavita, The Man With the Flower in His Mouth. Minerva Press (Funk & Wagnalls).

Seneca's *Oedipus.* Ted Hughes. Faber and Faber.

Three Plays. *Five Finger Exercise* by Peter Shaffer, *The Kitchen* by Arnold Wesker, *The Hamlet of Stepney Green* by Bernard Kops. Penguin. (Paperback.)

Three Tragedies. Federico Garcia Lorca. *The House of Bernard Alba, Blood Wedding, Yerma.* Penguin. (Paperback.)

Treasury of the Theater from Henrik Ibsen to Robert Lowell. Volume Two. John Gassner and Bernard F. Dukore, editors. *Ghosts* and *Hedda Gabler* by Henrik Ibsen, *The Vultures* by Henri Becque, *The Power of Darkness* by Leo Tolstoy, *The Father* and *A Dream Play* by August Strindberg, *The Intruder* by Maurice Maeterlinck, *The Weavers* by Gerhart Hauptmann, *The Importance of Being Earnest* by Oscar Wilde, *Heartbreak House* and *Candida* by George Bernard Shaw, *Ubu the King* by Alfred Jarry, *Cyrano de Bergerac* by Edmond Rostand, *The Tenor* by Frank Wedekind, *The Cherry Orchard* by Anton Chekhov, *The Lower Depths* by Maxim Gorki, *Riders to the Sea* and *The Playboy of the Western World* by John Millington Synge, *The Tidings Brought to Mary* by Paul Claudel, *The Circle* by W. Somerset Maugham, *Six Characters in Search of an Author* by Luigi Pirandello, *The Cuttlefish* by Stanislaw I. Witkiewicz, *The Hairy Ape* and *A Moon for the Misbegotten* by Eugene O'Neill, *The Spurt of Blood* by Antonin Artaud, *The Plough and the Stars* by Sean O'Casey, *Elizabeth the Queen* by Maxwell Anderson, *Blood Wedding* by Federico Garcia Lorca, *Golden Boy* by Clifford Odets, *Our Town* by Thornton Wilder, *Purgatory* by William Butler Yeats, *The Good Woman of Setzuan* and *Galileo* by Bertolt Brecht, *My Heart's in the Highlands* by William Saroyan, *The Little Foxes* by Lillian Hellman, *The Madwoman of Chaillot* by Jean Giraudoux, *The Lark* by Jean Anouilh, *The Flies* by Jean-Paul Sartre, *The Glass Menagerie* by Tennessee Williams, *Death of a Salesman* by Arthur Miller, *Epitaph for George Dillon* by John Osborne and Anthony Creighton, *A Slight Ache* by Harold Pinter, *Who's Afraid of Virginia Woolf?* by Edward Albee, *Dutchman* by LeRoi Jones, *Benito Cereno* by Robert Lowell. Holt, Rinehart, Winston.

Twenty Plays of the No Theater. Donald Keene, editor.

Two Plays. Brian Friel. *Crystal and Fox* and *The Mundy Scheme.* Farrar, Straus & Giroux.

MUSICAL AND DRAMATIC RECORDINGS OF NEW YORK SHOWS

Title and publishing company are listed below. Each record is an original New York cast album unless otherwise indicated. An asterisk (*) indicates recording is also available on cassettes.

Bob and Ray. Columbia.
The Boy Friend (revival; original British cast). Stanyan.
Cactus Flower (movie sound track). Bell.*
Cry for Us All. Project 3.
Darling Lili (movie sound track). RCA Victor.*
Follies. Capitol.
Gertrude Stein's First Reader. Polydor.
Hair (original Japanese cast). RCA Victor.
Hair (original French cast). Phillips.*
In Circles. Avant-Garde.
Me Nobody Knows, The. Atlantic.*
New Faces of 1952 (revival). RCA Victor.
No, No, Nanette. Columbia.*
On a Clear Day You Can See Forever (movie sound track). Columbia.*
Purlie. Ampex.*
Rothschilds, The. Columbia.*
Story Theater. Columbia (two records).
Tell Me That You Love Me, Junie Moon (movie sound track). Columbia.
Two by Two. Columbia.*
Where's Charley? (original London cast). Monument-Evergreen (two records).

THE BEST PLAYS, 1894-1970

Listed in alphabetical order below are all those works selected as Best Plays in previous volumes in the *Best Plays* series. Opposite each title is given the volume in which the play appears, its opening date and its total number of performances. Those plays marked with an asterisk (*) were still playing on June 1, 1971 and their number of performances was figured through May 31, 1971. Adaptors and translators are indicated by (ad) and (tr), and the symbols (b), (m) and (l) stand for the author of the book, music and lyrics in the case of musicals.

NOTE: A season-by-season listing, rather than an alphabetical one, of the 500 Best Plays in the first 50 volumes, starting with the yearbook for the season of 1919-20, appears in *The Best Plays of 1968-69*.

PLAY	VOLUME	OPENED	PERFS.
ABE LINCOLN IN ILLINOIS—Robert E. Sherwood	38-39	Oct. 15, 1938	472
ABRAHAM LINCOLN—John Drinkwater	19-20	Dec. 15, 1919	193
ACCENT ON YOUTH—Samson Raphaelson	34-35	Dec. 25, 1934	229
ADAM AND EVA—Guy Bolton, George Middleton	19-20	Sept. 13, 1919	312
ADAPTATION—Elaine May; and NEXT—Terrence McNally	68-69	Feb. 10, 1969	707
AFFAIRS OF STATE—Louis Verneuil	50-51	Sept. 25, 1950	610
AFTER THE FALL—Arthur Miller	63-64	Jan. 23, 1964	208
AFTER THE RAIN—John Bowen	67-68	Oct. 9, 1967	64
AH, WILDERNESS!—Eugene O'Neill	33-34	Oct. 2, 1933	289
ALIEN CORN—Sidney Howard	32-33	Feb. 20, 1933	98
ALISON'S HOUSE—Susan Glaspell	30-31	Dec. 1, 1930	41
ALL MY SONS—Arthur Miller	46-47	Jan. 29, 1947	328
ALL THE WAY HOME—Tad Mosel, based on James Agee's novel *A Death in the Family*	60-61	Nov. 30, 1960	333
ALLEGRO—(b, l) Oscar Hammerstein II, (m) Richard Rodgers	47-48	Oct. 10, 1947	315
AMBUSH—Arthur Richman	21-22	Oct. 10, 1921	98
AMERICA HURRAH—Jean-Claude van Itallie	66-67	Nov. 6, 1966	634
AMERICAN WAY, THE—George S. Kaufman, Moss Hart	38-39	Jan. 21, 1939	164
AMPHITRYON 38—Jean Giraudoux, (ad) S. N. Behrman	37-38	Nov. 1, 1937	153
ANDERSONVILLE TRIAL, THE—Saul Levitt	59-60	Dec. 29, 1959	179
ANDORRA—Max Frisch, (ad) George Tabori	62-63	Feb. 9, 1963	9
ANGEL STREET—Patrick Hamilton	41-42	Dec. 5, 1941	1,295
ANIMAL KINGDOM, THE—Philip Barry	31-32	Jan. 12, 1932	183
ANNA CHRISTIE—Eugene O'Neill	21-22	Nov. 2, 1921	177
ANNA LUCASTA—Philip Yordan	44-45	Aug. 30, 1944	957
ANNE OF THE THOUSAND DAYS—Maxwell Anderson	48-49	Dec. 8, 1948	286
ANOTHER LANGUAGE—Rose Franken	31-32	Apr. 25, 1932	344
ANOTHER PART OF THE FOREST—Lillian Hellman	46-47	Nov. 20, 1946	182
ANTIGONE—Jean Anouilh, (ad) Lewis Galantière	45-46	Feb. 18, 1946	64
*APPLAUSE—(b) Betty Comden and Adolph Green, (m) Charles Strouse, (l) Lee Adams, based on the film *All About Eve* and the original story by Mary Orr	69-70	Mar. 30, 1970	489
APPLE TREE, THE—(b), (l) Sheldon Harnick, (b), (m) Jerry Bock, add'l (b) Jerome Coopersmith, based on stories by Mark Twain, Frank R. Stockton and Jules Feiffer	66-67	Oct. 18, 1966	463
ARSENIC AND OLD LACE—Joseph Kesselring	40-41	Jan. 10, 1941	1,444
AS HUSBANDS GO—Rachel Crothers	30-31	Mar. 5, 1931	148
AUTUMN GARDEN, THE—Lillian Hellman	50-51	Mar. 7, 1951	101
AWAKE AND SING—Clifford Odets	34-35	Feb. 19, 1935	209
BAD MAN, THE—Porter Emerson Browne	20-21	Aug. 30, 1920	350
BAD SEED—Maxwell Anderson, based on William March's novel	54-55	Dec. 8, 1954	332
BARBARA FRIETCHIE—Clyde Fitch	99-09	Oct. 23, 1899	83

NECROLOGY

MAY 1970—JUNE 1971

PERFORMERS

Addison, Victoria (92)—April 9, 1971
Aguglia, Mimi (85)—July 31, 1970
Aherne, Patrick (69)—September 30, 1970
Albright, "Oklahoma" Bob (87)—April 30, 1971
Allen, Dorothy (74)—October 2, 1970
Allister, Claud (76)—July 26, 1970
Althouse, Earl F. (78)—February 6, 1971
Anderson, Bronco Billy (88)—January 20, 1971
Anderson, Robert W. (31)—September 15, 1971
Anthony, John J.—July 16, 1970
Astor, George (77)—Autumn 1970
Aubrey, Madge—October 21, 1970
Bamattre, Martha (78)—July 12, 1970
Barrett, Lester (68)—September 23, 1970
Barth, Belle (59)—February 14, 1971
Benstead, Fabbie—Autumn 1970
Benzell, Mimi (47)—December 23, 1970
Bernie, Dick (60)—February 7, 1971
Besant, Sonya (40)—July 30, 1970
Black, Lew (60)—January 26, 1971
Boese, Joachim (38)—April 25, 1971
Booth, Helen—February 5, 1971
Bourvil (57)—September 23, 1970
Bradford, Marshall (75)—January 11, 1971
Braun, Eric (46)—October 27, 1970
Breen, May Singhi (76)—December 19, 1970
Brisman, Chaim (67)—June 24, 1970
Brooks, Helen (60)—April 6, 1971
Bruce, Paul—May 2, 1971
Buchanan, Margaret—July 1970
Burns, David (69)—March 12, 1971
Burns, Edward—November 3, 1970
Bussey, Hank (80)—January 14, 1971
Calvert, Catherine (80)—January 18, 1971
Carminati, Tullio (77)—February 26, 1971
Casey, Ethel (49)—January 30, 1971
Cesana, Renzo—November 8, 1970
Chandler, Douglas M. H. (53)—October 22, 1970
Ciceri, Leo (46)—August 10, 1970
Clare, Mary (78)—August 29, 1970
Clarke, Albert (73)—April 8, 1971
Clarkson, George, Jr. (52)—July 21, 1970
Clement, Donald (29)—July 28, 1970
Clifton, Bernard (68)—July 1970
Clinton-Baddeley, V. V.—August 6, 1970
Cockshutt, Stanislaus (66)—June 9, 1969

Cole, Eddie (59)—June 17, 1969
Coleman, Frank 3d (35)—December 5, 1970
Colt, Phyllis (52)—April 9, 1971
Compton, Viola (85)—April 7, 1971
Cortez, Leon (72)—December 31, 1970
Court, Bob (68)—August 21, 1970
Craig, Miriam (54)—March 1, 1971
Cunningham, Ruby Hale White (79)—April 23, 1971
Curtis, Jack (44)—September 25, 1970
Dale, Pat (57)—July 1970
Dall, John (50)—January 15, 1971
Dames, Harry L. (82)—March 27, 1971
Daniels, Bebe (71)—March 16, 1971
Darling, May (83)—March 23, 1971
Darrel, J. Stevan (65)—August 14, 1970
Daw, Evelyn (58)—November 30, 1970
Dawley, Herbert M. (90)—August 15, 1970
Day, Edith (75)—May 1, 1971
Dean, Fabian (41)—January 15, 1971
Dee, Danny (48)—October 25, 1970
De Lon, Jack (40)—July 2, 1970
Dennis, Dorian (47)—December 8, 1970
Dermont, Paul (54)—August 1970
Diers, Eugene (70s)—September 15, 1970
Digges, Ernest—August 15, 1970
Dobritsch, Al (60)—March 11, 1971
Doner, Maurice (66)—February 21, 1971
Douglas, Milton (64)—September 16, 1970
Draylin, Paul (56)—May 19, 1970
Durieux, Tilla (90)—February 21, 1971
Earle, Jackson (69)—January 15, 1971
Elliott, Ruth (81)—February 15, 1971
English, Ralph (59)—May 18, 1970
Esser, Peter (84)—June 23, 1970
Fair, May (67)—May 24, 1971
Farkas, Karl (77)—May 16, 1971
Farmer, Frances (56)—August 1, 1970
Farrell, Glenda (66)—May 1, 1971
Feiler, Herta (54)—November 4, 1970
Feldman, Edythe A. (58)—February 28, 1971
Fernandel (67)—February 26, 1971
Finnegan, Edward (72)—February 7, 1971
Flaherty, Pat J. Sr.—December 2, 1970
Flippen, Jay C. (70)—February 3, 1971
Folwell, Denis (66)—April 26, 1971
Foran, Thomas F. (79)—August 19, 1970
Forbes, Earle (73)—August 12, 1970
Foster, Betty—June 1970
Foster, Preston (69)—July 14, 1970
Frey, Nathaniel (57)—November 9, 1970
Friedmann, Shraga (47)—July 1970

398

Fries, Helen Warnow (44)—December 28, 1970
Gale, Chet W. (52)—December 9, 1970
Garcia, Henry (66)—November 3, 1970
Gardiner, Patrick (44)—September 30, 1970
Genzmer, Hertha (74)—February 2, 1971
Gilbert, Louis (59)—August 18, 1970
Glaum, Louise (70)—November 26, 1970
Glenn, Roy, Sr. (56)—March 12, 1971
Glover, Thomas J.—January 16, 1971
Godderis, Albert (89)—February 2, 1971
Goldstein, Becky (94)—Spring 1971
Golub, Harry (74)—July 25, 1970
Gordon, Edith Althoff (65)—October 25, 1970
Gordon, Gavin (69)—November 18, 1970
Gordon, Oliver (67)—September 26, 1970
Gottlieb, Polly Rose—February 13, 1971
Grant, Billy—May 12, 1971
Grant, Earl—June 10, 1970
Gravey, Fernand (65)—November 2, 1970
Greenwood, Ethel (72)—December 8, 1970
Grew, Mary (68)—March 20, 1971
Grimm, Harry E. (72)—December 3, 1970
Grimshaw, Nicholas (69)—October 10, 1970
Grover, Myrtle—June 10, 1970
Hall, Bob (83)—August 13, 1970
Hall, Geraldine (65)—September 18, 1970
Hamper, Genevieve (82)—February 13, 1971
Hare, Mollie—February 6, 1971
Harkins, Jim (82)—October 23, 1970
Hart, Teddy (74)—February 17, 1971
Hartzell, Willard C. (60)—May 30, 1970
Hayden, Louis (56)—May 1971
Hendrix, Jimi (27)—September 18, 1970
Herlein, Lillian—April 13, 1971
Hernandez, Juan G. (74)—July 17, 1970
Hewett, Molly—September 8, 1970
Hoagland, Harland (75)—January 9, 1971
Hoey, W. H. (76)—December 7, 1970
Horton, Edward Everett (83)—September 29, 1970
Hoyt, Eileen (67)—July 19, 1970
Hynd, Colin (84)—August 1970
Jameson, House (68)—April 22, 1971
Jamin, Georges (64)—February 23, 1971
Johnson, Lonnie (70)—June 17, 1970
Johnson, Travis (64)—June 18, 1970
Joplin, Janis (27)—October 4, 1970
Joyce, Lind (51)—May 3, 1971
Keith, James (68)—December 27, 1970
King, Dennis (73)—May 21, 1971
Kinnaird, David (45)—April 2, 1971
Kirkham, Sam (48)—October 30, 1970
Kollmar, Richard (60)—January 9, 1971
Kortner, Fritz (78)—July 22, 1970
Krueger, Bum (65)—March 15, 1971
Kusell, Mrs. Harold (68)—May 18, 1971
Lake, Sue—July 16, 1970
Lancaster, Ann (50)—October 31, 1970
Lang, Harold—November 16, 1970
Lang, Jimmy (65)—Summer 1970
Latham, Joseph W. Sr. (80)—October 10, 1970

Lawrence, Elaine (28)—May 20, 1971
Ledford, Harrison C. (69)—June 19, 1970
Leeds, Florence (75)—September 29, 1970
Legat, Nadine (81)—February 4, 1971
Lenihan, Brigid (41)—June 11, 1970
Leonard, Murray (72)—November 6, 1970
Leonard, Patrick A. (82)—January 10, 1971
Leslie, Arthur (68)—June 30, 1970
Lightner, Winnie (71)—March 5, 1971
Lindsay, Lex (70)—April 24, 1971
Lloyd, Harold (77)—March 8, 1971
Lockwood, King (73)—February 23, 1971
Lombardo, Carmen (67)—April 17, 1971
Louchlamn, Gearold O. (78)—July 24, 1970
Lowe, Edmund (79)—April 21, 1971
Lulli, Folco (58)—May 24, 1970
Magley, Guy (79)—February 18, 1971
Mandia, Joe (45)—August 11, 1970
Maple, Audrey (72)—April 18, 1971
Maratier, Florence Tanner—October 13, 1970
Marks, Ben (72)—July 26, 1970
Marshall, F. Elmer (89)—April 12, 1971
Maxam, Louella Modie (74)—September 4, 1970
Maynard, Kermit (73)—January 16, 1971
McCurry, Jack Howard (94)—July 2, 1970
McHugh, Mathew (77)—February 22, 1971
Meggas, Joseph J. (53)—January 22, 1971
Meighan, James E. Jr. (66)—June 20, 1970
Melville, June (54)—September 15, 1970
Merlini (64)—March 1, 1971
Merritt, Lillie (90)—January 17, 1971
Middleton, Josephine (88)—April 8, 1971
Miller, Art (Smiley) (67)—April 27, 1971
Miller, Eddie (80)—March 9, 1971
Montfort, Stanley W. (67)—June 15, 1970
Moore, Del (53)—August 30, 1970
Morris, Chester (69)—September 15, 1970
Moubrey, Lilian (95)—November 11, 1970
Murphy, Audie (46)—May 31, 1971
Murphy, Delia (68)—February 13, 1971
Nelson, Edith (Dot) (78)—September 5, 1970
Nichols, Marjorie J.—September 28, 1970
O'Brien, Donnell—July 27, 1970
O'Brien, Terence (82)—October 13, 1970
Olivette, Nina (63)—February 21, 1971
Olp, Georgie—December 2, 1970
O'Neill, Carlotta Monterey (82)—November 21, 1970
Palmer, Jay (71)—August 14, 1970
Pankey, Aubrey (65)—May 1971
Pardave, Jose (68)—May 26, 1970
Parker, Cecil (73)—April 20, 1971
Perry, Mary (83)—March 6, 1971
Peters, Werner (52)—March 31, 1971
Pipo (68)—August 6, 1970
Porter, Mabel Butterworth (85)—May 23, 1970
Powell, Peggy (56)—October 26, 1970
Quinn, Miriam (71)—May 27, 1970
Quirk, Margaret C. (70)—January 12, 1971
Rafferty, Chips (62)—May 27, 1971
Rambeau, Marjorie (80)—July 6, 1970

Ranson, Herbert W. (87)—November 14, 1970
Ray, Estelle Goulding (82)—August 1, 1970
Reed, Carol—June 4, 1970
Richman, Lou (84)—June 8, 1970
Rigby, Arthur (70)—April 25, 1971
Riss, Dan (60)—August 28, 1970
Robles, Rud (60)—August 1970
Rogers, Cynthis (62)—May 1, 1971
Rose, Harry (61)—April 20, 1971
Ruggles, Charles (84)—December 23, 1970
Sandeman, Eleanor Brady (73)—March 26, 1971
Sarago, Theo (33)—August 28, 1970
Sawyer, Laura (85)—September 7, 1970
Schieske, Alfred (61)—July 14, 1970
Scott, Nan (72)—Autumn 1970
Shanahan, James A. Sr. (82)—September 19, 1970
Shannon, Ray (76)—January 4, 1971
Shaw, Dennis (50)—February 28, 1971
Shea, Jack (70)—October 13, 1970
Shelton, George (87)—February 12, 1971
Sherman, Joe (76)—August 20, 1970
Shillen, Joseph P. (55)—April 1, 1971
Shor, Miriam Craig (54)—March 1, 1971
Short, Sarah (95)—September 30, 1970
Shumlin, Carmen—December 13, 1970
Sidney, Irene (Sarli)—August 13, 1970
Silvera, Frank (56)—June 11, 1970
Skulnik, Menasha (79)—June 4, 1970
Soto, Luchy (50)—October 1970
Spivy (64)—January 8, 1971
Stephen, Stainless (79)—January 6, 1971
Stephens, Mrs. B. N. (78)—October 29, 1970
Stephenson, Robert Robinson (69)—September 8, 1970
Sterling, Frank B. (84)—September 19, 1970
Stewart, Fred (63)—December 5, 1970
Stratton, Chester (57)—July 7, 1970
Styler, Alan (44)—September 4, 1970
Taylor, Mabel—July 7, 1970
Teague, Brian (33)—May 30, 1970
Tershay, Joe—December 8, 1970
Tissot, Alice (81)—May 5, 1971
Tracey, Sid (70)—September 15, 1970
Trevor, Ann—July 1970
Tufts, Sonny (59)—June 4, 1970
Turner, Percy M.—January 17, 1971
Turner, Rob—October 16, 1970
Ulric, Lenore (78)—December 30, 1970
Valentine, Dickie (41)—May 6, 1971
Verney, Guy—September 19, 1970
Vilar, Jean (59)—May 28, 1971
Vladimiroff, Pierre (77)—November 26, 1970
von Meyerinck, Herbert (74)—May 13, 1971
Walker, Allan—September 2, 1970
Wall, Geraldine (57)—June 22, 1970
Warnow, Helen (44)—December 25, 1970
Warton, Elizabeth Hines (76)—February 19, 1971
Wayne, Naunton (69)—November 17, 1970
Weigel, Helen (70)—May 6, 1971
Weire, Sylvester (60)—July 7, 1970

Weiser, Grethe (67)—October 2, 1970
Westman, Nydia (68)—May 23, 1970
Whitman, Estelle—July 14, 1970
Wilkinson, Lillie M. (90)—January 17, 1971
Willard, Harry Francis (74)—June 28, 1970
Williams, Irene (38)—July 12, 1970
Wilson, Jack (76)—August 29, 1970
Wolff, Laura Sawyer (85)—September 7, 1970
Wood, Eugene (67)—January 22, 1971
Wood, George—June 24, 1970
Woollard, Robert (83)—March 24, 1971
Wymark, Patrick (44)—October 20, 1970
Wynn, Nan (55)—March 21, 1971

PLAYWRIGHTS

Archibald, William (53)—December 27, 1970
Baldwin, Earl (69)—October 9, 1970
Dazey, Francis Mitchell (78)—June 16, 1970
de Kruif, Paul (80)—February 28, 1971
Dix, Beulah M. (94)—September 25, 1970
Donovan, Alice Dougan (90)—March 28, 1971
Erdman, Nikolai R. (68)—August 10, 1970
Ervine, St. John (87)—January 24, 1971
Eunson, Katherine Albert (68)—July 26, 1970
Forster, E.M. (91)—June 7, 1970
Harris, Raymond (86)—April 10, 1971
Hunter, N. C. (62)—April 19, 1971
Jeanson, Henri (70)—Fall 1970
Kay, Jay (48)—October 3, 1970
Lennart, Isobel (55)—January 25, 1971
Nash, Ogden (68)—May 19, 1971
Pemberton, Madge (85)—September 23, 1970
Randolph, Clemence (81)—June 1970
Remarque, Erich Maria (72)—September 25, 1970
Steele, Wilbur Daniel (84)—May 26, 1970
Sully, Ruby (51)—January 15, 1971
Von Unruh, Fritz (85)—November 28, 1970
Wells, Malcolm (51)—December 9, 1970

COMPOSERS AND LYRICISTS

Brown, Russ (56)—February 18, 1971
Brunswick, Mark (69)—May 26, 1971
Buchwald, Julius (61)—August 9, 1970
Eardley-Wilmot, May (86)—June 1970
Forrest, John R. (62)—January 4, 1971
Forzano, Giovacchino (86)—October 28, 1970
Gallop, Sammy (55)—February 24, 1971
Gilbert, L. Wolfe (83)—July 12, 1970
Goodman, Harry—November 23, 1970
Gregory, Bobby (71)—May 13, 1971
Hayton, Lennie (63)—April 24, 1971
Henderson, Ray (74)—December 31, 1970
Hilliard, Bob (53)—February 1, 1971
Hosking, Arthur (96)—December 2, 1970
King, Karl L. (80)—March 31, 1971
Lana, Agustin (70)—November 5, 1970
Laslo, Alexander (75)—Autumn 1970
Lilley, Joseph J. (56)—January 1, 1971
Lorenzo, Ange (77)—April 22, 1971

McIntyre, Mark Walton (53)—May 13, 1970
McWhinney, Michael (39)—August 1, 1970
Pelman, Paul (81)—Spring 1971
Pepper, Harry S. (79)—June 6, 1970
Roig, Gonzalo (80)—June 13, 1970
Rose, Kenneth (74)—Autumn 1970
Schafer, John K. (51)—September 13, 1970
Scott, Kay (43)—January 1, 1971
Smith, Margaret Armstrong (73)—May 6, 1971
Stevens, Leith (60)—July 23, 1970
Stravinsky, Igor (88)—April 6, 1971
Tobias, George (72)—July 8, 1970
Tucker, Johnny (73)—February 14, 1971
Van Cleave, Nathan (60)—July 2, 1970
Van Parys, Georges (68)—January 29, 1971

PRODUCERS, DIRECTORS, CHOREOGRAPHERS

Clayton, Harold (68)—May 13, 1971
Cole, Alonzo Deen (74)—March 31, 1971
Du Ree, Meurisse (37)—November 12, 1970
Edens, Roger (64)—July 13, 1970
Farrell, Charles (78)—Autumn 1970
Gorall, Leslie (54)—December 26, 1971
Greene, Mary—May 23, 1970
Guthrie, Tyrone (70)—May 15, 1971
Hayward, Leland (68)—March 19, 19771
Hebertot, Jacques (84)—June 19, 1970
Hunt, Peter H. (55)—July 17, 1970
Lamy, Marcel (52)—October 1970
List, Kurt (57)—November 16, 1970
Lowe, K. Elmo (71)—January 26, 1971
Mangan, Francis A. (86)—January 6, 1971
Maxwell, Robert (61)—February 3, 1971
Meloney, William Brown (69)—May 4, 1971
Michie, Bryan (65)—March 25, 1971
Motyleff, Ilya (76)—November 30, 1970
Ott, Alexander (82)—December 13, 1970
Reiner, Ethel Linder (65)—February 8, 1971
Serlin, Oscar (70)—February 27, 1971
Tihmar, David (61)—April 16, 1971
von Ostfelden, Maria (75)—April 4, 1971
Westzel, Charles (Baldy) (79)—August 4, 1970
Wymetal, William (80)—November 7, 1970

CONDUCTORS

Barbirolli, John (70)—July 29, 1970
Braithwaite, Warwick (75)—January 18, 1971
Broza, Stan Lee (73)—December 15, 1970
Corelli, Alfonso (70)—October 10, 1970
Kurzweil, Frederic (57)—August 11, 1970
Lehmann, Otto (65)—April 29, 1971
List, Kurt (57)—November 16, 1970
Martin, Wolfgang (71)—June 17, 1970
Szell, George (73)—July 30, 1970

DESIGNERS

Boynes, Anthony—Autumn 1970
Flory, Julia McClune (89)—April 23, 1971

Forsyth, Gerald (90)—December 27, 1971
Hamrick, Burwell (64)—September 21, 1970
Heckroth, Hein (69)—July 6, 1970
Huneker, Erick H. (77)—May 4, 1971
Schlanger, Ben (66)—May 3, 1971
Sullivan, George—March 1, 1971

CRITICS

Arauz, Alvaro—December 22, 1970
Cater, Percy (73)—February 15, 1971
Cohen, Nathan (47)—March 26, 1971
DeMotte, Warren (60)—May 26, 1970
Dwight, Ogden G. (55)—September 23, 1970
Heimer, Mel (55)—February 8, 1971
Hoyt, Harlowe R.—October 24, 1970
Kaufman, Wolfe (65)—November 24, 1970
Kelly, Herb (71)—September 26, 1970
Knudsen, Hans (84)—February 4, 1971
Korman, Sey (60)—January 6, 1971
Koval, Francis W. (62)—December 26, 1971
Laird, Landon (75)—June 12, 1970
Mason, Colin (47)—February 6, 1971
Moora, Robert L. (58)—February 4, 1971
Murdock, Henry T. (69)—April 20, 1971
Perkins, Francis D. (72)—October 10, 1970
Ramirez, Arturo G. (62)—August 29, 1970
Reid, James MacArthur (70)—September 16, 1970
Rodriguez, Manuel Pena (63)—July 1970
Seldes, Gilbert (77)—September 30, 1970
Simon, Henry W. (68)—October 1, 1970
Smith, Oscar (74)—March 26, 1971
Strobel, Heinrich (72)—August 29, 1970
Tabachnik, Abraham Ber (68)—June 16, 1970
Whitlock, E. Clyde (84)—May 10, 1970
Wilson, Samuel T. (71)—January 10, 1971

MUSICIANS

Aaron, Abe (60)—November 17, 1970
Ayler, Albert (36)—November 25, 1970
Bagby, Harry (Doc)—September 3, 1970
Beer, Alex (73)—June 12, 1970
Blackwood, Roy E.—March 23, 1971
Brown, William F. Jr. (20)—December 1970
Carcares, Ernie (69)—January 10, 1971
Carry, George D. (Scoops) (57)—August 4, 1970
Cates, Gordon (63)—June 2, 1970
Clements, Harry—Winter 1970
Crosse, Gay S. (54)—March 9, 1971
Csirscu, Eugene G. (53)—July 3, 1970
Davis, Peter (90)—April 29, 1971
Dickinson, Hal (56)—November 18, 1970
Doege, Neil (21)—April 13, 1971
Driggs, Mrs. William King (81)—October 6, 1970
Ervin, Booker T. (39)—August 31, 1970
Ferrera, John B. (57)—February 6, 1971
Fuleihan, Anis (70)—October 15, 1970
Gobrecht, Harold (Whitey) (64)—June 24, 1970

Gusbeth, William (79)—March 30, 1971
Handy, "Captain John"—January 12, 1971
Hardwick, (Toby) Otto (66)—August 5, 1970
Harrison, Lionel E.—October 21, 1970
Johnson, Ernie (49)—December 14, 1970
Johnson, Joshua (67)—February 22, 1971
Johnson, Lonnie (81)—June 16, 1970
Johnson, Manzie I. (64)—April 9, 1971
Kane, Sherman (52)—September 29, 1970
Kelly, Monty (60)—March 15, 1971
Laskin, Caceil (Chuck) (40)—August 25, 1970
Lucarell, Joseph A. (63)—March 1, 1971
Milton, Georges (82)—October 16, 1970
Moriarty, Ruby (69)—October 10, 1970
Nutter, D. M. (Stix)—August 27, 1970
Olsen, George (78)—March 18, 1971
Peabody, Eddie (68)—November 7, 1970
Person, Irving L. (64)—August 17, 1970
Radlach, Karl—November 22, 1970
Rainbird, Paul (42)—Autumn 1970
Rapp, Barney (70)—October 10, 1970
Rogers, Mack—November 17, 1970
Roy, Harry (67)—January 30, 1971
Schoebel, Elmer (74)—December 14, 1970
Schubert, William A. (77)—November 5, 1970
Spitalny, Phil (80)—October 11, 1970
Tsfasman, Aleksandr (64)—Winter 1971
Ugarte, Pascal Louis (80)—Autumn 1970
Walton, Harry (Jack)—April 15, 1971
White, Sonny (53)—April 29, 1971
Wilson, Alan (27)—September 1970

OTHERS

Ackerman, Irving (85)—July 12, 1970
Theaterowner and legit booker
Alvord, Ned (87)—August 9, 1970
Theatrical publicist
Ashley, Arthur (85)—December 28, 1970
Manager of Percy Williams Home
Aylward, Keen (82)—January 31, 1971
Songplugger
Balaban, Barney (83)—March 7, 1971
Film industry leader
Bennett, George (53)—June 25, 1970
Movie and theater publicist
Berns, Charles A. (69)—February 20, 1971
Co-founder of 21 Club
Boyd, Alastair (50)—October 16, 1970
Theater publicist
Brill, Gene (38)—July 20, 1970
President of Brill Theatrical Agency
Brownstone, Joseph (50)—October 23, 1970
Production stage manager
Budde, Thom (37)—January 23, 1971
Hollywood manager
Campbell, Oscar James Jr. (90)—June 1, 1970
Shakespearean scholar
Carter, Frederick (70)—December 24, 1970
London theater executive
Clifford, Margaret (63)—May 4, 1971
Chairman of Drama Dept., Skidmore

Colby, Sidney J. (42)—August 31, 1970
Manager of Hotel Algonquin
Comstock, Mrs. F. Ray (80)—June 23, 1970
Manager of Booth Theater
Conners, James L. (72)—October 30, 1970
Variety correspondent
Cook, Howard (40)—June 15, 1970
Music publicist
Darrow, Whitney Sr. (89)—August 27, 1970
Secretary of The Players
D'Essen, Lorrain (51)—November 7, 1970
Animal talent agent
Diven, Mrs. Marjorie C. (77)—August 15, 1970. Secretary to Rudy Vallee
Dow, John W. (67)—February 3, 1971
Art Director, The Playbill
Doyle, Adrian Conan (59)—June 3, 1970
Son of Arthur Conan Doyle
Edwards, Steve—December 9, 1970
Movie publicist
Ehrle, August Emil (76)—September 23, 1970
Composing room foreman at Variety
Entratter, Jack (57)—March 11, 1971
President, Sands Hotel
Epstein, Dave (74)—September 8, 1970
Hollywood publicist
Fabian, Simon (71)—August 16, 1970
Builder of theaters
Fagan, Irene (86)—March 13, 1971
Theatrical costumer
Feder, Joseph (69)—September 28, 1970
Business manager
Fields, W. C., Jr. (60)—February 16, 1971
Son of W. C. Fields
Flanagan, Dick (56)—June 5, 1970
Theatrical publicist
Flory, Mrs. Walter (89)—April 24, 1971
A founder of Cleveland Play House
Fogler, Gertrude (91)—October 29, 1970
Diction coach
Foreman, Elliot S. (87)—March 10, 1971
Advance man
Fox, Robin (57)—January 21, 1971
Impresario
Gayle, Tim (57)—October 14, 1970
Publicist and song promoter
Geist, Irving (70)—November 28, 1970
Theatrical backer
Goldberg, Hyman (62)—September 19, 1970
Reporter, Sunday Mirror Magazine
Gould, Harry E. Sr. (72)—March 8, 1971
Showman, theaterowner
Grady, Bill Jr. (52)—August 27, 1970
Film Editor
Granik, Theodore (63)—September 22, 1970
Radio-TV moderator
Green, Jeanette F. (71)—December 13, 1970
Artists' representative
Gunther, John (68)—May 29, 1969
Journalist, author
Hackett, Charles M. (61)—September 27, 1970. Correspondent for Variety

NECROLOGY 403

Hall, Benjamin M. III (46)—December 1970
Editor of *Show Magazine*
Hampton, Gladys Neal (57)—April 29, 1971
Wife of Lionel Hampton
Harman, Homer H.—February 4, 1971
Publicity director of Roxy Theater
Hanley, Richard (61)—January 3, 1971
Executive assistant for Richard Burton
Harris, Catherine Richardson (80)—December 3, 1970. Widow of Victor Harris
Harvey, John (53)—December 25, 1970
Artists' manager
Helfer, Bobby (53)—June 13, 1970
Music contractor
Hemley, Jesse (63)—November 6, 1970
Theatrical lawyer
Henry, Dick (82)—September 15, 1971
Agent
Hess, Jack J. (78)—October 11, 1970
Publicist
Hogan, Charlie (67)—November 23, 1970
Theater booker, agent
Hollister, Paul M. (79)—July 27, 1970
Publicist
Hortop, Jack (57)—December 7, 1970
Lecturer, tour manager
Jones, Johnny (71)—March 17, 1971
Theater manager, columnist
Kenin, Herman (69)—July 21, 1970
President Amer. Federation of Musicians
Klein, Joseph (62)—November 8, 1970
Correspondent for *Variety*
Larkin, Lou (52)—December 10, 1970
Free lance writer, TV columnist
Lee, Manfred B. (65)—April 2, 1970
Ellery Queen
Levine, Marks (80)—May 29, 1971
Manager of musicians
Liebling, Estelle (90)—September 25, 1970
Singing teacher
Lilley, Joseph J. (57)—January 1, 1971
Music arranger
Londes, Nick (65)—December 13, 1970
Managing director, Olympia Stadium
McCormack, Lily F. (84)—April 26, 1971
Widow of John McCormack
McHugh, James W. (56)—May 5, 1971
Publisher, *Amusement Business*
Mayer, Jack W. (77)—February 13, 1971
Former owner of Liberty Theater
Mechanic, Emaline—April 12, 1971
Production assistant
Mersereau, Don (74)—September 18, 1970
General mgr, *Boxoffice*
Morgan, Richard (57)—December 17, 1970
Legal staff, Paramount Pictures
Morrow, Bill (63)—February 5, 1971
Writer for Jack Benny, Bing Crosby
Murphy, Frank M. (59)—September 17, 1970
Theater executive
O'Connell Thomas (96)—November 7, 1970
Theatrical publicist
Parke, James H.—August 31, 1970

Head of U. of Texas Drama Dept.
Parmenter, Al (69)—November 3, 1970
Film publicist
Pettebone, Jean (56)—July 11, 1970
Publicist
Phillips, Tommy (60)—September 30, 1970
Hollywood publicist
Piermont, Benny (82)—June 10, 1969
Fox Theater booker
Pils, Jacques (66)—Autumn 1970
Singing instructor
Polikoff, Benet Sr. (72)—December 18, 1970
Theater attorney
Quinn, Joe (54)—February 2, 1971
Toastmaster, publicist
Quittner, Joseph (83)—January 30, 1971
Theatrical lawyer
Reinheimer, Howard E. (71)—August 7, 1970
Theatrical attorney
Reynolds, Fred—Autumn 1970
British legit agent
Riley, Henry D. (71)—September 9, 1970
Agent for circus
Russell, Jay (57)—December 2, 1970
Theatrical publicist
Saucier, Ted (74)—October 16, 1970
Publicist for Waldorf-Astoria
Scanlon, Ed (77)—November 27, 1970
Business mgr for ATPAM
Schofield, Robert W. (69)—October 16, 1970
Production manager for *March of Time*
Schultz, Cecelia (92)—March 4, 1971
Impresario, promoter
Schwerin, Herman (68)—October 2, 1970
German film producer, lawyer
Shea, Joe (72)—December 21, 1970
Theatrical publicist
Shine, J. Myer (78)—May 8, 1971
Theater owner
Shurr, Lester H.—March 2, 1971
Talent agent
Smith, Charles E. (64)—December 17, 1970
Pioneer jazz writer
Smith, Lester (77)—June 29, 1970
Theatrical publicist
Spachner, Leon (87)—March 13, 1971
Theatrical manager
Stein, Mrs. Ann R. (72)—December 25, 1970
William Morris Agency lawyer
Sturm, Mrs. Justin (71)—May 8, 1971
Wife of playwright Justin Sturm
Tomsky, Aleksandr—September 27, 1970
Director of Bolshoi Ballet
Valdo, Pat (89)—November 6, 1970
Performance director of circus
Watson, George M. (51)—January 12, 1971
Publicist
Wayne, Timothy (22)—August 17, 1970
Son of actor David Wayne
Wear, (Mike) Millard (73)—July 9, 1970
Editorial staff of *Variety*
Wendling, Charles (72)—March 27, 1971
Talent agent

Westmore, Perc (65)—September 30, 1970
  Studio makeup artist
Spachner, Leon (87)—March 13, 1971
  Theatrical manager

Wilde, Al (60)—December 20, 1970
  Personal manager
Zeidman, Bennie E.—August 7, 1970
  Hollywood publicist

INDEX

Play titles are in **bold face** and ***bold face italic*** page numbers refer to pages where cast and credit listings may be found.

405